CONTESTING SPIRIT

CONTESTING SPIRIT

NIETZSCHE, AFFIRMATION, RELIGION

TYLER T. ROBERTS

PRINCETON UNIVERSITY PRESS

PRINCETON, NEW JERSEY

Copyright © 1998 by Princeton University Press
Published by Princeton University Press, 41 William Street,
Princeton, New Jersey 08540
In the United Kingdom: Princeton University Press,
Chichester, West Sussex

Library of Congress Cataloging-in-Publication Data

Roberts, Tyler T., 1960–

Contesting spirit : Nietzsche, affirmation, religion / Tyler T. Roberts.

p.   cm.

Includes bibliographical references and index.

ISBN 0-691-05937-3 (alk. paper). — ISBN 0-691-00127-8 (pbk. : alk. paper)

1. Nietzsche, Friedrich Wilhelm, 1844–1900—Religion.

2. Religion—Philosophy—History—19th century. I. Title

B3318.R4R63   1998   200'.92—dc21   98-14875   CIP

"Heaven" words and music by David Byrne. © 1979 Sire Records Co.,

p. 1979 Index Music, Inc. / Bleu Disque Music Co., Inc.

This book has been composed in Sabon

Princeton University Press books are printed
on acid-free paper and meet the guidelines for
permanence and durability of the Committee on
Production Guidelines for Book Longevity
of the Council on Library Resources

http://pup.princeton.edu

Printed in the United States of America

10 9 8 7 6 5 4 3 2 1

10 9 8 7 6 5 4 3 2 1
(Pbk.)

CONTENTS

ACKNOWLEDGMENTS

A FIRST BOOK carries with it more debts of gratitude than it is possible to remember, much less acknowledge in a page or two. This book is a revision of my dissertation, so I will begin by thanking my advisers at Harvard: Gordon Kaufman, Francis Fiorenza, and Fred Neuhouser. Each provided detailed, rigorous responses to my work. I would like to thank Gordon Kaufman in particular, not only for the support he gave me throughout my years as a doctoral student, but also for the generosity and guidance he has continued to offer as I have worked to revise the dissertation. Others who deserve thanks for helpful comments on drafts and stimulating conversation include Margaret Miles, Sharon Welch, David Lamberth, Alec Irwin, Charlie Stang, Brad Cullin, Mark Taylor, Charles Hallisey, and Anne Monius. Charles Winquist, Leslie Paul Thiele, and John Lysaker each read the penultimate draft and offered insightful challenges that have made this a better book. I also would like to thank the following for opportunities to present and discuss portions of the book: the Harvard Divinity School Theology Colloquium and the Mysticism, Nineteenth-Century Theology, and Philosophy of Religion groups of the American Academy of Religion. Ann Wald at Princeton University Press has been an informative and encouraging guide through the world of publishing. Lucinda Schutzmann was a great help in putting together the index.

In addition to those directly involved in the writing of the book, many others have offered support and inspiration. Early in my graduate studies, Sharon Welch demonstrated for me, and, I know, for many others, the model of an impassioned and affirmative scholar and teacher. Diana Eck and my colleagues at the Committee for the Study of Religion at Harvard provided a stimulating and challenging environment for a new teacher and young scholar. Throughout the years, Richard Wright, Bill Zieff, Rooney and Sarah Self, and Jack and Audrey Berry have been great friends. I have to give special thanks to Rooney and Sarah for a quiet spot in the hills of New Hampshire, where I first sketched the basic ideas for this book. I also want to thank my family, particularly my mother, Jane Roberts, and my grandfather, Charles Tillinghast. They instilled in me and continue to exemplify in their lives the synergy of dreams and discipline.

Finally, I thank my colleague, friend, and wife, Kathleen Roberts Skerrett. She has been my most cherished intellectual companion: a partner in countless conversations that have been instrumental in shaping my thinking, and an unfailing and uncompromising editor who has read every word of this book—many times. Most important, though, Kathleen has graced my life with her laughter, her compassion, and her love. And with Madeleine, who has brought both of us immeasurable joy.

NOTE ON TEXTS AND CITATIONS

I HAVE INCORPORATED references to Nietzsche into the text. For Nietzsche's works, I have used *Sämtliche Werke. Kritische Studienausgabe in 15 Bänden*, edited by G. Colli and M. Montinari (Berlin: de Gruyter, 1980). For the most part I follow the translations listed below. Where I have made alterations, or where I have followed the translation but feel that no English word or phrase can render adequately Nietzsche's German, I have supplied the German in the text. I cite works that have been published separately in English by the initials of their English titles and the page number. Other citations are designated by SW, volume number, and page number (eg., SW 13: 127). There are a few citations from the *Nachlass* that I found in Kaufmann's translation of *The Will to Power*, and did not track down in the notebooks. Those are cited as WP.

At this point let me say a brief word about my use of Nietzsche's texts in this study. Since Nietzsche's sister and others collected notes and fragments from Nietzsche's *Nachlass* under the title of *The Will to Power*, and especially since Heidegger's magisterial four-volume study of Nietzsche, which relied heavily on *The Will to Power*, a debate has ensued as to whether Nietzsche's published works or his *Nachlass* hold the key to his thought. My own view is that we must begin with the texts Nietzsche either published in his lifetime or that he considered finished (*The Antichrist* and *Ecce Homo*), but that were not published until after his breakdown. Nietzsche was not just a philosopher interested in taking a position or constructing clear arguments. He was also a writer who considered the style, the force, and the rhetoric of his writings to be of utmost importance in understanding his thinking. As I argue in this study, to ignore the strategies and styles of Nietzsche's writing is to ignore a key aspect of his philosophical task. It is necessary, then, for the interpreter of Nietzsche to attend first of all to the work that he considered ready for publication, the work that was written and rewritten, not just jotted down or sketched. This does not mean, however, that Nietzsche's notes and letters, as with those of any thinker, are not helpful for illustrating ideas and concepts for which he argues in his finished texts. This is particularly true in studies, such as the present one, that attempt not only to establish and evaluate certain ideas in Nietzsche, but also to emphasize and explore his ambivalences and ambiguities. Thus, for example, the notes are extremely suggestive on the question of religion. In my study, then, I refer to the *Nachlass* sparingly, either when I am satisfied that a note synthesizes or illustrates ideas or arguments I find in Nietzsche's finished texts, or when a note suggests directions in which we might take ideas further than Nietzsche himself did.

I list here the abbreviations used in the text and the works to which they refer, followed by the date(s) that best reflect when the book was actually written and the publication information for the English translations. Note that instead of a date, the German *The Will to Power* is designated by (PH). This reflects the fact that this text not only was not published by Nietzsche, but was assembled from his notebooks by others after his death. *Thus Spake Zarathustra* was written, in four parts, between 1883 and 1885, but while the first three books appeared during Nietzsche's lifetime, it was not published in the form we have it today, with a fourth part, until after Nietzsche's death. Finally, *Dithyrambs of Dionysus* are poems written throughout Nietzsche's life and assembled by him in 1888.

Nietzsche's Texts

AC   *Der Antichrist* 1888: *The Antichrist*. Translated by R. J. Hollingdale. London: Penguin Books, 1990.

BG   *Jenseits von Gut und Böse* 1886: *Beyond Good and Evil*. Translated by Walter Kaufmann. New York: Vintage Books, 1989.

BT   *Der Geburt der Tragödie* 1872: *The Birth of Tragedy*. Translated by Walter Kaufmann. New York: Vintage Books, 1967.

D   *Morgenröte* 1881: *Dawn*. Translated by R. J. Hollingdale. Cambridge: Cambridge University Press, 1982.

DD   *Dionysos Dithyramben* 1888: *Dithyrambs of Dionysus*. Translated by R. J. Hollingdale. Redding Ridge, Conn.: Black Swan Books, 1984.

EH   *Ecce Homo* 1888. Translated by Walter Kaufmann. New York: Vintage Books, 1969.

GM   *Zur Genealogie der Moral* 1887: *On the Genealogy of Morals*. Translated by Walter Kaufmann and R. J. Hollingdale. New York: Vintage Books, 1969.

GS   *Die fröhliche Wissenschaft* 1882 (Part 5, 1887): *The Gay Science*. Translated by Walter Kaufmann. New York: Vintage Books, 1974.

HH   *Menschliches, Allzumenschliches* 1878: *Human, All too Human*. Translated by R. J. Hollingdale. Cambridge: Cambridge University Press, 1986.

NC   *Nietzsche contra Wagner* 1888. Translated by Walter Kaufmann, in *The Portable Nietzsche*. New York: Viking Penguin, 1954.

PTG *Die Philosophie im tragischen Zeitalter der Griechen* 1873: *Philosophy in the Tragic Age of the Greeks*. Translated by Marianne Cowen. Washington, D.C.: Regnery Publishing, 1962.

SP   *Nietzsche, A Self-Portrait in His Letters*. Edited by Peter Fuss and Henry Shapiro. Cambridge, Mass.: Harvard University Press, 1971.

SW   *Sämtliche Werke. Kritische Studienausgabe in 15 Bänden*. Edited by G. Colli and M. Montinari. Berlin: de Gruyter, 1980.

TI   *Götzen-Dämmerung* 1888: *Twilight of the Idols*. Translated by R. J. Hollingdale. London: Penguin Books, 1990.

UM   *Unzeitmässige Betrachtungen* 1873–76: *Untimely Meditations*. Translated by R. J. Hollingdale. Cambridge: Cambridge University Press.

WP   *Der Wille zur Macht* (PH): *The Will to Power*. Translated by Walter Kaufmann and R. J. Hollingdale. New York: Vintage Books, 1968.

Z   *Also Sprach Zarathustra* 1883–85: *Thus Spake Zarathustra*. Translated by Walter Kaufmann. London: Penguin Books, 1978.

CONTESTING SPIRIT

Introduction

NIETZSCHE AND RELIGION

> If we are to think anew it must be from a new stance, one
> essentially unfamiliar to us; or, say, from a further perspective
> that is uncontrollable by us.
> (Stanley Cavell, "Time after Time")

IN 1886, at the height of his powers as writer and thinker, Friedrich
Nietzsche wrote a series of prefaces for new editions of his early
works.[1] As autobiography, they embellish the plain facts of his life;
as philosophy, they say more about what Nietzsche was thinking in 1886
than about the early texts with which they are concerned. Still, they disclose a vibrant and paradoxical vision of Nietzsche as a thinker. Read
together, the new prefaces narrate the trajectory of Nietzsche's writing
and thinking as a life that transpired between hopeless disillusion and the
joy of love's recovery. In the new preface to *The Gay Science*, Nietzsche
exults in "the saturnalia of a spirit who has patiently resisted a terrible,
long pressure—patiently, severely, coldly, without submitting, but also
without hope—and who is now all at once attacked by hope, the hope
for health, and the *intoxication* of convalescence" (GS: 32). Here, and
throughout his writing, Nietzsche imagines philosophy as a practice of
shaping a life—as the struggles and failures and ecstatic surges of energy—
that turned him from the malaise of idealism through myriad dark nights
and toward the reaches of an impassioned health.

Perhaps the greatest modern critic of religion, Nietzsche would with
these prefaces subtly activate the conventions of classic religious narratives: the discovery of a deep-seated sickness unto death; scales falling
from eyes; brave and bleak periods of isolation; daily martyrdoms; the
bite of hard-heartedness, of discipline and desire; the flaming spirit; and,
finally, the grace of renewal where one finds one's life and one's world

---

Epigraph: Cavell 1995: 6.

[1] Nietzsche wrote prefaces for new editions of the following: *The Birth of Tragedy*, originally published in 1872; *Human, All too Human*, first published in 1878; *Dawn*, published
in 1881; and *The Gay Science*, published in 1882. Having finished *Thus Spake Zarathustra*
in 1884, Nietzsche published *Beyond Good and Evil* in 1885, the prefaces and the remarkable fifth book of *The Gay Science* in 1886, and *On the Genealogy of Morals*
in 1887.

transformed. If one reads Nietzsche carefully, one finds throughout all his writing a glancing equivocation between religion and antireligion. From the romanticism of *The Birth of Tragedy* through the cold "chemistry" of *Human, All too Human*, and *Dawn*, to the rapture of *The Gay Science* and "no-saying" of his final works, Nietzsche led a philosophical life that resisted the religious traditions that have shaped Western civilization only at the same time that he accomplished a transformative renewal of their disciplines and passions.

Since the early 1960s in France, and a decade or so later in the United States, scores of books and articles have been published on Nietzsche's thought and life. For a thinker who brazenly transgressed modern disciplinary boundaries, it is not surprising that these studies have emerged from a wide range of academic fields, and from between fields, including philosophy, literary criticism, political science, sociology, and women's studies. Some commentators continue to elaborate the existentialist, anti-Christian Nietzsche—the Nietzsche of the will to power and eternal recurrence—familiar since the turn of the century.[2] Many others, however, have explored the multiple faces of the "new Nietzsche." This Nietzsche is the prototype of the postmodern thinker/writer, writing on the boundaries of academic discourse, flaunting his extravagant style, and sweeping away the renunciatory ethic—the "spirit of gravity"—that has tied Western thought to metaphysics and religion.[3] For still another group of commentators, finally, neither the old nor the new Nietzsche offers anything to celebrate. Few figures in the tradition of Western thought have aroused as much antipathy as Nietzsche has. From the beginning of this century, defenders of Western cultural, philosophical, and religious traditions have pointed to Nietzsche as the most visible symptom, or even a source, of the decline of Western culture. For them, Nietzsche's relativism contributes to the undermining of any coherent sense of the value of Western cultural traditions, and his apparent reduction of reason to interest and power supports the politically dangerous antihumanism of postmodern thought.[4]

His work having been scrutinized from almost every imaginable perspective and from radically different intellectual commitments, it is surprising how, in at least one respect, the same Nietzsche reappears so often in the secondary literature: most commentators—modernists and postmodernists, supporters and detractors alike—agree that Nietzschean suspicion and Nietzschean affirmation are definitive modes of antireligious

[2] Walter Kaufmann's (1974) remains the most influential interpretation along these lines. Karl Jaspers's (1961) *Nietzsche and Christianity* is less influential (though it was instrumental for Kaufmann) but is superior to Kaufmann's on the issues of Christianity and religion.

[3] See Deleuze 1983, Nehamas 1985, and Allison 1985.

[4] See Habermas 1986, MacIntyre 1984, and Bloom 1987.

thought.[5] On this point, the new Nietzsche is the same as the old. Not without good reason, of course, for Nietzsche's polemics against religious consolation and illusion mark him as one of modernity's foremost despisers of religion. However, as Friedrich Schleiermacher reminded his contemporaries at the beginning of the nineteenth century, it is one thing to be a cultured despiser of religion and another thing to think and write without or beyond religion. I suggest that if we move too quickly from Nietzsche's attacks on religion to assimilate him to modern secularism, as most of his commentators do—the gesture is now almost automatic—we miss a great deal of his complexity, and we fail to think carefully about religion. Such assimilation may be useful as a blunt hermeneutical instrument for various ideological and polemical interests: for committed secularists with a furious view of the degradations of religious life; or for defenders of the faith who can point to Nietzsche's ideas on power and morality to demonstrate the dark logic of secular modernity. But such assimilation fails to think *with* Nietzsche, for it does not think with sufficient genealogical self-consciousness; it does not adequately resist the temptation to position Nietzsche rather than follow the dynamic movement of his thought; and it fails to recognize that to think with Nietzsche is to think against him.

The Question of Religion

The place of religion in Nietzsche's writing begs to be reexamined. Nietzsche announces the death of God, but with Dionysus, the eternal return, and affirmation, he invokes a new spiritual sensibility—a new reverence, a new joy—that has yet to be fully explored by his interpreters. Even if it is undeniable that Nietzsche is highly critical of a certain religiosity—which he sometimes, but not always, equates with "religion" in general—and regardless of how we want to view Nietzsche's "final" conception of religion (whatever "final" might mean for a thinker like Nietzsche), his thought suggests ways to distance ourselves from the ossi-

---

[5] This is not to say that commentators never remark on a certain spiritual, prophetic, or even religious pathos in Nietzsche's thought. But even among those who do, very few studies have treated this aspect of Nietzsche's thought in any real depth, and most seem satisfied that this sensibility has little impact on the overall anti-religious nature of his ideas. Exceptions are Jaspers 1961 and, more recently, Valadier 1975 and Figl 1984. There remains no sustained examination of the issue in English. Stambaugh 1994 examines some of the mystical tendencies of Nietzsche's writing and Makarushka 1994 offers an analysis of religious language in some of Nietzsche's texts. Neither study, however, undertakes a detailed and comprehensive exploration of the problem of religion in Nietzsche. There are a number of theological thinkers who find Nietzsche a valuable resource for postmodern religious thought, though they also have not supplied any detailed studies of Nietzsche's thought. See especially Altizer and Hamilton 1966, Taylor 1984, Winquist 1995, and Raschke 1996.

fied conceptual dichotomy so instrumental for modernity: secular/religious. In this book, I endeavor to specify a certain equivocation in Nietzsche's writing between religion and antireligion, the religious and the secular. My purpose is not to ease the strains or difficulties caused by this equivocation. It is, rather, to ask whether these equivocations might be regarded as productive, helping us to gain more insight into Nietzsche's thought and, in addition, to gain more insight into ourselves by offering us an opportunity to explore the meaning of religion at the end of the twentieth century.

We cannot understand Nietzsche, in other words, without questioning the way we depend upon the construct of "religion" in order to order and settle our world, and within it, the modern study of religion.[6] This is a book about Nietzsche, but it is also an exercise in what Jonathan Z. Smith has called "imagining religion" (1982). Imagining and reimagining religion becomes a particularly important task not just as new forms of spiritual life emerge, but as scholars of religion become more and more aware of the degree to which "religion" is a construct of modern Western thought. As various genealogies of religion have shown, *religion* is a word with a history, in the course of which it has taken on specific meanings in specific contexts. Most important for my purposes here, *religion* is a word that took shape in the medieval and modern periods as, first, the Christian Church exerted its authority to distinguish Christian practices as "true religion" from paganism, and then, second, as early modern political thinkers, scientists, and philosophers sought to distinguish the religious from the secular.[7] Especially with respect to the latter, *religion* as a noun rather than an adjective comes to the fore to refer to cultural complexes marked by rituals, beliefs, books, and gods. The word takes its modern meaning at the intersection of the encounter between Christianity and what came to be called "other religions," and between Christianity and the antitraditional and naturalistic impulses of modernity. It is enmeshed, therefore, with issues of power, politics, and culture as it is deployed to mark these differences.[8] *Religion* becomes a highly charged term, playing a crucial role in negotiating giant encounters and shifts of worldviews, the ramifications of which are felt in the very way we understand modernity, enlightenment, progress, pluralism, and tradition.

[6] In *Desiring Theology*, Charles Winquist states, "Secular discourse has to risk wandering out of mind if it is to let go of reductionistic strategies" (1995: 43).

[7] See the accounts of W. C. Smith 1978, Robert Markus 1990, and Talal Asad 1993.

[8] Asad criticizes the "insistence that religion has an autonomous essence" and wonders, with a heavy dose of irony, whether it is "a happy accident that this effort of defining religion converges with the liberal demand in our time that it be kept quite separate from politics, law, and science—spaces in which varieties of power and reason articulate our distinctively modern life." He also points out that it can be a strategy on the part of liberal Christians for defending religion (1993: 28).

Religion, therefore, has meant different things at different times to different people. And it has meant nothing at all—because it could not be translated into their language—for many others whom modern Westerners, without hesitation, call "religious." This is not to imply that such people are not religious, or that the word somehow falsifies their reality—though this danger is a real one. It is to say, instead, that to the extent that "religion" is a category that human beings in the West have constructed for exploring and understanding their world, they should strive to be self-conscious about how they use it. We should ask what these particular categories have allowed us to see, think, do, and imagine—and we should consider the ways in which they may have blinded us to other possibilities of understanding and experiencing.

Nietzsche plays a significant role in the genealogy of religion, through his own criticisms of religion and through the assimilation of his thought to the ideology of secularization. The rhetoric of this ideology makes it easy for most readers to identify religion in Nietzsche's texts as the embodiment of a nihilism to be overcome; in turn, this makes it difficult to see that the questions he raises and the possibilities he imagines are far more complex than is allowed by a simplistic reading of the pronouncement, "God is dead," which Nietzsche made in *The Gay Science* (GS: 167, 181). Often the consequence of ignoring the question of religion is to force Nietzsche into a secularizing and/or philosophizing mode that misses deep tensions in his thought and the deep resonance of Greco-Roman and Christian ideas and practices that pervade his imagination—whether he acknowledges it or not. It is interesting, for example, that so many interpreters of Nietzsche assume that the "religious" has simply a negative place in his thought, while "art" and "philosophy" hold places of honor. In fact, from his earliest writings, Nietzsche problematized each of these categories. Though it is true that he was more generally critical of religion than of philosophy or art, Nietzsche sought to subvert and reimagine each of them, looking ahead to new philosophers, new artists—and even new saints (GS: 346). He did so in such a way that, properly speaking, what emerges from his thinking is not "philosophy," "art," or "religion" in the modern senses of these terms, but something else, something Nietzsche never really named. However, by reintroducing the complex of ideas and practices that the concept *religion* allows us to deploy, and by critically interrogating this concept, one can follow the complexity of Nietzsche's vision with more precision than a simply secular reading affords.

Religion and Affirmation

Nietzsche's madman declares the death of God, and his Zarathustra urges his disciples to "remain true to the earth." But those who mock the madman are those "who did not believe in God." And Nietzsche's "earth" is not simply the ordinary, disenchanted world as experienced by the "men of today" whom Zarathustra dismisses as "sterile," "incapable of faith," and "unbelievable" (Z: 120). Neither the madman nor Zarathustra feels at home with such unbelievers precisely because they are too much at home in their modern malaise. They have not understood or been willing to experience the full force of the madman's pronouncement because it demands a far greater engagement with life than they can imagine. They refuse the true message of the death of God: the end of the illusory ideal that has hidden a deathlike despiritualization of humanity and the difficult demand to affirm the homelessness implicated in the death of God. In fact, where the death of God is both terrifying and exhilarating for the madman, to the "men of today" it is old news, like all news.

But even if the madman means something far more profound than those unbelievers can grasp, if, in some significant sense, God is dead, how does the category *religion* help us to understand Nietzsche?

The rejection of the moral cosmos implicated in Nietzsche's pronouncement of God's death is a hard teaching, for it means that human beings must confront a certain blankness, or muteness, in the fabric of the universe. This elicits different responses. One might fall into a despairing nihilism that yearns nostalgically for some ultimate grounding or meaning—as Nietzsche, at times, seemed tempted to do. Or, granting this impossibility, one might embrace the modern humanist self-assertion that appears indifferent to metaphysical grounds and offers human foundations instead—whether scientific progress, moral autonomy, or social consensus. But this too, for Nietzsche, is ultimately nihilistic. He points in a different direction, affirming the meaninglessness of the universe without existentialist angst, modernist self-assertion, or postmodern indifference. In the will to power—in life itself—Nietzsche finds what he calls "the affirmation of life" or "the eternal joy of becoming." To the extent that the will to power is simply the pulse of striving, amoral, endless life, however, he finds joy only at the same time that he encounters a deep anonymity and insecurity. The Nietzschean philosopher must bring him- or herself to the edge of the abyss of meaninglessness, and there must learn to dance. Such dancing, writes Nietzsche, is the philosopher's "ideal," "art," and "finally his only piety" (GS: 346). This dance proclaims a "faith" (GS: 340) that holds gracefully the affirmative tension between joy and meaninglessness. This is not faith as blithe assurance or even as fear and trembling—it is the affirmation of holiness without familiarity, and life without consolation.

Again, if God is dead, what kind of "faith" are we talking about? In some respects, it is a relatively simple matter to define religion in terms of the belief in gods; that is, in terms of superhuman beings that exist independently of human beings, are not accessible to them in the same way natural phenomena are, and exert some kind of control over or influence on them. If we define religion and gods in this way, then I think there would be little debate that Nietzsche is an atheist and an enemy of religion. But scholars of religion are not at all in agreement that religion always has to do with gods as they have just been defined, either because scholars want to include as "religions" nontheistic traditions (Theravada Buddhism, for example, generally has been understood to be nontheistic), or because the concept *god*, when considered carefully, can be just as difficult to pin down as the concept *religion*. One response to this difficulty has been to define religion not in terms of gods, but, more abstractly, in terms of a kind of experience of ultimate or divine force, the "Holy" or the "Sacred." But what actually constitutes such experience has been notoriously hard to define.[9] As Ninian Smart (1979) argues, it is not clear that descriptions of religious experience that focus on an "Other" that exists over against one, or that descriptions of some power, even if not personalized as a god, account for all kinds of religious experience.

Even in contexts where gods or other superhuman entities are invoked, it is a mistake to assume automatically that they are "believed in" in the sense of propositional statements about the existence of certain kinds of beings. Such an assumption leads one to reduce the mythical, literary, and ritualistic use of god language and symbol to the propositional language of doctrine. Even Nietzsche's writing, in spite of the madman's declaration, is full of the language of the divine: apart from criticizing Christian notions of God, he writes of feeling divine, of creating gods, of Dionysus. Following the protocols of modern critical thought, it might be easy to dismiss the language of divinity in Nietzsche as merely metaphor or as a poeticizing of all-too-human psychological states. But, from Nietzsche's perspective, I will argue, this reduction to the psychological is simply one more form of dogmatism, one that fails to understand the power and the source of metaphor and poetry. As numerous commentators have contended, even "body" and "psyche" are metaphors for Nietzsche, ways of tracing the boundaries of human life and human knowledge. From this perspective, the language of the divine in Nietzsche serves to designate neither independently existing beings or forces, nor "mere" projections that can be traced to foundational psychic causes. Instead, such language traces the unrepresentable limits of the human, emerging in the practice and experience of these limits.

Whether or not religion has to do with gods or other superhuman forces or experiences, many scholars of religion treat it primarily in terms of its social function, where religious beliefs are a reflection of social values or

[9] For a more detailed criticism of the category of the Sacred, and its place in the study of religion, see Penner 1989.

meanings and religious rituals are the means by which these binding forces are affirmed. Karl Marx and Emile Durkheim offer two prominent examples of this approach. Nietzsche, too, can be read this way: thus, the madman's bewildered, frightened gloss on his pronouncement of God's death: "Are we not straying as though through an infinite nothing? Do we not feel the breath of empty space?" (GS: 181). After the death of God, in other words, there is no longer anything to hold us together, or hold us in place, and so circumscribe our world as a meaningful one: Where will we find meaning? What shall we value? If we view religion as a force for stabilizing social meaning, the death of God as Nietzsche understands it would mean the end of religion. Robert Torrance has recently argued, however, following anthropologists such as Victor Turner, that religion and ritual are creative forces, not simply serving to reinforce already existing values, meanings, or social structures, but anticipating new ones and so making possible the transformation of both community and individual: "Religion reveals the intrinsic incompleteness of all human attainments by holding out the possibility of an order transcending the approximative actual: the indispensable if unreachable goal of an all-encompassing nomos, all-embracing communitas" (1994: 15). If we think about religion and ritual in terms of such transformation of meaning, instead of simply its maintenance, and if we adjust for Torrance's totalizing language, then we might be better prepared to note the ritualistic tones of Nietzsche's madman: "What was holiest and mightiest of all that the world has yet owned has bled to death under our knives: who will wipe this blood off us? What water is there for us to clean ourselves? What festivals of atonement, what sacred games shall we have to invent?" (GS: 181).

There is something common to these approaches to religion, even if we acknowledge the doubts about the centrality of gods or stabilizing human meaning, value, and community. In both cases, there is an orientation to transcendence: thus Smart argues that the most we can say in trying to define religion along these lines is to employ the rather general idea of the "transcendentally unseen" as that with which religious myths, concepts, and rituals typically deal. In various ways, and to varying degrees of intensity, religious belief and practices point us beyond the manifest, even the meaningful world in ways that can either legitimize it or relativize it, or both (1979: 34). I would add to this, however, by qualifying the idea of the "transcendentally unseen" with the idea of "truth" or "reality." Relating to that which is unseen, human beings, in some sense or another, relate themselves to what is ultimately true, or ultimately meaningful, or salvific. Religion involves discourses and practices that attend to the limits of the human in the cultivation of the fullness of human life: religion brings us to the limits, the "borderland" of what is us and what is not.[10] As they say to the man with the blue guitar, in the poem by Wallace Stevens: "But play, you must,/A tune beyond us, yet ourselves,/A tune upon the blue guitar/Of things exactly as they are" (1982:165).

I highlight this common factor in two influential but problematic approaches to the study of religion not in order to assert a new essence of religion by salvaging something common from them, but to indicate, heuristically, a point of linkage between Nietzsche's thought and the way religion in the West has been imagined. As writer and thinker, Nietzsche finds himself at the limits of the human in his effort to imagine and practice an affirmative humanity. Paraphrasing Clement Rosset, one way to describe affirmation is as an unconditional commitment to the real and the practice of continually reorienting oneself to it (1993: 25). For Nietzsche, the "real" is not "merely" the world we find in front of us in our daily, ordinary lives. Instead, "reality" is this world experienced through the transfiguring awareness of the becoming, shifting flux or chaos "beyond" the world we ordinarily perceive and think. Again, Stevens writes: "Things as they are/Are changed upon the blue guitar." Nietzsche seeks to intensify the awareness of the flux of life by living life as "becoming": in this awareness exists a connection with the power of life, which finds its force in the tension between the organizing, shaping forces of language and culture and the unlimited striving of will to power.

Some of the most poetic and reverential writing in Nietzsche is to be found in passages expressing, discussing, imagining an affirmative life, a life that refuses to shrink before life's demands and sufferings but embraces them with love and joy. It is here that we need to think seriously about how Western religious traditions offer paradigms that can help us understand, through contrast and comparison, Nietzsche's affirmative project. And it is here, I argue, that we find resources in Nietzsche for reimagining religion. For if we acknowledge the valid objections to casting traditions and spiritual virtuosos commonly called "religious" in terms of belief in God or gods, or in terms of faith in the ultimate salvation

---

[10] J. Z. Smith argues that when we study religion, we are studying "one mode of constructing worlds of meaning . . . the passion and the drama of man discovering the truth of what it is to be human." He goes on to say that "religion is the quest, within the bounds of the human, historical condition, for the power to manipulate and negotiate one's 'situation' so as to have 'space' in which to meaningfully dwell . . . [and] so as to guarantee the conviction that one's existence 'matters.' Religion is a distinctive mode of human creativity, a creativity which both discovers limits and creates limits for humane existence . . . through the use of myths, rituals and experiences of transformation" (1993: 290–91). George Steiner claims that one of the two main senses of religion is "a root-impulse of the human spirit to explore possibilities of meaning and of truth that lie outside empirical seizure or proof." (1989: 225).

of the individual beyond his or her worldly, temporal life, then we might consider Nietzsche's affirmation as a form of reverence. This is surely not an "otherworldly" faith, but one that cultivates the passionate, eternal affirmation in and of this life through a certain—both critical and affirmative—practice of the limit of the human. Nietzsche does not "believe," but he performs a worshipful dance that exemplifies Emerson's dictum: "Let a man learn . . . to bear the disappearance of things he was wont to reverence without losing his reverence" (1982: 336).

Affirmation, Negation, Nihilism

Nietzsche's reputation as a despiser of the otherworldly promises of religion is well deserved. His deft and merciless unmasking of the need for power and consolation at the root of religious life has exerted enormous influence on philosophical, psychological, and sociological studies of religion. Of course, such unmasking by itself does not necessarily make one an antireligious thinker, for many past "masters of suspicion" have been passionately religious—one need think only of the prophets of the Hebrew Bible, or, more recently, prophetic theologians, such as Kierkegaard and Karl Barth.[11] But of course Nietzsche is not simply suspicious of the reasons some people embrace religion; he connects Christianity and religion, God, worship, and faith with the nihilistic hatred of life. He rejects belief in God and most other forms of community, ritual, and reverence generally associated with the religious life. His reasons for this are various; most importantly, he finds that religion has been one of the most potent sources of the "denial of life" that has infected humankind.

In this respect, as so many have noted, Nietzsche exhibits affinities with other modern unmaskers of religious illusion, such as Marx and Freud.[12] But these affinities are limited by a crucial difference. Marx and Freud sought to guide human beings to a more rational conduct of life by enlightening them about their irrationality. What makes them distinctively modern is that they sought to ground their unmaskings "scientifically," by isolating the material codes or mechanisms by which human society or the human psyche works. Marx thought the way to the future was opened by demystifying human social and economic relations; Freud, despite a certain resignation, was relentless in asserting the need for the mastery of Logos and ego. Nietzsche, however, was more ambivalent than either with respect to the modern project of enlightenment. He did not reject the value of enlightenment, but he insisted on its limits, and on the

---

[11] See Westphal 1993.

[12] See Paul Ricoeur's famous characterization of Freud, Marx, and Nietzsche as "masters of suspicion" (1970: 32).

value of cultivating attention to these limits and to that which lies beyond them. As such, Nietzsche was as suspicious of the modern idealization of rationality, and its humanistic faith in enlightenment, as he was of metaphysical values, religion, and morality.

It is precisely at this point that many commentators, whether they are persuaded or not by Nietzsche's analysis, find Nietzsche's own thought nihilistic.[13] And it is true that a certain groundlessness seems to haunt all Nietzsche's attempts to put forward positive claims or "solutions." Nietzsche veered from the humanistic ideals of modernity with a groundless—"abyssal"—suspicion that refused to anchor itself in reason, science, and/or morality. Some critics accuse Nietzsche of moral or epistemological nihilism; others go further to argue that such nihilism, paired with his glorification of power, culminates in a sort of monstrous fascism—or in French postmodernism. And, indeed, despite his claims to be an affirmative thinker, it is impossible to ignore the fact that there is much about this existence that Nietzsche despised and from which he yearned to be free; denial and negation played such a formative role in his thought and rhetoric that they at times smothered the affirmative impulse. Nietzsche denounced the mediocrity and bankruptcy of Western culture; he ridiculed the moral thinkers of his day and of past generations; he honored the Dionysian "joy in destruction"; he exhibited an unapologetic streak of misogyny, and he expressed disgust at humankind in general: he was, in many respects, a vituperative naysayer. At times, there seems to be little about human life that Nietzsche was able to affirm except possibly the strength that allowed him to endure in his misanthropic solitude.

Nietzsche himself, however, insisted on a close, even paradoxical relation in his thought between negation and nihilism on the one hand, and affirmation on the other. Zarathustra proclaims, "Deeply I love only life—and verily most of all when I hate it" (Z: 109); and he preaches that the creation of new values requires both a "sacred 'No'" and a "sacred 'Yes'" (Z: 27).[14] Tensions between love and hate, yes and no, hope and despair, meaning and nihilism strain the problem of affirmation in Nietzsche's thinking. How does one affirm life in the depths of abyssal suspicion? How does one simultaneously affirm life and demand that it be transformed? How does one love life in hating it? When Nietzsche distanced himself from both the metaphysical traditions of religion and the critical modernity exemplified by Marx and Freud, he was one of the first Western

---

[13] See, for example, Milbank 1990. Although I disagree with some of his conclusions about the echo of idealism in Nietzsche, the best work on Nietzsche and nihilism is in Gillespie, *Nihilism Before Nietzsche* (1995).

[14] Nietzsche also asserts that "the desire for *destruction*, change, and becoming can be an expression of an overflowing energy that is pregnant with future" (GS: 329).

thinkers to think the postmodern, or, in what might be a less loaded and more precise term, the *postcritical*. Like Freud, Nietzsche undertook what Paul Ricoeur describes as an *"ascesis* of the necessary." But unlike so many modern thinkers, Nietzsche refused to stop with the critical, demystifying move and insisted on the affirmative embrace of life: where Freud commends a stoic resignation in the face of the necessary, Nietzsche imagines affirmation as the ecstatic, joyful embrace of a life that holds no hope for metaphysical salvation. In *Zarathustra*, and also later, in more critical and somber writings, life is loved and praised, even revered: not simply accepted or nobly borne. What enabled Nietzsche to make the move to affirmation instead of resignation?

The question of the relation of negation and affirmation in Nietzsche is not solved simply by invoking the historical labor of the negative, whether through Hegelian or Marxist dialectic, or through the struggle of a quasi-Darwinistic evolution. Metaphysical morality and religion are, for Nietzsche, responses to the problem of existence that promise to solve the problem once and for all. Yet, it is precisely in this attempt to find a *solution* to existence that, for Nietzsche, nihilism is most clearly and dangerously manifested. In the final analysis, Nietzsche's critical attack on religion—which gains its full force as an attack on Christianity—is secondary to his confrontation with nihilism. As I explain in the first chapter, for Nietzsche nihilism is rooted in the attempt to ground and secure one's being, to master it in a way that excludes boredom, suffering, and tragedy. But this grasp for mastery is self-defeating, for in the end it leaves one with nothing: unable to acknowledge the reality of this world of suffering, one puts one's faith in something beyond the real (for instance God or Truth), in what for Nietzsche literally is *nothing*.

The dynamic of Nietzsche's thought is one that continually prevents us from holding too tightly to any perspective, any ideal, any meaning. Some of the most profound suffering in human life arises for Nietzsche precisely in confronting the fact that any definitive meaning of life continually escapes our grasp. He presents this poetically, if not philosophically, with his idea of eternal recurrence. Eternal recurrence signals the definitive rejection of an economy of redemption that would give life meaning by offering an ultimate meaning for suffering. Affirmation, as Nietzsche's response to nihilism, is not a kind of salvation in the sense of a solution or justification of the difficulties and pain of human existence. Nietzsche imagined an affirmation that eschews the need for promises of paradise or purity, certainty and security—or even more mundane promises of "improvement" or "progress." For him, the problem of affirmation becomes the problem of how we affirm a life without the hope that the negative—evil and suffering—will slowly wither away to nothing. To affirm life only in the hope that we are able to end suffering—or to affirm life only from the perspective of that goal ("it was difficult, but it was worth it")—is not to affirm *this* life.

Nietzsche thinks, therefore, that we must embrace a certain meaning-lessness, a certain muteness in existence, instead of wishing it or thinking it away with "solutions" such as God or Truth; nihilism, he contends, can be a "divine way of thinking." But such divine nihilism must be contrasted with the exhausted, life-hating nihilism of the Western tradition. As he explored the nihilism of modernity and imagined a joy that transcends the rational ego-centered consciousness, Nietzsche's thinking recovered certain religious concepts and practices. His ambivalence toward modernity is mirrored by an essentially ambivalent attitude toward religion. It is possible to specify the ways in which Nietzsche saw specific forms of religion implicated with nihilism; but it also is possible to then highlight those aspects of religious life that Nietzsche continues to affirm and to specify certain forms of religious life that help us illuminate Nietzsche's "Yes and amen" to life.

Philosophy as Spiritual Practice

Nietzsche was convinced that philosophy as he knew it in nineteenth-century Germany was one of the many symptoms of nihilism. He sought therefore to transfigure philosophy, in part by looking to its past. When he writes of himself as a philosopher, or about the philosophers he imagines for the future, Nietzsche's model is not the respected academic philosopher of the Kantian or Hegelian tradition, but the ancient philosopher, whom Nietzsche the philologist and classicist had studied closely. For ancient philosophers, philosophy was enmeshed in regimens and practices of life and spirit: it was "a way of life," as Bernard McGinn puts it, "more than a mode of discourse" (1995: 63). Working with this ancient model, Nietzsche writes a new, embodied philosophy, one that is both more passionate and more literary than the philosophy of his time. As with so many of the dichotomies central to modern thought—like the "religious" and the "secular"—Nietzsche interrogates and unsettles the distinction between the philosophical and the literary, between theory and practice, and between writing as argument and writing as performance. The philosopher for Nietzsche is a shaper of self and culture. Like the figure of the ascetic saint, with which Nietzsche was so fascinated, the philosopher is a figure that represents, in body, soul, and practice—not simply in thought or text—the powers and possibilities of human life.

The complexity of Nietzsche's thought and style demands flexibility with respect to the methodological resources one brings to bear on his texts. Nietzsche is a thinker who calls us to see things in a new way and in doing so tears down many of the concepts and methods we use to view and understand our world. This causes certain problems for the reader, especially since Nietzsche gleefully uses categories and concepts at the same time that he is denouncing them. He writes, in many respects, against himself. This suggests the limitations of a hermeneutic strategy that would be satisfied with the univocal philosophical determination of his concepts and arguments. To borrow from contemporary deconstructive criticism, the necessity emerges out of Nietzsche's own thinking to read him against the grain of closure. When confronted with Nietzsche's contradictions, or evasions, or metaphors, it is not enough just to attempt to make his thinking cohere or to conclude that he was confused. One must also ask, what is he doing by writing this way? Or, how is he performing? In part, my reading of Nietzsche rests on the claim that he enacts affirmation precisely in undermining philosophy as he considers it to have been established in the West since Socrates. Nietzsche's abyssal suspicion is not, from this perspective, a failure of intellect or a misguided nihilism, but a practice of self-resistance through which Nietzsche is able to write an affirmative joy. Philosophy, as Nietzsche understands it, is a spiritual path *of* (not simply *to*) affirmation, the only path he sees available for those of us living in the West at the end of modernity. The possibility of affirmation rests on something beyond philosophical investigations and justifications, for affirmation wells from out of the body as much as from the mind, compelling one to live vibrantly rather than assuredly. Ultimately, Nietzsche does not simply discuss and analyze affirmation philosophically; instead, he exemplifies affirmation in his philosophical practice, in a performance of an ecstatic, figurative, affirmative thinking and writing.

There are significant dimensions of Nietzsche's thought that come into view only when we treat his work as the expression of a spiritual practice. I use the term *spiritual* with some hesitation, which emerges directly from the questions of religion this book seeks to address. Used with some specificity, the term can be helpful. For example, Pierre Hadot (1995) has defined the *spiritual* as a person's "whole way of being"—the existential unity of intellect, emotion, and psyche—and *spiritual exercise* as a process of self-transformation and reorientation of this existential unity. This definition helps us distinguish, for instance, between the spirit and the psyche or the spiritual and the psychological. *Spirit* indicates something more comprehensive than *psyche*: cultivating the spiritual, a person opens him- or herself to something beyond the psychological unity we refer to as the personal self. To be spiritual, in this sense, is not simply to be well integrated within oneself and one's community, but to be able to view oneself and one's web of interpersonal relationships from a perspective of "not-self," a perspective from which one can be forced to resist and seek to transform certain aspects of self and community. As David Halperin glosses Hadot, the "spiritual self" is "not the locus of a unique and private psychological depth (on the model of bourgeois humanism) but the side of a radical alterity: it is the space within each human being where she or he encounters the not-self, the beyond" (1995: 75).[15]

In this sense, the term *spirit* is important for understanding Nietzsche, who makes great use of the concept *Geist*, the German word most often translated by the English word *spirit*. At times, Nietzsche uses *Geist* to refer to mind, intellect, or consciousness. But he also uses it in a more open, dynamic sense to identify one of the most important ways in which the "will to power" increases in the human being through a certain capacity for self-reflexivity and self-resistance: spirit, in this sense, is something by which life "cuts into itself" in order to grow into strength and beauty. Moreover, when Nietzsche writes that philosophy is the "most spiritual will to power" (*der geistigste Will zur Macht*; SW 5: 22), he says something more about spirit and about philosophy. In and through the capacity for self-reflection and self-cultivation, one's whole being becomes stronger. And I will argue that "stronger" in this case means far more than the power to manipulate or control; it means "beautiful" and "exemplary." The powerful self is one that shines. Philosophy, then, is for Nietzsche more than an academic discipline: it is a practice by which he cultivates, strengthens, and beautifies the self and its relationship to the world and cosmos; it is the spiritual exercise *par excellence*. Philosophy is the "art" of spiritual cultivation—or, to use Nietzsche's word, the art of *transfiguration* in which one continually refines and beautifies body and mind in the "spiritualization" of oneself. To be spiritual, for Nietzsche, is to learn to live in pain and paradox, even exacerbating these, with an affirmative intensity and celebration.

The terms *spirit* and *spiritual*, however, are not without their problems. In contemporary Western culture, many people use the word *spiritual* when they want to say something like *religious*, but cannot quite bring themselves to do it, largely because of the authoritarian, traditionalist, dogmatic connotations religion has for them, or because, in our naturalistic age, it is simply impossible for them to find any real meaning in a term like "God" or to believe in anything "supernatural." In addition, for good historical and conceptual reasons scholars tend to be wary of the term. The current use of "spiritual" owes much to the modern, Protestant attempt to distinguish the "faith" of a vibrant inner, "spiritual" life from the "religion" of dead dogmatic (read Catholic) tradition or rote ritual.

---

[15] Halperin's work is especially illuminating for the link it makes between the spiritual and the political. This use of "spiritual," and its implication with self-transformation and politics, is also conveyed by Iris Murdoch's term *moral*: "I can only choose within the world I can see, in the moral sense of 'see' which implies that clear vision is a result of moral imagination and moral effort" (1970: 37).

But then in contrasting the spiritual and the religious, it is easy to ignore the dogmatic roots of the former and lend support to a thin, problematic—and quintessentially modern—understanding of religion. As such, the term *spiritual* also reflects the rise of modern, Western individualism, based in the valorization of the autonomous, rational self for whom tradition and ritual can be nothing more than hindrances to the full, free development or realization of the self. Closely connected with such individualism is the modern split between the public and the private. Traditional religion, in the modern view, is dangerous in large part because it is public, and so threatens the autonomy of the political and economic realms. Spirituality, on the other hand, is private, and more easily avoids the temptations of public pronouncement and influence faced by modern institutional religion. With *spiritual*, then, one can point to something inward, profound, deeply or ultimately important; one can even invoke some sort of connection with a transhuman or divine reality, though not one that can be circumscribed or regulated in the institutional setting of a "religion"; one can distinguish (crudely) between a set of discourses, institutions, hierarchies, and practices, centered on the idea of God and functioning as a social authority or ideology, and a nondogmatic, nonauthoritarian commitment to the practice of self-transformation; one can contrast religion, tradition, and ritual as vehicles by which human beings close off and regulate human experience from spirituality, by which one cultivates a dynamic openness to experience.

These kinds of distinctions function polemically in Nietzsche's writing. Thus, he rails vehemently against Paul and the tradition of "Christianity," while, in the same pages, honoring Jesus as a "free spirit" who "stands outside all religion" (AC: 155). At the same time, though, it is easy to imagine Nietzsche scoffing at what "spirituality" has become today. Being spiritual today is easy; for Nietzsche becoming a free spirit was the most difficult thing a human being could undertake. Nietzsche loved the insouciance of the gay scientist, the lightness of dancing feet, the cheerfulness of the noble disregard for suffering—but he loved these not because they are ways of living free from severe discipline and deep suffering, but because they are the refined expressions of a life that is religiously passionate in its confrontation with life's difficulties. The problem with any sharp distinction between the religious and the spiritual, Nietzsche's included, is that it tends to rely on a distorted, one-sided view of religion, ignoring the close interweaving of discourses of authority and community on the one hand, and practices of self-transformation and piety on the other, that one finds in any religious tradition. As Robert Torrance has argued, the world's religious traditions are means by which human beings have negotiated the dialectic of openness and closure, dynamism and stability, both of which are necessary for meaningful, vibrant human life (1994: 261–

22). Throughout this book, then, I invoke the term *religious* pragmatically, in an effort to push the contemporary use of "spiritual" toward a balance between these two poles. Nietzsche too easily ignored the way in which religious traditions, especially Christianity, offer resources for the affirmation of spiritual searching and researching. The contemporary use of "spiritual" too easily ignores the difficulty, discipline, and structure that must be embraced in such a quest.

Asceticism and Mysticism

This study examines Nietzsche's philosophy in terms of the ascetic and mystical elements of Nietzsche's philosophical spiritual practice.[16] His joyous, Dionysian "dance of life" is grounded in intellectual and bodily disciplines that have close affinities and connections with the ascetical and mystical practices of Western religious traditions. Despite his vehement criticisms of the ascetic ideal and religious intoxication, Nietzsche cultivates an affirmative self in a transfiguration of ascetic and mystical practices. For example, certain forms of self-denial and discipline are central to Nietzsche's self-image as a philosopher: the quest for knowledge is based on the renunciation of much that is comfortable and peaceful in human life—particularly the renunciation of consolation—and his philosophical life is made possible by highly disciplined "practices of the self," which attend to the smallest details of body, mind, and will and to the intimate connections between nature, spirit, and culture. While Nietzsche criticizes Christianity for its life-denying "ascetic ideal," he sees philosophy as a kind of self-discipline and renunciation, which he describes as the "asceticism" of "the most spiritual human beings" (AC: 188). It might appear paradoxical that the affirmation Nietzsche celebrates could be based in the serious and painful labor of asceticism, which he so often denounced as an expression of the hatred of life. But Nietzsche recognized that the ascetic had discovered a key to power and spirit. Instead of repeating the paradigmatic gesture of the ascetic ideal by extirpating asceticism, Nietzsche refigured asceticism as an affirmative discipline of spiritualization.

Nietzsche's influence as an antireligious thinker has contributed to the specifically modern connotation of *asceticism* as a term of abuse, epitomizing the otherworldly, life-denying aspects not only of religion—Christianity in particular—but also of Western culture in general. Images of emaciated, verminous hermits or of parsimonious, repressed Puritans have been composed, with more or less subtlety, by great modern think-

---

[16] By writing about ascetic and mystical "elements," I want to avoid the ultimately uninteresting issue of whether Nietzsche is a mystic or an ascetic. I follow Bernard McGinn's example in his study of Christian mysticism (1994: xv–xvi).

ers, such as Rousseau, Weber, and Freud, in addition to Nietzsche. More recently, such images have been reactivated by postmodern and feminist thinkers who seek to celebrate the unrepressed body and desire. There is a strong correlation between the construction of asceticism as religious grotesque and the ideology of healthy, vibrant secularization. To put it crudely, the ascetic stands for repression and denial in an age when self-definition is understood to be a task of freeing oneself from such barriers to self-realization.

But some scholars have recently argued that it is a mistake to view all forms of asceticism as pathological phenomena. Instead, they suggest we think about asceticism as *ascesis*, as an empowering means of re-creating mind and body. Despite his role in the modern construction of asceticism, I argue that Nietzsche himself offers resources for such a rethinking of asceticism. By attending to the dynamic of self-denial and self-affirmation in the process of exercising a specific self, one begins to appreciate the kinetic relationships between "no" and "yes," suffering and affirmation, discipline and freedom that energize the uncanny "logic" of Nietzsche's thinking. Rethinking asceticism with and against Nietzsche means rethinking ourselves, engaging in a kind of spiritual discipline. In this way, this book is an attempt to indicate how Nietzsche calls us to such discipline.

Nietzsche's ascetic discipline is the means by which he cultivates certain practices of ecstasy crucial to his affirmative vision. In the book he valued above all his others, Nietzsche portrays Zarathustra as undergoing experiences of self-transcendence in which he realizes the joy of eternity, a joy that involves the affirmation of the necessity of worldly, suffering life.[17] In *Ecce Homo*, and scattered throughout his other works, Nietzsche invokes a kind of ecstatic thinking and writing constitutive of the restless logic of his philosophical style and method. In each of these cases, Nietzsche offers powerful reasons for bringing the lenses of mystical experience and mystical writing to bear on his work.

The study of mysticism offers another angle on the tension between affirmation and negation in Nietzsche. In the literature of certain Christian mystics one finds a paradoxical intertwining of joy and suffering that helps me to follow the links Nietzsche forges between suffering, ecstasy, and affirmation. Most accounts of Nietzsche's affirmation have either avoided his difficult attitude toward suffering, explained it away, or simply rejected it as perverse and ethically problematic. None have tried to explain it in terms of mystical transcendence and participation. Nietzsche views suffering as necessary for the cultivation of the noble soul; yet his affirmation of suffering is not merely instrumental, it is also ecstatic. That is, although he finds in suffering a certain kind of meaning for his own

---

[17] "So rich is joy that it thirsts for woe, for hell, for hatred, for disgrace, for the cripple, for world—this world, oh, you know it!" (Z: 323).

life, this meaning is inextricably bound up with a movement of self-transcendence that simultaneously renders the individual insignificant. There are some difficult epistemological and ethical questions involved here, which may be enlivened (if not answered) by displaying Nietzsche's consonance with mystical traditions. Like many mystics, Nietzsche's disposition to and for suffering composes a particular kind of responsiveness to the world and to others, what I will call a "passion for the real." I will argue that we need to suspend common and seemingly obvious ideas about action, command, and power in Nietzsche in order to take full measure of the kinds of responsiveness his philosophy articulates. His passion for the real is a strange and vibrant disposition, not far removed (though absent the theistic inflection) from what Simone Weil, herself a fierce opponent of Nietzsche's, describes as the "gift" of suffering: "Each time that we have some pain to go through, we can say to ourselves quite truly that it is the universe, the order, and beauty of the world and the obedience of creation to God that are entering our body. After that how can we fail to bless with tenderest gratitude the Love that sends us this gift? Joy and suffering are two equally precious gifts both of which must be savored to the full" (1951: 131–22).

Questioning Religion, Questioning Nietzsche

I utilize historical and theoretical studies of asceticism and mysticism to generate a novel hermeneutical approach to Nietzsche's writing. Although I rely on current scholarship to argue that we need to resist and rethink common modern constructs of asceticism and mysticism, I do not seek simply to cull alternative definitions that I might then "apply" to Nietzsche in order to argue that he "is" an ascetic or mystic. Such an exercise would be uninteresting, for it would only play with definitions. It also would ignore the fact that concepts such as *asceticism* and *mysticism*—like *religion*—are constructs, which, in their contemporary usage, are generated in large part through the debates that constitute the modern study of religion. Their status as intellectual and social constructions, in addition to Nietzsche's own polemical contribution to those debates and his indelible impress on the terms themselves, will chasten any aspirations to use the terms definitively. Thus, in deploying these terms, I do not seek to prove that Nietzsche is a particular kind of ascetic or meets the criteria of an authentic mystic—or that he is or is not religious. Nor do I seek to dispute the usefulness of the concepts by exposing them as "mere" constructions. To view them as constructions is not to invalidate them, but to use them strategically and pragmatically, in a way that enables questions and comparisons that might not be obvious when contemporary constructions are used uncritically. Thus, all three terms are useful as lenses, through which I identify certain central modes of discipline, self-transcendence, and piety, which enable scholars to identify and compare practices and ideas across historical and cultural contexts. In the case of Nietzsche, they carry a constructively subversive force, resisting the assimilation with secularism by illuminating productive tensions in his thought. The relevant question is not whether Nietzsche "is" or "is not" a religious thinker, or whether he is a "religious" rather than a "secular" thinker. I do not want to dispute that in many respects his thinking is radically "worldly" and "historical"—*secular* in the most literal sense of the word. Instead, the question I want to ask is whether the concept of religion—and more generally the web of concepts that religion leads us to deploy, such as reverence, piety, and god—makes it possible to perceive and analyze something in Nietzsche's thinking that has not received adequate attention.

In addition, I use these terms to read Nietzsche against himself, ironically, to show not only the kinetic sources of Nietzsche's positive vision, but to exhibit the polemical limitations of the essentializing rancor of his criticisms of religion. This ironic hermeneutics is intended sincerely, however, for it seems to me that illuminating Nietzsche's thought in this way raises questions about some of the fundamental distinctions and dichotomies we use to map our modern world. My objective, then, is twofold: to undertake a critical study of Nietzsche and to explore the categories by which we endeavor to understand human religiosity. These objectives depend on one another, and work through each other, for as Nietzsche challenges us to examine our desire for religious consolation, the question of religion, raised in a way that resists certain modern constructions of the category, challenges us to reread Nietzsche.

This demands a three-step hermeneutic. It is necessary, first, to explore the way Nietzsche determines the concepts of asceticism, mysticism, and religion. I examine Nietzsche's critical perspective on religion in Chapters 1 and 2 and his views of asceticism and mysticism in the opening sections of Chapters 3 and 4. These chapters and sections lay the textual groundwork for my study. Second, I will examine contemporary studies of asceticism and mysticism that challenge or complicate modern constructions of the concepts, particularly with respect to the way modern thinkers have, after Nietzsche and Weber, constructed asceticism and mysticism as two forms of flight from or denial of the world. In other words, I explore the ways in which ascetic and mystical practices can be said to be affirmative in the Nietzschean sense. This is the task of Chapters 3 and 4. Finally, the third step is a comparative and evaluative process by which I use the lenses of asceticism and mysticism to compare Nietzsche to his self-declared enemy, Christianity. In doing do, I argue that in certain specific ways Nietzsche is closer to Christianity than is commonly thought. I must emphasize from the start, however, that the point of this comparison is *not* to claim that Nietzsche is Christian or that the Christian thinkers I examine are Nietzscheans. Instead, the point is to bring them together as closely as possible, utilizing the lenses of asceticism and mysticism, to determine precisely where they are similar and where they differ on the question of denial and affirmation. This allows me to articulate the limitations of Nietzsche's criticisms of religion and to argue that rethinking or reimagining religion through a certain resistance to the modern distinction between the religious and the secular allows us to gain new perspectives on Nietzsche's affirmation. In particular, it allows us to appreciate the significance of the slender but brilliant threads of thanksgiving, reverence, and love woven into the fabric of Nietzsche's writing.

Nietzsche has become a familiar icon, a strong and unmovable signpost for the division between the religious and the secular. Perhaps we have not wanted to question why we are so content, even determined, to have him do this. Yet, like any great thinker, Nietzsche can provoke us to rethink our common sense, to remap the familiar terrain of our world and experience, by looking, once again, at how he constantly unsettled his own convictions. Reading Nietzsche as he asks us to read him is to engage in a sort of ascetic discipline, a discipline by which the reader repeats the tension that springs the dynamic of his writing—the tension between close, slow attention and a letting go of the mastery that demands progression, coherence, and resolution. Nietzsche asks us to resist the desire for such mastery in an effort to read with him—and against him—as he opens himself to the plurality of forces by which one becomes who one is. Such discipline opens us to new questions and new insights on persisting questions; it lures us into the labyrinth of ourselves and our time as we think with and against Nietzsche, with and against ourselves.

Chapter One

TOO MUCH OF NOTHING: METAPHYSICS
AND THE VALUE OF EXISTENCE

> It's hard to imagine, that nothing at all could be so exciting,
> could be this much fun.
> (David Byrne, "Heaven")

> There is not enough love and goodness in the world for us to be
> permitted to give any of it away to imaginary things.
> (Nietzsche, *Human, All too Human*)

THE VALUE OF EXISTENCE

Introduction

IN THE 1886 preface to his first book, *The Birth of Tragedy* (originally published in 1872), Nietzsche offered a critical review of that book's attempt to grapple with the question, What is the value of existence? By 1886 the significance of the question had changed for him, yet it continued to occupy his reflections on affirmation. The new preface recalls how he had tried to pose the problem of the value of existence by contrasting the "pessimism" of Greek tragedy and the "optimism" of Socratic philosophy. Nietzsche had claimed that with the demise of tragic sensibility Western culture had lost a fundamental connection with the primal forces of life. This was not, however, simply a historical or scholarly problem, for Nietzsche was looking forward to a recovery of a tragic sensibility as the key to the renewal of European culture. The new preface reflects back:

> You will guess where the big question mark concerning the value of existence had thus been raised. Is pessimism *necessarily* a sign of decline, degeneration, waywardness, weary and weak instincts—as it once was in India and now is, to all appearances, among us "modern" men and Europeans? Is there a pessimism of *strength*? An intellectual predilection for the hard, gruesome, evil, problematic aspects of existence, prompted by well-being, by overflowing

Epigraphs: Talking Heads, "Heaven," from the album *Fear of Music*; Nietzsche, HH: 69.

health, by the *fullness* of existence? Is it perhaps possible to suffer precisely from overfullness? (BT: 17)

When he was writing *The Birth of Tragedy*, Nietzsche was still very much engaged with the thoughts of Schopenhauer.[1] He had been convinced, and would remain convinced, of one of Schopenhauer's fundamental claims: all life consists in suffering. In tragedy, Nietzsche believed he had discovered the way in which pre-Socratic Greeks had confronted suffering while continuing to affirm life. Tragedy, he argued, had provided a "metaphysical comfort" for those who had glimpsed the terrifying "Dionysian" depths of life. Tragedy, in other words, was a dramatic ruse by which life preserved itself in the face of the stark revelation that the life of the individual is never released from suffering.

By 1886, Nietzsche's ideas about the significance of tragedy had changed. His emphasis was not on metaphysical comfort, which he now rejected, but on what he called, in a new formulation, the "pessimism of strength." Nietzsche contrasted the pessimism of strength with a pessimism of decline. By now, he had Schopenhauer in mind as an exemplar of declining pessimism, for Schopenhauer had thought that the ultimate response to suffering was to deny the value of life by turning from it in mystical transcendence. The new preface disparaged this kind of response, and raised questions about the possibility of another, one without metaphysical comfort or consolation, one grounded in a willingness, a settled disposition, or even desire ("predilection") to seek out *positively* the difficult and dangerous aspects of existence. Nietzsche continued to affirm pessimism because he continued to believe that suffering was fundamental to life. But where Schopenhauer recommended turning from this life, Nietzsche now sought to affirm life in its radical implication with suffering.

The rejection of Schopenhauer's weak pessimism entailed more than a different response to the problem of suffering and to the question of the value of existence. By 1886, Nietzsche had concluded that the question of value could not be adjudicated philosophically: as he would bluntly state in a later text, "The value of life cannot be estimated" (TI: 40). But this did not prevent him from finding the question, and the attempts philosophers had made to answer it, of great interest, for he viewed the philosophical disposition that questioned the value of existence as symptomatic of a certain kind of soul. The question of the value of life thus became a psychological question, to be explored in terms of the health

[1] It is generally accepted that it was only after *The Birth of Tragedy* that Nietzsche began to move away from Schopenhauer. In two very different studies, both of which have shaped my reading of Nietzsche on metaphysics, Jörg Salaquarda (1989) and John Sallis (1991) challenge this interpretation, arguing that Nietzsche had already had deep reservations about Schopenhauer's metaphysics by the time of *The Birth of Tragedy*.

that "prompts" the question of value in the first place. This particular question, and more generally all modes of valuing, register for Nietzsche significant features of a people's psychocultural condition.

Affirmation and Denial in Schopenhauer

The problem of affirmation takes shape in Nietzsche's efforts first to understand, then to resist, Schopenhauer's philosophy. Schopenhauer's position on suffering can be traced to his basic metaphysical claim that "will" is the true inner nature of all that is, the "thing-in-itself," of which all that we are and experience, all phenomena, are representations. This fundamental reality is not divine, but only blind, endless striving, suffering in its eternal conflict with itself. "All willing," according to Schopenhauer, "springs from lack, from deficiency, and thus from suffering" (1969a: 196). This lack never can be filled: the will wills endlessly, always seeking new satisfactions, always finding that its satisfactions don't satisfy the endless hunger. Thus Schopenhauer's "pessimism."[2] It is not surprising that the young Nietzsche, who broke with Christianity in his adolescence and already had intimate experience with chronic pain and isolation, would find truth in this pessimism.[3]

As evidenced by the distinction between phenomenon and the thing-in-itself—in this case, between the will as it appeared in the individual will and "Will" as metaphysical reality—Schopenhauer's philosophy was deeply indebted to Kant. He agreed with Kant that our knowledge of phenomena, ourselves included, is determined by the "principle of sufficient reason" and thus is subject to the conditions of space and time (1969a: 173). He also rejected post-Kantian speculative attempts to reconcile the Kantian distinction between things as we know them and things in themselves through a philosophy of consciousness, particularly Hegel's. But Schopenhauer took issue with Kant on a crucial issue by claiming that the will, as thing-in-itself, can be known; more specifically, can be "intuited." Following Plato instead of Kant on this point, he thought that through the intuitive grasp of the will, in what he describes as "con-

---

[2] Schopenhauer writes that optimism, "where it is not merely the thoughtless talk of those who harbor nothing but words under their shallow foreheads, seems to me to be not merely an absurd, but also a really *wicked*, way of thinking, a bitter mockery of the unspeakable sufferings of mankind" (1969a: 326).

[3] Hayman (1982: 72 ff.). Hayman quotes from a memoir, in which Nietzsche remembered his first encounter with Schopenhauer's *The World as Will and Representation*: "Each line cried out with renunciation, negation, resignation. I was looking into a mirror that reflected the world, life and my own mind with hideous magnificence." Schopenhauer was one of the first major Western philosophers to take seriously Hindu and Buddhist thought, which no doubt influenced his view that the willing self must be extinguished in order to end the inevitable misery of life.

templation," we can come to the knowledge not of individual, phenomenal things, but of "Ideas" themselves (1969a: 179, 199). The "Idea," as the principle of form, is the purest and most "adequate" representation, or objectification, of the will and is on this account to be distinguished from "concept." Ideas are the original, living, unified objectifications of the will, whereas concepts are the abstract unities constructed by human intellectual effort out of our perceptions of the plurality of the world. Ideas are not constructed and manipulated, but apprehended in the "metaphysical glance" (1969a: 279) of intuition that is afforded the "genius" (1969a: 235). Schopenhauer argued that such intuition is grounded not in consciousness but in the body, in its desires and passions, and that it could be brought to the point of knowledge in an act of pure, will-less knowing. Because in contemplation human beings are freed from the strivings and struggles of willing, Schopenhauer considers this state the most blissful one that human beings can experience (1969a: 196). This position would be an important point of departure for Nietzsche in *The Birth of Tragedy.*

Schopenhauer's major work, *The World as Will and Representation,* which Nietzsche first read in 1865, examines in great detail the affirmation and denial of life. There, Schopenhauer writes that the "willing or not willing of life" is "the great question" (1969a: 308). In one sense, he argues, such willing is the very nature of will: the will *is* "the will-to-live" and it affirms itself in its representations, the phenomena. But Schopenhauer distinguishes between this natural, blind self-affirmation of the will from the self-conscious affirmation to which human beings can ascend in contemplation. Attending only to phenomena, human beings are easily struck by the inevitability of suffering and the pain of individuation. But they continue to will as individuals, desiring the end of their suffering. It is only in a certain overcoming of the individual will, thinks Schopenhauer, that life can be genuinely affirmed. He is particularly interested in two types of overcoming. In the artist, Schopenhauer sees the paradigmatic affirmer of life. The true artist is able to grasp intuitively the selfless knowledge of the will, participating in a particularly vivid way in the will's suffering, yet doing so in such a way that he or she finds pleasure and consolation in the spectacle created in this activity. In contemplation, the artist, as a pure subject of knowledge, sees beyond his or her own misery and death to comprehend the greater movement of life, the "eternal justice" by which all suffering and destruction is balanced by the creation of new life (1969a: 330). In artistic creation the will comes to know itself in such a way that "this knowledge does not in any way impede its willing" (1969a: 285).

Taken one step farther, however, knowledge of the will actually enables the will to turn against itself. According to Schopenhauer, this step, the will's self-transcendence, the denial of life, is taken by the religious virtuoso. The life of the virtuoso is characterized not simply by transient experiences of aesthetic bliss, but by the cultivation of a life turned against the ever-striving will, by the denial of the will to live. Schopenhauer makes three basic distinctions between the artist and the religious virtuoso. First, the latter ascends farther in a contemplative knowledge of the will not just as objectified Idea, but in the full reality of its fundamental discord and suffering: the saint loses the self and becomes the will in encountering the highest truth: that "constant suffering is essential to all life." Second, this knowledge is grounded in a certain kind of conduct toward others, a self-transcending love for all beings in their suffering (1969a: 309). Schopenhauer is difficult to interpret on this point, but he seems to be suggesting that while aesthetic contemplation discerns the reality of the will as Idea, that is, the reality of the will in its most fundamental objectification, the religious virtuoso, in taking on the suffering of others, intuits the "inner nature" of the will as suffering. The artist, in other words, comes to know the will simply through contemplation, but the saint's intuition of the will also involves the experiential knowledge that comes through pity. Third, the saintly denial of life, the will's self-renunciation, liberates: coming to contemplative and experiential knowledge of the ultimate truth that all that we desire is grounded in discord and conflict, the will turns against itself, stripping the human being in whom this happens of the motives for desiring or willing (1969a: 402). This is a turn in which one "abandons all knowledge of individual things as such . . . and, by means of knowledge of the Ideas, sees through the *principium individuationis*. An actual appearance of the real freedom of the will as thing-in-itself then becomes possible, by which the phenomenon comes into a certain contradiction with itself, as is expressed by the word self-renunciation" (1969a: 301).

This, claims Schopenhauer, is the saint's state of holiness, ultimate freedom of the will. His pessimism thus leads to a vision of the end of all striving and desiring.

Soon after *The Birth of Tragedy*, Nietzsche came to question the metaphysical pretensions of this vision and valuation and became more and more convinced that to affirm life, human beings had to affirm the suffering of existence—not transcend it—and even find joy in it. In "Schopenhauer as Educator," from 1874, Nietzsche paid homage to his teacher, but also hinted at a fundamental break on the questions of suffering and value. Praising Schopenhauer's resistance to the vacuous optimisms of Christianity and liberal modernism, Nietzsche asserted that simply by asking the question of the value of existence, Schopenhauer had taught him the way of "struggling against [one's] age" (UM: 153). For this, Nietzsche would always admire Schopenhauer. But without directly confronting his teacher's answer to that question, Nietzsche suggests a way of asking and answering it that puts him once and for all at odds with Schopenhauerian resignation. "Do you affirm this existence in the depths of your heart? Is it sufficient for you? Would you be its advocate, its redeemer? For you have only to pronounce a single heartfelt Yes!—and life, though it faces such heavy accusations, shall go free" (UM: 146).[4] Nietzsche imagines freedom in the "Yes" rather than in the "No." This "Yes" marks the beginning of a philosophical journey that would find one of its culminating statements in the new view of tragedy Nietzsche articulated in the preface from 1886. There, tragedy is viewed as a pessimism of strength, an affirmative insistence on the depths of human suffering that *desires* the "hard, gruesome, evil, problematic aspects of existence." The question of affirmation is the question of this desire.

METAPHYSICS AND THE DENIAL OF LIFE

Metaphysics, Philosophy, and the Value of Existence: Human, All too Human

Nietzsche began to take his distance from Schopenhauerian pessimism in a thorough rethinking of the goals and methods of philosophy. This effort brought him to the conclusion that certain ways of doing philosophy are in themselves either life-denying or life-affirming. Specifically, in *Human, All too Human*, *Dawn*, and *The Gay Science*, Nietzsche criticized what he called "metaphysics" and experimented with a new philosophical method. He poses the problem—with an allusion to Schopenhauer—in the first chapter of *Human, All too Human*, from 1878, entitled "First and Last Things": "almost all the problems of philosophy once again pose the same form of question as they did two thousand years ago: how can something originate in its opposite, for example . . . disinterested contemplation in covetous desire?" (HH: 12). This "question" points to the fundamental philosophical dualism that Nietzsche will continue to struggle against, under the names of metaphysics, morality, and the ascetic ideal, for the remainder of his active life.[5]

---

[4] Nonetheless, Nietzsche would continue to struggle with his own pessimism. "The conviction that life is worthless and that all goals are delusions comes over me so strongly, above all when I'm lying sick in bed." Letter to Carl Von Gersdorff, 13 December 1875 (see Fuss and Shapiro 1971: 30). He offers another insight into his feelings in a note from 1888: "Since I was a child, I felt in my heart two contradictory feelings: *l'horreur de la vie, et l'extase de la vie*" (SW 13: 81).

[5] In the preface to GM (1887), Nietzsche looks back on *Human, All too Human*, as an attempt to free himself from Schopenhauer's influence. "What was especially at stake was the value of the "unegoistic," the instincts of pity, self-abnegation, self-sacrifice, which Schopenhauer had gilded, deified, and projected into a beyond for so long that at last they be-

Philosophers and priests, sages of all types, Nietzsche argues, have always been offended by the idea that those things they value most highly might have an origin that is less than pure and perfect. When he uses the term *metaphysics*, Nietzsche refers to a philosophy based in the dualistic conviction that things of the highest value have an origin altogether distinct from the origin of the things of lower value. This dualism draws this absolute distinction in values in a particular way: things of the highest value are unchanging, unconditioned, eternal, and harmonious, while things of lowest value are changing, conditioned, transitory, and dissonant. "Metaphysical philosophy has hitherto surmounted this difficulty [of origins] by . . . assuming for the more highly valued thing a miraculous source in the very kernel and being of the 'thing in itself' " (HH: 12). Later, in *Beyond Good and Evil*, Nietzsche will designate as the "faith in opposite values" the assumption that

> things of the highest value must have another, peculiar origin—they cannot be derived from this transitory, seductive, deceptive, paltry world, from this turmoil of delusion and lust. Rather from the lap of Being, the intransitory, the hidden god, the "thing-in-itself"—there must be their basis, and nowhere else. This way of judging constitutes the typical prejudgment and prejudice which give away the metaphysicians of all ages; this kind of valuation looms in the background of all their logical procedures; it is on account of this "faith" that they trouble themselves about "knowledge," about something that is finally baptized solemnly as "the truth." (BG: 10)

Human, All too Human, like all Nietzsche's subsequent philosophy, proceeds from a different premise: the origin of all values are to be found *in* and not *beyond* the contingencies and dissonances of human life—in the "human, all too human." Under the influence of his friend Paul Ree and of F. A. Lange's *History of Materialism*, Nietzsche sought to bring a rigorous scientific and empirical sensibility to philosophy.[6] He moved from there to a radical historicizing project that looks to the body, psychology, and society to develop a "chemistry" and history of moral feelings and values. This methodological interest grounds one major aspect of his critique of metaphysics. Nietzsche was not interested in proving that all the claims made by metaphysicians are wrong—he even acknowledges that "there could be a metaphysical world" (HH: 15). But, he con-

---

came for him "value-in-itself," on the basis of which he *said No* to life and to himself" (GM: 19).

[6] Ree, a close friend of Nietzsche's, especially in the late 1870s, had written a book entitled *Psychological Observations*, which Nietzsche thought was an excellent example of the scientific way of thinking he was pursuing in *Human, All too Human*. Nietzsche thought Lange's *History of Materialism and Critique of Its Significance for the Present* was one of the most important philosophical works of the nineteenth century.

tends, there are no good philosophical grounds for supposing that there is such a pristine, otherworldly origin for our highest values. More generally, Nietzsche argues that metaphysical explanations are methodologically suspect. He writes that they have "been begotten in passion, error and self-deception; the worst of all methods of acquiring knowledge, not the best of all, have taught belief in them." Exposing these methods, as far as Nietzsche is concerned, is enough to refute the systems developed out of them (HH: 15).

Nietzsche also argues, however, that such philosophical criticism of the methods of metaphysics is limited, for though it can undermine the philosophical pretensions of metaphysics, it cannot understand the value of metaphysics. Compared to the question of value, the issue of the origin of beliefs is relatively unimportant; as Nietzsche would claim in *Dawn*: "The more insight we possess into an origin, the less significant does it appear" (D: 31).[7] His point is not that we should not investigate origins, but that origins do not determine the value or worth of ideas, beliefs, or practices. Nietzsche therefore brings another type of examination to bear on the question of metaphysics: a psychological hermeneutic of value that anticipates what he would come to call "genealogy."[8] This is a genuinely critical method of demystification, one that not only tries to determine whether a belief is mistaken or not, but one that examines how even a mistaken idea can exert a powerful hold on human beings by virtue of the role it plays in their lives.

The "philosophical liberation" that Nietzsche seeks to achieve through the criticism of metaphysics is therefore a complex one, for it demands both philosophical clarity, with respect to the propositional claims of metaphysical beliefs, and psychological and sociological analyses of the value of metaphysics for human life. This aspect of Nietzsche's investigation is diagnostic and therapeutic, rather than strictly philosophical; "overcoming metaphysics" is achieved only through a rigorous philosophical regimen or therapy designed to "eliminate metaphysical needs" (HH: 26, 82). Most important, this means eliminating the need for what Nietzsche calls "consolation." For Nietzsche, the value of metaphysics can be attributed, in large part, to its function as an interpretation of suffering, one that directs human concern away from worldly sources of misery and to a future or ultimate state where suffering will be redeemed or ended (HH: 60). Metaphysics promises a certain kind of control over the contingencies and disasters of human life, consoling human beings and offering them security. This control is ultimately unverifiable, but this itself, as Nietzsche would come to recognize more and more, contributes to the power of its interpretations. Nietzsche believes this immense power

[7] See also GS: 285.
[8] See Schrift's discussion of Nietzsche's "psychogenealogy" (1990: 53 ff.).

of consolation is dangerous, for it alleviates certain forms of human suffering only at the expense of creating other, more terrible forms of suffering, which undermine and weaken engagement with this life.

To further complicate matters, Nietzsche refuses to level a blanket condemnation of metaphysics. When he claims that origin does not determine value, Nietzsche has in mind not only the fact that the criticism of an origin will not necessarily free us from an error, but he also is asserting that something rooted in error can come to have great value and produce great beauty. Or that something can be both valuable and destructive. To understand metaphysics, one must take a "retrograde step" in order to understand the historical and psychological significance of metaphysical ideas, a process by which one comes to realize not only the danger of consolation, but that, in certain respects, metaphysical ideas "have been the most responsible for the advancement of mankind" (HH: 23). Nietzsche's project here echoes Feuerbach's: although religious ideas and feelings are based in mistakes, only through these ideas have human beings been able to develop to the present level of culture (HH: 26). This suggests that the practice of liberation involves recognizing the historical continuity of human life, and further, that it is impossible simply to start afresh with new ways of valuing and living. Rather, it is necessary to build on the past, so as not to be deprived "of the best that mankind has hitherto produced" (HH: 23; D: 32).

The existential implications of his own philosophical "chemistry" frighten Nietzsche. For even assuming one could succeed in undermining false ways of thinking, if "every belief in the value and dignity of life rests on false thinking" (HH: 28), how then is one to renew the sense of meaningfulness? How can human beings say "Yes" to their existence? How can they affirm their dignity? Will genuine philosophical vigilance undermine life? One might derail these questions by supposing that Nietzsche is only making a historical claim here; that, *to this point*, all belief in dignity and value have rested on false thinking, but that with "right thinking," Nietzsche's thinking, new, more solid, grounds for human dignity can be established. But Nietzsche does not see it this way in *Human, All too Human*, for although philosophy can strip us of our consolations by arriving at knowledge of the errors and sources of previous ways of valuing life, philosophy conducted with proper respect for the limits of reason and the nature of human valuing cannot determine or discover new value. The reason is that valuing is not a matter of knowing as much as it is of feeling, mood, and desire (HH: 28). The human being, therefore, is torn between knower and valuer. The most the intellect can do is tell us that we are necessarily unjust and illogical, that we depend on errors; this, writes Nietzsche, "is one of the greatest and most irresolvable discords of existence" (HH: 28).

By 1878, then, Nietzsche already had brought himself to the impasse with which he would struggle for the rest of his active life. Honest thinkers cannot but see through humanity's most cherished ideals and values—but it is not clear how they can establish new ones, for it seems that science and philosophy resist all affirmations of the value of existence. "Will our philosophy not thus become a tragedy? Will truth not become inimical to life, to the better man?" (HH: 29). Faced with this prospect, Nietzsche offers some tentative answers in fragments scattered throughout *Human, All too Human*. Two are of interest here. At one point, he wonders whether there is an alternative to philosophical despair, at least for persons with a particular kind of "temperament," in a kind of liberating, contemplative detachment. Such detachment would enable one to live "as in nature, without praising, blaming, contending, gazing contentedly, as though at a spectacle, upon many things for which one formerly felt only fear" (HH: 30). This solution shows traces of Schopenhauer's continuing influence (and of a traditional Platonic vision of philosophical transcendence), for it requires a reorientation of desire in a shift from relationships and ordinary forms of valuing to a "free, fearless hovering over men, customs, laws, and the traditional evaluations of things," a freedom from things of the world that is itself "most desirable" (HH: 30).

At the same time, Nietzsche's antimetaphysical perspective requires that the objects of his contemplation not be eternal ideas or God, but human life and nature themselves. Nietzsche suggests that such philosophical liberation is only possible through a practice of knowing in which one is continually reimmersing oneself in life—in order to again transcend it. This philosophical practice is a kind of "wandering," which involves being "a noble traitor to all things that can in any way be betrayed (HH: 203).⁹ The object of wandering is not to transcend one's humanity in any final sense, but to distance oneself from oneself, gaining some degree of freedom from passions, needs, and conviction. As wandering, philosophy is a matter of utilizing one's life—one's "unjust" and "illogical" perspectives on life—to gain knowledge about oneself and about humanity: one can come to some knowledge of oneself *as* unjust and illogical. One's experiences, passions, and moods become the stuff of philosophy; one looks into oneself and takes from oneself: one's "own life will acquire the value of an instrument and means of knowledge," and "the clouds of affliction hovering over you will yet have to serve you as udders from which you will milk the milk for your refreshment" (HH: 135). And, in opposition to Platonic philosophizing, the tragic motif continues to play a role in Nietzsche's thinking, for he has here interiorized the tragic stage by envisioning a kind of self-relation in which one gains enough

⁹ What became the second part of *Human, All too Human*, was originally a separate work, entitled *The Wanderer and His Shadow*.

distance from oneself to be able to turn back and view, as a "spectator," one's own passionate struggles and sufferings. In the spectacle of suffering life, as achieved by the philosopher, one finds equanimity and joy.

Nietzsche offers a second response to the conflict between knowledge and value. This one, however, throws into question the precise extent of Nietzsche's hopes for overcoming metaphysics, for he poses the possibility of establishing a creative and fruitful tension between science and metaphysics by addressing the conflicting demands of the "drives" toward science, on the one hand, and "poetry, religion and metaphysics," on the other. Where his contemplative solution demands the overcoming of the latter in favor of the former, here he claims that "higher culture" demands something different.

> Such a situation between two so different demands is very hard to maintain, for science presses for the absolute dominance of its methods, and if this pressure is not relaxed there arises the other danger of a feeble vacillation back and forth between different drives. To indicate the way towards a resolution of this difficulty, however, if only by means of a parable, one might recall that the *dance* is not the same thing as a languid reeling back and forth between different drives. High culture will resemble an audacious dance. (HH: 130–31)

There is a hint in this passage of a perspective on science that belies the critical attitude Nietzsche affirms in most of the rest of the text, for science here is more than a means to knowledge and even more than an "attachment" that one might find desirable. It is, instead, a drive that seeks absolute dominance. It appears that Nietzsche senses the need to resist this drive. This passage, then, raises two questions. How does the figure of the dance help Nietzsche conceive of a relation to both science and metaphysics that both resists and affirms them? And, does this figure suggest the affirmation of a certain kind of metaphysics, poetry, or religion?

Nihilism as the Will to Nothing: On the Genealogy of Morals

Nietzsche criticizes metaphysics because its object of value and its goal are, in reality, "nothing." The human need for consolation, the inability to will or desire the reality of suffering, has meant for millennia that this nothing has been the object of humanity's greatest desires: "Have all the great passions of mankind not hitherto been as these are, passions for a nothing? And all their solemnities—solemnities about a nothing?" (D: 197). Reflecting on this "nothing," Nietzsche was led in his later works, and especially in the essay on the ascetic ideal in *On the Genealogy of Morals* (1887; hereafter *Genealogy*), to grapple with the problem of nihilism.

In this essay, Nietzsche argues that in order to live, human beings need a goal for their will, an ideal. When life has a goal, he asserts, it has meaning. The essay shows how the dualism of a metaphysical, religio-moral ideal—the ascetic ideal—has been able to inspire countless people by giving them "nothingness" to will. Nietzsche claims that to this point in human history this ideal has been the *only* goal that the human will has had so far.

> Apart from the ascetic ideal, man, the human *animal*, had no meaning so far. His existence on earth contained no goal . . . the *will* for man and earth was lacking. . . . *This* is precisely what the ascetic ideal means: that something was *lacking*, that man was surrounded by a fearful *void*—he did not know how to justify, to account for, to affirm himself; he *suffered* from the problem of his meaning. He also suffered otherwise, he was in the main a sickly animal: but his problem was *not* suffering itself, but that there was no answer to the crying question, "*why* do I suffer?" (GM: 162)

The ascetic ideal holds power because it makes human suffering bearable—even desirable—by giving it meaning: specifically, suffering becomes the sign of the promise that, at some point, in some other realm of existence, suffering will end once and for all.

So strong is the need, for ideal or meaning, that human beings "would rather will nothingness than will nothing at all." This distinction goes to the heart of Nietzsche's mature critique of metaphysics as the "faith in opposite values" and as nihilism. To "will nothingness" is still to will, in this case, to will a metaphysical "beyond." By contrast, "to will nothing at all" means that the will finds nothing, not even the illusory beyond, to strive for: it simply does not will. This echoes the problem that Nietzsche had already anticipated in *Human, All too Human*: struggling to expose the nothingness of the metaphysical will to the beyond, he confronts the calamitous possibility of being left with nothing to will. The primary question Nietzsche raises in the *Genealogy*, therefore, can be posed in an initial formulation: when we see the ascetic ideal for what it is—a will to nothingness—is it possible to find a new ideal, a new way of willing or valuing, or does the philosophical search for the truth of our most cherished values and meanings leave us with nothing?

However, in the period between *Human, All too Human*, and the *Genealogy*, Nietzsche had come to look at the power of metaphysics in a new way. With the formulation "will to power," Nietzsche began to think toward a philosophical monism in which all reality was understood in terms of forces of life striving for power. As a result, Nietzsche began to treat the power of metaphysics not simply in terms of a conscious need for security and control, but as a deep instinctual response of self-preservation. The ascetic ideal gives meaning to life by denying the value of the world and nature, but this denial is a ruse of the life force itself. Its vehicle is the priest. Through this figure, Nietzsche deepened his grasp of the intertwining of sociological and psychological forces in the creation of human value.

Nietzsche contrasts two perspectives on the ascetic ideal. On the surface is the valuation of life acknowledged by the "ascetic priest," who "juxtaposes [life] (along with what pertains to it: "nature," "world," the whole sphere of becoming and transitoriness) with a totally different mode of existence which it opposes and excludes, *unless* it turn against itself, deny itself: in that case, the case of the ascetic life, life counts as a bridge to that other mode of existence" (GM: 117).

The ascetic priest is a self-conscious dualist: one lives this life and undergoes its suffering, glories in its suffering, for the sake of another—better, truer, more divine—mode of existence. Nietzsche's priest believes that it is possible to lead a life that will make it possible for one to enter this different mode of existence; as with Schopenhauer's saint, this involves a way of stepping beyond life, in the course of life, so as find a place from which one can turn against life. For Nietzsche, however, this is the characteristic misunderstanding of value committed by those enslaved to the faith in opposite values, and it is the characteristic hope of those for whom the absence of suffering is the highest value. Reading values genealogically, as expressions of historical forms of "life," of will to power, Nietzsche probes to a different perspective: "*The ascetic ideal springs from the protective instinct of a degenerating life* which tries by all means to sustain itself and to fight for its existence; it indicates a partial physiological obstruction and exhaustion against which the deepest instincts of life, which have remained intact, continually struggle with new expedients and devices" (GM: 120–21).

Nietzsche's monism gives him a way of rejecting the priestly (and Schopenhauerian) idea of a transcendent freedom by means of which something that lives can turn against the principle of life itself. The ascetic ideal, from this perspective, is not a denial but an affirmation, the means by which the instinct of self-preservation of a particular kind of life accomplishes its purpose. The ascetic priest works as the tool of a will to power. The will to nothingness, in other words, is for Nietzsche the manifestation of "the deepest instincts of life" struggling to preserve themselves. And the priest, "this apparent enemy of life, this denier—precisely he is among the greatest conserving and yes-creating forces of life" (GM: 120–21). Nihilism, as the will to nothing, has been a force for the preservation of life at the same time that it is a route to power for the priest.

Yet Nietzsche still wants to talk about the ascetic ideal's "denial" of life; more specifically, its "hostility" to life, and he conveys the impression that he wants humanity to find a different meaning for life. Despite the fact that it is a "yes-creating" force, Nietzsche sees three fundamental, interconnected problems with the ascetic ideal. First, one who follows the ascetic ideal gives meaning to his or her life only through a self-deceptive, dualistic refusal to acknowledge his or her own rootedness in life or motives in adhering to the ideal. The desire to transcend this life can be justified, and be successfully self-deceptive, only if it posits a realm of absolute truth and value. Otherwise the weak must face the fact that their desire for another mode of existence is rooted in their own weakness and their own desire, not in God's command. Claiming to worship God, one really seeks to be free of suffering. Thus the ascetic ideal can no longer grasp those who see through this self-deception, those who are compelled to "honesty." Second, the ascetic ideal has preserved a specific kind of life— a declining, weak, exhausted life—for those who are bewitched by the promises of a life without suffering. Third, and most important: the ascetic ideal has been the means by which the weak, led by the priest, have prevailed over the strong in a battle of values. This victory deserves careful attention.

The weak have been victorious, according to Nietzsche, through a revaluation of values, or, more precisely, by instituting a new mode of valuation. In the first essay of the *Genealogy*, Nietzsche argues that the ascetic ideal finds its source in the *ressentiment* of the priest and all those who, out of one form of weakness or another, hate and envy self-affirming humanity. The self-affirmers are the strong and noble, who find the source of all value in themselves and all that is an extension of themselves: valuing, here, begins in designating themselves as the "good." In contrast to this active self-affirmation, the weak value through the reactivity of *ressentiment*.[10] That is, their mode of valuation begins in the reaction to the strong, determining them as "evil"; "good," in this scheme, is the derivative concept, used to designate the victim of evil—oneself. When Nietzsche writes of the revaluation of values, he has in mind this essential difference between the active valuing of health and affirmation, on the one hand, and the reactive valuing of *ressentiment*, on the other.

For it to have any force, the mode of valuing rooted in the distinction between evil and good must be made absolute:

> They monopolize virtue, these weak, hopelessly sick people, there is no doubt of it: "We alone are the good and the just," they say, "we alone are *homines bonae voluntatis*." They walk among us as embodied reproaches, as warnings to us—as if health, well-constitutedness, strength, pride and the sense of power

[10] See the first essay in the *Genealogy*, especially Section Ten, for Nietzsche's discussion of these issues. See also Deleuze (1983: 1–36) for a detailed discussion of the concepts "active" and "reactive."

were in themselves necessarily vicious things for which one must pay some day, and pay bitterly: how ready they themselves are at bottom to *make* one pay; how they crave to be *hangmen*. . . . The will of the weak to represent *some* form of superiority, their instinct for devious paths to tyranny over the healthy—where can it not be discovered, this will to power of the weakest. (GM: 123)

The ascetic ideal allows the weak to affirm life through self-deception and the active hostility to ascending, vital life. Paradoxically, the will to nothingness, as a last gasp of the weak, has found the power of domination: nihilism has held sway under "the holiest of names." The particular configuration of metaphysics, morality, and religion employed by the ascetic priest not only gives meaning to suffering, but with the claim that its evaluation of life has an otherworldly, divine source, it supports its moral absolutism. The power of this hostile absolutism is supported by the fact that there are so many people who need this interpretation. The ascetic ideal thereby undermines any "will for man and earth" and idealizes the passion for nothingness. Through the ascetic ideal, life can simultaneously be affirmed and despised. It is not affirmed or loved for itself, but only as a means to peace beyond this life and absolute mastery in this life. Nietzsche attacks the ascetic ideal because it undermines those who would affirm this life here and now.

The Ascetic Ideal and the Will to Truth

Religion and morality are the most prominent initial targets in Nietzsche's attack on the ascetic ideal. It is therefore surprising, at least at first, that near the end of the essay on the ascetic ideal, Nietzsche leaves off his discussion of the ascetic priest to argue that the ascetic ideal finds its "strictest, most spiritual formulation" not in Christianity, but in the atheistic and scientific spirit of modernity (GM: 160). As he had shown in *Human, All too Human*, Nietzsche's criticisms of metaphysics, religion, and morality lead him to a position in which he questions his own embrace of the scientific, worldly spirit of the age. In that earlier book, however, Nietzsche had been concerned primarily with the possibility that the critical consciousness would undermine the ability of human beings to value their existence. Thus, he had imagined the possibility of being able to find joy and dignity in scientific, philosophical detachment, in the enjoyment of the spectacle produced by the insistence on truth. By the time of the *Genealogy*, however, Nietzsche had refined his understanding of the metaphysical presuppositions of philosophy itself, and he had found the metaphysical consciousness more uncanny than he had thought. Near the end of the *Genealogy*, Nietzsche argues that the antimetaphysical spirit is itself metaphysical, a manifestation of the ascetic ideal. "Unconditional and honest atheism (and its is the only air we breathe, we more spiritual men of this age!) is therefore not the antithesis of the ideal, as it appears to be; it is rather only one of the latest phases of its evolution" (GM: 160).[11]

Nietzsche bases this claim on the argument that at the core of the ascetic ideal, of both the metaphysical and "anti-metaphysical" spirit, one finds a moral imperative—the "will to truth." This will has been the driving force of the ascetic ideal, and continues to drive the secularism and atheism of modernity.[12] Nietzsche thus brings into sharp relief the fundamental characteristic of metaphysical dualism. The key to the will to truth lies not in epistemological problems regarding truth or knowledge—their existence or human access to them—but in the moral/religious problem of the belief in the absolute value of truth. The "will to truth" is

> faith in the ascetic ideal itself, even if as an unconscious imperative—don't be deceived about that—it is the faith in a metaphysical value, that absolute value of truth, sanctioned and guaranteed by this ideal alone. . . . The truthful man, in the audacious and ultimate sense presupposed by the faith in science, *thereby affirms another world* than that of life, nature, and history; and insofar as he affirms this "other world," does this not mean that he has to deny its antithesis, this world, *our* world? (GM: 151–52)

The will to truth affirms a value qualitatively different from all other values, an otherworldly value that subordinates all "natural" human values to itself. Those who adhere to the will to truth do not necessarily require that all natural values are in fact valueless, only that their value consists in the extent to which they make possible the realization of truth: this world only has value to the extent that it leads us to the "true world." Like the theist, the unconditional atheist is an absolutist, who refuses to question the value of truth.

Throughout the *Genealogy*—and in the fifth book of *The Gay Science*—Nietzsche identifies himself with the "men of knowledge" who have held truth to be divine.[13] Yet in these texts, pursuing the will to truth into the ascetic ideal, Nietzsche has found the men of knowledge, there with the rest of those remorseless introspectors and vivisectors who up-

[11] A few pages earlier, Nietzsche is even more explicit, quoting a passage from the fifth book of *The Gay Science*: "It is still a *metaphysical faith* that underlies our faith in science—and we men of knowledge of today, we godless men and anti-metaphysicians, we, too, still derive our flame from the fire ignited by a faith millennia old, the Christian faith, which was also Plato's, that God is truth, that truth is *divine*" (GM: 152).

[12] See GS: 282–83 for Nietzsche's discussion of the connection between will to truth and morality.

[13] See also Nietzsche's discussion of the "self-sublimation" of morality in the preface to *Dawn*.

hold the ascetic ideal. These truth seekers have remained ignorant of their own constituting ideals and drives; the will to truth has masked a certain will to ignorance about the souls that cleave to the will to truth. "We are unknown to ourselves, we men of knowledge—and with good reason. We have never sought ourselves—how could it happen that we should ever find ourselves?" (GM: 15). The will to truth, Nietzsche perceives, "has become conscious of itself as a problem in us" (GM: 161).

Nietzsche finds the face of the ascetic in the mirror of his own philosophical inquiry. To discover the ascetic ideal as the condition of one's own philosophical spirit mortifies the genealogist. Thus the will to truth attacks itself; the ascetic ideal mortifies its highest objectives. Paradoxically, Nietzsche's genealogy epitomizes, to the furthest degree, as it were, the self-mortifying reflex of the ascetic ideal. And yet at the furthest degree of this torment, the philosopher is able to look beyond. He sees a possibility that has not been broached before: the possibility that the value of truth, the "kernel" of all absolute values, is not absolute. The will to truth turns its merciless gaze on itself to give Nietzsche insight into the fate of the absolutism of metaphysics: the nihilism of a historical trajectory in which the highest values—God, the Good, Truth—devalue themselves.

> All great things bring about their own destruction through an act of self-overcoming: thus the law of life will have it, the law of the necessity of "self-overcoming" in the nature of life. . . . After Christian truthfulness has drawn one inference after another, it must end by drawing its *most striking inference*, its inference *against* itself; this will happen, however, when it poses the question *"what is the meaning of all will to truth?"* (GM: 161)

At the end of the *Genealogy*, Nietzsche appears to leave us with the hope that this question—"What is the meaning of all will to truth?" or "What is the value of truth?"—may provide the means to extricate ourselves from the ascetic ideal. Turning truth on truth, the ascetic ideal betrays itself. But this betrayal holds familiar dangers, for if God dies, if truth is not an absolute value, how can human beings determine the value or the meaning of life? From what perspective, or with what criterion, will they be able to determine what is or is not valuable? If they, with Nietzsche, look beyond the ascetic ideal, they are confronted with a new intensification of nihilism, no longer the will to nothingness, but, more terrifying, the state of having nothing to will.

One of the most uncanny things about the *Genealogy* is that it is not at all clear that, out of these discoveries, Nietzsche is able to present us with a definitive alternative, a vision of the "opposing ideal." One might argue that he has given us this vision in *Zarathustra*, as he suggests at the end of the second essay and confirms in *Ecce Homo*. This position is, I think, essentially correct, yet it must be qualified by his assertion that the will to truth has only now risen to consciousness "as a problem," which will take "centuries" to work through (GS: 280–83). In other words, Nietzsche discovers a problem, not a solution; in fact, he claims to find his meaning not in an ideal that solves the problem of the ascetic ideal, but in the *problem* of the old ideal itself. " '*What does all will to truth mean?*' . . . and here I touch on my problem again, on *our* problem, my unknown friends . . . : what meaning does our being have, if it were not that will to truth has become conscious of itself *as a problem* in us?" (GM: 161).

One solution to this problem would be to consider whether it is possible to give meaning to life with an ideal or highest value that is not absolute in the life-denying way of the ascetic ideal. Along these lines, Maudmarie Clark has argued that Nietzsche's critique of the will to truth does not involve the claim that there is no longer any value in searching for truth. Questioning truth as absolute value is not the same as claiming that truth does not exist or that it has no value. As Clark argues, one can pursue the truth of truth without conceiving of this pursuit as the most important thing one can do, or, at least, without thinking that this search has its end in itself (1990: 200). Clark proposes, therefore, that Nietzsche's task is to find a new ideal, for the sake of which one searches for truth. As Nietzsche asks, "Where is the opposing will that might express an opposing ideal?" (GM: 146). Finding their meaning in the absolute value of truth, human beings will find their meaning in some other ideal, which as Clark rightly points out, will be an ideal that affirms this-worldly life.

But what makes an ideal life affirming or life denying? In the *Genealogy*, Nietzsche neither poses an explicit answer to this question, nor proposes an alternative to the ascetic ideal. While he points to Zarathustra as the "man of the future, who will redeem us . . . from the hitherto reigning ideal" (GM: 96), he only takes us as far as the "problem" of the old ideal. One partial explanation for this is that Nietzsche finds himself still captive to the ascetic ideal. He finds himself on a threshold, at a place where values that have reigned heretofore are devaluing themselves and where the future remains unclear because the will to truth remains a problem. But he also claims that this problem of the will to truth *is* the meaning of "our being." Is Nietzsche suggesting that the *question* of the will to truth and the ascetic ideal—"the only meaning offered so far"—is itself a new meaning? If we follow *Genealogy's* identification of "meaning" and "ideal," do we find that the new ideal for which Nietzsche is searching is the search itself?

Morality as Mastery

For Nietzsche, "morality," strictly speaking (though he will use the term more loosely at times), is the mode of valuing rooted in *ressentiment* and the metaphysical faith in opposite values. The priest, the guardian of morality, proclaims the ultimate value of selflessness and the virtue of surrender. Nietzsche, however, unmasks priestly morality as an uncanny, and intricately deceptive drive for power. It has been braided out of secret and obsessive mutterings of the need for vengeance on all that constrains or hurts the vulnerable self; it arises in the tenderly nurtured desire to have more power than the rapacious oppressors; power, as I have indicated, that is incontestable, absolute, inhuman. Nietzsche's attack on the ascetic ideal is an attack on the priestly attempt to master "life itself," revealing the fundamental nature of Nietzsche's concept of nihilism: seeking absolute mastery, this mode of idealizing and valuing in essence eviscerates the very ground of value—life itself—and so produces highest values that must always consume themselves (GM: 117–18).[14] At the same time, however, this insidious "will to power of the weakest" is able to triumph over the "noble morality" of the strong.

As the philosopher of the will to power, Nietzsche affirms the way all life strives for power. Nevertheless, he attacks morality because it is based in a quest for unworldly power: unable to exercise the power of life, it seeks power over life. Adherents of the ascetic ideal, on this view, nurture twists of self-deception, which permit them to evade knowledge of their hatred for life and ground their claims to power not in their own will, but in a "divine" will to which they "surrender" themselves. Since their morality exalts self-surrender, they must never admit how this ruse disguises their hunger for limitless power. Nietzsche perceives that adherents of the ascetic ideal find relief from the human condition by bathing in the intoxicating righteousness of *moral* condemnation, which derives not from the puny, insignificant self, but from infinite God, who upholds the weak and mortifies the strong. Through morality, one denounces one's own finite power in a self-deceptive orgy of self-denial only in order to wield or be comforted by absolute, divine power.

The problem of nihilism as Nietzsche poses it in the *Genealogy* is primarily a moral problem—not just one moral problem among others, but the problem of morality itself. It is not a religious problem. Evidence for this can be found in the fact that Nietzsche does not find the slave revolt in values only in the emergence of Judaism and Christianity, or in religion in general, as one who has read only the *Genealogy* might suppose.

---

[14] Cf. Kristeva (1987: 63): "It is the height of nihilism to claim in the name of the rights of man—or superman—rights over life itself."

Nietzsche's critique of the "slave revolt in values" is also at the heart of his criticism of Western philosophy since Plato. In *Twilight of the Idols* (1888), he traces the trajectory of *ressentiment* and morality through the philosophical revaluation accomplished by Socrates. There, Nietzsche returns us to the victory of Socratic philosophical optimism over the pessimism of Greek tragedy, an optimism he had described in an earlier book as the "delusion of limitless power" (BT: 111). He argues that Socratic dialectic was a tool of the "rabble" by which Socrates completed the destruction of the aristocratic mode of valuation. With the Athenian nobles already mired in decadence, their instincts in a state of anarchy, forces from the lower social order embodied in Socrates asserted themselves to impose a new mode of valuation grounded in morality and reason (TI: 39–44). Nietzsche condenses this mode of valuation in the formula "reason = virtue = happiness." Socratic *ressentiment* expresses itself by endowing reason with absolute value. Reason as moral imperative overrides the instincts of self-affirmation and dominance that had characterized the Greeks of the tragic age. All instincts and desires now had to *justify* themselves before the tribunal of reason, all that Nietzsche will come to call "the body" now had to submit itself to the mastery of consciousness. This mastery becomes the obsession of Western philosophy—a philosophy of consciousness—from Plato to Kant and Schopenhauer.

For Nietzsche the critique of nihilistic mastery shakes the foundations of modern, Western morality, which means, ultimately, the seat of this morality in the concept of the ego or the "I." In his later work, Nietzsche returns again and again to the concept of the "I," criticizing priestly philosophers who have been bewitched by grammar into believing that "I" refers to some kind of substantiality, some autonomous consciousness, underlying all acts and feelings. As Nietzsche puts it in the *Genealogy*, the priest understands the "I" as a "neutral substratum" behind all actions, as their cause. This belief, Nietzsche thinks, is an error with great consequences (TI: 48). For the priest, "evil" implies the judgment that those so designated can choose not to be as they are, that they are responsible for their "evil" (GM: 45). The "I" is the ground of this responsibility: because its neutrality means it can "choose" to act in one way or another, it is the condition for the ideas of free will and responsibility, ideas without which morality would not have been possible (GM: 45). And for the resentful priest the idea of a self with free will becomes a powerful weapon in the battle with the nobles because it allows the priest to claim that the nobles are responsible for the harm they visit upon the weak.

Philosophers have followed the priest by attaching to this "I" the thought not just of freedom but also of holiness. This is especially clear in Kant, for whom morality is concentrated in a freely reasoning and willing "I" that can divorce itself from body, instincts, desire, relationships—from the whole of its material and historical matrix—in order to will solely on rational/moral grounds. Such willing is definitive of holiness. The imaginary unified consciousness is set over against the body and desire, expressing freedom and holiness by subjugating those imponderable forces of energy and fecundity. The moral self, the holy self, is the self who masters that part of itself that changes. Although, as we have seen, Schopenhauer takes issue with Kantian epistemology, both are in essential agreement with respect to morality and holiness. As in Kant, Schopenhauer identifies holiness with the freedom of the will by which the will detaches itself from the life of the body and the passions. For both, then, the self, as holy—as spirit—exists only in a certain curved cipher, whose sharp edges cut against the suffering body. Nietzsche despised this domesticated holiness that opposes in principle the wildness of the body, for it expresses the philosophical baptism of a pathological will to mastery. Such holiness no longer breathes in the element of mysterious attractions, births, transformations, deaths, which disclose the permeability of the self, its radical constitution through unbiddable forces; holiness as a certain abashed and exalted piety before the necessities of one's life is overthrown. Instead, now, the holiness of the self is readily located in the imaginary, yet utterly transparent, point of the impassive free will.

It is from the perspective of this critique of morality as "anti-nature" (TI: 52) that Nietzsche rejects moral concepts of "responsibility," "freedom," and "spirit." These concepts drive the stake of responsibility deep into the body of human beings, dividing them from themselves with the idea that it is their finitude and animality that are responsible for their suffering. To this spectacle of human beings tearing themselves apart from guilt, Nietzsche can offer only an agonized lament: "Oh, this insane, pathetic beast—man! What ideas he has, what unnaturalness, what paroxysms of nonsense, what *bestiality of thought* erupts as soon as he is prevented just a little from being a *beast in deed*!" (GM: 93). Responsibility as a moral category, suspended between guilt and innocence, registers the ideal of primordial mastery, given to human beings, a mastery over suffering itself, over life itself. This, finally, is God's mastery, devolved upon human beings in the moment of creation. Yet despite his provocative claims about the nonexistence of free will, the illusion of the ego, and the sickness of morality, Nietzsche does not seek to deny certain possibilities of freedom, self, or responsibility. His objective is to combat the psychological and sociological uses to which these ideas have been put in service of the morality of the ascetic ideal. And he seeks to imagine a human self whose freedom and holiness are not premised on the grammatical "I," nor lorded over the heterogeneous regions of suffering, desire, and contingency, which philosophers designate, "the body." Although Nietzsche thinks a certain kind of self-mastery is the mark of the noble, affirmative self, such mastery must be distinguished from the absolute mastery over life.[15] Self-mastery, as Nietzsche affirms it, is always mastery within life, thus vulnerable to the inescapable conditions of life and growth. It must affirm this vulnerability, not seek to hide or flee from it.

CONCLUSION

From the time of *The Birth of Tragedy*, Nietzsche, in one way or another, grappled with the question of the value of life. In his later work, however, he was convinced that the question itself was symptomatic of a perverse will to master life. Discussing "The Problem of Socrates," in *Twilight of the Idols*, Nietzsche writes: "One must reach out and try to grasp this astonishing *finesse, that the value of life cannot be estimated.* Not by a living man, because he is party to the dispute, indeed its object, and not the judge of it; not by a dead one, for another reason.—For a philosopher to see a problem in the *value* of life thus even constitutes an objection to him, a question-mark as to his wisdom, a piece of unwisdom" (TI: 40). The value of life cannot be estimated by the living, which includes the deadened priest who absolutizes self-surrender or the deadened philosopher who seeks to master life through consciousness. A will to mastery over life underwrites both these demands, tearing human thought and expression from body, nature, and history.

In Nietzsche's rethinking of mastery, selfhood, and responsibility, one begins to apprehend the extent to which his search for a "Yes" to life changes the whole issue of value. The revaluation of all values is not simply a matter of a new set of values, but of a new way of valuing altogether, as Deleuze points out when he argues that the revaluation of values means

---

[15] To reiterate, Nietzsche does not equate this morality of mastery—the morality of the weak or the slaves—with religion per se. He does correlate it with the priestly revaluation made possible in the monotheistic religions of the Hebrews, but he also correlates life-affirming self-mastery with the religious roots of Greek tragedy. These correlations are evident in his contrast between the concepts of "sin," rooted in Judaism, with the Greek concept of "sacrilege." "Sin" is based in a conception of the divine as totally separated from the human, a dualistic vision of power, such that all transgressive expressions of human power are seen as utterly evil. By contrast, the concept of "sacrilege" does not assume an absolute distinction between human power and divine power. Transgression against the divine in this case, as evidenced in Greek tragedy, is punishable, but it is not without nobility (GS: 188). Thus tragedy is, for Nietzsche, alien to monotheistic religious traditions and Western philosophical morality alike.

"not a change of values, but a change in the element from which the value of values derives" (1983: 170). This element can be either the active "Yes" or the reactive "No." These are not judgments for or against life, but fundamental stances toward the alterity of existence from which all valuing emerges. For Nietzsche, the modern soul finds itself caught between the two.

He argues further that for centuries the "No" has been implicated in the will to truth. But now the will to truth unmasks itself to itself as an aversion to life. How can Nietzsche, himself a "man of knowledge" and— so I will argue—an ascetic, move from this "No" to the noble "Yes"? I have indicated that the inconclusiveness of both the *Genealogy* and *The Gay Science* suggests that for Nietzsche the "Yes" must begin here and now, in the midst of the problem of the ascetic ideal itself, not in the solution to the problem. Is it possible to live the problem of life turned against itself, valuing the search for its own sake, not for the sake of the destination? Nietzsche, on this reading, is not looking to settle the issue of life, but to dance with life, eschewing the rigid posture of philosophical and moral "positions" in the fluid choreography of gesture and motion. Nietzsche seeks to envision a mastery or self-discipline that is aesthetic rather than moral, the self-discipline and freedom of a dancer, for whom freedom and holiness emerge from the beauty of body and spirit in motion: "I would not know what the spirit of a philosopher might wish more to be than a good dancer. For the dance is his ideal, also his art, and finally also his only piety, his 'service of God'" (GS: 346).

This holiness entails its own practices, psalms, laments, deprivations, and raptures. It will involve, as we will see in the following chapters, characteristically religious themes. The question of religion has not been treated in any detail in this chapter, in part because I sought to demonstrate that Nietzsche's critique of nihilism is directed primarily at a certain way of valuing and devaluing life. Of course, Nietzsche argues that religious beliefs and institutions have been instrumental in sustaining the nihilistic dualism of the faith in opposite values, and, in certain instances, he comes close to identifying religion with nihilism. And in his later work, as he became more explicitly concerned with the problem of nihilism, Nietzsche's polemic against Christianity became sharper and more relentless, to the point where in two of his final works, Christianity is identified as *the* enemy of his positive Dionysian vision. If we want to talk about the religious character of Nietzsche's philosophical vision, we are clearly faced with the conundrum of identifying the instrumentalities of his vision with the very tropes he vehemently denounced.

It will be necessary, then, to determine the nature and scope of Nietzsche's criticism of religion. What, precisely, is the link between religion and nihilism? What distinctions need to be drawn between Christianity, in particular, and religion, in general? And what is one to make of the "remainder" of religious language and imagery in Nietzsche's writing? Why, for example, does he leave us, at the end of *Ecce Homo*, not with Zarathustra—the "godless"—but with a confrontation between gods— "Dionysus vs. the Crucified"?

Chapter Two

FIGURING RELIGION, CONTESTING SPIRIT

> The stories of saints are the most ambiguous literature in existence . . .
> (Nietzsche, *The Antichrist*)

> The Christian conception of God—God as God of the sick, God
> as spider, God as spirit—is one of the most corrupt conceptions
> of God arrived at on earth: perhaps it even represents the low-
> water mark in the descending development of the God type. God
> degenerated to the *contradiction* of life, instead of being its
> transfiguration and eternal *Yes!*
> (Nietzsche, *The Antichrist*)

> Have I been understood?—*Dionysus vs. the Crucified.*
> (Nietzsche, *Ecce Homo*)

THE POWER OF RELIGION

WITH FREUD AND MARX, Nietzsche is widely regarded as one of the modern period's original and most influential "masters of suspicion." Like their Enlightenment predecessors, each of these thinkers held the critique of religion as an important key to overcoming the discontents of humankind and realizing human autonomy. At the same time, each went beyond Enlightenment conceptions of reason and superstition to develop deep critical readings of religion that sought to account for the hold it exerted on human beings. In the case of Nietzsche, the quintessential modern vision of the liberation from religion leading to human progress is especially evident in the pre-*Zarathustra* works, where he seeks to accomplish a movement from a philosophy still bound by metaphysics, morality, and religion to a "truly liberating philosophical science" (HH: 26). His later work, however, complicates this vision, not only on the matters of philosophy and affirmation, but on the matter of religion as well. Religion in Nietzsche's text is multivalent—both with respect to the meaning of the concept itself and with respect to his judgments about the value of particular religious traditions and figures.[1] This multivalence, however, has not been satisfactorily acknowl-

---

Epigraphs: Nietzsche, AC: 150; AC: 138; EH: 335.

[1] Nietzsche entitles the third chapter of *Beyond Good and Evil*, "*Das Religiöse Wesen.*"

edged by Nietzsche's commentators: in this chapter, I chart the contours of this multivalence to show that it demands a rethinking of Nietzsche's critique of religion.

Consoling Powers

In *Human, All too Human*, and in *Dawn*, Nietzsche explores the question of religion from two methodological perspectives, following the pattern I isolated in the previous chapter. First, he attacks the speculative origin of religion. For example, he suggests that it originated in the attempt to regulate nature through the mistaken belief that nature is controlled by invisible spirits. For those with a modern, intellectual conscience, he argues, it is no longer possible to believe in supernatural beings or forces. "Thus the daemon of Socrates too was perhaps an ear-infection which, in accordance with the moralizing manner of thinking that dominated him, he only interpreted differently from how it would be interpreted now" (HH: 68). Second, following his protogenealogical claim that "the more insight we possess into an origin, the less significant does it appear" (D: 31), Nietzsche critically examines the value of religion by asking how this speculative, intellectual "error" could exert such a hold on human imagination and life.[2] Nietzsche forges a psychological link between the philosophical and genealogical approaches to religion with the ideas of fear, suffering, and power. He believes that metaphysical, religious errors take hold of the human imagination in situations of fear or suffering, developing as powerful ways of coping with the uncontrollable exigencies of human life. These ideas and practices are more than errors, they constitute a hermeneutic through which one comes to view and experience life and suffering. As Nietzsche writes in the opening of his chapter on religion

---

One might translate this as "the essence of religion" (Walter Kaufmann's translation turns it into the question, "What is religion?"). Nietzsche identifies this *Wesen* as the *religiöse Neurose*—the religious neurosis. Does Nietzsche, in the end, essentialize religion, despite his genealogical method and the numerous meanings that "religion" takes on in his work? And does he connect the essence of religion with the misery of a human neurosis he seeks to overcome? Gilles Deleuze, whose *Nietzsche and Philosophy* has had an enormous impact on poststructuralism and the "new Nietzsche," makes such an argument. Deleuze recognizes quite clearly that Nietzsche claims there are active and affirmative gods and religions. However, he also argues that Nietzsche nonetheless holds that religion is essentially tied to bad conscience, and, from bad conscience, also to *ressentiment* and guilt (1983: 143–44). On this reading, religion is essentially allied to all the "reactive forces" that for Deleuze are at the root of the nihilistic negation of being that Nietzsche's affirmation seeks to overcome. As I argue below, however, it is a mistake to move so quickly from bad conscience to guilt. Moreover, this identification of religion and *ressentiment* does not leave adequate room for religion as "gratitude," which Nietzsche attributes to the Greeks.

[2] For example, his discussion of "metaphysical need" (HH: 62) and the uses of "revelation" (D: 38).

in *Human, All too Human,* when people suffer, they "can dispose of it either by getting rid of its cause or by changing the effect it produces in our sensibilities" (HH: 60). To address its effects on our sensibilities is to interpret suffering, in this case by interpreting life and world religiously (and, Nietzsche adds, artistically and metaphysically).

Thus, Nietzsche raises three basic objections to religion, where religion is understood as the belief in metaphysical entities that determine the fortunes and misfortunes of human life. First, it is an intellectual error to posit metaphysical causes, since, by definition, we can have no evidence of such causes. Second, by positing metaphysical causes of suffering and developing methods of calling to and persuading divine power(s) to address their woes, human beings ignore real, worldly causes. Consequently, suffering is only ameliorated through a "narcotic" effect, not eliminated or healed. Finally, as with any narcotic, religious (and moral) interpretations only grant the alleviation of suffering by intensifying other kinds of suffering. For example, Christianity alleviates meaninglessness and hopelessness by infecting people with the belief in sin and guilt, which only further alienates them from the reality of human life. Ultimately, Nietzsche thinks, religious interpretations of suffering make the human condition worse.[3] "The worst sickness of mankind originated in the way in which they have combated their sicknesses, and what seemed to cure has in the long run produced something worse than that which it was supposed to overcome" (D: 33).

Religion as a hermeneutic of suffering has succeeded, Nietzsche argues, in large part because it has been able to impart to human beings a sense of power in the face of fear and suffering.[4] Even in *Human, All too Human,* and *Dawn,* before Nietzsche began to write of the "will to power," the nature of divine power was crucial for his hermeneutic of religion. Of particular importance here is the distinction between polytheism and monotheism. Nietzsche admired the polytheism of the Greeks. He saw the Greek gods as idealized versions of humans, standing in close relationship to them, "as though two castes lived side by side, a nobler and mightier and one less noble; but both somehow belong together in their origins and are of *one* species" (HH: 65). Although these gods are in one sense metaphysical because they "exist" beyond the physical, they are not metaphysical in the sense that, as values, they oppose and negate the physical world. Such gods develop as an idealizing expression of noble self-affirmation. Moreover, Nietzsche finds in polytheism's affirmation

---

[3] See, for example, HH: 60, where Nietzsche claims that religion, art, and metaphysical philosophy are interpretations of suffering that serve only as narcotics and cannot address the real problem of suffering.

[4] Nietzsche ascribes the origin of religion to various factors, for example, the struggle with nature (HH: 65) and of fear and need (HH: 62). See also D: 16, 19.

of plurality the roots of later positive developments of humanity. In *The Gay Science*, he writes of polytheism's "wonderful art and gift of creating gods" and considers its affirmation of plurality a great advantage over monotheism. Polytheism was the preliminary form of the "free-spiriting and many-spiriting of man [which cultivated] the strength to create for ourselves our own new eyes" (GS: 191). In other words, polytheism provides a certain kind of model for a philosophy of "free spirits" and "perspectivism." In this affirmation of plurality and difference, polytheism also provides Nietzsche with a model for affirmative love. "What is love but understanding and rejoicing at the fact that another lives, feels and acts in a way different from and opposite to ours. If love is to bridge these antitheses through joy it may not deny or seek to abolish them" (HH: 229–30).

By contrast, in monotheistic visions of absolute power Nietzsche isolates the key to the metaphysical faith in opposite values and its devaluation of the human. The monotheistic notion of divinity, he claims, is based in an absolute, metaphysical gulf between God and human. I have already indicated how, from this theological perspective, when human beings compare themselves with this almighty God, they see themselves as "totally depraved," "crushed and shattered" beneath the weight of divine perfection. The god of monotheism therefore reflects not an idealization of the human, but is a negative reflection of a lack, representing all that we are not but should be. Given this distinction between polytheism and monotheism, then, it is not surprising that as his thinking develops, Nietzsche's most detailed and incisive criticisms of "religion" come more and more to focus on what is for him the most completely developed form of monotheism: "Christianity." This suffering of the soul in sin, instilled through the Christian conception of divine power, horrifies Nietzsche and becomes the target of a bitter polemic. Reaching its peak in his final months of frenzied writing, the target of his polemic against sin, punishment, and responsibility "becomes Christian."[5]

Nietzsche's critical view of Christianity focuses on the concept of sin, which he links to the figure of Paul. For Nietzsche, Paul is the true founder of Christianity as tradition and dogma. (Interestingly, as I discuss below, the intensity of Nietzsche's contempt for Paul is matched by his admiration for Jesus.) Nietzsche's interpretation of Paul is, in key respects, traditionally Protestant, concentrating on Paul's struggle with the Law and the theological genius that was able to "discover a signpost of consolation in [his] own personal distress" (D: 39). But Nietzsche attributes this struggle

[5] Though after *Dawn* Nietzsche's primary target remains Christianity, in the *Genealogy* he places the original revaluation of all values at the feet of the Jews. In the *Antichrist*, Nietzsche also casts Buddhism as a development of nihilistic resignation. Throughout, the Greeks and the "Brahmans" hold a more positive position.

and its success less to Paul's piety than to his yearning for distinction and power. Paul discovers that his guilt over his inevitable sinning can be eliminated by "accepting" the fact that the Law is overcome with the crucifixion of Jesus. Dying with Christ, Paul can die to the Law; and to die to the Law is to die to the flesh.[6] Dying to the world and the flesh, Nietzsche writes, Paul becomes one with Jesus in an "intoxication" of divinity where "all shame, all subordination, all bounds are taken from [the importunity of his soul] and the intractable lust for power reveals itself as an anticipatory reveling in *divine* glories" (D: 42).

Nietzsche's Paul reinterprets the suffering of guilt and sin as signs that one must turn against the world. This does not eliminate one's guilt; in fact, it intensifies it as one begins to see—more and more clearly, the harder one tries to turn away from the world—how deeply one remains enmeshed in it. Rather than relieving guilt, the Pauline strategy is to bring it to a nearly unbearable pitch in the recognition of one's worthlessness— and in preparation for surrendering to the power of grace. On this reading, suffering and worldly misery are signs of future happiness. "[M]an sees in every feeling of indisposition and misfortune a punishment, that is to say, an atonement for guilt and the means of getting free from the evil spell of a real or supposed injustice" (D: 15). The idea of a moral God consoles only by casting suffering as a sign of future bliss, and requiring that it be intensified in order to gain that future state. Suffering itself is not healed, but, at the price of one kind of suffering from suffering— guilt—another—the feelings of helplessness and uncertainty—is ameliorated. Suffering is "healed" only in its transformation into hatred for this world and desire for the next.

Nietzsche's treatment of Paul establishes the basis of his attack on Christianity as an attack on religious monotheism. The monotheist devalues finite human power in an intoxicating, self-deceptive contrast with the absolute power of God. The way to new life is accomplished not simply by cultivating a path of suffering, but by systematically devaluing and renouncing all that is human. Nietzsche will pursue this argument in great depth in the *Genealogy*, where he shows that the power of the ascetic ideal finds a foothold in a decadent, exhausted culture. In such a context, the goal of another life enables decadents to live, it relieves boredom and exhaustion by giving them something to strive for: the rest and peace they want more than anything else.

In *Dawn*, however, Nietzsche develops a different part of his analysis, one that is always presupposed in his later work. Instead of concentrating on the religiosity of followers, Nietzsche analyzes the paradigmatic reli-

---

[6] As part of his critical insistence on a dualistic interpretation of Christianity, Nietzsche flatly interprets "flesh" as carnality, thereby equating it with nature in general. As I discuss in Chapter 3, many Christian thinkers do not equate "flesh" and body or nature.

gious virtuosos—the saint, the ascetic, and the priest—to show how they thrive on the metaphysical interpretation of power that becomes Christianity. This attention to the religious virtuoso coincides with the development of Nietzsche's ideas about power in the years leading up to the writing of *Zarathustra*. In *Human, All too Human*, Nietzsche seems to be operating with an essentially hedonistic view of human motivation: human beings are motivated by the desire to maximize pleasure and minimize pain. But even there, and more and more in *Dawn*, Nietzsche refers to the "lust for power" as that which drives human beings (D: 16). He argues that suffering is of little consequence because human beings do not strive after happiness or pleasure, but after power. This issue dominates the opening pages of *Dawn*, to the point where Nietzsche appears no longer interested in the intellectual errors at the origin of religion, but in the way religion originates in the lust for power. He continues to stress the need for consolation, but now the promise of a better life is not simply a consolation that allows one to *bear* suffering in the present, but, to the extent that one is able to strive for that future by imposing suffering in the present, one also is able to experience the intoxication of power. Put differently, power itself consoles (D: 15, 19). And it does so in two ways: through "madness" and "voluntary suffering," both of which are means to power perfected in the saint.

The Saint

Following Schopenhauer, the saint is for Nietzsche the paradigm of the religious virtuoso or genius: as in Schopenhauer, the saint is both mystic and ascetic. Nietzsche argues that ecstatic states and ascetic practices enable certain people to exercise great power. In the "madness" of ecstasy, one appears to lose oneself in the immediate and to experience the overwhelming power of the "divine," in a way that rids one, at least temporarily, of fear and anxiety. "By devoting yourself with enthusiasm and making a sacrifice of yourselves you enjoy the ecstatic thought of henceforth being at one with the powerful being . . . to whom you dedicate yourself" (D: 134). Moreover, through such experience, the metaphysical interpretation of the cosmos is confirmed. One can see that an extraordinary power exists, a power unlike anything one can produce oneself and through which one feels united with all. One finds, in the ecstatic state, the transcendent goal of human life, the true state of the human soul, in comparison with which the life of finitude and change stands condemned (D: 27, 33). The self-deception of this stance is at the root of Nietzsche's critique of mysticism.

This power promises those who have ecstatic experiences, as well as those who observe them, that it is possible for human beings to possess, in being possessed, divine powers and "pure spirit." Ecstasy, in this case, literally is the loss of oneself, but it is a loss repaid with a gain. The ecstatic, by means of this possession, is able to separate him- or herself from the domination of custom and law that binds the community together, for the feeling of power serves as a divine warrant for the rejection of the communal norm; it becomes the guarantee that the voice urging one to depart from custom is not the voice of a mere human, but the voice of a god. The display of ecstasy or madness also can convince the rest of the community of the presence of divine power, concentrating that power in the saint. Nietzsche invokes the concept of "spectacle" and "performance" to explain the cultural power of ecstasy: madness becomes a dramatic struggle between the divine and the human.

In addition to madness, sometimes in the context of madness, "cruelty" plays a crucial role in the drama of power because, as Nietzsche puts it, "to practice cruelty is to enjoy the highest gratification of the feeling of power" (D: 16). In the spectacle of cruelty, human beings find power in forgetting the suffering of their own lives. They also imagine that the gods enjoy cruelty, so it becomes necessary to have in the community people who suffer. The ascetic is originally so fascinating for Nietzsche because religious leaders can stand out from and lead the community if they take upon themselves a certain amount of "voluntary suffering" in order to appease the gods (D: 17). Because most people cannot comprehend how others can impose suffering upon themselves, they assume that those who can, those who overcome the power of natural human desire and display their self-denial in excess and ecstasy, are empowered with divinity. Self-imposed suffering produces a feeling of power in the ascetic as well—as with Paul, there is a unique feeling of power that comes with absolute submission, submission to the point of inflicting suffering upon oneself. In fact, Nietzsche argues, "happiness, conceived of as the liveliest feeling of power, has perhaps been nowhere greater on earth than in the souls of superstitious ascetics" (D: 68).

In a fundamental sense, the power of the ascetic is based in an illusion. As "this riddle of self-conquest and final renunciation" (BG: 65), the ascetic certainly is a powerful human being. But Nietzsche, unlike Schopenhauer, does not believe that any "final renunciation" or absolute self-transcendence is possible. "The truth of the matter is that you only seem to sacrifice yourselves: in reality you transform yourselves in thought into gods and enjoy yourselves as such" (D: 139). Nietzsche acknowledges the feeling of the divine as a feeling of power, but points out that the idea of "self-sacrifice" is self-deceptive. Without dismissing the value of ecstasy or renunciation and without dismissing the usefulness of the concept of the divine, Nietzsche contends that as long as ecstasy and renunciation are interpreted as indications of metaphysical power, they hide the fact that fundamentally they are ways of increasing power that is "human, all too human." The distinction between finite human power and absolute divine power is a false one. The religious illusion that propagates the power of the ecstatic/ascetic saint helps also to propagate destructive ideas about guilt, responsibility, and the corruption of the "natural" human condition.

But the saint remains for Nietzsche an ambiguous figure. Even after turning away from Schopenhauer, Nietzsche continues to be fascinated with the idea of self-denial. This leads him to rethink the vague psychological hedonism that marks *Human, All too Human*, in favor of a more complex understanding of the psychology of power. Any simple understanding of pleasure and pain is inadequate for explaining the "happiness" that can result from the denial (which for Nietzsche is, in fact, always the deferral) of pleasure, the embrace of surrender or weakness (D: 36), and, most important, the striving for freedom. Although Nietzsche finds that ecstatics and ascetics deceive themselves as to the source of their power, he recognizes that their freedom, their departure from the stupid pleasures and consolations of the herd, could be purchased only at the price of great pain. "Every smallest step in the field of free thought, of a life shaped personally, has always had to be fought for with spiritual and bodily tortures . . . change of any kind has needed its innumerable martyrs" (D: 17). Madness and suffering, suffering in madness, are means by which those chosen by the gods are identified to stand apart, with the power of distinction, from the community. In this respect, the saint is a force of alterity within the human and a precursor to Nietzsche's free spirit. In his own striving for freedom of thought, genuine philosophy, and individuality, Nietzsche encounters his own pain and power and inquires whether he might not find some direction along this path from the saint.

The Priest

The saint is the central religious figure of Nietzsche's early work, but after *Dawn* the figure of the priest begins to play an equal, if not more important, role.[7] The emergence of the priest in Nietzsche's texts is tied to the increasing vehemence of his attacks on Christianity, as well as the growing subtlety of his conception of the workings of power in individual and society. With respect to the saint, Nietzsche argues that religion is a means by which individuals cultivate and interpret extraordinary experi-

[7] There is no final way to demarcate the priest from the ascetic or the ecstatic saint, for a priest could be a saint and vice versa. One might say that "priest" for Nietzsche is a socioreligious category and has to do primarily with religion as institution, while "saint" is primarily a spiritual category.

ences and disciplines of power through which they distinguish themselves from the herd. But already in the analysis of the saint, Nietzsche saw how such power could be used not just to tear the individual away from the constraints of the community, but also to exercise power over the community. The saint, in other words, can be a force for alterity but also a force for new community and conformity. Nietzsche articulates this possibility in his discussions of the priest, complicating the figure of the saint by showing how one class of people exerts social power by investing itself with the aura of the divine, and also, in the process, by infecting others with the self-doubt and self-hatred of guilt and sin. These analyses are not unrelated: as the Paul of *Dawn* found an intoxicating sense of the divine in the depths of sin, the priest of the later work transforms impotence—the inability to express oneself in "deeds"—into a "spiritual" strength. But Nietzsche's later analysis is distinguished by the addition of the concept of *ressentiment*, a "most spiritual and poisonous kind of hatred" (GM: 33). With this development, the later Nietzsche, particularly in the *Genealogy*, exposes the means by which priestly power in the west has accomplished a "revaluation of values."

Nietzsche describes *ressentiment* as the hatred of "all that represents the *ascending* movement of life, well-constitutedness, power, beauty, self-affirmation on earth." He goes on to say that, as priestly hatred of such affirmation, *ressentiment* "becomes genius" and

> invent[s] *another* world from which that *life–affirmation* would appear evil, reprehensible as such. . . . [For the] *priestly* kind, *decadence* is only a *means*: this kind of man has a life-interest in making mankind *sick* and inverting the concepts "good" and "evil," "true" and "false," in a morally dangerous and world-calumnating sense. (AC: 144–45)

Reflecting on this hatred and on the sociological conflict between masters and slaves (or the noble and the base) leads Nietzsche to develop his most complex genealogical account of the origin of priestly religion—of which Christianity is the logical culmination. In the second essay of the *Genealogy*, Nietzsche distinguishes a fundamental psychological self-alienation he calls "bad conscience" from the idea of guilt before God. Bad conscience has its origin in the "internalization" of aggressive impulses required for the preservation of social structures. Guilt has a dual origin, first, in economic relationships of indebtedness, and, second, in the concept of "god" that grows out of the gradual intensification of the feeling of debt and fear toward ancestors. Here is where the priest steps in, finding in the concept of "god" a perfect tool for bringing the self-hatred of the bad conscience to its highest pitch. The priest transforms the feeling of debt before ancestors/gods into an unredeemable guilt before God.

This man of the bad conscience has seized upon the presupposition of religion so as to drive his self-torture to its most gruesome pitch of severity and rigor. Guilt before God: this thought becomes an instrument of torture to him. He apprehends in "God" the ultimate antithesis of his own ineluctable animal instincts; he reinterprets these animal instincts themselves as a form of guilt before God . . . he stretches himself upon the contradiction "God" and "Devil." (GM: 92)

Nietzsche is concerned here not with the power of the free spirit struggling against the morality of mores, but with a social revolution, an uprising of the "weak," led by the priest, who wield the weapon of the morality of good and evil. This distinction between good and evil, and, implicit in that distinction, the concepts of individual responsibility and guilt, corrupts the spontaneous self-affirmation of the nobles and makes self-denial an ideal. Through this ascetic ideal, Nietzsche argues, the priest has exerted great power in Western civilization and has given great numbers of exhausted, decadent people a reason to live, thus playing a significant role in the preservation of the human species.[8] Denying human power, invoking divine power, the priest institutes the mastery of the will to power of the weakest.

RELIGION AND THE FREE SPIRIT

Religion in Nietzsche I: Christianity and Totality

In the period between *Human, All too Human*, and the *Genealogy*, Nietzsche shifts emphasis from the saint to the priest. Correlatively, he comes to focus more and more on the development of monotheism in the Jewish and Christian traditions, and on the moral and social consequences of this trajectory. In the process, his critique of "religion" becomes, strictly speaking, a critique of monotheism, and particularly of Christianity. These trajectories are crucial parts of the more general movement of Nietzsche's thought, described in the previous chapter, toward a critique of Western nihilism. The focus on Christianity does not mean that there are not resources in both Nietzsche's early and late writing for a comprehensive critique of religion, or that it is impossible to define religion in such a way as to make Nietzsche's mature thought deeply opposed to "it." However, in his mature work Nietzsche's main problem is the nihilistic religio-moral revaluation of the "priest" who uses the monothe-

---

[8] Already, in *The Gay Science*, Nietzsche argues that every individual—even the most apparently harmful individual—inevitably serves the "preservation" of the human race. His main point concerns an "instinct," that is, the instinct to preserve the human race, which Nietzsche claims is the "essence of our species, our herd" (GS: 73).

istic God of Christianity and Judaism to form a conception of the human emptied of any sense of self-worth. The priest relies on the idea of human depravity as strategy for worldly power. In this way, Christianity has "carried" Western nihilism for two millennia.

On these points, it is instructive to compare Nietzsche's thought to that of some of the other "masters of suspicion" of the nineteenth and early twentieth centuries. Marx, Nietzsche, and Freud, as well as Feuerbach, all offer methods of interpreting religion beyond the ostensive meaning of religious ideas, symbols, and practices. As critics of religion, they do not simply dismiss religion as superstition or error, they "read" religion: its signs have meanings and logics, or, alternatively, its signs are symptoms; in either case, religion can be read in a way that leads us to a greater understanding of the ills and the possibilities it holds for human life.

Of these thinkers, Feuerbach and Nietzsche developed the most genuinely critical readings of religion.[9] Neither simply rejects religion, like some of their Enlightenment predecessors, as simply a mistake; each explores the complex roles, both constructive and destructive, that religion has played in human culture. Their thought exhibits interesting parallels with respect to the concepts of projection and alienation, and to the place of Christianity in a developmental scheme of religions. In these respects, Hegel and the historicizing temper of the nineteenth century stand in back of both of them. Feuerbach argues that the idea of god originates when human beings "project" their species consciousness, creating belief in a separate, transcendent reality. This projection, more literally, this "objectification" (*Vergegenständlichung*) gradually results in the alienation of humanity from its powers and possibilities as humanity weakens itself to the same degree that the projected god becomes more and more perfect. Obviously, there is some similarity here to Nietzsche's claims about religion and power, for he too, as I have argued above, claims that belief in a perfect, all powerful God drains human beings of their ability to affirm their own power.[10] To borrow the term *alienation* to describe the effects of metaphysical and moral religion in Nietzsche is to acknowledge the point that for him, as for Feuerbach, human beings can lose themselves through belief in God.

[9] Ultimately Feuerbach is more concerned than Nietzsche with the question "What is religion?" Here, I confine my remarks to the Feuerbach of *The Essence of Christianity*. For the definitive treatment of Feuerbach on religion, see Harvey 1995. Wagner, at least before his conversion to Christianity, was strongly influenced by Feuerbach and encouraged Nietzsche to read him. Surprisingly, Nietzsche mentions Feuerbach fewer than ten times in his notes, though, according to one of contemporaries, Nietzsche was discussing Feuerbach with friends and acquaintances in the period leading up to *Zarathustra* (see Gilman 1987: 114).

[10] "He ejects from himself [*wirft . . . aus sich heraus*] all his denial of himself, of his nature, naturalness, and actuality, in the form of an affirmation, as something existent, corporeal, real, as God, as the holiness of God, as God the Judge, as God the Hangman" (GM: 92).

In distinction from Feuerbach, however, Nietzsche claims that Christians do not project their possibilities and perfections into God, but rather their impossibilities. In other words, God becomes a perfect omnipotence that humans could never achieve. This impossible perfection makes their own finite power seem worthless.[11] Where for Feuerbach the concept of God *is* human possibility, for Nietzsche the concept destroys genuine possibility. For Feuerbach, therefore, the danger of alienation lies in the loss of that which human beings have projected into God; that which has been alienated must be recovered. The Hegelian Feuerbach sees a universal process of projection, alienation, and reconciliation as the history of the development of human self-consciousness. Like Hegel, he sees the history of religion as involving a necessary alienation by which human destiny is achieved. History, coming to its culmination in modern self-consciousness, testifies to the redemption of alienation in this self-consciousness: alienation and religion have been the means by which human beings have come to know and become themselves. For Nietzsche, by contrast, God becomes a means to self-torture. The function of alienation consists in the priestly preservation of the weak. The genealogical Nietzsche sees the concept of god being used in a particular way in a particular historical trajectory by which human beings alienate themselves in the worship of God. Although Nietzsche does think that it has brought some benefits to human culture, this historical trajectory does not represent the necessary movement of spirit or human self-consciousness.

Despite this difference, Nietzsche, like Hegel and Feuerbach, does think that we can understand the significance of the history of alienation only in a reading of Christianity, one that attends especially to the correlation between Christ's crucifixion and the atheism of the present. In each of these thinkers, the concept of alienation is worked out in the logic of the concept of the monotheistic God, which reaches its culmination in the Christian narrative of the death of God in the crucifixion of Christ. The crucifixion is the self-sacrifice of God. For Hegel, and especially for Feuerbach, this self-sacrifice is an act of love by which God gives autonomy to human beings, an autonomy realized, paradoxically, in the atheism of the nineteenth century. For Nietzsche, matters are more complicated and ambiguous. He argues that the crucifixion marks the culmination of religious self-hatred insofar as it reflects the recognition that the debt to God could never be repaid by human beings, that only God could pay the

---

[11] It must be kept in mind that Nietzsche's criticism only goes for monotheism. In fact, it seems that the Feuerbachian idea of "objectification" might be more properly applied to Nietzsche's claims about polytheism. For Nietzsche, monotheists project their fears and their lack into God; polytheists project their ideals, that is, their strengths. This is objectification in a strict sense, that is, without the detrimental, alienating effects that Feuerbach describes.

wages of sin. In this respect, the crucifixion points to the ultimate power-lessness of human beings. Moreover, the death of God in modernity does not automatically lead to autonomy, for, as I have discussed, atheism it-self, for Nietzsche, can be a form of religious nihilism. Yet, Nietzsche does recognize in himself, and thus in a certain trajectory of modern Western thought, a turning point in the development of human self-consciousness. He finds in himself the kernel of the ascetic ideal—the will to truth—and, in doing so, becomes aware of himself as a point in the history of nihilism, an awareness that holds some promise for the overcoming of the denial of the world. There is, then, as in Feuerbach and Hegel, the promise of "redemption" in the death of God (TI: 64). God's overcoming of God—the highest value devaluing itself—is the high point of nihilism.

Christianity, in short, is ultimately more radically self-effacing for Nietzsche than it is for either Hegel or Feuerbach. Hegelian logic, to which at least the early Feuerbach is still indebted, demands that the es-sence of Christian truth and love be fully realized in the death of God. Feuerbach, for example, argues that God's sacrifice for love shows us that it is more important to love one another than to love God: love conquers faith. More generally, Christianity essentially realizes its morality in its own self-dissolution, or kenosis. Thus both Hegel and Feuerbach adhere to the modern tendency to find the positive content of religion in morality, content that can be purified of tradition and dogma by philosophical rea-son. This idea is of a piece with their interpretation of the history of hu-manity as a history of an alienation ultimately reconciled. And to the extent that they propose an ultimate reconciliation, their visions are closed, totalizing. For both, and for Marx as well, this reconciliation is marked by the "end" of religion, where the "end" of religion is religion's goal, accomplished in Christianity's self-overcoming.

By contrast, Nietzsche claims that Christian love is based in self-hatred and that the overcoming of belief in God (which also is the overcoming of the will to truth) is not simply a demythologization but also demoral-ization. In other words, for Nietzsche, the completion of the devaluation of the highest values must involve a revaluation. The teleological vision of universal love and self-consciousness is, for Nietzsche, mere romanticism, more nihilism; he urges revaluation rather than reconciliation. He claims that human beings can never be reconciled to themselves if they will con-tinue to grow, if they are going to be able to affirm life. Reconciliation, the end of all alienation, means the end of striving and struggle, which, for Nietzsche, means the end of power, growth, life. Thus, he does not envision the final overcoming of bad conscience or asceticism, does not reject self-denial or self-imposed suffering. On the contrary, he values these as means to power, understood as the means to spiritualization, the creating of "distance" within the soul. Affirmation for Nietzsche thus is not a kind of reconciliation of the human being with him- or herself, an overcoming of self-hatred, the struggle of the self with itself, or suffering. Affirmation does overcome the alienation of believing oneself to be sinful, but Nietzsche's affirmation does not overcome a certain distance within the self, a self-aversion that keeps the self constantly striving.

In this respect, Nietzsche is closer to Freud, than to Hegel, Feuerbach, or Marx, for both Nietzsche and Freud reject a vision of a human consciousness and human community at peace with itself. But Nietzsche also resists the kind of resignation Freud exemplifies, finding self-aversion constitutive of joy and envisioning a "redemption of the earth" in a joyous, exuberant play of body and mind. One question, then, is how Nietzsche finds his way between resignation and reconciliation, how his thinking exemplifies Zarathustra's hope for a will that can "will something higher than any reconciliation" (Z: 141).

Religion in Nietzsche II: Affirming Alterity, Freeing the Spirit

A more general question needs to be addressed first. In one sense, at least, Nietzsche's rejection of Christianity, and of moral-metaphysical religion generally, is more complete than that of Feuerbach or Marx, because Nietzsche finds that there is no real promise in the Christian promise— only nihilism and decadence. But should we equate Nietzsche's polemic against Christianity with a polemic against religion in general? Much of what Nietzsche writes makes such an identification seem unproblematic; and it cannot be denied that in numerous places he claims that the answer to the nihilistic crisis of the modern West lies beyond religious belief and practice. Still, the issue can be contested on two grounds. First, even though Nietzsche does make some apparently sweeping rejections of "religion," he is not consistent on this point, as his comments on polytheism show. Second, even to the extent that Nietzsche does reject "religion," there is no prima facie reason that one should simply accept his claims about what does or does not count as "religion." If Nietzsche never develops a coherent or systematic theory, nor offers a comprehensive critique of "religion" in general, then even if one wants to argue that on his own terms Nietzsche does reject religion, one might want to question those terms. It may be that there are elements of his thought and his practice of philosophy that one might want to call religious, or, at least, that can be more fully comprehended when one attends to the way they are positively informed by religious traditions and practices. It becomes necessary, therefore, to elaborate Nietzsche's hints of a different, affirmative conception of religion by relating them to other aspects of his thought, and in light of a critical reading of his treatment of both religion and Christianity.

It is possible to distinguish at least three uses of "religion" in Nietzsche's texts. The dominant one is critical, and refers to priestly, monotheistic religion as a social force—most importantly, Christianity.

But alongside this conception are two others—polytheistic religion and saintliness—each of which reflects the value Nietzsche places on difference and affirmation. Neither conception is necessarily canceled out or rendered inconsequential by Nietzsche's attack on Christianity. On the contrary, Nietzsche considers both to be instrumental for understanding his "free spirit."

Nietzsche expresses a consistent admiration for pagan religion and polytheism. Though his admiration is in most respects muted compared with his condemnation of Christianity, his late invocations of Dionysus occupy a crucial place in his thought. As I have remarked, for Nietzsche polytheism's belief in a multiplicity of gods is an idealizing expression of gratitude for human life and for the differences that constitute it. Nietzsche invokes paganism and polytheism at crucial points in his work, thus qualifying his tendency to offer blanket condemnations of "religion" or the concepts of "divinity" or "god." For instance, at the point in the *Genealogy* where his attack on the Christian concept of guilt nears its rhetorical peak, Nietzsche pauses to reflect on "nobler uses" of the conceptions of gods in Greek religion (GM: 93).[12] Despite some of his own claims to the contrary, the distinction between monotheism and polytheism complicates the relation of religion and metaphysics in Nietzsche's writing. For it makes it impossible to say that Nietzsche simply defines religion in terms of metaphysics in the full, nihilistic sense. Even as he was writing *The Antichrist*, his notes reflect another attitude, one in which he could reflect on the possibility of a "yes-saying religion" and exclaim "and how many new gods are still possible!"[13]

In *The Gay Science*, Nietzsche writes of polytheism as the "preliminary form" of free spiritedness: "The wonderful art and gift of creating gods—polytheism—was the medium through which this impulse [to individualism] could discharge, purify, perfect and ennoble itself. . . . In polytheism the free-spiriting and many-spiriting of man attained its first preliminary form" (GS: 191–92). *Beyond Good and Evil* allows a more thorough comparison between such free spiritedness and the monomania of Christianity, for Nietzsche devotes the second chapter to the "free spirit" and the third to the "Religious Essence," especially as exemplified in Christianity. The chapter on spirit concentrates on the necessity of error for life, the masks and solitudes of the free spirit, and the philosopher as "attempter" who breaks with the herd's previous valuations and experiments with values and new ways of life. The "spirit," in this context, is defined as a capacity for "invention and simulation" (BG: 54), which enables the free spirit to cultivate the difference that marks his own life

[12] See also HH: 65 to 66; D: 129; BG: 49, 64; AC: 144.

[13] See SW 13; in the same volume of notes Nietzsche writes: "We believe in the Olympians, not in the "Crucified" (487).

and to become a force for difference in the culture. By contrast, in the next chapter the "Christian faith" is seen as the "sacrifice of all freedom, all pride, all self-confidence of the spirit" (BG: 60). As such, religion is "a bond that unites rulers and subjects and betrays and delivers the consciences of the latter, that which is most concealed and intimate and would like to elude obedience, to the former" (BG: 72–73). Where free spirits lead a life of cultivating and creating beauty out of difference—that which is "most concealed and intimate" about themselves—the *homines religosi* preach a life of conformity through self-denial.

As his polemic against Christianity grew in volume and rancor, particularly in his final year of writing, Nietzsche came more and more to oppose Christianity with the figure of Dionysus. In what turned out to be his final book, *Ecce Homo*, Nietzsche ends with the formula, "Dionysus versus the Crucified." This contrast is fleshed out in a note from the spring of 1888. There, Nietzsche compares the deaths and resurrections of Christ and Dionysus. The "Crucified" symbolizes the hope for final redemption from the human condition, the romantic wish for a life without suffering, resurrection into a *new* life. Dionysus, on the other hand, affirms suffering, because he is born back into *this* life. "One will see that the problem is that of the meaning of suffering: whether a Christian meaning or a tragic meaning. In the former case, it is supposed to be the path to holy existence; in the latter case, being is counted as *holy enough* to justify even a monstrous amount of suffering" (SW 13: 265–67). In both *Twilight of the Idols* and *Ecce Homo*, Nietzsche ties this concept of Dionysus to human creativity and the creative urge of life itself, suggesting a non-monotheistic, immanent conception of divinity.

"The stories of saints are the most ambiguous literature in existence" (AC: 150). With this observation, Nietzsche begins his most detailed and passionate treatment of the figure of Jesus and the concept of free spirit. In doing so, he articulates with some precision another aspect of his multivalent view of religion: the saint as a force of alterity and blessedness. Nietzsche's saint, though an ambiguous figure, is potentially a force for difference and affirmation because the saint finds the power to separate him- or herself from the herd, to affirm a different set of values, and to find a liberating blessedness in this life.

In the Gospels one finds Jesus as both preacher of the Sermon on the Mount and as fierce opponent of the Jews. How does one interpret such an ambiguous text to understand who Jesus really was? Nietzsche dismisses the historical-critical search for the "historical Jesus" as incapable of comprehending such ambiguity, arguing instead in favor of a "psychological" examination of the issue. And such, Nietzsche claims, can be conducted only by "we emancipated spirits" who possess the requisite insight and discipline to distinguish "Jesus" the man from "Christ" of the tradition. For my purposes, what is most significant about this claim is that Nietzsche thereby asserts a certain identity between himself and Jesus. Jesus is himself a kind of free spirit: "[H]e cares nothing for what is fixed: the word *killeth*, everything fixed *killeth*. . . . He speaks only of the inmost thing: 'life' or 'truth' of 'light' is his expression for the inmost thing—everything else, the whole of reality, the whole of nature, language itself possesses for him merely the value of a sign, a metaphor" (AC: 154).[14]

Nietzsche can be one of the first in almost two thousand years to really understand Jesus because, as free spirit himself, he also finds life in the movement of metaphor and death in the fixed conformity that so easily befalls community and language. Nietzsche, too, is an "evangel" (the label he thinks best fits Jesus) of affirmation, seeking to bring the "glad tidings" (EH: 327) of a spiritual perspective that "transfigures" all of reality: as Karl Jaspers put it, "The problem of the presence of eternity, of experiencing bliss, which Jesus solved by his way of life, is Nietzsche's own problem" (1961: 89).

In light of his vehement criticisms of Christianity, and of the "Christ" figure produced by the Christian tradition, Nietzsche's identification with Jesus, as only a few commentators have noted, is remarkable.[15] This is not to say that Nietzsche's portrait of Jesus is wholly positive. Nietzsche attributes to Jesus as "redeemer" an "instinctive hatred of reality" that forces him to take refuge in an unchangeable, impervious inner reality. He also sees Jesus as childlike, in fact more "idiot" than "hero." And Jesus is a "decadent." But the apparent harshness of such characterizations must be qualified with care. It is necessary, for one, to distinguish the physiological aversion to reality Nietzsche attributes to Jesus from the *ressentiment* of his followers. That is, the love that Jesus proclaims does not emerge from the subterranean twistings of hatred and envy that Nietzsche so brilliantly explores in the *Genealogy*. Jesus loves with a child-like innocence. This makes him, in Nietzsche's eyes, an idiot in the sense of Dostoevsky's Prince Myshkin—"sick" and "childish" but also "sublime." And one must keep in mind that for Nietzsche, decadence is always equivocal: indicative of a disruption and decline of the strength of the instincts, but also the prerequisite condition for change, growth, and enhancement.

There are other important differences between Nietzsche's Jesus and Nietzsche's philosophical free spirit. As he does with Jesus, Nietzsche characterizes the affirming spirit in terms of a kind of childlike play; it is a child who can proclaim the "sacred Yes" (Z: 139) and who embodies

[14] It is instructive to compare Nietzsche's treatment of Jesus in these pages with Emerson's in his "Address" to students from Harvard Divinity School, which Nietzsche had read (Emerson 1982: 114 ff.).

[15] See Jaspers 1961; Makarushka 1994; Stang 1997.

the "great health" (GS: 347). But, as he makes clear in *Zarathustra*, one must *become* a child, one must first bear the burdens of the camel and learn to say "No" like the lion (Z: 26). Nietzsche's affirmer has passed through the fires of suspicion and nihilism; Nietzsche's Jesus, by contrast, has not. He is a child by nature, he has never matured. This difference decisively marks their respective affirmations. For Nietzsche, Jesus is incapable of resisting, and he is incapable of experiencing enmity and the sense of distance between people; his affirmation is therefore unable to discriminate between types of people or kinds of lives. As Nietzsche writes in his notes, for Jesus "everything is good" (WP: 128). Jesus's spirit is in this respect stunted, without the intellectual perspicacity or joy in struggle characteristic of the Nietzschean spirit. This is not the case for the Nietzschean affirmer. One way to put the difference is that the Nietzschean affirmer is "noble," that is, is an affirmer of "distance" between things and people, and he places different values on things. The affirmation of Jesus falls back into a kind of totalizing way of thought; Nietzsche's noble affirmation affirms differences that the former cannot acknowledge.

Still, Nietzsche's identification with Jesus remains significant, particularly as it relates to the question of "religion." Note that it is not symbols such as "God" or "Kingdom of God" that Nietzsche finds problematic or necessarily life-denying in Jesus. For Jesus, this symbolism is precisely an expression of the freedom of spirit; that is, of the "idealizing" or "transfiguring" capacity Nietzsche finds so wonderful in human beings. What is significant about Jesus for Nietzsche is not the metaphysical reality of Father, Son, and Kingdom of Heaven, but this "condition of the heart" (AC: 157). This condition makes blessedness possible here and now by the *practice* of a divine life. What Nietzsche finds so compelling in Jesus is that "he knows that it is through the *practice* of one's life that one feels 'divine,' 'blessed,' 'evangelic' at all times a 'child of god.' It is *not* 'penance,' *not* 'prayer for forgiveness' which leads to God: *evangelic practice alone* leads to God, it *is* God!" (AC: 156). Jesus shares his blessedness; as evangel he teaches that "blessedness is not promised, it is not tied to any conditions: it is the *only* reality, the rest is signs for speaking of it," and that the Kingdom of God is within (AC: 155). Paul and the other disciples of Jesus were unable, psychologically, to comprehend this intimacy of the divine. Consequently, for them, Jesus became the Christ and blessedness become a function of a metaphysical God's promise for the future. The key to this Christ was not the life Jesus practiced, but the promise contained in his death. The living spirit of Jesus' symbolism became petrified into dogma and institution, to which one must adhere through "faith"; the Jesus who, for Nietzsche, is the "holy anarchist" and "stands outside all religion" (AC: 155) becomes the dogmatic Christ of the Christian religion. As free spirit, however, Jesus practices a life of blessedness—without sin, without *ressentiment*—and understands all reality as a symbol of this blessedness.

Where the saint and the polytheist are, for Nietzsche, forces of alterity, the priest represents the resentful drive for totality. Like the saint (even as a saint) the priest is able to find the power to distinguish himself from the herd; unlike the saint, however, the priest does not affirm this difference in itself, but seeks to master the herd, strengthening the ties that bind the herd together, in order to wage war against the nobles.[16] Using this contrast between the saint and the priest, it is possible to trace two trajectories of "religion" in Nietzsche's thought. The first, the priestly line, has its contemporary manifestation in Christianity and the scientific spirit. The second, the saintly line (along with polytheism's affirmation of multiplicity) has produced something that is not obviously religious, the philosophical free spirit.[17] The saint, in other words, is the figure in whom the distinction I made in the introduction between the "religious" and the "spiritual" is particularly relevant. Here is where we see that, for Nietzsche, "religion" designates discourses and institutions of authority and conformity, valuing totality and unity and structured around a strict correlation between the unity, perfection, and omnipotence of a monotheistic god, the peace and harmony of the social body, and the unity and rationality of the subject. "Spirit," on the other hand, specifically, the "free spirit," is based in the valuation of difference, and is manifested precisely in spiritual exercises in which the totalizations of society and self are resisted, where spirit disrupts totality to reinvigorate and empower human life by opening the self to the undomesticated power of life.[18]

TRANSFIGURING RELIGION, CONTESTING SPIRIT

I argued in the introduction that although the distinction between the spiritual and the religious has its uses, it depends on a problematic view of religion. This problem, I think, is reflected in Nietzsche's provocative,

[16] In a similar vein, both Hegel and Feuerbach see the trajectory of Christianity as one in which humanity finds the possibility of unification and reintegration through demystification and reason. Nietzsche's reading of Christianity, however, both exposes the lie of such reconciliation, and challenges the ideal of reconciliation itself by positing difference and struggle as necessary for human life.

[17] For one account, see GM: 115.

[18] This is an extremely complex distinction and marks a place of deep ambiguity in Nietzsche's writing. For instance, in *The Antichrist* Nietzsche describes the free spirit as one who wages war on "holy lies" (158), but, later in the book, he seems to affirm the holy lie (185), if it is told for the sake of the right "ends." On the one hand, Nietzsche develops this concept of free spirit as a force of difference; on the other, those who are free spirits, he

but ultimately absurd, claim that Jesus "stands outside all religion." On the contrary, even if we agree with Nietzsche's view of the free spiritedness of Jesus, the fact remains that the metaphors Jesus employs and the religious structures he both honors and resists are made possible only in the context of a religious tradition. Moreover, Jesus, or any "saint," only can realize free spiritedness by embodying and inspiriting both the structuring and the liberating potentials of a religious tradition or traditions—even if it means realizing the potential in revolutionizing or overcoming a particular tradition.

The same is true for Nietzsche, for his affirmative self takes shape in a "transfiguration" or "spiritualization" of the religious self. I take the term *transfiguration* from Nietzsche's description of philosophy as a practice of creative spiritualization: "A philosopher who has traversed many kinds of health, and keeps traversing them, has passed through an equal number of philosophies; he simply *cannot* keep from transposing [*umzusetzen*] his states every time into the most spiritual form and distance: this art of transfiguration [*Transfiguration*] is philosophy" (GS: 35).

With the idea of "transfiguration," Nietzsche's conceptions of art, philosophy, and religion converge to determine his task as a thinker. On the one hand, transfiguration is a philosophical practice in the sense that it is an attempt to articulate the body in language, to bring the truth of life to thought. On the other hand transfiguration is an art, more specifically a divine art, in the sense that in the course of bringing the body to thought, the body (and life and world) shines forth in idealized, perfected form.

Nietzsche describes this art of philosophy in terms of the "transposition" and "transfiguration" of body into spirit. His choice of these words is significant. As a musician and music lover, Nietzsche would have been attuned to the technical sense of *transposition* as the reiteration of a piece of music in a higher or lower key. When a piece of music is transposed, it both changes and remains the same, not through a kind of evolution or growth into a mature state, not through a purifying of something into its essence, but rather in a kind of translation that allows the same melody to be heard in a different way, or played on a different instrument, producing some of the same impressions or feelings, but new ones as well. Different keys are more or less able to convey different moods: music played in minor keys, for instance, is generally sadder or more haunting than music in major keys. Hayden's choice of C major as the key that ushers in God's light in *Die Schöpfung* is far from arbitrary. If we think of transposition, then, in terms of the connections between philosophy, health, body, and

---

envisions, will also be the rulers of the future, those, who for the sake of the order of rank may use the holy lie, may impose a total culture on others. A similar tension can be found in *Beyond Good and Evil* between Chapter Two's discussion of the free spirit and Chapter Three's treatment of the uses to which religion may be put to create culture.

spirit that Nietzsche utilizes in this passage, it suggests that philosophy's spiritualization is not an overcoming or purifying of body by spirit, but body in a different key. It also suggests that the body is not the "ground" of spirit, but that these are modulations of one another. As transposition, Nietzsche's philosophy expresses in its method and form a reconceptualization of the relation between body and spirit.

The character of this transposition is made more precise through the term *transfiguration*. As the scion of generations of Lutheran pastors, Nietzsche would have been aware of the episode of "The Transfiguration" in the New Testament. There, Jesus ascends a mountain, talks with Moses and Elijah, and is "transfigured" so that "his face shone like the sun and his garments became white as light."[19] Theologically, this epiphany echoes the baptism of Jesus and foreshadows both the Passion and Parousia. In German, this episode is generally referred to as *die Verklärung*. Beyond its specifically Christian use, *Verklärung* means "glorification," and as a verb (*verklären*), it means to rise above the earthly or to appear in clear light. This word is commonly associated with religious phenomena, but Nietzsche used it most often in the context of his discussions of art. In *The Birth of Tragedy*, for instance, he writes of the "*Verklärungsschein* of art" (BT: 143). Kaufmann translates this as "transfiguring illusion," a concept that many commentators treat as central in their discussion of Nietzsche's aesthetics.[20] But, as Kaufmann points out in a footnote, "*Verklärungsschein*" might also be translated as "transfiguring halo" (BT: 143, n. 2). And to support the idea that we should attune ourselves to such religious resonances in Nietzsche's writing, it is the case that Nietzsche uses the term *Verklärung* in his discussion of Jesus in *The Antichrist*. As I noted, the blessedness that Jesus practices is a "transfiguration of all things."

Because Nietzsche had used the word *Verklärung* frequently in the past, and would continue to do so, it is remarkable that in defining philosophy in the preface to *The Gay Science* he uses *Transfiguration*, the Latin cognate (from *transfiguratio*), instead of *Verklärung*. This is a word that is used rarely in German and then *only* to refer to the transfiguration of Christ.[21] What this suggests is that in this brief definition of philosophy,

---

[19] Gospel of Matthew 17:1–8, as translated in *The New Oxford Annotated Bible*, Revised Standard Version. The episode also appears in Mark and Luke.

[20] See Schacht 1983: 476 f.

[21] *Transfiguration* does not even appear in many German dictionaries, including the Grimm edition of 1935. In D. Sanders's *Wörterbuch der Deutschen Sprache* (Leipzig: Otto Wigand, 1876), it is defined simply as "the *Verklärung* of Christ or a painting of it." In a contemporary dictionary, it is defined, first, as "the *Verklärung* of Christ and the change in his form [*Gestalt*] into that of a heavenly being," and, second, as "a representation of the Transfiguration." (Duden: *Deutsches Universalwörterbuch* [Mannheim: Dudenverlag,

Nietzsche is telling us something crucial not only about the way he understands philosophy, but also about the relation between body and spirit, and, I will argue, about the religious sensibility implicated in his concepts of art and philosophy. "Transfiguration," first of all, helps specify the difference between body and spirit while suggesting, as with "transposition," that the relation between them is not fundamentally adversarial or hierarchical. In the biblical transfiguration, the spirit of Jesus does not leave the body; instead, *he*—body and soul—shines. As I will discuss in more detail in the next chapter, for Nietzsche spirit is not something opposed to body, but an aura or a shining, or raiment, by which the body and one's whole being is glorified. It is a manifestation of blessedness.

More generally, *transfiguration*—as either *Transfiguration* or *Verklärung*—can be applied to Nietzsche's notion of artistic idealization, which, for him, is the function of art—and the clearest expression of affirmation. Throughout his writing, as I discuss particularly in Chapter 6, Nietzsche draws close connections between transfiguration, art, religion, and affirmation; he in fact asserts that everything worth living for is "transfiguring, subtle, mad, and divine" (BG: 101). Such transfiguration is accomplished by the Greek gods, and, it seems, by the God of Jesus, but not the "Christian" God. The latter is "God degenerated to the *contradiction of life*, instead of being its transfiguration (*Verklärung*) and eternal *Yes!*" (AC: 138). Transfiguration does not affirm the ideal at the expense of reality, but is a way of rendering, shaping, "perfecting" reality so that it shines, so that one exalts it. To transfigure the body and the world is to affirm reality in transcending it; it is not to transcend the world in order to master it.

The meaning of transfiguration can be extended in another direction. At the same time that he criticizes Christianity and religion, Nietzsche acknowledges the crucial roles these have played in the development of human culture and the human soul. One might acknowledge this and still claim that Nietzsche's vision is nonetheless antireligious, following, for example, the model of Feuerbach, for whom religion has outlived its usefulness and is now a destructive force in human life. There is much in Nietzsche's writing to support this view. Yet, his view of the free spirit and the philosopher invoke and allude to practices, dispositions, and ex-

1989]). The only other uses of *transfiguration* in Nietzsche's published texts that I have found are D: 10, GM: 111, and TI: 83. In the first, Nietzsche writes of a "new transfiguration" that, it appears, would produce a new type of human being. In the second, sounding like Freud, Nietzsche writes of the transfiguration of sensuality into an aesthetic state. Finally, Nietzsche writes of Dionysian art and its powers of "representation, imitation, transfiguration [*transfiguriren*], transmutation." The word also appears in a few places in his notes. For example, he entitles a note from the spring of 1888, "The Transfiguration, the temporary Metamorphosis" (SW: 13, 309).

periences that, as Nietzsche is aware, are closely connected with asceticism and mysticism. He returns to the ascetic again and again, for the most part as a paradigmatic figure of life-denial, but also, in a more positive vein, as one who has great insight into the secrets of power and desire. Only by appropriating these insights is Nietzsche able to imagine the power to affirm life. In addition, and in spite of his criticisms of intoxication, Nietzsche testifies to the importance of ecstatic, even mystical states in the cultivation of an affirmative life, particularly in *Zarathustra* and in descriptions of the genuine philosopher.

Nietzsche assumes, in short, a kind of development or "metamorphosis" by which the disposition or the practices of the saint or ascetic are transformed to produce the free spirit or philosopher (GM: 115–16). Transfiguration is only possible given an overcoming of the self-deceptive misunderstanding of power that idealizes "communion" with transcendent divinity. The religious element of Nietzsche's thought takes shape in the transfiguration of the spiritual practices of asceticism and mysticism.

Spiritualization and Self-Denial

In subsequent chapters, I examine asceticism and mysticism in more detail; to conclude here, I establish concepts and definitions upon which this work will be based. First, Nietzsche's conception of spirit. Humanity, for Nietzsche, finds its meaning in spirit, that is, in the capacity for creative, intellectual shaping and beautifying of self and world: the capacity for transfiguration. But it will not do to rely only on the model of Jesus to understand spiritualization in the fullest Nietzschean sense, for Jesus was too naive and innocent. Nietzsche, the postcritical master of suspicion, knows that spirit in his day knows more, is more troubled, even sicker. There is always at least a hint of violence, cruelty, and dis-ease when Nietzsche writes of the spirit; and always some ambivalence when he writes about consciousness.[22] In *Zarathustra*, Nietzsche refers to spirit as "life cutting into life" (Z: 104). Walter Kaufmann points out that spirit thereby becomes "an instrument used by life in its effort to enhance itself" (1974: 271). Spirit is at once the sickness and the health of the human being, and tensions between nature, instinct, and spirit create a dynamic of the human soul that is the basis of Nietzsche's anthropology. Enhancement is painful, for spirit is based in an agonistic conception of life. This is to say that spirit *is* contest, ordeal, not to say that life is the contest between spirit and body, or that spirit attempts to master the body and all else that changes. In this sense, it is correct to see in Nietzsche an anticipation of the psychoanalytic concept of sublimation, but only if

---

[22] See, for example, AC: 134–35.

one keeps in mind that sublimation as Freud sees it is grounded in the repression of sexual instincts, which enables them to be expressed in socially acceptable ways; it is, in other words, a force for conformity or social acceptability. For Nietzsche, by contrast, sublimation, as spiritualization or transfiguration, involves an intensification or beautification of the instincts as it is expressed in freedom from conformity, in an agonistic relationship not just within the self, but between the individual and the community.

This is why the ascetic is such a crucial figure: it represents for Nietzsche an uncanny conjunction of power, spirit, and self-denial, which, he thinks, has much to teach us about the relation of renunciation and spiritualization. But how should we understand the self-denial involved in spiritualization, since so much of Nietzsche's thought denies denial? Basically, Nietzsche distinguishes spiritualization from the self-denial of the ascetic ideal, that is, from the idealization by which self-denial becomes a goal in itself and confers value on life.[23] This is the self-denial that dominates the *Genealogy*. The sophistication of this work lies in large part in the important distinctions Nietzsche makes between bad conscience, *ressentiment*, and guilt. As he indicates in the second essay, bad conscience is a "sickness" that results when human beings are forced to live together in peace by internalizing aggressive impulses and so directing them back upon themselves: this is the origin of bad conscience, and bad conscience is the origin of spirit. But for Nietzsche the bad conscience is a "promise" as well as a sickness (Nietzsche describes this sickness with a figure that has much meaning for him; it is a sickness like "pregnancy" is a sickness). In other words, it is only in bad conscience that human beings become capable of inward depth and self-cultivation.[24]

The danger of this condition, as Nietzsche writes in the first essay, is realized when the priest uses *ressentiment* and guilt to intensify bad conscience by *moralizing* the god-human relationship. Nietzsche argues that the ultimate perversion of bad conscience is the idea of a sin before God

[23] Clark (1990: 161) reads this turn back to this-worldliness as a turn back to "natural human existence." From the perspective of Clark's theory of truth, the term "natural human existence" is relatively unproblematic: it refers to the existence attested to by human senses and human experience. However, from the perspective of Nietzsche's claims about suffering and spiritualization, "natural human existence" is a strange matter, for spiritualization is only possible to the extent that nature turns against itself. The reader will note that I engage Clark's book on Nietzsche in a number of places in the following pages. I do so for the simple reason that I consider this book to be one of the best recent purely philosophical interpretations of Nietzsche.

[24] "Let us add at once that, on the other hand, the existence on earth of an animal soul turned against itself, taking sides against itself, was something so new, profound, unheard of, enigmatic, contradictory, and *full of future* that the aspect of the earth was essentially altered" (GM: 85).

that is so deep it can never be atoned for—except by God himself. This concept of sin radically separates the divine and the human, a separation that tears the human self apart in the hatred of all that in itself which causes the separation. The creative possibilities of spirit and bad conscience are subverted in this historical trajectory to the point where the enhancement and affirmation of the human itself becomes a sin.[25]

Though Nietzsche was an unwavering enemy of the power of the ideas of guilt and sin over the human soul, this did not lead him to envision a final reconciliation within the soul, an end to the painful internalization of bad conscience. In the months before his breakdown, Nietzsche claimed the essays in the *Genealogy* "are perhaps uncannier than anything else written so far" (EH: 312). This uncanniness lies, I think, in the way Nietzsche links the "sickness" of bad conscience with the enhancement of humanity. To understand Nietzschean affirmation requires that one grasp that human existence itself is "uncanny" (GM: 85) because its enhancement involves a turn against "natural" humanity.[26] Nietzsche mocks the Stoics' presumption to live according to nature when he asks, "Living—is that not precisely wanting to be other than this nature?" (BG: 15). His battle against sin and guilt do not involve the overcoming of bad conscience; instead, he imagines redirecting the bad conscience against "all the unnatural inclinations, all those aspirations to the beyond, to that which runs counter to sense, instinct, nature, animal, in short all ideals hitherto, which are one and all hostile to life and ideals that slander the world" (GM: 95). Nietzsche seeks to cultivate a "good conscience" that is able to revalue "nature," the "senses," and "instinct," yet he does not write of the *eradication* of "unnatural inclinations," nor of the fundamental self-alienation within human beings, "this animal soul turned against itself," that he calls the bad conscience. Cruelty directed against the self, for Nietzsche, remains essential to all human enhancement. He writes admiringly of "those well-constituted, joyful mortals who far from regarding their unstable equilibrium between 'animal and angel' as neces-

[25] As Nietzsche writes a few years later, "The concepts of guilt and punishment . . . [are] a priestly assassination! . . . *When the natural consequences of an act are no longer 'natural'* . . . *then one has committed the greatest crime against humanity.*—Sin, to say it again, that form par excellence of the self-degradation and self-desecration of man, was invented to make science, culture, every kind of elevation and nobility of man impossible; the priest rules through the invention of sin" (AC: 175–76).

[26] The English "uncanny" is used to translate Nietzsche's "*unheimlich*," which literally means something like "out of home," or "not homelike." Writing of the "free spirit," Nietzsche exclaims, "He looks back gratefully—grateful to his wandering, to his hardness and self-alienation, to his viewing of far distances and bird-like flights in cold heights. What a good thing he had not always stayed 'at home,' stayed 'within himself' like a delicate apathetic loafer! He had been *beside himself*: no doubt of that" (HH: 8). The uncanny becomes the ecstatic. I will pursue this link in later chapters, arguing that ecstasy, transcendence, and spiritualization all are involved in elaborating this turn against the natural.

sarily an argument against existence [find it] one more stimulus to life" (GM: 99). And he expresses disdain for nature unspiritualized with images such as the "herd," which he contrasts with his admired "free spirit." His "sovereign individual," one who is capable of making promises and taking responsibility for oneself, only gains this capacity by overcoming the "natural" tendency to forgetfulness (which Nietzsche figures as good "digestion").

The free spirit, the sovereign individual, and the philosopher, therefore, all represent forms of "sickness" that result when the will to power, the "unexhausted procreative will of life" (Z:115) is directed back against "human nature" in the process of spiritualization. The human being is a self-alienated being because, in the human, nature is torn, divided against itself. As Eric Blondel puts it, there is a "tragic gap between nature and itself *within man*" (1991: 48). In this respect "nature" and "spirit" are reflections of one another. Or, to put it differently, this gap *is* spirit, or what Nietzsche describes as the "distance" within the human soul. This self-alienation makes a certain kind (but not all kinds) of spiritual suffering inevitable; it also is the condition of possibility for human growth and spiritualization. Nietzsche's therefore is an uncanny "naturalism." It is true, of course, that Nietzsche seeks a reconciliation of human nature with itself, but only with the understanding that the term *human nature* itself refers to a conflict, a fundamental alterity—spirit—that forms the self: to be reconciled to human nature therefore is to affirm the conflict between "nature" and "anti-nature."[27] It is possible to deny life either by adhering to the faith in opposite values and the ascetic ideal, which locate the reality of life in a purely spiritual realm where consciousness masters body and nature, *or* by believing that human beings can somehow return to nature and live a life free of the conflict between spirit and nature. Both visions hope for a peace of soul that Nietzsche in the later writings calls "romanticism." Nietzsche, by contrast, speaks "of a 'return to nature' although it is not really a going-back but a *going-up*, up into a high, free, even frightful nature and naturalness" (TI: 111).

In the final section of the essay on the ascetic ideal, Nietzsche claims: "Man, the bravest of animals and the one most accustomed to suffering, does *not* repudiate suffering as such; he *desires* it, he even seeks it out, provided he is shown a *meaning* for it" (GM: 162). In *Beyond Good and Evil*, Nietzsche offers one way of thinking about how suffering might be desirable by attributing the enhancement of humanity to "great suffering."

> The discipline and cultivation of suffering, of *great* suffering—do you not know that only *this* discipline has created all enhancements of man so far? That ten-

[27] See, for example, BG: 159 f.

sion of the soul in unhappiness which cultivates its strength, its shudders face to face with great ruin, its inventiveness and courage in enduring, persevering, interpreting and exploiting suffering, and whatever has been granted to it of profundity, secret, mask, spirit, cunning greatness—was it not granted to it through suffering, through the discipline of great suffering? In man *creature* and *creator* are united: in man there is material, fragment, excess, clay, dirt, nonsense, chaos; but in man there is also creator, form giver, hammer hardness, spectator divinity, and seventh day: do you understand this contrast? And that *your* pity is for the "creature in man," for what must be formed, broken, forged, torn, burnt, made incandescent, and purified—that which *necessarily* must and *should* suffer? And *our* pity—do you not comprehend for whom our *converse* pity is when it resists your pity as the worst of all pamperings and weaknesses? (BG: 154)

Nietzsche's affirmation of "instinct," and "nature" does not preclude this harsh forging of the self in a certain kind of self-inflicted suffering. His problem, then, is not the elimination of suffering in general, or the suffering of the soul in particular; it is, rather, a problem of revaluing suffering, of transforming the self-denial of the ascetic into an affirmative practice of renewal and enhancement. Nietzsche looks beyond the ascetic ideal by reinterpreting the conflict between "nature" and "anti-nature" within the human soul with the understanding that there is no pure nature, instinct, or body; there is only the constant interchange that constitutes body and spirit. Nietzsche's affirmation does not consist in a simple "yes" to nature or "this world," but in their painful, empowering enhancement.

Power and Ecstasy

There is something ironic about Nietzsche's own glorification of power and the way that glorification has been received by his readers (or by those who do not read him). For it is precisely because human beings have been enamored and driven by the promise of absolute, divine power, and/ or the power of the masterful ego, that Nietzsche's glorification of human power, with its limitations and conflicts, becomes so important. Nietzsche's attack on the idea of sin and his affirmation of will to power and egoism are crucial components of the view that there is *no* absolute power, that human beings are finite, vulnerable, and of limited power. Tearing ourselves apart with sin and guilt has meant turning vulnerability and limitation into absolute powerlessness and depravity and, in response, worshiping absolute power. From this perspective, Nietzsche does not pathologically absolutize human power; to the contrary, he attempts to affirm, beautify, and maximize the power that is our lot as human beings. When he does write about the divinization or perfection of humanity, then, Nietzsche is not elevating the self or humanity to the place or power of the Christian God. Instead, he is writing about spiritualization and the capacity human beings have for feeling great power and joy in striving beyond themselves, in creating beyond themselves, and so blessing themselves and their world. Such striving can be affirmative only if it resists the temptation to claim absolute power; that is, only on the condition that it recognize that joy is found in the striving and creating of desire itself, not in any eschatological totality.

Nietzsche denounces Christianity for its denial of the value of human power. But in the midst of his histories of guilt and the self-laceration of the soul, he invokes the Greeks and Jesus to show how "the conception of gods in itself need not lead to the degradation of the imagination," and that it is possible to "deify" the "animal in man" (GM: 93; AC: 157). This possibility depends on a contrast between the metaphysical dualism of power brought to its logical extreme in the Christian tradition and an affirmative, god-creating instinct that idealizes the human, and even a plurality of types of humanity (GS: 191). The god concept, in this sense, involves idealization and worship as affirmation: the nobles idealize themselves in their gods, and they give thanks for their life. Such idealization is not absolute, for there is a kind of mutuality between gods and humans; the gods are more human, humans more godlike than they are in monotheistic traditions. And here, one can see how even Nietzsche's Jesus undermines the monotheistic trajectory by embodying the divine here and now. In both cases, the complete human, with its conflicts and fallibilities, and the life of body and nature itself, is being idealized by being made beautiful and noble. The mutuality between god and human allows the fullness of human life—rather than only the "spiritual"—to be reflected in the divine ideal.

In his final year of writing, Nietzsche compares Dionysus and "the Crucified" and reminds us that paganism was "a form of thanksgiving and affirmation of life . . . a type of well-constituted and ecstatically overflowing spirit." "Dionysus" is the name for Nietzsche's spiritualization, qualifying it religiously. The Dionysian, Nietzsche claims, is the "religious affirmation of life" (TI: 120), a healthy, grateful intoxication that results in a creative, affirmative spiritualization of self and world. In such a state, one feels blessed, feels oneself and one's world as perfect, divine. There is a strong aesthetic sense, and a corresponding devaluation of the "moral," in Nietzsche's concept of pagan idealization or "deification." It is important to make the link with creativity here, for the feeling of blessedness is made possible through the difficult process of artistic creativity as spiritualization. As I will argue below, one must be careful not to simplify Nietzsche's notion of the "religious" as a feeling by making it a purely subjective state. It is also a practice, an encounter with the world in which one participates in shaping the world, in making it divine in an affirmative overflowing.

Nietzsche's late (re)turn to tragedy and Dionysus represents a transfiguration of the ecstasy and creativity he finds in pagan religion. "Before me this transposition of the Dionysian into a philosophical pathos did not exist: tragic wisdom was lacking" (EH: 273). Nietzsche seeks to inscribe the Dionysian into philosophy. Dionysian ecstasy is a path—philosophy as a spiritual practice—by which one finds oneself in a renewed relationship with earth and life. Though Nietzsche is profoundly suspicious of the human need for intoxication, with Dionysian ecstasy, as a participation with the power of life, he isolates an ecstasy, even a mysticism, that is the key to understanding affirmation.

Chapter Three

NIETZSCHE'S ASCETICISM

> Growing heavy.—You do not know him: though he hang many
> weights on himself he can nonetheless lift them with him into the
> heights. And you, judging him by the beating of your own petty
> wings, conclude that, *because* he hangs these weights on himself, he
> wants to stay *below*.
> (Nietzsche, *Dawn*)

> They greatly afflict their bodies, not because they do not love their
> bodies, rather, they want to bring their bodies to Eden in glory.
> (Ephraim the Syrian, "On Hermits and Desert Dwellers")

NIETZSCHE AND ASCETICISM

THE MONSTROUS, mad power of the ascetic fascinated
Nietzsche. In one of his earliest discussions of asceticism—from
Dawn—Nietzsche writes with the piercing voice of a "solitary and
agitated mind":

Ah, give me madness, you heavenly powers! Madness, that I may at last believe
in myself! Give deliriums and convulsions, sudden lights and darkness, terrify
me with frost and fire such that no mortal has ever felt, with deafening din and
prowling figures, make me howl and whine and crawl like a beast: so that I
may only come to believe in myself!. . . Prove to me that I am yours; madness
alone can prove it. (D: 15)

Nietzsche's fascination with asceticism developed into the point of his
attack on Christianity, most famously in the *Genealogy's* essay on the
ascetic ideal. This essay has exerted a huge influence on modern critics of
religion, for many of whom asceticism has become the paradigmatic gesture of religious madness—a cramped, dour rejection of earthly delight
and worldly power and passion. In intellectual circles, *asceticism* has become a pivotal term for comprehensive critiques of Western culture:
Weber finds in the innerworldly asceticism of Puritanism the mechanism
of modernity's "iron cage" (1985); Foucault argues that the monastic cell
is reinstituted in the modern prison and factory (1979); feminist philosopher Mary Daly identifies asceticism as the "sadospirituality" through
which patriarchy has formed the world's major religious traditions

Epigraph: Nietzsche, D: 97; Ephraim the Syrian, "On Hermits and Desert Dwellers," in
Wimbush 1990: 72.

(1984).[1] Such diagnoses seek to disclose the pervasiveness, pathology, and ideological functions of socially constructed ascetic ideals in which forms of self-scrutiny, self-denial, and self-sacrifice are considered to be of supreme moral worth.

Despite the continuing power of the antiascetic critique, in recent years historians and religionists have begun to contest the simplistic association of asceticism with masochistic madness by attending to the empowering, liberating potential of ascetic practices.[2] Their work can help us distinguish between "asceticism" and the "ascetic ideal," a distinction significant for two reasons. First, it can be used as a critical lens to isolate and evaluate some of the shortcomings of Nietzsche's reading of Christianity, which essentially reduces it to the ascetic ideal. Second, it can help us see that Nietzsche himself offers resources for rethinking asceticism in a more constructive fashion, that he in fact anticipates the reevaluations of asceticism that some scholars and spiritual thinkers are undertaking today.

It is a mistake to read Nietzsche as simplistically as he reads Christianity, for despite his polemic against the ascetic ideal, his writing does not reject but transfigures asceticism. Living in the late twentieth century, we have become enlightened about the dangers and evils of repression and self-denial, but there is a tendency today, in the name of liberation, to equate all discipline and all forms of denial with life-suffocating repression. Nietzsche is more subtle than this, for he is convinced that life only grows through suffering and the "sacrifice of its highest types." Though he seeks an end to otherworldly goals and dreams, Nietzsche demands a discipline of affirmation that vies with the ascetic ideal in its severity of self-denial and self-mastery. Comparing these disciplines of the self, I argue that the self-cultivation Nietzsche develops in (and through) his writing is closely related to traditional forms of religious ascetic practice, and has particularly striking affinities with practices of body and soul developed in the same Christian tradition of which he was so critical.

Nietzsche as Ascetic

To suggest that Nietzsche is an ascetic is nothing new: Walter Kaufmann points out that "Nietzsche, unlike many of his readers, never loses sight of the fact that he was an ascetic" (1974: 258). But what is asceticism?

[1] For Nietzsche's influence on Weber and Foucault, see Stauth and Turner (1988). For the modern Western aversion to asceticism and to the spiritual significance of pain in the Christian tradition, see Asad (1993) and Rieff (1987). In *Saints and Postmodernism*, Edith Wyschogrod discusses the criticism of asceticism in Enlightenment naturalism (1990: 14). From the beginning of Enlightenment, and through the nineteenth century, the criticism of asceticism was an integral part of many attacks on religion, but with Nietzsche one begins to see the figure of asceticism play an important role in more general interpretations of Western culture.

[2] See especially Wimbush 1990 and Wimbush and Valantasis 1995.

For the most part, Nietzsche's commentators, though offering subtle interpretations of his "ascetic ideal," have failed to give equally careful consideration to his "asceticism." As recent examples, the insightful commentaries of Nehamas (1985) and Clark (1990) are each limited by the tendency to conflate asceticism and the ascetic ideal. This leads each of them to connect the ascetic ideal with a religious (read, simply, *other-worldly*) denial of life, power, and body. They can then distinguish moral and religious practices of self-discipline (ascetic ideal/asceticism) from Nietzsche's practices of self-mastery, which, they contend, are nonmoral and nonreligious (i.e., *this-worldly*)—and so, nonascetic. While both are thereby able to make sense of Nietzsche's effort to envision a new, affirmative way of life, they fail, I think, to account for the complexity of Nietzsche's attitudes not just toward asceticism, but toward religion in general.[3]

Clark offers what is perhaps the most challenging counter to the claim that Nietzsche is an ascetic by arguing that asceticism requires the self-deception made possible through a dualistic faith in opposite values. She recognizes the importance of discipline and even the internalization of cruelty in Nietzsche, but argues that the ascetic "needs the valuation and interpretation of life offered by the ascetic ideal in order to get a sense of power from self-denial." That is, the ascetic only gets power from self-denial by believing in a "true world," a life beyond this one, toward which one moves through self-denial. Since, however, as Clark argues, Nietzsche's monism locates all power in the power of life, in the will to power, the idealization of self-denial that depends on a metaphysical power is impossible and ascetic practices pointless (1990: 234). In short, Clark argues that it makes no sense to speak of an asceticism that is not self-

---

[3] Another strategy for dealing with asceticism in Nietzsche, one found in certain "postmodern" readings, is to underemphasize the central place of suffering and self-denial in his work. See, for example, Deleuze 1983. While, with Deleuze, I think we have to read Nietzsche as a thinker of affirmation, part of my purpose in arguing that Nietzsche is an ascetic is to counter those readings of Nietzsche that overemphasize the themes of style or play in Nietzsche's work at the expense of the themes of suffering and discipline. Such readings do not adequately thematize the "great seriousness" that grounds all his play. One interpreter who treats Nietzsche's asceticism in some depth is Geoffrey Harpham 1987. Harpham's reading acknowledges Nietzsche's asceticism but claims that Nietzsche is an ascetic in spite of and precisely because of his resistance to asceticism (as the ascetic ideal). "Although Nietzsche tries in the *Genealogy* to imagine the nonascetic, he can only replicate it" (219). In contrast to Harpham, I show that Nietzsche recognizes and affirms a "natural" asceticism. Leslie Paul Thiele writes that Nietzsche's skepticism and atheism are basically "spiritual, and even religious" positions and that the Dionysian faith that emerges from this religious passion is "the force behind Nietzsche's own ascetic tendencies" (1990: 143–46). Thiele offers a broader understanding of asceticism than any of Nietzsche's other interpreters when he treats it as knowing "the powers of the passions and the instincts" and says that Nietzsche made "their investigation, development, and sublimation his life's work" (146–47).

deceptive or that gains power without the metaphysical idealization of self-denial. From this perspective, the asceticism of the ascetic priest is the only sensible way to think of asceticism.[4]

Approaches like Clark's, which concentrate so exclusively on the issue of self-denial and its idealization, miss a number of crucial points. I will mention one important one here, and flesh out others in the remainder of the chapter. I do not want to claim that Nietzsche idealizes self-denial or that there are not religious figures we would want to call "ascetic" that do. But a careful examination of the phenomenon of asceticism in Christianity reveals practices of renunciation and self-discipline undertaken for complex, often psychologically and physiologically astute reasons far more subtle—and realistic—than critics of asceticism usually assume. To put it more succinctly, not all Christian ascetics are the dualists that Clark's conception of asceticism requires. If that is the case, then to confine our definition of asceticism to those who do self-deceptively idealize self-denial construes the term far more narrowly than the Christian tradition has.

A similar problem can also be found in attempts, such as Pierre Hadot's, to decisively distinguish asceticism from *ascesis* as it was understood in the Greek philosophical context. (This would be a strategy open to Clark as a way of acknowledging the importance of discipline for Nietzsche.) Hadot defines *ascesis* as "spiritual exercise" and contrasts it with asceticism defined as "complete abstinence or restriction in the use of food, drink, sleep, dress, and property, and especially continence in sexual matters" (1995: 128). This approach has the advantage of recognizing the affirmative significance of strenuous modes of self-discipline for ancient philosophers such as the Stoics, and even for early Christian ascetics, and for philosophers such as Nietzsche. At the same time, though, it only makes this distinction by defining asceticism (as in Clark) in such a way as to render it both relatively uninteresting and inherently self-deceptive. Such an approach either leaves us with few actual ascetics or requires us to radically simplify the practice of Christian ascetics. Moreover, Hadot seems to be placing great weight on the distinction between "spiritual exercise" as predominantly intellectual, and ascetic practices, like those listed above, which concentrate on the physical body. Again, while such a distinction is useful in certain contexts, it is not adequate, as I will explain, for understanding either the Christian or the Nietzschean case, where ascetic practice works precisely at the boundaries—and in fact works to open up the boundaries—between body and soul.

None of this is to say that there are not are warrants in Nietzsche's writing for a kind of conflation of asceticism and the ascetic ideal, for

---

[4] I respond to Nehamas at the end of this chapter.

he never settles on a clear distinction between them. In the essay on the ascetic ideal, Nietzsche almost always uses the terms *ascetic ideal* and *asceticism* interchangeably. In the essay's first discussion of the ascetic priest, Nietzsche argues that the priest's "monstrous" mode of valuation is the defining characteristic of asceticism as a whole; he writes about the earth as the "distinctively ascetic planet," and about the "ascetic life" as a "self-contradiction" (GM: 116–17). In other places as well, Nietzsche treats asceticism simply as a negative phenomenon, describing it as a form of suicide (GS: 131), and writing that the ascetic seeks to "extirpate" (as opposed to spiritualize) the passions (TI: 52). But he also views asceticism more positively. In *The Antichrist* he describes asceticism as "nature, need, instinct" of the "most spiritual human beings" (AC: 188). The single exception to the conflation of asceticism and ascetic ideal in the *Genealogy* occurs in Nietzsche's discussion of "philosophical asceticism" (GM: 112). There he asserts that "a certain asceticism, a severe and cheerful continence with the best will, belongs to the most favorable conditions of supreme spirituality." And, in a note from that period, he writes: "I also want to make asceticism natural again: in place of the aim of denial, the aim of strengthening; a gymnastics of the will; abstinence and periods of fasting of all kinds, in the most spiritual realm too; a casuistry of deeds in regard to the opinions we have regarding our strengths; an experiment with adventures and arbitrary dangers" (SW 12: 386).[5] Despite his criticism of the ascetic ideal, Nietzsche makes room for a "certain asceticism," which he relates closely to spiritual power and the practice of philosophy.

Taking this cue from Nietzsche's notes, I will refer to this asceticism as "natural asceticism." As I argued in the previous chapter, however, Nietzsche seeks to return human beings to nature, but only as a way of cultivating an affirmative spiritualization: the "transfiguration" of body into spirit. "Natural asceticism" involves a cultivation of spirit through a struggle of "nature" with and against itself.[6] By contrast, in its refusal of the reality of suffering, in its imagined paradise of another world of Truth or Peace, the ascetic ideal denies the reality of the conflict *within* nature at the heart of the human soul—and must posit imaginary, and absolute, powers to offer an imaginary solution. Paradoxically, in order to overcome this conflict, the ascetic ideal exacerbates it, inflicting suffering upon the self that further tears apart spirit and nature. Its goal, however, is not the strengthening of both nature and spirit, but rather the mastery of spirit, as antinature, over nature. It does this through a self-surrender that

---

[5] See also the note entitled "On the Asceticism of the Strong" (SW 13: 476).

[6] Kallistos Ware also makes this point, and invokes the idea of "natural asceticism" in arguing that *enkratia* (self-control) does not necessarily involve "violence to our natural appetites" but can instead be a means to "transfiguration" (1995: 10). With respect to the idea of the transfiguration of the body, see Patricia Cox Miller 1995: 282.

is thought to open a space for the absolute power of the divine. The ascetic ideal depends on a dualistic, rather than a dialectic, relation between spirit and nature, human and divine. It is possible to distinguish between a dualistic, mortifying asceticism (the ascetic ideal, or priestly asceticism) and a dialectical asceticism of empowerment (natural asceticism).

Recent theoretical and historical work on asceticism helps us to think beyond asceticism as a dualistic denial of life or self. But this is not to deny that asceticism has attracted and offered a vehicle for some spectacular despisers of the body, self, and life. Rather it is to think about asceticism in a way that encompasses practices by which people can integrate bodily and spiritual life, explore contours of spirit and desire, and resist and transform powerful modes of socialization. More generally, with the term *asceticism*, I indicate a wide range of what Foucault calls "practices of the self," that is, practices and disciplines of desire by which a person cultivates his or her subjectivity within a web of relations between person, culture, and nature. With the help of these recent studies, I suggest one needs to take seriously the life-affirming possibilities of asceticism.[7]

I confine my discussion to scholarship on Western pagan and Christian ascetic traditions. My purpose is not to construct a universal definition of asceticism, nor even to isolate the essence of a phenomenon we might call "Western" or "Christian" asceticism (though I will suggest that we can make certain kinds of distinctions between ascetic traditions). Instead, I will sketch an "ascetic thematics" by which I elucidate certain central modes of discipline/renunciation/cultivation that theorists and historians have highlighted in constructing Western asceticism. I argue that asceticism, in this sense, becomes a useful heuristic for considering Nietzsche's work because it provides a perspective that allows us to see his relationship to Western religious traditions and his own constructive thought in a new light.

New Perspectives on Asceticism

Body, Dualism, and Self-Denial

It is rarely denied that asceticism expresses a certain "madness" with regard to the body. Yet, historians such as Margaret Miles, Peter Brown, and Caroline Walker Bynum point out that Christian asceticism does not and has not necessarily involved hatred or denial of the body. In general, they argue, ascetics have attended so closely to the body precisely because they have been highly attuned to its power in the spiritual life of human

---

[7] Foucault describes *ascesis* as "the labor that one undertakes by oneself on oneself in order to be transformed, or in order to have this self appear, which happily never happens" (James Miller 1993: 258).

beings. It is this spiritual life, and not the body, that is the primary focus of asceticism. While the body certainly is the *site* of many ascetic practices, the *object* of these practices is the liberation, salvation, or transformation of the person. For example, Margaret Miles argues that fundamental Christian doctrines—such as the doctrines of Creation, Incarnation, and Resurrection—affirm the permanent connectedness of the body and the soul, and so precludes metaphysical dualism (1990: 95). Thus, "Ascetic practice consonant with Christian faith requires that the only condition in which human beings can turn to the source of life and being is as unities of body and soul in which the body is always the 'spouse,' the soul's intimate companion" (1981: 35). Discipline imposed on the body can teach discipline to the soul, such that the experience of both becomes intensified. The body becomes "the intimate partner of the soul in learning, suffering, and salvation" (1981: 35) in enhancing life through a reorientation—a turning—toward "fullness of life," which is spirit.

The basic struggle within the Christian soul is not between the body and soul, but between "spirit and flesh."[8] These two conceptual pairs are not equivalent, for while the first might be seen in terms of a distinction between the material and the spiritual parts of the self, the second pair are not so much distinct parts of the human being as principles of orientation for the whole human being. Thus, as Miles points out, ascetics such as Saint Antony do not confine themselves to bodily disciplines but are always involved with disciplines of the soul or psyche as well. And the point of these disciplines (at least for some Christian ascetics) is not that denial is valuable in itself, but that it is a way of training and turning the body/soul to spirit instead of flesh. Asceticism, then, is not first of all a matter of castigation or punishment, but a matter of the liberation and empowerment that comes when one shifts one's orientation from the immediacy of a certain worldliness to the divine. Miles argues that it is the attempt to "break the hegemony of the flesh over the body so that the spirit, hitherto uncultivated, unexercised, and unstrengthened, can begin to possess it" (1981: 48).

Caroline Walker Bynum also argues that interpreting Christian asceticism as inherently dualistic does not do justice to Christian spirituality, even in the case of some of the intense and sometimes revolting ascetic

[8] Like Miles, Peter Brown acknowledges that despite the theological affirmation of the body in Christian doctrine, the opposition between spirit and flesh developed, in practice, to a dualism separating body and soul. Brown argues that the distinction between spirit and flesh articulated in the letters of Paul found many conflicting interpretations in the early Church, some of which led this complex distinction to be simplified into the distinction between body and soul. Consequently, the body took on the threatening aspects of the flesh and became the focus of Christian fears, pitting body and soul against one another and making possible a theological affirmation of ontological dualism that does not follow necessarily from the distinction between spirit and flesh (1988: 148).

practices she has found in the eucharistic piety of medieval women mystics. Bynum follows Max Weber in defining asceticism in terms of "discipline and method" rather than dualism and self-punishment: she argues that asceticism can be "a systematic, disciplined, determined self manipulation" aimed at meaning and empowerment (1991: 73). Even practices such as self-starvation, rolling in broken glass, and self-flagellation, she claims, cannot be construed simply as an internalization of misogyny, the hatred of the female body, or simply a misguided attempt to inflict as much pain as possible for pain's sake. These spectacular practices, according to Bynum, were rooted in a complex web of motivations and ideas. Among them, these practices were means by which women could gain some control over their environment—like contortionists, turning their narrowly circumscribed roles and lives into spectacular "gymnastics" of the spirit. Their practices also resisted moderating influences on the spirituality of the medieval Church. And through the body, these ascetics cultivated spiritual union with God, "plumb[ing] and realiz[ing] all the possibilities of the flesh" in a "profound expression of the doctrine of the Incarnation" (1987: 245, 294–95). That is, their suffering was an imitation of Christ, and not for the purpose of saving themselves, but, like Christ, for the purpose of saving others. These women "fus[ed] with a Christ whose suffering saves the world" by making the body the site of a spiritual practice in which pain and pleasure are experienced simultaneously (1987: 211).

"Living Flame": Ascetic Desire

Quoting Abba Joseph, one of the Desert Fathers, Bernard McGinn reminds us that ascetics often figured the perfection of spirit in terms of "fire" or "flame": "If you will, you could become a living flame" (1994: 137). This supports the view that concern with spirit is more fundamental to ascetic practice than denial of the body; more generally, it suggests that asceticism is aimed not at the repression but at the reorientation of desire. As Geoffrey Harpham argues, asceticism is "a meditation on, even an enactment of desire" (1987: 45).

Michel Foucault and Peter Brown have delineated useful distinctions between ascetic attitudes toward desire in Greco-Roman culture and Christianity.[9] Both take issue with the common notion that "the pre-

[9] Making such distinctions is hazardous business. Given the great variety of practices and spiritualities in paganism and Christianity, and the continuities between these cultural complexes, I use historians like Foucault and Brown simply to distinguish patterns and tendencies. Though both argue that a unique form of asceticism emerges with Christianity, I do not claim that this is the only possible form of asceticism compatible with Christianity.

Christian Roman world was a sunny 'Eden of the unrepressed' " (Brown 1988: 21) and with the contrast with "repressive" Christianity that this notion implies. Like their Christian counterparts, Greco-Roman thinkers reflected extensively on issues of sexuality and desire and instituted careful ascetic regimens of body and spirit. But the visions of self, nature, and culture that provided a context for Greco-Roman and Christian ascetics did differ. Foucault writes of two "forms of subjectivation": a Greco-Roman "aesthetics of existence" and a Christian "hermeneutics of desire." Greco-Roman discourse on the "care of the self" posited *ascesis* as "an exercise of freedom" and "self-mastery" centering on the struggle with desire (even to the point of its complete extirpation) (1990: 69). In this context, there was not the suspicion of desire that would later mark Christian asceticism, for desire and the needs of the body were understood to be a natural part of the human being. What mattered most was that one had the strength, achieved through the training of body and soul, to be able to master desire and decide when and how it was to be satisfied, expressed, used. Such self-mastery was an attitude, evident to others, that would mark one as a free and noble man through the display of "a relationship with oneself [that] would become isomorphic with the relationship of domination, hierarchy, and authority that one expected, as a man, a free man, to establish over inferiors" (1990: 83, 93). As an "aesthetics of existence," asceticism was cultivation and performance of the (free, male) self, marking his preeminent place in society.

The Christian "hermeneutics of desire," according to Foucault, was based on a radically different view. Rather than conceptualizing the problem of desire in terms of a disorderly but natural aspect of human life, Christian thought and practice reflected the idea that the self had been invaded by an "Other," which had corrupted desire and will. Concupiscence was "alien" and traceable to the Fall, but it was also so completely enmeshed with the human heart that it was difficult to determine what belonged to one's "true" self and what was a result of corruption. The self thus became a battleground. "The conceptual link between the movement of concupiscence, in its most insidious and most secret forms, and the presence of the Other, with its ruses and power of illusion, was to be one of the essential traits of the Christian ethics of the flesh" (1990: 68). Consequently, ascetic practice centered on the minute inspection of desire: one had to peer into the depths of one's heart, "reading" it in order to determine the various sources of different desires. This Christian hermeneutics served an ascetic regime of purification and transformation through which all desire would be directed to God (1990: 70).[10]

[10] See also an essay by Foucault entitled "Technologies of the Self" (1988b: 16–49). In this connection, Bernard McGinn notes that, for Origen, the soul is transformed "in the very act of reading and appropriating the scriptural text" (1995: 64).

Brown uncovers a complexity of attitudes and ideas toward desire and purification in early Christianity, which Foucault does not address. Nevertheless, Brown's study of the body and sexual renunciation depends on a similar distinctions. Most important, he gives evidence to support Foucault's claims with respect to the Christian hermeneutics of desire. Brown writes:

> The monk's own heart was the new book. What required infinitely skilled exegesis and long spiritual experience were the "movements of the heart," and the strategies and snares that the Devil laid within it. . . . The shift from a culture of the book to a *cultura Dei* . . . was rightly hailed as the greatest and the most peculiar achievement of the Old Men of Egypt: it amounted to nothing less than the discovery of a new alphabet of the heart. (1988: 229)

Self, Society, and the Cultivation of Subjectivity

Miles, Brown, and Bynum each argue that Christian ascetic practices have served as means of resistance to the powerful socializing forces of human culture. Central to Brown's thesis in *Body and Society* (1988) is the claim that Greek and Roman writers understood human beings and their societies to be a part of the "great chain of being." The conception and practices of the body that proceeded from this *Weltanschauung* could be severe, but the strong connection with nature meant that the relationship between nature, self, and culture was mutually reinforcing. Foucault's claims for the "aesthetics of existence" illustrates this point nicely. Human society was built on the hierarchies and orders thought to be dictated by nature. The free, self-mastering male stood at the summit of this hierarchy and displayed this mastery through his *ascesis*.

Christian attitudes toward the body were based on a view of nature and of mastery that differed significantly from Greco-Roman views. For Christians, nature, like humanity, had been corrupted in the Fall. Thus human desire could be transformed only by removing the body from fallen nature's chain of being, only by removing it from striving for human or natural forms of mastery and submitting to God's mastery. While Greco-Roman ascetic thought and practice was organized around the idea that human desire could be "harnessed" or "administered," Christians demanded a "transformation" of desire. Brown's history shows that, up to Augustine, Christians thought that participation in society supported one's slavery to desire and sin (the flesh), and so tempted one to remain tied to a nature alien to the state of paradise.[11] Like their Greek counterparts, Christian thinkers saw Greco-Roman society as an extension of nature, part of the chain of being; since Christians sought to escape this

---

[11] According to Brown, part of Augustine's great significance was that he brought to

"fallen nature," the transformation of body and soul could be accomplished only through some sort of distancing from society.

Brown's argument focuses on the eschatological basis of the early Christian practice of virginity: human beings could participate in God's new creation (announced by Christ) by breaking the bonds to the old creation, "wrench[ing] the body free from ancient solidarities." For Christians of the first two centuries, this often involved sexual abstinence, and, in the later cases of the desert ascetics, it meant leaving the villages of Egypt for the barren vastness of the desert (1988: 436). Such physical denial and separation, however, were only a first step in the attempt to free oneself from the bonds of fallen nature, society, and sin. For it was only once "the florid symptoms of greed and sexual longing, associated with the ascetic's past habits, had subsided, [that] he was brought face to face with the baffling closedness of his own heart" (1988: 225). The move to the desert was therefore not primarily a gesture of denial; rather, it was the attempt to remove oneself from certain habits and temptations in order to be able to attend more carefully to one's own heart and the voice of God. And it was an attempt to break the cycles of nature on which human culture depended and to anticipate the coming Kingdom in the creation of a countersociety.

By removing themselves to the desert in order to be able to attend more carefully to the self and to the self's relationships with nature, ascetics became examples and inspirations to those who remained within society. Many ascetics did not completely abandon the society they had left behind, but returned, in person and in books about their lives, to inspire others to follow their quest. The ascetic in Christian Egypt became a "hero of the settled land" (Brown, 1988: 227). As Harpham points out, their exhaustive efforts to remake themselves in the image of Christ made them, in turn, images for others to follow (1987: xiv). As with the *ascesis* in the Greco-Roman context, Christian ascetic practices were performances representing an ideal self and its relations to nature and culture.

There were important differences between the ways in which pagan and Christian ascetics served as ideals. The differences are especially evident when one considers the asceticism of the pagan *philosopher*. In many respects, the boundaries between Greco-Roman philosophy and Christian asceticism are difficult to draw, and involve different issues depending on whether one is talking about Platonism, Stoicism, or Cynicism. Most important, it is necessary to keep in mind that early Christian monastics, especially in the Greek-speaking context where Christian monasticism

---

dominance that strand of Christian thought that rejected the flight from society. A similar reading of Augustine's influence on the tradition in terms of asceticism and martyrdom can be found in Elaine Pagels's book on the early centuries of Christianity, *Adam, Eve, and the Serpent* (1989).

originated, understood themselves to be leading a philosophical life, along the model of the Greco-Roman philosophers. Hadot has described classical philosophy as "a way of life" rather than simply a mode of discourse, a spiritual way of life founded upon *ascesis* and *theoria theou* (vision of the divine). As Arnold Davidson describes Hadot's position, this practice was "so radical and all-encompassing as to make the philosopher *atopos*, unclassifiable, since he is in love with wisdom, which makes him strange, and foreign to the world of most mortals" (1995: 23). Both the pagan philosopher and the Christian ascetic therefore performed and embodied certain kinds of ideals through their renunciations and withdrawals. Brown, however, points out that although the philosopher of early antiquity renounced many of the ideals and ways of life of the citizen, he nonetheless "had made his own an ideal of the self whose potential other educated men had realized only imperfectly or fitfully." The classical philosopher, then, was *atopos* in the sense of transcending the social categories that constituted society, but this meant primarily that he was able to avoid some of the compromises to virtue required of those who actively participated in the life of politics and social power. He still represented the ideal of virtue for the citizen, and so played a valued role for the dominant culture (1980: 12). By contrast the early Christian ascetics, especially by embracing poverty and dwelling in the desert, identified with the marginalized of the culture of the Roman Empire, not with its leaders. In this sense, their asceticism was a more radical practice of the limits, one that "took up [a] position in the zone of anti-culture" (1980: 15).

Ascetic performances from the zone of anticulture can subvert modes of socialization and offer new ideals for human selfhood. They can provide a critical means with which to reflect on and resist forms of socialization, and they can be ways of experimenting with new constructions of self and community. Miles draws a distinction between the "socially conditioned self" and the "religious self," which, she argues, is a "consciously chosen self . . . created by the strategy of systematically dismantling the self automatically created by socialization" (1990: 95). The body plays a crucial role in this work as the "site and symbol of resistance" to society (1989: 57; 1990: 102–3). Herein, for certain scholars and activists, lies much of the historical and contemporary relevance of asceticism as a constructive and affirmative practice. In their studies of women in the Christian traditions, both Miles and Bynum point to the importance of ascetic practices in enabling women to resist dominant gender roles and refigure their lives as women. David Halperin (1995) has given shape to Foucault's suggestions for a "homosexual ascesis" or "queer mode of discipline" by which dominant modes of sexual identity can be resisted and new possibilities for pleasure, relationship, and embodied life can be explored.

Summary

Asceticism involves practices of self-discipline—both bodily and spiritual—by which relations between nature, culture, and self are articulated and enacted, transformed and performed.[12] To understand asceticism simply in terms of practices of self-denial is to extract particular acts and practices from their philosophical, religious, and cultural contexts and so to misunderstand the complex motivations and worldviews that ascetics embraced. To understand it *only* as the idealization of self-denial (which, in some, maybe many, cases it might be) is to ignore the role of desire in asceticism and its constructive aspects: asceticism as the empowerment or reorientation and reconstruction of desire and the self (Valantasis 1995: 547).[13] In both the Greco-Roman and Christian contexts, one finds practices in which the one's relationship to desire and culture is the object of highly self-conscious regimens of self-scrutiny and self-cultivation and/or transformation. Such an attitude toward self and culture must be distinguished from the relatively unself-conscious way in which many of us conduct our lives, even if we engage in practices of self-cultivation—from physical exercise, to education, to psychoanalysis. To be an ascetic is to self-consciously enact and embody a self on the cultural stage, a self that expresses the ideals of a culture or counterculture and offers a model for imitation and inspiration for others. Harpham, Brown, and Foucault all emphasize the display of the ascetic self and the importance of the ascetic's communication of his or her life, "in the flesh" or in writing. In its most general sense, asceticism is the cultivation and performance of an ideal self.

Apart from these continuities, the work I have summarized permits some general distinctions between Greco-Roman and Christian forms of asceticism. This involves, first, a distinction between Greco-Roman self-mastery, where one seeks to *control* or *administer* desire and nature, and Christian renewal, where one seeks to *transform* them. In the Christian context, human fallenness meant that many of the natural desires and impulses of the self were attributed to an "Other," the "enemy within" or "flesh." Thus, human nature and culture became problematic for Christians in ways that they were not for pagans because the break in the immediate connection between God and God's creation had twisted self and culture. Thus, a second distinction: where pagan *ascesis* occupies a space at the center of Greco-Roman society, Christian ascetics occupied

[12] For further reflections, see Richard Valantasis, "A Theory of the Social Function of Asceticism" (1995: 544).

[13] Valantasis argues, "At the center of ascetical activity is a self who, through behavioral changes, seeks to become a different person, a new self; to become a different person in new relationships; and to become a different person in a new society that forms a new culture."

the boundaries of society. Before Constantine and Augustine, Christian ascetics resisted society through practices of virginity or solitude; in the period of Christendom, they occupied the margins as monastics or mendicants. They sought a transformation that involved a struggle between fleshly desire and spiritual desire; here, the model of self-cultivation is not (simply) the creation of a beautiful, serene self, but a battle within the self against an enemy that must be isolated and eradicated. This battle is waged in close, persistent reading of the heart that enables resistance to corruption and the turning toward a new Kingdom. Although Christian asceticism does not necessarily entail (and theologically should never entail) a dualism that divorces the physical and the spiritual, the tension within the Christian ascetic is drastically intensified in comparison with the Greco-Roman ascetic.

ASCETIC THEMES IN NIETZSCHE'S THOUGHT

It would be easy to assume that Nietzsche—anti-Christ and lover of antiquity—would be more closely aligned with Greco-Roman than with Christian forms of discipline and self-fashioning. But a closer look at asceticism in Nietzsche's writing will show that his relation to Christian forms of asceticism is a complex one. Although there is much about inherited notions of Christian asceticism that Nietzsche rejects and much about Greco-Roman practices of the self that he embraces, certain themes I have delineated above as characteristic of Christian asceticism play a powerful role in Nietzsche's thought. This is not to say that Nietzsche is a "Christian ascetic," but simply to suggest that Nietzsche's understanding of the self and of the way "one becomes what one is" is indebted, in a positive way, to Christian asceticism.

The Body and Philosophy: Transfiguring Spirit

Following Schopenhauer, Nietzsche was one of the first philosophers of the modern era to write with seriousness about the body. He generally condemns the treatment of the body in Western philosophical thought: "The unconscious disguise of physiological needs under the cloaks of the objective, ideal, purely spiritual goes to frightening lengths—and often I have asked myself whether, taking a large view, philosophy has not been merely an interpretation of the body and a *misunderstanding of the body*" (GS: 34–35). For Nietzsche, this misunderstanding has less to do with a failure to treat the body as an important philosophical topic than with a failure to recognize how the body penetrates all thinking and all spirit.

By thinking against the body, the philosophical tradition has attempted to think without the body, following the Socratic imperative to a mastery of consciousness. Nietzsche, by contrast, attempted to think with and through the body, reflecting closely on how his body enlivened and shaped his thinking. Doing so, he found one must attend to the "small things" of life—such as climate, diet, and physical exercise—to discover and cultivate the optimal conditions of spiritualization; he apprehended fluent transpirations between movement and thought (EH: 256); he correlated philosophical positions to specific bodily states; and he wrote in a style that resisted—vehemently, joyously, passionately—the bloodless composure and coherence of traditional philosophical style.[14] As Zarathustra puts it: "The awakened and knowing say: body am I entirely, and nothing else; and soul is only a word for something about the body. . . . Behind your thoughts and feelings, my brother, there stands a mighty ruler, an unknown sage—whose name is self. In your body he dwells; he is your body" (Z: 34).

For Nietzsche, soul and spirit are bodily through and through, not separate entities grafted onto or into the body. We might conceive of them as refined and lambent expressions of the bodily will to power, or what Zarathustra, in this passage, calls "self."[15] But Nietzsche's attention to the body does not yield physiological reductionism: he does not juxtapose spirit to material body, where the latter would imply an animal machine and the former a mere expression determined by the operations of that machine. Although he often writes "physiologically" and appeals to the pressure of instincts or drives in human life, he does not imagine a given bodily nature, nor does body serve as a philosophical foundation for his arguments.[16] Nietzsche resists such foundations by imagining a dialectical relationship between body and spirit. These are not discrete realities, but modulations and complications of each other. We might conceive of this body and this spirit as heterogeneous, overlapping fields of the self, which energize and shape one another. With reference to the experience of writing *Zarathustra*, Nietzsche comments on the way spirit affects the body:

[14] Stauth and Turner explore the significance of Nietzsche's attention to these "small things" in *Nietzsche's Dance* (1988).

[15] For Nietzsche, "soul" (*Seele*), as it is employed in this context, is a vague, almost romantic term that serves to designate the inner life—conscious and unconscious—of the human being (e.g., GM: 84). It is roughly equivalent to, and as vague as, the figurative use of "heart" in English. As I have indicated, "Spirit" (*Geist*) is a more important, though not always more precisely defined, term for Nietzsche. It can mean "reason" or "mind," but its full meaning for Nietzsche is broader and more dynamic, involving, most importantly, the ideas of self-consciousness and self-transcendence.

[16] For instance, see Nietzsche's discussion of the vital role the drives play in philosophy (BG: 13–14).

"The suppleness of my muscles has always been greatest when my creative energies were flowing most abundantly. The *body* is inspired" (EH: 302–3). Spirit invigorates the body, not as a ghost animating a machine, but as a piercing quality of responsiveness, the intensity and meaning of sensation, the focusing of awareness.

Nietzsche articulates the interplay between body and spirit with two concepts: "breeding" and "transfiguration." He argues that instincts and drives can be "bred" or "cultivated" in the interplay of body and spirit, culture and nature. Thus, he can write that Christianity destroyed the Greco-Roman "instinct" for knowledge and taste, and claim that his task is to regain the sensibility of antiquity "*not* as brain training" but as "body, as gesture, as instinct" (TI: 92).[17] This is one reason "interpretation" is so important to Nietzsche: interpretations are inscribed into the bodies that together compose culture—the Platonic-Christian culture of Europe *embodies* the ascetic ideal. Nietzsche's vision of "breeding" is possible because human nature and human bodies are malleable to interpretations and disciplines of spirit. Man is the "*as yet undetermined animal*" because human beings are still in the process of "ascending" to their nature (BG: 74).

Such ascent is manifested in the "transfiguration" of body into spirit. It is worth repeating, in a broader context, the passage on transfiguration I cited in the previous chapter:

A philosopher who has traversed many kinds of health, and keeps traversing them, has passed through an equal number of philosophies; he simply *cannot* keep from transposing his states every time into the most spiritual form and distance: this art of transfiguration *is* philosophy. We philosophers are not free to divide body and soul, as the people do; we are even less free to divide soul from spirit. . . . [C]onstantly we have to give birth to our thoughts out of our pain and, like mothers, endow them with all we have of blood, heart, fire, pleasure, passion, agony, conscience, fate and catastrophe. Life—that means for us constantly transforming all that we are into light and flame—also everything that wounds us; we simply can do no other. (GS: 35–36)

Like the desert ascetics of early Christianity, Nietzsche seeks the transfiguration of body into flaming spirit. Philosophy, as Nietzsche understands it, is a discipline of close attention to "all that we are," through which one gives birth to spirit; it is an ascetic project, but one that does not oppose body and spirit, even though it may exact severe discipline from body and spirit for the sake of the shining body of a keen spirituality.

Zarathustra says that he loves only what is written in the body's blood; but he also says, "Write with blood and you will experience that blood

---

[17] But Nietzsche also expresses a debt to the breeding of the spirit accomplished by Christianity (BG: 101, 210).

is spirit" (Z: 40). Writing is Nietzsche's most important transfigurative practice. Writing out of the body creates spirit—more precisely, writing out of the *suffering* body creates spirit. The preface to *Human, All too Human*, offers a horrible and delicate image. The philosopher as psychologist "takes a host of painful things . . . and as it were *impales* them with a kind of needle-point:—is it any wonder if, with such sharp-pointed and ticklish work, a certain amount of blood occasionally flows, if the psychologist engaged in it has blood on his fingers and not always only—on his fingers?" (HH: 210). There is here expressed the refined and exacting cruelty of the most voluptuous ascetic. The philosopher uses writing to tattoo a pattern into the wounded body. Writing is the means by which the will to power inscribes spirit into itself, and is "consecrated as a sacrificial animal" (Z: 104) for the sake of greater spirit.

Beyond Hermeneutics and Aesthetics

On this account, philosophy, as a particular practice of writing, is always implicated with pain.[18] Knowledge is fundamentally painful for Nietzsche because it involves seeing through human illusions in order to confront without consolation the deep recesses of the suffering body. Writing and philosophy are practices of attention to the suffering—that is, the living—body. But so is the ascetic ideal. Early on, Nietzsche had connected the pain of philosophy with the power of asceticism. In *Dawn*, he writes that "happiness, conceived as the liveliest feeling of power, has perhaps been nowhere greater on earth than in the souls of superstitious ascetics." Nietzsche links this happiness to the "basic disposition" of the ascetic, which involves the "triumph over oneself and revel[ing] in an extremity of power." He then moves directly to consider knowledge, more precisely, "knowledge acquired through suffering." This sequence links the power of the self-denying ascetic and the necessary suffering of the genuine philosopher (D: 69). The quest for knowledge and the creation of spirit involves painful renunciation: pain is, for Nietzsche, the "mother" of thought and spirit and philosophy is an ascetic practice of knowing and transfiguring the body.[19]

Nietzsche attacks the ascetic ideal for the way it holds the body culpable for its own suffering. It is not surprising, therefore, that in his attempt to

[18] Nehamas is right to point out that, for Nietzsche, "writing is perhaps the most important part of thinking"; that thinking "is an action" and that, consequently, "writing is also the most important part of living" (1985: 41).

[19] Compare Adorno: "The existent negates itself as thought upon itself. Such negation is mind's element." Walter Lowe cites this passage and adds, "It is almost as if thought itself were an implicit gesture of repentance." Lowe explicitly connects this gesture of thought to Western asceticism, indicating an inherently ascetic cast to thinking (1993: 143).

develop a new response to human self-alienation and its attendant suffering, Nietzsche sought to express his ideals in nonmoral or aesthetic terms.

> To "give style" to one's character—a great and rare art! It is practiced by those
> who survey all the strengths and weaknesses of their nature and then fit them
> into an artistic plan until every one of them appears as art and reason and even
> weaknesses delight the eye. . . . It will be the strong and domineering natures
> that enjoy their finest gaiety in such constraint and perfection under a law of
> their own; the passion of their tremendous will relents in the face of all stylized
> nature, of all conquered and serving nature. (GS: 232)

One might relate the complex attitude toward nature expressed in this
passage to that which Foucault describes as the Greco-Roman "aesthetics
of existence," for here Nietzsche expresses the value of a certain mastery
over nature. Nature is something to be worked with, it is material for an
artistic, philosophical creation; but at the same time, nature itself, as
spirit, is the creative force, cutting and sculpting itself. Simply because
nature is not confronted here by an ontologically distinct force or entity
does not mean that nature's stylization of itself is not a matter of painful
domination. To create, one must be able to master oneself the way an
artist masters his or her material and technique.

Nietzsche does not conceive of the cultivation of self and culture simply
in artistic terms, however. Whereas his artistic love of form and surface
leads him to idealize the creation of a beautiful self, his pursuit of the
history of values turns him into a "subterranean man," who mines the
depths of human moralities in order to extricate and expose to light our
twisted self-deceptions. Thus, he holds a tension between an artistic adoration of the surface and the disciplined removal of the "veils" that cover
that surface (GS: 38). Along with, even at times apparently in conflict
with, his praise of the "profound superficiality" of the Greeks, Nietzsche
is impelled to look beneath the surface to uncover the historical and physiological conditions underlying desire, value, and culture. His goal is to
"explore the whole sphere of the modern soul, to have sat in its every
nook": "We modern men are the heirs of the conscience-vivisection and
self-torture of millennia: this is what we have practiced longest, it is our
distinctive art perhaps" (GM: 95).

As Nietzsche digs down into the modern soul, his closest subject—hid-
eously exposed on the table—is himself. As a subterranean man, engaged
in a project he describes as "my ambition, my torture, my happiness"
(WP: 532), Nietzsche explores both the dark recesses of his culture and
of his own soul as a product of that culture. "I have a subtler sense of
smell for the signs of ascent and decline than any other human being
before me: I am the teacher *par excellence* for this—I know both, I am
both" (EH: 222). Although he seeks to avoid a decadent moralizing that

would sneer at the bad smells he excavates, he cannot avoid the techniques that Western culture has perfected for laying open the soul. Nietzsche sees in Christianity "the means through which the European spirit has been trained to strength, ruthless curiosity, and subtle mobility" (BG: 101). His attempt to think and write beyond the ascetic ideal cannot be undertaken solely through the regular exercise of an "aesthetics of existence," but must also mobilize the more scrupulous "hermeneutics of desire," fostered in the Christian tradition.

Though for Nietzsche the "will to truth" is not exclusively of Christian or Jewish origin, it has been developed in Christianity in a particularly subtle and ruthless direction, becoming a will to self-scrutiny that is matchless in its suspicious resourcefulness. Nietzsche is critical of the "evil eye" that people of Western civilization have cast on their natural inclinations. Yet, in reflecting on the courage required of the philosopher who strives for self-consciousness, Nietzsche argues that it is precisely through ruthless questioning, which cuts into the soul, that philosophers will gain insight into new human possibilities.

> Our attitude towards *ourselves is hubris*, for we experiment with ourselves in a way we would never permit ourselves to experiment with animals and, carried away by curiosity, we cheerfully vivisect our souls: what is the "salvation" of the soul to us today?. . . We violate ourselves nowadays, no doubt of it, we nutcrackers of the soul, ever questioning and questionable, as if life were nothing but cracking nuts; and thus we are bound to grow day-by-day more questionable, *worthier* of asking questions; perhaps also worthier—of living? (GM: 113)

Nietzsche is concerned to diagnose not only contemporary culture, but also his own entanglement, as a "man of knowledge," with the temptations of the will to truth and the ascetic ideal. By undertaking the tortuous untwisting of insidious desires and motives in himself, he reaches within to bring to light his intransigent temptations and illusions. Paradoxically, only by means of such ruthless techniques will the modern men of knowledge be able to discern and oppose the ascetic ideal. But the techniques are themselves ascetic.

They are also philosophical in a more modern sense. Contemporary philosophical commentators have devoted considerable energy to examining and debating the epistemological and historical ramifications of Nietzschean "perspectivism" and "genealogy." Such endeavors are certainly justified. Nietzsche's ideas about the different bodily and spiritual perspectives that shape the way we know, and the particular historicization of desire and meaning he accomplishes through genealogy, have significance apart from the particular way they were deployed by Nietzsche himself. However, to understand them in the context of Nietzsche's own writing requires careful attention to their status as "practices of the self" aimed at a transformative spiritualization. Nietzsche is less interested in developing detailed theories of knowledge (so see, for example, his numerous snide comments about epistemologists) than in cultivating and utilizing different perspectives in order to have access to every nook and cranny of the modern soul. Nietzsche's genealogies, whether historically accurate or not, serve as vehicles for imagining different possibilities to the extent that they defamiliarize and open to reconstruction concepts and values we think we know so well. To think with Nietzsche is not only to render philosophical judgments about the validity of his methods, but to find ways to think *differently* about self, community, and history.

Self, Community, and Power: The Free Spirit

To become a self is to be socialized: each of us is constituted as a self only to the extent that we are implicated in webs of particular desires, expectations, and relations. But to become a self is also to become self-conscious, with at least some ability to reflect on and direct the forces at play in the constitution of self and community. Cultivation of self and community involves what Margaret Miles describes as "difficult disciplines of self-definition," where old comforts, hopes, and ways of perceiving and relating are overcome and/or transformed through long, persistent practice, which involves disciplined experimentation with and embodiment of new ways of life. Herein, I think, lies not only the contemporary political and religious significance of asceticism as a means of criticism and liberation, but one of the most important aspects of Nietzsche's own asceticism. This is displayed vividly in Nietzsche's rejection of the comforts, values, and ideals that have shaped modern Europe, made possible by the "No" that he burned into his own soul, and in his celebration of the "free spirit" who says "Yes" to life.

Nietzsche describes *Thus Spake Zarathustra* as "a dithyramb on solitude." Zarathustra loves the freedom of his desert solitude as Nietzsche loved the "free spirit." In this frustrating and fantastic book, Nietzsche displays his preoccupation with the themes of wandering, communication, and the lures and temptations of society. In the process, he demonstrates, in concept, narrative, and metaphor (and, certainly, parody), the central place of ascetic themes in his vision. Like the desert ascetics, who saw their move to the wastelands of Egypt as an imitation of Christ's sojourn in the desert, Zarathustra spends years of solitude in his cave and proclaims that "[i]t was ever in the desert that the truthful have dwelt, the free spirits, as masters of the desert" (Z: 103–4). Like Saint Antony, Zarathustra struggles with temptations and demons who, in Nietzsche's case, take the grotesque forms of dwarfs, dogs, and snakes. Resisting these temptations, Zarathustra seeks a new self and a new hope. Like those early desert dwellers, Nietzsche saw solitude as an effort to break the grip of "nature"; it was the means by which he could distance himself from and resist a human society he called the "herd:" "this natural, all too natural . . . development of man towards the similar, ordinary, average, herdlike—*common*!" (BG: 217, 226).

The enmity Nietzsche posits between the philosopher and the herd means that one should not assume that his battle against the ascetic ideal is ever finished—it remains a problem. If the monotheism of the ascetic ideal tempts us to embrace the monomania of moral conformity, then the battle against it must be a constant one, not one that merely produces a new conformity. According to Nietzsche, the comfort of certainty and conformity is a permanent danger; it infiltrates our desires through the common language we speak and think (BG: 216–17). The weakness and sickness of the ascetic ideal idealizes a pure heart, without conflict, and the peaceable kingdom where all live with a common will. Nietzsche's resistance to the ascetic ideal is therefore also resistance to the forces in community that find their goal in peace and consensus. The struggle against the "common" is perennial, requiring the constant inspection of one's language and consciousness for the lures to conformity implanted within. There is a daunting tension in Nietzsche's work between, on the one hand, his vision of future society based on his "revaluation of values," and, on the other hand, a permanent overcoming, by the philosopher, of any stable regime of conformity.

In order to participate in the striving of life and the joy of desire, the philosopher must learn how to negotiate the line between culture and anticulture. The ability to struggle with this tension is for Nietzsche a sign of health and spirit—this struggle *is* freedom of the spirit. "The free man is a warrior.—How is freedom measured, in individuals as in nations? By the resistance which has to be overcome, by the effort it costs to stay *aloft*" (TI: 102). As he remarks in *Beyond Good and Evil*, a primary task of the philosopher is to be the "bad conscience" of his or her time, whose "enemy was ever the ideal of today." More positively, Nietzsche describes the philosopher engaged in searching "beyond good and evil" as a *Versucher*, a term that can be translated into English only by hovering between *tempter* and *attempter*. As the narrative of *Zarathustra* confirms, Nietzsche's solitude is not one that cuts him off from society, it is rather a means by which he occupies the boundaries or limits of human community in an effort to experiment with old and new values and to serve as an exemplar for those he lures away from the herd (Z: 23; HH: 8).

It is also a means by which he moves at the limits of the self, for there is a close parallel in Nietzsche between self and community. Indeed, he conceives the self as a kind of community: not a monarchy or dictatorship commanded by consciousness, but a "subjective multiplicity," where willing is "a question of commanding and obeying, on the basis . . . of a social structure composed of many 'souls'" (BG: 20). The self *is* a constant power struggle that the philosopher must negotiate and influence by departing and returning to the self in a wandering that mirrors his wandering on the limits of society and culture. "[The free spirit] looks back gratefully—grateful to his wandering, to his hardness and self-alienation, to his viewing of far distances and bird-like flights in cold heights. What a good thing he had not always stayed at home, stayed 'under his own roof' like a delicate apathetic loafer! He had been beside himself: no doubt of that" (HH: 8).

The purpose of such wandering, and a key to understanding the free spirit, is what Nietzsche calls "self-overcoming." In "On Self-Overcoming" from *Zarathustra*, his first published discussion of the will to power (and an anticipation of the essay on the ascetic ideal), Zarathustra speaks to "the wisest" (Z: 113–19). He questions their claim to be driven by the "will to truth," offering a different interpretation of their desire: they are driven, he claims, by the "will to power," which he identifies with the "unexhausted procreative will of life." He then offers his thoughts on power, obedience, and life.

> But wherever I found the living, there I heard also the speech on obedience. Whatever lives, obeys. And this is the second point: he who cannot obey himself is commanded. That is the nature of the living. . . . And life itself confided this secret to me: "Behold," it said, "I am *that which must always overcome itself* . . . where there is perishing and a falling of leaves, behold, there life sacrifices itself—for power. . . . Whatever I create and however much I love it—soon I must be an enemy to it and my love; thus my will wills it. . . . There is much that life esteems more highly than life itself; but out of the esteeming itself speaks the will to power. Thus life once taught me; and with this I shall yet solve the riddle of your heart, you who are wisest. . . . With your values and words of good and evil you do violence when you value; and this is your hidden love and the splendor and trembling and overflowing of your soul. (Z: 115–16)

Zarathustra solves the riddle in the heart of the wisest by showing them that their will to truth is actually a will to power. He also asserts an intimate link between love and the will to power. The wisest, like Zarathustra, recognize the value of self-overcoming, but they think that their overcoming is a mastering or transcendence of life, when, in actuality, it is the movement of life itself. This movement, as Zarathustra says, must be repeated "again and again" in the "overflowing" of love, value, and creation. Desire is doubled in this process of self-overcoming: it is expressed in the love that "esteems" and creates, but it then turns back on itself, now not as desire for the object created or esteemed, but as the desire for desire itself that Nietzsche calls "power."

The problem with the wisest, from this perspective, is not that they sacrifice their love or engage in ascetic practices of self-denial and self-overcoming, but that they cannot admit to themselves their own lust for power; they cannot justify themselves without a justification beyond life. Nietzsche identifies the will to power with life's self-overcoming but distinguishes between a self-overcoming that springs from priestly *ressentiment* against life and one in which the philosopher turns away from him- or herself for the sake of enhanced power and life. For Nietzsche, then, human life is enhanced (empowered) by a self-overcoming enacted through the denial or sacrifice of that which one loves and creates. He writes, "Deeply I love only life—and verily, most of all when I hate life." Nietzsche's asceticism involves a constant attempt to decipher or interpret the text of the self by taking sides against the self; in this process, the philosopher sacrifices love and self for the sake of the increased love and power of spirit. Nietzsche's asceticism cultivates "the craving for an ever new widening of distances within the soul itself, the development of ever higher, rarer, more remote, further-stretching, more comprehensive states—in brief, simply the enhancement of the type 'man,' the continual 'self-overcoming of man,' to use a moral formula in a supra-moral sense" (BG: 201).

The decadent self seeks to impose a false peace and conformity on the instincts through the mastery of consciousness and the goal of transcendent life (TI: 43). Nietzsche, by contrast, honors internal contradictions and the "enemy within" (TI: 54). The ascending self, in Deleuze's words, opens itself up "to the multiplicities that traverse it from head to toe" (James Miller 1993: 245). In one respect, this is an exercise in depersonalization and so an encounter with alterity. Yet it also is the precondition of the freedom of the spirit because it makes it possible for "strong" and "illiberal" instincts or wills to struggle against the decadent temptations of conformity. Nietzsche's social vision is constructed out of a tension between a culture with a strict hierarchy and the *Versucher* of the philosopher of the boundaries. Similarly, the self of the Nietzschean philosopher only finds its freedom in the transfiguring tension between the mastery of strong and affirmative drives and the de-selfing that makes knowledge and spirit possible.

Conclusion: Nietzsche's Asceticism

Nietzsche's vision of philosophy resembles closely the classical vision of philosophy as spiritual exercise. In at least one crucial respect, however, his spiritualization resembles more closely the turn from flesh to spirit in Christian asceticism than the imposition of reason's mastery in the Greco-Roman context. Like the Christian ascetic, Nietzsche moves to demolish established ideals and envisions new ones; he seeks a radical transformation or reorientation of desire and meaning. Thus, Nietzsche's spiritual-ization, like Christian asceticism, exacerbates a division within the self, and complicates the relations between self, nature, and culture. The ascetic digs his hermitage in the crevices among these shifting and plastic forces. Deploying the "ruthless curiosity" and suspicion, which he attributes to Christianity, Nietzsche explores the multifarious and insidious ways the ascetic ideal captures body and spirit. While it is true that Nietzsche does not conceive of this self-division in theological terms (such as fall, guilt, and sin), he does construct an "enemy" out of the natural aversion to pain and the inclination to conformity, for both generate the fear that underwrites the ascetic ideal.[20]

Nietzsche's asceticism also differs from both Greco-Roman and Christian forms. Rather than seeking an end to self-cultivation in the hierarchies of nature, as in Greco-Roman culture—or in the peace of God, as in Christianity—Nietzsche envisions a never-ending struggle for creation, a continual self-overcoming and spiritual growth. He calls this "life." Insofar as he conceives of human nature as structured around an irreconcilable tear or gap within human beings, Nietzsche precludes traditional forms of spiritual reconciliation. The self is a permanent battleground of conflicting wills and ideals. This battle is not something to be resolved, despite the suffering and bewilderment it causes, for it is the condition of freedom and spiritual enhancement. Spirit depends, therefore, on exacerbating *productively* the tension of the self's fundamental self-alienation. In contrast with the spirituality of the ascetic ideal, Nietzsche imposes suffering upon himself in order to live and grow as a human self in this world. To live life, instead of the living death of the ascetic ideal, one must resist the consoling promises of Truth or God. Only through a discipline in which the self is constantly turning on itself, questioning itself, and overcoming itself can it resist these temptations, and continue in the way of the free spirit.

• • • • •

In his influential book on Nietzsche, Alexander Nehamas dismisses the problem of Nietzsche's asceticism by describing Nietzsche's discipline and

[20] See BG: 217, 226. Although my primary purpose here is to draw some positive connections between Nietzsche and Christian asceticism, a more complete treatment would involve an exploration of Nietzsche's connections to the philosophical tradition of Cynicism. See Peter Sloterdijk's discussion of Nietzsche's cynicism (1987a, 1987b). In some of his final lectures, Michel Foucault claimed that Christian asceticism is directly connected to the Cynic's "agonizing and idiosyncratic approach to the truth": "The desert saint, like the pagan Cynic, wrenched himself away from everyday life and ordinary society, cutting the normal ties that bind a human being to family and friends. The goal . . . [was to] transfigure totally who one was and what one thought, creating, if necessary, through the most immoderate

self-denial as a simple case of "prudential self-control." This he distinguishes from the moralizing dogmatism of "asceticism" (as ascetic ideal) (Nehamas 1985: 116). Again, this attempt to save Nietzsche from the terrible specter of asceticism oversimplifies both Nietzsche and asceticism. It does correctly encompass the sense of *ascesis* as "training," which we might think of in terms of self-imposed discipline and pain for the sake of a certain fitness and health. And it helpfully points to Nietzsche's critique of morality. Yet it ignores important aspects of the ecstatic element of Nietzsche's thought, in two ways. First, it ignores the radically transformative character of Nietzsche's philosophy as spiritual practice. This practice, as I have indicated, requires severe practices of depersonalization or de-selfing in order to enable new possibilities of selfhood to be created. What, exactly, is "self-control" or "prudence" in this case? As radically transformative, Nietzsche's asceticism is much more than training, because it seeks not simply to maximize the possibilities of already existing capacities; it seeks new capacities and new possibilities. Moreover—possibly more disturbing and certainly less prudent—Nietzsche argues that human beings actually take pleasure in causing themselves pain, and experience an "over-abundant enjoyment at [their] own suffering." These are not simply "superstitious" or life-denying ascetics, nor, clearly, are they prudential utilitarians.

> The most spiritual human beings, as the *strongest*, find their happiness where others would find their destruction: in the labyrinth, in severity towards themselves and others, in attempting; their joy lies in self-constraint: with them asceticism becomes nature, need, instinct. They consider the hard task a privilege, to play with vices which overwhelm others a *recuperation*: . . . Knowledge—a form of asceticism [ellipses Nietzsche's]. (AC: 188)[21]

For Nietzsche, happiness and joy are found *in* the labyrinth and *in* self-constraint, not simply at the end of the labyrinth or as a result of power gained by self-constraint. A prudential asceticism is goal-oriented, but Nietzsche challenges us with a more complex perspective on renunciation and pain. He certainly is not rejecting the idea that his ascetic practices have a goal, but when the goal is "spirit" things get complicated. Nietzsche is saying something more, for when he celebrates the "pain of

and punishing of practices, a radically other sort of existence, manifest in one's body, unmistakable in one's style of life—turning one's bios, as such, into 'the immediate, explosive, and savage presence of truth' " (James Miller 1993: 361).

[21] For the will to knowledge as a spiritualized form of directing cruelty against oneself, see BG: 159. Nietzsche also expresses his distaste for prudence from a slightly different perspective: "But the genuine philosopher—as it seems to *us*, my friends?—lives 'unphilosophically' and 'unwisely,' above all imprudently, and feels the burden and the duty of a hundred attempts and temptations of life—he risks himself constantly, he plays the wicked game—" (BG: 125).

childbirth" and the "Dionysian mysteries" in which "pain is sanctified" (TI: 120), he brings religious considerations to bear. From a Dionysian perspective, the perspective of the process of creation, pain is experienced as an integral and necessary moment of life; in renunciation one experiences the power of life's creative force. This process Nietzsche describes as "the road to life . . . the sacred road." By celebrating the process—the way, the "labyrinth"—as sacred, Nietzsche consecrates each of its constituents as sacred, each signifying something necessary to life. That Nietzsche is not simply valuing pain because it is a means to creativity is also supported in the section immediately following the discussion of childbirth. There, continuing his reflections on the Dionysian, Nietzsche writes that the will to life rejoices in itself "through" the "sacrifice of its highest types" (TI: 120). In other words, the sacred nature of life is not experienced only in productivity or creativity, but also in the pain and destructiveness of sacrifice. In certain kinds of pain and suffering, Nietzsche's philosopher experiences the fullness and inexhaustibility of life; his asceticism thus is not simply calculation but celebration and worship, a way of realizing "in oneself the eternal joy of becoming." In the following chapters I take up the issue of mysticism and affirmation to make this connection more explicit.

Chapter Four

THE PROBLEM OF MYSTICISM IN NIETZSCHE

> In the Dionysian dithyramb . . . the entire symbolism of the body is
> called into play, not the mere symbolism of the lips, face, and speech
> but the whole pantomime of dancing, forcing every member into
> rhythmic movement.
>
> (Nietzsche, *The Birth of Tragedy*)

> Now I am light, now I fly, now I see myself beneath myself, now a god
> dances through me.
>
> (Nietzsche, *Thus Spake Zarathustra*)

> If you stand right fronting and face to face to a fact, you will see the
> sun glimmer on both its surfaces, as if it were a cimiter, and feel its
> sweet edge dividing you through the heart and marrow, and so you
> will happily conclude your mortal career. Be it life or death, we
> crave only reality.
>
> (Henry David Thoreau, *Walden*)

NIETZSCHE AND MYSTICISM

Introduction

I N THE REMAINING CHAPTERS of the book, I discuss the mystical
elements of Nietzsche's thought. These are central to Nietzsche's affirmative vision and are the proper context for understanding
Nietzsche's asceticism. Yet they are more difficult to specify than the ascetic aspects, for Nietzsche did not treat mysticism, even critically, in
nearly as much depth as he treated asceticism: one rarely finds the words
mystic or *mysticism* in his writing, and the issue of mysticism has not
been an important one for Nietzsche's commentators.[1] But I will argue

Epigraphs: Nietzsche, BT: 40; Z: 41; Thoreau 1991: 80.

[1] Nietzsche does explicitly mention mysticism at a few points: see GS: 182, 235, 269; BG
64; GM: 132. The mystical resonance in *Zarathustra*, or in Nietzsche's thought in general,
has been noted, but little sustained attention has been devoted to this topic. Examples are
Higgens (1987: 140–42) and Thiele (1990: 155). Joan Stambaugh has written a series of
essays that offer the most extensive and suggestive treatment of Nietzsche's mysticism, particularly with respect to their philosophical implications. Focusing on *Zarathustra*, Stambaugh calls Nietzsche a "poetic mystic" and analyzes the place of classic mystical motifs
such as *coincidentia oppositorum* and union with the cosmos in this work. Stambaugh
(1994) also discusses parallels between Nietzsche's mysticism and Eastern religious and philosophical traditions. Most importantly, she draws attention to the significant element of

that mysticism, properly understood, can give us great insight into Nietzsche's thought. Mysticism, for instance, was a problem central to Nietzsche's engagement with Schopenhauer because Schopenhauer explicitly linked asceticism and mysticism in the figure of the saint, who only achieves the denial of life in the *unio mystica*. Mystical imagery and questions continued to retain their fascination for Nietzsche beyond his turn from Schopenhauer, as a reading of *Zarathustra* shows, and as one sees in the essay on the ascetic ideal where Nietzsche considers how ascetic practices make possible the intoxicating, ecstatic feeling of divinity. Such intoxication serves both as a means to power for the religious virtuoso and as a kind of tranquilizing consolation for people in general. For the saint or the contemplative mystic, intoxication involves self-surrender in the ecstatic transcendence of individuality and the feeling of divine empowerment. When used to warrant human, all too human truths motivated by the desire for revenge and/or escape, Nietzsche finds such intoxication despicable and destructive. Nonetheless, Nietzsche placed a high value on "elevated," ecstatic states. The problem for the interpreter is to determine just how Nietzsche draws the fine line between life-denying narcosis and life-affirming ecstasy, how we should link Nietzsche's ecstasy to "mysticism," and just how ecstasy and/or mysticism plays a role in Nietzsche's philosophy.

Schopenhauer and The Birth of Tragedy

Nietzsche's engagement with the problem of affirmation and denial emerges directly from Schopenhauer's treatment of asceticism and mysticism as practices of saintliness. In his grandly bleak masterpiece, *The*

---

passivity in Nietzsche's conception of philosophical thinking and artistic creativity. To take seriously this passivity, especially in the context of the tension in Nietzsche's thought with respect to the relation of power and intoxication, requires some major adjustment of the popular understanding of "will to power." For all its suggestiveness, though, Stambaugh's work remains sketchy, more an indicator of problems that require attention than an attempt to work through any of them in depth. One particular issue that needs to be addressed in more detail, which I attempt below, is the significance of the "mystical poetry" of *Zarathustra* for Nietzsche's vision of philosophy and affirmation. Irena Makarushka offers a provocative analysis of Nietzsche's identification with Jesus in *The Antichrist*, comparing it with the mystical experience of union. She also cites Lou Andreas Salomé's discussion of eternal recurrence as a mystical idea (1994: 34, 47). Finally, Georges Bataille, in his inimitable way, treats Nietzsche as a mystic. I will not attempt to summarize Bataille's ideas, but will simply cite a few passages that he attributes to Nietzsche, but which I have not been able to locate. "The new feeling of power is the state of mysticism; and the clearest, boldest rationalism is only a help and a means toward it.—Philosophy expresses extraordinarily elevated states of soul" (1992: 175). "The definition of a mystic: someone with enough happiness of his own, maybe too much, seeking a language for his happiness because he wants to *give away* that happiness."

World as Will and Representation, Schopenhauer argued that the highest ethico-religious expression of life is its denial: all that is good, noble, and holy is made possible only insofar as one intuits the fundamental fact of suffering and, as a result, becomes the vehicle by which the will to life freely "turns" against itself. This turn is the paradigmatic ascetic gesture, a renunciation that Nietzsche would come to argue is impossible. Defined narrowly, asceticism for Schopenhauer is the "deliberate breaking of the will . . . the voluntarily chosen way of life of penance and self-chastise-ment, for the constant mortification of the will" (1969a: 392). But, as will be the case for Nietzsche, in Schopenhauer's treatment, asceticism is bound up with mysticism and sainthood. The intuition of the real nature of the will, the liberating insight upon which ascetic denial ultimately depends, is the basis of Schopenhauer's "mysticism" (1969a: 390). More-over, the denial of the will and the mystical insight depend on saintly acts of pity: the renunciatory practices of the ascetic involve not just a turn against the self, but also the turn toward the suffering of others. Through pity, the ascetic/mystic/saint takes the world's suffering upon him- or her-self and so truly comes to know—in mystical insight—the nature of the will in the experience of suffering.

Nietzsche's first book, *The Birth of Tragedy*, emerges from his own reflection on Schopenhauer's central problematic: individuality as the source of pain and misery. Nietzsche proposed that the power of Greek tragedy was to be found in the way it made available the promise of indi-viduality's blissful dissolution (BT: 73). In this respect, the mystical impli-cations of the book are unmistakable. Later in his life, however, Nietzsche had harsh criticisms for the book, particularly for what he saw as its otherworldly escapism and the Schopenhauerian metaphysic that sup-ported it. In the 1886 preface to the book, entitled "Attempt at Self-Criti-cism," Nietzsche claims that he had mistakenly identified the tragic effect in terms of "metaphysical comfort," an illusion-producing capacity that allowed the Greeks to forget the pain of existence. Looking back, Nietzsche counsels his readers to "learn the art of this-worldly comfort first" and "dispatch all metaphysical comforts to the devil" (BT: 26). Do his later criticisms of the book, and attacks on intoxication, attest, then, to a complete rejection of mystical sensibility? If so, how does one explain the presence, especially in the late writings, of a positive vision of artistic intoxication and of Dionysus—the god of intoxicated ecstasy? How does one explain the "dithyramb" *Thus Spake Zarathustra*?[2] It is worth exam-

---

[2] In *Ecce Homo*, Nietzsche describes *Zarathustra* as a "dithyramb." Walter Burkert in-forms us that the *dithyrambos* was a genre of choral lyric associated with the festival of Dionysus. The name *Dithyrambos* refers "equally to the god, his hymn, and his dance," and the Dionysian revelers were recognized by their "wild shouts" of "*dithyrambe*" (1985: 74, 102, 163).

ining *The Birth of Tragedy* to begin thinking about the place of mysticism in Nietzsche's thought.

The Birth of Tragedy is an examination of Greek tragic theater and the development of Greek art and philosophy. Nietzsche argues that tragedy developed from lyric poetry and the tragic chorus and links the death of tragedy to the rise of Socratic philosophy. His research led Nietzsche to challenge Aristotle's influential definition of tragedy. Where Aristotle claimed that tragedy effects a purgation of the emotions of fear and pity in the spectator, Nietzsche wrote of the "metaphysical comfort" created by the dissolution of and return to individuality. In these respects, *The Birth of Tragedy* was a work in classics and the science of aesthetics, Nietzsche's first major scholarly project (and, for all intents and purposes, his last) following his appointment as Professor of Philology at Basel University in 1869.

Yet from his first line it is clear that what Nietzsche means by "art" and his approach to its study has a decidedly nonscholarly element and radically expands the boundaries of modern aesthetics. He writes: "We shall have gained much for the science of aesthetics, once we perceive not merely by logical inference, but with the immediate certainty of vision" (BT: 33). This line anticipates Nietzsche's criticism of a philosophy divorced from the instincts and intuition, and it is closely linked to his early conviction that art is not just a human activity, but a metaphysical force. The book approaches art in "the metaphysical, broadest, and profoundest sense" (BT: 93). It also views art as religiously significant, for the gods Dionysus and Apollo are "artistic energies which burst forth from nature herself." This view of art and aesthetics rests on two fundamental claims. First, while tragedy as dramatic art form develops out of lyric poetry, the origin of tragedy as a Dionysian phenomenon ultimately lies in the Greek mystery cults. Second, the artist is a kind of mystic, a "medium through which the one truly existent subject celebrates his release in appearance" and returns to the bosom of the "primordially One" (BT: 52, 132).

The link between the mystery cults and tragedy is not simply a matter of the appropriation of certain divine figures and themes for the use in drama; the cults are much more intimately related to tragedy understood as a religious phenomenon based in "a mystic feeling of oneness" (*eine mystische Einheits Empfindung*). Nietzsche does not discuss the mystery cults at great length in *The Birth of Tragedy*, but in his notebooks from the period he describes the secrecy and ritual of the mysteries as a proto-dramatic form.[3] Specifically, he locates the origin of tragedy in the "orgias-

---

[3] More recently, Albert Henrichs (1993: 21) has written that "in the Bacchae, epiphany becomes theater, and the stage becomes the *locus sacer* for divine revelation, miracles, and visions."

tic festivals of Dionysus," where participants were possessed by the god
and experienced the blissful shattering of the boundaries of the self. As
drama, he sees tragedy as a kind of civic-religious ritual, no longer the
cult of initiates but a citywide, dramatic vision of the god. Thus, his claim
that "art and religion in the Greek sense are identical" (SW 7: 311). In *The
Birth of Tragedy* itself, he argues that the origins of tragedy are "purely
religious," and writes of the "mystery doctrine of tragedy," namely, "the
fundamental knowledge of the oneness of everything existent, the conception of individuation as the primal cause of evil, and of art as the joyous
hope that the spell of individuation may be broken in the augury of a
restored oneness" (BT: 56, 74).

This "pessimistic" doctrine, however, is not fully communicated in the
"tragic effect" that Nietzsche identifies. He argues that all tragic heroes
are images of Dionysus, the "primal one," the "contradiction born of
bliss and pain." But tragedy is not simply a Dionysian phenomenon. The
portrayal of Dionysus can be achieved only through Apollo, the god of
image and illusion. Dionysus is always masked, his revelation is always
also a concealing. The tragic effect of metaphysical comfort itself depends
on this simultaneous revealing and veiling of the pain of ultimate reality:
the terrible made sublime. Here is the occasion for Nietzsche's famous
pronouncement that life is justified only aesthetically. As a vision of Dionysus, tragedy shatters individuality in a mystical communion with the
joyful/painful contradictions of the primal one. In this communion, one
becomes aware of the ultimate terror, amorality, senselessness of existence. But, as art, tragedy also seduces one to this existence through the
sublimity of Apollonian image, which, for the spectator at least, "cast[s]
a spell over his eyes and prevent[s] him from penetrating deeper" (BT:
140). Rather than being left with the terror of ultimate reality, the spectator is left with an "overwhelming feeling of unity" (BT: 59). There is
fusion with the primal being, but the magic of art is to relegate the pain
of this unity to oblivion.

As a religious and dramatic phenomenon, the key to tragedy is the
chorus and its music. Nietzsche's interpretation of the chorus blurs the
boundaries between spectator, actor, and artist and so separates even further the Greek and modern conceptions of art. The "chorist lives in a
religiously acknowledged reality under sanction of myth and cult" (BT:
58) and represents human beings as "timeless servants of their god" (BT:
64). The chorist, then, is an extension or development of the Dionysian
initiate (BT: 62). The music of the chorus is the "dithyramb." In its proto-
typical form, tragedy is not "drama" in the narrow sense, but simply the
dithyrambic dance of the chorus, a "community of unconscious actors
who consider themselves and one another transformed." The chorus is

possessed by Dionysus and, in its music and dance, casts forth the god's image on the stage. The tragic drama is in this respect more like a religious ritual than a "show" or "production."

This possession, the union with Dionysus, is the "presupposition of all dramatic art" (BT: 64), for in the dithyramb "man is incited to the greatest exaltation of all his symbolic faculties" and so is able to express symbolically "the essence of nature" in both word and movement (BT: 40). Thus, the interesting link between the chorus and the dramatist/poet. The dramatist, Nietzsche argues, is both a "religious thinker" (BT: 68) and, like the chorus, also a "medium" for the voice of the primal one. Here, Nietzsche departs from Schopenhauer, for the latter's conception of the artist as affirmer of life relies on the idea of artistic contemplation in which the artist is dissolved *only to some extent* in the Will. The artist therefore protects himself from full experiential knowledge of the reality of metaphysical suffering, not penetrating as deeply as the saint. Nietzsche contends, by contrast, that the true artist *completely* "coalesces" with the "primordial artist." Moreover, he conceives of the expression of the primordial artist, for which the human artist is a medium, as a "celebration." In other words, it seems, Nietzsche is working with the idea that the "one truly existent subject" *affirms itself* through art, celebrates itself through the medium of the artist.

Where it is easy to see how Schopenhauer's conception of art might be subject to Nietzsche's 1886 rejection of "metaphysical comfort," it is not as clear that Nietzsche's is. The idea of celebration unsettles the idea of "metaphysical comfort," introducing an ambiguity into the concept that reverberates throughout the text and makes its effects felt in the rest of Nietzsche's work. Nietzsche describes "the mystery doctrine of tragedy" as pessimistic. But where Schopenhauer's philosophy is pessimistic to the point of complete denial of life, Nietzsche's is caught between the desire to escape individuality and the will's affirmation of itself. He thus finds wisdom in tragedy more positive than Schopenhauer's or the wisdom of Silenus'. To the extent that it involves hope for a "restored oneness," tragedy does provide metaphysical comfort. But this is not the only wisdom Nietzsche thinks tragedy expresses, for he at least offers hints of a different wisdom, which he describes in terms of the characteristic "cheerfulness" of the Greeks. He rejects the idea that this cheerfulness is a state of "unendangered comfort" (BT: 67) and argues instead that it emerges in a knowing confrontation with the suffering of life, that "the best and highest possession mankind can acquire is obtained by sacrilege and must be paid for with consequences that involve the whole flood of sufferings and sorrows" (BT: 71). To the extent that the artist presents this idea in the tragic hero, art comforts not through a forgetting, but through an affirmation, specifically of the idea that suffering, as an effect of wisdom, leads to blessedness—for example, the blessedness that Oedipus finds in the final play of the Oedipus trilogy. This blessedness is not so much a "hope" for restored oneness as a recognition of the fact of oneness, of the fact of the close link between suffering and joy, pain and wisdom. The early Nietzsche is clearly more "metaphysical" than the late Nietzsche will allow, but, at the same time, he is already anticipating his mature vision in which the highest expression of life is not Schopenhauerian denial, but celebratory affirmation.

Tragedy and Philosophy

Nietzsche's first book was as much about the death of tragedy at the hands of philosophy as its birth in the spirit of music. The death of tragedy comes about with the "typical non-mystic," Socrates (BT: 88). It was Socrates, claimed Nietzsche, who inspired Euripides to make tragedy intelligible; that is, to replace the "instinctual" or "mystical" process of creativity, with a self-conscious, intelligible dramatic production. Where Greek religion and dithyrambic art had been the means by which the forces of nature and instinct had given voice to themselves and by which human beings could become these voices, with Socrates, art and philosophy are given a new basis in consciousness and consciousness becomes the *critic* of nature. This meant not only the end of tragedy, but the end of Greek religion and myth, for Nietzsche's Socrates represents optimistic faith in reason and the corrigibility of the wound of nature. Such a loss of myth inevitably means for a culture the loss of "the healthy natural power of its creativity" (BT: 135). Socratic philosophy is opposed to the instincts and to the intuitive connection with nature expressed in a positive relation with the instincts. In his "Philosophy in the Tragic Age of the Greeks," an unpublished but completed essay from the same period as *The Birth of Tragedy*, Nietzsche had reflected on the different vision of philosophy he found in the pre-Socratics. For those philosophers, intuition and rapture still played a positive role. Thus Nietzsche writes that Heraclitus grasps truth in intuition rather than logic and "in Syballine raptures gazes but does not peer, knows but does not calculate" (PTG: 69).

The distinction between the gaze of tragic wisdom and the lucidity of Socratic knowledge was for Nietzsche of crucial concern for his own nineteenth century. In what he perceived to be a time of cultural, religious, and philosophical crisis—a time of the loss of guiding myths—Nietzsche optimistically championed the rebirth of tragedy in the operas of Richard Wagner. Philosophically, Nietzsche saw the beginnings of this rebirth in Kant and Schopenhauer, because these intrepid philosophers had drawn the limits of optimistic, Socratic science (BT: 112). Though Kant vigorously resisted the idea of knowledge beyond phenomena, Schopenhauer, as I have indicated, claimed that certain kinds of intuition into the very nature of things were possible. The early Nietzsche followed Schopenhauer with his claims about the rebirth of tragedy in a new Dionysian wisdom. But Nietzsche forges a closer link between art and religion, creativity and mysticism, than does Schopenhauer. This is especially apparent in the figure of the "artistic Socrates" for which Nietzsche expresses hope in *The Birth of Tragedy*. This figure unites the philosopher with the Schopenhauerian artist, saint, and mystic, one who possesses a wisdom that "turns with unmoved eyes to a comprehensive view of the world, and seeks to grasp, with sympathetic feelings of love, the eternal suffering as its own" (BT: 112). The rebirth of tragedy is the rebirth of philosophy as wisdom rather than science: "But how suddenly the desert of our exhausted culture . . . is changed when it is touched by the Dionysian magic! . . . Yes, my friends, believe with me in Dionysian life and the rebirth of tragedy. The age of the Socratic man is over. . . . Prepare yourselves for hard strife, but believe in the miracles of your god" (BT: 124).

Within a few years of writing this exhortation, Nietzsche broke with Wagner and increased his distance from Schopenhauer, turning to an at times skeptical, at times quasi-positivistic style of thinking in his works of the early 1880s. He grew more and more suspicious of "intoxication" and "romanticism" and began forging an antimetaphysical philosophy. The fruits of these years led Nietzsche, in 1886, to call for "this-worldly comfort" rather than "metaphysical comfort." Given the link between metaphysical comfort and mysticism in *The Birth of Tragedy*, it is tempting to dismiss the relevance of Nietzsche's early mystical sensibility for understanding his later work. To bolster such a reading, one might point out that with the rejection of Schopenhauer came a rejection of the idea of a primordial will into which one can dissolve one's individuality, and with Nietzsche's criticisms of Christianity and romanticism came the rejection of a metaphysical, dualistic faith in an otherworldly realm of existence, by means of which one can articulate hope for future bliss. It is tempting to read Nietzsche's late preface as a wholesale rejection of Dionysian ecstasy as grounded in a metaphysical, otherworldly hope. Turning from his early mentors, Nietzsche turns to a relentless philosophical attack on all forms of religious intuition, transcendence, faith.

But there remains the ecstatic dance and the dithyramb. Even in a work as adamantly "this-worldly" as *Human, All too Human,* one finds Nietzsche continuing to figure his philosophical journey in terms of ecstatic, magical moments. There, Nietzsche writes of "The Wanderer" who does not "let his heart adhere too firmly to any individual thing," and so often experiences "dreadful" nights. But the wanderer finds recompense, once and a while, in "joyful mornings," in which the Muses come dancing by him in the mist of the mountains, when afterwards, if he relaxes quietly beneath the trees in the equanimity of his soul at morning, good and bright things will be thrown down to him from their tops and leafy hiding-places, the gifts of all those free spirits who are at home in mountain, wood, solitude and who, like him, are, in their now joyful, now thoughtful way, wanderers and philosophers. Born out of the mysteries of dawn, they ponder on how, between the tenth and the twelfth stroke of the clock, the day could present a face so pure, so light-filled, so cheerful and transfigured. (HH: 204)

Two closely related patterns are inscribed in this passage. One is familiar; both will be repeated, often, in Nietzsche's writing; they will figure centrally in considering the place of mysticism in Nietzsche's later work. First, note the echo of *The Birth of Tragedy* in the close link of the dread of abyssal night and the shining gifts of the dawn. Second, the skeptical philosopher—the "free spirit"—finds, in the midst of a long journey of "searching and researching," a journey filled with renunciation and suffering, the gift of joyful creativity. Such gifts do not indicate that the wanderer has reached his destination—there is none, save, possibly, this dawn itself, that gives the wanderer the strength and resources to continue.[4]

The Study of Mysticism

Constructing Mystical Experience

Before moving to Nietzsche's later work, it will be helpful to consider in some detail how to use the term *mysticism*. As with *asceticism*, it is a mistake to rely uncritically on common modern conceptions of mysticism in evaluating Nietzsche's thought. This is not to say that Nietzsche's conception of mysticism is not implicated with modern views of religious experience and mysticism, only that these should not determine how we use the term *mysticism* or this evaluation. Rethinking religion means rethinking mysticism. I seek to open up the issue by problematizing common received notions of mysticism, in the hope that this will offer some lines of comparison with Nietzsche and others whom we might not, at first glance, see as comparable.

When I invoke the "modern" conception of mysticism, I refer to the widespread use of the term to indicate a dramatic experience of unity with

---

[4] This second pattern is reinscribed, along with some strategic remarks, in the notebooks from the period of *The Gay Science*.

Are you prepared? You must have lived through every grade of skepticism and have bathed with joy in ice-cold streams—otherwise you have no right to these thoughts; I want to protect myself from the easy-believing and foolish. I want to *defend* my thoughts in advance. It should be the religion of the most free, cheerful and elevated soul—a loving ground of wisdom between golden ice and pure skies. (SW 9: 573) or absorption in God, the divine, or ultimate reality, where one has access to some kind of ultimate knowledge. But it is only in the context of a long history of Platonic and Christian thought that we go from the Greek *mystikos* to this contemporary *mysticism*. Traced philologically through the root *my(s)*, which means "I close my eyes," the history of mysticism begins with the Greek mystery religions. In this context, *mystikos* referred to one who kept silent about the secrets of the initiations into the cult. Walter Burkert warns that it is misleading to think of the mystery religions as mystical in the contemporary sense of the word, for they did not necessarily involve "the transformation of consciousness" (1987: 7). He does claim, however, that they made possible the "encounter with the divine" (1987: 90). Pierre Hadot supports this idea, following Aristotle's claim that the initiates of Eleusis did not learn anything about the divine, but did experience it (1995: 28).

In the early Christian context, and particularly at the point of intersection between Christianity and Platonism, the term *mystical* comes to refer to certain ways of thinking about, writing about, and understanding God. This is "mystical theology," not, it must be emphasized, modern "mysticism." Specifically, the term refers to a way of interpreting the Bible by looking below its surface meanings to find the "spiritual" or "mystical" meaning of the text. It is clear that this use of the term retains the sense of something hidden and secret from the Greek mystery religions. But it also represents a kind of reversal, for in the early Christian context the point is not an "experience" of God, but an intellectual realization or revelation. Both Grace Jantzen and Denys Turner emphasize this point in their studies of Christian mystical traditions. Jantzen points out that in the early mystical hermeneutic, God, as Christ, is revealed in a way not accessible to ordinary readers of the Bible, but intellectually, not experientially (1995: 69, 138–39). Only in the context of late-medieval love mysticism, and specifically that practiced by women such as Hadewijch and Julian of Norwich, do we begin to see a pronounced experiential component in Christian mystical traditions. Turner concentrates on the medieval apophatic mystical theology stemming from the influential writings of Denys the Aeropagite. Turner's primary contention is that apophatic mysticism should not be construed experientially, whether as an experience of negativity, or of the absence of God. Instead, it should be viewed in terms of the *absence* of experience of God, the recognition that God is precisely that which is hidden from experience. For Turner, "It is better to say, as expressive of the apophatic, simply that God is what is on the other side of anything at all we can be conscious of, whether of its presence or of its absence" (1996: 264).

Michel de Certeau has argued that, although the adjectival use of "mystical" has a long tradition in Greek and Christian traditions, the noun "mysticism" is a modern term that in some respects reflects the secularization resulting from the breakdown of the institutional and ontological horizons of Christendom (1992: 76, 121, 299). As such, it finds a significant parallel in the emergence of empirical science: in both, one sees a turn to experience, instead of tradition or institution, as the locus and authority of knowledge, both of the world and of God (1992: 129). Thus it is only in the modern period that mysticism has become largely a private, experiential phenomenon.[5] And, although mysticism develops as a Christian phenomenon, as personal experience of God comes to be valued, and as traditional or institutional structuring of the revelation of the divine weakens, the possibility emerges of an experience of the divine apart from the particularities of Christianity, or apart from religious traditions in general. The question then can be asked whether in mystical experience a truth beyond the traditions is experienced, something universally human that can be compared across traditions. The place of a generalized mysticism, a way of being "religious," or "spiritual" beyond all religious traditions, has been created.

Mysticism has occupied a privileged place in the study of religion from its beginnings in the late nineteenth century. In part, this is due to the modern fascination with religious experience; in part, it is due to increasing encounters between different religious traditions, for scholars and religious figures have been intrigued by the idea that in mystical experience something is encountered that transcends the particularity of religious traditions: truth and/or divinity beyond the interpretations provided by those traditions. In the "perennial philosophy"—the idea of a single, divine reality accessible only in the mystical transcendence of human particularity—resources have been found for comparing religious traditions and asserting a fundamental human unity. Recently, however, some scholars have begun to problematize "mysticism" as a construction and category, raising questions about the perennialist project and about mystical experience. Steven Katz, for example, has devoted numerous studies to showing the consequences and mistakes involved in failing to pay sufficient attention to the very particular contexts in which different mystical experiences take place.[6] The result of not attending to such contexts, he argues, has been to overemphasize, or simply assume, the similarity between experiences taking place in different times and places and traditions; or, as I have indicated, to claim that underneath all the "extraneous" additions of tradition and dogma, all mystical experiences—across

[5] De Certeau connects this shift with the emergence of empirical science and the breakdown of Christendom. However, Grace Jantzen's work (1995) on women's medieval love mysticsm suggests that such a shift may already have been occurring as women, disempowered by the tradition, looked to experience as a source of spiritual authority.

[6] See Katz, ed., 1978, 1983, 1992.

culture, time, and tradition—are essentially identical. Studying accounts of mystical experience from representatives of different traditions, and arguing that all experience is culturally and linguistically mediated, Katz takes the position that persons from different traditions have different "mystical" experiences. Thus, a Christian will experience Jesus Christ and a Buddhist will experience Nirvana; it is not simply the case that these people use "Jesus Christ" and "Nirvana" because they are the only terms they have to interpret an experience that, underneath the interpretations, is the same.[7]

This is not to say, however, that comparison between different experiences across time and tradition is useless or misguided, though Katz and others may imply or even assert such a position. It is to say instead that such comparison requires attention to detail and context, as well as a certain degree of abstraction from specific, in some respects very different, experiences. As Wayne Proudfoot argues, we can "employ the results of phenomenological analyses without subscribing to the conviction that these represent some fundamental uninterpreted experience" (1985: 124).[8] Since trying to assert a common object of mystical experience is a sure way to reduce the complexity and richness of individual experiences and their role in different lives and traditions, one way to accomplish such abstraction is to focus instead on the dynamics of mystical consciousness. For example, Jeffrey Kripal points out that a "dialectical approach" to mysticism can take seriously the different contexts of mystics—the different ontologies, histories, techniques, objects of their experience—*as well as* a common apophatic level of the experience "of" nothingness. To take seriously the latter is to acknowledge that at some level one must "withdraw the 'what'" of the experience; that is, prescind from claiming that one can offer an exhaustive account of the mystical experience by focusing on the *object* of experience. Doing so, one can avoid identifying a common core experience "of something" without rejecting the possibility that there are certain states or dynamics of consciousness common to different traditions and different times (1995: 19). Thus I am inclined to find some comparative use in approaches to mysticism such as Louis Dupré's, who writes of "the self [which] expands beyond its ordinary boundaries and is passively united with a reality which transcends its normal state" (1979: 361). This is vague, but it helpfully points to a dynamic of experience rather than an object of experience. If we are careful to allow for different meanings of "union" and other concepts such as "self," it provides some heuristic guidance for thinking about mysticism. I return to this issue below.

[7] For a critical response to Katz, see Forman 1990.

[8] For an example with respect to the issue of oneness or unification, see Gimello 1978, 177.

A careful use of "mysticism" as a category in the study of religion will be attentive to history and context, but we should not renounce the category in a misguided attempt to protect particularity. To do so would not only prevent comparison across traditions, but within them. Within Christianity, for instance, there are a multiplicity of mysticisms. Bernard McGinn has considered this multiplicity and argues that if we hold to a strict idea of union with God as the defining criterion of mystical experience, there are very few mystics in the Christian tradition. He suggests, as an alternative to union, the "presence" of God, and he points out that such presence has taken many shapes, including, in addition to "union," "contemplation," "ecstasy," and "birth of the Word in the soul." McGinn emphasizes the adjective "mystical" rather than the noun "mysticism" to indicate that we do not find *mystics* in Christianity, but *Christians,* whose lives have a more or less pronounced "mystical element." The mystical element of Christianity is "that part of its belief and practices that concerns the preparation for, the consciousness of, and the reaction to what can be described as the immediate or direct presence of God" (1994: xvii). McGinn thus lays the groundwork for comparison within the Christian tradition without sacrificing detailed attention to context.

In part, he is able to do this because he stresses the mystical life rather than a single Christian mystical experience. Indeed, he shows that for many Christian mystics, the mystical element of their thought and practice is not focused on dramatic experiences as the goal or the essence of their religious life. Many Christian mystics, such as Meister Eckhart, have been quite critical of the preoccupation with such experiences and are suspicious of their own. The point is not any particular experience, but rather the transformation of consciousness or awareness (McGinn 1994: xviii). Thus, McGinn prefers to speak of "mystical consciousness" rather than "mystical experience," and, with his emphasis on the mystical life, this means not a transitory state of consciousness, but the cultivation of habits or ways of consciousness. What happens on either "side" of any particular experience, the preparation for and response to all the experiences that make up one's life, is as significant for understanding mysticism as those particular experiences themselves. Acknowledging the preparation for mystical experience, one notes the intimate connection between mysticism and ascetic practices that concentrate desire and consciousness. And, looking beyond "mystical experience," one notes that the ultimate significance of any experience can be understood only in the context of the religious life as a whole—no single experience by itself completes the Christian life or can tell us anything definitive about God. Eckhart suggests that the proper cultivation of one's relation to God should result in God's presence in all experience. In support, contemporary historian and theologian Rowan Williams argues that the key to Christian spiritual life is not any particular "mystical experience," but the way the mystic is able to lead a life of bringing God's love into the world (1990: 122, 136). Robert Gimello makes the point more generally. "The mysticism of any particular mystic is really the whole pattern of his life. The wonderful 'peaks' of experience are a part of that pattern, but only a part, and their real value lies only in their relations to the other parts, to his thought, his moral values, his conduct towards others, his character and personality, etc." (1983: 85).

In sum, I am charting a tendency in contemporary studies of mysticism to focus on practices by which one reorients the dynamics or modes of his or her experience in general. This reorientation is made possible when the boundaries of self and other, self and world, are disrupted or transformed in the context of being opened to the divine, or to "reality." This is not to deny dramatic experiences as part of the mystical life, or to say that such a life does not involve some kind of awareness or knowledge of the divine or ultimate reality or truth. But such awareness should be thought of in terms of a transformation of consciousness, not resulting simply from a particular experience, but deliberately cultivated in a life of study, discipline, and spiritual practice in which one transforms the way one experiences self, world, and God. In short, it is helpful to differentiate between "ecstatic experience" and "mystical life." In his study of the Hindu mystic Ramakrishna, Sudhir Kakar offers the ideas of "creative experiencing" and "experiencing experience" to point to a kind of openness to experience, a kind of *responsiveness*, that takes shape in the mystic's encounter with the divine. In the Hindu context, Kakar describes this responsiveness—"which is done 'with all one's heart, all one's soul, and all one's might' "—with the Sanskrit term *bhava*, which can be translated as "feeling" or "mood." *Bhava* is a *way* of experiencing, not a particular experience. In Ramakrishna's case, it is a way of "rekindl[ing] the world with fresh vision, discovering or rather endowing it with newfound beauty and harmony. . . .[It] deepened his sensate and metaphysical responsiveness" (1991: 18–19). In the Christian context, the analogy to the responsiveness of this *bhava* is love. At least some Christian mystics do speak of experiences of union, but more important, from the perspective I am suggesting, is the way the mystic becomes open to and so a vehicle for the love exemplified in Christ. In and through such love, the mystic moves toward the world and all experience, in a new, creative responsiveness to it.

What Does the Mystic Know?

If we think of mysticism as a transformation of experience in general toward an increased responsiveness, and de-emphasize the significance of particular experiences of particular "objects," then we also need to rethink some of the difficult issues surrounding mystical knowledge. In his treatment of mysticism as the most important form of religious experience, William James was influential in raising the problem of the "noetic" element of mysticism. As James notes, mystical experiences are often reported to be "inexpressible" or "ineffable" and so "are more like states of feeling than like states of intellect."[9] At the same time, though, mystics also claim that these are states of knowledge, "states of insight into depths of truth unplumbed by the discursive intellect" (1985: 380). Following up on the long tradition in which the "mystical" resonates with a sense of mystery, secret, and hidden knowledge, this knowledge, as James puts it, is in some sense not accessible to our normal ways of understanding and not able to be articulated by our normal ways of speaking. What kind of knowledge or truth is at stake here? Much recent philosophical interest in mysticism is related to the question of what kinds of knowledge claims mystical or religious experience provide. Indeed, the modern construction of mysticism takes shape in large part through a confrontation with philosophical knowledge claims. As early as Kant, we find a philosopher protecting the boundaries of the knowable from extravagant mystical claims to a kind of privileged, immediate access to God. Kant's epistemological revolution forecloses knowledge of God in confining knowledge to the empirical world, to that which we "experience" through the senses. Kant rejects what he calls "intellectual intuition" and dismisses as spurious "mystical" claims to knowledge received in ways other than through the senses. The God Kant left room for was the God who was an idea of pure reason, a God we could think but not know. On Kantian grounds, the idea of mystical knowledge, as knowledge of God, becomes incoherent. Thus, relatively early in the modern period, mysticism is cast as the "other" of philosophy.[10]

As part of his historical critique of the experientialist approach to Christian mysticism, Denys Turner (1996) warns that it is a mistake, on mystical grounds, to try to comprehend Christian mysticism as an "experiential positivism." In other words, we should not view mysticism along the lines of an experience of the divine, which, if not sensory, is at least directly analogous to sensory experience in terms of an encounter between subject and object and in terms of the knowledge such an encounter produces. At least from the perspective of the apophatic tradition Turner examines, mysticism does not challenge the knowledge claims of philoso-

[9] For the continuing debate on the usefulness of the concept of ineffability, both with respect to the attempt to describe mystical experience and the process of cultivating certain kinds of experience, see Katz 1978, Proudfoot 1985, and Sells 1994.

[10] Apart from the fundamental philosophical claims made by Kant in his *Critiques*, see also Kant's essay "What Is Orientation in Thinking" (1991). As I have already indicated, Nietzsche, in *The Birth of Tragedy*, characterizes Socrates as an antimystic. See also Habermas's treatment of Derrida in *The Philosophical Discourse of Modernity* (1986: 182–84).

phy. One of the common claims made by mystics and their interpreters is that mystical experience is ineffable; that is, always more than language can say. Indeed, mystical texts are often written in such a way as to point away from themselves or to subvert their own descriptive or conceptual function. Does this mean that there is actually propositional knowledge there, "in" the mystic, that he or she simply cannot communicate to others? Or does it suggest, instead, that the model of propositional scientific or philosophical knowledge is not an appropriate model for what the mystic "knows"? Consider James's assertion that mystical experiences are "more like states of feeling than like states of intellect" (1985: 380). Is there knowledge involved in being in a state of love or a state of joy? We would, I think, agree that the feeling of being in love entails far more than the knowledge that "I am in love with X." In fact, one may never "know" that one is in love, but may eventually find that such knowledge is not crucial, that what is crucial is a developing relationship, a certain "feel" for a particular way of being in the world. Again I would employ the distinction between specific experiences and "ways" of experiencing. Mysticism involves, primarily, a sense, both in body and mind, of *how* to experience; less crucial is knowledge gained from or grounded by particular experiences. If we were to think of mysticism along these lines, as a kind of opening or expanding of experience, a new awareness, other possibilities emerge for thinking about what mystics can and cannot know.

To elaborate, I turn to the work of philosopher Stanley Cavell. Cavell's thought emerges from encounters with thinkers whom one often sees described as mystical: Wittgenstein and Heidegger, and especially Emerson and Thoreau (whom Cavell does describe as a mystic). One way of placing Cavell as a philosopher is through his contributions to the romantic response to Kant and the problem of skepticism. Kant described his project as limiting knowledge to make room for faith, which among other things meant separating human beings from any direct knowledge of world and God as things in themselves. The romantic response to Kant sought to overcome the Kantian gulf between human beings and things in themselves. For my purposes, Cavell's most important contribution to this confrontation is the concept of *acknowledgment*, a concept with which he articulates a relation to the world that is more "primary" than Kantian knowledge (1981: 106). Cavell basically accepts Kant's view of knowledge as a constructive activity based in material provided by the senses. But he also develops the idea of a mode of thinking—acknowledgment— which is a kind of intellectual receptivity (1990: 39). Cavell argues that in Emerson and Thoreau we find resources for conceptualizing a kind of intuitive intimacy with the world which is neither Kantian "immediacy" nor knowledge, not concepts one constructs of any particular aspects of the world, but rather an openness or responsiveness to the world as a whole, as something other than me (1981: 107). Cavell posits a "mutual attraction" between human and world, a form of "romance"; following Thoreau, he calls this relation a nextness, a neighboring of the world (1981: 106).

Cavell argues that the skeptical dissatisfaction with the lack of direct knowledge of things in themselves is part of the human condition as finite creatures. The traditional philosophical response to this condition has been to try to satisfy this desire through a better, more exacting foundation for our knowledge, or the replacement of our ordinary language with a special, exact set of words, or with something beyond language altogether. Cavell argues, however, that such strategies not only cannot succeed but end up obscuring the intimacy with the world that we have through acknowledgment. The more we try to grasp the world through knowledge, the more, to use an image from Emerson, it slips through our hands. With Heidegger, Cavell envisions a kind of thinking that is not grasping, but receptive: thinking as thanking.

The distinction Cavell makes between intimacy and immediacy reflects his debt to ordinary language philosophy, and especially to Wittgenstein. Where certain philosophers view the mediation of our ordinary language as precisely that which separates us from the world and each other, Cavell, following Wittgenstein, argues that language connects us to the world and to each other. Words, on this view, represent an "agreement" between human beings and the world. Only in and through ordinary language do humans encounter the world and each other at all. Language constitutes, rather than limits, our relation to the world (Cavell 1990: 22). It affords us intimacy. Philosophy, then, is not the search for a transparent language or foundations for knowledge, but a kind of "therapy" (Cavell's word, after Wittgenstein) or "spiritual exercise" (my word), a testing and contesting of word and self by which human beings realize their intimacy with the world. This intimacy is "deeper" than knowing; it is a condition of knowing. So Cavell argues that we must struggle with words by living them beyond habit and necessity, hearing them from all sides, listening for their resonance, resisting, as Nietzsche recognized, the conformity to which they tempt us. We must examine with the thoroughness of a philosopher all the conditions of our words, not simply our habitual, narrow uses of them (1988: 14). When we do not test our words by examining their conditions, we face a double danger: either we repudiate our conditions altogether, desiring an inhuman intimacy; or, alternatively, we believe ourselves too narrowly constrained by conditions, subjecting ourselves to various kinds of false necessity. The task of philosophy, therefore, is to examine the conditions of our words, the conditions of our relation to the world. Clarifying them, returning to them out of our desire to transcend our conditions, means acknowledging ourselves and our relation to the world.

In this sense, then, it is important not to romanticize (too much) the concept of acknowledgment by casting it as a kind of fuzzy, "mystical," extrasensory capacity (1988: 8). It is first of all a discipline that attends carefully to the way we use and abuse language; a way of locating ourselves in relation to language and the world. And certainly, if one is convinced that mysticism is all about extraordinary experiences beyond words, Cavell's orientation to the problem of language and the ordinary seems to take us in precisely the opposite direction from mysticism. Cavell immerses us in words, in everyday words, telling us not to try to escape the way they condition us and so deny our humanity. Insofar as the skeptic desires and the mystic accomplishes a closer relationship to the world and/or God, more immediate than our words, and tries to realize this relationship, he or she denies language and the human.

But is not such denial the first move of the mystic? Yes and no. Cavell does not deny that a certain denial of the human and a certain desire for transcendence moves the search for immediacy. But in striving for immediacy, the skeptic, the foundationalist (and, I would add, certain mystics), deny intimacy, the deepest relationship with reality that human beings can have. This does not mean that Cavell denies transcendence. On the contrary, he seeks to refigure it as a movement more deeply into our humanity and its relation to what is external to it, Other. This is a movement toward finding fullness of life *within* the ordinary, not in a flight to the extraordinary. There is a turn toward the extraordinary in Cavell, but this turn has to be accompanied always by a return to the ordinary, in what he describes as a reinhabiting of the world.

It may seem that this intimacy is not enough to be counted as mystical, that, indeed, a more complete, even an absolute immediacy is what is called for. Discussing Thoreau's "neighboring," Cavell writes: "You may call this mysticism, but it is a very particular view of the subject; it is not what the inexperienced may imagine as a claim to union, or absorption in nature" (1981: 106). As I have argued, though, this concern with experiential immediacy is largely a product of the modern encounter between philosophy and religion. What I find so provocative about Cavell—and I will develop this further below—is that he is trying to conceive of a kind of receptivity that is part of all experience. This receptivity is shaped in an acknowledgment of the otherness of the world, a world apart from me. This I think is close to the mystical idea of God as Denys Turner presents it: "God is what is on the other side of anything at all we can be conscious of, whether of its presence or of its absence" (1996: 264). Cavell helps us think of mysticism as a practice of placing oneself in the life of the world by encountering it in the reality of its otherness, which is a precondition for acknowledging it in its relation to us. In doing so, he provides resources for thinking about an affirmative (in Nietzsche's sense) mysticism.

What Does the Mystic Write?

Also suggestive in this context, and also to be picked up again below, is Cavell's focus on testing and contesting of words—acknowledgment as a practice of reading and writing. The issue of the reading and writing of mystical texts is a crucial one. Scholars of mysticism, for the most part, unless they are mystics themselves, do not have direct access to the mystical life or experience, but rather to "mystical" texts. Thus some scholars define mysticism not in terms of certain types of experience, but in terms of certain kinds of writing. Carl Keller has defined "mystical writing" as "texts that deal with ultimate knowledge," and he has specified a number of literary genres in which such writing is found, including aphorism, biography, report on visions, instruction, prayer, religious poetry, and fiction (1992: 77, 79). This list already suggests that defining such texts as "dealing" with ultimate knowledge is ambiguous. How does a poem or a prayer "deal" with ultimate knowledge? Do they make propositional knowledge claims—about God, for example—that can be tested for their validity? There is a similar problem with relating such writing to mystical experience. Keller argues that it is "impossible to chart the passage from the text to the experience." Taking a less extreme position, McGinn (1994: xiv) argues that it is necessary to articulate a "mystical hermeneutics," for it is rarely a simple matter to determine what is "experience" and what is "interpretation," "elaboration," or "reflection" of or on that experience.[11]

This problematic can be illustrated by Nietzsche's writing. Below, I concentrate on the way Nietzsche writes about certain kinds of extraordinary experience. Many of these are to be found in *Zarathustra*, and the questions one must raise with respect to mystical poetry should be raised here as well. Are Zarathustra's speeches and songs *accounts* of experience? If so, whose? Nietzsche's? Zarathustra's? Both in *Zarathustra* and elsewhere, Nietzsche surrounds his "accounts" of experience with warnings about the difficulty of being able to capture one's experience in words:

[11] Kevin Hart puts it nicely when he claims that mystical experience is "refracted" rather than "reflected" in texts and that "the texts themselves are endlessly refracted by other texts, by entire traditions of textual practices. Although what we may take to be a preexperience may institute a text it cannot function as the origin of the text's significations" (1989: 180–81).

"Our true experiences are not garrulous" (TI: 92). If, then, Zarathustra does not provide a description of his experiences, are his songs and speeches, like much mystical poetry, better seen as a *product* or *expression* of such experiences and/or of a particular kind of life? If so, are they simply expressions of the joy or awe that accompanies the experience, or are they an attempt to communicate some sense of the experience to others, or to provoke them toward their own experience through a certain kind of linguistic performance? Finally, one also might ask whether Nietzsche's writing is in some sense *constitutive of* his experiences or of a mystical way of experiencing. In other words, can writing itself be a kind of mystical practice?

There is no simple correspondence between mystical writing and mystical experience. Mystical language is liminal language, particularly in apophatic traditions. Michael Sells has examined apophasis in his fascinating study, *Mystical Languages of Unsaying* (1994). For Sells, the apophatic writings of figures such as Plotinus, Ibn Arabi, and Marguerite Porete struggle with the issue of divine transcendence of a monotheistic God: as the absolutely unlimited, how can God be referred to in language, which, as reference, always delimits? Conceptually, apophatic writing is often doctrinally radical, or, better, adoctrinal, for it twists itself away, in complex series of affirmations and negations, from the categories and definitions that it is the purpose of doctrine to maintain. This interweaving of affirmations and negations, argues Sells, moves toward the "transreferential"— without dispensing with naming the ultimate, this writing continually "unnames" and "unsays" and thereby points beyond reference.[12] This has the effect of unsaying distinctions between presence and absence, transcendence and immanence, divine and human, ordinary and extraordinary.

For Sells, apophasis is not simply writing that struggles conceptually with this problem of unnameability and unsaying, it *performs* it. This is a performance of "referential openness," in which reason is allowed "to lead beyond itself" (1994: 58) to the "mystery" to which so many mystical texts refer. This Sells describes as a "meaning event," which "does not describe or refer to mystical union but effects a semantic union that recreates or imitates the mystical union" (1994: 9). It is this event, and not any presumed experience or knowledge of author or reader, that defines a text for Sells as apophatic or mystical. The "meaning" of an apophatic

---

[12] Derrida (1992b) and others argue that Christian mystics, even the most radically apophatic, must posit God as a hyperessentiality and thus do not escape ontotheology. For a well-informed discussion of Derrida's text, which essentially supports Derrida's major claim, see Caputo 1997: 33 ff. Kevin Hart, however, writing before Derrida's essay, argues that apophasis is a form of deconstruction and thus is a "supplement" of positive theology, rather than simply playing a role within it (1989: 202). This position would seem to raise questions for Derrida's assertions about negative theology's "hyperessentiality."

text, therefore, can only be glimpsed in the constant movement and referential openness pointing toward mystery. The mystery is not a secret doctrine, which could be stated—to the right person at the right time—but an openness, an abyss of groundlessness, at the heart of a tradition's doctrine (1994: 8).[13] To say, nonetheless, that meaning is in some sense there—glimpsed—is to say that the assertions of doctrines, despite the tension caused by their negation, give a point of departure, a perspective on the boundary of meaning and nonmeaning, knowledge and mystery. Sells shows, for example, that the turns of John the Scot Eriugena's writing lead language to "overflow" with meaning so that the "reified and substantial deity momentarily recedes," affording a glimpse of God as a "nonentified divinity" (1994: 62).

Apophatic writing is, for Sells, a kind of performance designed to evoke a certain experience in the reader. For Michel de Certeau, it is something more, actually a practice or exercise—an *ascesis*—by which the writer shapes, concentrates, and even experiences his or her relation to the divine. De Certeau treats mystical discourse as a "labor of transcending limits" and—influenced by both Lacan and Derrida—he suggests that the object of the mystical life is to be found *within* the text of speaking and writing, and not prior to it. "The Other that organizes the text is not an outside the text. It is not the (imaginary) object that one might distinguish from the movement by which it is sketched" (1992: 15).[14] This is not to deny that mysticism involves a kind of experience, but to note that such experience is shaped in and through utterance. What de Certeau calls "mystics"—as opposed to traditional mystical theology—involves the production of a new language, an "experimental knowledge," which takes shape in a new kind of speaking and writing no longer grounded in the institutions and doctrines of the past. Mystics, a form of writing, seeks to speak in a way that is *founded* in being, rather than *adequate* to being; in other words, mystical language is not first of all theological description or reference; it is, instead, language that speaks out of a certain way of life and through which, at least in part, that life is shaped and led (1992: 113, 135). "Mystics *is* a 'manner of speaking,' figured as a kind of 'walking' or 'gait,' especially as a 'wandering': he or she is a mystic who cannot stop walking and, with the certainty of what is lacking, knows of every place and object that it is *not that*; one cannot stay *there* nor be content with *that*."

This wandering language marks its destination at every moment in pointing beyond itself through an unsaying. Sells claims that the funda-

---

[13] For the importance of the "secret" in mystical writing, see also Sells 1994: 216, de Certeau 1986: 82, 91, and McGinn 1994: 1, 319.

[14] See also his claim that "the beginning of the mystic experience is thus to be found in the very operation . . . by which discourse takes up position" (1992: 187).

mental semantic unit of mystical discourse is the confrontation of two sentences in paradox; de Certeau argues that the fundamental unit is the trope, specifically the metaphor—a single word or phrase in which two meanings collide. For both, then, the smallest semantic unit is always doubled—and it is in the strain and strangeness produced in this doubling that a glimpse of the "beyond" is produced. For de Certeau the trope or figure is a turning, a conversion, that departs from the "proper" sense of our words and introduces deviation into discourse. This deviation or departure allows the glimpse of a different meaning. Metaphor, then, "is exit, semantic exile, already ecstasy," tropes are "machines for voyages and ecstasies outside of received meanings" (1992: 142–48). Such figures are at once signs of desire and detachment: desire for the beyond and the means of setting oneself "adrift" from past connections. They are therefore not just expressions of a particular kind of desire for that which is beyond language and the subjectivity constructed in that language; they are a way of connecting with that which is beyond language through language, of "*being* language's *other*" (1986: 96–97).[15]

With this, let me return to Cavell, for he develops the concept of acknowledgment in elaborating reading and writing as spiritual practices. Viewed this way, and through Cavell's reading of Emerson, the significance of metaphor as both apophatic and affirmative becomes evident. Cavell uses "reading" and "writing" in both literal and figurative senses. Reading is the way of receiving the world and our language, a discipline of attention to the conditions of our words. We are always already embedded in both language and the world, in the world through language and specifically through the conditions or agreements that make possible the intimacy between word and world (1988: 38). In reading we test and contest our words, our inheritance of language and the world, and, following Wittgenstein, our form of life. We thereby find ourselves in the world, locating ourselves in and through the conditions of language, which are our conditions for being in the world.

Writing, for Cavell, is a process of giving inflection to the language we receive. In this way language lives, and we find ourselves, as this voice, here and now, in the present. Reading and writing, on Cavell's view, are therefore not separate activities, but implicated with one another. Language is only fully received in our taking it up, in enacting our part of the relation with the world, bringing it to life.[16] Writing too, then, is a contest:

[15] De Certeau himself notes a link between Nietzsche and his mystics. Writing of Saint Teresa, he reflects on "a disappearance (ecstasy) or death that constitutes the subject as pleasure in the other. 'I is an other'—that is the secret told by the mystic long before the poetic experience of Rimbaud, Rilke, or Nietzsche" (1986: 96).

[16] Like Katz, Cavell is concerned with our inheritance of language, but articulates, I think, a deeper, more complex relationship with language than Katz's constructivism allows. He is thereby able to say more about the way a certain receptiveness to language games is also the way to transfiguring self and language.

our inflections of language, the active component of our reception of language, is a way of testing language by expanding it, not simply resigning ourselves to its conditions. As is the case in many mystical traditions, and especially in apophatic traditions, Cavell is aware of the ways in which words trap us, habituate us, and tear us away from reality, making intimacy impossible. Our words continually lead us to desire a grasping relationship with the world, so we must just as continually unsay them, silence them, so that we may listen to the world and through this relationship bring new words to life. Cavell considers the relation, or the mutual implication, of philosophy and poetry. Where the skeptic seeks to transcend conditions, and where one enslaved to habit contracts his or her conditions, the philosopher-poet tests conditions and expands them in figure and metaphor (which, of course, depend on mutual agreement as to the literal meaning of words, their conditions, in order to work). "In the realm of the figurative, our words are not felt as confining but as releasing, or not as binding but as bonding" (1988: 148). Metaphor, so to speak, pushes against the conditions of language without rejecting them, represents, therefore, the tension between the ordinary and extraordinary, through which we try to bring life to our intuitions, to our reception of the world. For Cavell, the way we find oneself alive in language is to keep language alive, by finding oneself reborn into language at every moment.

In this context, it is important to think carefully about what apophasis is. As Michael Sells treats it, apophasis makes signification possible only in the tension created between saying and unsaying: statements do not have their significance in themselves, as self-contained propositions, but only in the dynamic of the process of alternation between saying and unsaying, and for Cavell, departure and return. The apophatic movement is not so much the exhaustion or transcendence of language, but a mode of thinking and writing by which the deadening habits of language are resisted so that words are able to continually relate us to the world here and now. And apophasis is mysticism not as extraordinary experience, but as practice, a way to live deliberately.

A Mystical Hermeneutic: Passion for the Real

Of the mystical life, Meister Eckhart wrote: "If a man thinks he will get more of God by meditation, by devotion, by ecstasies or by special infusion of grace than by the fireside or in the stable—that is nothing but taking God, wrapping a cloak round His head and shoving Him under a bench. For whoever seeks God in a special way gets the way and misses God, who lies hidden in it" (Forman 1990: 113).

In both the Christian and the Buddhist traditions, spiritual practices of transcending self and intensifying life enable, ideally, a spontaneous commitment to living beings (enacted in love or compassion). To the extent that we can talk about transcendence in each case, transcendence does not involve a release or escape from the world as such, but from the habits and words that construct the world according to self-centered needs and anxieties: one transcends a certain way of being in the world, one is released toward the other. There are numerous concrete figures in these traditions who exemplify a fruitful and complex tension between transcendence and immanence, the desire for salvation from the "world" and a loving, affirmative engagement with it.[17]

Thoreau writes that "God himself culminates in the present moment" (1991: 79). Can we reimagine mysticism, then, in terms of a process of placing or finding the human in relation to that which is really real? A transcendence that is not transport to another realm, but to another inhabitation of this realm (Cavell 1989: 107), not an effort to remove oneself from the world, not encountering God or ultimate reality as an escape from the world, but a way of intensifying and realizing life here and now? A transformation of the way one experiences the world instead of an otherworldly experience? We find such mysticism in Eckhart's counsel to seek God in the stable, in the Beguines and their loving service to others, and in Thomas Merton's insistence that "it is in the ordinary duties and labors of life that the Christian can and should develop his spiritual union with God" (1996: 9). From this perspective, the precise outlines of the "object" of mystical experience are less important than a dynamic of "transcendence" and "immanence" by which one returns, awakened, to the world, through a departure from it.

For de Certeau, mystic discourse is a wandering writing based in the turning of the trope, a "manner of speaking" about a passion and a manner of speaking passionately. The object of this passion is clear: it is a passion *for* God—which, as it works toward union, also becomes a passion *of* God. I find a similar "manner of speaking" in Nietzsche's writing, though I will not attempt to argue that we find there a passion for God. The issue, though, is not the object of the passion, but the passion itself. Even de Certeau is caught between passion and the object of the passion. On the one hand, he distinguishes between the form and content of mys-

---

[17] The best comparison along these lines would be between Christian love mysticism and Mahayana Buddhism. Thus, Robert Gimello writes: "Mahayana enlightenment is said to be a way of life, a pattern of conduct, a manner of acting. The human ideal of Mahayana, the bodhisattva, is precisely the being who does not abide in or succumb to his own salvific experiences, but rather turns them compassinately to account in his work among and for all sentient beings" (1978: 190). And Louis Dupré on Christian love mysticism: "As the incarnational consciousness spread to all creation, divine transcendence ceased to imply a negation of the created world. Thenceforth God's presence has been found within rather than beyond creation. Precisely this immanentization of the divine accounts for the earthly quality of Christian love mysticism and for its followers deep involvement with human cares and worldly concerns" (1987: 255).

tics, the form being a language of departure, the content being God. Yet his analysis of mystic language leads him to acknowledge that the object of this language "is never anything but the unstable metaphor for what is inaccessible. Every 'object' of mystical discourse becomes inverted into the trace of an ever-passing Subject" (1992: 77). Mystic texts, he writes, "tell of a passion of what *is*," yet "the Other that organizes the text is not an outside of the text" (1992: 15). With respect to Nietzsche's work, I will use the term *passion* to point to a form of desire and a way of speaking, writing, living this desire, and which, as a translation of "affirmation" or "the eternal joy of becoming," I will call "a passion for the real." The passion for the real does not make an object of the real (as apophasis refuses to make an object of God), but, as passion, as a form of suffering, it is a responsiveness to the real, a participation with it.

Where de Certeau's mystics write a passion for God that is always at the same time a departing from any positive statement about God, Nietzsche writes passion for an affirmative relation to this world and one's own life that always both invokes and turns away from the real. Much of the passion of Nietzsche's writing is reflected in its "unsaying," in the multiple voices that shake the idea of a unified philosophical voice, in the hyperbole that casts suspicion on "Nietzsche's" seriousness, and in the clash between measured philosophical prose and other forms of writing. All this represents a kind of "letting go" and a certain transcendence of "self" and "truth" by which Nietzsche aligns himself with, speaks with the voice of, life. In the intensity of its concentration and the explosiveness of its release, Nietzsche's writing figures a certain kind of ecstasy; in its liminality it points away from its own truth claims by alerting us to the tension between concealing and revealing that it harbors. In both de Certeau's mystics and in Nietzsche, one finds such passions of self-transcendence lived in a wandering and a writing that involve at once a search for and an inscription/evocation of a "real." This "real" cannot be circumscribed as an object; it is as much a "how" of becoming as a "what" of being.

Mysticism, as I am construing it here, is not about the human *achievement* of the nonhuman, but about a *meeting* between the human and what is other than human—here and now. One of the paradoxical things about mysticism is that it involves both activity and passivity; even though it involves rigorous human practice, it also involves a kind of passivity that is not so much achieved as happens. The passion for the real is not accomplished in grasping it, in knowing it, but in a certain kind of awakening to or receiving of it. The practice involved is a matter of confronting one's false necessities and false hopes—one's fantasies, as Iris Murdoch would call them. Cavell, like Murdoch and Freud, and like mystics from various religious traditions, sees spiritual practice as a process of confronting and overcoming the narcissistic fantasies that separate us from reality. This is a painful process of purification, a process that involves surrendering to the facts of human existence without hope for reward or consolation, but simply for "truthful obedience."

It is necessary to take seriously mystical forms of engagement with the world. It also is necessary to consider Nietzschean forms of transcendence. Both manifest complexities that defeat any simple distinctions between "this-worldliness" and "other-worldliness." In 1883, as he was making notes for the third book of *Zarathustra*, Nietzsche cited a passage from Emerson's "Circles": "The one thing which we seek with insatiable desire is to forget ourselves, to be surprised out of our propriety, to lose our sempiternal memory, and to do something without knowing how or why; in short to draw a new circle. Nothing great was ever achieved without enthusiasm. The way of life is wonderful: it is by abandonment" (SW 10: 486).

I locate the mystical element of Nietzsche's thought in the way he writes a certain insatiable desire, abandonment, and creativity on the limits of his philosophical discourse. Emerson's abandonment is Nietzsche's "forgetting." To "forget" the self, the "I," is to forget philosophy's attempt to grasp and comprehend the world; self-forgetting is a limit, an ecstasy, an abandon by which the world and self are released in an experience of reality beyond the intentionality of the philosophical reach. It is to step into the mode of "creative experiencing": "Oh, how we now learn to forget well, and to be good at *not* knowing, as artists!" (GS: 37).

In the remainder of this chapter, I discuss the central place of ecstatic, mystical experience in *Thus Spake Zarathustra*. In Chapter 5, I examine the way Nietzsche writes "the eternal joy of becoming" into his philosophy. In Chapter 6, I return to the problem of suffering to argue that especially in Nietzsche's approach to this problem, one finds a complex interweaving of transfiguration, transcendence, and immanence.

ZARATHUSTRA AND MYSTICISM

Nietzsche writes:

He must yet come to us, the redeeming man of great love and contempt, the creative spirit whose compelling strength will not let him rest in any aloofness or any beyond, whose isolation is misunderstood by the people as it were a flight *from* reality—while it is only his absorption, immersion, penetration *into* reality, so that, when he one day emerges again into the light, he may bring home the *redemption* of this reality. (GM: 96)

Despite Nietzsche's philosophical shifts after *The Birth of Tragedy*, there remains a significant mystical element in his thought. This is most obvious in *Thus Spake Zarathustra,* which Nietzsche himself described as a "dithyramb" (EH: 306) and as "devotional literature" (SP: 82).[18] *Zarathustra* contains numerous episodes that read like mystical poetry; it returns again and again to dramatic experiences of ecstatic vision and communion, and it is the book in which Nietzsche's writing finds its most poetic and celebratory expression as it strains between exuberant Yes-saying and prophetic denunciation. The book narrates the "searches and researches," the trials and the joys, of a teacher/sage who struggles with his hopes for humanity, with the difficulty of communicating with his fellow human beings, and with his love of life. This love gains depth and strength in the course of the narrative. At the heart of *Zarathustra,* as Nietzsche later claimed, is the difficult "idea" of eternal recurrence. Some commentators have treated *Zarathustra* as a philosophical text with a veneer of poetry and narrative that can be wiped away to reveal a "doctrine" of eternal recurrence at the center of the text. I will argue, however, that before thinking about the philosophical significance of a doctrine or concept of eternal recurrence, it is necessary to consider Zarathustra's experience of eternity.

Zarathustra's Eternity

Thus Spake Zarathustra is divided into four books, in which Nietzsche draws and redraws lines between "supreme experience" and "suffering, pain and agony" in varying figures of ecstasy. Among the comings and goings and the speeches of Zarathustra in the first two books, Nietzsche includes a number of episodes that relate experiences and visions, setting a mystical tone and anticipating later, climactic events.[19] At the very start, Zarathustra's proclamation of the *Übermensch* also proclaims Dionysian ecstasy. "Behold, I teach you the *Übermensch*: he is this lightning, he is this frenzy" (Z: 14). And, with his announcements of the "coming" *Übermensch,* with his own comings and goings, and with his dancing, Zarathustra himself is a mask for Dionysus, as Nietzsche points out in *Ecce Homo*: "My concept of the 'Dionysian' [in *Zarathustra*] became a *supreme deed*" (EH: 304).

Zarathustra's wisdom and vision are of heroic proportions, and as the book progresses this wisdom leads him to the terror of his most "abysmal thought." In the third book, intimations of this thought force Zarathustra to return to the solitude of his mountaintop and cave, where he can "con-

[18] One should also note Nietzsche's *Dithyrambs of Dionysus*. In "Fame and Eternity," he writes "eternal Yes of being, eternally am I thy Yes: for I love thee, O eternity" (DD: 67).

[19] "O heaven above me, pure and deep! You abyss of light! Seeing you, I tremble with godlike desires. To throw myself into your height, that is *my* depth. To hide in your purity, that is *my* innocence" (Z: 164).

verse with his soul." This conversation portrays deep a struggle within Zarathustra's soul, which finally leaves him in a deep trance. When he awakens, we learn for the first time that his abysmal thought concerned his realization that the small man, the sort of human being he had hoped to overcome, will recur eternally.[20] He tells his animals of his ordeal: "The great weariness with man—this choked me and had crawled into my throat. . . . 'Eternally recurs the man of whom you are weary, the small man'. . . All-too-small, the greatest!—that was my disgust with man. And the eternal recurrence even of the smallest—that was my weariness with all existence. Alas! Nausea! Nausea! Nausea!" (Z: 219).

Earlier, Zarathustra had struggled with the past, with the fact that while the future remains open, the will is constrained by its inability to change what has already happened. The will must therefore teach itself to embrace the past and say, "Thus I willed it." But in the abysmal thought, Zarathustra encounters a different despair, for the thought of eternal recurrence seems to have closed off not the past, but the future. Despite Zarathustra's great will for the transforming Übermensch, he comes to realize that the "smallest" is going to recur eternally. The thought of this specific recurrence brings Zarathustra to the point of nausea. His quest for an affirmative humanity, his will for a new humanity, is seemingly at an end as he comes to realize that his will cannot, in a fundamental way, change the future.

But this point of despair and nausea is also a turning point for Zarathustra: finding his hopes for the future dashed, he turns to "eternity." In the final sections of Book Three, we find songs about the overcoming of despair and about love for life and eternity in "The Other Dancing Song" and "The Seven Seals (Or, The Yes and Amen Song)." In the course of "The Other Dancing Song," Zarathustra dances and converses with life—personified as a woman—and displays newfound wisdom that has resulted from his confrontation with the most abysmal thought. This song actually finds its first expression in Book Two's "The Dancing Song," where Zarathustra had despaired over his inability to "fathom" life. There, Zarathustra is looking for answers, and blames life when he cannot find them, putting a series of accusatory questions that serve as that song's refrain: "Why? What for? By what? Whither? Where? How? Is it not folly still to be alive?" (Z: 110). By contrast, in "The Other Dancing Song," Zarathustra no longer hurls penetrating questions at life, but follows life's labyrinthine lead, dancing *with* her. It seems that Zarathustra, as Nietzsche does in *Human, All too Human*, views the dance itself as a kind of answer to the problem of life—not an answer in the sense of a solution, but in the sense of a response. That is, Zarathustra has discovered, by the time of this second dance, that the important thing is not distanced,

---

[20] Nietzsche's original intention was for Book Three to be the end of *Zarathustra*. See Hayman (1982: 270).

objective knowledge that "fathoms" life, but rather engagement with life in a letting go of the boundaries of the knowing self, which enables one to participate with and love life. Zarathustra shows evidence of a new, and more complex, attitude toward life, one that involves a dance of love and hate, joy and suffering. "I fear you near, I love you far; your flight lures me, your seeking cures me: I suffer, but what would I not gladly suffer for you? . . . Who would not hate you. . . . Who would not love you" (Z: 225). After this dance/song, Zarathustra and Life pledge their mutual love for one another, Life claiming she loves Zarathustra on account of his wisdom, and Zarathustra saying, "Then life was dearer to me than all my wisdom ever was."

At this point of Book Three, something strange happens. The dialogue with Life comes to a halt, and the figures of Zarathustra and Life recede. The reader is left with only a short, untitled poem/song, whose words come forth from no apparent source. For convenience's sake, I will call it "the midnight song":[21] "One! O man, take care! Two! What does the deep midnight declare? Three! I was asleep—Four! From a dream I woke and swear: Five! The world is deep. Six! Deeper than day had been aware. Seven! Deep is its woe; Eight! Joy—deeper yet than agony: Nine! Woe implores: Go! Ten! But all joy wants eternity—Eleven! Wants deep, wants deep eternity. Twelve!" (Z: 227–28).

The "midnight song" tolls in stillness and anonymity, hollowing out a space in the text for a cryptic song of woe and joy. The tolling will recur at the end of Book Four, and below I will attempt to draw out some of its significance. Here, I simply remark on an anomaly. In each of the sections of *Zarathustra*, with the exception of this song and the one that follows it ("Seven Seals"), the speaker/singer is identified clearly in the text. These sections, however, are conspicuous for the absence of a specified voice.[22] This can be explained by the fact that Zarathustra, after his

[21] The importance of the midnight setting for this song should not be underestimated, especially by those interpreters of Nietzsche who place so much emphasis on his epistemological reflections in *Twilight of the Idol's* "How the 'Real World' at Last Became a Fable" (TI: 50–51). The climax of this fable is described by Nietzsche as "Mid-day; moment of the shortest shadow; end of the longest error; zenith of mankind; INCIPIT ZARATHUSTRA." This, then, is the "great noon" that Nietzsche celebrates in other writings as a moment of great affirmation. But the climaxes of *Zarathustra* in Books Three and Four take place at midnight, the "opposite" of the great noon, and usher in a new dawn. As always, enlightenment in Nietzsche is haunted by darkness and passion. Cf. Ricoeur on the "tragic view of the divine": "The sphere of the sacred, then, admits the polarity of night and day, the passion of night and the lawfulness of the day" (1967: 220).

[22] In *Zarathustra* each chapter ends in one of three ways: the vast majority are speeches or songs spoken/sung by Zarathustra, all of which conclude with either "Thus spake Zarathustra" or "Thus sang Zarathustra"; alternatively, some end with the voice of the narrator, describing, for instance, Zarathustra's journey; finally, a few sections end in conversation, either Zarathustra's internal dialogue or a conversation between Zarathustra and another character. In all these cases, the voice is identified clearly.

confrontation with his abysmal thought, after his dance with life and his pledge with love, undergoes an ecstatic experience, born of the painful experience of the abyss.

The tolling of the midnight bell is a prelude to a song of love, "The Seven Seals (Or, the Yes and Amen Song)." This is a song about the love for eternity: each section of the song ends with the refrain, "Oh, how should I not lust after eternity and after the nuptial ring of rings, the ring of recurrence? Never yet have I found the woman from whom I wanted children, unless it be this woman whom I love: for I love you, O eternity. *For I love you, O eternity!*" It is also a song of affirmation: the singer sings of watching a "heavy cloud . . . prepared for lightning and the redemptive flash, pregnant with lightning bolts that say Yes and laugh Yes." Finally, it is a song of participation: the singer "hangs on the mountains," dances "star-dances," sails on the sea, jumps into "rose slopes and hedges of lilies," and soars in the sky. In each of these respects—love, affirmation, and participation—the song attests to Zarathustra's ecstasy, even to the experience of a mystical union with all that is: he is lost to himself, he, Zarathustra, is no longer singer or agent, rather he is being sung, the anonymous voice of life is singing *through* him.[23]

Or dancing through him: "Now I am light, now I fly, now I see myself beneath myself, now a god dances through me" (Z: 41). Zarathustra has been struck by the frenzy, the Dionysian lightning bolt, precisely at the point of the descent into the abyss that causes him to surrender or radically refigure his hopes for the *Übermensch*: in this surrender, he finds himself beyond himself. These final sections of Book Three inscribe the pattern of Dionysian ecstatic vision/dance that Nietzsche had delineated in *The Birth of Tragedy*: "In song and dance man expresses himself as a member of a higher community; he has forgotten how to walk and speak and is on the way toward flying into the air, dancing. . . . He feels himself a god, he himself now walks about enchanted, in ecstasy, like the gods he saw walking in his dreams" (BT: 37).

For some commentators, the crucial event at the end of Book Three is not this ecstatic experience but the doctrine of eternal recurrence articulated earlier, when Zarathustra awakes from his abysmal dream. Yet it is the animals, not Zarathustra, who, at this point, declare a "doctrine" of

---

[23] Peter Berkowitz (1995) argues that ultimately Zarathustra turns away from the visions represented by the climaxes to Books Three and Four. With this, he argues, Nietzsche shows how the self-deification and absolute mastery represented by Zarathustra's *Übermensch* is not attainable. But note that the ecstatic vision of Book Three comes only *after* Zarathustra confronts the abysmal thought that essentially defeats his original hope for the *Übermensch*. In contrast to Berkowitz, I argue that Nietzsche embraces the visions at the end of Books Three and Four, and that it is precisely there that we see a self-transcendence that undermines not deification, but the idea that the self, as an individual, can be perfected and become god. In other words, the deification represented here does not take the form of a human being assuming the mastery of the monotheistic God.

eternal recurrence. When he wakes, Zarathustra speaks of nausea and the eternally recurring small man. His animals respond to this by declaring Zarathustra the teacher of eternal recurrence: "Behold, we know what you teach: that all things recur eternally, and we ourselves too; and that we have already existed an eternal number of times, and all things with us." The animals continue, in words that form an interpretation of eternal recurrence as a cosmological doctrine. But Zarathustra's response to the declaration is evasive. He avoids affirming or denying the abstract, even metaphysical language used by the animals, first teasing the animals for having "made a hurdy-gurdy song" of his struggle by calling them "buffoons and barrel organs" and, then, falling into silence.[24]

This silence returns, in the form of a secret, one section later in "The Other Dancing Song." After Life has declared her love for him, and has scolded him for not loving her from the heart, Zarathustra whispers a secret to her, to which the reader is not privy. We only observe Life's surprised reaction: "Nobody knows that." At which point Zarathustra declares his love for life. Nietzsche portrays Zarathustra as having discovered something in his struggle and convalescence, but does not put it into words—or, more subtly, as secret, puts it into words that do not speak. One might speculate that Zarathustra's secret is that life recurs eternally. In the context, it does make sense that Zarathustra's most affirmative encounter with life would follow directly on his climatic encounter with his abysmal thought and that the key to his transformation would be his knowledge of eternal recurrence. But, again, Nietzsche veils Zarathustra's realization in the silence of the secret, refusing to have him state eternal recurrence—or whatever it is that he has learned—in a discursive, philosophical way. Aside from the secret, Nietzsche offers only ecstasy and poetry: Zarathustra's realization is "experienced," but only ecstatically; that is, as something that happens when one is not oneself; therefore, it can be figured or symbolized—in a dance or a song of love—but it cannot be the stuff of philosophical doctrine. The point, then, is not to articulate what lies behind the secret, but to follow the dance and the desire.

Questions remain nonetheless. In "The Seven Seals," the singer sings of "Yes-saying" and the love of eternity. What does love for "eternity" signify? In "The Other Dancing Song," Zarathustra had sung of the love of "life." Is the love of eternity also a love of life, or does this song express some remaining reluctance or inability on Zarathustra's part to fully affirm earthly, temporal life, as Heidegger suggests?[25] Such a suspicion might be supported by the central image of a birdlike spirit soaring above

[24] This point is made by both Shapiro (1989: 82) and White (1990).

[25] Heidegger (see Allison 1985) argues that rather than escaping the desire for revenge, Nietzsche's doctrine of eternal recurrence, and his thought as a whole, is the culmination of a tradition of Western thought that expresses the spirit of revenge.

all that is heavy and earthbound. Despite Nietzsche's many polemics against "otherworldliness," is it possible that this love for eternity is a desire to escape the earth and life? To answer these questions, it is necessary to turn to the fourth and final book of *Zarathustra*.

Joy

In Book Four, Zarathustra encounters the despair of various "higher men" and gathers them in his cave to converse and celebrate with them in a last supper. In the process, he engages in yet another struggle: to overcome his pity (*mit-leid*, or "suffering-with") for these higher men. The book is filled with absurd, comical characters and, on the whole, seems a parody. Yet the laughter that Zarathustra recommends to the higher men is not his final teaching. Following the riotous supper, in which much wine is consumed, Zarathustra undergoes another visionary experience in "The Nightwandering Song."[26] This song reprises the ecstatic songs at the end of Book Three: as it opens, Zarathustra's spirit flies ahead and comes to rest on the "high ridge" that was the scene for the opening lines of "The Seven Seals" (Z: 318). And again, the midnight bell tolls, drawing Zarathustra to mysterious depths where he experiences a moment of perfection: "Did not my world become perfect just now?" When the moment passes, Zarathustra speaks to the higher men, not in his own words, but whispering the "words" of the bell. "Here," says Zarathustra, "things are heard that by day may not become loud."

This is another vision bounded by deferral and silence, in which the reader and the higher men are told of suffering, joy, and eternity. Still, it is possible to draw some conclusions about the relation between eternity and the world left obscure by the end of Book Three. The song contrasts experiences of suffering and joy.

> All that is unripe wants to live: woe! Woe entreats: Go! Away, woe! But all that suffers wants to live, that it may become ripe and joyous and longing—longing

[26] This title of the song, *Das Nachtwandler-Lied*, suggests more than Kaufmann's translation, "The Drunken Song." Of course, Kaufmann's translation captures the important doubling of Zarathustra and Dionysus. But when Nietzsche writes that Zarathustra stands "like a drunkard," the German is unambiguous: Zarathustra is *wie ein Trunkener*. By contrast, *Nachtwandler* has the primary meaning of "sleepwalking." Significantly, *wandeln* means "to change" or "to walk," and *die Wandlung* is a "change" or, as a religious term, a "transubstantiation" or a "consecration." In this section, the wandering, the transformation, and even the consecration ("did not my world become perfect?") are as important, I think, as the drunkenness. After hearing the tolling of the midnight bell, Zarathustra calls to those around him, "Let us wander in the night" (*lasst uns in die Nacht wandeln*). It is worth noting, with respect to note 22 above, that Nietzsche also invokes sleepwalking at a crucial point of *The Gay Science*, where he considers the tension between the Enlightenment imperative to daylight and the "spirit and power of the dream": "We somnambulists of the day! We artists! We ignore what is natural. We are moonstruck and God-struck" (GS: 123).

for what is farther, higher, brighter. "I want heirs"—thus speaks all that suffers; "I want children, I do not want *myself*." Joy, however, does not want heirs, or children—joy wants itself, wants eternity, wants recurrence, wants everything eternally the same. (Z: 322)

Nietzsche figures two modalities of desire: suffering desires life, though not its own, and joy desires eternity. In its desire to be rid of itself, woe becomes a creative, striving force; joy, on the other hand, wants everything to remain "eternally the same." Suffering wants what is not; joy affirms what is. In fact, joy gives us the simplest definition for Nietzsche's affirmation: the desiring embrace of what is, saying "Yes" in declaring all that is to be good.

As the song progresses, however, these different desires become related in a moment of perfection in which this "Yes" embraces suffering itself.

Just now my world became perfect; midnight too is noon; pain too is a joy; curses too are a blessing; night too is a sun—go away or you will learn; a sage too is a fool. Have you ever said Yes to a single joy? O my friends, then you said Yes to *all* woe. All things are bound together, entangled, enamored; if ever you wanted one thing twice, if ever you said, "You please me, happiness! Abide, moment!" then you wanted *all* back. All anew, all eternally, all bound up, entangled, enamored—oh, then you *loved* the world. Eternal ones, love it eternally and evermore; and to woe too, you say: go, but return. *For all joy wants eternity* . . . so rich is joy that it thirsts for woe, for hell, for hatred, for disgrace, for the cripple, for *world*—this world, oh, you know it. . . . All eternal joy longs for failures. For all joy wants itself, hence it also wants agony. (Z: 323)

From beyond his perfect moment, Zarathustra signals that joy's love for eternity includes the desire for suffering; this is desire as love for the process, the eternal cycle by which it comes to be, a cycle that includes growth, flowering, and death, this love is constitutive of joy. Joy "longs" for failure and agony, it desires the struggle and conflict out of which suffering becomes creative: in this final song, Zarathustra, therefore, comes to love and affirm the recurrence of even the small man. The perspective of eternity and the experience of joy are more inclusive than the perspective or experience of woe; implicated in the experience of joy is the recognition of the way in which joy and woe are bound up together. Love for eternity is, *at the same time*, love for the becoming of the world. Thus, in *Ecce Homo*, Nietzsche writes that Zarathustra is one who "having being, dives into becoming; the soul that has, but wants to want and will" (EH: 305). Joy, world, and eternity are bound up momentarily in a perfect, fruitful union of love. In the perfect moment, the joy of eternity floods the present of the world, so that the present is affirmed by all that leads to it and from it.

Immanent Transcendence

Note the "listening" and the "wandering" in "The Nightwandering Song": Zarathustra is being overtaken by something over which he has little control and which throws his identity into confusion. The common image of the strident, ever-wakeful, invulnerable Nietzschean *Übermensch* is radically qualified in these pages through the tenderness, hesitancy, and even passivity that are part of Zarathustra's ecstasy.[27] In and through this experience, Zarathustra overcomes the temptation of pity for the higher men, but he renounces his pity not in a self-aggrandizing, Darwinian assertion of superiority, but in a mystical declaration of love for the world. In contrast to interpretations of Nietzsche's will to power that see it (correctly) as a principle of immanence but that conclude (incorrectly) that this means that it is only a never-ending drive to historical self-transcendence, Zarathustra's mysticism involves a notion of transcendence in which the surpassing is not forward in time but toward a timeless grounding in the eternity of joy and love.[28]

Nietzsche describes a movement of transcendence toward eternity that is completed only in a return to the world and the finite self. Through this transcendence, one inhabits a transfigured self and world, seen through the eyes of love. Such love does not distort the reality of self and world, for "woe," "hatred," and "the cripple" remain: the love for eternity is mystical love for the real.[29] "The world" is not transcended as false or incomplete, as it would be in certain monistic religious systems (or as it is in Nietzsche's own, mature reading of *The Birth of Tragedy*); nor is the experience of eternity seen as a hint of better things to come, as it might be in certain understandings of Christianity. In other words, this transcendence is not a movement of self or spirit away from the earthly and finite. It is instead an expansion of awareness in which one's life in the earthly

[27] Earlier in the book, Zarathustra attributes the phrase "just now the world became perfect" to the happiness of the woman who "obeys out of entire love" (Z: 67).

[28] Yovel introduces the helpful term "inner transcendent dimension" in his discussion of transcendence in Hegel, Spinoza, and Nietzsche (1989: 111–2; 126). Yovel also is right to point out that Nietzsche rejects Hegel's telos and Spinoza's, "eternal substance and laws of nature" as the ground underlying the world of flux; that is, as the inner transcendent dimension of existence. Yet, in his attempt to preclude all pantheistic and mystical elements from Nietzsche's thought, Yovel attributes to Nietzsche a "defiant affirmation" that places him at odds with the universe. This claim does not do justice to the experiences of ecstasy in *Zarathustra*. There certainly is a kind of defiance in Nietzsche's affirmation, but it is the defiance of a certain kind of love, of *amor fati*, one that refuses resentful conclusions of suffering, pain, and disappointment. I develop this theme in Chapter 6.

[29] Rosset claims that "beatitude," "blessedness," *Seligkeit*, is the central theme of Nietzschean philosophy. This is "the simple and unadorned experience of the real" (1993: 25).

and finite is experienced differently, from a new center "beyond" itself or "deeper" than itself. "Eternity" is not a different realm of existence more real than our illusory, worldly realm, but rather the space of the "eternal joy of becoming" (TI: 120). Although Nietzsche rejects the comfort of metaphysical dualism, he continues to value an ecstatic abandon that has as its goal a certain reoccupying of the self, a resettling of or rebinding of the self to itself and world. An abyssal movement, a distancing of self from self, an ecstasy: a movement at/of the limits of the self through which one participates with the world's becoming.

Chapter Five

ECSTATIC PHILOSOPHY

> The music hoped for and heard, echoes in the body like an inner voice
> that one cannot specify by name but that transforms one's use of
> words. Whoever is "seized" or "possessed" by it begins to speak in a
> haunted tongue. The music comes from an unknown quarter, inaugu-
> rates a new rhythm of existence—some would say a new "breath," a
> new way of walking, a different "style" of life. It simultaneously capti-
> vates an attentiveness from within, disturbs the orderly flow of
> thought, and opens up or frees new spaces. There is no mystics with-
> out it. The mystic experience therefore often has the guise of a poem
> that we "hear" the way we drift into a dance.
> (Michel de Certeau, *The Mystic Fable*)

> Everything I have so far written is foreground; for me myself it always
> begins with the dashes.
> (Nietzsche, in a letter to his sister, Elisabeth Förster Nietzsche)

INTRODUCTION: MYSTICS AND METAPHYSICS

IT IS ONE THING to claim that *Zarathustra* contains writing that
one might describe as mystical or ecstatic poetry, it is another to claim
that there is a mystical element pervading Nietzsche's thought in general. What is the relevance of *Zarathustra* for Nietzsche's later work? One
might argue that the ecstatic poetry of Nietzsche's enigmatic "gift" is
actually a parody of mystical affirmations, or an ironic warning against
overexuberant hopes and loves. Given Nietzsche's attack on ascetic practices and mystical states in the *Genealogy*, such an interpretation cannot
be dismissed. Yet, Nietzsche's later writing, viewed with a discerning eye,
also supports a different interpretation. Nietzsche sought to rethink the
task of philosophy. It is not surprising, then, that his writing stands out
from the canon of Western philosophy—especially as that canon existed
in his lifetime—for its stylistic diversity and resistance to straightforward
argumentation, studied objectivity, and system. Nietzsche's is writing
highly controlled in image and in the concentrated insight and thought of
the aphorism; it is also writing that at least appears to let go of many of
the restraints that determined "good taste," "scholarship," and "philoso-

Epigraphs: de Certeau, 1992: 297; Nietzsche, 20 May 1885.

phy" in nineteenth-century Europe. Nietzsche possessed, as he himself commented, "the most multifarious art of style." The reader is vividly reminded of this not only by the presence of *Zarathustra* at the center of his corpus, but also by the poems and songs at the margins of his "philosophical" texts, as well as the irony, hyperbole, and metaphor that figure throughout them. Nietzsche's writing draws attention to itself as liminal writing: writing situated at the boundary between philosophy and poetry, body and consciousness, emotion and reason; writing that in a significant and precise sense seeks to create an opening whereby the philosopher brings self and culture beyond themselves. Thus I name Nietzsche's revision of philosophy "ecstatic philosophy." In this chapter, I examine Nietzsche's ecstatic philosophy and then, in the final section of the chapter, begin the move from ecstatic philosophy to mystical writing. The mystical writing I have highlighted in *Zarathustra* should be taken seriously because it is inscribed in Nietzsche's later texts as well.

The mystical element of Nietzsche's affirmation is closely related to his antimetaphysical view of philosophy, which he continued to refine in the works that span the last four years of his active life and which finds its definitive statement in the attack on metaphysical dualism in *Twilight of the Idols*. To counter this dualism, expressed in the west's millennia-long religious and philosophical obsession with "being," Nietzsche invokes "becoming." As he does so, however, Nietzsche recognizes that the philosophical criticism of being recoils back on the mastery of philosophy, forcing the philosopher to acknowledge the limits of conceptualization. This ecstatic opening takes Nietzsche's writing in a mystical direction, to the figures of eternity and Dionysus. These figures do not occupy the central conceptual place of the books in which they appear; they are drawn at the edges and ends of Nietzsche's writing. There, they turn Nietzsche's philosophy out into the intoxicated overflowing of affirmation, and they qualify by deepening, not negating, the worldliness and historicity of Nietzsche's genealogical unmaskings.

In *The Birth of Tragedy*, Nietzsche charged Socrates with antipathy to mysticism, yet also expressed the hope that one day an "artistic Socrates" would be possible (BT: 92). He wondered, in other words, about a philosophy that does not deny the positive and productive role of the Dionysian, or the "instincts," in the apprehension of reality and the living of life. Does Nietzsche's late philosophy embody this hope? Dionysus is all but absent from the writings Nietzsche published between 1872 and 1884.[1] By the time of *Ecce Homo*, however, he could proclaim, "I have the right to understand myself as the first tragic philosopher—that is, the most extreme opposite and antipode of a pessimistic philosopher. Before me

[1] However, Laurence Lampert (1986) persuasively argues that in many respects Zarathustra is a Dionysian figure.

this transposition [*Umsetzung*] of the Dionysian into a philosophical pathos did not exist: tragic wisdom was lacking" (EH: 273). In the mature works, the artistic Socrates becomes the Dionysian philosopher—the philosophical "disciple" of Dionysus. To understand the Dionysian as a philosophical pathos is to understand Nietzsche's writings as "gay science," where the cold demystifications of philosophy become woven into the practice and expression of the "eternal joy of becoming." And it is to understand how "tragic wisdom" is Nietzsche's expression for an affirming acknowledgment with which he supplants the pessimistic "wisdom of Silenus."

BECOMING DIONYSIAN

Dionysus

In a provocative study of *The Birth of Tragedy*, John Sallis argues that Nietzsche, even in his first book, was already engaged in a critique of Schopenhauer and a "twisting away" from metaphysics (Sallis 1991). Working from the philosophical ground cleared by Deleuze, and, above all, by Derrida, Sallis argues that the opposition between Apollo and Dionysus is one of tension rather than sublation or reconciliation. The crucial concepts for Sallis are *excess* and *ecstasy*. Dionysus determines the course of tragedy through a "logic of ecstasy" in which limits—of individuality, of reason, of metaphysics—are at once transgressed and delimited in an ecstatic movement. As a "state" of being outside oneself, ecstasy is a state in which the limits of the self are exceeded. But in this very transgression, ecstasy disrupts the opposition that distinguishes inside from outside, the self from the not-self; it disrupts as well, therefore, the opposition between self and other and self and thing.[2] More generally, then, ecstasy is in tension with the concept of being that structures metaphysical dualism.

Since limits themselves are a function of the Apollonian, the principle of individuation or determination, the Dionysian blurs the opposition that separates it from the Apollonian: the Dionysian disrupts "itself." But Sallis argues that from the perspective of the logic of ecstasy, there is no "itself," no being, as such, to the Dionysian. As that which is "opposed" to the Apollonian, the Dionysian "is" only as excess, in ecstasy: it "is" movement "beyond." The Dionysian cannot be experienced *as such*, but only in the flashing, excessive space on the margins of its Apollonian man-

---

[2] I might add the opposition between the religious and the secular. Sallis's (1991) is a brilliant reading of *The Birth of Tragedy*, but it also is a perfect example of a certain blindness among Nietzsche's commentators. Sallis writes of ecstasy, mysticism, gods, personifications of nature, healing, revelation, redemption—but registers no recognition of the possibility that a religious problematic could be involved in unpacking the text.

ifestation. The identity of the Dionysian, writes Sallis, is "abysmal": realized only in "the movement, the figure," not "in some originary being
over against the individual, who in Dionysian ecstasy would then return
to this origin. For there is no origin." There is no origin, there "is" abyss;
there is no primal "one," there "is" excess. It might even be said, to elaborate on the discussion of mystical experience in the previous chapter, that
the ecstatic, excessive experience of the Dionysian is no experience at all,
since the "I," that which "has" experience, is disrupted in this excess.
"Ecstatic experience" is an oxymoron; ecstasy takes place in the anonymity of the "event," rather than in experience.

In its abysmal disruption of metaphysics, Nietzsche's first book anticipates his later work: Dionysus returns as a figure of ecstasy or excess.
The late Dionysus is not a concept that Nietzsche subjects to analysis
or speculation, but rather an invocation that marks the limits between
becoming and what can be thought or said. And it is the figure with which
Nietzsche marks his efforts to exceed the deadening dogmatism of "the
Crucified."

Accordingly, Dionysus appears almost exclusively at the end of the texts
in which he appears, specifically, *Beyond Good and Evil*, *Twilight of the
Idols*, and *Ecce Homo*. At the end of *Beyond Good and Evil*, in an exceptionally lyrical passage, Dionysus appears as a philosopher and an (at)-
tempter god (or "god of experimenters), leading "every soul" deeper
within itself and into new hopes and new dissatisfactions. As Kaufmann
points out, the portrait Nietzsche draws here—Dionysus as philosopher-
god—evokes Socrates as much as it evokes the Dionysus of *The Birth of
Tragedy* (BG: 234, n. 43). But aspects of the early Dionysus remain, for
this later one is "the great ambiguous one . . . to whom I once offered, as
you know, in all secrecy and reverence, my first-born—as the last, it seems
to me, who offered him a sacrifice" (BG: 235). More specifically, as
tempter and attempter, this Dionysus leads one beyond established ways
of thinking and valuing and into one's own depths where one finds oneself
"newer to oneself, broken open . . . full of new will and currents, full of
new dissatisfactions and undertows" (BG: 234). Dionysus takes one deep
within oneself, confronts one with the excess, the alterity within. In this
opening to new voices and new thoughts, which pluralize and energize,
Dionysus teaches one how to listen.

At the end of *Twilight of the Idols*, Dionysus is the subject of some of
the most explicitly religious passages in Nietzsche's published writing.
There, he writes of a "faith" (*Glaube*) he has "baptized" (*getauft*) with
the name of Dionysus and which he describes as a "joyful and trusting
fatalism." He invokes the will to life of the pre-Socratic Greeks as an
affirmative will to "eternal life" and claims that in the name *Dionysus*,
this will is "experienced religiously" (*religiös empfunden*). In a text that

argues conceptually against the privilege of *being* over *becoming* in philosophical discourse, Dionysus registers an experience of becoming that subverts the boundaries of self and time: in the Dionysian state, Nietzsche writes, one realizes "in oneself the eternal joy of becoming." As in *Beyond Good and Evil*, Dionysus represents an experience/event of becoming and renewal, a religious experience of gratitude and joy. This religiosity is further defined, through contrast, in *Ecce Homo*, where Dionysus marks the end of Nietzsche's writings. The final line of Nietzsche's final work reads, "Have I been understood—*Dionysus versus the Crucified.*—"

Dionysus makes another appearance in *Ecce Homo*, this time in the middle of the text, in the discussion of *Zarathustra*. Here, Dionysus names a certain excess of *Zarathustra*, a text that resists assimilation to Nietzsche's philosophical work and that, from Nietzsche's own hyperbolic point of view, is of ultimate importance not only for his own work but for all of humankind. In *Ecce Homo*, Zarathustra is now interpreted in the name of Dionysus. "My concept of the 'Dionysian' here became a *supreme deed*; measured against that, all the rest of human activity seems poor and relative" (EH: 304). Nietzsche relates Dionysus to Zarathustra in two ways. First, Dionysus/Zarathustra is a soul on the boundary of being and becoming, a soul that "having being, dives into becoming; the soul that *has*, but *wants* to want and will" (EH: 305). Second, Dionysus/Zarathustra is the spirit who bears the heaviest weight and stares into the deepest abysses, yet is "the lightest and most transcendent," "a dancer" who finds in the most abysmal idea—eternal recurrence—"one reason more for being himself the eternal Yes to all things, 'the tremendous, unbounded saying Yes and Amen' " (EH: 306).

Becoming

I am exploring the connections between the mystical sensibility in *The Birth of Tragedy*, the visionary and affirmative writing of *Zarathustra*, and Nietzsche's later philosophy. Attention to the role the figures "eternity" and "becoming" play in his attack on metaphysics will help articulate these connections. In an elusive and highly condensed chapter of *Twilight of the Idols*, entitled, "How the 'True World' Finally Became a Fable: The History of an Error," Nietzsche draws the broad outlines of a "history" of the metaphysical opposition between the true (*wahre*) and apparent (*scheinbare*) worlds.[3] In just over a single page, Nietzsche adumbrates six stages of the religious and philosophical history of this opposition, from *ressentiment* and metaphysics in Plato to "the high point of humanity," which he designates "INCIPIT ZARATHUSTRA." The final three stages

---

[3] He had treated this opposition previously as a key to understanding the faith in opposite values (BG: 1, 9–10, 46–47).

mark the decline of the idea of the true world: the fourth stage is characterized by the positivist claim that the concept of the true world is unthinkable;[4] the fifth by the recognition that the concept of the true world has become useless and, "consequently," refuted; and the sixth—"INCIPIT ZARATHUSTRA"—by the fact that "with the true world we have also abolished the apparent world" (TI: 51).[5] With these three latter stages, Nietzsche registers his rejection of positions that, at one time or another, he had seriously considered, particularly Kant's: although we can no longer claim to know anything about the true world, we still must posit one; and Schopenhauer's: we can intuit the "true world" of the will.

This history presents many difficulties and complexities; here I will confine myself to the final stage and the question of appearance. What does Nietzsche mean by overcoming the true-apparent distinction? This can be answered only by placing the "Fable" in the context of the immediately preceding section of the book. There, Nietzsche claims that to distinguish between the true and apparent worlds, and to value the former, is a sign of decadence. This is because a philosophy of stable oppositions and eternal truth, of faith in opposite values, places ultimate value on a dualistic stasis whereby "the higher [truth, beauty, consciousness] must not be allowed to grow out of the lower" (TI: 47). Nietzsche's frequent characterizations of Western philosophy as "vampirism" or "Egyptianism" convey his belief that philosophy preserves the illusion of eternity and order only by alienating thought from its origins in the body and life. To abolish the "true world," therefore, is to avoid the bewitching lures of consciousness and language, which depend on a degree of stasis in order to work at all, and to return to the living, growing, healthy body as the origin of thought. Every philosophical "position" or "word," as Nietzsche puts it in an earlier text, is a "mask" (BG: 229). But philosophy masks the excess of becoming, not a true world or thing-in-itself

As an exemplification of the healthy body, Nietzsche extols the "Dionysian artist." In doing so, he complicates matters, for he writes that this artist "esteems appearance [*der Schein*] higher than reality." That is, at the same time that Nietzsche rejects the opposition between the true and apparent worlds, he puts another distinction and another concept of appearance into play: the distinction between appearance and "reality."

---

[4] I use "unthinkable" in the Kantian sense of "thinking." For Kant, the true world can be thought, but it cannot be known. In discussing the fourth stage, Nietzsche uses the term *unbekannt*, which Hollingdale translates as "unknown." In German, though, there is a distinction between knowing in the sense of knowledge (*Erkenntnis*) and knowing in the sense of familiarity (*bekannt*), which English is not as adept at indicating. In the third stage, Nietzsche seems to indicate the true world as thinkable in the Kantian sense; in the fourth stage, then, *Bekannt* seems to indicate something like unimaginable.

[5] For insightful treatments of this crucial and controversial text, see Clark 1990; Heidegger 1991a, 1991b; and Rosen 1993.

Given Nietzsche's rejection of the apparent world/true world opposition, the appearance he attributes to the Dionysian artist must be something other than simple untruth or illusion. He confirms this by describing this new appearance as "reality *once more*, only by way of selection, reinforcement, and correction." Thus, rather than invoking two oppositions, Nietzsche contrasts an *opposition* between the philosophical sense of appearance and philosophical truth, on the one hand, with the relative *difference* between an artistic appearance and reality, on the other: artistic appearance *is* "reality once more." In *Beyond Good and Evil*, Nietzsche offers a sense of what such a difference might entail when he posits a relative difference between truth and falsity. There, he had opposed metaphysical dualism by treating the true-false distinction in terms of "different degrees of apparentness, and, as it were, lighter and darker shadows and shades of appearance—different 'values,' to use the language of painters" (BG: 46–47). Nietzsche substitutes for the absolute metaphysical opposition between true and apparent worlds, a relative, artistic distinction between appearance and reality. To the extent that he does this as a philosopher, however, Nietzsche's nonmetaphysical, artistic "concept" of appearance also ultimately subverts the distinction between philosophy and art.[6]

Complications remain, however, for Nietzsche views artistic appearance as a "correction" of reality. But is not the idea that one can "correct" reality not indicative of weakness for Nietzsche? This issue needs to be approached from two perspectives, one is metaphysical/epistemological, the other is psychological.

First, the metaphysical/epistemological issues. Nietzsche's appeal to a Dionysian conception of art undercuts the philosophical distinction between truth and appearance by rejecting the idea that there is any intelligible ground or transcendent reality—Truth—"beneath" the process of appearance. As he puts it in *The Gay Science*:

> This youthful madness in the love of truth, [has] lost [its] charm for us: for that we are too experienced, too serious, too merry, too burned, too *profound*. We no longer believe that truth remains truth when the veils are withdrawn; we have lived too much to believe this. . . . Those Greeks were superficial—*out of profundity*. And is not this precisely what we are again coming back to, we daredevils of the spirit who have climbed the highest and most dangerous peak of present thought and looked around from up there—we who have looked *down* from there? Are we not, precisely in this respect, Greeks? Adorers of forms, of tones, of words? And therefore—*artists*? (GS: 38)

[6] Below, when I write of Dionysian art, it should be understood that such an artist is also a philosopher.

There is no ground; for Nietzsche there is only "becoming," a never-ending movement or flux out of which all phenomena appear. In countering philosophical claims about Being with his ideas about becoming, Nietzsche asserts a vision of what he describes as "the total character of the world" (*der Gesammt-Charakter der Welt*; GS: 168), which he calls "chaos." *Becoming*, as Nietzsche understands it, avoids metaphysics, at least in two specific senses of the term. First, becoming is not the ontological ground of appearance in the sense that it serves as a foundation or source to which all being can be traced. Instead, becoming is always both a concealing and a revealing, a shifting and a layering of surfaces, a continuous flux: becoming "is" abyss. Second, becoming is not the epistemological ground of appearance, understood as the means for comprehending and explaining the reality of appearances: becoming "is" chaos.[7] These claims point us in the direction of Cavell's concept of acknowledgment: one acknowledges, one does not know, "the total character of the world" as "chaos." Acknowledging becoming as our condition, the artist-philosopher relates to the world in a way that does not force him or her to think in terms of a dualistic contrast between reality and appearance. Acknowledgment thinks beyond what Emerson calls a "paltry empiricism," which would locate reality only in that which can be grasped by the senses, for, as "reality *once more*," becoming is something more than "mere appearance," more than that particular empirical reality that one ordinarily encounters as "this world." Though Nietzsche argues that there is no (metaphysically) true *world*, this does not exclude the position that there is something about our relation to this world that is not grasped by sense capacities and constructed by our understanding, but which still can, nonetheless, inform our use of reason and language.

Still, to the extent that Nietzsche does posit a "total character of existence," one might argue that he posits an "essence" of reality, and so remains a metaphysician.[8] As such, he substitutes for the philosophical and religious dualisms that have dominated Western thought what I will call an ecstatic monism. But this monism does not involve "essence" in the strict philosophical sense, for its "character" is to be without character or

---

[7] The figures of abyss (*Abgrund*) and chaos (*Chaos*) figure throughout Nietzsche's books and notes, particularly from the first edition of GS. For abyss, see GS 290. For chaos, see GS 168.

[8] Stanley Rosen (1993: 141) distinguishes between metaphysics in the Aristotelian sense as the study of Being *qua* being (which, for Nietzsche, is already committed to dualism) and metaphysics as claims about the whole beyond the empirical. It is in this last sense that Nietzsche remains a metaphysician. Salaquarda makes the related claim that Nietzsche rejects metaphysics as dualism, but follows F. A. Lange's idea of metaphysics as "*Begriffsdichtung.*" Salaquarda also argues that Nietzsche differs from Lange in that the scientifically thematized world is itself not "given" but the product of interpretation (1989: 267).

principle. In Sallis's sense of the word, it "is" excess: reality is always "more." Thus it is an *ecstatic* monism: because "knowledge and becoming exclude one another" (WP: 517), because becoming is no-thing, is abyss, "it" cannot be known or held by the philosophical gaze. Nietzsche does, however, suggest that it can be glimpsed like a flash of lightning, in an awareness marked by the "once more." This insight is not the product of philosophical reflection or scientific objectivity; it does not comprehend reality. It is not even something "experienced" or "had" in the full, subjective sense of these words. It is something acknowledged in the course of, as the condition of, a certain kind of practice of relating to self and world. The real can only be embodied or performed in a practical, artistic engagement, a participation in the flux of life. This participation, claims Nietzsche, is a sign of the Dionysian artist, who "realizes" in himself "the eternal joy of becoming," who "adores" appearance.

Below, I will suggest that a key to this practice or performance is to be found in the role of metaphor in Nietzsche's writing. In and through metaphor, the artist who affirms reality "once more" maintains a tension between the particularity of appearance and the awareness of the abyss of becoming at the boundary of each and every appearance. Appearances, phenomena, are reality, yet there is for Nietzsche always a "more," there is always that which is *between* (not behind or above) different appearances.

Nietzsche continues to use a conception of reality, but it is one that does not function as a ground or foundation for his thought; instead, it demands the constant movement of thought. Thus, the question of the "correction" of reality is not, in the end, an epistemological or metaphysical question. It is only resolved for Nietzsche through the psychological distinction between a Dionysian affirmation of "appearance" and a weak, metaphysical condemnation of appearance. Appearance, Nietzsche's revised, nonmetaphysical, idea of appearance, *is* reality—"once more." Reveling in the eternal reiteration of the "once more," the Dionysian artist renounces the mastery over life sought by the philosopher-priest and so the morally inflected choice between the true and the false. In an early section of *Twilight of the Idols*, Nietzsche treats the pretension to be able to evaluate and correct life as the paradigmatic gesture of Socratic philosophy. For the philosopher, correcting life means taking a position outside of life, or, in what amounts to the same thing, finding the ground of reality, in order to judge and correct life. As we have seen, Nietzsche rejects this pretense and argues that to assert a ground that "is" reality, is to reveal the decadent fear of life at the heart of one's vision of reality. By contrast, the affirmation of the groundlessness of becoming is a sign of the health of one who lives wholly and enthusiastically—and realistically, that is, in the acknowledgment that we live by our interpreting, valuing, creative activity.

Artistic "correction," then, does not pretend to stand outside the flux of becoming, but rather is a certain kind of response to the flux from within it. The Dionysian artist-philosopher is committed to life as an endless process of reinterpreting, revaluing, transfiguring that finds its goal precisely in the constant "once more" of this process of creation. Such activity does not "correct" reality with Truth, but instead corrects one appearance/reality with another by creating out of the first, affirming it in a movement of idealization, what Nietzsche describes as "deification." Thus Nietzsche makes a psychological distinction between two kinds of the artistic "will to immortalize." This will, he asserts, can find its origin in the "tyrannical" and vengeful will of one who "would like to turn what is most personal, singular, and narrow, the real idiosyncrasy of his suffering, into a binding law and compulsion." Or, it can be an expression of "gratitude and love," a "dithyrambic . . . art of apotheosis" (GS: 329). Rather than asserting mastery, such art affirms; it says "*Yes* to all that is questionable and terrible in existence" (TI: 49).

This distinction between wills makes possible, finally, a clear statement of the difference between the Dionysian artist/philosopher of Nietzsche's later work and the Dionysus of *The Birth of Tragedy*. Consider the passage cited above from the preface to *The Gay Science*. There, truth is experienced as abyss, not as ground. For the philosopher, who needs ground to stand on, preferably ground that is "nowhere," this experience is terrifying and confusing. But in the return from the abyss to the surface, the artist "adores." In *The Birth of Tragedy*, Nietzsche had claimed that one is "comforted" by the spectacle of the hero, by the shining beauty of the Apollonian image of primal suffering. This beauty makes one forget the pain of primal suffering. In the late work, however, Dionysian art celebrates the "once more" by deifying appearance without excluding other appearances, other deifications. Thus, it celebrates the plural, dynamic character of reality. This reality is not a world of *mere* appearance, as if there were some thing or world more real behind the appearance, but of *affirmed* appearance, that is, appearance created out of an affirmative stance toward becoming. In contrast to Nietzsche's first book, this return is not made out of necessity in order to hide from view the terrible truth of Dionysus; it is a return out of love and gratitude for this world.

There is a second crucial difference between the Dionysian of *The Birth of Tragedy* and that of the late work. In his first book, Nietzsche had not freed himself completely from Schopenhauerian pessimism: thus, life is suffering, but metaphysical comfort seduces us to live. He later rejects this pessimism, not by rejecting the idea that life is suffering, but by rethinking suffering.[9] For Schopenhauer, suffering comes from lack, a desire or need one yearns to fulfill. Nietzsche poses an alternative: a "suffering from overfullness." "There are two kinds of sufferers: first those who suffer from *the overfullness of life*—they want a Dionysian art and likewise a tragic view of life, a tragic insight—and then those who suffer from *the impoverishment of life* and seek rest, stillness, calm seas, redemption from themselves" (GS: 328). The vectors of these two kinds of suffering are distinct. The suffering from impoverishment leads one to seek satisfaction, fulfillment, or completion: suffering desires to end desire, it seeks rest. By contrast, suffering from overfullness leads one to desire desire, to desire want; the Dionysian soul "*has*, but *wants* to want and will" (EH: 305). Becoming, therefore, does not mark the end of philosophy or writing, as the goal to which they are the means, but marks instead the love and desire out of which one philosophizes and writes in the first place.

AT THE BOUNDARIES OF PHILOSOPHY

Michel de Certeau has argued that mysticism is less a discourse on God than a "manner of speaking" that follows the "excess" of desire and the rhythm of the dance (1992: 113, 299). Nietzsche's Dionysus, the excess or ecstasy of the "once more," is revealed in a way of writing. Nietzsche does not so much philosophize *about* Dionysus or the eternal joy of becoming; rather, he enacts the Dionysian in writing that performs the ecstatic nonthought, nonexperience of the "once more." At the center of Nietzsche's corpus is *Zarathustra*, a book that Nietzsche describes as "dithyrambic." The excess of the dithyramb is, in a sense, the model for all of Nietzsche's writing, for even his philosophical texts are unusual for their celebration of metaphor, figure, narrative, for their cryptic, fragmentary style, and for their overt, often polemic engagement. They also are in many places interrupted and bounded by nonphilosophical or nonargumentative, nonconceptual writing such as poetry, song, and quasi-autobiographical narrative. These devices help Nietzsche to trace and exceed the boundaries of philosophical thought in his writing.

Experience and Text: Moments from the Life of Philosophy

Nietzsche often invokes and even offers some accounts of what he calls his "elevated states." It appears that Nietzsche during his lifetime did undergo at least one dramatic experience that we might call mystical: the moment, in August of 1881, "6,000 feet beyond man and time," when

---

[9] Because he continues to hold this position on suffering, he sometimes still refers to his position as pessimistic, though he is not consistent on this point.

he first "receives" the thought of eternal recurrence.[10] But whether or not we agree that Nietzsche did have "mystical experiences," it is clear that invoking "tremendous moments" or elevated states plays a crucial role in his writing. These are present in the series of prefaces he wrote in 1886–87, in the heavily stylized, autobiographical *Ecce Homo*, in the closing sections of his later writings, and in his notebooks—that is, generally on the boundaries of his "philosophy." While they do not play an active role "in" Nietzsche's philosophy—as warrants for truth-claims, for example—they do serve as sources for thought and help to define the philosopher: "A philosopher is a human being who constantly experiences, sees, hears, suspects, hopes, and dreams extraordinary things; who is struck by his own thoughts as from outside, as from above and below, as by *his* type of experiences and lightning bolts" (BG: 230).

Nietzsche offers one of the most extended and revealing of these accounts when he describes the experience of writing *Zarathustra*, a time during which, as he tells us, the "Yes-saying pathos *par excellence*, which I call the tragic pathos, was alive in me to the highest degree" (EH: 296). Nietzsche recalls that "Zarathustra overtook me," and that the main idea of the book, eternal recurrence, struck him like lightning (EH: 298).[11] From this, he describes "*my* experience of inspiration."

> If one had the slightest residue of superstition left in one's system, one could hardly reject altogether the idea that one is merely incarnation, merely mouthpiece, merely a medium of overpowering forces. The concept of revelation—in the sense that suddenly, with indescribable certainty and subtlety, something becomes *visible*, audible, something that shakes one to the last depths and throws one down—that merely describes the facts. One hears, one does not seek; one accepts, one does not ask who gives; like lightning, a thought flashes up, with necessity, without hesitation regarding its form—I never had any choice. A rapture whose tremendous tension occasionally discharges itself in a flood of tears—now the pace quickens involuntarily, now it becomes slow; one is altogether beside oneself. . . . Everything happens involuntarily in the highest degree but as in a gale of a feeling of freedom, of absoluteness, of power, of divinity.—The involuntariness of image and metaphor is strangest of all; one no longer has any notion of what is an image or a metaphor: everything offers itself as the nearest, most obvious, simplest expression. It actually seems, to allude to something Zarathustra says, as if the things themselves approached and offered themselves as metaphors. ("Here all things come caressingly to your

[10] See Kaufmann 1974: 323f.

[11] I have already remarked on the difficulty of asserting connections between mystical experience and mystical writing, and I will reassert that here I am interested in identifying those aspects of Nietzsche's "philosophy" that warrant the ascription of mystical writing. Still, it is not completely besides the point to note hints of Nietzsche's own "mystical" experience.

discourse and flatter you; for they want to ride on your back. On every metaphor you ride to every truth. . . . Here the words and word-shrines of all being
open up before you; here all being wishes to become word, all becoming wishes
to learn from you how to speak"). (EH: 300–301)

Nietzsche traces two kinds of boundaries in this passage: between time
and eternity and between writing and experience. The lightning of inspiration is powerful, striking in the flash of an instant, in the "Moment," it
opens one to eternity. The "Moment" for Nietzsche is a brief but deeply
significant event in one's life to which he returns again and again in his
writing. "Life consists of rare individual moments of the highest significance and countless intervals in which at best the phantoms of those moments hover about us" (HH: 189). The Moment is ecstasy, for in the
Moment one is overtaken, stricken—"I never had any choice"—and one
experiences a flowing beyond the boundaries of the self. In a late notebook entry, Nietzsche writes: "Five, six seconds and not more: you suddenly feel the presence of the eternal harmony. . . . You seem to be in
contact with the whole of nature and you say, 'Yes, this is true!' as God,
when he created the world, said 'Yes, this is true, this is good' at the end
of every day" (SW 13: 146).[12]

The Moment is fleeting, yet, in the sense that it contacts all of "nature"
or "world," it is also eternal: both in and out of time, the flashing of
eternity in the present. The first mention of eternal recurrence in *Zarathustra* takes place in a dream in which Zarathustra encounters a gateway
called "Moment," where two paths meet, one going backward into eternity and the other forward (Z: 157–58). As Alan White has argued, eternity in this sense is not the eternity of time stretched out to recur over and
over, not a cosmological recurrence, but "the omnipresence, the ubiquity
of the moment within my earthly life, which is my only life" (1990: 100).
Nietzsche elaborates on this idea in a famous passage from *The Gay Science*, in his first extended reference to eternal recurrence in his published
writing. The reader is asked to imagine being visited by a demon who
tells us that "this life as you now live it and have lived it, you will have
to live once more and innumerable times more." Nietzsche then poses a
question: "Would you not throw yourself down and gnash your teeth
and curse the demon who spoke thus? Or have you once experienced a
tremendous moment when you would have answered him: 'You are a god
and never have I heard anything more divine' " (GS: 273–74).[13] In both
of these dreamlike scenarios, Nietzsche is asking us to attend in a concentrated way to our life; that is, to concentrate our life into a moment.
In particular, he is asking whether we have experienced a "tremendous

---

[12] See also GS: 231 and SW 9: 554.
[13] I shall return to this question in the next chapter.

moment" that can transform a demonic scenario into an occasion for a declaration of divinity. Such moments, he thinks, raise a question for the whole of one's life: can the affirmation of the moment be carried through one's life, and, if so, how? In this sense, they are present at every other moment of life.

Nietzsche's account of inspiration also invokes the boundary between experience and writing, for it blurs the line between Nietzsche's own elevated, inspired state and the ecstatic experiences of the character Zarathustra. Nietzsche borrows images central to the ecstatic songs of joy in *Zarathustra*—lightning, the flood of tears—to describe the inspiration under which he wrote the book.[14] He even writes into this account one of the most clearly mystical passages from *Zarathustra*, where "all being" and the "things themselves" speak through the writer. Numerous boundaries are laid down and exceeded here: between self and not-self—Nietzsche-"overpowering forces," Nietzsche-Zarathustra, Zarathustra-being—and between writing and experience. As he writes about writing *Zarathustra* and about Zarathustra's mystical experience, Nietzsche writes about his own experience of inspired writing. His ecstatic experiences strike in and through his writing.

One will be tempted, however, to invoke another boundary—between body and spirit—in order to point out how Nietzsche also undermines his accounts of ecstatic states. In general, his philosophical writing is strongly characterized by a radical suspicion of intoxication, ecstasy, and mysticism. And this suspicion is clearly present in the passage cited above: Nietzsche qualifies his discussion of inspiration with tortured, ambiguous phrases such as, "If one had the slightest residue of superstition left in one's system, one could hardly reject altogether the idea that one is merely incarnation"; he notes that concepts like "revelation" are merely descriptive; and he will say only that one "seems" to be in contact with the whole of nature. In short, Nietzsche may, in places, describe his experiences in terms that gesture toward the mystical and the divine, but this does not entail that, as a philosopher, he would argue that such experiences are what they "seem" to be. By the same token, however, Nietzsche never in any definitive way reduces his "spiritual" experiences to bodily or material states.[15] He may write that words such as *revelation* only "describe" the experience, but he is far from offering an "explanation" of the experience, especially one that would reduce one's experience to a single, master-interpretation: "It is perhaps just dawning on five or six minds

---

[14] Recall that in the first section of the "Seven Seals," the singer tells of "lightening bolts that say Yes and laugh Yes, soothsaying lightning bolts" (Z: 228).

[15] Eric Blondel argues that "where we might expect a physiological reductionism [Nietzsche deploys] epistemologically a metaphysics of interpretation, whose 'physiological' discourse in reality is merely metaphor" (1991: 219).

that physics, too, is only an interpretation and exegesis of the world . . . and not a world-explanation" (BG: 21).[16] Indeed, in this passage from *Zarathustra*, Nietzsche seems to be pointing to the very moment of creativity, where the critical faculties are suspended, and, insofar as "things themselves" present themselves as metaphor, the world speaks of its plurality.

Suspicion has its place in Nietzsche because experience is always ambiguous. But one should not forget that chronic suspicion of one's own ecstatic and visionary states is far from alien to the mystical life. The greatest mystics have often been exceptionally acute psychological observers and analysts who insisted on the need to examine one's own experiences with great care and realism—they generally did not use any particular experience as a theological warrant, nor did they find the goal of the mystical life in these experiences themselves. As Meister Eckhart indicates, attachment to such experiences, making them the goal of life or desiring them as a way of removing oneself from the everyday, is a temptation to be resisted: "If a man were in rapture like Saint Paul, and knew a sick man who needed some soup from him, I should think it far better if you abandoned rapture for love" (Williams 1990: 136). Though ecstasies and raptures may mark the "tremendous moments" of life, one must know how to give them up, how to live through them and beyond them.

Nietzsche's suspicion is directed not toward experience itself but to the way such experiences reflect and are integrated into one's life. The point of his suspicion is not to reduce ecstatic experiences to physiological causes, but to examine the way of life connected to them: Is it a declining or ascending life, an overfull or needy life, an affirmative or denying life? In the case of the ascending life, suspicion is an ascetic practice, integrating transforming ecstatic experience with the whole of one's life through persistent, methodical, and realistic reflection on that experience. Such reflection must resist the temptation to turn any experience into an idol. For Nietzsche, life strives for expression, language, consciousness and, in doing so, seeks beautiful "word-shrines" for itself; but, for it to "become" and remain alive, it must destroy its shrines with insistent unmasking, a demystifying that reduces shrines to ashes for the sake of rebirth.

Nietzsche's Dionysian wisdom, the "knowledge" that emerges out his "mysticism," is not contained in any particular experience. Rather, it

---

[16] See also GM: 129 and GS: 335–36, where Nietzsche writes: "Do we really want to permit existence to be degraded for us like this—reduced to a mere exercise for a calculator and an indoor diversion for mathematicians? Above all, one should not wish to divest existence of its *rich ambiguity*. . . . Assuming that one estimated the *value* of a piece of music according to how much of it could be counted, calculated, and expressed in formulas: how absurd would such a 'scientific' estimation of music be! What would one have comprehended, understood, grasped ot it? Noething, really nothing of what is 'music' in it!"

manifests itself as a comprehensive awareness, cultivation, and communication of the context or life in which rapturous moments of creativity take place. It is a practical knowledge, a way of life and a way of writing—which Nietzsche calls "philosophy"—by which one continually orients oneself to the real, even though an integral part of that orientation is knowing that the real is always "beyond," not something to be grasped. Nietzsche's elevated states are only moments, flashes in which the real overtakes one on the boundaries of awareness, text, and self.

Wandering and Abandonment: At the Boundaries of Time and Culture

For Nietzsche, another way of saying that the philosophical life is a life of writing is to say that it is a life of wandering. The philosopher is a "wanderer": "restlessly and aimlessly on his way as if in a desert" (HH: 8); "homeless" (GS: 338); one of the "argonauts of the ideal" (GS: 346); and one of "the most spiritual human beings . . . [who] find their happiness . . . in the labyrinth" (TI: 140).[17] As wanderer, the philosopher is one who occupies many different points of view or perspectives, and who experiments with different ways of life. Wandering, then, as a process and as a practice, is a focal point for considering Nietzsche's complex, deeply ambiguous vision of the relation of the philosopher to his or her time and culture.

Consider the narrative of sickness and convalescence that Nietzsche relates in numerous places, particularly in the preface to *Human, All too Human*. It tells a "passionate history of the soul," a tale of wandering through different conceptions of the philosophical life and different values. On this journey, Nietzsche experiences both sickness and health. Together, these experiences enable him to overcome the sickness of "his time." In this sense, wandering refers to the exploration of human life and culture from different perspectives—different bodies and different lives. The knowledge gained thereby enables the philosopher to develop a comprehensive and masterful soul, to take a certain kind of metaperspective and rank human experiences and types. All this is necessary for the development of the genuine philosopher, one who can create and give new values and so lay the foundation for a new, healthy culture. On this account, Nietzsche's wanderings (he describes his early works as "travel books") take the shape of a journey, one with many detours, but, nonetheless, one with a definite beginning and end. Thus, in *Beyond Good and Evil*, the "beyond" of the book's title might indicate a future culture and the future philosophers who will usher in this new stage of human history.

---

[17] Cf. de Certeau: "He or she is a mystic who cannot stop walking and, with the certainty of what is lacking, knows of every place and object that it is not that; one cannot stay there nor be content with that" (1992: 14, 299). See also Mark Taylor 1984: 149–57.

It is the task of the philosopher to find worthy companions with whom to turn away from the decadence of the present and begin the task of imagining and embodying the future.

There is, however, another vision of philosophical wandering traced in Nietzsche's texts. When Nietzsche invokes Dionysus as the "tempter god" and the philosopher as the *Versucher*, the tempter-attempter, who "lures" many away from the herd, another kind of "beyond" beckons, one in tension with the first. Dionysus tempts the philosopher to a departure, a detachment, that is not simply the beginning of a journey destined to discover a new culture in a new time, but is a wandering, attempting, or searching that is its own end.

At the end of the fifth book of *The Gay Science*, Nietzsche writes of being "homeless" and departing from the shores of the present and familiar into uncharted waters, "new seas." He casts himself and his hoped-for companions as the "argonauts of the new ideal" who, by means of a "great health," distance themselves from their "time" in undertaking this search (GS: 342–43). This great health, however, is not something that one simply attains, as a means to an end, or as the end itself, for it is something that "one does not merely have but also acquires continually, and must acquire because one gives it up again and again, and must give it up" (GS: 346). Nietzsche complicates the search for the new ideal, as I already suggested with respect to the *Genealogy*, by demanding the continual departure from the established and secure for the passion of the new and unknown. This is a "strange" ideal that beckons Nietzsche and his companions, always running ahead, luring them to announce and renounce the great health. The constant departures and reversals of Nietzsche's writing indicate, in fact, that the ideal is "discovered" precisely in never being fully achieved, in the constant renewal of the passion that finds joy and strength in the attempt, in the experiment. The ideal, then, is not any particular creation or achievement, not a future that is ever "present," but rather a capacity of openness or responsiveness to the future and the unknown. To wander, as Nietzsche notes as a prelude to the discussion of the great health, is not to journey, but to dance (GS: 346; HH: 204). The philosopher, on this reading, is not one to institute or rule a new culture, but a figure of the boundaries, an "untimely" figure of instability, transgression, creation, writing against the ideas and values of his time. "Whenever a great thinker wants to make of himself a binding institution for future mankind, one may be certain that he is past the peak of his powers and is very weary, very close to the setting of his sun" (D: 216; GS: 131).

Nietzsche's is a struggle against the complacency, even the death, of the "common," which constitutes culture. The inertia toward the common is manifested in the idealism of philosophy that always reduces the strange to the familiar, and in language, which is only possible, on Nietzsche's account, on the basis of common experience. Language and consciousness on this view do "not really belong to man's individual existence but rather to his social or herd nature." Thus, "given the best will in the world to understand ourselves as individually as possible, 'to know ourselves,' each of us will always succeed in becoming conscious only of what is not individual but average" (GS: 299). Culture and language—even consciousness itself—therefore depend on and reinforce commonality while devaluing, and even counting as "evil," experiences that are genuinely individual. Nietzsche seeks to disrupt "the common," attempting himself and tempting others to cultivate rare elevated states of creativity and lives of affirmation. As I have argued, this requires an ascetic's disciplined resistance to the "natural" tendency of the herd. "One must invoke tremendous counter-forces in order to cross this natural, all too natural *progressus in simile*, the continual development of man toward the similar, ordinary, average, herdlike—common!" (BG: 217).

There is a constant tension in Nietzsche's thinking, therefore, between the timeliness of his analysis—both its orientation to a future and its sense of the present as a turning point in history—and the timeless joy of eternity that continually overtakes him. Writing both within and without time, Nietzsche writes both for and against culture. He seeks a future for Western culture, yet he pursues a philosophical practice that seeks to make the familiar strange, resisting habit in an effort to inspire creative participation in becoming. This disruption is never stable or final, for Nietzsche must always return to words and concepts. To live beyond the ascetic ideal is therefore to hold to the boundaries of culture and meaning, on the verge of meaninglessness or nihilism. Nietzsche finds life in the act of giving meaning and striving for goals, but he finds a certain death in being imprisoned by that which he gives and creates. If one tries to maintain meaning, to rest in stability, one is no longer living in the striving, growing sense that Nietzsche values as becoming; if one sacrifices that which one loves and values—that which is meaningful, one's own "great health"—then the process of bestowing meaning can begin again. The philosopher must be a "tragic artist" who manifests "the will to life rejoicing in its own inexhaustibility through the sacrifice of its highest types" (TI: 120). Or, as Nietzsche writes, in a poem entitled *Ecce Homo*: "I consume myself, and glow" (GS: 67). While the philosopher as value giver cultivates the most comprehensive perspective, the philosopher as tragic artist and abysmal thinker finds power in the eternal joy of becoming.

Thinking the Abyss, Writing Unsaying

"Our true experiences are not garrulous. They could not communicate themselves if they wanted to, they lack words. We have already grown beyond what we have words for" (TI: 92). The problem of communication reverberates through all Nietzsche's writing: he despairs over his failure to make himself heard by his contemporaries, yet he insists on silence, masks, secrets, and the inability of language to communicate elevated states. Communication, for Nietzsche, is not futile, but it always conceals as much as it reveals. In his drama of communication, Nietzsche performs a self trying to maintain its connection with the Dionysian "beyond." The reader is lured by this performance, continually forced back to the boundaries of concept, argument, perspective, forced to think again, to think "once more." Nietzsche describes his writing as having "a knack for seeking out fellow-rhapsodizers and for luring them on to new secret paths and dancing places" (BT: 19). He seeks to communicate the joy of becoming by transfiguring the dancing of the Dionysian ecstatic into the dancing of the pen (TI: 75).

This dance communicates as a kind of apophatic writing. Conceptually and graphically, with suspicion, shifting perspective, and aphorism, Nietzsche surrounds his writing with silence and space. In the crossing of his affirmations and his demystifying unmaskings, in the movement from one aphorism to the next, he points us to something other than what is said. The profound man is one who "instinctively needs speech for silence and for burial in silence and who is inexhaustible in his evasion of communication" (BG: 51). To hold onto the experience of eternal joy that marks Nietzsche's most elevated states, to hope that such states are the "truth" or the "end" of life is for Nietzsche just one more consolation and falsification. Nonetheless, as I argued above, it is a mistake to assume that he simply wants us to confront the bland, human, all too human "reality" of ordinary life. Instead, these moments in Nietzsche's writing resist one another, performing a kind of "unsaying" that continually brings the reader back to the movement of life—its cycle of joy and suffering, its becoming. Like the ascetic, as Geoffrey Harpham puts it, this writing on the boundaries addresses the problem of "how to be alive to the spirit and dead to the world at the same time. In other words, how to be both living and coherent" (1987: 16).

There are some rather obvious modes of unsaying in Nietzsche's texts. In the final section of both *The Gay Science* and *Beyond Good and Evil*, Nietzsche looks back on what he has written—in one case with humor, in the other sorrow—to take leave of the ideas he has lived through in the text. Having been "said," that is written, "immortalized," Nietzsche says that they are on the verge of losing their life. So, he takes his departure from them, continues his wandering. In each case, Nietzsche leaves his philosophical writing and moves to poetry and song, repeating, in a different register, the movement, at the end of Book Three of *Zarathustra*, from "abysmal thought" to joyous song. Nietzsche abandons philosophy for affirming song, but it is only through his philosophy that he gets to that point.

Nietzsche also writes unsaying within his philosophical texts, especially with respect to the problem of (the impossibility of) self-knowledge. Dionysian self-knowledge is "knowledge" of the self as strange to itself, divided from itself in a way that disrupts Socratic self-knowledge in ecstatic awareness and abandonment of love, value, ideal.[18] If one attempts to know oneself as a persisting entity or as a soul, one only becomes "entangled in the snares of grammar," for the stabilizing force of language, reason, and thought continually takes us away from that which is most ourselves. Knowing oneself as becoming, one knows oneself as already having become "something else." Self-knowledge, therefore, insofar as it can be mediated by language at all, requires an apophatic subversion of language. What Nietzsche's unsaying tries to communicate are not concepts, but rather the elusive experience of the emergence of language and thought from the chaos of becoming, the moment and the power of creation.[19] In this experience, one finds oneself—over and over—just as often as one loses oneself.

MYSTICISM AND METAPHOR: CONTESTING SPIRIT

> Upward flies our sense: thus it is a parable of our body, a parable of elevation. . . . Thus the body goes through history, becoming and fighting. And the spirit—what is that to the body? The herald of its fights and victories, companion and echo. . . . Watch for every hour, my brothers, in which our spirit wants to speak in parables: there lies the origin of your virtue. There your body is elevated and resurrected; with its rapture it delights the spirit so that it turns creator and esteemer and lover and benefactor of all things. (Z: 75–76)

[18] In a poem from the series that opens *The Gay Science*, entitled, "The Solitary," Nietzsche writes: "Even to lead myself is not my speed / I love to lose myself for a good while, / Like animals in forests and the sea, / To sit and think on some abandoned isle, / And lure myself back home from far away, / Seducing myself to come back to me (GS: 53–54).

[19] And such experiences are not only not communicable to others, but even to oneself. In the preface to GM, Nietzsche seems to echo Emerson's "Experience." Emerson's essay begins, "Where do we find ourselves?" and one of its central themes is the elusiveness of "reality," the difficulty of grasping and feeling the "sharp peaks and edges of truth." Nietzsche begins the preface to the *Genealogy* with what could well be taken for a reply to Emerson: "We are unknown to ourselves, we men of knowledge—and with good reason. We have never sought ourselves—how could it happen that we should ever *find* ourselves?" (GM: 15). As in Emerson, the theme here is experience, the experience of "we knowers," one that knowers find difficult to grasp because they are always too immersed in themselves—which really means too far outside of themselves, "away from home"—to see what is happening to them and around them. As knowers, then, it is precisely "our" experience, "ourselves" that we find most elusive; we are "necessarily strangers to ourselves."

On Reading and Writing

In his reading of *Walden*, Stanley Cavell shows Thoreau reading and writing as he lives, deliberately. Cavell takes note of the way that Thoreau tests and contests words and syntax as a way of attending to the conditions of his words, unsaying them, as it were, in order to make them speak. "We must be reborn again in order to speak" (Cavell 1981: 15). Thoreau's mysticism, for Cavell, is found not primarily in the moments of absorptive ecstasy that Thoreau describes, but in the way all experiences of the world are shaped through the incessant demand to make life come alive in each moment—to make real, to realize the real. In fact, the "experiences" of ecstatic absorption, Thoreau writes, function as figures for something he tries to bring to every moment of life in the process of finding oneself in words and wording forth the world. That is, in reading and writing Thoreau endeavors to find the way each word he reads or writes links him, here and now, to the world and so to his life. "To discover what is being said to us, as to discover what we are saying, is to discover the precise location from which it is said; to understand why it is said from just there, and at that time" (Cavell 1981: 64).

But to be reborn to words and world also means to die to old words and old meanings. Reading and speaking our conditions, our words, we find ourselves "face to face to a fact." At the same time, the flow of words, the succession of time is always carrying us away from that present (Cavell 1981: 63): it is lost just as it is found and so must always be recovered, reinhabited. As Cavell reads it, Thoreau's "experiment" ("for the present was my next experiment of this kind") requires a constant turning, a constant disinvestment of the past, a dying to the past, as a precondition to rebirth. "It is through words that words are to be overcome. (Silence may only be the tying of the tongue, not relinquishing words, but gagging on them. True silence is the untying of the tongue, letting its words go)" (1981: 44). Writing relinquishes words, in a surrender that is at the same time a liberation. "Not till we are lost, in other words, not till we have lost the world do we begin to find ourselves, and realize where we are and the infinite extent of our relations" (1981: 50). In contrast to religious or philosophical (skeptical) repudiations of this condition, Thoreau accepts the loss of the world, and so, disinvesting himself of the past, acknowledging its otherness, is able to acknowledge the world that is always newly dawning (Cavell 1988: 172; 1989: 84). It is only in this loss that one finds life, because it is only in this loss that one opens oneself for new words, a new place of inhabitation. Always departing, "the writer is always coming to us from a sense of loss" (1981: 51).

Departing, the writer is always also turning back toward the world and the dawn: as Thoreau writes, the world is always "revealing itself by turns"; that is, by turnings of speech, tropes. This brings us to Emerson and his dismissal of a "paltry empiricism" (Emerson 1982: 310) and mere "aesthetics" in favor of a grand empiricism, "a science of the real" (1982: 265). Cavell notes that with this distinction between empiricisms, Emerson is warning us to be careful about what we count as experience. The experience that Emerson wants us to take seriously is the "seeing" or the "intuition" of the poetic imagination, for in such seeing we are most intimate with the world, sharing in its reality. Emerson wants "every touch of nature [to] thrill" (1982: 260), and it is the poet, "one step nearer the world," reading and writing the world, who has the power to receive this thrill and impart it by releasing it for all of us. Thus the experience upon which Emerson models the science of the real is not the experience of detached observation, but the experience of love, in which poet and nature animate one another: "The simplest words,—we do not know what they mean except when we love and aspire" (Cavell 1988: 24).

Poetry, Cavell argues, is the means by which we find and create the words to release and realize our feelings and so come to know ourselves. Poetry gives voice to humanity by reaching into the unknown in order to push and expand its language.[20] On this reading, one can say that, for Emerson, in the act of placing oneself in relation to the real, through the transition from intuition to tuition, the poet brings the words and world to life in mystical participation. Emerson distinguishes between the poet and the mystic, but only to make the distinction between living and dead religion. The poet lives in the turning and troping of language, but the mystic, insofar as he or she is dependent on the dogmas of the tradition to the point where the words no longer live, "nails a symbol to one sense, which was a true sense for a moment, but soon becomes old and false" (Emerson 1982: 279).[21] One should not repeat words senselessly for the sake of tradition, but neither should one simply imitate the words of the great poet. At best these are "provocations," which can only spur one to write/voice one's own world in reading it. "Every man is so far a poet as to be susceptible of these enhancements of nature" (Emerson 1982: 267). The life is not in the word itself, but in the process, the transition, of bringing the word to speech. In the next instant, the same word will not have the same life. What is crucial is not that which the words name or represent, but how reading and writing in the broadest sense enact our relationship to reality.

[20] In an early essay on acknowledgment, Cavell (1976) suggests that we might think about God not in the Freudian manner, as a kind of childish fear, but instead, as the sense of the inarticulate unknown from which words and meanings emerge. But then the movement toward God would not be finished in confronting the fact that there is an unknown, but in the effort to bring the unknown to words, not words that grasp, but words that release.

[21] This is not a simple rejection of all symbols because they are old. In "The Poet," Emerson writes, "We are far from having exhausted the significance of the few symobls we use. We can come to use them yet with a terrible simplicity" (1982: 269).

Body as Metaphor

The boundaries that separate the poet, the mystic and the Nietzschean philosopher are impossible to stabilize, because the effect of Nietzsche's writing is to constantly exceed such boundaries. It is not insignificant that it is in a speech entitled "Reading and Writing" that Zarathustra declares: "Now I am light, now I fly, now I see myself beneath myself, now a god dances through me" (Z: 41). The Nietzschean philosopher renounces the mastery of consciousness in the performance of becoming and body. This is not to say that he or she forsakes consciousness, for philosophy on this view is a discipline of consciousness and language. It is a discipline, however, that mortifies the philosophical temptation—one might argue that it is the philosophical imperative—to stabilize and hold language in the permanence of conceptualization. This is a life-giving mortification, for the resistance to concept inspires and liberates language. The Nietzschean philosopher turns to metaphor as a means of wandering beyond received meanings and reawakening, inspiriting word, thought, and life.

Paul Ricoeur has written that "poetic language alone restores to us that participation in or belonging to an order of things which precedes our capacity to oppose ourselves to things taken as objects opposed to a subject" (1980: 101).[22] Eric Blondel follows Ricoeur's claim that metaphor is fundamental to the ability of poetic language to redescribe reality. Metaphor, he writes, "is like a world made dynamic by a play of attraction and repulsion that continually creates interaction and intersection among different movements . . . without this play ever coming to rest in an absolute knowledge that would reabsorb all the tensions" (1991: 245). From this perspective, Blondel offers the most incisive and comprehensive of the many treatments of metaphor in Nietzsche's thought.[23] He argues that

[22] Charles Winquist gives the definition of poesis a slightly different, but closely related, spin: "Poesis is a refiguring of discourse to make space for the incorrigibility of the other within discourse" (1995: 138).

[23] The place of metaphor in Nietzsche's thought has drawn much attention, particularly in poststructuralist thinkers fixated on Nietzsche's early essay, "On Truth and Lie in an Extramoral Sense," with its famous passage that has generally been interpreted as accomplishing the reduction of concept to metaphor. Though this essay is crucial for Nietzsche's concept of metaphor, and its relation to philosophy, it is too easily assumed that this essay represents Nietzsche's mature position. See, for example, Kofman 1993 and Barker 178, 180. Blondel does not depend on this essay to the extent that others do. This is significant, because with his emphasis on the metaphor of body, I think Blondel (1991) helps show us why Nietzsche is closer to the Cavellian perspective on language, metaphor, and reality than to the Sausserian vision of language that posits a completely arbitrary relation between language and the world, such that the system of language operates completely without any reference to reality. As Nietzsche suggests through Zarathustra, in the turning of metaphor we do see language related to reality: "Here all being wishes to become word, all becoming wishes to learn from

metaphor for Nietzsche is the paradigm of interpretation and that "body" is Nietzsche's fundamental metaphor. Through this metaphor, Nietzsche's hermeneutics resist the conceptual reductionisms of both materialism and idealism: "body" is not a concept that serves as a physiological foundation for Nietzsche's thought, but is a way of designating the irreducible plurality of drives that themselves are already interpretations (1991: 219). "Body" is the "intermediary space between the absolute plural of the world's chaos and the absolute simplification of intellect" serving as a scheme of interpretation, the "metaphorical imagination" (1991: 207, 245–47). Metaphor and concept represent different degrees of the simplification of, or, better, orientation to chaotic becoming. They are, however, fundamentally different types of simplification: where concept is oriented to viewing the world as an ordered unity, metaphor can be utilized for an "interrogative pluralization," which allows different perspectives, different aspects of becoming to be examined without the pressure toward unifying reduction exerted by the concept.

Through metaphor, one is able to indicate and perform becoming without arresting it conceptually in any final way—and without sacrificing the positivity of perspective. Metaphor enables one to say, at the same time, that something both "is" and "is not"; it brings together and holds in tension the ordinary and the extraordinary (1991: 247). Where Ricoeur decisively distinguishes metaphor from concept, Nietzsche, without reducing one to the other, does not; he does not, in other words, write poetry instead of philosophy—he writes conceptual thought constantly dissolving in apophasis and turning back to metaphor, thus philosophy constantly beside itself, opening itself to the "heterogeneity of the 'body' " (Blondel 1991: 308): ecstatic philosophy.

Metaphor, in other words, enacts immanent transcendence. Figuring and transfiguring self and world, one points beyond this particular configuration of things and ideas: the "beyond" is the "once again" of the ever-shifting surface of life. Any particular metaphor offers a new, particular perspective on something familiar, but in doing so it also inscribes or acknowledges this "beyond." For Nietzsche, "body" is a metaphor that gathers and focuses the chaotic becoming of the world, and "spirit" is a metaphor for the shining, transfigured power of the body. These considerations allow a more refined grasp of Nietzsche's ideas on power and self-overcoming. Self-overcoming involves a kind of mastery over oneself. But when linked with metaphor, this Nietzschean mastery contrasts sharply with the Socratic mastery of consciousness. The mastery made possible

---

you how to speak" (EH: 301). This is not to posit a one to one correspondence between words and things, for it is precisely through the emphasis on metaphor that we see that for Nietzsche, as for Cavell, the reference, or the speaking of the world, is fleeting and momentary, taking place in the movement of words and not in the words themselves.

by metaphorically based thinking is one that organizes and spiritualizes without unifying or totalizing (Schrift 1990: 94). Metaphorically based thinking is fundamentally plural; it is without the foundational concept or "transcendental signified" that would bring a halt to the play of word and world. Nietzsche's self-overcoming therefore means, first of all, the power to resist the temptations to rest and unity. It demands the organization and beautification of the self, it demands the enhancement of the self, where to enhance means to enliven, which means to create and re-create, lose and regain the great health. Emerson suggests—as Nietzsche would have known—that power resides in the transitions or turnings that participate with becoming. If metaphor—between chaos and stasis—enacts these transitions, then the body as metaphor is the inspirited, transfigured body: the body turning, receiving, and speaking; not the static, mute body of naturalism but the body that powers the imagination and is, in turn, empowered by it. Spiritualization, as transfiguration, is a process in which the body's reception of the world becomes refined in metaphorical renewal, empowering the body in its relations with the world, others, and itself.

Metaphor and Mysticism: Desiring the World

As the moment of transition and excess on the boundaries of consciousness and conceptualization, metaphor is the means by which Nietzsche writes his passion for the real. In and through metaphor, Nietzsche's writing aims not at a conceptual grasp of becoming, but at the dance that participates with it. "On every metaphor you ride to every truth. . . . Here the words and word-shrines of all being open up before you; here all being wishes to become word, all becoming wishes to learn from you how to speak" (EH: 301). In the moment of transition from being to word, in a writing of and on the boundary, Nietzsche, like Zarathustra, finds eternity and divinity.

Nietzsche's is a mysticism of metaphor. Like Zarathustra, like Dionysus, Nietzsche's writing "lure[s] many away from the herd" (Z: 23); as the errant voice of ecstasy and abandonment, a voice opens self and culture to new thoughts and new words. But it is necessary to take care with terms such as *abandonment* and *ecstasy*, for they refer first of all not to a swooning surrender of all one's faculties, but rather to a disciplined, deliberate practice of writing. Again, the point is not whether or not Nietzsche had dramatic mystical experiences, but it is the way he inscribes becoming into his texts, practicing an ecstatic philosophy by which he opens himself and the reader to a new responsiveness.

Carl Raschke points to Nietzsche's invocation of the mask and notes that "in Greek drama the mask, or disguise, is the 'sacramental' element that renders the theatrical—that which is 'envisioned'—*religious*. It is religious, because it is 'mimetic' not of the things of the everyday world, but of the 'beings of the other world,' beings 'holy' and 'horrific' " (1996: 179). Raschke is right to make these connections between mimesis, religion, and Nietzsche's conception of tragedy: Nietzsche's writing is a dramatic performance of/at the boundaries of thought, body, spirit. However, this beyond is not the beyond of another world, but of the "holy" and "horrific" faces, the extraordinary faces, of this world. Nietzsche's writing seeks to renew all things by resisting the idealistic need for the familiar and common and by seeking out the strange and extraordinary—new conjunctions and relations, new differences that make the familiar new. This is a wandering writing, which finds, in each of its returns, that "what is nearest and everyday here speaks of unheard of things" (EH: 305).

> It seems to him as if his eyes are only now open to what is close at hand. He is astonished and sits silent: where had he been? These near and nearest things [*Diese nahen und nächsten Dinge*]: how changed they seem! what bloom and magic they have acquired! He looks back gratefully—grateful to his wandering, to his hardness and self-alienation, to his viewing of far distances and bird-like flights in cold heights. What a good thing he had not always stated "at home," stayed "under his own roof" like a delicate apathetic loafer! He had been beside himself: no doubt of that. (HH: 8)

I will have occasion, below, to ask whether Nietzsche gives adequate emphasis to this return. For now it is enough to assert that in a fully affirmative mystical writing there is always return; in the return, the ordinary is transfigured, the extraordinary or the "magical" in the ordinary is reawakened. This extraordinary experience of the everyday is a way of being "faithful to the earth." This is mysticism as a continual reconnecting or rebinding with the reality of things in a cycle of departure, wandering, and return.

Chapter Six

NIETZSCHE'S AFFIRMATION:
A PASSION FOR THE REAL

> I Zarathustra, the advocate of life, the advocate of suffering, the
> advocate of the circle.
> (Nietzsche, *Thus Spake Zarathustra*)

> A full and powerful soul not only copes with painful, even terrible
> losses, deprivations, robberies, insults; it emerges from such hells
> with a greater fullness and powerfulness; and, most essential of all,
> with a new increase in the blissfulness of love.
> (Nietzsche, *The Will to Power*)

SUFFERING AND AFFIRMATION

The Meaning of Suffering

THROUGHOUT HIS LIFE, Nietzsche remained wedded to the
Schopenhauerian idea that suffering was constitutive of the
human condition. As he puts it in *Twilight of the Idols*, "all becoming and growing . . . postulates pain" (TI: 120). Yet, Nietzschean affirmation takes shape in the resistance to Schopenhauer's conclusion that
the denial of life is the ultimate human response to this condition and that
such denial—exemplified in the saint—is definitive of holiness. Nietzsche
did not share Schopenhauer's estimation of the Christian saint, but he
nevertheless remained fascinated with the way that the religious virtuoso
used renunciation, intoxication, and suffering to forge happiness and
power; and he continued to believe that spiritual insight and power were
intimately linked to human suffering. It is not surprising, therefore, that
the Schopenhauerian saint and the Nietzschean philosopher are closely
related. But where the saint finds in suffering both the reason and, ultimately (the saint imagines), the power to deny life, the Nietzschean philosopher affirms by forging a new orientation to the suffering implicated in
all human life.

Epigraphs: Nietzsche, Z: 215; WP: 532.

One reason Nietzsche rejects Schopenhauerian denial is simply that he believed such denial to be impossible: "denial" does not deny, it defers, it spiritualizes. But there is another, ultimately more interesting, reason. To understand precisely how Nietzsche's philosophy takes shape in response to Schopenhauer, it is not enough to see how he seeks to affirm life instead of denying it; one must also see how he twists himself away from Schopenhauer's approach by rethinking the significance of suffering for human life. For Nietzsche, suffering continues to be constitutive of human life, but he no longer sees suffering as a problem to be overcome or a condition to be transcended.

I have argued that we must be careful in considering what exactly Nietzsche means in the *Genealogy*, when, upon exposing the life-denial of the ascetic ideal, he asks: "Where is the opposing will that might express an opposing ideal?. . . Where is the other 'one goal'?" (GM: 146). In the essay on the ascetic ideal, Nietzsche equates, at least for adherents of the ascetic ideal, the meaning of suffering with the meaning of life: life becomes meaningful when such human beings have an answer to the question: "Why do I suffer?" (GM: 162). We must be careful in considering Nietzsche's alternative to this view because he never directly answers the question of this other ideal or will; at the end of the book, he seems only to have succeeded in reimmersing himself in the new problem of the meaning of the self-overcoming of the will to truth. He leaves us with questions and a search, not a solution. This in itself, I think, is a kind of answer: the search itself as a new ideal. But, of course, this is not simply a new ideal, it is a new *kind* of ideal. Where the ascetic ideal involves a solution to suffering as the meaning of life, Nietzsche suggests the ideal of a search, which demands more questions and a reimmersion in suffering life. Nietzsche does not offer an alternative to the ascetic ideal as much as he twists away from viewing suffering as a "problem."

The ascetic ideal gives meaning to life by answering the question, Why do we suffer? On this view, the ideal human life is defined in relation to suffering. For precisely this reason, however, Nietzsche considers the ascetic ideal to be essentially reactive: human beings find meaning in life only in reaction to the way in which life injures them. Suffering, life itself, then becomes a problem that one must solve in order to live. From the genealogical perspective, the hope for a final liberation from suffering is ultimately the expression of exhaustion, the nihilistic hope of an impoverished life able to will only nothingness, life *without* suffering. Like the nobles at the beginning of the *Genealogy*, Nietzsche's view of suffering is active: suffering results inevitably from the engagement with life; however, it does not determine the relation between self and life. The question "Why do we suffer?" therefore does not hold such a central place in the noble conception of life and its meaning—the noble does not need an answer to the question of suffering in order to find meaning in life.[1] Where adherents of the ascetic ideal seek a life different from the suffering life of the human condition, specifically the cessation of desire in "rest, stillness, calm seas," the noble desires to continue desiring, it "*wants* to want and will" (EH: 305) even to the point of desiring the worst of the human condition. In short, the noble affirms the return, not the cessation of desire, and so the return of suffering.

The problem of suffering often holds a key place in both the stories and the systematic thought of different religious traditions. In fact, religion is often characterized in terms of the overcoming of suffering in healing or salvation. In Christian intellectual circles, the problem of suffering is articulated in the theological enterprise of theodicy. For close to two millennia, Christian thinkers have grappled with the question of why God—as omnipotent and loving—allows evil and suffering. For many it follows that evil and suffering must be necessary for some greater purpose of God's. John Hick, for example, argues that it is only through a historical process of struggle with good and evil in freedom that human beings can achieve genuine moral goodness; human beings would not be as good if God had created them morally perfect (1981: 44). Kenneth Surin describes the project of theodicy more generally as "the attempt to provide a teleology of evil and suffering, to slot occurrences of evil and suffering into a scheme of things consonant with the essentially rational workings of divine providence" (1987: 53). Theodicy is an attempt, then, to determine the economy of evil and suffering.

Even in cases where one is not justifying God, or in defending the "essentially rational workings of divine providence," the term *theodicy* is often used, beyond the strictly Christian context, to describe efforts like Nietzsche's to provide a conceptual framework for assessing the significance of suffering and evil. It is in this sense that some commentators have construed Nietzsche's project along the lines of theodicy.[2] Nietzsche himself actually uses the word *theodicy* on occasion. "The pessimism of

---

[1] I am indebted to John Lysaker's comments on this chapter for impressing upon me the importance of the active-reactive distinction for understanding Nietzsche's, and the noble's, perspective on suffering.

[2] Kathleen Higgens argues that the doctrine of eternal recurrence provides a theodicy to the extent that it "provides a framework in which tragic events and moral atrocities take their place beside life's lighter contents, a framework in which the overall significance of such horrors can be assessed" (1987: 198). Rosset compares Nietzsche to Leibniz, arguing that Nietzsche goes beyond Leibnizian theodicy with an affirmation not of God, but of "chance," an affirmation, in other words, of the way of the cosmos (1993: 27). Similarly, Deleuze (1983) writes of a "cosmodicy," thereby distinguishing Nietzsche's project from theodicy's justification of God yet drawing the parallel that Nietzsche remains concerned to demonstrate the "justice" of the cosmos.

strength ends in a theodicy, i.e. in an absolute affirmation of the world. . . . [It leads] to the conception of this world as the actually achieved highest possible ideal" (WP: 527). But, for at least one important reason, it is misleading to think of Nietzsche's project in terms of theodicy: theodicy, like few other theological projects or religious practices, exemplifies the reactive potential of Christianity. As in Schopenhauer, most theodicies begin with the presumption that suffering is a problem to be solved, a problem that touches the deepest meaning of God and of life. Suffering, as Nietzsche saw so well, can therefore easily become the point of departure for one's understanding of and relationship to God— God as that which somehow redeems or helps us overcome suffering. Such a God emerges from a lack, from the need to find an answer to suffering.

The conception of God as an answer to suffering is reactive in the deepest sense. When, in the first essay of the *Genealogy*, Nietzsche contrasts active and reactive modes of valuing as characteristic of strong and weak forms of life, he narrates a process whereby the priestly class uses the power of reactivity to transmute their weakness into an insidious strength, which defeats the nobles in a revaluation of values. The weak accomplish this revaluation by locating the source of value beyond themselves and beyond humanity, in the metaphysical will of God. With this power, then, as Nietzsche writes in the third essay, the priest not only succeeds in mastering the strong, but seeks also to master life itself. Reactivity, in short, powers the metaphysics of mastery. Theodicy reflects this drive to absolute mastery, not only in the insistence on the omnipotence of God, not only in its assumption that human consciousness should be able to comprehend the workings of this omnipotence, but also in its deep need for all suffering to have a purpose or reward, thus to be cashed out in a divine economy.

It should be noted that in the passages where Nietzsche invokes theodicy, he is describing attitudes—pessimism of strength and tragic profundity—that "end" in a "theodicy." That is, Nietzschean "theodicy" is a consequence, or an expression, of a more a fundamental attitude or disposition: the "conception of the world" *follows* the affirmation, it is not a means *to* affirmation. Nietzsche's theodicy is less an attempt to assert ("discover") the metaphysical meaning of suffering and life than another way of saying "Yes" to life.[3] To understand Nietzsche's affirmation, attention must be directed to something other than the reactivity of the effort

---

[3] One might make the same point about certain Christian theodicies, that they are expressions of faith, of "faith seeking understanding," and not attempts to judge or define God outside the circle of faith. Often, however, this boundary is not recognized and theodicy becomes a general philosophical problem. The reactivity of theodicy reflects, as I said, the reactive *potential* of Christianity.

to determine the meaning or the economy of suffering. This suggests, as my work in Chapter 1 has anticipated, that the "new ideal" Nietzsche hints at in the *Genealogy* is far more than a new answer or a new meaning for suffering. While I do think that in some significant sense Nietzsche finds new meaning in suffering, he does so only against the background of an affirmation that embraces not just the meaning, but also the meaninglessness of suffering. Nietzsche's new ideal, I will argue, is a new way of practicing suffering as a response to the real.

At this point, the series of themes I have traced in the book so far come together to make possible a final approach to affirmation. Nietzsche's asceticism is not the life-denying asceticism of the ascetic ideal, suffering practiced for the sake of ending all suffering, but a practice of opening oneself to the conflicting, painful reality of life and world in active engagement with them. This asceticism recognizes and affirms the power of suffering in the creation of spirit; it is a practice of suffering. The mystical element of Nietzsche's thought offers a different perspective on the practice of suffering, yet is intimately linked to his asceticism. As a mysticism of metaphor, Nietzsche's is a practice of writing and thinking in which he cultivates the openness to, even the participation with, becoming. Rather than metaphysical mastery, Nietzsche as writer practices a responsiveness to the mystery and the power of the world—or, as I have put it, a passion for the real, passion in the sense of strong desire, and in the sense of the pain of submission to the real. Only with such passion is the creation of spirit possible: in Nietzsche's ascetic/mystical practice of transfiguration, suffering leads to joy, abysmal thought and bodily pain are transfigured into affirmative spirit.

Dionysus versus the Crucified

It is not by chance that I use the word *passion* in this context. For those attuned to the word's Christian resonance it may seem out of place, especially given Nietzsche's own comparison between "Dionysus" and "the Crucified." Nietzsche concludes *Ecce Homo*, written only months before his breakdown, with a question and a contrast: "Have I been understood?—*Dionysus versus the Crucified*." He elaborates in a notebook entry from this period.

> Dionysus versus the "Crucified": there you have the antithesis. It is *not* a difference in regard to their martyrdom—it is a difference in the meaning of it. Life itself, its eternal fruitfulness and recurrence, creates torment, destruction, the will to annihilation. In the other case, suffering—the "Crucified as the innocent one"—counts as an objection to this life, as a formula for its condemnation.—One will see that the problem is that of the meaning of suffering: whether a Christian meaning or a tragic meaning. In the former case, it is supposed to be

the path to a holy existence; in the latter case, *being is counted as holy enough* to justify even a monstrous amount of suffering. The tragic man affirms even the harshest suffering: he is sufficiently strong, rich, and capable of deifying to do so. . . . The god on the cross is a curse on life, a signpost to seek redemption from life; Dionysus cut to pieces is a *promise* of life: it will be eternally reborn and return home again from destruction. (SW 13: 265–67)

Dionysus and the Crucified: martyrs, sufferers, gods—but, for Nietzsche, their trials mean different things. "The Crucified," for Nietzsche, represents the suffering from impoverishment: one suffers from suffering itself because one feels that suffering is an objection to life. For this kind of person, "the Crucified" promises life beyond this one. The Dionysian suffers from overfullness; suffers not from suffering itself, but from engagement with life. Suffering, from this perspective, is not an objection to life; indeed, it is something to affirm because it is part of life.

Nietzsche's comparison raises numerous questions. This chapter revolves around two of them. What does it mean to affirm suffering? And how should we receive Nietzsche's comparison of Dionysus and the Crucified? After introducing the first question, I will argue that a critical comparison between Nietzschean and certain forms of Christian suffering will expose problems with Nietzsche's view of Christian suffering and suggest that he is much closer to certain Christian views on the question of the affirmation of suffering than he allows. The comparison, then, will be a helpful step in elucidating Nietzsche's affirmation. It will not, I must emphasize, leave us with the conclusion that Nietzsche is a Christian or that Christian mystics are Nietzschean, but it will allow me to define more precisely the relationship between two views on suffering and affirmation. From there, it will be possible to offer my final formulations of Nietzsche's uses and abuses of the ascetic ideal, the mystical element of his thought, and his affirmation.

"The advocate of life, the advocate of suffering, the advocate of the circle"

Nietzsche seeks to overcome the reactivity of the ascetic ideal, but he continues to insist on a close link between suffering and affirmation, between the vision of the abyss and the experience of eternal joy. In *Zarathustra* we observe the transfiguration of one to the other, from the abysmal thought to Zarathustra's songs to eternity. A similar dynamic is at the heart of the passage from *The Gay Science* entitled "The Greatest Weight."

What, if some day or night a demon were to steal after you in your loneliest loneliness and say to you: "This life as you now live it and have lived it, you will have to live once more and innumerable times more; and there will be nothing new in it, but every pain and every joy and every thought and everything unutterably small and great in your life will return to you, all in the same succession and sequence. . . ." Would you not throw yourself down and gnash your teeth and curse the demon who spoke thus? Or have you once experienced a tremendous moment when you would have answered him: "You are a god and never have I heard anything more divine." (GS: 273–74)

For the affirmer, the thought of recurrence is divine, not demonic, but, as *Zarathustra* indicates, this thought only becomes divine in the process of plumbing its abysmal depths. To say "Yes" to recurrence is not simply to say "Yes" to joy, but also to "every pain." To understand the link between suffering and affirmation in Nietzsche, it is necessary to examine the idea of eternal recurrence.

Numerous interpreters have examined Nietzsche's scattered and apparently sketchy claims about eternal recurrence in some detail.[4] Nonetheless, it remains one of the most enigmatic of Nietzsche's ideas. The difficulty is particularly pronounced when it is thought that the ideal entails the affirmation of all that has happened in the past, not only in one's own life, but in the entire web of history in which one was produced. This means affirming all of one's personal sufferings and, in addition, all sorts of horrific evils. Recently, Maudmarie Clark has grappled with this consequence of Nietzsche's idea in her powerful and in many respects persuasive reading of Nietzsche's eternal recurrence (1990). Her reading provides a useful discussion of affirmation as "affirming eternal recurrence." It also is instructive as an illustration of the way a relentlessly secular and philosophical approach to Nietzsche can lead one to misread the issue of affirming suffering.

Clark argues that many of the difficulties attributed to Nietzsche's idea of eternal recurrence are dissolved if one emphasizes its practical significance instead of its cosmological implications. On her reading, one can "affirm eternal recurrence" without believing in the truth of the cosmological version of eternal recurrence. She points out that when the demon approaches in one's "loneliest loneliness," one is not going to consider the metaphysical implications of the idea, nor the question of whether life will actually recur. Instead, one will grapple with the thought "What if. . .?" She compares this test to the question one spouse might ask another: "If you had to marry me again, would you?" Eternal recurrence, on this view, is a thought to be affirmed, though not a metaphysical doc-

---

[4] It is not the *Übermensch*, but eternal recurrence that Nietzsche describes as "the fundamental conception" of *Zarathustra* and "the highest formula of affirmation that is at all attainable" (Z: 295). Gary Shapiro points out that the term Nietzsche uses here—*Grundconception*—is significant, for, unlike *Begriff* or *Idee*, it refers not to what in English we would call *concept* or *idea*, but rather to "sketch" or "germ of a story" (1991: 97).

trine to be believed or proposed. The idea of the endless repetition of one's life in all its detail serves as an exercise of the imagination that tests one's fundamental attitude toward life: if one finds joy in the thought of eternal recurrence, then one is living affirmatively because one evaluates life only from the perspective of the very process of living it. Nietzsche, Clark argues, challenges the ascetic ideal with an ideal she terms "affirming eternal recurrence."

Part of the persuasive power of Clark's interpretation derives from her willingness to address the problem of the affirmation of suffering head-on. As Nietzsche's demon tells us, affirming eternal recurrence means affirming a life that may include agony—either suffering one has already undergone, or suffering that one may yet encounter; it means affirming a life in which those moments would be lived over and over again, without the hope that there would be an "end" to this life that would redeem its painful aspects in any final way. Clark elucidates precisely what this perspective on suffering entails. The idea of eternal recurrence tests what she calls the "intrinsic affirmation" of life, because by renouncing any end or reward, one finds the grounds for affirmation only in the process of living; this affirmation is truly a love for *this* life. But although the affirmer loves life for its own sake, no healthy person, according to Clark, can love suffering (or evil) in the same, unconditional, way. A distinction must be drawn, then, between the affirmation of life and the affirmation of any particular moment in that life. Clark contends that affirming eternal recurrence means that one is "willing to relive eternally even those parts of "this life" that one does not and cannot love" (1990: 279). In other words, the affirmer affirms suffering in the sense of being "willing," or assenting to it, but not in the sense of "loving" it. This means, for Clark, that even if one finds joy in the thought of living one's life over and over again exactly as it has been lived, one might also prefer an alternative life, one without the suffering or evil of one's actual life. She argues that preferring an alternative life does not negate one's affirmation of this life; indeed, she goes beyond simply suggesting that one can still affirm life even if one prefers that some things had not happened by claiming that it is "a greater affirmation of life to want the repetition of the past without the bad things" (1990: 281).[5]

---

[5] What does Clark mean by "bad things"? It is not clear. When she brings up the subject initially, she refers to the "painful experiences of one's life" and to the affirmation of "Hitler's atrocities" (1990: 279), apparently grouping together the affirmation of suffering (painful experiences) with the affirmation of evil (Hitler). As her argument progresses these become, simply, the "painful, horrible, and obscene events," and then, even more simply, "bad things" (1990: 279, 281). In fact, Clark appears to be eliding the significance of suffering because her examples appear to focus on the "horrible" and on the evil of Hitler. My concern here is primarily with Nietzsche's attitude toward suffering. However, it is the case that Nietzsche claims that we must affirm the eternal recurrence of everything. I think one aspect

With this argument, Clark finds genuine humanity in Nietzsche's vision of affirmation. If Nietzsche sought to affirm a life in which one loved each second with equal joy and gratitude, would he be affirming a *human* life? Does not a rich human life include regret and hatred; does it not involve the effort to resist suffering and evil? Even if I can see that in something terrible from the past—say the death of a loved one—I have learned much about myself and now lead a richer life, is it not part of the humanity we would want to affirm to still wish that that person was still with us? Given the choice in this instance, would we want to say that it is a denial of life to wish that our loved one was still alive? Or take the case of great evil, such as the Holocaust. Can we affirm *any* vision of affirmation that would refuse to change that particular part of our history? Clark makes the reasonable point that an affirmation which depended on either an even-handed acceptance of everything or on the love of suffering and evil would be inhuman. Simply because we have not loved every moment in our lives does not mean that we will not experience joy at the thought of repeating our life: affirmation, on this reading, requires only that we are joyfully willing, for the sake of the whole of our life, to relive those aspects of our lives we do not love; that, if given the choice, we would not choose to have happen again. To illustrate this point, one might compare the love of life with the love of a person. One does not necessarily love everything about a person one is in love with—being in love with someone does not depend on loving equally each and every aspect of the person, but on the love of the whole. Indeed, one might argue that the richest and most affirming love is only possible when there are aspects of a person that one does not love. That is, love of an other is experienced fully only when one learns how to love the other as a person with faults, limitations, and differences.

Clark's attempt to interpret Nietzsche in such a way that his affirmation avoids the position of affirming "the bad things" unconditionally is useful and interesting. But it fails to satisfactorily account for a number of claims Nietzsche makes about suffering. If it is true that it is a greater affirmation of life to prefer a life without the bad things, then, it seems, suffering is rendered superfluous. This, however, precludes two positions that I contend Nietzsche holds: first, Nietzsche holds that suffering is *necessary* for a strong and affirmative life; second, the affirmer, in some sense, actually *desires* the painful or horrible aspects of his or her life.

---

of his affirmation of evil is evident, ironically, in his discussion of Jesus in *The Antichrist* (a figure who must be distinguished from "the Crucified"): "He does not resist, he does not defend his rights, he takes no steps to avert the worst that can happen to him—more, *he provokes it.* . . . And he entreats, he suffers, he loves *with* those, *in* those who are doing evil to him. . . . *Not* to defend oneself, *not* to grow angry, *not* to make responsible. . . . But not to resist even the evil man—to *love* him" (AC: 158).

At first glance, it does not seem implausible that Nietzsche should hold that at least certain kinds of suffering are necessary for a full, powerful, affirmative human life. He makes this explicit in the *Genealogy* when he describes "great health" in terms of a spirit "strengthened by war and victory, for whom conquest, adventure, danger and even pain have become needs" (GM: 96). But what could it possibly mean to "desire" suffering? That this is a significant question is suggested in a number of places in Nietzsche's writing. In "The Greatest Weight," Nietzsche writes that the idea of eternal recurrence is a question "in each and every thing"; that is, it is not just a question about life as a whole, but about each moment: "Do you desire *this* once more and innumerable times more?" (italics added). That Nietzsche is concerned with *desire* in this passage, and not simply *assent* (as in Clark's "being willing to"), is confirmed in numerous other passages: writing of the "suffering from overfullness" Nietzsche claims that it "craves the frightful" (*nach dem Furchtbaren verlangt*); he has Zarathustra proclaim himself "the advocate of life, the advocate of suffering, the advocate of the circle" (Z: 215), and sing an ecstatic song of eternity that contains the line: "So rich is joy that it thirsts for woe" (Z: 324); he writes of the Dionysian "sanctification" of pain, connecting it explicitly to the idea of eternal recurrence that he finds in Greek tragedy (TI: 120); he ridicules humanists for their aversion to suffering: "You want, if possible—and there is no more insane 'if possible'—to abolish suffering. And we? It really seems that we would rather have it higher and worse than ever" (BG: 153).[6] Finally, in a note from 1888, Nietzsche writes of "My new path to a 'Yes' " and of philosophy as a "voluntary quest for even the most detested and notorious sides of existence."

> Such an experimental philosophy as I live anticipates experimentally even the possibilities of the most fundamental nihilism; but this does not mean that it must halt at a negation, a No, a will to negation. It wants rather to cross over to the opposite of this—to a Dionysian affirmation of the world as it is, without subtraction, exception, or selection—it wants the eternal circulation. . . . The highest state a philosopher can attain: to stand in a Dionysian relationship to existence—my formula for this is *amor fati*. It is part of this state to perceive not merely the necessity of those sides of existence hitherto denied, but their desirability; and not their desirability merely in relation to the sides hitherto affirmed . . . but for their own sake. (WP: 536–37)

How does one explain these kinds of passages? Contrary to Clark, I think they mean that one must take seriously the idea that a Nietzschean affirmer would *not* prefer a life without moments of pain and terror, that this affirmer, in fact, *loves* them. I would qualify this immediately by

[6] See also Z: 87, 154, 162.

pointing out that to speak of the "desire" or "love" for suffering does not necessarily entail the claim that suffering is not aversive. Nietzsche certainly will admit that in moments of suffering one wishes that one could escape it: in the song at the end of *Zarathustra*, it is "joy" that wants agony, while "Woe entreats: go! Away woe!" (Z: 322). What he suggests with "The Greatest Weight," however, is that affirming eternal recurrence depends on a vision of divinity, that there is a perspective from which suffering is loved.[7] These passages push us therefore to explore what Clement Rosset calls the "secret alliance" in all of Nietzsche's work "between misfortune and bliss, the tragic and the jubilatory, the experience of pain and the affirmation of joy" (1993: 31). And they demand a closer examination of what I have described above as the transfiguration of suffering and the mystical element of Nietzsche's thought. Where Clark interprets "The Greatest Weight," and Nietzsche's view of recurrence in general, along resolutely secular lines, Nietzsche's invocation of the extraordinary and divine should not be ignored. Writing as the "advocate of suffering," Nietzsche brings to the idea of suffering a complex attitude where suffering yields something beyond the aversiveness of pain, perhaps beyond the experiences, needs, and values of the atomistic self. An adequate interpretation of suffering and affirmation in Nietzsche must examine, therefore, how he holds, at the same time, that such moments of pain and suffering are necessary for life, even that there are certain moments in life in which one actually "desires" suffering *and* that, in the midst of suffering, one wants to escape it.

CHRISTIAN MYSTICISM AS PASSION FOR THE REAL

Theodicy's Denial, Christian Economics

As I have suggested, I will approach this question through a comparison between Nietzsche's view of suffering and certain Christian views, specifically those exemplified in the mystical practice of suffering. Nietzsche, I argue, is wrong to condemn Christianity in itself with the claim that *the* Christian response to suffering is reactive. Through a certain "theology of the Cross," Christians demonstrate a practice of suffering that engages the reality of the world in a way that exhibits close affinities with Nietzsche's affirmation.

To begin, I return to the issue of theodicy. Certain Christian thinkers have criticized the project of theodicy by arguing that the real problem with it is not intellectual but practical. What is accomplished in trying to comprehend the ultimate significance of all evil and suffering? What

---

[7] See Klossowski 1985.

are the effects of this theological practice? Arguing that it is the responsibility of the theologian and the philosopher to be self-conscious about the
praxis their work mediates, Kenneth Surin claims that the project
of theodicy, in practice, is implicated with a denial of the concrete reality
of human suffering. As an intellectual attempt to give meaning to suffering
per se, theodicy must focus on the general question of evil and suffering,
and therefore cannot attend to the "radical particularity" of actual
instances of evil and suffering. Theodicy therefore mediates "a social
and political praxis which averts its gaze from all the cruelties that exist
in the world" (1989: 77). Paul Ricoeur, in a similar vein, argues that
the comprehensive and systematic approach to suffering and evil of Christian theodicy can achieve, at best, only a victory over the "aesthetic phan-
tom" of evil (1974: 312). Like Kierkegaard's systematizer who constructs
grand edifices of thought, but in actuality lives in the doghouse next door,
theodicy makes conceptual promises about the meaning of suffering and
evil, which do little, if anything, to respond to it concretely. Kathleen
Sands puts it plainly when she argues that "it is wasteful to feign evil's
resolution by 'thinking it through to the end,' when what is needed is
illumination, creativity, discernment, and transformation in evil's midst"
(1994: 29).[8]

There are religious considerations at stake here as well. Ricoeur employs the story of Job and the symbol of the Cross to affirm a worship
and love for God beyond lament and political struggle, beyond, that is,
active attempts to ameliorate suffering and resist evil (though, for Ricoeur,
this "going beyond" does not preclude the moral imperative to attend to
these crucial tasks). At the point marked by Job's confrontation with the
whirlwind and by Christ's death on the Cross, Ricoeur claims that one
renounces "the desire to be spared of all suffering," and escapes the cycle
of retribution by "loving God for nought." With this, Ricoeur captures
something profound about Christian worship. At its deepest level, worship of God is not a matter of economy, for one does not worship God
because God gives meaning to life, or *because* God promises eternal life,
or *because*, in loving God, one can overcome suffering. Instead, one wor-
ships because God is creator and life-giver.[9] But even putting it this way
is not quite right, at least as long as the word *because* designates some

---

[8] One will note that in many of these discussions of theodicy, the focus is on evil rather
than suffering. However, it is also the case that both Surin (1989) and Ricoeur (1974), when
discussing the shortcomings of theodicy, focus on the inability of theodicy to explain certain
kinds of suffering. It seems that part of the problem that theodicy is trying to grapple with
is the problem of just how we untangle evil and suffering from one another, especially in a
biblical context where there is always the temptation to see suffering as punishment for evil
or as a form of purification.

[9] I think H. R. Niebuhr (1970) is getting at a similar point when he argues that God is
not a value, but rather the center of value.

kind of utility, or some simple cause/effect relationship. Such terms miss the important point that worship and faith are, in the sense I am invoking, *active* forms of love and, as such, cannot be reduced to a *because*. I would suggest that it is part of the very definition of "divine" or "God" that that which we designate by these terms is beyond human meaning and human reason—is, to put it more positively, worshiped for its own sake, not ours. Calling something "divine" precedes the attribution of meaning or value.[10]

This is not to say that one can worship a God who seems to not care about human suffering: love is not blind; it does not simply refuse to question; it is not wholly without reason. The pull of theodicy consists in the fact that human beings are creatures who need to make at least some sense of their lives, who seek to understand God's care for them. Accordingly, neither Surin nor Ricoeur dismiss completely the theological attempt to address the mystery of evil and suffering. Instead, each displaces the theoretical imperative of theodicy by means of a practical theology of the Cross. Unlike theodicy's attempt to forge a speculatively totalizing account of evil and suffering, a theology of the Cross is a component of the practical participation in relationship to the God who suffers in and with the world. Such a theology articulates God's response to suffering without dwelling on the question of how God allows suffering in the first place, and it locates the human-divine encounter in suffering.[11] And, crucially, it grants priority to love rather than suffering. Thus a theology of the Cross directs human beings to a life, like Christ's, that, out of love, opens itself to the world and all its suffering and refuses to flee from it. This is a life of giving, even to the point of bearing suffering in one's own body: it shows us a divine life in suffering, not divinity as the means to transcend all suffering.

Is it possible (it certainly would be ironic) that in a theology of the Cross we might find a Christian perspective on suffering that escapes Nietzsche's criticisms of the ascetic ideal? Nietzsche's criticisms of the suffering and self-denial idealized by Christianity are directed to suffering as the price for or the way to heavenly bliss; the symbol of the Cross is a symbol for the "hatred of reality" (AC: 161). The question then is whether a theology of the Cross can articulate a Christian life that leads to engagement with reality through a deep love for *this* life. Such a theology would not empha-

[10] See Murdoch 1993: 106–7. Murdoch writes: "The 'true saint' believes in 'God' but not as a super-person who satisfies all our ordinary desires 'in the end.' (There is no end, there is no reward)."

[11] Surin is helpful on both these points. He rejects the impassability of God without sacrificing the idea of omnipotence, and he makes the interesting point that in the kind of theology of the Cross he is recommending theodicy resolves into a "suffering theophany" (1989: 77).

size the impassable, omnipotent God of metaphysical dualism, one whose apathetic response to pain and suffering becomes an ideal for human response, but a God that suffers with humanity, a God immersed in the this-worldly reality of the human, *out of love*. Here, imitating Christ on the Cross would not be a means to another life, but an expression of love for this life—a life in which the deepest suffering is intimately connected with the deepest affirmation.

By this route, one who is persuaded by Nietzsche's criticisms of the ascetic ideal might nonetheless see that there are other possibilities for understanding suffering within Christianity, and might agree that Christianity has more possibilities for affirmation than Nietzsche allows. Such possibilities are exemplified in certain forms of Christian mysticism.

Mystic Suffering

Hadewijch, the thirteenth-century Flemish beguine, mystic, and poet, writes:

> Hell is the seventh name
> of this Love wherein I suffer.
> For there is nothing Love does not engulf and damn.
>
> .   .   .   .
>
> As Hell turns everything to ruin,
> In Love nothing else is acquired
> But disgust and torture without pity;
> Forever to be in unrest,
> Forever assault and new persecution;
> To be wholly devoured and engulfed
> In her unfathomable essence,
> To founder unceasingly in heat and cold,
> In the deep, insurmountable darkness of Love.
> This outdoes the torments of Hell.

(Bynum 1987)

Caroline Walker Bynum observes that Hadewijch's poetic account of the torments of love describes a union with Christ "in a frenzy of suffering that included and transcended pleasure and pain" (1987: 154). Such mystical union in suffering was not uncommon in the spirituality of medieval, Western Christians, dominated as it was by the shadow of the Cross. Richard Kieckheffer has argued that for fourteenth-century saints "suffering was . . . the key to holiness" (1984: 121).[12] There was a flowering of

---

[12] Meister Eckhart writes: "If my suffering is in God and God is suffering with me, how then can suffering be sorrow to me . . . as I find pure suffering for the love of God and in God, I find my God suffering" (Sells 1994: 176).

such spirituality in the thirteenth and fourteenth centuries, though it has not been confined to this period of Christianity. In the sixteenth century, Teresa of Avila described an "agony" in which one "rejoic[es] with ineffable joy," an experience her follower and fellow mystic, Saint John of the Cross, also understood well:

> Oh that it may be perfectly understood how the soul cannot attain to the thicket and wisdom of the richness of God, which are of many kinds, save by entering into the thicket of many kinds of suffering, and by setting thereupon its consolation and desire. And how the soul that of a truth desires Divine wisdom first desires suffering, that it may enter therein—yea into the thicket of the Cross. (Katz 1983: 49)[13]

More recently, Simone Weil described a spiritual life grounded in the experience of "affliction," a state in which one is "nailed to the center of the universe" and there encounters divine love (1951: 135).

Nietzsche, of course, addresses such valorizations of suffering in the *Genealogy*. He mocks Christian claims about the love symbolized by the Cross, and he mourns those tortured by guilt so deep that they believe it can be atoned only by God's self-sacrifice. He also describes the "morbidly lascivious conscience" of the sinner who "thirsts" for pain as an antidote to this sense of guilt and as a way to make life "very interesting" (GM: 141). The power of Nietzsche's interpretation has been proved by recent scholarly interpretations of Christian suffering. Caroline Walker Bynum raises the possibility of a masochistic element in the ascetic and mystical practices of medieval Christian women. She does not reduce these practices to a "morbidly lascivious conscience," but she does point out the dangers of glorifying suffering in a spirituality of the Cross that excludes adequate consideration of the Resurrection (1987: 208f., 252 f.). And it is not too far from Nietzsche's general concern with the ascetic ideal as an expression of the will to power to Richard Kieckheffer's sociological argument that the practices of pain of fourteenth-century mystics were a means of achieving status within the saints' society (1984: 120).[14]

There are, however, interpretations of mystic suffering that challenge Nietzsche's. As my treatment of asceticism demonstrates, Christian suffering can be interpreted and practiced as an intensification and spiritualization, rather than as the extirpation, of desire. Grace Jantzen argues, with respect to the idea of "deification" in Hadewijch, that such desire is cultivated in union with Christ not as "a calm spiritual ascent" toward

---

[13] See Teresa of Avila 1957: 113, 141: "Yet at the same time this pain is so sweet, and the soul is so conscious of its value, that it now desires this suffering more than all the gifts that it used to receive."

[14] See also E. M. Cioran 1995. Cioran was strongly influenced by Nietzsche.

the otherworldly but in an identification with the humanity and love of Christ which directs them, in love, to this world (1995: 140–41). More generally, criticisms of Christianity's asceticism and otherworldliness, like Nietzsche's, have led contemporary Christian thinkers to look carefully at how they and their predecessors have treated the question of suffering. Dorthee Soelle and Rowan Williams are particularly helpful in this regard. Both argue that suffering can be a crucial element in a practice of love, and both appeal to Christian mystical traditions for insightful and practical reflections on the significance and place of suffering in human life.

Soelle works out of the radical theology of the Cross proposed by Japanese theologian Kazoh Kitamori. Writing of the "mysticism of pain," Kitamori articulates a complex dynamic of affirmation and resistance: "Our only desire is to become one in pain with God. Because of this desire we will seek and long for our pain. . . . We can conquer [pain] only when we seek it within ourselves and long for it" (Kitamori 1965: 81). In at least one specific respect, this brings Kitamori close to Nietzsche's Dionysian theology, for this view of pain requires a God that human beings experience not in victory *over* this life of suffering, but in the midst of it. Nietzsche argues that the will to power of the ascetic priest seeks to "master" life, and the Cross for Nietzsche is a sign of this final (illusory and deathlike) transcendence: the ascetic ideal finds its power in a worldly surrender for the sake of an otherworldly victory and mastery. But when Kitamori and Soelle write of "conquering" pain, they point to a different dynamic: not the reactive search for redemption from or elimination of pain, but the discovery, in the very longing for pain, of the healing presence of Christ. To "conquer" pain, on this view, is not to make oneself free of pain, but rather to recognize in pain one's own responsiveness to the world; it is to love pain in the same way that Jesus insists one must love one's enemies: in active, giving responsiveness. Soelle argues that the acceptance of reality hinges on the affirmation of suffering, that affirming life means making ourselves vulnerable to the pain of which so much earthly reality consists, and in which the creative God participates. The Cross is the symbol of this reality (1975: 163). Spiritual life understood as a *practice of suffering* is an insistence on bearing reality in one's body and soul.

I want to emphasize here a particular kind of openness or responsiveness to reality as the fundamental characteristic of mystical affirmation. Iris Murdoch, who, like Soelle, owes much to Simone Weil's reflections on suffering, usefully elaborates this point. For Murdoch, one of the most difficult things about suffering is actually to see or perceive it. This may sound counterintuitive, and there certainly are many forms of extreme suffering that are brutally present to the senses. But it also is the case that human beings employ manifold means to hide suffering, their own and especially the suffering of others, from themselves. In our efforts to avoid suffering, we create all kinds of illusions for ourselves to the point where it becomes extremely difficult to see, feel, and respond to many of the worst kinds of sufferings that human beings experience. For Murdoch, the mystical path is first of all a path of purification by which one strips oneself of all such self-centered illusions in an effort to learn how to *attend* to the world before one. Mysticism, for Murdoch, is a practice of attention. She notes that Simone Weil was particularly concerned with attention to suffering, which Weil believed was possible only on the basis of an attention obedient to the mystery of God; that is, willing to face the deep pain of forsakeness in the midst of suffering. Weil thereby identifies pain with an openness to or, in the full sense of the word, a *passion* for the real. "Each time that we have some pain to go through, we can say to ourselves quite truly that it is the universe, the order, and beauty of the world and the obedience of creation to God that are entering our body. After that how can we fail to bless with tenderest gratitude the Love that sends us this gift? Joy and suffering are two equally precious gifts both of which must be savored to the full" (Weil, 1951: 131–33).

To suffer in a mystical way, on this view, is to practice the passion for the real. Soelle finds such love demonstrated in the lives of Christian mystics whose "love for reality . . . avoids placing conditions on reality" or on God. Mystical love exceeds the need to explain reality or God in the way of theodicy—it is not an economical love. Thus "the theodicy question"—the question of the meaning, justification, or economy of suffering—"is superseded by an unlimited love for reality" (1975: 91). Such unconditional loving immerses one in reality to the point where one loves beyond the omnipotent God who promises redemption, loving only the God who is no less than love itself. It is from this perspective that one can understand Eckhart when he writes: "I pray God to rid me of God."[15]

This mystical love is different from forms of Christian transcendence that seek a final end to suffering, from platonically inflected contemplation that seeks the invulnerability of communion with Ideas, or from Stoic tranquillity that transmutes suffering in the transcendence of finite attachments. In the intensification of love, the Christian mystic becomes more vulnerable to the pain of reality. Yet this cultivation of vulnerability, this loving openness to reality, transforms suffering in "submitting" to it. It is neither simply submission nor resistance. Soelle describes the practice of suffering undertaken by mystics as the attempt to "turn all suffering into labor pains and to abolish all senselessness" (1975: 91). This love does

---

[15] Nietzsche quotes this passage (GS: 235).

not resist suffering in general, or condemn life because it suffers; it resists
a certain response to or consequence of suffering: destruction, depression,
and muteness, the deadening that results from the inability to bear suffering and the consequent refusal to engage life for fear of suffering. Love,
as compassion, bears the suffering of oneself and others in a practice by
which the contours of suffering are discerned and creatively transformed.
Suffering, on this account, is not something to be justified or explained
theoretically, but something to be embraced by love: love precedes justification and demands action.

Rowan Williams's survey of Christian spirituality offers historical support for this view of mysticism and suffering and articulates a soteriology
grounded in a decidedly this-worldly view of Christian life. At the beginning of his survey, Williams asserts, "If we believe we can experience our
healing without deepening our hurt, we have understood nothing about
the roots of our faith" (1990: 11). Properly understood, Williams argues,
the greatest figures of the tradition themselves saw the Christian life as a
life of "the fellowship of God with human beings in their humanness"
(1990: 30). The meeting place for this fellowship is the Cross (1990: 83).
One bears the Cross not in order to suffer, but as an expression of love;
one thereby joins with God in joining with the suffering of others. God is
a "worldly reality," experienced in the here and now, always, therefore,
as both present and absent. Williams finds in Martin Luther's view of
God as a "negative theologian" the exemplification of this attitude: this
God is present as God only in the godlessness of the world, only in that
which "negates and mocks all human conceptions of God" (1990: 149).
Christian experience is human experience; union with God is an experience of glory and bliss only as it also is an experience of anguish and
alienation.

For Williams, as for Soelle, all forms of suffering are, in their depths,
manifestations of the human encounter with the otherness of reality. This
is the "pain of not being able to evade the constraints of reality, the 'giv-
enness' of events." To desire suffering, then, is to understand suffering as
a sign of reality and reality as a gift from God (1990: 72). One therefore
experiences pain as the mark of God's "companionship" with us in that
reality.[16] Or, as Soelle puts it, suffering becomes an "object of burning
love." This love of suffering, as Williams stresses, is neither masochism—
it does not involve the anticipation of the voluptuousness of pain itself,
nor glorification of suffering—nor does it seek pain as a good in itself. As
either, pain simply would become a comfort and consolation, neutralized

---

[16] Williams cites Ruth Burrows, a contemporary Carmelite: "Below the level of consciousness we know that our pain is the effect of God's closeness; we know it when the pain
is withdrawn. We know we have lost for a time that profound companionship which was
there in our pain" (1990: 171).

of its aversiveness, and thus no longer able to move one to growth and love. Pain would become an idol. Mystical love avoids these dangers in a delicate and passionate balance, yearning for God's presence but only through a disciplined suspicion of illusions of complacency or self-aggrandizement that would dissipate the mystic's concentrated desire.

As I have indicated, even desire for "mystical experience" can be an attachment that defeats love. Mystical love is more important than mystical "experience." Williams and Soelle each write of "mysticism" and "spirituality," but they both stress that what is of utmost significance for the spiritual life is not extraordinary experience of union with God—in pain or in bliss—but activity in the world grounded in divine love. If we are going to continue to speak of mystical union, one could say that God is present in every moment of such activity. This mystical tradition thus shares with Nietzsche real suspicion about the way extraordinary states of consciousness become escapist consolation. Moreover, the mystic must renounce the sense and meaning of suffering, the temptation to integrate it completely to the economy of human growth and becoming. Though love seeks to transform all suffering into meaning, suffering is excessive and challenges the human will to affirm God without conditions, in an affirmation that does not ask of suffering, "What is in it for me?" (1975: 96). The affirmation of suffering, therefore, takes place only by holding a tension between struggle and surrender. On the one hand, human beings strive to give voice to suffering, to name and make suffering meaningful, shaping themselves out of suffering. On the other hand, to use a concept from Eckhart, they must cultivate the attitude of *Gelassenheit* (letting be) in an obedience to a reality that cannot be mastered. The Cross defeats consolation: Christ experiences himself as forsaken or, as Williams puts it, "God is born in the hell of abandonment" (1990: 141). We must read the multivalence of the word abandonment here: on the one hand, it is abandonment as forsakeness; on the other hand, it is abandonment as "letting go," which, as Thomas Merton writes, is not an act but a gift: "The final step on the way to holiness in Christ is then to completely abandon ourselves with confident joy to the apparent madness of the cross. . . . This madness, the folly of abandoning all concern for ourselves . . . is a twisting, a letting go, an act of total abandonment. But it is also a final break-through into joy" (1996: 119).

At stake here is not simply a different conception of Christian suffering than that offered by Nietzsche, but a different conception of the Christian God. Traditional Christian theodicies that attempt to comprehend the economy of suffering generally depend on the God of metaphysical dualism, whose apathetic response to pain and suffering becomes an ideal for human response. By contrast, a theology of the Cross can affirm a God who suffers with humanity, who is immersed, out of love, in the worldly reality of the human. This God is closer to the repeated suffering and dying of Nietzsche's Dionysus than the impassable God who supports the dualism of the ascetic ideal. Contrary to Nietzsche's assertion, such a mystical theology would find in the imitation of Christ on the Cross not a means to another life, but an expression of love for this life—a life in which the deepest suffering is intimately connected with the deepest affirmation.

From Suffering to Affirmation

I carry the blessings of my Yes into all abysses. (Z: 164)

"Dionysus versus the Crucified": as Nietzsche sees it, an affirmation of rebirth into this life versus an accusation against life in the hope for a resurrection to eternal bliss. But the contrast is not as stark as Nietzsche claims. Since his attack on Christianity develops out of his critique of the monotheistic vision of absolute divine power and human abjection, a Christian vision concentrating on God's vulnerability avoids the blows of Nietzsche's idol-smashing hammer. Soelle and Williams show us how Christian mysticism creates an affirmative dynamic out of suffering, love, and responsiveness. Indeed, not only is Nietzsche's criticism off the mark, but there are some strong affinities between Nietzsche and the Christian mysticism they articulate: in both, affirmation is made possible only by a practice of suffering by which the self explores the contours and depths of vulnerability in the course of a loving embrace of reality. At this point, other affinities suggest themselves, which lead me to examine the degree to which Nietzsche's affirmative vision depends on vulnerability, responsiveness, and love, ideas not ordinarily associated with Nietzsche. Exploring these ideas, and so attending carefully to the similarities and differences between Nietzsche and Christian mysticism, I interpret Nietzsche's affirmation as a disposition of joy and love.

Suffering

Nietzsche conceives of philosophy itself as a practice of suffering, one that embraces and transfigures suffering. This dynamic is a key to affirmation, for only in the disciplined responsiveness to suffering—what Saint John of the Cross calls the "dark night of the soul" and Nietzsche the "abysmal thought" or "midnight"—are joy, creativity, and love made possible. "A full and powerful soul not only copes with painful, even terrible losses, deprivations, robberies, insults; it emerges from such hells with a greater fullness and powerfulness; and, most essential of all, with a new increase in the blissfulness of love" (WP: 532). Nietzsche figures his philosophical path in the descents and ascents of *Zarathustra*, which do not have an "end" in final knowledge or contemplation, but constitute Zarathustra's "work" (Z: 237). This work, this love of the world, is always accompanied by the experience of eternity and love we find at the end of both Books III and IV. In *Zarathustra*, the transfiguration of suffering finds its clearest expression in the pages leading up to Zarathustra's first declaration of love for eternity, near the end of Book III. In the chapter that falls between "The Convalescent"—in which Zarathustra wakes from the trance in which he dreamt of the recurrence of the small man—and the ecstatic songs that end Book III, Zarathustra converses with his soul in a chapter entitled "On the Great Longing." Here, Nietzsche narrates an act of self-overcoming in which the despair of the abysmal thought is transfigured into the joy of affirmative vision.

> O my soul, your smile longs for tears and your trembling mouth for sobs. "Is not all weeping a lamentation? And all lamentation an accusation?" Thus you speak to yourself, and therefore, my soul, you would sooner smile than pour out your suffering—pour out into plunging tears all your suffering over your fullness and over the vine's urge for the vintager and his knife. (Z: 223)

At the end of Zarathustra's greatest struggle with himself, a struggle in which he has had to resist his desire for any final overcoming of "man," his soul is characterized by "longing" and "overabundance." It suffers from overfullness of insight and wants to express this suffering, but without accusation. Zarathustra tells his soul: "But if you will not weep, not weep out your crimson melancholy, then you will have to sing, O my soul. Behold, I myself smile as I say this before you: sing with a roaring song till all seas are silenced, that they may listen to your longing." Instead of pouring out tears that accuse the world, Zarathustra transfigures his suffering into longing, beauty, and celebration, offering a dance with life and a song of love. His song, a hymn to eternity, is a declaration of love and affirmation. The encounter with the "abysmal thought" produces an overflowing joy and creativity.

In the preface to *The Gay Science*, Nietzsche puts the matter of philosophy as suffering and suffering's transfiguration a bit more prosaically. He honors his "fickle health" because it has put him at odds with life—it has made him suffer—and so has opened the space of philosophical reflection. Philosophy, as Nietzsche understands it in this context, is the transfiguration of "everything that wounds us" into "light and flame" (GS: 36). As a practice of suffering, philosophy, like sickness, demands an encounter with the real, which is always an encounter with suffering. Like Zarathustra, the philosopher "goes down," descending into the "subterranean" world of "the modern soul" to examine all-too-human reality of its highest ideals and its deepest sufferings.

Nietzsche's vision of suffering centers on the close relation, even ambiguity, that always exists between suffering and desire. Generally, we use "suffering" to designate the aversiveness experienced in need or in pain, and "desire" to designate the direction toward the goal of filling the need or stopping the pain. In a sense then, suffering is a condition of desire; the pleasure and power of desire needs the aversiveness of suffering. Nietzsche imagines a mode of desire that seeks out confrontation with the otherness and painfulness of reality in the knowledge that it is only in such aversiveness, in resistance to it and creating out of it, that desire has its force. "Suffering from overfullness" is a particular, active way of suffering: it renounces the search for the object or the way of life that will fill or stop suffering and desire once and for all because it knows the desire for desire and so "wants to want and will."

"Wanting to want," desiring desire, is a key to Nietzsche's affirmation. John Caputo has taken issue with Deleuze's reading of Nietzsche by characterizing the affirmation of Deleuze's Nietzsche as follows: "True affirmation does not affirm anything in-itself, anything other-than-itself, i.e. anything *other*. What is other will weigh the will down. . . . So, if affirmation affirms itself, then that is Being affirming itself, which is why, if affirmation affirmed something *other* than itself, that would be nihilism." Caputo points out that Deleuze's affirmation sounds suspiciously like a philosophy of "pure act or pure presence"; that is, like a philosophy of *parousia par excellence* (1993: 45–46). For Deleuze, the affirmative will is only creative and only wills itself in what Edith Wyschogrod describes as a "desire that streams without restriction."[17] The affirmer must, for Deleuze, know how to say "no," but this negation is only the negation of all the forces of reactivity.

Nietzsche's negation is more complex and uncanny than this. For him, the person is constructed out of the dynamics of a conflict with itself. Affirmation must affirm this conflict by spiritualizing it rather than dissolving it or turning it into guilt. This entails a turn to otherness. When Zarathustra proclaims his love for eternity and shows us that this means that joy wants to want and will, we see joy negating itself in a return to the world. Joy sacrifices its bliss for the sake of more desire: it wants to want. In one respect, as Deleuze says, Nietzsche's affirmation does take place in the will willing itself, in the desire for desire. But it can only do this through another kind of desire, the finite desire expressed in the will to creativity, the will to create and love things in the world. In creating, the suffering will expresses the desire for something other than itself ("Woe says, Go!"). At the peak of the creative moment, however, in the accomplishment of beauty, the will finds itself in the eternal moment,

[17] Wyschogrod describes as "saints of depravity" those who exemplify the unconstrained desire affirmed by Deleuze, but "in whom the altruistic impulse remains intact" (1990: 215).

wanting only itself. But that also is the moment of sacrifice, the turn to the world and its desires. Joy sacrifices its self-sufficiency and self-containment, opens itself to the finite and to suffering.[18]

The conflict at the heart of the self, then, is mirrored in the conflict between two kinds of desire: the desire for things of the world—and satiation—and the desire for desire itself. The former depends on the sacrifice of the latter. Where Deleuze argues that Nietzsche's affirmation poses an unresolvable conflict with the Hegelian dialectic, I think it is more helpful to consider the alternative Nietzsche poses to a certain Platonic vision of pure presence. Suffering involves a complex interplay between intense concentration on the self, in all the excruciating details of its pain, and the desire to be free of this self in pain, the desire for something beyond. In suffering, then, a space of resistance of the self to itself, of the self "beyond," to the self in pain, is opened up. In Western thought since Plato, the desire for transcendence inherent in pain has often been conceptualized and practiced as a philosophical or religious path toward contemplation of God, in which one gradually detaches oneself from "the mass of perishable flesh" to turn toward the permanent and eternal. One turns away, that is, from all that causes pain, including the self as finite body; one seeks to master the suffering body and life itself. In the *Symposium*, Plato's Socrates describes the invulnerable love that transcends all finite attachments. But Plato also allows Alcibiades to speak of his passionate and beautiful love for a particular human being—Socrates. Martha Nussbaum has argued that even if we read Plato as affirming the self-sufficient, unchanging love of the divine, the attractiveness of Alcibiades tells us something important (1986: 165–99). It makes clear the very real sacrifice of the particular, the human, the finite, which the love for the eternal entails.

What I find so interesting in Nietzsche's alternative to this vision is not simply that he embraces the necessity of tragic sacrifice, but that he does so while also arguing that love for eternity and love for the finite do not exclude one another but depend on one another. Affirmation as love for life emerges out of a sacrificial dynamic that, for the sake of the fundamental dynamism of love, resists any attempt to hold too tightly to the love of eternity, the love of the world, or the love of self. Affirmation consists in the simultaneous recognition of the aversiveness and the fruitfulness of pain, the desire for transcendence, and the desire for return. This is not simply a matter of accepting the suffering that is one's lot for the sake of

---

[18] This process is sung not just in the climaxes of Zarathustra, but in the narrative itself as the quest for the *Übermensch* gives way to the affirmation of the recurrence of the small man. Zarathustra gives up his desire for the complete transcendence of humanity not because he gives up striving and overcoming, but in the recognition that the joy is in the striving itself and not in the accomplishment.

the whole of one's life, but it involves, at the very least, the active cultivation of the vulnerability and empathy that can affirm the inevitability of suffering. On this view, suffering is integral to the affirmative life, it is the ground in which such life can be cultivated. Nietzsche thus "justifies" suffering.

The Madness of Affirmation

To acknowledge that suffering is necessary for the affirmative life is not all Nietzsche means by "advocating suffering" or "thirsting for woe." Put differently, this justification does not fully account for *affirmation*, understood as the uncalculating *desire* for the real. The Nietzschean philosopher does make affirmation to the meaning of suffering, in the sense that suffering is the means to affirmation. But this does not mean that one opens oneself to suffering in order to become affirmative; rather, one does so because one affirms. Affirmation, in other words, is the condition, not the consequence, of meaning: affirmation takes place "beyond" meaning, and, in that sense, is nihilistic.

To make this clearer, I return to the meaning of the *Genealogy*. This book maps one of Nietzsche's descents, his exploration of the suffering of the modern soul. On this journey, Nietzsche finds that human beings would rather will nothing than not will at all. Human beings submit themselves to the suffering and self-hatred of sin, willing a kind of self-destruction, rather than facing the suffering of meaninglessness. Nietzsche, by contrast, in exposing the nihilism of the ascetic ideal as the will to nothing of Western humanity, takes the nihilism of meaninglessness upon himself, as "my problem." He thereby brings himself (and us?) to the place where Zarathustra arrives when he faces the terror of "the most abysmal thought," or where Nietzsche's madman comes when he proclaims the death of God: "Are we not straying as though through an infinite nothing? Do we not feel the breath of empty space?" (GS: 181).

There are no easy or clear answers to Nietzsche's problem, because he offers no answers that promise the definitive overcoming of nihilism. The will to the definitive overcoming of nihilism, would merely reinscribe the metaphysics of mastery, as Blanchot recognizes: "Nihilism would be identical with the will to overcome Nihilism *absolutely*" (1985: 126). Instead of offering a solution to nihilism, Nietzsche *responds* to nihilism. The abyss of the death of God, Nietzsche's encounter with nihilism, is a "dark night of the soul," or, as Rowan Williams describes it: "not just a sequence of decisions to do without spiritual consolation; it is the actual felt absence of consolation" (1990: 170). From one perspective, such absence of consolation might be described as the "suffering of suffering," as suffering without meaning, the suffering at being forsaken even by God. Yet precisely in making this nihilism "my problem," Nietzsche transfigures it. The problem of meaning becomes a philosophical adventure and task, Nietzsche finds joy at this boundary of Western culture and human life. Nihilism as meaninglessness now becomes a space in which creativity is possible, a space of freedom where the turn to affirmation can be accomplished: it becomes, as Nietzsche puts it in a note, "a divine way of thinking" (SW 12: 354). This affirmation is not consolation but a difficult joy that takes shape in the tension between the renunciatory "No" of nihilism and the "Yes" of creativity.[19] And it is precisely in the rejection of "purpose" and the embrace of chaos and chance that Nietzsche finds the possibility of blessing and affirming (Z: 166).

Affirmation, as Nietzsche writes it, is a kind of madness. It is the madness of a surrender to that which lies outside of knowledge or reason, to the chaos of becoming. Like the Christian mystic enacting the anarchy of love—loving through his or her suffering and beyond God, meaning, and all human hierarchies—Nietzsche's affirmation is ultimately grounded in a "hidden Yes." The madness of this "hidden Yes" is a theme of the final pages of *The Gay Science*. There, the "playful spirit" (GS: 346) that is Nietzsche's new ideal is moved not by *reasons*, Socratic grounds developed, asserted, and confirmed in the broad daylight of consciousness, but by a "hidden Yes," by "will," a passion emerging from body and shining in spirit—amoral, nonmetaphysical, unreasonable. Here, Nietzsche invokes madness and play, enthusiasm and ecstasy, to help envision a passionate way of life, one that does not sacrifice the joy of the moment for the sake of deliberation about and achievement of certain ends. This does not mean that Nietzsche forsakes all goals and ideals—he obviously does not, because he *seeks* to cultivate an affirmative life. But at the same time that one hopes for affirmation, it must in some way be embodied and lived in the now, in the passion of the problem and the experience of the experiment. Genuine affirmation finds its source in a movement of the soul that cannot be willed or forced, for it is an embrace of life out of love; it is an "inspiration," a feeling "of freedom, of absoluteness, of power, of divinity" (EH: 300). Ultimately, the source of affirmation is as mysterious as the source of faith.

In one sense, Nietzsche demands the joy of affirmation, as an act of what Soelle calls "mystical defiance," willing affirmation from the abyss and enacting it in creative praise of life and eternity. But despite the

---

[19] Here, the term "joy," in Clement Rosset's sense, becomes a key concept for understanding affirmation. For Rosset, joy is "unconditional rejoicing for and with respect to existence," in the full realization of the tragic nature of existence. Joy does not overcome tragedy or suffering, but is "eminently attentive to calamity" and thus paradoxical. "There is no true joy unless it is simultaneously thwarted, in contradiction with itself"(1993: 15–17).

emphasis Nietzsche puts on the individual will, Zarathustra does not simply call on "his own" will. Note that Zarathustra's transfiguration of the abysmal thought into the joy of eternity takes place in the context of a conversation between "Zarathustra," as voice, as ego, and his soul, which Zarathustra describes in both personal and cosmological terms, as both "mine" and, variously, "sea," "destiny," and "umbilical cord of time." This conversation takes place, in other words, at the boundary where self and "beyond"—something more fundamental and more comprehensive than the ego—meet. Zarathustra's affirmation is not the result of a calculating knowledge that determines it is better to affirm than to deny, for it takes place only as the boundaries of the self are broken, as the self is overtaken by the "Yes." This "Yes" is not something he controls, but something that occurs in him, an affirmation that strikes in "lightning bolts that say 'Yes' and laugh 'Yes.' " Zarathustra gives all he has to the soul, and he bids it to say "Yes," but it is only the soul that can make the affirmation. Zarathustra is beyond himself in this "Yes." He cannot grasp affirmation, he cannot master it and have it. He can will it, but this will must be enacted as a joyful love by which Zarathustra moves beyond himself in a receptivity to life and through which life affirms itself in him.

"To Share not Suffering but Joy": Nietzsche's Affirmation

This "Yes" is not all there is to affirmation, however. It makes affirmation possible, but affirmation as a mode of life, a way of living, is more complex. To articulate in more detail what Nietzsche means by affirmation, it is necessary to consider Nietzsche's view of love and joy. The suffering that the Nietzschean practices is not only personal suffering, but a more generalized human suffering. As I have argued, Nietzsche's philosophical methods—such as the "hermeneutics of desire" or, more generally, "perspectivism"—are as much spiritual practices of discernment and transformation as they are exemplifications of epistemological theory. Specifically, when he writes of philosophy understood as wandering or traveling in "many distant, terrifying worlds," viewing life from different perspectives, Nietzsche signals that he is less interested in philosophy as constructing a coherent theory of knowledge than in inhabiting different points of view as a way of learning about others and about oneself. As suffering drives him to explore the depths of his own life, and so to open himself to further suffering, Nietzsche encounters many different possibilities of suffering and philosophy. "A philosopher who has traversed many kinds of health, and keeps traversing them, has passed through an equal number of philosophies" (GS: 35). These enable him to understand the suffering of many different kinds of people.

Anyone who manages to experience the history of humanity as a whole as his own history will feel in an enormously generalized way all the grief of an invalid who thinks of health, of an old man who thinks of the dreams of his youth, of a lover deprived of his beloved, of the martyr whose ideal is perishing, of the hero on the evening after a battle that has decided nothing but brought him wounds and the loss of his friend. (GS: 268)

As psychologist (and artist), the genuine philosopher is able to make many types of people come to life in his own "underworld." The "reality" to which such a philosopher has access in suffering is not a metaphysical reality, but the reality of one's own suffering body and soul and, in this process, the bodies and souls of others.

Nietzsche's practice of suffering, then, depends on a kind of empathy. True, he calls this empathy "enormously generalized," less empathy with particular individuals than with types. One might therefore accuse Nietzsche of knowing suffering in the kind of generalized or aestheticized way that Surin and Ricoeur criticize. But a consideration of Nietzsche's critique of pity opens up a different way to look at the issue. Nietzsche was vituperative in his attack on Christian pity—*mitleid*, literally, suffering-with. But to suffer-with admits of at least two meanings. One can suffer-with in a way that shares with the other your knowledge of his or her suffering, or you can suffer-with from a distance, recognizing the suffering of the other, even experiencing it yourself, without communicating that knowledge or feeling to that person in any direct way. It is the former kind of suffering-with that Nietzsche rejects as pity. In part, he does so because he believes that sharing suffering shames the one who suffers, and he believes that shame is the worst form of suffering there is. Pity, on this view, *imposes* upon the other a particularly wasteful and demoralizing form of suffering. Speaking through Zarathustra, Nietzsche writes: "Thus speaks he who has knowledge: shame, shame, shame—that is the history of man. And that is why he who is noble bids himself not to shame. . . . If I must pity, at least I do not want it known; and if I do pity, it is preferably from a distance" (Z: 88). More importantly, however, Nietzsche rejects pity because when one responds to another in pity, one threatens to tear the sufferer away from his or her suffering:

Is it good for you yourselves to be above all full of pity? And is it good for those who suffer?. . . Whenever people notice that we suffer, they interpret our suffering superficially. It is the very essence of the emotion of pity that it strips away from the suffering of others whatever is distinctly personal. . . . They wish to help and have no thought of the personal necessity of distress, although terrors, deprivations, impoverishments, midnights . . . are as necessary for me and you as their opposites. It never occurs to them that, to put it mystically, the path to one's own heaven always leads through the voluptuousness of one's own hell. No, the "religion of pity" (or "the heart") commands them to help, and they believe that they have helped most when they have helped most quickly. (GS: 269)

Pity, for Nietzsche—both in extending it and receiving it—tempts one away from oneself, it distances one in a deadening way from the suffering body. In his view, it is only in moving through suffering—through one's own "hell"—that one finds one's own path and one's own joy.

Nietzsche rejects pity as sharing and shaming, but this does not mean that he refuses to suffer or to recognize or feel the suffering of others. In fact, it is only because he can feel the suffering of others that the philosopher is, according to Nietzsche, always tempted by pity: "The more a psychologist—a born and inevitable psychologist and unriddler of souls—applies himself to the more exquisite cases and human beings, the greater becomes the danger that he might suffocate from pity" (BG: 217). Though he does so from a distance, Nietzsche does practice a kind of empathy or compassion. Consequently, his view of suffering must be distinguished from the stoicism, or simply the cruelty and callousness, with which he is sometimes identified.[20]

There is, nevertheless, a connection with others that is missing from Nietzsche's vision, one that has both ethical and philosophical consequences. Zarathustra suffers with the higher men but resists pity. And in the end, he is alone, having turned from the higher men to seek his true companions. Nietzsche's writing resounds—in vain, it seems—with the call for those who can "hear" him. But who can hear him? Who are his true companions? The difficulty interpreters have in discerning the genuine compassion in Nietzsche's thought results in part from his refusal/inability to communicate compassion except in the most oblique manner. To the extent that he seeks to communicate only to select, noble souls, this indirection is intentional on Nietzsche's part, and it is of a piece with his tendency to focus only on suffering to which one can respond out of one's own strength. His ideal is the tragic hero who struggles valiantly and alone against inexorable fate, and he is critical of the demand to "suffer with" those who cannot fend for themselves against the misfortune or the evil they encounter. Nietzsche claims, correctly, that the Christian idea of sin threatens to turn all suffering into punishment and destructive self-condemnation. However, he fails to acknowledge the danger of his approach to suffering: turning *all* suffering into a test of spirit. Nietzsche's legitimate concern for the superficiality of pity leads ultimately to a failure to recognize the value of community and human love as compassion, a failure that prevents the affirmation of full human relationship.

[20] See Nussbaum 1993 and Tillich 1952.

Each of us, at least to some extent, is alone with our suffering. Compassion, like all powerful spiritual practices, can therefore be used stupidly, because it can undermine self-reliance. But this does not mean that all compassion—not from a distance, but fully engaged with the sufferer—tears us away from or prevents us from reaching that place—the dark night of the soul—that both Nietzsche and the Christian mystics find so important. Compassion can be a powerful mode of attention to the other that seeks to discern when another is being overwhelmed to the point of physical or spiritual paralysis—as Nietzsche knows is all too possible. Thus, as Soelle argues, compassion, expressed in both "spiritual" and "material" ways, can in many instances be that which enables certain people to discover or rediscover the strength that allows them to go on to confront and affirm their own suffering. Nietzsche seems blind to the strengthening power of a certain kind of love, and so does not distinguish suffering that will make one more powerful in love and spirit from suffering that destroys.

There is, however, a way to respond to this criticism on Nietzsche's behalf, for he is not without a positive vision of human relationship. He has a strong appreciation for the value of friendship as the Greeks understood it, the noble, self-full love of *philia*, rather than the self-less love of *agape*. Moreover, his attack on pity is accompanied by the claim that his goal is to teach others how "to share not suffering but joy" (GS: 271).[21] Love between friends consists primarily, for Nietzsche, in sharing joy. To what extent might sharing one's joy with one who suffers do more to empower him or her than sharing suffering? Is it possible that sharing joy is more compassionate than sharing suffering?

Nietzsche argues that pity is a means of erasing the differences between self and other and holding the deepest sufferings at bay. When one pities, one assimilates the suffering of the other to one's own experience, in part, no doubt, out of genuine concern to communicate, but also in part, thinks Nietzsche, to save ourselves from facing the concrete particularity—and the difficulty—of the other's suffering. The effect, then, is actually to silence the sufferer. Genuine friendship, for Nietzsche, is different, because it is based in the recognition of difference between self and other. To be able to have a friend is to be able to see the other as other, as different. Friendship, claims Nietzsche, is therefore intimately linked with enmity, not in the sense of envious hatred, or a desire to conquer, but in the sense of resistance that refuses to assimilate the friend to oneself, that keeps the differences alive. Ever critical of liberal tolerance, Nietzsche holds that the genuine response to difference, on some very fundamental level, is resistance, but an attentive resistance. Friendship requires resistance because one should become for one's friend a beacon for overcoming, be-

---

[21] "[Men of] antiquity knew better how to rejoice: we how to suffer less. . . . Perhaps we are only constructing the foundations upon which [to] again erect the temple of joy" (HH: 259).

cause friendship is based in "a *shared* thirst for an ideal above [the friends']" (GS: 89). And this means that one should hide one's "compassion . . . under a hard shell" in order to encourage the friend to find his or her own resources for self-overcoming. Resistance in this sense also means keeping enough of a distance so as to be able to continue to recognize difference and so truly to relate to the other as other. "In a friend one should have one's best enemy. You should be closest to him with your heart when you resist him" (Z: 56).

As he imagines it, then, Nietzsche's *philia* is a love constituted out of tensions and differences. For that very reason it is a genuine bond between persons, to be distinguished from forms of love in which difference is erased, love that finds reason only in an engulfing intoxication such as the surreptitious love of oneself, or love that seeks to lose oneself in the other. "What is love but understanding and rejoicing [*freuen*] at the fact that another lives, feels and acts in a way different from and opposite to ours? If love is to bridge [*überbrucke*] these antitheses through joy [*Freude*] it may not deny [*aufheben*] or seek to abolish them.—even self-love presupposes an unblendable duality (or multiplicity) in one person" (HH: 229–30).

Love is a form of joy—"rejoicing" in the encounter with the other as other, whether the other is another person or an aspect of oneself. Again, we see that Nietzsche thereby refuses a certain kind of mastery of consciousness and knowledge that assimilates the other to oneself, attempting to unify the multiplicity and difference even within the self. This refusal, viewed positively, is love. In this sense, love is an expression of the passion for the real because it demands the attention that allows the other to be and therefore allows one to experience the other as other. Clement Rosset has emphasized this point with respect to the significance of music for Nietzsche as a "witness to the world." Rosset (1993) cites *The Gay Science*:

> This is what happens to us in music: First one has to *learn to hear* a figure and melody at all, to detect and distinguish it, to isolate it and delimit it as a separate life. Then it requires some exertion and good will to *tolerate* it in spite of its strangeness, to be patient with its appearance and expression and kindhearted about its oddity. Finally there comes a moment when we are *used* to it, when we wait for it, when we sense that we should miss it if it were missing; and now it continues to compel and enchant us relentlessly until we have become its humble and enraptured lovers who desire nothing better from the world than it and only it. But that is what happens to us not only in music. That is how we have *learned to love* all things that we now love. (GS: 262)

To suffer, in the most general sense, is to find oneself impinged upon by that which is other. Love is thus a practice of suffering, though not a sharing of suffering. To speak of love in this manner, however, is also to point out that it involves not only the passivity of being impinged upon by the other, but also the activity of *desiring* the other as other. Desiring the suffering that this entails is, as we find in the mystics, an expression of the love for the real.

"Joy" is that which one gives and shares in friendship (HH: 180). Nietzsche places immense value, in his writing, on giving: his affirmer is an "overflowing" spirit whose creations are gifts given out of fullness, gratitude, and love.[22] In the final speech of Book One, Zarathustra proclaims the "gift-giving virtue" as the highest virtue. He explains this virtue by distinguishing two kinds of selfishness: first, a selfishness that proceeds from a powerful self-love overflowing in gifts of love; second, a "sick selfishness" that is greedy and needy, taking simply to fill an endless lack that can never give freely. Each form of selfishness corresponds to a kind of selflessness. With respect to sick selfishness, selflessness is always reluctant and instrumental, giving (of) oneself only under the threat of punishment—the "spasm of the scourge"—or the lure of reward. It is a calculating virtue, giving in order to receive, seeking its own best interest. "And now you are angry with me because I teach that there is no reward and paymaster? And verily, I do not even teach that virtue is its own reward" (Z: 93–94). Healthy, powerful giving, by contrast, gives itself in the overflowing of love; this is *active* giving, giving out of the urge to create, without regard to itself or thought to reward. To the extent that one gives without calculation of reward, one gives selflessly. It is only selfish in the sense that what is given comes out of one's fullness, made possible by a loving cultivation of oneself. For Nietzsche, one must give freely and be willing to lose oneself, to let go of oneself at least to some degree, in order for giving to be genuine.[23] There is an ecstatic element to Nietzsche's conception of giving and creativity, and he writes, "It is in this *state of consecration* that one should live" (D: 223).

This sharing of joy is also the basis for the Nietzschean ethic. Zarathustra invokes love to explain virtue, finding the origin of all such virtue in the grace of "the lover's will" (Z: 76), and he proclaims that when we learn to feel joy "we learn best not to hurt others or to plan hurts for them" (Z: 88). He even warns against a pathos of heroism that takes pride in the self-denial of self-overcoming. Such pathos leads only to hatred and gloom, and cannot discover the blessedness of joy. Instead of asserting one's heroism, Zarathustra counsels, one should learn "beauty," "laughter," and "kindness" (Z: 118). Nietzsche's power, on this reading, is not

---

[22] Zarathustra says that he leaves his solitude in order to "give away and distribute" his wisdom. "Behold, this cup wants to become empty again, and Zarathustra wants to become man again" (Z: 10).

[23] For related reflections on giving, reciprocity, and ethics, see Derrida 1992a and 1995. For a response to Derrida, see Milbank 1995.

a violent explosion of dominating will. It is far too simplistic to view his "will to power" in terms of some kind of egoistic, self-aggrandizing power over others. On the contrary, it involves an elevated, ecstatic state of "will-lessness," a state where one's personal will is transcended in a graceful giving. It is not too much of a stretch to find here in Nietzsche a version of the Augustinian ethic: "Love, and do what you will."[24] This joyful will-lessness is the essence of mystical love for the world.

Williams and Soelle demonstrate in their reading of the Christian mystical tradition that what persists through the dark night of the soul, the suffering encounter with the real, is love, not God the Redeemer, but God the lover experienced as one's own love for the world. As Nietzsche conceives it, the analogous experience is the experience of creative love, which both connects us with the concrete reality of the world and also detaches us from it. One must give oneself, in love, to the other. However, in order to continue willing and loving, one must also be able to detach oneself from that which is created and loved, in order to maintain the awareness of the greater movement of love and creativity. "Verily, through a hundred souls I have already passed on my way, and through a hundred cradles and birth pangs. Many a farewell have I taken; I know the heartrending last hours. But this my creative will, my destiny, wills it" (Z: 87). The Nietzschean self, as portrayed in these sections from *Zarathustra*, finds itself enmeshed in relations of creativity and love that, however crucial and constitutive of the self, are relativized in a broader or deeper connection with a process of power/creativity that Nietzsche calls "life." In order to maintain the positive intensity of life, Zarathustra claims that all one's creations and loves—all that is oneself—have to at least in some way be overcome or abandoned.

"Love," as Nietzsche understands it, is a rejoicing in the other, a directionality toward or desire for the other manifested in creative giving. "Joy" is a more generalized state of relation to the whole of world and life. To put it in terms of love, joy is that element of love that joins the lovers in something beyond themselves, the transcendent aspect of love that makes "sharing" possible even as the friends resist one another. As such, joy is a complicated, even paradoxical state or mood. Wanting itself and the agony of the world, joy is more comprehensive than the feeling of rejoicing in or desiring of some particular object. Nietzsche isolates two movements of the will, two registers of mystical abandonment: the abandonment of an overflowing giving that forges relations of love, and the abandonment of oneself as invested in that love. With respect to each,

[24] Henri Birault, in his essay "Beatitude in Nietzsche," quotes Nietzsche's notebooks: "What must I do to be happy? That I know not, but I say to you: Be happy, and then do as you please" (1985: 222). Nietzsche also writes: "An action compelled by the instinct of life has in the joy of performing it the proof it is a right action" (AC: 132).

Nietzsche is concerned with the way the self finds itself subject to a will to power that is both within it and beyond it. This will compels the self always to move beyond itself in acts of giving and self-transcendence. On this view, the self is not an atomistic soul, but a dynamic movement of will, ever reaching out and beyond itself. At the heart of this movement is a relation between the self, as ego, and the will to power, as that which both grounds the self and transcends the self. Embracing the will to power, one lives intensely and affirmatively in a continual re-creating and overcoming of the self, a new casting forth of the self in the world. In the end, this is what I think Nietzsche means by affirmation: not simply the love that perseveres through dark nights of the soul, but the flowering of this love into an embrace of the whole, in all its joy, in all its pain. In Nietzsche's terms, such flowering is the manifestation of the divine. This transfiguration of the human into the divine is not a matter of attaining a superhuman, overhuman omniscience or omnipotence, but a matter of active love that blesses all of existence. For the affirmer, in the affirmer, life says "Yes" to itself: "eternal Yes of being/eternally am I thy Yes:/for I love thee, O eternity!" (DD: 67). Affirmation is mystical participation.

A Divine Way of Thinking

The rhetoric of secular ideology makes it easy for most readers to identify religion in Nietzsche's texts as the embodiment of a nihilism to be overcome. In turn, this has made it difficult to see that the questions he raises and the possibilities he imagines with respect to religion are far more complex than is allowed by a simplistic reading of his attack on religion. But the secular reading of Nietzsche results from far more than ideological struggle (and than Nietzsche's own ambivalences). The pronouncement of the madman—"God is dead"—has resonated with the temper of the late-nineteenth and twentieth centuries because Western culture during that period has been deeply informed by a sense of loss of what people imagine to have been a richer, more cosmic, more meaningful way of being in the world. The fear expressed by the madman in the face of his own pronouncement speaks clearly to the culture shaped by nostalgia for God, or faith, or simply meaning.

One of the first, and among the most important, of the intellectual figures to be deeply influenced by Nietzsche was Max Weber. In his own conceptual idiom, Weber treated the loss proclaimed by Nietzsche's madman as "disenchantment," understood as a historical trajectory in which magic and religion are lost to human beings in the face of increasing rationalism. In this process, "the world's processes become disenchanted . . . and henceforth simply "are" and "happen" but no longer signify anything." (1978: 506). Thus Nietzsche's early despair in the face of a demystifying rationality whose imperative he could not and would not escape; thus Weber's lifelong struggle with the problem of meaning; thus the nihilism of modernity: as human beings perfect reason, they lose the reason to live. For Weber, the loss of such signification led to an intensification of the importance of meaning: "It is the intellectual who conceives of the 'world' as a problem of meaning. . . . As a consequence [of disenchantment] there is a growing demand that the world and the total pattern of life be subject to an order that is significant and meaningful." Since the meaningful order of the world was no longer simply "there" or self-evident, no longer inhered in the relation of one's god or gods to the world in a relatively unproblematic way, meaning became an articulate problem and demand. The modern fascination with meaning, and the modern study of religion's tendency to cast religion as a meaning-creating force, are consequences of this demand. Lost sight of in this process of intellectualization is the fact that meaning, when it is most meaningful, is not an intellectual, self-conscious sense of the world's significance as much as it is a lived, embodied, practiced relation to the world: the world "is" meaningful, the natural and the cultural are much closer together than they become in the modern period.

The mature Nietzsche, the Nietzsche who already had expressed a yearning for "Dionysian magic" and dancing muses in his first books, and who had written *Zarathustra*, suggests a new way to enchantment, through affirmation. On the one hand, Nietzschean enchantment is based in the recognition that after the death of God, meaning does not inhere in the cosmos as objective reality, but is created in and through human beings. On the other hand, however, Nietzsche is not paralyzed by the modern illusion that human creation emerges simply out of the autonomous subject. Creation happens—it is as much, maybe more, an event than an intentional action. Nietzsche's enchantment does not renounce the imperatives of modern rationality, however, but works only through close attention to the real and the natural. For the real, as Nietzsche sees it, happens at the interstices of imagination, creation, and nature. Nietzsche's mysticism is a discipline of finding/creating magic in the "closest things."

In the spring of 1888—as he was preparing to write *Twilight of the Idols* and *The Antichrist*—Nietzsche wrote an extended entry in his notebooks, entitled "On the History of the Concept of God." There he identifies the concept of god with the will to power of a people, he distinguishes between decadent and ascending gods, and he rejects the popular nineteenth-century claim that the development from the God of ancient Israel to the Christian God of pure goodness represents an advance. This last, he claims, is "God degenerated to the contradiction of life, rather than its transfiguration [*Verklärung*] and eternal 'Yes.' " Christianity, he complains, has prevented the creation of new gods: "Almost two thousand years: and not a single new god!" He ends, however, on a hopeful note.

> And how many new gods are still possible! As for myself, in whom the religious, that is to say god-forming instinct occasionally becomes active at impossible times—how differently, how variously the divine has revealed itself to me each time! So many strange things have passed before me in those timeless moments that fall into one's life as if from the moon, when one no longer has any idea how old one is or how young one will yet be—I should not doubt that there are many kinds of gods. (SW 13: 523–26)

Nietzsche proclaims the death of the Christian God, but, as he attests here, more gods are still possible. And, in one of his "Dionysian Dithyrambs," he speaks to one of these, whom he describes only as an "unknown god."

> No!
> Come back!
> *with* all your torments!
> All the streams of my tears
> run their course to you!
> and the last flame of my heart,
> it burns up to you.
> Oh come back,
> my unknown god! my *pain*!
> my last happiness!
>
> (DD: 57)[25]

As an expression of a passion and praise for life, Nietzsche's affirmation is a declaration of divinity. When one says "Yes" out of the deepest suffering and the deepest joy, when one says to the "demon" who proclaims eternal recurrence, "You are a god," one declares divinity. The divine reveals itself to the affirmer in the sense that to affirm is to deify. After the death of God, the point for Nietzsche is not to discover new gods, nor to determine a new eternal will or order, but to find his own will, deep beyond his personal self, out of which he desires and creates gods.

These considerations raise the question of the significance of the "divine" in discourses such as Nietzsche's. Nietzsche writes of feeling divine; he invokes Dionysus. In doing so, is he simply using figurative language to communicate something human, all too human? Can the intensity he

---

[25] See also GS: 117, where Nietzsche describes the particular passion that defines nobility of soul as "offering sacrifices on altars that are dedicated to an unknown god . . . a self-sufficiency that overflows and gives to men and things."

experiences in his "inspiration," even if it cannot be reduced to any single materialist or naturalistic interpretation, at least be generally comprehended in terms of the relation between the intensity of body and significations of consciousness without involving any third term, such as "god"? In short, is divinity for Nietzsche simply a subjective, psychological state or, as in Feuerbach, a projection?

This question must be approached carefully, and I can only begin to do this here. First, the "divine" for Nietzsche is not realized in an independently existing entity or force—"Dionysus" is not a being. As creator and affirmer, Nietzsche is not interested in the metaphysical question of whether gods "exist" or not, nor whether reality, or "will," or "life," is divine "in-itself." Second, even if one therefore wants to call Nietzsche's divinity a projection, one must also recognize that it is not pathological, or alienating projection, for it is not an expression of need or the production of a lack. It is, instead, an expression of celebration and gratitude. Third, it is a mistake to move from these two points to the position that "divinity" in Nietzsche is "merely" a figure of speech that can, for all intents and purposes, simply be eliminated in a strict analysis of his ideas.

To encounter reality as perfection by creatively and lovingly living in it is to enact a divine transfiguration. In general, Nietzsche describes transfiguration in terms of art and philosophy rather than religion. But it should be clear that "art" and "philosophy" as we ordinarily understand them—creating beautiful things and careful thinking about important things—are not what Nietzsche had in mind here. Instead, philosophy and art are spiritual practices in which the highest possibilities of human life are realized—precisely because they are ways of living in which affirmation is enacted. The divine aspect of this affirmation is strongest in some of Nietzsche's comments on art. In his late work, the primary question is not how art comforts, but how certain kinds of art (most importantly, tragic philosophy) express certain elevated states of soul. "Dionysian art," Nietzsche's ideal, is the "transfiguring power of intoxication" rooted in the noble soul's overabundant "gratitude and love" (GS: 328). He therefore rejects the decadence and deadness of Kantian and Schopenhauerian idealizations of a disinterested "*L'art pour l'art.*" The artist as lover "becomes a squanderer . . . he believes in God again, he believes in virtue, because he believes in love" (SW 13: 299–300).

As John Sallis (1991: 71) writes, the identity of the Dionysian is "abysmal": it is realized only in a certain movement of creativity and not "in some originary being over against the individual." In part, this means that that which the artist/philosopher produces—works of art/philosophy—are ultimately less important than the process of growth and spiritualization by which they are generated. Dionysian art/philosophy is a process by which life speaks in and through one. This requires both a responsive listening and a creativity. For Nietzsche, the divine resides in this living relationship between self and reality by which one connects with that which is beyond oneself—"timeless moments that fall into one's life as if from the moon." Dionysian creation is participation. In this participation one "creates" gods. But, again, what is significant here is not the particular creation—divinity comes alive as neither projection nor object—but the state, the feeling of divine participation and gratitude, out of which the creation emerges. To reimagine religion in a Nietzschean key, one must take seriously the de-emphasis or subversion of god as entity that has persisted in apophatic mystical traditions, and which, for Nietzsche, is even evident in the life of Jesus. In *The Antichrist*, he writes: "*Evangelic practice alone* leads to God, it *is* God!" Religion, then, as a certain openness or responsiveness in which divinity is not so much encountered as realized.

In his final polemic against Wagner, Nietzsche asserts that the essence of all "great" art is "gratitude [*Dankbarkeit*]" (CW: 191–92). In the same note in which he affirms the possibility of new gods, Nietzsche describes religion as a "form of gratitude." He is more specific on this point in *Beyond Good and Evil*, for there he asserts that it is the noble religion of the Greeks that is characterized by gratitude (BG: 64). To qualify nobility in terms of such gratitude complicates the picture of the noble Nietzsche often gives us, particularly in the first essay of the *Genealogy*, for there the noble is simply active, blindly imposing himself on all around him. But when he describes nobility as thankful, he suggests that there is a way to be both active *and* receptive. The idea of gratitude also complicates Nietzsche's concept of art. It is only through the disciplined attention of the artist, a determined seeing, feeling, hearing of the real, that true creativity is possible. Nietzsche rejects the romantic cult of genius in favor of the "severe, noble, conscientious training in the service of art" (CW: 182). The artist does not assign meaning to the world as an autonomous consciousness, on the model of God the Creator. Often, it seems, the artist is as unsure about what a creation means as is his or her audience. Meaning emerges, and it is as much visceral and sensual as intellectual; creation, in a way, takes place beyond intention and meaning. Only through a certain abandonment of the self is the world experienced as enchanted and is one able to enchant the world. This is one reason why we should hesitate before locating mysticism in peak experiences. Is the word "experience" helpful in illuminating what happens in artistic creation? Is it not more illuminating to talk about a kind of event or interaction between artist and world or the artist and God?

The religious, mystical element in Nietzsche's thought is expressed in reverence as gratitude, not pious awe, but the active thankfulness for existence that is the active blessing of transfiguration—the art of apotheosis, the declaration of divinity (BG: 213; Z: 164; GS: 328). This declaration of divinity is a kind of deification, for such art, writes Nietzsche, is not only the "essentially *affirmation, blessing, deification of existence*"; it is itself "perfection of existence, [the] production of perfection and pleni-tude" (WP: 434). The point is a way of existing, a way of desiring and creating that attributes perfection to this life, here and now, that finds perfection in the creative, self-affirming surge of life always beyond itself. Divinity, for Nietzsche, is realized in the affirmative human being, in the transfiguration of reality accomplished in and through the reality of an affirmative life, in a love that reaches beyond, beneath the self and turns even the encounter with the demonic into a declaration of the divine. Nietzsche's reflection on Jesus applies equally to his affirmer. "[H]e knows that it is through the *practice* of one's life that one feels 'divine,' 'blessed,' 'evangelic,'. . . The profound instinct for how one would have to *live* in order to feel oneself 'in Heaven,' to feel oneself 'eternal' while in every other condition one by *no* means feels oneself 'in Heaven': this alone is the psychological reality of 'redemption.'—A new way of living, *not* a new belief" (AC: 156).

Conclusion

ALTERITY AND AFFIRMATION

> Is not this remythicizing a sign that the discipline of reality is nothing
> without the grace of imagination? that the consideration of necessity is
> nothing without the evocation of possibility?. . . What carries this
> mytho-poetic function is another power of language, a power that is
> no longer the demand of desire, demand for protection, demand for
> providence, but a call in which I leave off all demands and listen.
> (Paul Ricouer, *Freud and Philosophy*)

> Religion in the mind is not credulity and the practice is not forms. It is
> a life. It is the order and soundness of a man. It is not something *else*
> *to be got*, to be *added*, but is a new life of those faculties you have.
> (Ralph Waldo Emerson)

MADNESS

I BEGAN WITH THE PREFACES of 1886 and Nietzsche's celebration of a life rejuvenated in the recovery of health and love. By the turn of the new year 1889, Nietzsche had fallen into madness, where he would remain for the final ten years of his life. In the months leading up to his collapse, Nietzsche had been working at a feverish pace, and at times had experienced intense feelings of euphoria. Some of his most "affirmative" statements come out of this period, particularly in *Ecce Homo*. We do not know why Nietzsche went mad—whether he suffered from a congenital illness, whether he had contracted syphilis, or whether he simply broke down from the strain of various physical ailments and excessive mental effort. Whatever the cause, one cannot help wondering: how intimately are his ideas about human life and affirmation bound up with the excesses and deprivations of a life that ended in madness? Does Nietzsche simply think from a place that most of us will not or should not go? Alan Megill (1985) describes Nietzsche and some of his poststructuralist successors as "prophets of extremity." Nietzsche's was extremity practiced at the boundaries of the self, humanity, and the divine. His writings illuminate these brilliantly. But if he was a kind of prophet, one can imagine him speaking—to himself? to an other?—in a voice like that of Jeremiah, who laments before the Lord of the pain he suffers at being un-

---

Epigraphs: Ricoeur, 1970: 525; Emerson, as quoted in *Emerson: Mind on Fire* (Richardson 1995: 126).

ALTERITY AND AFFIRMATION 203

heard.[1] For Nietzsche's was also an extremity of solitude. He was a lonely, sickly man without home, without community. He celebrates his solitude, but he suffers from it as well. And in the end, it closed in on him, leading him to megalomania and, finally, to silence.

I have tried to turn our attention to the extremity of responsiveness that I believe is integral to Nietzsche's affirmative vision. It has too long been ignored, and it is a primary reason why I believe we are compelled to rethink the question of religion in Nietzsche. But when I look squarely at his life and his writing, I also find myself compelled to ask whether it was precisely with respect to the issue of responsiveness that both his life and his affirmative vision fail. In his life, Nietzsche was not able to practice relations with others that could support his affirmation; in his writing, such relations are, at the very least, muted—which is a very good reason they have been all but ignored. Nietzsche sought to find "bloom and magic" in the "near and nearest things" (*Diese nahen und nächsten Dinge*; HH: 8); he strained to hear, in "what is nearest and everyday," "unheard of things" (*das Nächsten, das Alltäglichen redet hier von unerhörten Dinge*; EH: 305). But relations of affirmative responsiveness are possible only in a spiritual practice that is as extreme in its embrace of the ordinary as it is in its desire to open itself to the extraordinary; a practice that is able to turn us back to the world renewed, invigorated, alive with the desire to be a human being in this world with other human beings. In the end, Nietzsche was unable to do this.

There are resources in Nietzsche for thinking such a turn. I have already discussed, briefly, his ethic of joy. In conclusion, I want to consider some of these resources by reflecting on how they help us rethink religion. But, in conclusion, I also remain unable to refrain from equivocating with respect to the question of religion in Nietzsche. A certain equivocation is the trade of the genealogist or the deconstructionist, for it is precisely the "is" of any definition, any essence, any philosophical conclusion, that one is interrogating. But ultimately my equivocation is not particularly sophisticated: I simply find myself caught between the recognition that, on the one hand, Nietzsche is far removed from any traditional and most commonly used conceptions of "religion," and, on the other hand, his thought exemplifies and expresses an embrace—even a faithful embrace— of existence, which I believe finds its closest analogs in particular expressions of Nietzsche's professed enemy, Christianity. Moreover, unlike many writers who embrace certain "postmodern" ideas and methods, or at least in contrast to the assurance with which they write the "undecidable," I find myself frustrated by the necessity of such equivocation. I am

[1] Jeremiah 20:7–8: "O Lord, thou has deceived me, and I was deceived; thou art stronger than I, and thou hast prevailed. I have become a laughingstock all the day; every one mocks me. For whenever I speak, I cry out, I shout, 'Violence and destruction!' For the word of the Lord has become for me a reproach and derision all day long."

tempted to relax my resistance to the "is" by stating flatly that Nietzsche is a religious thinker.

At the same time, I feel the need to resist this temptation. One way to do this, though it still frustrates the desire to take position or possession, is to declare Nietzsche a "postreligious" thinker. Certainly this has been implied in my claim that he can lead us to think beyond the secular/religious distinction.[2] Such a gesture at once asserts and withdraws a claim about the religiosity of Nietzsche's writings. It may be a self-serving gesture; but it does reflect Nietzsche's own practice of articulating possibilities which he then, in full view of the reader, subverts. He does this not so that the reader is forced to choose in the manner of an either/or. Instead, he does it to push the reader to think beyond. With this in mind, then, I resist positioning Nietzsche by attempting to explain how his own resistance to position can help us rethink religion in a postmodern age. This is a necessary task, for there are many who find themselves "beyond" religion, not as antireligious, modern secularists, but as postmoderns; that is, in no simple sense with or without religion.

To invoke the "postreligious" or the "postmodern" is to make explicit a form of equivocation. The prefix "post-" must be used with trepidation, subject as it is to many silly polemics, on the one hand, and to sloppy generality, on the other. Rather than simply invoke it, then, I will endeavor to explain here precisely how it can help us to reflect with some precision on Nietzsche and religion. I can summarize this effort by saying that I want to work toward a conception of the postmodern that can think and say "Yes," to ourselves and to alterity—that which is other than ourselves, or other than the human.

ON THE BOUNDARIES OF RELIGION

> The soul becomes the place in which that *separation of self from itself* prompts a *hospitality*, now "ascetic," now "mystic," that *makes room* for the other. (de Certeau 1992: 195)

Embodying Dionysus

I have argued that Nietzsche writes on the boundaries of philosophy and the boundaries of religion. Another way to put this is to say that he writes on the boundaries of representation: writing to represent, he also writes

---

[2] Leslie Paul Thiele claims that Nietzsche "secularizes piety" by distinguishing between religion as belief and affirmation as reverence (1990: 143). This is helpful if "secular" is taken simply to mean "this-worldly." But, as I have argued, the problem with contrasting secular in this sense to religious is that the temporal significance of "secular" helps prevent

resistance to representation. In the metaphorical turn of his writing, Nietzsche enacts a practice of the real in which words do not represent the real but rather perform the excess of becoming out of which human beings construct significance and meaning. Nietzsche thus moves toward the postmodern as the "aesthetic of the unrepresentable." For Nietzsche, the unrepresentable "is" Dionysus. Nietzsche's attention is critical and active, yet his thinking more generally only takes shape in an opening to something beyond the critical manipulations of the ego and consciousness—the voice of Dionysus. Dionysian thinking does not think from the metaphysical belief in God or gods, but it does think out of what may be called a postreligious practice of the declaration of divinity.

One of the polemical strategies employed to keep the difficulties of postmodernism at bay, and one often used to dismiss Nietzsche, is the accusation of "nihilism"—as if it were self-evident what nihilism entails. Modernist suspicions of postmodern nihilism are not without grounds, for much self-identified postmodern discourse is composed in the key of negativity. But whether such rhetoric necessarily excludes the "Yes" is, I think, an open question. At the very least, it is possible to distinguish different postmodernisms. Here, I follow Carl Raschke, who appropriates terms from David Levin to distinguish the "analytic postmodern" from the "metaphorical postmodern" (1996: 11). The former, Raschke argues, is in fact a reinscription of modernist antimetaphysics and is characterized by its own form of totalization: the nihilistic "exhaustion" of signification. This postmodernism, however, is no more than a hypermodernism: an intensification of the critical impulses of modernity minus the grounds of modern rationality or the hopes of modern humanism. Beyond hypermodernism, though, Raschke argues that a "metaphorical postmodern" offers a far more successful attempt to think the boundaries of modernity, for it both embraces the critical impulses of modernity and offers new possibilities for signification and value.

Metaphorical postmodernity makes this positive move by rooting itself in a "fundamental ontology of the body" in a manner akin to Julia Kristeva's semiotics of the body. Whereas analytic postmodernity relegates all significations to the ultimately meaningless play of signifiers, metaphoric postmodernity reconnects the signifier to the signified through the body: signification is not purely linguistic; it is somatic, it speaks desire. How-

us from acknowledging the key role of "eternity" in Nietzsche's thought, and, more generally, from thinking carefully about what "affirmation as reverence" might mean. As I have argued, this element of eternity transfigures the worldliness and the temporality of Nietzsche's thought. Once we are going to talk about a world reenchanted beyond the natural-supernatural distinction, the secular/religious distinction loses its force. But why exclude a different kind of piety, one that does not look beyond the temporality of this life, but to the passionate, eternal affirmation in and of this life?

ever, in order to avoid thinking of this body as a conceptual ground or a naturalistic foundation, it is important to consider how this body "speaks." Charles Winquist, close to Raschke on this point, explains by means of the psychoanalytic distinction between primary and secondary processes. We have no direct access to the primary processes of body and desire; these can only "speak" as mediated by the secondary processes of conscious reflection. To explore the connections between signification and desire, in other words, is to attempt to think the unthought or say the unsaid, to create, through metaphor and metonymy, a discourse at the limits of representation: "Any discourse about primary process is heuristic and provisional. To think of it as foundational is self-admitted irony . . . since whatever figurations represent the primary process are themselves simulacra, the achievement . . . is not that we now have principles for grounding discourse but that we have principles for turning discourse" (1995: 93). The metaphorical postmodernist seeks to open consciousness and language to the body, to the forces and intensities beyond meaning that help to shape and figure consciousness, forces and intensities that the dominant subjectivity of modernity seeks to repress or decode once and for all. The Dionysian body of metaphorical postmodernity is both material and metaphorical: body as the "dance" or "rhythm" of a multiplicity of drives and instincts, which, in their alterity, resist any final appropriation or reduction by consciousness. The body as metaphor is the body as a matrix of interpretation, nature suffused with culture to produce culture.

Within the "metaphorical postmodernism" the body and desire become heuristics for interpreting the relationship between consciousness and world. The body is the most immediate "other" to consciousness, and it is through the body and its primary processes that the world impinges upon consciousness and so upon language.[3] The body, in other words, is the site of suffering. The metaphorical postmodern is an opening to suffering. This opening of consciousness make possible a kind of listening that connects consciousness to the rhythms of signification and life, language and desire. This results in a new kind of discourse, metaphorical or poetic rather than simply conceptual; as Charles Winquist puts it: "a mixed genre of force and meaning. . . . Texts are places of meeting, theaters of conjunction and confrontation between the incorrigibilities of mind and body" (1995: 39). The point is not to exhaust meaning but to intensify force. This is accomplished by loosening the weave of discourse as meaning without unraveling it, interrupting consciousness with the entrance of intensity that brings the life of the body to the spirit of meaning. In one sense, this intensification of force destabilizes meaning, because it pre-

---

[3] See Winquist 1995; see Scarry 1985.

cludes totalization and rationalization. But in another sense, bringing the force of body and desire to meaning intensifies its meaningfulness. Emerson, as I have noted, found power in transition, which, when put in terms of writing, is the power of metaphor. The renunciation of representational or conceptual mastery, then, finds its positivity in the affirmation of the power of metaphor and body, the transfiguring dance by which the body is spiritualized and consciousness embodied.

Mastery and the Ends of Humanism

The critique of modern humanism found in certain Continental thinkers of the twentieth century—particularly in structuralists and poststructuralists—finds a key predecessor in Nietzsche.[4] His dismissal of the idea of social progress, his antidemocratic elitism, and, most important, his subversion of the philosophy of consciousness and the dominant subject constitute a kind of "antihumanism." Reflecting on Nietzsche and antihumanism is a complex matter, for there are two or three sides to every issue. For all his attacks on the ideals of modernity and humanism, Nietzsche seeks, on his own terms, to affirm, even to glorify the human. It should not be forgotten that he is an admirer of the Renaissance and of the humanistic impulses of that period that honored human intellect and creativity. And implicated in my very preliminary treatment of Nietzsche's ethic of joy in the previous chapter is the claim that he was not without hopes for greater human love and flourishing. But Nietzsche's glorification of the human appears politically and ethically problematic, to say the least. He does not believe in human equality—in either a political or a spiritual sense—and it is questionable whether one could extrapolate any basic human rights from his work. He imagines a social structure that has as a primary purpose the enhancement of the most spiritual individuals. There are obvious elitist and even oppressive implications in many of his political and ethical ideas. Even here, however, there is more to consider, as recent Nietzscheans, like Foucault, have reminded us. Such thinkers have exposed the dark side of the politics and ethics of the modern humanistic presumption to assert a fundamental, normalizing human nature upon which ideals of equality can be based. For Nietzsche, such concerns are intimately tied to his attack on monotheism and its "doctrine of one normal human type" and ideal (GS: 143).

Here, though, I want to emphasize a different perspective on the question of humanism, one figured in the invocations of "beyond" in the figures of the *Übermensch* and eternal recurrence. It is simplistic and distorting to read the *Übermensch* as a post-God apotheosis of the modern,

[4] See Frank 1989.

secular, that is, *humanist* project, for Nietzsche's *Übermensch*, to the extent that we can even call it an ideal, is not a "man" of the future. That is, the *Übermensch* is not an ideal emerging out of hopes for a future of increasing human autonomy and humanly engineered progress.[5] Instead, the *über* in *Übermensch* is a figure of transcendence, the "beyond" of "beyond good and evil." More literally, as Cavell reminds us, it is the *über* of *Übermorgen*—the day after tomorrow, as in "the philosopher is the man of tomorrow and the day after tomorrow" (Cavell 1995: 7). Nietzsche certainly is not without concern and hope for the future, but the day after tomorrow is always beyond, the philosopher is always turning toward a new dawn. The beyond of this *über* is the beyond of alterity, striking Zarathustra like lightning. It seems that the more Zarathustra tries to preach and grasp the ideal, the more it recedes from him. In the narrative of *Zarathustra*, the hope for the *Übermensch* is overtaken and shaken by the abysmal thought of the eternal recurrence of the small man. At this point, the *Übermensch*, at least as an ideal for the future, seems to disappear from the narrative; it no longer represents a new humanity, an evolution of the human into something bigger and better. What has happened instead is that the hope for the *Übermensch* opens up in Zarathustra a region of alterity; his imagination and poetic capacities have become receptive to dreams and visions inhabited by dwarfes, snakes, and strange, fantastic, and absurd "higher men," as well as moments of bliss and harmony. Occupied by something other than himself, Zarathustra is led on his quest by something(s) other. His quest does not end with the assertion or reassertion of Zarathustra's mastery: instead, he overcomes pity and finds eternity—and also finds that a new dawn awaits, and with it, more work to be done.

On this quest, Zarathustra not only refigures his relationship to himself, but also his relation to time. As many commentators have discussed, the embrace of eternal recurrence involves the ability to will the past, to view the past, no matter what has happened, as something one has willed. In one respect, this seems like a desperate assertion of the power of the will, an attempt to dominate time at least as wild as any modern attempts to take hold of the future. But when we reflect on how this refiguring of the past involves a refiguring of the future, things look different. Zarathustra's willing of the past involves the renunciation of a certain way of hoping for the future. After Book Three, Zarathustra must let go, to some degree, of his hopes for the future in order to embody the formula for greatness that Nietzsche articulates in *Ecce Homo* as "*amor fati*": "that one wants nothing to be different, not forward, not backward, not in all eternity" (EH: 258). Since he continues on with his work, this is not to

[5] In Derrida's words, the *Übermensch* "affirms play and tries to pass beyond man and humanism" (1978b: 292).

say that Zarathustra becomes resigned to whatever happens, only that this hope is less articulate, less determined, than it was at the beginning of the book. By the end of Nietzsche's self-acclaimed masterwork, as at the end of the *Genealogy*, it becomes very difficult to determine what the protagonist hopes for, though it is clear that a kind of hope remains alive. As much as Zarathustra wishes to create a future, he must also learn to "await" it.

Cavell finds a strong link between Nietzsche and Emerson with respect to this perspective on the future. Learning to await the future requires a new thinking, a kind of receptivity, a creativity that is not simply an assertion of the human, but something that happens, an event. "To learn to await, in the way you write, and therewith in every action, is to learn not to despair of opportunity unforeseen. That was always the knack of faith" (1981: 61). Such faithful receptivity to the future shows that the willing of the past is less a desperate assertion of the will than a liberation from fixation on the past, a detachment or departure from the past in a way that may only be possible by viewing the past as willed or in some sense determined. Nietzsche might say it is a way of "forgetting." Such receptivity opens up the present and the future, allowing one to see all opportunities.

Nietzsche thinks beyond humanism in thinking a new kind of transcendence, one with many contemporary echoes. Cavell describes this movement into the future as "steps, but without a path" (1995: 8). Elsewhere he invokes a passage from Emerson: "I shun father and mother and wife and brother when my genius calls me. I would write on the lintels of the door-post, *Whim*. I hope it is somewhat better than whim at last, but we cannot spend the day in explanation" (Emerson 1982: 179). Like Kierkegaard's Abraham, Emerson renounces communication, assurance, and even self-knowledge in the face of the call. One hopes the call is more than the voice of whim—Abraham hopes it is God—but that cannot be guaranteed or controlled; nor can the future wait. Faith, in this sense, is a response within a radical kind of uncertainty and within a kind of responsiveness to that which is unknown. It requires a kind of passivity at odds with modern humanism's ideal of constructive, calculating agency. George Steiner also uses the figure of an unknown path to describe the transcendence of creativity: "a step beyond both moral good sense and the existentially empirical . . . a step embarrassing beyond words where 'embarrassment' must serve precisely as that which compels inference beyond words" (1989: 200). Finally, Maurice Blanchot (1992) writes of *Le Pas Au-Dela*, or, the "step/not beyond." The duality of this title invokes a transcendence or transgression (the step beyond), only at the same time, and in an undecidable manner, that it recognizes a prohibition against such a step (do not go beyond). One does not "take" the step beyond, for transcendence happens precisely at the point where the self exceeds itself, is beyond activity. As Caputo puts it: "The step beyond, *le pas au-dela*, the pas-sage, the transcendence, or the 'transgression,' is . . . a passivity more passive than passivity. . . . [It is] the worklessness of patience, not the doing of an *agens* but the suffering of a *patiens*." (1997: 82).

One might read this as a counsel to quietism, a dangerous provocation to which we must respond with the redoubling of activity, vigilance, and responsibility. But for critics of modern humanism, such a response only threatens to reinforce the totalizing ethic of action that must control. Given the totalitarianisms that have been politically realized in this century, such antihumanism may seem like so much irresponsible hyperbole. Yet, it seems to me that the point is not to equate humanism with, say, Nazism, but to inquire carefully into the multifarious ways that humanistic injunctions to agency and control may be implicated in humanity's seeming rush to consume itself and the planet of which it is a part. It is to ask whether such injunctions prevent us from thinking and practicing a "passivity" that would create the silence and space that is indispensable for the responsiveness of genuine responsibility.[6] How do we respond to what is other, whether that be another person, an animal, or an ecosystem? Before we can even ask that question, another has to be posed. How do we see the other or listen to the other *as* other?

Paradoxically, we might begin with ourselves. It is clear that Nietzsche sees the self as a multiplicity, and in this he anticipates a central tenet of contemporary antihumanism. Nietzsche affirms humanity, then, only at the same time that he radically rethinks human subjectivity. Where Kantians and Romantics each posited a subject that in key respects inherited the unity, creative autonomy, and even freedom of the Christian God, Nietzsche asserts a subject that is subject to the ruptures and fissures of the body and necessity. This subject is creative, but it is not the master of its creativity; it seeks power, but it is human, finite power, not power modeled on the submission-omnipotence model of Christianity.[7] Nietzsche's is not a wholehearted rejection of subjectivity, agency, or intentionality, but, as Charles Winquist (1995) puts it so nicely, a "drift of subjectivity," as if the self awoke from its Cartesian/Kantian dream of foundational, unified selfhood to find itself afloat, washed about on the sea of the desiring body. To begin with ourselves and that alterity closest to us—the material body inaccessible to any direct conscious representation—we might begin to develop a practice of listening without (immediately) knowing or acting, attending without self-assertion. Opening one-

---

[6] See Welch 1989 and Niebuhr 1970.

[7] To follow through on this claim, which I cannot argue for here, would lead one, I think, to raise some important questions about recent treatments of the problem of autonomy in Nietzsche. See Rorty 1989 and Pippin 1991.

self to body is not simply opening ourselves to the material matrix out of which one's particular consciousness emerges—one's physical body. Body is metaphor, or, in this case, it may be more accurate to say, metonymy: the body stands for all that which is other, existing independently of me. To write out of the body, then, is to engage in a practice of responsiveness to that which is other. Passivity, in this sense, is not quietism, but passion, suffering oneself as another. It is what Nietzsche means by "becoming what one is": exposing oneself to the otherness within and without.

Nietzsche is not alone in the experience of this passion, as thinkers as different as Augustine—"I have been made for myself a land of difficulty and of great sweat and tears"—and Heidegger—"I have become a question unto myself"—attest. We might begin, in other words, with a kind of confession. Nietzsche's ideal is not some superhuman self that can say "Yes," but rather the ability to be able to say "Yes" to who one is. Nietzsche rejects the concept of responsibility to the extent that it presupposes a unified subject that ultimately is the cause of all thought and action; yet he practices another kind of responsibility—a responsiveness—as the conscious and deliberate meditation on the multiplicity at the heart of the subject. Nietzsche, as Sloterdijk (1987b) says, is a "thinker on stage," performing, creating a spectacle of and for himself by creating a space or a stage where the conflicts, desires, relations, and ideas from which he is constituted find their voice and character. He sets in play, with thought and imagination, forces of good and evil, excess and discipline, hate and love, blindness and insight. The discipline involved in this project requires the courage and strength to allow the different characters within one to take shape and improvise; it is a matter of resisting the temptation to direct them too forcefully to follow the script. Such spectacle provides a model of spiritual and ascetic practice in which one learns to explore oneself in order to set in play one's intellect and imagination, cruelty and perversity, in order to find out who one is and to learn how to take responsibility for oneself.

To take responsibility for oneself in the way I am describing does not mean to follow through indiscriminately on one's desires, hopes, and perversities in the world—to act the anarchy one is in all one's day-to-day relations with others. Part of the practice involved is learning how to think and feel one thing and do another. Nietzsche insists on creating a beautiful character through self-mastery. But such self-mastery does not seek to extirpate or deny the "turmoil of delusion and lust" that makes up the human self. Just because one thinks about and tries to do what is right or good does not mean that one should think and feel what is right or good. To try and make these the same is to engage in the kind of religious or humanistic asceticism that tries to forge a pure heart out of the fissures and resistances that make up the human self. Integrity in action is one thing, integrity of heart another. At the same time, however, I am not suggesting that to "become who you are" means to engage in a process of nonjudgmental, therapeutic self-discovery. What makes the Nietzschean spectacle so fascinating is that there are parts of the self that one does not like, that one hates and fears, that one knows are evil. The discipline involved here is to allow these aspects of oneself to have life and access to one's imagination, to resist the inclination to push these parts of oneself away, to distance them from oneself with labels like "neurosis," "false consciousness," "prejudice." For one thereby separates them from oneself, recognizing them as "problems" or "issues," and, in that very act, imagines that, "in reality," one is essentially good and whole—and meant for a different life. Through such strategies, one constitutes a reactive relationship to oneself and others. By contrast, an active relationship to oneself embraces who one is. Such an affirmation of the otherness of oneself is, in a sense, a submission, but it is a submission that, like sacrifice, is both passive and active. It requires a certain kind of ascetic discipline, or self-mortification, that resists the desire to separate oneself from one's otherness; but it also requires affirmation, an active submission, a "Yes" to who one is that submits without succumbing to a numbing self-hatred or resignation.

The question of faith, the "knack of faith," resurfaces. To say "Yes" to what is other in oneself, and in others, is to embrace a certain fatedness—not in order to resign oneself or submit to what must be, but in order to liberate oneself from the fixations that result from the need to control. And it is to take a certain risk, for the "Yes" only proceeds from the way of love, not the way of control. To become what one is does, then, entail a process of purification and transformation: a process of embracing, not excising or extirpating, a process of learning to love what (one) is.

Thinking Religiously: The Passion of Affirmation

It has been easy to assume that the pathos of Nietzsche's writing has its source in his reaction to the death of God: after this disaster, Nietzsche finds himself confronted with the prospect of meaninglessness and so asks how human beings can find or create new meaning. It would follow, then, that if one sought to articulate the religious significance of Nietzsche, one might explore the ways he creates new meaning. In the past century, it has been common for scholars of religion to find the key of religion in the creation of meaningful worlds.[8] In some respects, this would be right—

---

[8] See J. Z. Smith 1993: 290. Irena Makarushka has argued that the "inner desire" at the heart of Nietzsche's writing "can be interpreted as religious insofar as it is directed toward the creation of meaning." She argues that Nietzsche's desire is rooted in the "lack" that results from the death of God: after this disaster, Nietzsche sees the necessity of "creating the conditions for a meaningful life" (Makarushka 1994: 28).

Nietzsche is concerned with the meaningfulness of life after the death of God. But he imagines a creativity emerging not out of lack, but out of overabundance, out of the activity of affirmation rather than the reactivity of *ressentiment*. That is, Nietzsche does not react to the death of God, but, in fact, seeks to complete the act of God's murder as a condition, not the cause, of the creation of new meaning. After the death of God the meaning of meaning is decisively changed because it can no longer be seen simply to inhere in the nature of things, in the nature of God's cosmos. Human beings must now realize what we might call the finite and plural anthropocentrism of meaning: there is no single, eternal, God-given meaning because meaning is born and dies with humanity. Among other things, this entails for Nietzsche that meaning and value are to be loved as they are being created, but particular meanings are not to be held as absolute and turned into idols.

What is religious in Nietzsche is not meaning itself or even the creation of meaning, but affirmative reflection/practice with respect to the limits of meaning and the limits of the human. Which, as I have argued, means confronting and embracing the meaninglessness that inheres in all genuine alterity, and from that point searching for the bonds that allow some kind of response to it. Meaning emerges out of this search, but only in the context of the affirmation—we might call it the transfiguring, divinizing piety—that enables one to move forth, passionately, toward the other as other. Saying "Yes" out of love, one wills to let go of "the meaning of it all," one steps beyond, on a new path.

John Caputo writes that "Yes" is an elemental religious word (1997: 255). Nietzsche recognized this as well, for instance in *Ecce Homo*, when he pairs "Yes" with "Amen," and also in his notes when he writes, "Five, six seconds and not more: you suddenly feel the presence of the eternal harmony. . . . You seem to be in contact with the whole of nature and you say, 'Yes, this is true!' as God, when he created the world, said 'Yes, this is true, this is good' at the end of every day" (SW 13: 146). This is not to say that "Yes" is the essence of religion, for, as Nietzsche shows so well, powerful religious forces can also be set in motion by a "No." But insofar as it is an opening to both self and other, "Yes" is the first step in attending to and embracing existence, the first step in living an active passion for life. In this respect, the "Yes" decisively determines Nietzsche's conception of spiritualization and, I think, points in the direction of a religious thinking beyond the death of God, a way to think the religious (or to think religiously) after religion.

The attempt to envision or cultivate an affirmative humanity—finding ourselves in and through the elemental "Yes"—moves beyond modernity. Specifically, it moves beyond the endlessly critical impetus of the modern, demystifying mind. Despite the exhausting self-consciousness, the evasive writing, the constant undermining of ideals—all hallmarks of what

Raschke (1996) calls hyper-modernity—I cannot read Nietzsche, and I have tried to show in this book why no one should read Nietzsche, without being struck by the passion he writes and, more to the immediate point, by the *wonder* and *hope* he writes. Nietzsche's is far from the debilitating nihilism of the modern critical perspective that laments the loss of meaning. He moves us through this perspective, affirming the discipline of demystification, but out of a passion for the real, not hatred for the unreal, out of a "Yes" prior to any "No." The affirmative impetus of Nietzsche's critical writing engages and enlivens by bringing us before the real, which we can so easily hide from ourselves and others if we insist that it must be meaningful. Such insistence is yet another way of assimilating the other to ourselves. But by beginning in the "Yes," one allows the openness of wonder. We then can see things anew, as a child. "The child is innocence and forgetting, a new beginning, a game, a self-propelled wheel, a first movement, a sacred 'Yes.' For the game of creation, my brothers, a sacred 'Yes' is needed" (Z: 27).

To see things anew might mean thinking, once and for all, beyond religion. But with his unsettling passion, with the life that bursts from Nietzsche's writing even as it undermines and questions our aspirations and our common sense, life, this life, as he says, "becomes interesting again." In the elemental Yes, and in the practice of keeping this Yes before us and alive, life hears the demanding call of the depth of mystery and enchantment.

BIBLIOGRAPHY

Allison, David B., ed. 1985. *The New Nietzsche*. Cambridge, Mass.: MIT Press.

Altizer, Thomas J. J. 1985. "Eternal Recurrence and the Kingdom of God." In *The New Nietzsche*, ed. David B. Allison. Cambridge, Mass.: MIT Press.

Altizer, Thomas J. J., and William Hamilton. 1966. *Radical Theology and the Death of God*. Indianapolis: Bobbs-Merrill.

Antonaccio, Maria, and Schweiker, William, eds. 1996. *Iris Murdoch and the Search for Human Goodness*. Chicago: University of Chicago Press.

Asad, Talal. 1993. *Genealogies of Religion*. Baltimore: Johns Hopkins University Press.

Athanasius. 1980. *The Life of Anthony*, trans. Robert C. Gregg. New York: Paulist Press.

Augustine. 1961. *Confessions*, trans. R. S. Pine-Coffin. New York: Penguin Books.

Barker, Stephen. 1992. *Autoaesthetics*. Atlantic Highlands, N.J.: Humanities Press.

Barth, Karl. 1977. *Epistle to the Romans*, trans. Edwyn Hoskyns (from the 6th German edition). Oxford: Oxford University Press.

Bataille, Georges. 1992b.*Theory of Religion*, trans. Robert Hurley. New York: Zone Books.

———. 1992a. *On Nietzsche*, trans. Bruce Boone. New York: Paragon House.

Behler, Ernst. 1991. *Confrontations: Derrida, Heidegger, Nietzsche*. Stanford: Stanford University Press.

Berkowitz, Peter. 1995. *Nietzsche: The Ethics of an Immoralist*. Cambridge, Mass.: Harvard University Press.

Birault, Henri. 1985. "Beatitude in Nietzsche." In *The New Nietzsche*, ed., David B. Allison. Cambridge, Mass.: MIT Press.

Blanchot, Maurice. 1992. *The Step Not Beyond*, trans. Lycette Nelson. Albany: State University of New York Press.

———. 1985. "The Limits of Experience: Nihilism." In *The New Nietzsche*, ed. David B. Allison. Cambridge, Mass.: MIT Press.

Blondel, Eric. 1991. *Nietzsche: The Body and Culture*, trans. Sean Hand. Stanford: Stanford University Press.

Bloom, Allan. 1987. *The Closing of the American Mind*. New York: Simon and Schuster.

Boothby, Richard. 1991. *Death and Desire*. New York: Routledge.

Brown, Peter. 1988. *The Body and Society*. New York: Columbia University Press.

———. 1980. "The Philosopher and Society in Late Antiquity." In *The Center for Hermeneutical Studies, Colloquy 34*. Berkeley: Graduate Theological Union and University of California.

Burkert, Walter. 1987. *Ancient Mystery Cults*. Cambridge, Mass.: Harvard University Press.

———. 1985. *Greek Religion*, trans. John Raffin. Cambridge, Mass.: Harvard University Press.

Bynum, Caroline Walker. 1991. *Fragmentation and Redemption*. New York: Zone Books.

——. 1987. *Holy Feast, Holy Fast*. Berkeley: University of California Press.

Caputo, John. 1997. *The Prayers and Tears of Jacques Derrida*. Bloomington: Indiana University Press.

——. 1993. *Against Ethics*. Bloomington: Indiana University Press.

——. 1986. *The Mystical Element in Heidegger's Thought*. New York: Fordham University Press.

Carr, Karen. 1992. *The Banalization of Nihilism*. Albany: State University of New York Press.

Cavell, Stanley. 1995. "Time after Time." *London Review of Books*, 12 January.

——. 1990. *Conditions Handsome and Unhandsome*. Chicago: University of Chicago Press.

——. 1989. *This New Yet Unapproachable America*. Albuquerque, N. Mex.: Living Batch Press.

——. 1988. *In Quest of the Ordinary*. Chicago: University of Chicago Press.

——. 1981. *Senses of Walden: An Expanded Edition*. Chicago: University of Chicago Press.

——. 1976. "Knowing and Acknowledging." In *Must We Mean What We Say?* Cambridge: Cambridge University Press.

Cioran, E. M. 1995. *Tears and Saints*, trans. Ilinca Zorifopol-Johnston. Chicago: University of Chicago Press.

Clark, Maudmarie. 1990. *Nietzsche on Truth and Philosophy*. Cambridge: Cambridge University Press.

Coward, Harold, and Foshay, Toby, eds. 1992. *Derrida and Negative Theology*. Albany: State University of New York Press.

Daly, Mary. 1984. *Pure Lust*. Boston: Beacon Press, 1984.

Davidson, Arnold. 1995. "Introduction: Pierre Hadot and the Spiritual Phenomenon of Ancient Philosophy." In Pierre Hadot, *Philosophy as a Way of Life*, ed. Arnold Davidson. Oxford: Basil Blackwell.

Davis, Steven, et al., eds. 1981. *Encountering Evil: Live Options in Theodicy*. Atlanta, Ga.: John Knox.

de Certeau, Michel. 1992. *The Mystic Fable*, trans. Michael B. Smith. Chicago: University of Chicago Press.

——. 1986. *Heterologies*, trans. Brian Masumi. Minneapolis: University of Minnesota Press.

Deleuze, Gilles. 1983. *Nietzsche and Philosophy*, trans. Hugh Tomlinson. New York: Columbia University Press.

de Man, Paul. 1986. *The Resistance to Theory*. Minneapolis: University of Minnesota Press.

——. 1979. *Allegories of Reading*. New Haven: Yale University Press.

Derrida, Jacques. 1995. *The Gift of Death*, trans. D. Wills. Chicago: University of Chicago Press.

——. 1992b. "How to Avoid Speaking: Denials." In *Derrida and Negative Theology*, ed. Harold Coward and Toby Foshay. Albany: State University of New York Press.

——. 1992a. *Counterfeit Money: Given Time I*, trans. P. Kamuf. Chicago: University of Chicago Press.

Derrida, Jacques. 1987. *Of Spirit*, trans. Geoffrey Bennington and Rachel Bowlby. Chicago: University of Chicago Press.

———. 1981. *Positions*, trans. Alan Bass. Chicago: University of Chicago Press.

———. 1978b. *Writing and Difference*, trans. Alan Bass. Chicago: University of Chicago Press.

———. 1978a. *Spurs: Nietzsche's Styles*, trans. Barbara Harlow. Chicago: University of Chicago Press.

———. 1974. *Of Grammatology*, trans. Gayatri Chakravorty Spivak. Baltimore: Johns Hopkins University Press.

Dodds, E. R. 1965. *Pagan and Christian in an Age of Anxiety*. Cambridge: Cambridge University Press.

Dupré, Louis. 1993. *Passage to Modernity*. New Haven: Yale University Press.

———. 1987. "Mysticism." In *Encyclopedia of Religion*, ed. Mircea Eliade. New York: MacMillan.

———. 1979. *The Other Dimension*. New York: Seabury Press.

Durkheim, Emile. 1965. *The Elementary Forms of Religious Life*, trans. Joseph Ward Swain. New York: Macmillan.

Eagleton, Terry. 1990. *The Ideology of the Aesthetic*. Oxford: Basil Blackwell.

Emerson, Ralph Waldo. 1982. *Selected Essays*, ed. L. Ziff. New York: Penguin.

Faure, Bernard. 1991. *The Rhetoric of Immediacy*. Princeton: Princeton University Press.

Feuerbach, Ludwig. 1957. *The Essence of Christianity*, trans. George Elliot. New York: Harper and Row.

Figl, Johann. 1984. *Dialektik der Gewalt*. Düsseldorf: Patmos Verlag.

Forman, Robert K. C. 1990. *The Problem of Pure Consciousness*. Oxford: Oxford University Press.

Foucault, Michel. 1990. *The Use of Pleasure*. Vol. 2, *The History of Sexuality*, trans. Robert Hurley. New York: Vintage Books.

———. 1988b. "Technologies of the Self." In *Technologies of the Self*, ed. Luther H. Martin, Huck Gutman, and Patrick H. Hutton. Amherst: University of Massachusetts Press.

———. 1988a. *The Care of the Self*. Vol. 3, *The History of Sexuality*, trans. Robert Hurley. New York: Vintage Books.

———. 1980. *An Introduction*. Vol. 1, *The History of Sexuality*, trans. Robert Hurley. New York: Vintage Books.

———. 1979. *Discipline and Punish*. New York: Vintage Books.

Frank, Manfred. 1989. *What Is Neostructuralism?* trans. Sabine Wilke and Richard Gray. Minneapolis: University of Minnesota Press.

Fuss, Peter, and Shapiro, Henry, eds. 1971. *Nietzsche, A Self-Portrait in His Letters*. Cambridge, Mass.: Harvard University Press.

Gasche, Rodolphe. 1986. *The Tain of the Mirror*. Cambridge, Mass.: Harvard University Press.

Gillespie, Michael Allen. 1995. *Nihilism before Nietzsche*. Chicago: University of Chicago Press.

Gilman, Sander, ed. 1987. *Conversations with Nietzsche*. Oxford: Oxford University Press.

Gimello, Robert. 1983. "Mysticism in Its Contexts." In *Mysticism and Religious Traditions*, ed. S. Katz. Oxford: Oxford University Press.

Gimello, Robert. 1978. "Mysticism and Meditation." In *Mysticism and Philosophical Analysis*, ed. S. Katz. Oxford: Oxford University Press.

Graybeal, Jean. 1990. *Languge and the Feminine in Nietzsche and Heidegger*. Bloomington: Indiana University Press.

Gutman, Huck, Patrick H. Hutton, and Luther H. Martin, eds. 1988. *Technologies of the Self*. Amherst: University of Massachusetts Press.

Habermas, Jürgen. 1986.*The Philosophical Discourse of Modernity*, trans. Bruce Lawrence. Cambridge, Mass.: MIT Press.

Hadot, Pierre. 1995. *Philosophy as a Way of Life*, ed. Arnold Davidson. Oxford: Basil Blackwell.

Halperin, David. 1995. *Saint Foucault*. Oxford: Oxford University Press.

Harpham, Geoffry G. 1987. *The Ascetic Imperative in Culture and Criticism*. Chicago: University of Chicago Press.

Hart, Kevin. 1989. *The Trespass of the Sign*. Cambridge: Cambridge University Press.

Harvey, Van. 1995. *Feuerbach and the Interpretation of Religion*. Cambridge: Cambridge University Press.

Hayman, Ronald. 1982. *Nietzsche: A Critical Life*. New York: Penguin Books.

Heidegger, Martin. 1991b. *Nietzsche*, Vol., II, trans. David Farell Krell. San Francisco: Harper.

———. 1991a. *Nietzsche*, Vol., I, trans. David Farell Krell. San Francisco: Harper.

———. 1985. "Who Is Nietzsche's Zarathustra?" In *The New Nietzsche*, ed. David B. Allison. Cambridge, Mass.: MIT Press.

———. 1971. *Poetry, Language, Thought*, trans. Albert Hofstadter. New York: Harper and Row.

———. 1968. *What Is Called Thinking?* trans. J. Glenn Gray. New York: Harper and Row.

———. 1962. *Being and Time*, trans. John Macquarrie and Edward Robinson. NewYork: Harper and Row.

Heller, Erich. 1988. *The Importance of Nietzsche*. Chicago: University of Chicago Press.

Henrichs, Albert. 1993. "He Has a God in Him." In *Masks of Dionysus*, ed. Thomas H. Carpenter and Christorpher A. Farone. Ithaca: Cornell University Press.

Hick, John. 1981. "An Irenaean Theodicy." In *Encountering Evil: Live Options in Theodicy*, ed. Steven Davis et al. Atlanta, Ga.: John Knox.

Higgens, Kathleen. 1987. *Nietzsche's Zarathustra*. Philadelphia: Temple University Press.

Hodgson, Peter. 1989. *God in History*. Nashville, Tenn.: Abingdon Press.

Irigaray, Luce. 1991. *Marine Lover of Friedrich Nietzsche*, trans. Gillian Gill. New York: Columbia University Press.

James, William. 1985. *The Varieties of Religious Experience*. New York: Penguin Books.

Jantzen, Grace. 1995. *Power, Gender, and Christian Mysticism*. Cambridge: Cambridge University Press.

Jaspers, Karl. 1961. *Nietzsche and Christianity*, trans. E. B. Ashton. Washington, D.C.: Henry Regnery Co.

Jones, L. G., and S. Fowl, eds. 1995. *Rethinking Metaphysics*. Oxford: Basil Blackwell.

Kakar, Sudhir. 1991. *The Analyst and the Mystic*. Chicago: University of Chicago Press.

Kant, Immanuel. 1991. "What Is Orientation in Thinking." In *Kant: Political Writings*, ed. Hans Reiss. Cambridge: Cambridge University Press.

———. 1960. *Religion within the Limits of Reason Alone*, trans. Theodore M. Greene and Hoyt H. Hudson. New York: Harper and Row.

Katz, Stephen. 1978. "Language, Epistemology, and Mysticism." In *Mysticism and Philosophical Analysis*, ed. S. Katz. Oxford: Oxford University Press.

Katz, Stephen, ed. 1992. *Mysticism and Language*. Oxford: Oxford University Press.

———. 1983. *Mysticism and Religious Traditions*. Oxford: Oxford University Press.

———. 1978. *Mysticism and Philosophical Analysis*. Oxford: Oxford University Press.

Kaufmann, Walter. 1974. *Nietzsche: Philosopher, Psychologist, Antichrist*. 4th ed. Princeton: Princeton University Press.

Keller, Carl. 1992. "Mystical Literature." In *Mysticism and Language*, ed. S. Katz. Oxford: Oxford University Press.

Kieckheffer, Richard. 1984. *Unquiet Souls*. Chicago: University of Chicago Press.

Kierkegaard, Søren. 1983. *Fear and Trembling*, trans. and ed. H. V. Hong and E. H. Hong. Princeton: Princeton University Press.

———. 1980. *The Concept of Anxiety*, trans. and ed. Reidar Thomte. Princeton: Princeton University Press.

Kitamori, Kazoh. 1965. *Theology of the Pain of God*. Richmond, Va.: John Knox.

Klossowski, Pierre. 1985. "Nietzsche's Experience of the Eternal Return." In *The New Nietzsche*, ed. David B. Allison. Cambridge, Mass.: MIT Press.

Koelb, Clayton, ed. 1990. *Nietzsche as Postmodernist*. Albany: State University of New York Press.

Kofman, Sarah. 1993. *Nietzsche and Metaphor*, trans. Duncan Large. Stanford: Stanford University Press.

Krell, David Farrell. 1986. *Postponements: Woman, Sensuality, and Death in Nietzsche*. Bloomington: Indiana University Press.

Kripal, Jeffrey. 1995. *Kali's Child*. Chicago: University of Chicago Press.

Kristeva, Julia. 1987. *In the Beginning There Was Love: Psychoanalysis and Faith*, trans. Arthur Goldhammer. New York: Columbia Univeristy Press.

Lampert, Laurence. 1986. *Nietzsche's Teaching*. New Haven: Yale University Press.

Lowe, Walter. 1993. *Theology and Difference*. Indianapolis: Indiana University Press.

MacIntyre, Alistair. 1984. *After Virtue*. Notre Dame, Ind.: University of Notre Dame Press.

Makarushka, Irena. 1994. *Religious Imagination and Language in Emerson and Nietzsche*. New York: St. Martin's Press.

Markus, Robert. 1990. *The End of Ancient Christianity*. Cambridge: Cambridge University Press.

McGinn, Bernard. 1995. "Asceticism and Mysticism in Late Antiquity and the Early Middle Ages." In *Asceticism*, ed. V. Wimbush and R. Valantasis. London: Oxford University Press.

———. 1994. *The Foundations of Mysticism*, New York: Crossroad.

Megill, Alan. 1985. *Prophets of Extremity*. Berkeley: University of California Press.

Merton, Thomas. 1996. *Life and Holiness*. New York: Image Books.

Milbank, John. 1995. "Can a Gift Be Given? Prolegomena to a Future Trinitarian Metaphysic." In *Rethinking Metaphysics*, ed. L. G. Jones and S. Fowl. Oxford: Basil Blackwell.

———. 1990. *Theology and Social Theory*. Oxford: Basil Blackwell.

Miles, Margaret R.. 1992. *Desire and Delight: A New Reading of Augustine's Confessions*. New York: Crossroad.

———. 1990. *Practicing Christianity*. New York: Crossroad.

———. 1989. *Carnal Knowing*. Boston: Beacon Press.

———. 1981. *Fullness of Life*. Philadelphia: Westminster Press.

Miller, James. 1993. *The Passion of Michel Foucault*. New York: Simon and Schuster.

Miller, J. Hilles. 1979. *Deconstruction and Criticism*. New York: Seabury Press.

Miller, Patricia Cox. 1995. "Dreaming the Body: An Aesthetics of Asceticism." In *Asceticism*, ed. V. Wimbush and R. Valantasis. London: Oxford University Press.

Montinari, Mazzino. 1980. "Nietzsche's Nachlass von 1885 bis 1888." In *Nietzsche*, ed. Jörg Salaquarda. Darmstadt: Wissenschaftliche Buchgesellschaft.

Most, Otto. 1977. *Zeitliches und Ewiges in der Philosophie Nietzsches und Schopenhauer*. Frankfurt: Vittorio Klosterman.

Murdoch, Iris. 1993. *Metaphysics as a Guide to Morals*. New York: Penguin Books.

———. 1970. *The Sovereignty of Good*. London: Routledge & Kegan Paul.

Nehamas, Alexander. 1985. *Nietzsche: Life as Literature*. Cambridge, Mass.: Harvard University Press.

Niebuhr, H. Richard. 1970. *Radical Monotheism and Western Culture*. New York: Harper and Row.

Norris, Christopher. 1987. *Derrida*. Cambridge: Harvard University Press.

Nussbaum, Martha, C. 1993. "Pity and Mercy: Nietzsche's Stoicism." In *Nietzsche, Genealogy, Morality*, ed. Richard Schacht. Berkeley: University of California Press.

———. 1990. *Love's Knowledge*. Oxford: Oxford University Press.

Oliver, Kelly. 1995. *Womanizing Nietzsche*. New York: Routledge.

Otto, Rudolf. 1950. *The Idea of the Holy*, trans. John W. Harvey. Oxford: Oxford University Press.

Pagels, Elaine. 1989. *Adam, Eve, and the Serpent*. New York: Vintage Books.

Parkes, Graham, ed. 1991. *Nietzsche and Asian Thought*. Chicago: University of Chicago Press.

Penner, Hans. 1989. *Impasse and Resolution: A Critique of the Study of Religion*. New York: P. Lang.

Perkins, Judith. 1995. *The Suffering Self*. New York: Routledge.

Pippen, Robert. 1991. *Modernism as a Philosophical Problem*. Oxford: Basil Blackwell.

Proudfoot, Wayne. 1985. *Religious Experience*. Berkeley: University of California Press.

Raschke, Carl. 1996. *Fire and Roses*. Albany: State University of New York Press.

Richardson, Robert D. Jr. 1995. *Emerson: Mind on Fire*. Berkeley: University of California Press.

Ricoeur, Paul. 1980. *Essays on Biblical Interpretation*, ed. Lewis S. Mudge. Philadelphia: Fortress Press.

———. 1974. "The Hermeneutics of Symbols and Philosophical Reflection: I." In *The Conflict of Interpretations*," trans. Don Ihde. Evanston, Ill.: Northwestern University Press.

———. 1970. *Freud and Philosophy*, trans. Denis Savage. New Haven: Yale University Press.

———. 1967. *The Symbolism of Evil*, trans. Emerson Buchanon. Boston: Beacon Press.

Rieff, Philip. 1987. *The Triumph of the Therapeutic*. Chicago: University of Chicago Press.

Rorty, Richard. 1989. *Contingency, Irony, and Solidarity*. Cambridge: Cambridge University Press.

Rosen, Stanley. 1993. *The Question of Being*. New Haven: Yale University Press.

Rosset, Clement. 1993. *Joyful Cruelty*, trans. and ed. David F. Bell. Oxford: Oxford University Press.

Salaquarda, Jörg, ed. 1989. "Nietzsche's Metaphysikritik und ihre Vorbereitung durch Schopenhauer." In *Krisis der Metaphysik*, ed. G. Abel and J. Salaquarda. Berlin: Walter de Gruyter.

———. 1980. *Nietzsche*. Darmstadt: Wissenschaftliche Buchgesellschaft.

Sallis, John. 1991. *Crossings: Nietzsche and the Space of Tragedy*. Chicago: University of Chicago Press.

Sands, Kathleen. 1994. *Escape from Paradise*. Minneapolis: Fortress Press.

Scarry, Elaine. 1985. *The Body in Pain*. Oxford: Oxford University Press.

Schacht, Richard. 1983. *Nietzsche*. London: Routledge & Kegan Paul.

Schleiermacher, Friedrich, 1958. *On Religion: Speeches to Its Cultured Despisers*, trans. John Oman. New York: Harper and Row.

Schneider, Mark. 1993. *Culture and Enchantment*. Chicago: University of Chicago Press.

Schopenhauer, Arthur. 1969b. *The World as Will and Representation*, Vol. 2, trans. E.F.J. Payne. New York: Dover Publications.

———. 1969a. *The World as Will and Representation*, Vol. 1, trans. E.F.J. Payne. New York: Dover Publications.

Schrift, Alan D. 1990. *Nietzsche and the Question of Interpretation*. New York: Routledge.

Scott, Charles. 1990. *The Question of Ethics*. Bloomington, Ind.: Indiana University Press.

Sells, Michael. 1994. *Mystical Languages of Unsaying*. Chicago: University of Chicago Press.

Shapiro, Gary. 1991. *Alcyone*. Albany: State University of New York Press.

———. 1989. *Nietzschean Narratives*. Bloomington: Indiana University Press.

Sloterdijk, Peter. 1987b. *Thinker on Stage: Nietzsche's Materialism*, trans. Jamie Owen Daniel. Minneapolis: University of Minnesota Press.

———. 1987a. *Critique of Cynical Reason*, trans. Michael Eldred. Minneapolis: University of Minnesota Press.

Smart, Ninian. 1979. *The Philosophy of Religion*. Oxford: Oxford University Press.

Smith, J. Z. 1993. *Map Is Not Territory*. Chicago: University of Chicago Press.

———. 1982. *Imagining Religion*. Chicago: University of Chicago Press.

Smith, W. C. 1978. *The Meaning and End of Religion*. San Francisco: Harper and Row.

Soelle, Dorthee. 1975. *Suffering*. Philadelphia: Fortress Press.

Sprung, Mervyn. 1991. "Nietzsche's Trans-European Eye." In *Nietzsche and Asian Thought*, ed. G. Parkes. Chicago: University of Chicago Press.

Stambaugh, Joan. 1994. *The Other Nietzsche*. Albany: State University of New York Press.

Stang, Charles. 1997. "Nietzsche, Socrates, Jesus." Senior honors thesis, Harvard University.

Stauth, Georg, and Bryan S. Turner. 1988. *Nietzsche's Dance*. Oxford: Basil Blackwell.

Steiner, George. 1989. *Real Presences*. Chicago: University of Chicago Press.

Stevens, Wallace. 1982. *The Collected Poems*. New York: Vintage Books.

Surin, Kenneth. 1989. *The Turnings of Darkness and Light*. Cambridge: Cambridge University Press.

———. 1987. *Theology and the Problem of Evil*. New York: Basil Blackwell.

Taylor, Charles. 1989. *Sources of the Self*. Cambridge, Mass.: Harvard University Press.

Taylor, Mark. 1990. *Tears*. Albany: State University of New York Press.

———. 1987. *Altarity*. Chicago: University of Chicago Press.

———. 1984. *Erring*. Chicago: University of Chicago Press.

Teresa of Avila. *The Life of Saint Teresa by Herself*. New York: Penguin Books.

Thiele, Leslie Paul. 1990. *Friedrich Nietzsche and the Politics of the Soul*. Princeton: Princeton University Press.

Thoreau, Henry David. 1991. *Walden*. New York: Vintage Books.

Tillich, Paul. 1967. *Perspectives on 19th and 20th Century Protestant Theology*, ed. Carl E. Braaten. New York: Harper and Row.

———. 1957. *The Dynamics of Faith*. New York: Harper and Row.

———. 1952. *The Courage to Be*. New Haven: Yale University Press.

———. 1951. *Systematic Theology*. 3 vols. Chicago: University of Chicago Press.

Torrance, Robert. 1994. *The Spiritual Quest*. Berkeley: University of California Press.

Turner, Bryan S. 1984. *The Body and Society*. Oxford: Basil Blackwell.

Turner, Denys. 1996. *The Darkness of God*. Cambridge: Cambridge University Press.

Valadier, Paul. 1975. *Nietzsche: L'Athée de rigeur*. Paris: Desclée de Brouwer.

Valadier, Paul. 1974. *Nietzsche et la Critique du Christianisme*. Paris: Les Editions du Cerf.

Valantasis, Richard. 1995. "A Theory of the Social Function of Asceticism." In *Asceticism*, ed. V. Wimbush and R. Valantasis. London: Oxford University Press.

Ward, Benedicta, ed. 1980. *The Lives of the Desert Fathers*, trans. Norman Russell. London: Mowbray.

Ware, Kallistos. 1995. "The Way of the Ascetics: Negative or Affirmative?" In *Asceticism*, ed. V. Wimbush and R. Valantasis. London: Oxford University Press.

Weber, Max. 1985. *The Protestant Ethic and the Spirit of Capitalism*, trans. Talcott Parsons. London: Unwin.

———. 1978. *Economy and Society*, ed. Guenther Roth and Claus Wittich. Berkeley: University of California Press.

Weil, Simone. 1951. *Waiting for God*, trans. Emma Crauford. New York: Harper.

Welch, Sharon. 1989. *A Feminist Ethic of Risk*. Minneapolis: Fortress Press.

Westphal, Merold. 1993. *Suspicion and Faith*. Grand Rapids, Mich.: W. Eerdman's.

White, Alan. 1990. *Within Nietzsche's Labyrinth*. New York: Routledge.

Williams, Rowan. 1990. *The Wound of Knowledge*. Cambridge, Mass.: Cowley Publications.

Wimbush, Vincent, ed. 1990. *Ascetic Behavior in Greco-Roman Antiquity*. Minneapolis: Fortress Press.

Wimbush, Vincent, and Richard Valantasis, eds. 1995. *Asceticism*. London: Oxford University Press.

Winquist, Charles. 1995. *Desiring Theology*. Chicago: University of Chicago Press.

Wyschogrod, Edith. 1990. *Saints and Postmodernism*. Chicago: University of Chicago Press.

Yovel, Yirmiyahu. 1989. *Spinoza and Other Heretics*. Princeton: Princeton University Press.

INDEX

abandonment, 162, 195–96

abysmal thought, 130, 132, 183–84, 189, 208

Adorno, Theodor, 93n

"aesthetics of existence," 85–86, 94

affirmation, 8, 11–16, 29, 32, 45–47, 60–61, 102, 166–201; and asceticism, 70, 74–78, 88; in Christianity, 174–83, 195; and denial, 13–15, 20, 41, 104; and eternal recurrence, 169–74; and love, 51, 192–96; and mysticism, 127, 174–201; in Nietzsche's Jesus, 65; and philosophy, 16, 139; and religion, 5, 48, 61–66, 69, 75, 196–201, 212–14; in Schopenhauer, 25–29; and suffering, 166–201; in *Zarathustra*, 131–35 alterity, 17, 61–66, 99, 204–14

Altizer, Thomas J. J., 5n

amor fati, 208

antihumanism, 4, 207–12

Antony, Saint, 83, 96

apophasis, 112, 122–25, 155–57

Apollo(nian), 106–7, 140

appearance, 143–48

art: Dionysian, 143–48; and divinity; in Greek tragedy, 105–9; in Schopenhauer, 27; and transfiguration, 67–69, 199–201

Asad, Talal, 6n

ascesis, 80, 82n, 85; of the necessary, 14

ascetic ideal, 19, 52, 57, 78–92, 93, 95, 97, 100, 155, 165–66, 169, 179, 187; essay on, 73–74; and meaning, 35; in modernity, 38–41; Nietzsche's critique of, 37–41; as will to truth, 60

asceticism, 19–23, 77–102; Christian, 80, 82–90; and critique of western civilization, 19, 77–78; and gender roles, 88; and incarnation, 84; modern construction of, 19–23, 38–41, 78, 82–90; natural, 81–82; Nietzsche's, 19–21, 40, 90–102, 168; and Nietzsche's concept of philosophy, 81, 90–100; pagan, 82–90; and power, 53–55; and saintliness, 15; in Schopenhauer, 105; as self-deception, 79–82; and selfhood, 86–90, 156; and society, 86–88; and spiritualization, 70–74, 99–100, 178; as transfiguration, 92–93

atheism, 59–60

Augustine, 86, 87n, 90

bad conscience, 56–57, 60, 71, 97

Barth, Karl, 12

Bataille, Georges, 104n

becoming, 11, 139, 142–48, 156, 160, 161, 162, 168, 188, 205

being, 139, 142

Berkowitz, Peter, 132n

Birault, Henri, 195n

Blanchot, Maurice, 187

Blondel, Eric, 73, 160–61

blessedness, 63–69, 75, 109, 136n

body, 27, 44–46, 80, 82–93, 157, 160–62, 205, 210

breeding, 92–93

Brown, Peter, 82–88

Buddhism, 9, 125–26, 126n

Burkert, Walter, 112

Burrows, Ruth, 181n

Bynum, Caroline Walker, 82–84, 86–88, 177–78

Caputo, John, 185, 210, 213

Cavell, Stanley, 118–21, 124–28, 158–59, 208–9; on acknowledgment, 118–21, 145; on language, 119; on the ordinary, 120; on philosophy, 119; on poetry, 125, 159; on reading and writing, 124–25, 158–59

chaos, 145

Christian love mysticism, 112, 126n, 180–83

Christianity: denial of human power in, 75; in Hegel and Feuerbach, 59–61; as hermeneutic of suffering, 51–53; as morality, 60; Nietzsche's criticism of, 12, 19, 46, 57–63, 77–78, 182–83; Nietzsche's relation to, 7, 26, 99–100, 183–96; and nihilism, 12, 58; as priestly religion, 56; as reactive, 167; slave revolt/revaluation, 42

Clark, Maudmarie, 41, 71n, 79–80, 170–74

common, 154–55, 163

communication, 156–57

community, 54–57, 64, 71, 96–100, 154–55, 163

comparison, 22–23

compassion, 191–92

confession, 211

conformity, 56, 63, 64, 66, 71

consolation, 5, 8, 12, 31, 34, 51–52, 53, 104

About the Author

TYLER T. ROBERTS is Assistant Professor of Religious Studies
at Grinnell College.

MIRROR OF HIS BEAUTY

JEWS, CHRISTIANS, AND MUSLIMS
FROM THE ANCIENT TO THE MODERN WORLD

SERIES EDITORS
R. Stephen Humphreys, William Chester Jordan,
and Peter Schäfer

Imperialism and Jewish Society, 200 B.C.E. to 640 C.E.
by Seth Schwartz

Beautiful Death: Jewish Poetry and Martyrdom in Medieval France
by Susan L. Einbinder

*Power in the Portrayal: Representations of Jews and Muslims in
Eleventh- and Twelfth-Century Islamic Spain*
by Ross Brann

*Mirror of His Beauty: Feminine Images of God from
the Bible to the Early Kabbalah*
by Peter Schäfer

MIRROR OF HIS BEAUTY

FEMININE IMAGES OF GOD
FROM THE BIBLE
TO THE EARLY KABBALAH

Peter Schäfer

PRINCETON UNIVERSITY PRESS

PRINCETON AND OXFORD

Library of Congress Cataloging-in-Publication Data

Schäfer, Peter, 1943–

Mirror of His beauty : feminine images of God from the Bible to the early Kabbalah /
Peter Schäfer.

p.   cm.   — (Jews, Christians, and Muslims from the ancient to the modern
world)

Includes bibliographical references and index.

ISBN 0-691-09068-8 (cloth : alk. paper)

1. Femininity of God—History of doctrines.   2. Femininity of God—Biblical teaching.
3. Cabala.   I. Title.   II. Series.

BT153.M6 S+

291.2′114—dc21   2001058512

British Library Cataloging-in-Publication Data is available

This book has been composed in Sabon Typeface

Printed on acid-free paper. ∞

www.pupress.princeton.edu

Printed in the United States of America

1   3   5   7   9   10   8   6   4   2

For my parents

Agnes and Josef Schäfer

✺ CONTENTS ✺

❖ FIGURES ❖

❀ ACKNOWLEDGMENTS ❀

THIS BOOK began with a number of seminars on the topic at both the Freie Universität Berlin and Princeton University. I recall with great pleasure the last of them, a graduate seminar on "The Feminine Side of God in Judaism," conducted together with my Princeton colleague Elaine Pagels during the spring term of 1999. It was during and after this seminar that most of the actual writing of this book took place. Only Chapter 6 was published in a preliminary version, as "Tochter, Schwester, Braut und Mutter. Bilder der Weiblichkeit Gottes in der frühen Kabbala" in the journal *Saeculum* (vol. 49, 1998, pp. 259–279) and in an updated English translation in the *Journal of the American Academy of Religion* (vol. 68, 2000, pp. 221–242).

Like *Judeophobia: Attitudes toward the Jews in the Ancient World*, this book was written completely in English and not translated from my native German. In this, I benefited greatly from the help of my research assistants at Princeton, first Hannah Schell and then Annette Yoshiko Reed. It was above all Annette, a budding scholar of late antique Judaism in her own right, who not only exercised her merciless criticism on my English style but forced me to clarify my thoughts and to express myself in the most simple (and brief) manner possible; in fact, the intellectual exchange with her during the writing process was among my most rewarding scholarly experiences.

At the final stages before submitting the manuscript to the Press, Tamara Everhartz, Thomas Streffing, and Klaus Herrmann of the Berlin Institut für Judaistik helped me with the arduous task of double checking and completing the references and footnotes. I am indebted to them for their efficiency and persistence in tracking down the quotations and references that, in the excitement of writing, I had forgotten to record properly.

I would also like to thank Princeton University Press for managing the production of the book with great professional care. I am particularly grateful to Brigitta van Rheinberg, the acquisitions editor, for her critical encouragement, and to Jonathan Munk, my copyeditor. Ivan Marcus and Israel Yuval took the trouble to serve as readers for the Press. They both provided me with a plethora of observations and constructive criticism of which an author can only dream.

❈ ABBREVIATIONS ❈

EJ	Encyclopaedia Judaica
HTR	Harvard Theological Review
IOS	Israel Oriental Studies
JAAR	Journal of the American Academy of Religion
JGS	Journal of Glass Studies
JJS	Journal of Jewish Studies
JQR	Jewish Quarterly Review
JSocS	Jewish Social Studies
JSQ	Jewish Studies Quarterly
N.S.	New Series
NT	Novum Testamentum
PAAJR	Proceedings of the American Academy for Jewish Research
PO	Patrologia Orientalis
PW	Paulys Real-Encyclopädie der Classischen Altertumswissenschaft
REJ	Revue des Études Juives

MIRROR OF HIS BEAUTY

❂ INTRODUCTION ❂

IT BELONGS to the cherished traditions of Western civilization that Judaism "invented" monotheism. In the eyes of most Jews and Christians, as well as numerous scholars of religion, the "monotheistic revolution" of the Hebrew Bible represents a radical break with the backward and underdeveloped abominations of the polytheistic cultures that surrounded—and continuously threatened—ancient Israel. As such, Jewish monotheism is considered to be a decisive step in the development of humanity towards ever higher forms of religion. According to the triumphalistic Christian view of history and its progress-oriented academic counterparts, this "evolution" reached its climax in Christianity (more precisely, in nineteenth-century Protestantism). Just as polytheism inevitably lead to monotheism, so the remote and stern God of Judaism had to be replaced by the loving God of Christianity. When Christianity adopted Jewish monotheism, it simultaneously softened it by including the idea of God's Trinity and his son's incarnation on earth. Only through this "extension" of strict monotheism, it is argued, could Christianity liberate true faith from Jewish ossification and guarantee its survival and perfection.

The notion of the necessary evolution of monotheism out of polytheism is as stereotyped as the conceit of its successful fulfillment in Christianity. Regarding the latter, the Christian doctrine of the Trinity can hardly claim, despite the efforts of the church fathers, to manifest the apex of monotheism. As for the former, the polytheistic religions of the ancient Near East were certainly not the embodiment of religious crudeness and unethical behavior, yearning to be saved by the dawn of biblical monotheism—an image that our Western tradition has impressed upon us since childhood. Nor did biblical monotheism represent the final and clear-cut break with polytheistic superstition that we have come to believe since Sunday school. The transitions were fluent and flowed in both directions. It was one of the great achievements of the Bible to adopt the abhorrent customs of its pagan neighbors and to domesticate them by integrating them in an evolving monotheistic system that became ever more dominant. But the many attacks that the authors of the Bible found necessary to launch against the polytheistic practices of their fellow country-men prove that these alleged "survivals" remained very much alive.

One case in point is the Canaanite goddess Asherah, well-known from the Ugarit pantheon as the consort of El. Literary and archeological evidence suggests that this goddess was wor-shiped as the consort of Ba'al in Israel as well (1 Kings 18:19). Whether or not the cultic installation of a wooden pole, which is also called "Asherah" in the Bible, symbolized the goddess of the same name, it clearly was a widely recognized object of worship (King Manasseh even brought it into the Temple of Jerusalem; 2 Kings 21:3,7), and only gradually banished from the official biblical cult.[1] Our picture of early Israelite religion has become even more diverse with the discovery of the inscriptions from Kuntillet Ajrud (near the road from Gaza to Eilat), which date from the time of the Judaean monarchy. They mention the God of Israel (using the classical biblical tetragrammaton YHWH) and, most likely, "his Asherah." This translation, of course, is controversial—it accords to the Jewish God a Queen consort, who is worshiped together with him—but such a reading cannot be easily dismissed.[2] Indeed, the Jewish mercenaries who settled at the military colony of Elephantine at the southern border of Egypt precisely during the reign of King Manasseh (about 650 BCE), not only built a temple of their own in Elephantine (in the immediate vicinity of the Egyptian god Khnum), but even wor-shiped two goddesses alongside Yahu (YHW) in their temple. Their cult obviously reflects—and preserves for more than two centuries[3]—a stage of the Judaean religion that can hardly be called monotheistic in the strict sense of the term.[4]

Judaeo-Christian monotheism, then, was neither "achieved" once and forever at a certain point in the history of Western reli-gions, nor is it the peak of any simple religious evolution. The term is not particularly helpful as a historical category, and much less as a moral indicator. Rather, we should consider "monothe-ism" as one pole of a broad spectrum, of which "polytheism" marks the other. Between these two poles there exists a wide range of possible combinations and configurations, which realize themselves in time and space—not in an ascending line from (primitive) polytheism to (higher and higher forms of) monotheism, but in movements back and forth between polytheism and varying degrees of monotheism. Such a dynamic model has the benefit of avoiding any value judgement. It does not favor monotheism over polytheism, but neither does it strive to exorcise the prejudice of the alleged superiority of Jewish-Christian monotheism with the attempted revival of ancient pagan values. The latter has become the prerogative of postmodern philosophers and historians of religion,[5] who extol ancient polytheistic religions as in harmony with nature, appreciate "paganism" as body- and life-affirming,[6] and claim to rediscover Egyptian "cosmotheism" as the ultimate salvation from the "Mosaic distinction," that epitome of monotheism.[7]

What is necessary is not to replace one cliché with another but to expose Jewish and Christian monotheism as a construct that encompasses more than the alleged end product, as a process continuously in flux, moving between the poles of a broad and varied spectrum. Such a revaluation of monotheism recognizes historical developments and shifts of emphasis *within* both Judaism and Christianity, and simultaneously allows for an examination of the relationship *between* both religions that liberates itself from the fatal pattern of the fulfillment of one religion in the other. From this viewpoint the notions of "orthodoxy" and "heresy" within one religion become less fixed,[8] and the boundaries between the two religions are seen to be permeable.

With the reform of King Josiah towards the end of the seventh century BCE—with its centralization of the cult of the one, unchanging, and male God worshiped in the one Temple in the one city, Jerusalem—Judaism definitely took up the path of an ever stricter monotheism. And yet nothing could be more mistaken than the assumption that the idea of the oneness of God is the quasi-dogmatic "essence" of Judaism. True, the daily *Shema' Yisra'el* prayer proclaims that "the Lord, our God, is one God alone" (Deut. 6:4)—and no one would ever contradict this solemn declaration, at least not openly—but the history of Judaism teaches us that this is only part of the story. Unless we want to ignore the other part and to dismiss any deviation from the strict monotheistic ideal as heresy, we must face the fact that the history of Judaism is much more complex and multifaceted than monotheistic zeal would have us believe.

The most salient example of an intra-Jewish movement that does not comply with the rules of a rigorous monotheism is Jewish mysticism, particularly the variety that bears the technical term "Kabbalah." It is a thorn in the flesh of all those who regard the liberal Judaism of the nineteenth century as the culmination of monotheism, and accordingly, has long been scorned or suppressed by Jewish and Christian historians of religion alike. But since the pioneering work of Gershom Scholem,[9] we know that the Kabbalah was one of the most powerful and vital movements in Judaism and that it began as the activity of a learned elite, eventually becoming a popular mass movement that shaped Judaism for centuries to come, up to this very day. To be sure, the Kabbalah is anything but a uniform phenomenon, having developed many faces during a long historical process; there can be no doubt, however, that it promoted some of the most radical ideas in the history of the Jewish religion, ideas that depart considerably from the paradigm of King Josiah and his "monotheistic reform." That the Kabbalists insisted that their theology was perfectly monotheistic, and that some of these ideas subsequently had to be domesticated to conform to the demands of a more orthodox image of the Jewish religion, only reinforces their radical and bold nature.[10]

The most daring innovation of the Kabbalah is its distinction between two "realms" within God: the hidden and transcendent God who is beyond any human comprehension, and the God who has revealed himself and his multiple inner structure to the initiate (the Kabbalist). The revealed God has a dynamic inner life that unfolds in ten potencies (Hebrew *Sefirot*), embodying different "facets" of the one God. The various systems of the Kabbalah develop different configurations of the ten Sefirot (and give them different names), but all agree that these potencies include one female Sefirah; nine are male and one is female. This female principle within God is called *Shekhinah* (literally "dwelling"), a term familiar from classical Rabbinical literature. There, it refers to the presence of God in the world and is always synonymous with God; as such it does not have any feminine characteristics. In the Kabbalah, however, the Shekhinah is not only included as a distinctive principle within the inner divine life, but this distinctive principle is explicitly, and quite graphically, described as female.

These two major innovations of the Kabbalah, in the technical sense of the term — the ten Sefirot and the inclusion among them of a female potency — emerge for the first time in history in a small book that appears in late twelfth-century Provence in Southern France: the book Bahir.[11] The earliest sources that we possess already attribute this book to R. Nehunya ben Haqana, a sage of the second century CE, but they disagree about the historical value of this early attribution. Whereas Isaac ben Jacob Cohen of Soria, a Spanish Kabbalist of the late thirteenth century, appeals to it in order to establish the book's origin from ancient Palestine and thus its "orthodoxy,"[12] Meir ben Simon, a Provencal Talmudist and opponent of the Kabbalah in the early thirteenth century, uses it to prove the opposite: that the Bahir is a forgery and the product of heretics,

who speak blasphemously of God and of the scholars who walk in the ways of the pure Torah and who fear God, while they themselves are wise in their own eyes, invent things out of their own minds and lean toward heretical opinions. . . . But God save us from the sin of heeding such heretical words, concerning which it would be better to keep silence in Israel. And we have heard that a book had already been written for them,[13] which they call Bahir, that is "bright," but no light shines through it. This book has come into our hands, and we have found that they falsely attribute it to R. Nehunya ben Haqana. God forbid! There is no truth in this. That righteous man, as we know him, did not come to ruin [by editing such a work] and his name is not to be mentioned in the same breath as sacrilege. The language of the book and its whole content show that it is the work of someone who lacked command of either literary language or good style, and in many passages it contains words which are out and out heresy.[14]

"Heresy" is the keyword of this fervent accusation, and the heresy against which Meir ben Simon fights is precisely the dreaded danger that the oneness and unity of God might be abandoned and replaced by a multitude of gods; in other words that polytheism, believed to be defeated for centuries, might rise from the dead. What we encounter in the Kabbalah looks indeed very much like the return of the repressed, a return that proved to be all the more forceful and explosive for the longer it had been prevented. And the polytheistic component of the Jewish religion had been repressed for many centuries. This is particularly true for the feminine element, the notion of goddesses as partners and consorts of the gods. Although Meir ben Simon does not specify this aspect of the detested heresy, it is obvious that he was aware of it and disapproved of it wholeheartedly. For those who had a static perception of the one God and his everlasting victory over the many gods, any supposed or real deviation from this ideal had to be denounced as heresy and to be condemned accordingly. The Kabbalists, however, propagated a different and much more dynamic view of the Jewish religion, boldly claiming that their "new" ideas were nothing but the revival of the "old." Perhaps they were more correct than they knew or would ever admit.

This book deals with the return of "polytheistic" tendencies in the Kabbalah or, more concretely, of the feminine manifestation of God in the earliest kabbalistic tractate, the Bahir. It takes as its starting point the question of whether the kabbalistic concept of God, with its emphasis on God's femininity, represents the innovation that it seems to be — despite all of its proponents' affirmations to the contrary. Or, to put it differently, the book tries to place the Bahir's concept of God in historical perspective and to demonstrate that its authors were right to claim that all they did and intended to do was reaffirm the "old," to reestablish the "Torah which was given to Moses on Mount Sinai." The problem, however, is what they conceived as "old." Most likely *not* what we today, after centuries of critical biblical research, have come to understand. They could have hardly been aware of the fact that what they offered as the Torah of Moses was in one sense a revival of polytheistic countertendencies in the monotheistic program of the Hebrew Bible, a new breaking up of an encrusted monotheism that had become all too secure of its superiority over "pagan" polytheism and, worst, had neglected or suppressed some of the basic needs of human beings.

In reopening the question of the origin of the bahiric concept of God and his feminine manifestation, I pursue two lines of inquiry. The first part of the book ("From the Bible to the Bahir") traces the development of the idea of God's femininity from the Hebrew Bible to the medieval Bahir. It begins in chapter 1 with a discussion of the early Jewish Wisdom tradition, which manifests itself in the canonical books of Job and Proverbs, and in the noncanonical books of Jesus Sirach (Wisdom of ben Sirach) and Sapientia Salomonis (Wisdom of Solomon). What all these texts have in common is that they connect Wisdom (Hebrew *hokhmah*, Greek *sophia*) with the process of creation and conceive "her" as the intrinsic structure of the created world, which can (in most cases) be obtained and understood by human beings.[15] Moreover, Wisdom is often personified and as such embodies God's revelation on earth. With the sole exception of Job, all of these texts envisage Wisdom as female, as God's beloved daughter (Proverbs) or even spouse (Sapientia Salomonis). Clearly in contact and interchange with surrounding Hellenistic cultures, Wisdom literature inaugurates (or rather reaffirms) the idea of a feminine manifestation of God within the received fabric of biblical monotheism.

The most courageous step in ancient Judaism towards the inclusion of the feminine in God was taken in the first century CE by Philo of Alexandria, the famous Jewish philosopher, who is the subject of the second chapter. Influenced both by the biblical Wisdom tradition and by the Greek philosophy of his time (particularly the Stoa and Platonism), Philo develops a complex network of relationships between God, his (female) Wisdom, his (male) Logos, and the human world. In adopting daughter and wife/mother imagery to describe Wisdom, he seems to combine the Proverbs and the Wisdom of Solomon traditions. Most conspicuously, however, he plays with Wisdom's gender and goes so far as to change deliberately her sex from female to male, apparently following the Platonic model of the active role of the masculine in contrast to the passive role of the feminine. As such, he embodies the culmination of the biblical and postbiblical Wisdom tradition, which would soon break off in Judaism and be taken up by Christianity.

The next chapter considers one of the most striking transformations of the heritage of the Wisdom tradition: the Sophia myth developed by so-called gnostic Christian groups that flourished in the second century CE. Among the most salient features of their doctrine belongs an elaborate narrative about the origin of the divine realm and of the mundane world. The material world of human beings is considered to be the result of a "mishap" in the divinity, a cosmic catastrophe inaugurated by an imperfect and "false" god, which needs to be mended through the abolition of all matter and the return of the spiritual human soul to its divine origin.

As in the early Jewish Wisdom tradition and in Philo, the gnostic Godhead contains a feminine power, which plays a prominent role in the gnostic myth of creation. According to the Apocryphon of John, one of the earliest and most succinct expositions of the gnostic myth that we now possess, Wisdom (Sophia) is held responsible for the break within the cosmic process and hence for the origin of the material world: she creates an imperfect image of herself who becomes the originator of the material universe outside of the divine realm, an evil counterworld, inhabited by all kinds of "rulers," "demons," and finally Adam and Eve with their offspring. In order to rectify her mistake, Sophia is sent down to earth to heal the rupture she caused and to redeem humanity. Here, the task of salvation is reserved for Wisdom, the feminine power of God — not the male Logos.

Quite a different picture emerges from the vast literature (Mishnah, Talmud, Midrash, Targum) passed on to us from the Rabbis, as we will see in Chapter 4. As the creators and leaders of what would become the "classical" and "normative" manifestation of late antique Judaism, the Rabbis presented themselves as *hakhamim* ("wise men," "sages"); they claimed to be the embodiment of the ideal of "Wisdom" developed in the biblical and postbiblical Wisdom tradition. More precisely, they took up the idea of Wisdom's identification with the Torah in Jesus Sirach and made it the essence and pivot of their thought. According to the Rabbis, Wisdom/Torah was simultaneously the blueprint of and God's tool for the creation of the universe; hence, the one who masters the Torah masters the world. It goes without saying that the Rabbis, with their concept of the dual ("Written" and "Oral") Torah revealed to Moses on Mount Sinai and transmitted to them, regarded themselves as the sole and true guardians of the Torah and its correct interpretation.

In adopting the equation of Wisdom with the Torah from Jesus Sirach, the Rabbis emphasized the availability of Wisdom on earth: Wisdom/Torah was given to human beings and is not only present among us, but at our disposal. Yet this increased availability was achieved at the expense of Wisdom's personality and her close relationship with God. Wisdom lost her persona and became a book, albeit a book revealed by God. Despite abandoning the biblical and postbiblical idea of Wisdom's personal presence among the people of Israel (as God's emissary), the Rabbis maintained and expanded the concept that *God* made himself present and available on earth. For this, they invented the term "Shekhinah" (from Hebrew *shakhan*, "to dwell, reside"), which denotes God's "indwelling" or "presence" on earth. But there is little in the vast literary corpus left to us by the Rabbis to indicate that this Shekhinah has any female attributes. On the contrary, despite the feminine gender of the Hebrew word "Shekhinah," the Rabbis went to great efforts to emphasize that the Shekhinah is no one else but the familiar (male) God of the Hebrew Bible. Even as a distinction between God and "his Shekhinah" was gradually introduced, leading to the increasing personification of the Shekhinah, they affirmed the unquestionable masculinity of their image of God. For the Rabbis, the feminine aspect of God seems to have been completely forgotten.

The most radical step in this direction was taken by the Jewish philosophy of the early Middle Ages, which developed under the influence of Islam and its adaptation of Greek philosophy. In fact, the early representatives of medieval Jewish philosophy are the most outspoken advocates of a rationalistic trend that was up in arms against anthropomorphic tendencies in the Hebrew Bible. In other words, the Jewish philosophers were concerned to recover what they believed was the original and pure form of Jewish monotheism, and they fought against what they feared was its all-too-human aberration. Theirs was the concept of a transcendent and spiritual God, dwelling not on earth but in the most remote heights of heaven or rather, even beyond the heavenly realm and certainly beyond human comprehension.

These philosophical and theological developments have important ramifications for the concept of the Shekhinah, as we will see in Chapter 5, which discusses the doctrines of Saadia Gaon (882– 942 CE), Judah ben Barzillai of Barcelona (ca. 1035–1105), Judah ha-Levi (before 1075–1141), and Moses Maimonides (1135– 1204). The image that these philosophers formed of God did not tolerate the Rabbinic concept of the Shekhinah as God's presence on earth. Since they could not simply eliminate this familiar and cherished Rabbinic tradition, they audaciously reinterpreted it, suggesting that the Shekhinah was not identical with God but on the contrary a created entity. With this move, they fended off the danger of positing any multiplicity within God and rejected latent polytheistic tendencies inherent in the concept of the Shekhinah. By "cleansing" God of any hint of corporeality, they simultaneously eliminated any trace of divine gender, whether male or female.

With Chapter 6, we reach the late twelfth century and the appearance of the Bahir, the kabbalistic counterpart of rationalistic Jewish philosophy. In many ways, the Bahir represents the return of the repressed: the recovery of an archaic and mythical world with a rich imagery that graphically depicts the dynamic inner life of the Godhead, the origin of evil, and God's relationship with his created world. Against the philosophers, it revives the Rabbinical concept of the Shekhinah as identical with God. It goes much further still, however, reintegrating the Shekhinah into God as one of the facets and aspects of his essence that can be fathomed and described by the initiate. And initiates they were, the editors of the Bahir and the heralds of its old/new doctrine. They knew that God, the heavenly King of the Rabbis, has "sons" who constitute, together with their father, the Godhead (the ten Sefirot) and that one of these "sons" is actually female, hence his "daughter." Moreover, they maintained that this "daughter" is simultaneously his "spouse"; in other words, that the "King" has a "Queen" with whom he procreates children (who are the people of Israel on earth).

It is this dynamic relationship between the manifold Godhead with its female component and the created world of human beings that constitutes the focus of the Bahir's creative interest. Within this interplay of divine and human forces, great importance is attached to the role of the Shekhinah. As the tenth and "lowest" among the Sefirot, the Shekhinah stands at the borderline between the heavenly and earthly realms and is sent down to earth as God's emissary. In her dual capacity as part of the Godhead and the "Oral Torah," she serves as God's "embodiment" on earth, with the sole task of leading Israel back to God and then, upon completion of her mission, reuniting herself with the Godhead. The bahiric Shekhinah is the bridge between both worlds, the true intercessor (*mediatrix*) between God and humanity.

In the chronological survey of the first six chapters, the bahiric concept of the Shekhinah has been located within the history of the suppression and reinterpretation of feminine images of the divine in Judaism and Christianity. This background, however, only serves to sharpen the problem of the origins of this concept, starkly exposing the kabbalistic notion of God's femininity as a radical departure from earlier Jewish models. It is to this problem that we turn in the second part of the book, "The Quest for Origins." I begin, in Chapter 7, with an examination of Scholem's explanatory model, which suggests that the concept originated in the gnostic systems of the first centuries of the Christian era. When we confront his theory with a fresh analysis of the gnostic sources, most of which were unavailable to Scholem, the result is quite paradoxical. Despite Scholem's dubious sources and particular prejudices, his intuition did not fail him. The bahiric idea of the Shekhinah comes closer to the gnostic myth than Scholem thought or was able to prove. This intensifies the problem posed by the fact that no historical connection between the "Gnosis" and the Bahir can be established.

However instructive and illuminating structural or phenomenological similarities may be, they are not particularly satisfying. In order to test the historical background more thoroughly, the eighth chapter turns to examine the immediate *Christian* context of twelfth-century France, the provenance of the Bahir itself. Scholem tried in vain to find some connection between the Bahir and the supposedly gnostic movements of the Cathari and Albigenses, but he completely ignored a more obvious and widespread phenomenon that profoundly shaped the Christian environment of the Jews in twelfth-century France: the veneration of the Virgin Mary. The chapter summarizes the evolution of the veneration of Mary from its beginnings in the Eastern church until it reached Western Christendom. Although Western theologians were initially hesitant to adopt Eastern Mariology, it is striking that their veneration of Mary would reach its climax in the twelfth century — at precisely the time when the Bahir was being edited.

When we examine the Marian doctrines of Peter Damian (1007–1072), Herman of Tournay (ca. 1090–ca. 1147), Bernard of Clairvaux (1091–1153), Godfrey of Admont (ca. 1100–1165), Hildegard of Bingen (1098–1179), and Peter of Blois (ca. 1135–1212?), we find striking parallels with the increased emphasis on the feminine aspects of divinity in the Kabbalah. All of these writers emphasize Mary's function as mediator (*mediatrix*) between God and humanity and as intercessor (*interventrix*) on behalf of humankind. Mary is essential for the success of God's plan of salvation; she "repairs" the first creation, which was spoiled by Eve.

As such she is praised as the "restorer" (*reparatrix*) of humanity and, together with her son Jesus, assumes the role of co-redeemer (*corredemptrix*). Hildegard even goes so far as to bestow on her the honorary title "savior" (*salvatrix*), usually reserved for Christ.

In her pivotal position, raised above human beings and angels alike, Mary is identified with biblical Wisdom. Her assumption into heaven not only reunites her with her son Jesus but elevates her into the holy Trinity. The eleventh and twelfth centuries thus saw the gradual deification of Mary—although often veiled with dogmatic considerations and frequently qualified by the superficial subordination of Mariology to Christology. It appears that the role and function of the Christian Mary comes very close to the role and function of the Jewish Shekhinah in the Bahir.

If the medieval Christian veneration of Mary is historically and geographically much closer to the Bahir than Scholem's proposed "Gnosis," can one seriously assume that the reemergence of God's femininity in Judaism was influenced by similar developments in Christianity? Such a proposal becomes all the more problematic in view of the long history of Christian polemics against the Jewish "stubbornness" in not believing in Jesus and Jewish polemics against Mary (Chapter 9). Christian sources transmit a number of legends that portray the Jews as full of hatred against Mary and her son Jesus: they disturb Mary's funeral in order to desecrate the holy body of the deceased Virgin, they dishonor the image of the Virgin by throwing it into a latrine, and they try to burn their own children who partake of the Holy Communion together with their Christian playmates. These stories originate in the Byzantine East and travel to the West, where they are readily adopted and widely publicized in both literature and art.

Such anti-Jewish legends and images could have hardly escaped the attention of the Jews. They responded with similarly unflattering narratives in which they polemicize against the Christian claim of Mary's virginity and the gradual process of her deification. Quite surprisingly, however, these responses are not as clear-cut and unambiguous as one might expect. The famous (or rather infamous) *Toledot Yeshu*, the best-known polemical Jewish tractate of Late Antiquity, reserves its polemical fervor for Jesus and to a large extent spares his mother Mary. A much more complicated story is told in the Apocalypse of Zerubbavel, a Byzantine-Jewish apocalypse from the early seventh century. Here the Christian narrative of the birth of the Messiah Jesus from the Virgin Mary is parodied in the counternarrative of the birth of the Antichrist Armilos from a beautiful statue with which Satan had intercourse. Yet the same text provides us with a mother of the Jewish Messiah, who plays an active role in the redemption process and helps her son to gain the final victory over the Antichrist. Thus the polemical rejection of Mary's function in the process of salvation is supplemented by the adaptation, or rather usurpation, of her role in a Jewish context.

This connection between Judaism and Christianity in an area in which it was the least expected makes the question of historical channels and trajectories of supposed mutual influences all the more pressing and disturbing. Such questions, however, raise major methodological problems that concern the nature of categories such as "origins," "dependence," "influence," and historical "evidence." In the last chapter I propose to reconsider these terms: instead of searching for the single mythical "origin" of a concept, I suggest that we focus our attention upon the dynamic interplay of the various factors under consideration in their historical dimension; and instead of defining "influence" as the interaction between two static entities, of which one is "active" and the other "passive," I present a dynamic model of "influence," in which both partners are engaged in a process of creative adaptation. Such a model rejects the myth of the "priority of origins" and instead draws our attention to the continuous *process* of the digestion, transformation, and recreation of traditions in ever-changing historical circumstances.

Applied to the Jewish and Christian view of God's femininity, such a dynamic theory of influence yields a much more colorful picture. It does not consider both religions as static and distinct entities but as two components of one religious discourse; it is not concerned with the origin of this idea in one or the other religion but with the process of its transformation in a shared cultural space, a process that gains its vitality through mutual exchange. Such a model takes into account a historical process extending over a longer period of time, as well as permitting a highly intensified exchange in the twelfth century, in particular. During this century, which marks the heyday of an entirely new view of the feminine both in the religious (veneration of Mary) and in the secular realm (love poetry of the troubadours), both Judaism and Christianity reach the climax of their high esteem for the feminine. This high esteem results from a long process, which is rooted in the shared Biblical Wisdom tradition, continues in different ways in Judaism and Christianity, and yet intersects at various points in history in mutual attraction and repulsion.

In proposing that the blossoming of the veneration of the Virgin Mary in the Christian world and the reintegration of the Shekhinah into the divinity in Judaism are neither accidental nor merely the results of parallel developments, I follow the increasing trend in recent scholarship to reject the static and erratic image of Judaism and Christianity as hermetically sealed against one another, forever frozen, as it were, in a perpetual state of hatred and fear.[16] The Jews of Southern France certainly did not live in a ghetto; they participated in a society that they shared with their Christian neighbors. To be sure, they were a minority culture dominated by a majority culture, but this does not necessarily mean that the minority culture defined itself solely in antipathy to the hegemonic culture. On the contrary, both communities lived in close proximity, and the common ground of daily life clearly facilitated a high degree of interaction. Ivan Marcus calls this phenomenon of cultural openness and adaptation "inward acculturation" and puts the emphasis on the often inverted and parodistic ways in which ancient Jewish traditions were fused with Christian themes and images.[17] This is certainly the case, but we will see that inward attraction and adaptation as the correlate of outward repulsion and rejection could come along in two disguises: as a parodistic counternarrative and as the naïve (or brazen) retelling of the same story.

The range of themes and texts, the span of time, and the geographical area covered in this book are alarmingly wide, and I gladly admit that each chapter merits a monograph of its own. Each has its own host of specialists within the scholarly community, and I am painfully aware that I cannot do justice to all of their manifold expectations. It is, however, not my aim here to write these many monographs and to fulfill the expectations that the specialists legitimately have. I take the deliberate risk of drafting a much broader picture, conscious of all the shortcomings that such an undertaking entails. It is my firm conviction that the time is more than ripe for such an enterprise, as daring as it may be, and that scholarly progress cannot and must not be restricted to ever-higher degrees of specialization.

I am also aware that it is a delicate venture for any "serious" historian to propose the possibility of the inward Jewish adaptation of Christian patterns. Not only does such research easily incur the reproach of being speculative and not providing sufficient evidence. Moreover, and more precariously, the historian is exposed to the danger of consciously or unconsciously bringing his/her own personal background into the sacred halls of scholarship and, depending on that background, betraying his/her own identity or oppressing the identity of the other. Woe to the historian of Judaism who happens to be Christian (Roman Catholic, no less) and to "discover" that the Christian veneration of Mary might have had an impact on the feminine manifestation of God in the Kabbalah! And yet, in the long run, I am confident in our ability to liberate ourselves, not only from medieval stereotypes, but also from modern ones.

PART I

FROM THE BIBLE TO
THE BAHIR

LADY WISDOM

THE CONCEPT of "Wisdom" (Hebrew *hokhmah*, Greek *sophia*), and the literature surrounding it, is one of the most distinctive and most discussed cultural phenomena in the history of ancient Israel. It is both a way of thinking and a way of life, deeply influenced by ancient Near Eastern, Egyptian, and Greek traditions. Its literary activity, first crystallized among professional scribes and members of the educated elite at Solomon's court, was subsequently attributed to the king himself. Among its most outstanding characteristics is its concern with the individual, rather than with the nation, and with his or her ethical behavior, rather than with the cult. The individual is understood as part of an encompassing and meaningfully structured cosmic order, which can be known and according to which the individual behaves properly; hence the emphasis put on knowledge, teaching, and education.

Among the most puzzling offshoots of Wisdom literature are the beautiful didactic poems in the books of Job (Chapter 28),[1] Proverbs (Chapter 8),[2] and Jesus Sirach (Chapter 24).[3] They are all part of the later development of Wisdom literature and can be dated to the third (Job 28, Prov. 8) and the second centuries BCE (Sirach) respectively. What they have in common is their highly poetical character, as well as the fact that they somehow connect Wisdom with the process of creation. In addition, at least Proverbs and Sirach for the first time present "Wisdom" not only as a personified figure, but also as a female person.

JOB: WISDOM CANNOT BE FOUND

I start with Job 28, since it is probably the most archaic formulation of the postexilic Wisdom tradition:[4]

> (1) There is a mine for silver,
> And a place where gold is refined.

(2) Iron is taken out of the earth,
And copper smelted from rock.
(3) He sets bounds for darkness;
To every limit man probes,
To rocks in deepest darkness.
(4) They open up a shaft far from where men live,
[In places] forgotten by wayfarers,
Destitute of men, far removed.
(5) Earth, out of which food grows,
Is changed below as if into fire.
(6) Its rocks are a source of sapphires;
It contains gold dust too.
(7) No bird of prey knows the path to it;[5]
The falcon's eye has not gazed upon it.
(8) The proud beasts have not reached it;
The lion has not crossed it.
(9) Man sets his hand against the flinty rock
And overturns mountains by the roots.
(10) He carves out channels through rock;
His eyes behold every precious thing.
(11) He dams up the sources of the streams
So that hidden things may be brought to light.

(12) But where can Wisdom (*ha-hokhmah*) be found;
Where is the place (*maqom*)[6] of understanding (*binah*)?

(13) No man (*enosh*) can set a value on it;
It cannot be found in the land of living.
(14) The deep says, "It is not in me";
The sea says, "I do not have it."
(15) It cannot be bartered for gold;
Silver cannot be paid out as its price.
(16) The finest gold of Ophir cannot be weighed against it,
Nor precious onyx, nor sapphire.
(17) Gold or glass cannot match its value,
Nor vessels of fine gold be exchanged for it.
(18) Coral and crystal cannot be mentioned with it;
A pouch of Wisdom is better than rubies.
(19) Topaz from Nubia cannot match its value;
Pure gold cannot be weighed against it.
(20) But whence does Wisdom come?
Where is the source of understanding?

(21) It is hidden from the eyes of all living,
Concealed from the fowl of heaven.
(22) Abaddon and Death say,
"We have heard a rumor of it with our ears."[7]
(23) God understands the way to it;
He knows its place (*meqomah*);[8]
(24) For He sees to the ends of the earth,
Observes all that is beneath the heavens.
(25) When He fixed the weight of the winds,
Set the measure of the waters;
(26) When He made a rule for the rain
And a course for the thunderstorms,
(27) Then He saw it (*ra'ah*) and gauged it (*yesapperah*);[9]
He set it up (*hekhinah*)[10] and searched it out (*haqarah*).[11]

(28) He said to man (*adam*),
"See! Fear of Lord is Wisdom;
To shun evil is understanding."

There can be no doubt that this poem has been secondarily inserted into the text. It clearly interrupts Job's long speech, with which it does not seem to be connected at all. The poem begins by describing the apparently unlimited power of humankind,[12] who search for and find all of the precious metals and stones in the deepest depths of the earth, discovering paths no animal would ever find. They even work their way through the hardest rock and, when necessary, stop the streams to reach their goal. But they do not know the location of the most precious "thing" at all: Wisdom and understanding. This sad conclusion is repeated twice in a refrain. Hence, the emphasis is clearly put on the place of Wisdom, not on its essence. It is not in the "land of living" nor in the "deep" nor in the "sea." Accordingly, the "eyes of all living," the "fowl of heaven" and the netherworld have not seen it; they have just heard "rumors" of it. Moreover, Wisdom cannot be traded for gold, silver, and all of the precious stones. If humankind possessed the wealth of earth in its entirety, they could not buy Wisdom with it.

In stark contrast to the deplorable inability and ignorance of humankind, so proud of mastering the resources of earth, is the omniscience and omnipotence of God, as described in verses 23–27. God alone understands (*hevin*, from the same root as *binah*, the synonym of "Wisdom" in the refrain) the way to Wisdom

and knows its place (v. 23). Why is this so? Because he sees everything and, more importantly, has seen it at a very precise and
concrete moment: when he "fixed the weight of the winds," "measured the waters," "made a rule for the rain," and "set a course
for the thunderstorms"; that is, at the very moment of creation.
Wisdom is connected with creation, or more precisely, it was created during the process of creation. The verbs used for Wisdom
("saw it," "counted it," "set it up," "searched it out") are unusual for the language of creation, but there can be no doubt that
they refer here to the creation of Wisdom. They seem to imply
some kind of "technical" knowledge — similar to the verbs used
for knowing the winds, waters, rain, and thunderstorms — depicting
God as a technician or craftsman.[13] One may even go a step further and argue that Wisdom is not only simultaneous with the
creation of the elements of nature, but rather functions as the
ordering principle that is inherent in the elements of nature and
in everything that is created. Wisdom is what determines the
weight of the winds, the measurement of the waters, the rule of
the rain, and the course of the thunderstorm. It represents the
order, structure, and pattern of the created world, the construction plan used by God. As Gerhard von Rad put it in his seminal
Wisdom in Israel, Wisdom is "the 'meaning' implanted by God in
creation."[14]

Nevertheless, the Wisdom portrayed in Job remains an abstract
category. It is certainly not personified, let alone an attribute or
even a hypostasis of God. If Wisdom represents the structure implanted by God in creation, it is related to God — but still created
and not part of him. Any further attempt to impose on the text
later philosophical or theological categories is thus meaningless.[15]
More important for our undertaking is another observation: there
is no hint whatsoever at a *female* character of Wisdom. To be
sure, the gender of the word *hokhmah* is feminine, but it would
be misleading to emphasize this fact since our text does not yet
depict Wisdom as a person. I therefore have constantly referred
to "Wisdom" in Job as "it" and not as "she."

One further step is yet to be made. Can we say more about the
relationship of Wisdom with humankind?[16] Wisdom dwells with
God, and God has "encoded" Wisdom into creation, but humankind has no access to it. With its technical skills, it may turn the
earth upside down, yet this will never lead it to Wisdom. This is

the blunt and quite pessimistic message of our poem. One possible way to get around this unsatisfactory result could be to argue that, if one cannot find Wisdom in the created world, one instead should turn to God, its creator. Evidently this is the conclusion reached by verse 28: if you fear God and shun evil you will have found Wisdom. But this is no doubt against the rationale of the poem, added by some pious editor who refused to accept the grandiose negative message: although God has encoded his Wisdom in creation, humans have no tool to decode it. Human beings cannot turn directly to God anymore—because God has given Wisdom away. All of their efforts to find Wisdom in the created world are futile—God does not want them to find it. It is this negative view of the world and of Wisdom (as well as of God) that finally may explain the insertion of our poem into the book of Job and into Job's desperate speech in particular. The question of how Wisdom reaches humankind remains unanswered.

PROVERBS: WISDOM AS GOD'S LITTLE DAUGHTER AND HIS EMBODIMENT ON EARTH

This attitude differs notably from that of our second poem, Proverbs 8. Here we find Wisdom suddenly standing on earth, making herself visible and audible, quite noisily audible, among human beings:

(1) It is Wisdom (*hokhmah*) calling,
Understanding (*tevunah*)[17] raising her voice.
(2) She takes her stand at the topmost heights,
By the wayside, at the crossroads,
(3) Near the gates at the city entrance;
At the entrance she shouts,

(4) "O men (*ishim*), I call to you;
My cry is to all humankind (*bene adam*).
(5) O simple ones, learn shrewdness;
O dullards, instruct your minds.
(6) Listen, for I speak noble things;
Uprightness comes from my lips;
(7) My mouth utters truth;
Wickedness is abhorrent to my lips.

(8) All my words are just,
None of them perverse or crooked;
(9) All are straightforward to the intelligent one,
And right to those who have attained knowledge.
(10) Accept my discipline (*musari*) rather than silver,
Knowledge (*da'at*) rather than choice gold.
(11) For Wisdom is better than rubies;
No goods can equal her.[18]

Wisdom asks humankind to listen to her and to follow her. Not only is she among them, she can and wants to be found, stating: "and those who seek me will find me" (v. 17). What she has to offer is much better than silver, gold, and rubies (probably a reference to Job's man searching the earth). Rather, she promises shrewdness, truth, justice, counsel, resourcefulness, understanding, courage (v. 14), and righteousness (v. 20), but also riches, honor, wealth, and success (v. 18)—everything that makes human life worth living, successful, and in accordance with the divine order. Whoever follows Wisdom is not only granted a full life, but also, and quite "naturally," adheres to the strictest ethical standard; for, "to fear the Lord is to hate evil; I hate pride, arrogance, the evil way, and duplicity in speech" (v. 13).

After this bold entrance Wisdom explains from whence she comes:

(22) The Lord created me (*qanani*) at the beginning (*reshit*) of His course
As the first (*qedem*) of His works of old (*me'az*).
(23) In the distant past (*me'olam*) I was fashioned (*nissakhti*),
At the beginning (*merosh*), at the origin of earth.
(24) There was still no deep when I was brought forth (*holalti*),
No springs rich in water;
(25) Before [the foundations of] the mountains were sunk,
Before the hills I was born (*holalti*).
(26) He had not yet made (*'asah*) earth and fields,
Or the world's first clumps of clay.
(27) I was there (*sham ani*) when He set the heavens into place (*bahakhino*);
When He fixed the horizon upon the deep;
(28) When He made the heavens above firm,
And the fountains of the deep gushed forth;

(29) When He assigned the sea its limits,
So that its waters never transgress His command;
When He fixed the foundations of the earth,
(30) I was with him as a confidant (*amon*),
A source of delight (*sha'ashu'im*) every day,
Playing (*mesaheqet*) in front of him all the time,[19]
(31) Playing (*mesaheqet*)[20] in His inhabited world,
Finding delight (*sha'ashu'ai*) with humankind (*bene adam*).

The first obvious observation to be made is that Wisdom describes herself as having been created. The verbs used here (v. 22: *qanani*, v. 23: *nissakhti*, v. 24: *holalti*) are not the standard terms for God's creation of heaven and earth (which are *bara* and *'asah*), but nevertheless there is no reason to infer from this any different meaning. Whereas *qanah* literally means "to acquire," it can also refer to the creation of heaven and earth (Gen. 14:19, 22) and of man/Adam (Ps. 139:13), particularly in poetical language and mythical context.[21] As to *nissakhti* in verse 23, which probably means "I was set up, dedicated" (lit., "I was poured out"), some scholars suggest to substitute *nessakoti* ("I was fashioned," lit. "woven").[22] But this does not make much of a difference in meaning and is indeed a matter of vocalization only. And finally *holalti* definitely means, "I was born, brought forth" and is used in this sense for human birth, too (Ps. 51:7). Thus Wisdom was brought forth into the world by God, her father.

Moreover, Wisdom was created by God at a certain point in time. The text makes it abundantly clear that she was present *before* the creation of heaven and earth. More precisely, she was the beginning of God's creation. Creation started with Wisdom; everything else was created after her. Yet the text does not state explicitly that Wisdom *participated* in this creation subsequent to her own: she was just "there" when God did all this, she was "with him." The whereabouts of her "there" and "with him" are not further explained. If one wants to press this point, one could perhaps speculate about some extraterrestrial place that she shared with God before and at the time of creation.

The Jewish Publication Society (JPS) translation of verse 30 as quoted above ("I was with Him as a confidant") does, however, presuppose the interpretation of Wisdom as somehow taking part in the act of creation (as God's counselor?). The only way to

determine whether or not this is correct is to look more closely at
the word *amon* and its context. Scores of scholars have written
on the meaning of the word *amon* as it occurs in Proverbs.[23]
Among the various interpretations, only two seem to deserve serious consideration, namely "work-master, craftsman" and "child."
The first is derived from the Akkadian *ummānu* ("craftsman")
and supported by the Septuagint (*harmozousa*, "as a fitting
[helper?]," "arranging [all things]"), as well as by Sapientia Salomonis (7:21; 8:6: *technītis*, "artist, worker"); the second is supported by Aquila (*tithēnoumenē*, "foster-child, darling") and presupposes the reading *amun* instead of *amon* (again a matter of
vocalization). Both interpretations are possible, and philological
considerations alone offer no definite proof in favor of one or the
other. There is, however, one argument that speaks decidedly in
favor of the translation "child," and this is the context. Wisdom
cannot have been "born" long before she is "with Him" during
the process of his creation. She literally must be a child when she
witnesses creation. And this, of course, is supported by what she
does when she is "with Him" as his *amon*: she is God's delight
and plays in front of him all the time. This fits the interpretation
of Wisdom as only a child, not a craftsman.

From this it becomes clear, too, that Wisdom is presented in
Proverbs as a person distinct from God, yet nevertheless very
close to him. The solemn "I" with which she speaks of herself
does not leave room for any other interpretation. Moreover, if
she is a child and God her father, there can be little doubt that
she is a female child, God's young daughter. This concept, the
personification of Wisdom and especially her depiction as female,
is completely new within the theological framework of ancient
Judaism. Scholars have argued for a long time that we are here
confronted with mythological ideas derived from other religions,
particularly from Egypt. It has been observed that Wisdom in
Proverbs (as well as in Jesus Sirach and in Sapientia Salomonis)
has been modeled along the lines of the Egyptian goddesses Maat
and, later, Isis.[24] Like Wisdom, Maat embodies primeval order,
truth, and justice. As in Wisdom, the world order encoded in
Maat has repercussions for the way of life of human beings, their
"ethical" behavior.[25] Maat was brought forth in primeval time by
God; she is the daughter of Re, the sun god.[26] In an image that
comes particularly close to Proverbs, it is said that her divine

father kisses his "daughter Maat," who is "before him," after he has "set her at his nose."[27] At the same time she is Re's consort, whom he "loves" and with whom he "unites."[28] Although created, she is eternal: "as long as you exist does Maat exist; as long as Maat exists do you exist . . . she is with you forever."[29] Maat, together with her brother Schu ("life"), are primeval forces latent in God that he emanates and that enable him to create the world and that simultaneously imbue him and his world with life.[30]

There can be little doubt that the appearance of Wisdom as God's daughter in Proverbs cannot be explained entirely from internal Jewish premises (although the idea of a female goddess was not completely alien to the Jewish religion). Thus, it is only reasonable to assume that the Egyptian Maat/Isis served as a model for the biblical Wisdom. To what extent the image of Maat/Isis was changed when adopted by the biblical author(s) is, however, a different question. There is no notion of God's sexual union with Wisdom in Proverbs. Moreover, the ambiguity of being created and at the same time eternal, which seems to characterize Maat,[31] is clearly resolved in Proverbs in favor of Wisdom's created status. Von Rad is right to emphasize this, but I am not sure whether he is equally right to maintain that Wisdom has "no divine status."[32] Wisdom comes very close to God, an aspect to which we will return when we look at Wisdom's function on earth. I therefore do not subscribe to von Rad's tactic of giving with one hand and taking with the other; namely, conceding that "Israelite teachers have been dependent on the idea of the Egyptian goddess of order" while at the same time asking, "But what does all this prove? Only that ideas which had their roots elsewhere came to Israel's help when she needed them, in order to be able to progress in her thinking within her own domain." If these "foreign ideas" helped Israel "to progress in her thinking," then these ideas cannot have been accidental and trivial; rather, one would want to know more about the progress they facilitated.

Following the description of Wisdom's origin the text takes an unexpected turn. Wisdom — God's little daughter, the first fruit of his creation — does not content herself with being with him, being his delight and playing in front of him. She plays (also) in God's inhabited world and finds delight with humankind; in other words, she turns her attention away from God and towards human beings. This surprising shift couldn't be better expressed than by the clear chiasm of *sha'ashu'im — mesaheqet : mesahe-qet — sha'ashu'ai* in verses 30 and 31. Wisdom is God's delight and plays in front of him, yet she plays in God's world and finds her delight with humankind. In obvious contrast to Job, Wisdom here is not hidden, inaccessible to and unattainable for human-kind. On the contrary, she wants to be recognized, she seeks out humankind, is immanent on earth. And what is her message? The text continues:

> (32) Now, sons, listen to me;
> Happy are they who keep my ways.
> (33) Heed discipline (*musar*) and become wise (*hakhamu*);
> Do not spurn it.
> (34) Happy is the man (*adam*) who listens to me,
> Coming early to my gates each day,
> Waiting outside my doors.
> (35) For he who finds me finds life
> And obtains favor from the Lord.
> (36) But he who misses me destroys himself;
> All who hate me love death.

The one who listens to her has to keep her ways and to heed discipline and, in turn, will become wise and happy. Moreover, what she has to offer is life, as opposed to nothing less than death. Presence of Wisdom is life; lack of Wisdom is death. Here Wisdom's claim clearly has a salvific quality. This is a bold and very self-confident expression of her message, which can only be explained by her divine origin. And yet Wisdom is not God; as we have seen, she is the firstborn of all his creatures. When she proclaims herself to be the source of life, which "normally" is the prerogative of God, this can only mean that she is God's mes-senger on earth or rather, his revelation. In other words: Lady Wisdom — the firstborn of God's creation, God's daughter — is God's revelation on earth. Proverb's Wisdom reveals what Job's Wisdom wanted to conceal: knowledge of the world order that leads to perfect harmony with the cosmos and with God.

In Proverbs, God no longer speaks through his human proph-ets. Instead, he reveals the mystery of his creation through his daughter of divine origin. The text does not say how Wisdom came down to earth. Rather, she is simply "there," as she was with him before, in this sudden turn from his presence to humankind (v. 30–31). It does not even explicitly say that Wisdom was sent by God, but there can be no doubt that her mission was endorsed by him. She is God's voice on earth, and more than that, as his daughter, she is God's embodiment on earth. In contrast to all the earlier biblical literature, we find here for the first time in Judaism an attempt to "materialize," to personify and to embody God's revelation on earth. That this embodiment takes place in the figure of his daughter is all the more surprising and, as we will see, an image that Judaism will soon abandon.

JESUS SIRACH: WISDOM AS GOD'S TORAH

The beautiful Wisdom poem in chapter 24 of Jesus Sirach, composed in Hebrew around 190 BCE and translated into Greek about 132 BCE by the author's grandson, clearly depends on Proverbs. After a brief introduction, which locates Wisdom "among her own people" and in the "assembly (*ekklēsia*) of the Most High," Wisdom explains her origin, again in the solemn "I" style:[33]

> (3) From the mouth of the Most High I came forth,
> and mistlike covered the earth.
> (4) In the heights of heaven I dwelt,
> my throne on a pillar of cloud.
> (5) The vault of heaven I compassed alone,
> through the deep abyss I took my course.
> (6) Over waves of the sea, over all the land,
> over every people and nation I held sway.
> (7) Among them all I sought a resting place:
> in whose inheritance should I abide?

This is similar to Proverbs in that it refers to Wisdom's creation before the creation of the world, when the universe was still in a chaotic state and slowly took shape as land and sea. As in Proverbs, Wisdom is personified, but there is no mention of her being God's daughter. She "came forth" from God's "mouth"; that is, she seems to be God's word, referring to the "Spirit of God" in Genesis 1:2, rather than to God's little child in Proverbs. Nevertheless, this "word" has taken shape in a female person, who speaks of herself as "I," who has a throne in heaven and takes her course through the newly created universe. Even more importantly, and quite in contrast to Proverbs, with its sudden shift from Wisdom playing in front of God to her immanence in the world, Sirach is much more concerned with Wisdom's move from heaven to earth. It explicitly states that Wisdom's wandering around in the universe has but one goal: she does not want to stay in heaven and is looking for a place in which to dwell. Moreover, it is now God who tells her what to do:

> (8) Then the Fashioner of all (*ho ktistēs hapantōn*) gave me his command,
> and he who made me (*ho ktisas me*) chose the spot for my tent,
> Saying, "In Jacob make your dwelling,
> in Israel your inheritance."
> (9) Before the ages, from the first, he created me (*ektise me*),
> and through the ages I shall not cease to be.

Emphasizing twice that Wisdom was created like any other creature, the text leaves no doubt that God himself ordered Wisdom not only to go down to earth, but also to settle among a certain people, those of Israel. This is again a clear departure from Proverbs (as well as Job). Whereas in Proverbs Wisdom finds her delight with humankind in general (*bene adam*) and demands that they (*banim*, "sons") listen to her, she now focuses her dwelling place and her attention on Israel and Israel alone. Of course, Wisdom immediately follows God's command:

> (10) In the holy Tent I ministered before him,
> and then in Zion I took up my post.
> (11) In the city he loves as he does me, he gave me rest;
> in Jerusalem is my domain.
> (12) I have struck root among the glorious people;
> in the portion of the Lord is my inheritance.

Wisdom takes residence among the people of Israel, first in the "holy Tent," which seems to refer to the Tabernacle in the wilderness, and then in Zion, certainly the Temple in Jerusalem. This is her final and permanent destination, and the text in no way suggests that she is supposed to leave the Temple. She is not God (since she was created), but she is nevertheless God's representative on earth. The author is firmly convinced that this happy "cohabitation" of Wisdom with her chosen people will last forever.

And then comes the proud self-praise of Wisdom, as she announces who she is and what she has to offer:

> (13) Like a cedar on Lebanon I am raised aloft,
> like a cypress on Mount Hermon.
> (14) Like a palm tree in Engeddi I stand out,
> like a rose garden in Jericho;
> Like a fair olive tree in the foothills,
> like a plane tree I am lofty beside the water.
> (15) Like cinnamon, or fragrant cane, or precious myrrh,
> I give forth perfume;
> Like galbanum and onycha and mastic,
> like the odor of incense in the holy Tent.
>
> (16) I spread out my branches like a terebinth,
> my branches so bright and so graceful.
> (17) I bud forth delights like the vine,
> my blossoms yield to fruits fair and rich.
> (19) Come to me, you that yearn for me,
> and be filled with my fruits;
> (20) You will remember me as sweeter than honey,
> better to have than the honeycomb.
> (21) He who eats of me will hunger still,
> he who drinks of me will thirst for more;
> (22) He who obeys me will not be put to shame,
> those who work with me will never fail.

Wisdom is like everything beautiful and delightful that has ever
been promised in the Bible, like all the famous trees and fragrances, not least like the odor of incense in the Temple. But she
exists not just for herself: she bears fruits, and she offers these
fruits to those who "yearn" for her. From verses 16–22 alone it
might seem as if her fruits are accessible to anyone who wants
them. It has been made only too clear, however, that she dwells
exclusively in Israel, so there can be no doubt that her fruits are
for the people of Israel and no one else. Moreover, we learn that
her fruits are not only inexhaustible, but also that those who
enjoy them are insatiable.

Then the text takes an unexpected turn; the image shifts from
enjoying Wisdom's fruits to obeying her (v. 22). This is clearly the
transition to what follows:

(23) All this (*tauta panta*) is true of the book of the Most High's
    covenant (*biblos diathēkēs*),[34]
the law (*nomon*) which Moses enjoined on us
as a heritage for the community of Jacob.
(25) It is brimful, like the Pishon, with Wisdom (*sophia*) —
like the Tigris at the time of the new crops.
(26) It runs over, like the Euphrates, with understanding (*synesis*);
like the Jordan at harvesttime.
(27) It floods, like the Nile, with knowledge (*paideia*);
like the Gihon at vintage time.
(28) The first human never knew Wisdom fully,
nor will the last succeed in fathoming her.
(29) Deeper than the sea are her thoughts;
her counsels (*hē boulē*), than the great abyss.

"All this," which has been said before by Wisdom and about
Wisdom, is identified, here, as the book of the covenant between
God and his people Israel, namely the Torah (Greek *nomos*). All
that Wisdom has to offer is to be found in the Torah, or rather
and more precisely: Wisdom *is* the book of the Torah. Thus Wisdom, God's personified messenger on earth (his daughter in Proverbs, his *logos* in Jesus Sirach), becomes embodied in a book —
the book, the Torah. The Torah is now abundant in Wisdom's
fruits, which can never be exhausted. For the first time in Jewish
history the rich imagery of Wisdom is tied to and concentrated in
a written document, which contains everything that God wants
to convey to humankind (or, more specifically, Israel) and that
humankind (again, Israel) needs to know. Wisdom, knowledge,
and all of the secrets of the cosmos are now contained in the
Torah and available (although never fully understandable) to
those — Israel — who have access to "her." This is the path subsequently taken by the movement in ancient Judaism that would
become the predominant school of thought, that of the Rabbis.

In the last paragraph of Jesus Sirach's Wisdom poem, apparently the speaker is a Torah teacher (the author, Jesus Sirach), the
"sage" (*hakham*), who has made Wisdom his profession. God no
longer reveals himself through his prophets, nor does he send his
personified Wisdom down to earth. Rather, Wisdom now spreads
through the teachings and instructions of the sage, who knows
how to make use of her, to expound her, and to transform

her (the Torah) into a mighty sea of knowledge for all future generations:

(30) Now I, like a rivulet from her stream,
channeling the waters forth into a garden,
(31) Said to myself, "I will water my plants,
my flower bed I will drench";
And suddenly this rivulet of mine became a river,
then this stream of mine, a sea.
(32) Again will I send my teachings (*paideia*) forth shining like the
dawn,
to spread their brightness afar off;
(33) Again will I pour out instruction (*didaskalia*) like prophecy,
and bequeath it to generations yet to come.

WISDOM OF SOLOMON: WISDOM AS THE MEDIUM OF DIVINE ENERGY AND GOD'S BELOVED SPOUSE

In the Wisdom of Solomon (Sapientia Salomonis), to which I now turn, we have the latest (first century BCE) and most elaborate treatment of the Wisdom tradition in the Bible and its surrounding literature. Within the triad God/man/creation-cosmos the emphasis has shifted entirely to man. "Man" now promulgates Wisdom's secret, and "man" is not just anyone but a very specific and outstanding man, King Solomon, who has been associated with Wisdom in a peculiar way: Solomon becomes the embodiment of Wisdom par excellence on earth. The one who speaks now is no longer Wisdom herself but Solomon: "What Wisdom (*sophia*) is, and how she came into being, I shall tell you; I shall not conceal her mysteries from you. I shall trace out her course from her first beginnings, and bring the knowledge of her into the light of day; I shall not leave the truth untold."[35] Hence the text, and Solomon as its speaker, is mainly concerned with "what Wisdom is" and what she does. This is what Solomon describes in rich detail and interweaves with his answer to the second part of the question, "how she came into being."

From the very beginning of his royal career, Solomon knew that Wisdom is the most precious of all the goods a king can possess, more precious than precious stones, than silver and gold,

than health and beauty (7:8–10). Yet her possession miraculously
bestows on the one who follows her all of the wonderful things
he has renounced in order to obtain her: "So all good things together came to me with her, and in her hands was wealth past
counting" (7:11). She is the "source" (*genetis*)³⁶ of all these good
things. This is similar to the Wisdom of Proverbs, but she is—
again as in Proverbs and also as in Job—more than that: she
gives insight into the structure of the cosmos. Strictly speaking,
however, it is not Wisdom who gives this insight, but rather God
himself. In a remarkable change the subject of Solomon's address
shifts from Wisdom to God, who is called "Wisdom's guide" (*tēs
sophias hodēgos*), and again back to Wisdom:

> (17) He [God] it was who gave me true understanding of things as
>   they are:
> a knowledge of the structure of the world (*systasin kosmou*) and
>   the operation of the elements;
> (18) the beginning and end of epochs and their middle course;
> the alternating solstices and changing seasons;
> (19) the cycles of the years and the constellations;
> (20) the nature of living creatures and behaviour of wild beasts;
> the violent force of winds and human thought;
> the varieties of plants and the virtues of roots.
> (21) I learnt it all, hidden or manifest,
> for I was taught by Wisdom, by her whose skill made all things
>   (*pantōn technitis*).³⁷

The link with Proverbs is obvious. It seems as if our author wants
to interpret the difficult *amon* in Proverbs, and if so, he apparently opts for the interpretation of "craftswoman" instead of
"daughter." As in Proverbs, however, it is God who is the creator
of the universe, not Wisdom. Wisdom is the order inherent in the
structure of the cosmos, which was created by God. This is made
very clear in 9:9: "With you [God] is Wisdom, who is familiar
with your works and was present when you created the universe"
(*parousa hote epoieis ton kosmon*). And although Wisdom teaches
man/Solomon all of this, the author leaves no doubt that it is
God who is the source of his understanding and knowledge.

Now, in verses 22b ff., the subject shifts to Wisdom's essence
and her relationship to God. Although it does not depict Wisdom
as God, Sapientia Salomonis is clearly the one among our Wis-

dom texts that moves Wisdom closest to God. Possibly referring back to Jesus Sirach (24:3),[38] but much more explicitly, it introduces another term explaining the delicate relationship between God and his Wisdom: Spirit (*pneuma*). Wisdom is not just Wisdom, but also the "Spirit of Wisdom" (*pneuma sophias*). Solomon prays for her, and she is given to him as a "Spirit of Wisdom" (7:7).[39] Similarly, at the end of his long prayer for Wisdom in chapter 9, Solomon confirms that a human being cannot possibly know the purpose of God's creation, "unless you had given him Wisdom (*sophia*) and sent your holy Spirit (*to hagion sou pneuma*) from heaven on high" (9:17). So apparently Wisdom is Spirit and simultaneously has a Spirit,[40] and this is exactly what 7:22 states: "In Wisdom there is a Spirit (*esti gar en autē pneuma*) intelligent and holy, unique in its kind and yet made up of many parts, subtle, free-moving, lucid . . . etc." (the qualities of Wisdom enumerated here, precisely twenty-one in number, seem to be composed deliberately of 3 × 7).[41] The same overlapping of "Wisdom," "(holy) Spirit," and "Spirit of Wisdom" appears already at the very beginning of Sapientia Salomonis (1:4–6), where Wisdom enters human beings because she loves them (*philanthrōpon*) and hates sin. At the same time, this Wisdom/Spirit is almost equated with God himself (1:7): "for the Spirit of the Lord (*pneuma kyriou*) fills the whole earth, and that which holds all things together knows well everything that is said." Again, she is not God, but she is very close to him. Through Wisdom/Spirit, God reaches into the world, permeates it, and transforms human beings.

The most elaborate description of Wisdom's origin in, and intimate relationship with, God follows immediately after the enumeration of her qualities (7:25–26):

(25) Like a fine mist she rises from the power of God,[42]
a clear effluence (*aporroia eilikrinēs*)[43] from the glory of the
  Almighty;
so nothing defiled can enter into her by stealth.
(26) She is the radiance (*apaugasma*)[44] that streams from everlasting light,
the flawless mirror of the active power of God (*tēs tou theou energeias*),
and the image (*eikōn*) of his goodness.

The imagery used here is that of energy being transmitted from its source (God) to its recipient (Wisdom). God is power, glory, light, energy; Wisdom is the steam or vapor, the effluence and radiance that goes forth from the divine power source, the mirror that reflects it. Wisdom receives, connects, and reflects the divine energy; she is the medium through which it enters the world. Thus, as close as this mediated energy is to its source (almost inseparably close), it is not this relationship between, in the terminology of modern science, secondary and primary energy that is our author's major concern, but rather that (and how) this energy is mediated with respect to the world of human beings. The final metaphor of verse 26 already refers to this, thereby leading into what follows (7:27–28):

> (27) She is but one, yet can do all things,
> herself unchanging, she makes all things new;
> age after age she enters into holy souls,
> and makes them friends of God and prophets,
> (28) for nothing is acceptable to God
> but the person who makes his home with Wisdom.

God enters human beings through Wisdom, his effusion and reflection, and she transforms them in such a way that they become his "friends"; that is, his "image and likeness" (Gen. 1:26). She directs the divine energy down to earth and enables humankind to redirect it to God.

The same chiasm between the divine and the mundane world is expressed in yet another image, which has long occupied scholars. Wisdom is finally described as the one who "sits beside your [God's] throne" (9:4); she is the *parhedros*, "coadjutor" of God. Moreover, as coadjutor, she is clearly depicted as a woman (8:3): "She adds lustre to her noble birth, because it is given her to live with God (*symbiōsin theou echousa*);[45] the Lord of all things loved her (*ēgapēsen autēn*)."[46] This is not a neutral, almost physical energy radiating from God, but God's beloved wife. And again, precisely the same image is transferred to Solomon. Solomon, too, falls in love with her and takes her home as his wife to live with him: "Wisdom I loved (*ephilēsa*); I sought her out when I was young and longed to win her for my bride; I was in love (*erastēs egenomēn*) with her beauty" (8:3). "So I determined to take her home to live with me (*pros symbiōsin*)" (8:9). Here the same word is used as in Wisdom's living together with God: *symbiōsis*. God gives Wisdom, his beloved spouse, to live with Solomon (the ideal archetype of all human beings), "for nothing is acceptable to God but the person who makes his home with Wisdom (*ton sophia synoikounta*)" (7:28).

The similarities of this image of Wisdom as God's spouse and the Isis/Osiris myth, specifically in its Hellenistic adaptation, has long been observed. In particular Burton L. Mack has pointed to many parallels:[47] Isis is the spouse and sister of the sun god Osiris; even the term *parhedros* is used in her relationship to Serapis, the Hellenistic Osiris.[48] Isis is the goddess of earth and nature, the "female principle of nature" (*to tēs physeōs thēly*),[49] the mother of the cosmos (*mētēr tou kosmou*).[50] In Plutarch's *De Iside*, in particular, Mack finds some striking terminological parallels with Sapientia Salomonis. Osiris, the "origin" (*archē*), "first" (*prōtos*), "good" (*tagathon*), "essence" (*ousia*) does not come in contact with the visible world but radiates his energy through "effluxes, emanations" (*aporroai*), "likenesses" (*homoiotētes*), "images" (*eikones*), "ideas" (*logoi*) and "forms" (*eidē*). These "radiations," however, remain in heaven,[51] where Isis, the goddess of the moon and Osiris's female partner,[52] receives them and channels them to the mundane world:

> "Thus Isis is the female principle of nature and that which receives all procreation (*hapasa genesis*), and so she is called by Plato the Nurse (*tithēnē*) and the All-receiving . . . because she is transformed by reason (*logos*) and receives all corporeal and spiritual forms. . . . [F]or both she is indeed a possible sphere and material, but she inclines ever of herself to what is better, offering her-self to it for reproduction and for the fructifying in herself of effluxes (*aporroai*) and likenesses (*homoiotētes*). In these she rejoices and she is glad when she is pregnant with them and teems with procreation. For procreation in matter is an image of being (*eikōn ousias*), and what comes into being is an imitation of what is."[53]

Thus the order and structure of the world, "the well-ordered (*to kekosmēmenon*), the good (*agathon*) and the useful (*ōphelimon*)," is the "work of Isis (*Isidos ergon*)," and as such the "image (*eikōn*), imitation (*mimēma*) and reason (*logos*) of Osiris."[54]

These parallels between Sapientia Salomonis and Plutarch are striking, indeed. The drawback of any comparison between Plutarch's *De Iside* and Sapientia Salomonis, however, is that for purely chronological reasons one can hardly argue for a possible influence of the former (written towards the end of the first century CE)[55] on the latter (written in the first century BCE). Mack is aware of this and attempts to explain the similarities on the basis of common Egyptian ideas.[56] But he nevertheless concludes: "No doubt, the author of Sapientia Salomonis did know the Hellenistic interpretation of Isis-Sophia."[57] This still remains to be proven. What is much more likely is that the author of Sapientia Salomonis developed ideas that later find a similar expression in Plutarch's *De Iside*, and that both are informed by Platonic and Stoic, as well as Egyptian, concepts of image, *anima mundi*, and Isis. It is this peculiar mixture of Platonic, Stoic and Egyptian elements that gives Wisdom/Spirit in Sapientia Salomonis her distinctive tinge.

To sum up briefly, the biblical and early postbiblical Wisdom literature displays a wide panorama of Wisdom traditions. Wisdom is the structure encoded in God's creation. Human beings are painfully aware of it, but, alas, do not have the necessary tool to decode it (Job). Most likely under the influence of Hellenized Egyptian ideas, this abstract code becomes personalized and turns into a created being, the firstborn of God's creation, who functions as the witness of creation and simultaneously as God's representative on earth. As such, Wisdom is decidedly and daringly described as female, God's "little daughter," who "plays" in front of him. Not (yet) identical with God, she is nevertheless a divine agent, who communicates the plan of God's creation to humanity. As God's spokeswoman, she bridges the gap between the heavenly and earthly realms which has opened up through the very act of creation (Proverbs). Wisdom's female character and her care for the human world is retained in Jesus Sirach, but at the same time she becomes depersonalized again and materializes herself in the form of a book—the Torah. The most complex picture of Wisdom is drawn in Sapientia Salomonis where she remains the order inherent in the structure of the cosmos and yet enters a very intimate relationship with her creator. Not only does she collect the divine energy and reflect it down to the earth, she is even elevated to the position of God's beloved spouse. This is the boldest step in a tradition that would be continued and enriched by Philo.

❊ 2 ❊

PHILO'S WISDOM

PHILO OF ALEXANDRIA (ca. 20 BCE–50 CE) is the most prominent Jewish philosopher of antiquity known to us. In fact, he is the first Jewish philosopher at all in the proper sense of the word and the only one in the ancient period who deserves this title. Some scholars even regard Philo as the archetype and father of all subsequent Jewish philosophy.[1] He was also one of the most distinguished members of the Jewish community in Alexandria, brother of the alabarch Alexander Lysimachus, the Roman official responsible for the fiscal administration of Egypt, and uncle of Tiberius Julius Alexander, who served as procurator of Judea from 46–48 CE. In 40 CE, Philo was the head of the Jewish embassy sent from Alexandria to Rome to present to the emperor Gaius Caligula the Jewish view concerning the battle among Greeks and Jews over citizenship (*politeia*) in Alexandria.[2]

As a philosopher, Philo was heavily influenced by the Greek philosophy of his time, in particular that of Stoa and Platonism.[3] He did not, however, develop a systematic philosophical doctrine of his own. Rather, he cast his philosophical ideas into the mold of an extensive exegesis of the Bible and an allegorical interpretation of its heroes. When investigating his concept of Wisdom,[4] one can easily see how deeply he is imbued with both "canonical" and "noncanonical" Jewish Wisdom traditions. He knew the book of Proverbs and quotes it, and, although he does not seem to quote Jesus Sirach and the Wisdom of Solomon, his writings definitely offer some parallels to these books. Jean Laporte, who has analyzed Philo's relationship to Wisdom literature in detail, concluded that there is a "continuity of ideas and language between Wisdom literature and Philo,"[5] and that "among the biblical books after the Pentateuch, the Wisdom literature has the greatest attraction for him."[6]

GOD AND HIS WISDOM

Let us begin by looking at the connection between Wisdom and God — although it should be emphasized from the outset that this is not what most interests Philo; he is much more concerned about how Wisdom reaches down to earth and manifests itself/herself in human beings. The most prominent passage appears in his tractate on drunkenness (*De Ebrietate*). Philo here refers to the biblical text in Deuteronomy 21:18–21 about the son who has gone astray and who has to be brought by his parents before the tribunal of the town, which in turn sentences him to be stoned to death. The mention of parents ("father" and "mother") in this passage induces Philo to reflect on the different meanings of "father and mother," the first of which is the "parents of the universe":

> Now "father and mother" is a phrase that can bear different meanings. For instance, we should rightly say and without further question that the Architect (*dēmiourgos*) who made this universe was at the same time father of what was thus born, while its mother was the knowledge (*epistēmē*) possessed by its Maker. With this knowledge God had union (*synōn*), though not as human beings have it, and begat created being. And knowledge, having received the divine seed (*ta tou theou spermata*) and when her travail was consummated, bore the only beloved son who is apprehended by the senses (*aisthētos*), the world which we see (*ton kosmon*). Thus in the pages of one of the inspired company [the author of Proverbs], Wisdom (*sophia*) is represented as speaking of herself after this manner: "God obtained me first of all his works and founded me before the ages" (Prov. 8:22). True, for it was necessary that all that came to the birth of creation should be younger than the mother and nurse (*tithēnē*) of the All.[7]

Philo here quotes Proverbs 8:22 explicitly and emphasizes Wisdom's old age: she was with God before the creation of the universe.[8] Interestingly enough, his translation comes closer to the Hebrew text than does the Septuagint (LXX): that God "obtained"(*ektēsato*) her is a more precise translation of *qanani* than *ektise* ("he created me") in the LXX, which can be found also in Aquila, Symmachus, and Theodotion.[9] Moreover, his interpretation of Wisdom as a "nurse" (*tithēnē*)[10] may echo Aquila's translation of *amon* as *tithēnoumenē*, "foster-child, darling."[11]

Unlike Proverbs, however, Philo clearly understands Wisdom here not as a child, God's daughter, but as his spouse, the mother of the (his) visible world. Whereas Wisdom, God's little daughter, in Proverbs witnesses the creation of the universe, yet does not take any active part in this creation, here she is God's spouse with whom he has union to produce the world. (Although he makes it clear that this union is "not as men have it," he nevertheless uses strongly sexual—perhaps Stoic?—language.) In relation to their creation, the universe, God and Wisdom are father and mother; in relation to each other, they are husband and wife (although Philo does not mention these terms here), God being the "architect" and Wisdom his "knowledge" (*epistēmē*). In stressing the intimate matrimonial bond between God and Wisdom, Philo seems to take up ideas developed in Sapientia Salomonis, rather than in Proverbs.

Wisdom and Logos

The graphic sexual imagery Philo uses in describing the relationship between God and Wisdom during the process of creating the world becomes all the more apparent if we compare it with other passages referring to creation. Following the Platonic pattern, Philo generally distinguishes between the *kosmos aisthētos*, the world perceived by our senses (often called, according to the father/son metaphor, *hyios aisthētos*, "the son apprehended by the senses"), and the *kosmos noētos*, the world discerned by the mind or the intellect. Both are related to each other like "archetype" and "image" or "copy," the former being the world of eternal and unchangeable "ideas," the latter our temporal, changeable and visible world. In *Quod Deus* 31f., Philo describes both forms of cosmos as God's two sons, one younger and one elder:

> For this universe, since we perceive it by our senses (*kosmos aisthētos*), is the younger son of God. To the elder son, I mean the intelligible universe (*noētos d'ekeinos*), He assigned the place of firstborn, and purposed that it should remain in His own keeping. So this younger son, the world of our senses (*hyios ho aisthētos*),

when set in motion, brought that entity we call time to the brightness of its rising.

Thus it becomes clear that the *kosmos aisthētos* in *De Ebrietate* is not the only beloved son of God in the sense that it is the only and one son, but rather the only beloved son who is apprehended by the senses, insofar as there is another beloved son, the *kosmos noētos*, who is apprehended by the mind. How these two sons (worlds) of God came into being is not related in *Quod Deus*: we only learn that God is their father and that he decided to keep his firstborn, the *kosmos noētos*, within his own realm. That there is also a mother we understand from *De Ebrietate*, where Wisdom (*epistēmē*) is clearly the mother of the *kosmos aisthētos* only (at least there is no mention, with respect to her, of the *kosmos noētos*).

We learn more about the origin and place of the *kosmos noētos* from the tractate on the creation of the world (*De Opificio Mundi*). Philo here presents his famous parable about the architect who first conceives the city he intends in his mind before he translates this plan into reality:

> Just such must be our thoughts about God. We must suppose that, when He was minded to found the one great city [the world], He conceived beforehand the models of its parts, and that out of these He constituted and brought to completion a world discernible only by the mind (*kosmos noētos*), and then, with that for a pattern, the world which our senses can perceive (*kosmos aisthētos*). As, then, the city which was fashioned beforehand within the mind of the architect held no place in the outer world, but had been engraved in the soul of the artificer as by a seal; even so the universe that consisted of ideas (*ho ek tōn ideōn kosmos*) would have no other location than the divine word (*ton theion logon*), which was the author of this ordered frame.[12]

God, the creator of the world, is like the architect, the builder of the city. Just as the true "place" of the city is in the mind or soul of the architect, so is the true "place" of the world in the mind of God, the divine Logos. Or, more precisely, since the world of ideas does not hold a place in the outer world but is kept within the divine realm, the *kosmos noētos* is identical with the divine Logos:

Should a man desire to use words in a more simple and direct way, he would say that the world discerned only by the intellect (*ton noēton kosmon*) is nothing else than the word of God when He was already engaged in the act of creation (*theou logon ēdē kosmopoiountos*).[13]

Hence it is the divine Logos that is the origin *and* place of the *kosmos noētos*. If we relate this with Wisdom as the origin (not place) of the *kosmos aisthētos*, we might conclude that there is a neat division of labor between Logos and Wisdom, with one responsible for the world of ideas and the other for the visible world. Unfortunately things are not that easy. Philo is not very explicit about the relationship between Logos and Wisdom,[14] but there is clear evidence that they may be closely related, if not identical. For instance, in *Legum Allegoriae* Philo interprets Genesis 2:10 ("A river goes forth from Eden to water the garden: thence it is separated into four heads") as follows: "Eden" is the Wisdom of God (*tēs tou theou sophias*), the "river" is "generic virtue" (*hē genikē aretē*) or "goodness" (*agathotēs*), and the four "heads" or branches of the river are the four cardinal virtues (prudence, self-mastery, courage, and justice).[15] As becomes immediately clear, Philo is not concerned here with the relationship between God and Wisdom but rather with Wisdom's influx into the world, through generic virtue and the four cardinal virtues; he is interested in how Wisdom's bounty is channeled down into the world of human beings. Nevertheless, within this context, he makes two important statements about the nature of Wisdom. First, he explains, the Wisdom of God "is full of joy, and brightness, and exultation, glorying and priding itself only upon God her Father (*tō patri autēs . . . theō*),"[16] and second, he says explicitly: "This [generic virtue/goodness] issues forth out of Eden, the Wisdom of God, and this is the Logos of God (*hē de estin ho theou logos*); for after that [the Logos: *kata gar touton*] has generic virtue been made."[17]

The first explanation once again draws Philo closer to Proverbs: God is Wisdom's father, and consequently Wisdom is God's child or, more precisely, God's daughter (although Philo does not emphasize here her female character). Her main purpose is, as in Proverbs, to be full of praise in front of God (cf. Prov. 8:30) and to channel God's goodness down to the world, as well. Since, however, generic virtue belongs to the *kosmos noētos*, the world discernible only by the mind, and since this world originates from, and is located in, the divine Logos, he has to make clear that ontologically Wisdom is identical with the Logos of God! In other words, we have here two overlapping streams of thought, which cannot be completely harmonized: the archetypal world of ideas in the divine mind and the mediation of these ideas in the world of human beings. When the emphasis is put on the former, the (male) Logos comes to the fore; when it is put on the latter, Philo prefers to talk about (female) Wisdom.[18]

Yet again, this insight should not mislead us into believing that Logos alone has an ontological quality, and Wisdom only an epistemological quality. Both Logos and Wisdom are at the same time ontologically connected with, as well as disconnected from, God and serve in the latter capacity as epistemological agents of God.[19] The following interpretation of the "spring of water from the flinty rock" and the "manna in the wilderness" in Deuteronomy 8:15f. stresses the epistemological quality of both Wisdom and Logos:

> . . . until God send forth the stream from His strong Wisdom (*tēs akrotomou sophias*) and quench with unfailing health the thirst of the soul that has turned from Him. The flinty rock (*akrotomos petra*)[20] is the Wisdom of God (*hē sophia tou theou*), which he marked off highest and chiefest from His powers, and from which He satisfies the thirsty souls that love God. And when they have been given water to drink, they are also filled with the manna, the most generic of substances (*tou genikōtatou*)—for the manna is called "somewhat" (*ti*), and that suggests the *summum genus* (*ho pantōn esti genos*)—but the supremely generic (*to de genikōtaton*) is God, and next to Him is the word of God (*ho theou logos*), but all other things subsist in word only.[21]

Both Wisdom and Logos quench the thirst (Wisdom: water) and satisfy the hunger (Logos: manna) of the human soul; that is, they fill it with God's spiritual bounty. But whereas the manna is called the "most generic of substances" and as such is directly related to God, the "supremely generic" (the Greek text uses the same word for God and manna: both are *genikōtatos*), the water is not qualified more precisely. Accordingly, the Logos as the source of the manna is drawn very closely to God (he is "next to him", *deuteros*, lit. "second"), whereas Wisdom is the highest and chiefest among his "powers" (*dynameis*). This does not mean, however, that Wisdom is inferior to Logos. In a parallel that uses the same imagery—the rock as Wisdom and manna as Logos—Philo explicitly equates "rock" and "manna": "In another place he [Moses] uses a synonym for this rock and calls it 'manna.' Manna is the divine Logos (*logon theion*), eldest of all existences (*ton presbytaton tōn ontōn*), which bears the most comprehensive (*to genikōtaton*) name of 'somewhat' (*ti*)."[22] Thus Logos and Wisdom are indeed ontologically identical but describe different aspects of God, as also of his creative activity. God, his Logos, and his Wisdom are one, while they simultaneously reflect distinct qualities within God and in relation to the created world.

WISDOM'S GENDER

If we return now to the question of gender, it goes without saying that Logos is male and Wisdom female. Indeed, it is precisely Wisdom's female quality that allows Philo to proffer much more detailed statements about the relationship of Wisdom to God and to the created world. We have noted already the husband/wife, the father/mother, and the father/daughter relationships, and we will see that this difficult kinship can be further complicated by a shift in, or rather a complete inversion of, the gender.

The husband/wife relationship is expounded in more detail in *De Cherubim* 49–51. Philo distinguishes here between "greater" and "lesser" mysteries, and although the prophet Jeremiah's mysteries are less than those of Moses, the God-beloved, Philo argues that Jeremiah, too, was a "worthy minister of the holy secrets" and became his disciple. Jeremiah's oracle "Did you not call upon Me as it were your house, your father and the husband of your virginity (*andra tēs parthenias sou*)" (Jer. 3:4)[23] is to be interpreted, he argues, as God speaking to virtue (*aretē*), the "all-peaceful":

> Thus he implies clearly that God is a house, the incorporeal dwelling-place of incorporeal ideas, that He is the father of all things, for He begat them, and the husband of Wisdom (*sophias anēr*), dropping the seed of happiness for the race of mortals into good and

virgin soil (*sperma . . . eudaimonias eis agathēn kai parthenon gēn*). For it is fitting that God should hold converse with the truly virgin nature, that which is undefiled and free from impure touch.[24]

Here we have again the almost paradoxical mixture of sexual language and asexual content: Wisdom is God's wife, and they have intercourse. But this wife is, and remains, a virgin. Since, as we have seen, it is actually the Logos who is the appropriate locus of the incorporeal ideas, one would expect the Logos rather than Wisdom to be God's partner. But Philo obviously wants to use the graphic imagery of sexual intercourse, and for this he has to employ Wisdom instead of the Logos. He makes it very clear, however, that one should not be misled into imagining divine "beings" behaving like "humans." On the contrary, he insists, God does not have intercourse, in the usual sense of the word, with the virgin Wisdom:

> Therefore the oracle makes itself safe by speaking of God as the husband not of a virgin (*parthenos*), for a virgin is liable to change and death, but of virginity (*parthenia*), the idea which is unchangeable and eternal. . . . It is fitting and right therefore that God the uncreated, the unchanging, should sow the ideas of the immortal and virgin virtues in virginity which changes not into the form of woman.[25]

The image of mother/nurse, as well as of daughter, expresses the epistemological aspect of Wisdom, her creative activity in the souls and minds of human beings. God is the "father of the created world" (*ton gennēsanta kosmon*),[26] of the "universe" (*tōn holōn*),[27] and Wisdom is the "mother of all things" (*tōn sympantōn*),[28] "by whose agency the universe (*to pan*) was brought to completion."[29] As parents of the created world, God and Wisdom are equal partners: they create the same world, not different parts of it (the terms used for "world" or "universe" are interchangeable).[30] Yet it is Wisdom's task to reach down to the created world, to channel the divine gifts of goodness, virtue, and knowledge to the realm of human beings. In other words, Wisdom, as in the canonical and noncanonical Wisdom literature, is the way God reaches down to earth. In an interpretation of Deuteronomy 32:13 ("He fed him honey from the rock, and oil from the flinty rock") Philo again relates the "rock" to Wisdom, and the "honey" and "oil" to the nourishment of the soul:

He [Moses] uses the word "rock" to express the solid and indestructible Wisdom of God (*sophian theou*), which feeds and nurses
and rears to sturdiness all who yearn after imperishable suste-
nance. For this divine Wisdom has appeared as mother of all that
are in the world (*tōn en kosmō*), affording to her offspring, as
soon as they are born, the nourishment which they require from
her own breasts. But not all her offspring are deemed fitting for
divine food, but such as are found worthy of their parents; for
many of them fall victims to the famine of virtue, a famine more
cruel than that of eatables and drinkables. The fountain of the
divine Wisdom (*hē tēs theias sophias pēgē*) runs sometimes with a
gentler and more quiet stream, at other times more swiftly and
with a fuller and stronger current. When it runs down gently, it
sweetens much as honey does; when it runs swiftly down, it comes
in full volume as material for lighting up the soul, even as oil does
a lamp.[31]

Human beings are Wisdom's offspring and nourished by her with
the most precious divine food she has to offer: virtue.[32] In a powerful image, Philo compares Wisdom with an ever-bubbling fountain that pours into adequate human receptacles: the souls. The
soul cannot get enough of it, but the effect is different, depending
on how the water runs down. Running down slowly it sweetens
the soul gently; running down swiftly and with full power, it en-
lightens the soul in a sudden flash (Philo comes very close here to
what is called electricity in modern terminology).[33]

In order to receive the spiritual gifts of Wisdom, soul and mind
have to renounce "sense-perception" (*aisthēsis*), the worst enemy
of Wisdom and of a life pleasing to God and to the purpose of his
creation. Interpreting Genesis 2:24 ("Hence a man leaves his father and mother and clings to his wife, so that they become one
flesh"), Philo applies "father" and "mother" to God and Wisdom
respectively, while equating the "wife" with sense-perception:

For the sake of sense-perception the mind, when it has become her
slave, abandons both God the father of the universe, and God's
excellence and Wisdom, the mother of all things, and cleaves to
and becomes one with sense-perception so that the two become
one flesh and one experience. Observe that it is not the woman
that cleaves to the man, but conversely the man to the woman,
mind to sense-perception. For when that which is superior, namely
mind, becomes one with that which is inferior, namely sense-

perception, it resolves itself into the order of flesh which is inferior, into sense-perception, the moving cause of the passions. But if sense the inferior follows mind the superior, there will be flesh no more, but both of them will be mind.[34]

The dichotomy of (male) mind and (female) sense within man has to be overcome and resolved in favor of mind, if man wants to have his share in the bounties of Wisdom, his mother.[35] Just as Wisdom is the true mother of all human beings, so is sense-perception (*aisthēsis*) "the nurse and foster-mother (*tēn trophon kai tithēnēn*) of our mortal race." When Adam (mind) called his wife *zōē* ("Life"), he was mistaken because she was not, as he believed, "the mother of all things living" (Gen. 3:20), but rather "of those who are in truth dead to the life of the soul. But those who are really living have Wisdom for their mother, but sense they take for a bond-woman (*doulē*), the handiwork of nature made to minister to knowledge (*epistēmē*)."[36]

GOD'S DAUGHTER

Turning now to the notion of Wisdom as God's daughter, we find a completely different kind of imagery. It cannot be harmonized with the metaphor of wife and mother, because, on the level of kinship, Wisdom can hardly be at the same time God's spouse and Israel's mother, as well as God's daughter (unless one wants to imply some incestuous relationship).[37] Of course, this is not Philo's problem: he could easily juxtapose different metaphors, although it seems that the father/daughter relationship is rarer than that of father-mother/husband-wife. The most striking text regarding Wisdom as God's daughter[38] is an explanation of Genesis 28:2 ("Rise up and flee away into Mesopotamia, to the house of Bethuel your mother's father, and take a wife there to yourself from the daughters of Laban your mother's brother"). The speaker is Rebecca, who requests her son Isaac to go to her father's house and to find there a wife for himself. Philo's interpretation equates her father's house with the house of Wisdom and Bethuel with Wisdom herself:

> For you shall find the house of Wisdom (*ton gar sophias oikon*) a calm and fair haven, which will welcome you kindly as you come

to your moorings in it; and it is Wisdom's name that the holy
oracles proclaim by "Bethuel," a name meaning in our speech [in
Hebrew][39] "daughter of God" (*thygatēr theou*); yea, a true-born
and ever-virgin daughter, who, by reason alike of her own modesty
and of the glory of Him that begot her, has obtained a nature free
from every defiling touch.[40]

This sounds quite innocent: Wisdom is God's daughter, and as
such is a virgin, free from any "defiling touch." In fact, the state
of virginity fits her status as daughter much better than that as
wife in the text quoted above, where Philo had to resort to God's
intercourse with the idea of virginity rather than with a virgin.[41] But fortunately enough (for Philo's true intention) things
are more complex, because the biblical text explicitly says that
Bethuel is Rebecca's father. He therefore continues:

He [Moses] called Bethuel Rebecca's father. How, pray, can Wisdom, the daughter of God, be rightly spoken of as father? Is it
because, while Wisdom's name is feminine (*onoma men thēly sophias estin*), her nature is masculine (*arren de hē physis*)? As indeed all the virtues have women's titles, but powers and activities
of consummate men. For that which comes after God, even though
it were chiefest of all other things, occupies a second place (*deu-
teran chōran*), and therefore was termed feminine to express its
contrast with the Maker of the universe who is masculine, and its
affinity to everything else. For pre-eminence always pertains to the
masculine, and the feminine always comes short of and is lesser
than it.[42]

Here, Philo lets the cat out of the bag and reveals what he
really thinks about Wisdom's gender. At first sight it might seem
as if he, out of misogyny, wants to explain away Wisdom's femininity and turn her into a male being. But this view is much too
simplistic (and I will return to it). Rather, he makes a most important distinction between Wisdom's essence (her relationship with
God) and her function (her relationship with the human world).
In her essence Wisdom is feminine (which for Philo is clearly a
passive quality), but in her function she is masculine (an active
quality).[43] Although she is ontologically identical with God, she is
at the same time distinct, as we have seen above, and this distinction (her second place within the divine realm) can aptly be

expressed by her feminine quality. Interestingly enough, Philo completely disregards here the male Logos (who is also called "second," *deuteros*),[44] because it does not fit the ambiguity of his gender concept. Instead, he concludes with the masculine function of Wisdom:

> Let us, then, pay no heed to the discrepancy in the gender of words, and say that the daughter of God, even Wisdom, is not only masculine but father (*arrena te kai patera*), sowing and begetting in souls aptness to learn, discipline, knowledge, sound sense, good and laudable actions. It is from this household that Jacob the Practiser seeks to win a bride (*gamos*, lit. "wedding"). To what other place than to the house of Wisdom shall he go to find a partner (*koinōnos*), a faultless judgement (*gnōmē*), with whom to spend his days forever.[45]

This is the climax of Philo's description of Wisdom. Wisdom is simultaneously mother and spouse, daughter and father, female and male. As God's spouse and Israel's mother, she is female; as God's daughter, she is paradoxically male, insofar as she takes over God's creative activity,[46] implementing in human souls his divine gifts. And, finally, as man's companion she is female again: Jacob marries her as the embodiment of "faultless judgement," to accompany him all his life.[47] In the end, Wisdom becomes the property of humankind.

DIVINE AND HUMAN WISDOM

Let us now briefly look more closely at the effect Wisdom has on human beings, in order to further elucidate Wisdom's essence and function. We have seen already that she nourishes humanity and that she can be compared with overflowing water, as well as with light. No doubt, she is humankind's highest achievement, a gift from God that must be accepted or rejected by them. Those who are blessed with her are enraptured by her beauty[48] and are taken up into close proximity with God:

> This is why those who crave for Wisdom and knowledge with insatiable persistence are said in the Sacred Oracles to have been called upwards (*anakeklēsthai*); for it accords with God's ways that those who have received His down-breathing (*tous hyp' autou katapneusthentas*) should be called up to Him. For when trees are

whirled up, roots and all, into the air by hurricanes and tornadoes . . . it is strange if a light substance like the mind is not rendered buoyant and raised to the utmost height by the native force of the divine spirit (*tou theiou pneumatos*), overcoming as it does in its boundless might all powers that are here below.[49]

Humanity, enraptured by Wisdom (note the almost synonymous use of "Wisdom" and "spirit"), is elevated to God like the biblical heroes of old. To be sure, humanity must crave for Wisdom, but once she is granted to them, they are completely overwhelmed by the experience. It is not something that can be "learned" in an orderly way, step by step. Rather it is bestowed upon humanity as a gift, which transforms them completely.[50] Hence the difference, which Philo emphasizes over and over again, between traditional knowledge and the knowledge of Wisdom:

No doubt it is profitable, if not for the acquisition of perfect virtue (*aretēs teleias*), at any rate for the life of civic virtue (*politeian*), to feed the mind on ancient and time-honoured thoughts, to trace the venerable tradition of noble deeds, which historians and all the family of poets have handed down to the memory of their own and future generations. But when, unforeseen and unhoped for, the sudden beam of self-inspired Wisdom (*automathous sophias*) has shone upon us, when that Wisdom has opened the closed eye of the soul and made us spectators rather than hearers of knowledge, and substituted in our minds sight, the swiftest of senses, for the lower sense of hearing, then it is idle any longer to exercise the ear with words. . . . We must not indeed reject any learning that has grown gray through time, nay, we should make it our aim to read the writings of the sages and listen to the proverbs and old-world stories from the lips of those who know antiquity, and ever seek for knowledge about the men and deeds of old. Yet when God causes the young shoots of self-inspired Wisdom (*neas . . . blastas autodidaktou sophias*) to spring up within the soul, the knowledge that comes from teaching (*ek didaskalias*) must straightway be abolished and swept off. Ay, even of itself it will subside and ebb away. God's scholar, God's pupil, God's disciple . . . cannot any more suffer the guidance of men.[51]

Human wisdom and divine Wisdom are as essentially different as are the ways by which they are acquired and the effects that they elicit. The effects are *aretē teleia*, "perfect virtue," as opposed to *politeia*; that is, everything that is connected to the proper life of a citizen. The latter is clearly subordinated to the former, and this statement is all the more remarkable if we take into consideration the historical context in which Philo writes: the Hellenistic city of Alexandria with its almost sacred ideal of *politeia* (in which the Jewish residents so desperately wanted to share). Most conspicuous are the ways by which one acquires human and divine Wisdom. The one is obtained by teaching and learning, containing the cultural memory of generations, the "venerable tradition" cultivated through the ages by our historians and poets. The other cannot be taught and learned: it is "self-taught" (this is the literal meaning of *automathēs* and *autodidaktos*). One should not, however, take this notion of "self-teaching" too literally. Wisdom is "self-taught" in the sense that it does not rely on the resources of traditional education, but emerges in the soul without recourse to "conventional Wisdom." Yet the soul is not its source: God, who "causes" its "young shoots to spring up within the soul," is its originator. And, most importantly, in contrast to human Wisdom, which is not only "old" and has grown "gray," but also needs a lifetime to be acquired, divine Wisdom is fresh and new and manifests itself suddenly, in a sudden act of cognition. Moreover, the new Wisdom does not supplement the old one, but rather substitutes it completely. The happy student of God bestowed with God's Wisdom no longer needs human wisdom; he has entered an entirely different realm of reality and cognition.

In making this distinction between traditional learning and "self-taught" Wisdom, Philo does not even hesitate to equate Wisdom and Logos again and to cast them both into the image of marriage:

> For to those who welcome training, who make progress, and improve, witness is borne of their deliberate choice of the good, that their very endeavour may not be left unrewarded. But the fitting lot of those who have been held worthy of a Wisdom that needs no other teaching and no other learning (*tois d' autodidaktou kai automathous sophias axiōtheisin*) is, apart from any agency of their own, to accept from God's hands Logos as their plighted spouse (*eggyasthai logon*), and to receive knowledge as partner in life of the wise (*tēn sophōn symbion epistēmēn*).[52]

Those who are worthy of self-taught or self-inspired Wisdom are given her ("knowledge," *epistēmē*, of course is Wisdom) in marriage by God. Interestingly enough, the word used for the partnership between Wisdom and the wise (*symbios*, "living together," "companion, partner," "husband, wife") is precisely the one used in Sapientia Salomonis for the "living together" (*symbiōsis*) of Wisdom with God and with Solomon![53] Moreover, this Wisdom is obviously identical with the Logos because God gives both (Wisdom and Logos) to the worthy wise, and both are given by God, the father, as a wife (*eggyasthai*, used for the Logos, means to have a woman plighted or betrothed to someone).

The wise man, who has chosen Wisdom as his spouse, enters a state of perfect happiness: "For when God delivers to us the lore of his eternal Wisdom (*tēs aidiou sophias*) without our toil or labour we find in it suddenly and unexpectedly a treasure of perfect happiness (*thēsauron eudaimonias teleias*)."[54] To be sure, one should not despise traditional learning, which compares to divine Wisdom as Hagar the handmaid compares to Sarah the mistress. Indeed, it may be necessary for some to turn first to the handmaid: " 'Go in, then,' she [Sarah/Wisdom] says, 'to my handmaid [Hagar], the lower instruction (*tēn . . . mesēn paideian*) given by the lower branches of school lore, that first you may have children by her,' for afterwards you will be able to avail yourself of the mistress's company to beget children of higher birth."[55] But only Wisdom's children (perfect virtues) are the source of true happiness and lead the way back to God: "For Wisdom is a straight high road, and it is when the mind's course is guided along that road that it reaches the goal which is the recognition and knowledge of God (*gnōsis . . . kai epistēmē theou*)."[56] Following Wisdom on the way to God means not only abandoning her handmaid, lower instruction, but also (and quite literally) giving up the pleasures of the flesh and the body.[57] An outstanding example of this ideal are the virginal Therapeutae who are married to Wisdom:

The feast [of the Therapeutae] is shared by women also, most of them aged virgins, who have kept their chastity not under compulsion, like some of the Greek priestesses, but of their own free will in their ardent yearning for Wisdom (*dia zēlon kai pothon sophias*). Eager to have her for their life mate (*symbioun*) they have spurned the pleasures of the body and desire no mortal offspring but those immortal children which only the soul that is dear to God can bring to the birth unaided[58] because the Father has sown in her spiritual rays enabling her to behold the verities of Wisdom (*theōrein ta sophias dogmata*).[59]

Philo leaves no doubt that the Therapeutae provide prime examples of those who seek Wisdom as their mate. They are by no means an exception however; rather they practise what he expects of any pious Jew. Marriage with Wisdom is a virgin marriage, inasmuch as the soul that marries Wisdom follows the example of Wisdom and turns into a virgin:

> For the union of human beings that is made for the procreation of children, turns virgins into women. But when God begins to consort with the soul, He makes what before was a woman into a virgin again, for he takes away the degenerate and emasculate passions which unmanned it and plants instead the native growth of unpolluted virtues. Thus He will not talk with Sarah[60] till she has ceased from all that is after the manner of women (Gen. 18:11).[61]

SUMMARY — AND ONCE AGAIN GENDER

Philo's concept of Wisdom is a dense and complex network of established Jewish traditions and contemporary philosophical influences. His Wisdom stands in close relationship to God and to God's Logos, as well as to the human world; she is simultaneously wife, mother, daughter, and father. In using both the wife/mother and the daughter imagery, Philo appears to deliberately combine the Proverbs (daughter) and the Sapientia Salomonis traditions (spouse).[62] In playing freely with her gender and changing her sex from female to male, he seems to follow his Platonic predilections — as well as the inclinations of his own misogyny.

The most recent discussion of Philo's idea of Wisdom has been presented by Joan Chamberlain Engelsman in her chapter on "The Repression of Sophia in the Writings of Philo" in *The Feminine Dimension of the Divine*.[63] Engelsman starts from the presupposition that the Philonic concept of Logos entered into competition with the older and established view of Wisdom, and that the Logos gradually displaced Wisdom and eventually was successful in demoting it. This process was facilitated, she argues, by Philo's "symbolic misogynism," which granted Wisdom "a station more befitting her sex."[64] Even the synonymous usage of the two terms "Logos" and "Sophia," she proposes, was aimed "to reinforce the right of Logos to replace Sophia."[65] Philo could not suppress Wisdom completely, however, because he felt bound to the biblical Wisdom tradition and at the same time to the Egyptian Isis/Osiris/Horus myth (Isis being the model of Wisdom and Horus that of Logos).[66] What could he do? He relegated Wisdom to her place in heaven, where she was allowed to retain her feminine qualities, while consigning her role on earth to Logos! As her main proof for this view, Engelsman cites the passage in which Logos is described as descending from the "fountain of Wisdom,"[67] which she takes as evidence that "Sophia becomes the mother of Logos."[68]

Philo's desire to restrict Wisdom — supposedly "a pale and sickly copy of her sister Isis" and "even a far cry from the Sophia of Proverbs" — to "the rarefied air of heaven" was enforced by contemporary philosophy (Plato), as well as Philo's "unhappy view of the feminine."[69] As an entirely heavenly figure, she was "protected from the contamination of the flesh"[70] and could remain a perpetual virgin. It is this "distaste for anything feminine,"[71] Engelsman argues, that also compelled him to change Wisdom's gender in the famous passage in *De Fuga et Inventione*.[72] In Wisdom's elevation to heaven, Philo finally "helps prepare the way for the Mariology which is elaborated in the Christian tradition. But it also may suggest why Mary can never be a full-blown goddess figure in the style of Isis or Demeter, or even the Sophia of the Jewish Wisdom tradition. Philo's Sophia is already a truncated and weakened version of the goddess — remote and not immanent, heavenly and not earthly, unifaceted and not multidimensional."[73]

This description of the Philonic Wisdom concept is quite a sweeping blow. First of all, Philo's Sophia is much more complex and variegated than Engelsman allows — as is the Wisdom of the biblical and postbiblical Wisdom tradition. To begin with the latter, we have seen already that the concept of "word" (Logos) seems to penetrate into the Wisdom tradition; at least in Jesus Sirach, a certain overlapping of "Wisdom" and "Logos" becomes apparent (while in Sapientia Salomonis "Wisdom" seems to overlap, at least partly, with "Spirit"). It would be difficult to reduce as "distaste for anything feminine" this gradual penetration of Logos into the realm of the earlier (?) Wisdom. Furthermore, and more importantly, it is simply wrong to maintain that the Logos *replaces* Wisdom in Philo and relegates her to the heavenly realm. This imposes too simplistic and biased a view upon Philo's sophisticated epistemology. As we have seen, both Wisdom and Logos belong to the heavenly, as well as to the earthly, worlds and are interrelated in a most complex fashion. If at all, there might be a preference for Wisdom's rather than for the Logos's epistemological aspect; and the sole metaphor of the Logos descending from the "fountain of Wisdom" does not adequately establish a mother/son relationship between Wisdom and Logos, in which Wisdom is supposedly confined to heaven and Logos assumes her role on earth. Philo's many descriptions of Wisdom are no less sympathetic than those of the Logos. Indeed, there can be no doubt that he takes up and integrates the biblical Wisdom tradition in a most deliberate and careful manner.

But what, then, about the delicate question of gender? Philo clearly follows the Platonic model of the active role of the masculine in contrast to the passive role of the feminine; this can be taken for granted and has nothing or little to do with whether or not he was a misogynist and had a "distaste for anything feminine" (a judgement that is as hard to prove as it is clichéd). But this gender dichotomy within the divine as well as the human realm is depicted as a complex interplay of forces.[74] Whether the masculine or the feminine, the active or the passive, the positive or the negative aspect predominates depends on the perspective and on the question of essence versus effect. Rather than simplistically delineating the masculine from the feminine in Philo and thus uncovering his repression of the feminine, it is much more important to realize that Philo considers not only the human but also the divine world as composed of masculine and feminine forces, depicted — despite his emphasis on the idea of virginity — in graphic sexual terms. Moreover, in describing Wisdom's creative activity and her operation on earth, Philo very much remains within the confines of the canonical and noncanonical Wisdom literature. Wisdom, in her interplay with Logos, functions as God's active force on earth, and it is her sole destiny to lead man back to his initial and original place in God. Philo's

Wisdom is not "a far cry from the Sophia of Proverbs" but, on the contrary, the climax and summary of the biblical Wisdom tradition, enriched by the Stoic and Platonic philosophy of his time.

As we will see, Philo evinces the culmination of a fruitful and multifarious tradition in Judaism, which accords Wisdom and femininity a prominent role in the dynamic interplay of divine and human forces, at least for the time being. To a large extent this line of thought breaks off in Judaism and is taken over by Christianity. Yet it is not just an idle game to speculate as to what would have happened if Philo had been granted a more positive and momentous reception in Judaism. In any case, Engelsman is correct in pointing out that the Christian veneration of the virgin Mary in particular has at least some of its roots in the culmination of the Wisdom tradition as presented by Philo. Her idea of Mary, however, is unfortunately as simplistic as her idea of Sophia. It is not Philo's relegation of Sophia to the remote realm of heaven, nor his image of Sophia as the "truncated and weakened version" of the pagan goddesses Isis or Demeter, that paves the way for the Christian Mary. Rather, like her precursor, Sophia, Mary is as much or more on earth as she is in heaven, and she definitely absorbs as much or more of the veneration devoted to her pagan rivals as does Sophia.[75]

☀ 3 ☀

THE GNOSTIC DRAMA

NOT MUCH LATER than Philo, at the beginning of the second century CE at the latest, there emerged a Christian movement, consisting of different "groups" and "schools of thought," whose members gave themselves the strange name *gnōstikoi*, "gnostics."[1] Derived from the Greek word *gnōsis* ("knowledge," "act of knowing") this term generally denotes "(those who are) capable of attaining knowledge." In claiming that they possessed a particular and exclusive "knowledge" that was not shared by other Christians, the members of these groups cultivated a strong sense of group identity, underlined by the development of a distinctive set of doctrines and practices, a special vocabulary, and a peculiar body of writings. Traditionally, these groups are lumped together under the rubrics of "Gnosis" or "Gnosticism,"[2] but recent scholarship has highlighted the problematic nature of these terms.[3] Not only do they lack ancient equivalents, but they imply a uniformity that never existed among the groups themselves, but rather only in the eyes of their opponents. Despite the problems with these categories, what can be safely said is that much of the literature we call "gnostic" is quite transparently based on exegeses of passages from the Hebrew Bible, most notably from the book of Genesis.[4] In labeling the gnostic schools as "Christian," modern scholarship takes into account that most, yet by no means all, of these exegeses bear distinctively Christian marks.

The origins of the gnostic schools are shrouded in the mists of history.[5] We possess two different sets of their literary production. First are their original writings, the majority of which have not come down to us in their original language (Greek) but in Coptic translation. The most famous among these are the Nag Hammadi codices, named for the town of Nag Hammadi on the Nile River in Egypt in the vicinity of which the codices were hidden around 350 CE and rediscovered in 1945. Our second set of evidence is comprised of extensive quotations by church fathers, most notably by Irenaeus of Lugdunum (modern Lyon). Probably as early as 170 CE, Irenaeus summarized the gnostic doctrines in his polemical masterpiece *Adversus Haereses*, focusing primarily upon the teachings of the "gnostic" Valentinus (ca. 100–ca. 175 CE) and his school.⁶ Irenaeus seems to have known several gnostic writings, including a version of the *Apocryphon of John*, the fullest rendering of the gnostic myth, now preserved only in Coptic. From this it becomes clear that, although the literary production of the gnostics extended over a long period of time, spanning at least until 350 CE, some of the works generally called "gnostic" clearly date from before 170 CE.

Although the beginning of the second century CE represents the earliest date that can be established by literary evidence, this does not mean that any gnostic group(s) did not exist earlier. On the contrary, some evidence may suggest an earlier origin. Scholars have pointed to the fact that the gnostic myth of creation depends on a peculiar blend of Plato's *Timaeus* (or rather its Middle Platonic interpretation) with the biblical book of Genesis—a blend that is also characteristic of Philo's philosophical thought. Hence, one might conclude with Bentley Layton⁷ that "since the gnostic myth seems to presuppose this speculative tradition, it *might* be as old as Philo Judaeus." Notably, Layton hastens to add cautiously: "Yet nothing proves that it *must* be so old. Scholars are therefore unable to say exactly how much older than Irenaeus (AD ca. 180) the gnostic sect actually must be."⁸

Whereas this qualification is well warranted, the real issue is not so much the question of origin and dating (that is, how many years before Irenaeus or Valentinus did "gnostic schools" or "gnostic myths" originate—not to mention "Gnosticism" or "the" gnostic myth), but rather the exact nature of the religious milieu (Christian or Jewish or other) in which they emerged. This fundamental question has yet to be decisively answered, but recent research seems to be more open to the possibility of a primarily Jewish background.⁹ That originally Jewish works were later revised from a Christian point of view is almost routine in the history of Jewish literature (some apocalypses are prominent examples), and one has certainly to reckon with this possibility in the case of the gnostic writings, too. The assumption of a Jewish origin of "Gnosticism"—or more cautiously: of certain branches of gnostic schools—also allows a much simpler and less forced explanation of Gnostic works that do not bear any traits of Christian influence.

The Creation Myth According to the Apocryphon of John

The Apocryphon of John presents one of the most succinct expositions of what may be labeled the classic gnostic myth. It is embedded in a clearly Christian frame story (a revelation of the resurrected Christ to John, the son of Zebedee), but its true subject concerns the gradual development of the cosmic drama: the description of God, "the Father of the All"; the structure of the divine world; the creation of the material world, of Adam, Eve, and their children; and finally the salvation of humanity. As such, it presents a most intriguing gnostic interpretation of the first chapters of the biblical book of Genesis, following the biblical story up to the birth of Seth (Gen. 4:25) and, briefly, Noah and the Flood (Gen. 6). Because of the prominent role given to Seth — the third son of Adam, after Cain had killed Abel — scholars regarded the book to be part of the so-called Sethian gnosis. Considerable emphasis is put, however, on the very first stage, the unfolding of the divine pleroma *before* the beginning of creation; that is, before the beginning of the Bible. The book can be dated sometime before Irenaeus's summary — before ca. 170 CE. In the following, I will outline some of the major ideas, with special emphasis, of course, on the role of Sophia, the feminine element within the divine world.[10]

The book begins with the self-revelation of the One who calls himself Father, Mother, and Son, who is a unity with nothing above it, the Father of the All, the invisible One. He is above the All, pure light, invisible Spirit, more than a god: eternal, totally perfect, illimitable, unsearchable, immeasurable, invisible, ineffable, unnamable, and so forth.[11] This notion of a God above everything, actually "more than a god," is clearly influenced by the Platonic Supreme Being, the First Principle or the Ultimate Intellect above and beyond everything that can be grasped by human cognition. This pure and perfect divine being desires nothing but himself alone;[12] he contemplates himself,[13] and this self-contemplation is symbolized, or rather visualized, in the medium of light and water: he perceives his own image (*eikōn*) in the water/light or light/water that surrounds him.[14] In desiring and perceiving himself, however, the self-sufficient "god," who rests in perfect silence,[15] releases something that goes beyond his perfect self. His desire and perception "materialize"; he emits another, second being, which in turn emits other spiritual beings — "aeons" in gnostic terminology — that in turn release the material world:

> And (27) [his thought (*ennoia*) became] actual and she came forth,
> (28) [namely] she who had [appeared] before him (29) in [the radiance of] his light.
> This is (30) the first [power, which was] before the All,
> (31) and [which came] forth from his mind.
> She (32) [is the Providence (*pronoia*) of the All]
> — her light (33) [shines like his] light —
> the [perfect] (34) power
> who is [the] image (*eikōn*) of the invisible, (35) virginal (*parthenikon*) Spirit (*pneuma*)
> who is perfect.
> (36) [The first power,]
> the glory of Barbelo,
> the perfect (5:1) glory in the aeons,
> the glory of the (2) revelation;
> she glorified the virginal (*parthenikon*) (3) Spirit (*pneuma*)
> and it was she who praised him,
> for because of him (4) she had come forth.[16]

Barbelo

The Second Principle, the realization of the thought and the "materialization" of the *eikōn* of the First Principle, comes very close to what we know about the Jewish Wisdom tradition.[17] To be sure, she is not called "Wisdom" here, but bears the strange name of "Barbelo" — probably a Coptic word of Egyptian origin meaning "emission, projectile" and "great," hence something like "the great emission."[18] The figure of "Wisdom" (*sophia*) is left to a later stage of the development of the cosmic drama; actually, as we will see below, the "split" between Barbelo and Sophia is one of the most significant characteristics of the gnostic myth as pre-

served in the Apocryphon of John. Nevertheless, the parallels between Barbelo and the early Jewish Wisdom are striking. First of
all, her gender is feminine, although the question of gender and
sex is more complicated (see below). Secondly, she is the "first
power" to be emanated from the First Principle "before the All";
that is, before anything else was brought into being. The text
does not explicitly state that she was "created" as in Proverbs,
but rather that she "came forth" and "appeared before him" (the
shorter version has the probably better reading "attended him").[19]
She is with him, obviously not always, but at a certain stage of
"God's" self-perception. And her first "reaction" after she had
come forth is praise: she praised him "for because of him she had
come forth." This "ceremonial-liturgical attendance"[20] clearly
points to a Jewish context. The question of whether this context
is a "Jewish angel engaged in the characteristically Jewish liturgical activity of glorifying"[21] or Wisdom praising her creator is of
secondary importance—although the image of Wisdom praising
her creator does not seem to belong to the predominant characteristics of the Jewish Wisdom tradition, since Wisdom is just
"there," and as such a source of God's "delight" (Prov. 8:30).

Finally, and most importantly, Barbelo is distinct from "God"
and yet still almost identical with him: "her light shines like his
light," and she is his "image" (*eikōn*)—in other words, when he
perceives himself, he sees her! The parallel that immediately comes
to mind is Sapientia Salomonis's version of Wisdom's relationship
with her creator:

> She is the radiance (*apaugasma*) that streams from everlasting
> light,
> the flawless mirror of the active power of God (*tēs tou theou
> energeias*),
> and the image (*eikōn*) of his goodness.[22]

The intimate relationship between First and Second Principle,
God and Wisdom, could not be expressed more forcefully. And
yet—as in the Jewish Wisdom tradition, with its different em-
phases in Proverbs, Jesus Sirach, and Sapientia Salomonis—
immediately following the description of the Second Principle's
origin and close connection with the First Principle, the text describes its function for the subsequent stages of emanation:

This is the first Thought, (5) his image (*eikōn*);
she became the womb (*mētra*) of everything,
(6) for it is she who is prior to them all,
the (7) Mother-Father (*mētropatōr*),
the first Man,
the holy Spirit (*pneuma*),
(8) the thrice-male,
the thrice-powerful,
(9) the thrice-named androgynous One,
and the (10) eternal aeon among the invisible ones,
and (11) the first to come forth.[23]

In her distinctiveness from the First Principle, Barbelo becomes the "starting-point" of all the subsequent emanations, the mediator between "God" and the "All." The powerful image of her "womb" emphasizes her female quality: she is the "womb of everything" because she precedes everything.[24] Barbelo's female quality is more complex than just this, however. First of all, in relation to her "originator," the perfect "invisible, virginal Spirit," her femininity is not particularly stressed. She is the "materialization" of his thought and of his image, and as such identical and distinct, but she is not represented as his wife (as in Sapientia Salomonis). Her femininity expresses itself most graphically in her role as mother of the All, of the entire spiritual (and material?) world. But it is precisely this femininity that is ambiguous. She is not just mother but rather "Mother-Father," the "first Man," the "thrice-male," the "thrice-named androgynous One." In other words, she is both male and female. As the Father's identical image she is male, and as his distinct counterpart she is female. "She is both the father *and* herself."[25]

This is reminiscent of the distinction we encountered in Philo's application of Bethuel, Rebecca's father, to Wisdom.[26] Like the Apocryphon of John, Philo distinguishes between two aspects of Wisdom: her identity with God and her distinctness from him. In her former quality she is male, and in her latter quality she is female; consequently, she is both male and female. Whereas Philo emphasizes Wisdom's male quality in the subsequent process of creative activity, the Apocryphon of John seems to stress Barbelo's role as mother ("womb") of all of the subsequent emanations. But this differentiation is probably only superficial. In its designation of Barbelo as "Mother-Father," the Apocryphon of John makes it very clear that she, too, retains her masculine quality; she too is both male and female.

The Self-Generated/Christ

With Barbelo's appearance the process of emanation is set in motion. At first Barbelo unfolds into the triad of "foreknowledge" (*prognōsis*), indestructibility, and eternal life, after requesting these attributes from the "invisible, virginal Spirit," who grants her request. Together with her first two attributes, "thought" (*ennoia*) and "providence" (*pronoia*), they form the "pentad of the aeons of the Father"[27]—the five aeons that actually are ten because they are androgynous like Barbelo herself.[28] The next step of the unfolding of the divine world is the birth of the son, the "only-begotten-One (*monogenēs*) of the Mother-Father,"[29] the "Self-Generated" (*autogenēs*),[30] the "first-born Son."[31] This birth of the Self-Generated is described differently in the long and the short versions of our text. Whereas in the long version the Father "looked into Barbelo," and "she conceived from him,"[32] it is Barbelo in the short version who "gazed intently into him [the Father]" and "gave birth to a spark of blessed light."[33] Thus either the Father or Barbelo takes the initiative, which makes a significant difference. In the light of the first step of emanation, where the Father sees his own image (Barbelo), it makes sense to argue in favor of the short version: now Barbelo perceives the Father, and this perception brings forth the son, the third aspect of the triad Father/Mother/Son.

Whereas Barbelo is identical with her originator and as such his female/male equal, however, the "offspring" of Barbelo and the Father is different; "he does not equal his [and her][34] greatness."[35] But nevertheless, he is the authentic image of the Father (and Barbelo), and the Father happily acknowledges his existence:

And (19) the invisible, virginal Spirit
rejoiced (20) over the light who had come into being,
who had proceeded (21) from the first power (22) of his Providence
    (*pronoia*),
which is Barbelo.

(23) And he anointed him with his Christhood/goodness[36]
(24) until he became perfect (*teleios*).[37]

Now the son, the divine Self-Generated, is put in charge of the next step of emanation. He requests "a fellow worker, which is the Mind (*nous*),"[38] from the invisible Spirit, the Father, and — through the triad Mind/Word/Will — he "created the All"[39] (the first time that the word "create" is here used):

And the invisible, (23) virginal Spirit
installed the (24) divine true Self-Generated (*autogenēs*) over the
   All.
(25) And he subjected to him every authority (*exousia*)
(26) and the truth which is in him,
(27) that he may know the All.[40]

Sophia and Her Offspring

The invisible Spirit gives the Self-Generated/Christ the power to emit four great lights (four aeons). These are characterized by the four powers of "Understanding" (*synēsis*), "Grace" (*charis*), "Perception" (*aisthēsis*), and "Prudence" (*phronēsis*), and are ruled by the four angels Armozel, Oriael, Davieithai, and Eleleth. At the same time these four aeons are the embodiment of four biblical archetypes: Pigera-Adamas, the heavenly Adam; Seth, the heavenly prototype of Adam's son; the seed (*sperma*) of Seth, which is the prototype of the spiritual community on earth; and "the souls (*psychē*) of those who do not know the Pleroma (*plērōma*) and did not repent at once, but who persisted for a while and repented afterwards"[41] — obviously the opponents of those whose conversion they expected. Finally, each of these four aeons generates three further aeons, making twelve aeons altogether.[42] To the last group of three belongs "Wisdom" (*sophia*), together with "Perfection" and "Peace."[43] Interestingly enough, the reference to "Wisdom" interrupts the carefully built structure of the twelve aeons. Whereas one of the four afore mentioned powers belongs to each of the first three groups of three aeons ("Grace" to the first, "Perception" to the second, and "Understanding" to the third), "Prudence" would be expected in the fourth group, but is missing. Instead, "Wisdom" appears, and as the very last of the twelve aeons.

Here we encounter, at last, the technical term so well-known from Jewish Wisdom literature. Wisdom is located at the boundary of the spiritual, divine world. Beyond her, and through her, as we shall see, begins the creation of the mundane world, the material universe. Up to her extends the divine power, expanding from the Father through Barbelo and her ten aeons to the Self-Generated/Christ and his four/twelve aeons, with her as the last one. But then a mishap or break within the cosmic drama takes place, and something unfortunate and unexpected occurs, not only disturbing, but also terminating the uninterrupted expansion of the divine power. The cause is Wisdom:[44]

> (16) Our fellow-sister, Wisdom (*sophia*), being an (17) aeon,
> conceived a thought (18) from herself,
> and in the conception (19) of the Spirit[45] and (20) Foreknowledge.
> She wanted to bring forth the (37:1) likeness out of herself,
> although the Spirit had not agreed (2) with her (3) nor consented,
> nor (4) had her consort (*syzygos*) approved,
> (5) namely, the male (6) virginal Spirit.
> She, however, did not find her (7) partner
> as she was about to decide
> (8) without the good will of the Spirit
> (9) and the knowledge of her own partner,
> (10) and as she brought forth
> because (11) of the sexual knowledge (*prounikon*) which is in her.[46]

The text starts solemnly with some kind of direct speech by the twelve aeons, to which Wisdom belongs. Wisdom is different from all of the others in that she "conceived a thought from herself" and "wanted to bring forth the likeness out of herself" without the knowledge and consent of the invisible Spirit and her own male syzygy. This is a clear and fatal break with the cosmological pattern of emanation. Barbelo had requested the pentad/decad of her aeons (in particular her son, the Self-Generated) from the Father, and the Father had granted her request. When she "conceived" the Self-Generated, she "gazed into" the Father. Similarly, the Self-Generated had been granted "all authority" from the Father. Wisdom, in sharp contrast to her precursors, relies solely on herself: not only does she not ask for permission, but she also generates her offspring out of herself, without any collaboration of her male partner. And the reason for this is that she is *prounikos*, most often translated as "lewd" and even "whore." Some scholars have argued that the word, in addition to its sexual tinge, has also the connotation of "untamable, impetuous, disruptive."[47] Hence Wisdom, and only Wisdom among all the aeons, is driven by a disruptive and sexually "independent" nature, which is not in accord with the cosmic and spiritual harmony set in motion by the Father and which results in the realization of her own "selfish" will.[48] Such an attempt, however, can only prove to be abortive:

> (12) Her thought could not remain (13) idle
> and her product came forth (14) imperfect,
> foreign in his (15) appearance,
> because she had made him without (16) her consort (*syzygos*).
> And he was not similar (17) to the likeness of the Mother,
> for he has (18) another form (*morphē*).[49]

The product of Wisdom's restless and independent thought is an imperfect image of his mother, Sophia—quite different from Barbelo, who is the perfect image of the Father, and from the Self-Generated/Christ who (although he is not equal to Barbelo and the Father) still remains the authentic image of them. With Sophia's offspring, dissimilarity and difference enter the process of emanation. Sophia, frightened by her rebellious act, casts him away from her and from her place within the spiritual realm of divine beings:

> And she saw him (19) in her deliberation
> that he was taking on the (20) form of another likeness,
> having the face of a (21) snake and the face of a lion.
> His (38:1) eyes were shining with fire.
> She (2) cast him away from her, outside (3) those places,
> that (4) none of the immortal ones might (5) see him,
> because she had given birth to him (6) in ignorance.[50]

Sophia's imperfect offspring, whom she names Ialdabaoth (probably "begetter/parent of Sabaoth"; that is, of the heavenly armies),[51] becomes the originator of a new material universe, of aeons outside the spritual realm—a counterworld to the world set in motion by the invisible Spirit/Father and Barbelo. Ialdabaoth is the Chief Ruler who creates other "rulers," "powers," "angels" or "demons" (365 in all), who are all driven by the ignorance, selfishness, and madness that he inherited from his mother, Sophia. Because of the power he still shares with his mother and because of his ignorant arrogance, he considers himself not only a god but the *only* god (a clear allusion to Exod. 30:3/Deut. 5:7).[52] Meanwhile, his mother repents that she has created Ialdabaoth and given away part of her power, and the invisible Spirit takes pity on her and moves her to "the ninth (heaven) until she has corrected her deficiency."[53] Ialdabaoth and his rulers proceed with creating Adam (and later Eve). Their product remains inactive and immovable because it lacks spirit/life, until Sophia, with the help of Barbelo, tempts Ialdabaoth to blow some of his spirit — the power he had "stolen" from his mother, Sophia — into Adam's face. This procedure animates Adam, who becomes stronger and more intelligent than his creators. With fury and envy Ialdabaoth and his entourage cast Adam down into the realm of matter and provide him with a material body.

Sophia's Descent

Now comes Sophia's great moment. In order to rectify her mistake, she is sent down into the material world by Mother-Father/ Barbelo:

But the blessed One, the Mother-Father [Barbelo],
(10) the beneficent and merciful One,
(11) had mercy on the power (*dynamis*) of the Mother [Sophia]
(12) which had been brought forth from the Chief Ruler [Ialdabaoth],
(13) for they [the rulers] might gain power
over the (14) psychic and perceptible body [Adam].
And he (15) sent, through his beneficent (16) Spirit
and his great mercy,
a helper (*boēthos*) (17) to Adam,
a luminous Afterthought (*epinoia*),[54]
(18) who comes out of her[55] [Barbelo],
(and) who is called (19) Life (*zōē*).
And she [Afterthought] assists the whole creature [Adam],
(20) by toiling with him,
and by restoring (21) him to his perfection (*plērōma*)
and by (22) teaching him about the descent of his (23) seed
   (*sperma*)
and by teaching him about the way of ascent,
(24) [which is] the way he[56] came down.
(25) And the Afterthought of the light was hidden in Adam,

(26) in order that the rulers (*archōn*) might not know [her],
(27) but that Afterthought might be a correction (28) of the deficiency of the Mother.[57]

The text does not state explicitly that it is Sophia herself who is sent down to help Adam and to rectify the cosmic disaster she had caused. It rather speaks of the "Afterthought of light" who is called "Life." But other passages indicate that Afterthought and Sophia are identical. Already at the very beginning of the drama that she initiated, and immediately after she had created Ialdabaoth, Sophia is called "Mother of the living."[58] After the creation of Eve, the connection between her and "Life" is made explicit: "And our sister Wisdom (*sophia*) [the sister of the other aeons] (is) she who came down in innocence (*akakos*) in order to rectify her deficiency. Therefore she was called Life (*zōē*), which is the Mother of the living, by the Forethought (*pronoia*) of the sovereignty (*authentia*) of heaven."[59] "Afterthought" ("Life") is Sophia, and the name "Life" is given her by "Forethought" (*pronoia*) who is Barbelo.[60] There is obviously a clear terminological symmetry between *ennoia* ("Thought" = invisible Spirit/Father), *pronoia* ("Forethought/Providence" = Barbelo), and *epinoia* ("Afterthought/Reflection" = "Wisdom," *sophia*), thus emphasizing the close relationship between Sophia and Barbelo.[61]

It is Sophia who heals the break and who functions as the revealer of the hidden knowledge and the redeemer of humanity, the descendants of Adam and Eve. Her abused power is still present in Adam's third son, Seth, and all of his offspring. It is the redeemer's task to secure them against the evil forces of Ialdabaoth and to lead humanity (or rather Seth and his descendants, the true "gnostics") back to their heavenly realm, the spiritual universe of the Father and Barbelo. The present time of the narrator of our story represents the final act of this cosmic drama of emanation, catastrophe, and deliverance.

Sophia and Barbelo

In this grandiose myth Wisdom plays a crucial role. She appears in dual form, as Barbelo and as Sophia. As Barbelo she is the Father's companion, his identical male/female image, through which the Father turns toward a realm outside himself and initiates the process of emanation; as Sophia she is the last stage of the emanation of the spiritual universe and the beginning of the material world, as well as the redeemer who leads the material world back to its spiritual origin. As such, this Wisdom myth is very similar to the Jewish Wisdom tradition, as outlined in particular in Proverbs and Sapientia Salomonis. Like its precursors, it explains how the world has been created and proposes that Wisdom, God's female principle, is essential in God's dealings with the world. It is only through his identical/separate image that something outside himself could come into existence. But there is one problem with this concept, which the Jewish Wisdom tradition has hardly broached, much less solved: the world, which was created through Wisdom, is not exactly as it was supposed to be. Jewish Wisdom literature is not particularly explicit about the question of how the imperfect and deplorable condition of humankind and the world came into being, what happened, and why the world is not entirely "good," as promised in the Bible (cf. Gen. 1:31)—despite the fact that it was created by God through his Wisdom, and despite the fact that Wisdom remains in the world and among humankind.

Here the innovation of the gnostic myth comes into play. Although it is certainly not the first to raise this problem, it poses the question of the origin of evil in a remarkably pointed way, through its account of the creation of the world. In order to keep God wholly separate from evil, it introduces a break between the spiritual and material world, as well as between Barbelo and Sophia—that is, essentially within God himself. It is only Sophia, not Barbelo, who is responsible for the creation of the material world and its contamination with evil. This departs radically from the classical Wisdom tradition, in which we find no trace of any separation between a positive, "higher" Wisdom in her heavenly form and a negative, "lower" Wisdom in her earthly manifestation. The classical Jewish Wisdom is always one and the same (Proverbs does know the "strange" and "alien woman"[62] as the counterimage of Wisdom, but this woman is a mundane figure and not heavenly Wisdom in her earthly form).

This split between Barbelo and Sophia is not, however, as definite as it might seem (and as some scholars want us to believe). As we have seen, the text does not draw the boundary between Barbelo and Sophia very sharply, to such an extent that it is not always clear whether certain epithets refer to Barbelo or to Sophia. Moreover, it is Barbelo who sends Sophia down to Adam as a helper and redeemer, thus maintaining the close relationship between her and Sophia even after Sophia's disruptive act of creating Ialdabaoth. Therefore, La Porta goes as far as to reconstruct an original version of the gnostic myth, in which there was no distinction between Barbelo and Sophia; accordingly Sophia first emanated from the Father, not Barbelo, similar to the Jewish Wisdom tradition.[63] Whether or not La Porta's rather elaborate reconstruction of the development of the myth from the classical Wisdom tradition to the Apocryphon of John is correct,[64] it is evident that the images of Barbelo and Sophia are so closely entwined that it makes little difference whether only Sophia was originally responsible for the cosmic drama, including the origin of evil, or whether (and when) Sophia was bifurcated into Barbelo and Sophia.

The very end of the book again emphasizes this close relationship between Barbelo and Sophia. Here, Barbelo praises herself in a beautiful poem, which could have been written by the author of Proverbs and of Jesus Sirach (aside from its peculiar gnostic flavor). In this poem it is Barbelo, instead of Sophia, who descends into the material world to perform the task of the redeemer. All speculations as to whether at some stage of the redactional process Sophia has been displaced by Barbelo[65] become futile: for the final editor of the book,[66] Barbelo is Sophia and Sophia is Barbelo:

> I [Barbelo], (12) therefore, the perfect Forethought (*pronoia*) of the All,
> (13) changed myself into the seed (*sperma*),
> for I existed (14) first, going on every road.
> (15) For I am the richness of the light;
> (16) I am the remembrance of the pleroma (*plērōma*).
> And I (17) went into the realm of darkness
> and (18) I endured till I entered the middle (19) of the prison.
> And the foundations of the chaos (20) shook.
> And I hid myself from them because of (21) their evil (*kakia*),[67]
> and they did not recognize me.
>
> Again (22) I returned for the second time (23) and I went about.
> I came forth from those who belong to the light,
> (24) which is I, the remembrance of the Forethought (*pronoia*).

(25) I entered into the midst of darkness and (26) the inside of
   Hades,
since I was seeking [to accomplish] (27) my task.
And the foundations of the chaos (28) shook,
that they might fall upon those who (29) are in chaos and might
   destroy them.
(30) And again I ran up to my root of light
(31) lest they be destroyed before (32) the time.

Still for a third time (33) I went
—I am the light (34) which exists in the light,
I am (35) the remembrance of the Forethought (*pronoia*)—
that I might (36) enter into the midst of darkness and the inside
   (31:1) of Hades.
And I filled my face with (2) the light of the contemplation of their
   aeon.
(3) And I entered into the midst of their prison
(4) which is the prison of the body. . . .

And (11) I said:
"I am the Forethought (*pronoia*) of the pure light;
(12) I am the thinking of the virginal (13) Spirit,
who raises you up to the honored (14) place.
Arise and remember (15) that it is you who hearkened,
and follow (16) your root, which is I, the merciful One,
and (17) guard yourself against (18) the angels of poverty
and the demons (19) of chaos and all those who ensnare you,
(20) and beware of the (21) deep sleep and the enclosure of the
   inside (22) of Hades."

And I raised him up (23) and sealed him
in the light (24) of the water with five seals,
in order that (25) death might not have power over him from this
   time on.
And (26) behold, now I shall go up to the perfect (*teleion*) (27)
   aeon.
I have completed everything for you (28) in your hearing.[68]

One final observation regarding the structure of the Wisdom
myth as presented in the Apocryphon of John: there is almost
nothing in the book that lends support to the well-known theory — spread mainly through Hans Jonas's *Gnosis und spätan-*

tiker Geist (later translated as *The Gnostic Religion*),[69] as well as through his ardent followers (prominent among them Gershom Scholem) — of the fall of Sophia into the material world. The only allusion to such a fall can be found in the fact that Sophia, after she repented Ialdabaoth's creation, "was taken up, not to her own eternal aeon but (to a place) above her son, that she might be in the ninth (heaven) until she has corrected her deficiency."[70] But to read into this Wisdom's fall into the material world (because of her "sin"), out of which she was elevated by the Father (or rather by the Father through Barbelo) seems to be an over-interpretation. The despairing and confused Wisdom, who no longer knows her proper place in the divine realm, is assigned a place higher than her previous aeon because she repented and because it is her task to play a crucial role in the process of redemption. And indeed, *this* is her descent (not her fall) into the material world: to rescue humankind from the evil inaugurated by her offspring, Ialdabaoth.[71]

The Valentinian Creation Myth According to Irenaeus

If we take a look now at the Valentinian version of the Wisdom myth as preserved in Irenaeus's account,[72] we enter a similar, but at the same time quite different, world. To begin with, Valentinus's version is less mythical, much more elaborate and rationalized, expounding a rather complicated philosophical system. Moreover, and most importantly, it is deeply Christian — not just displaying a Christian veneer but thoroughly Christianized and lacking many of the clearly Jewish features of the gnostic myth presented by the Apocryphon of John. This pertains, as we will see, mainly to the role of Wisdom and the function of the redeemer/savior.

The spiritual world consists of a first and second tetrad, which together form an ogdoad, ten aeons, and twelve aeons, altogether "30 silent and unrecognizable aeons."[73] This world is carefully structured in bisexual terms; that is, male and female, androgynously. The "First-Beginning" (*proarchē*) [1][74] emits, through his consort "Thought" (*ennoia*) [2],[75] his "Firstborn" [3]: "Mind" (*nous*)/"Only-Begotten" (*monogenēs*)/"Father" (*patēr*), together with "Truth" (*alētheia*) [4]. They form the first tetrad, similar to what we know from the Apocryphon of John, although much less emphasis is put on "Thought," the equivalent of Barbelo, with features taken from the classical Jewish Wisdom tradition. Then "Mind" emits the next pair: "Word" (*logos*) [5] and "Life" (*zōē*) [6], who subsequently bring forth "Man" (*anthrōpos*) [7] and "Church" (*ekklēsia*) [8]. The next step is the emission of ten aeons out of "Word" and "Life," and finally of twelve aeons out of "Man" and "Church," all of them in androgynous pairs of two. The very last of these twelve aeons is "Wisdom" which forms a pair together with her companion, the "(Divinely) Willed" (*thelētos*).

Passionate Sophia

Now, as in the Apocryphon of John, Wisdom forgets herself and disturbs the predetermined pattern. But the cosmic drama she inaugurates is here described quite differently. Whereas all of the other aeons long for their originator, the "Emitter of their seed" (the First-Beginning = First-Father), "more or less in stillness," Wisdom behaves differently:

> But "Wisdom" (*sophia*) — the very last, most recent aeon of the group of twelve that had been emitted by "Man" and "Church" — charged forward and experienced passion (*epathe pathos*) without the involvement of her consort, the "(Divinely) Willed."
>
> The passion originated in the region of "Mind" and "Truth"; but it accumulated[76] in this (last aeon), which had been diverted — ostensibly out of love but really out of recklessness — because she had not communicated with the "Perfect Father" as "Mind" had.
>
> The passion consisted of a search for the "Father";[77] for — they say — she wanted to comprehend his magnitude. She was unable to do so, for she had tried to accomplish the impossible. And she became engaged in a very great struggle, owing to the magnitude of the "Deep," the unsearchability of the "Father," and her longing for him.
>
> Then she strained forward more and more. And she would have been swallowed by his sweetness and would have dissolved into universal essence (*eis tēn holēn ousian*) had she not encountered a power that established the All and kept it outside of the ineffable magnitude. And this power they call "Limit" (*horos*). By it she was

held back and fixed. With difficulty, she turned back to herself and became convinced that the "Father" was incomprehensible: and so she put off her former thinking, along with its consequent passion, which had come from that amazing admiration (for the Father).[78]

Sophia's improper behavior consists of having too much passion and of releasing this passion in order to search actively, without the consent of her consort, for the object of her boundless desire: the First-Father. Her passion and desire is not negative in itself; what is negative about it is the fact that Sophia does not restrain it, as the other aeons do. In fact, poor Sophia is the weakest of all the aeons because passion, although originating in Mind and Truth, is accumulated in her and makes her the most "passionate" among the aeons. So it is almost inevitable that Sophia seeks the impossible, to comprehend the Father. But — and this is Sophia's true mistake — due to her unbridled desire to know the Father, she eventually risks being dissolved into his universal and undivided essence. In other words, she attempts to reverse the process of emanation inaugurated by the First Principle. One could even go a step further and argue that, in the original intention of the Father, it was Sophia's task to continue the process of emanation — with the involvement of her consort — and to emit further aeons. Instead, Sophia acted independently and tried to return to her origin. To stop this, the Father emits another principle or aeon, Limit (also called "Redeemer"), which restrains Sophia at her proper place and saves the work of emanation. Now restless Sophia has finally been put to rest and does not try to break out of the predestined system again.

With this, the story could have come to an end. But there is still one problem: what happens to Sophia's exuberant passion? Sophia could only be restored as a full partner within the realm of spiritual aeons by excreting the excesses of her passion: "For, thinking and its consequent passion were separated from her: she remained inside the fullness; but her thinking and the passion were bounded apart by Limit, were fenced off with a palisade, and existed outside the fullness."[79]

Thus Sophia excretes her thinking and passion (or rather, her thinking and passion are excreted and separated from her), and this becomes the starting point of the lower, and in the end material, universe. Before this process is set in motion, the Father seals and shields his spiritual universe from any other possible disruption by emitting a final pair of aeons, the guardian pair of "Christ" and "Holy Spirit": "After it [passion] had been bounded outside the fullness of the aeons and its mother [Sophia] had been restored to membership in her own pair, the Only-Begotten emitted another pair by the Father's foresight, for the fixing and establishment of the fullness, lest any of the aeons should experience the same as she [Sophia] had. This consisted of Christ and the Holy Spirit; by them the aeons were set in order."[80] This Christ is also called the "first Christ" because all the aeons together, in praise of the Father, emit yet another one, the "second Christ," or Jesus.

Sophia and Achamoth, Upper and Lower Wisdom

The unfolding of the material world is described in terms similar to those we know from the Apocryphon of John. But there are two crucial differences, which are closely interrelated. First, unlike the Apocryphon of John, where the Wisdom imagery is shared among Barbelo and Sophia, who both remain within the spiritual world (except for Sophia's salvific task), this version of the Valentinian Gnosis clearly divides Wisdom into an "upper" and a "lower" Wisdom; one that belongs to the spiritual realm, and another belonging to the lower world. The upper Wisdom is Sophia, who has no contact at all with the material world, and the lower Wisdom is the materialization of Sophia's thinking and passion that was excreted from her. It is called "Achamoth," a clear allusion to the Hebrew *hokhmah* ("Wisdom"): "she—they say—accounts for the genesis and essence of the matter out of which this world came into being."[81] Hence what in the Apocryphon of John is Ialdabaoth, Sophia's offspring, is here the lower Wisdom who, to be sure, later generates the demiurge, the true creator of the material world with its "rulers," "demons," Adam, and so forth. As in the Apocryphon of John, the demiurge believes, out of his ignorance, that he is the only god and that he creates the lower worlds out of his own power, rather than through the spiritual essence that he has inherited from his mother.

Second, Sophia has lost her salvific quality that plays such an important role in the Apocryphon of John. It is not Sophia who comes down into the material world to redeem it from the evil power of Ialdabaoth, but rather Christ, the savior. Sophia has been restored to the divine realm; and her lower counterpart, Achamoth, although located above the demiurge, at the highest point of the mundane realm,[82] nevertheless belongs to it and therefore cannot intervene as redeemer. This task is left to Christ — a clear indication of the predominantly Christian flavor of the text — who appears as both the first and the second Christ. The first Christ deals with Achamoth only, whereas the second Christ is responsible for the redemption of the material world below Achamoth and the demiurge. Thus Christ the savior will eventually redeem even Achamoth: "When all the seed has grown to maturity, Achamoth their mother will — they say — leave the place of the midpoint [the highest point of the mundane world, between the upper and the lower worlds], enter the fullness, and receive as her bridegroom the savior, who derives from all [the aeons], so that a pair is produced consisting of the savior and Wisdom (*sophia*) who is Achamoth: they are the bridegroom and bride, and the entire fullness is the bridal chamber."[83]

Achamoth then returns, together with the second Christ, to the place she belongs, the spiritual world of the aeons. It is not clear whether she reunites with Sophia, her divine mother, or whether she, together with Christ, forms a new pair of aeons. In favor of the latter possibility is the fact that the second Christ originally did not have a consort in the spiritual world; in favor of the former is the fact that Sophia is here explicitly identified with Achamoth. In any case, whether or not she reunites with Sophia, Achamoth herself is redeemed and restored to her proper place. Sophia/Achamoth's salvific function has been taken from her and transferred to the Christian savior figure.

In sum, the gnostic Wisdom myth in its earliest form is an adaptation of the classical Jewish Wisdom tradition, enriched by (Middle) Platonic philosophy. Wisdom's role as God's companion, his witness and partner in the process of creation, her turning to the world and her commitment to its inhabitants, her effort to lead the world back to its creator — all of this has been largely expanded by gnostic mythology and tinted with its particular color. The female character of Wisdom has given way to a fully structured androgynous universe. And above all, into the somewhat naïve or optimistic worldview of the Jewish Wisdom, the pressing question of the origin of evil within the process of emanation has been integrated. Jewish Wisdom has lost, so to speak, her innocence. But contrary to widespread assumptions, gnostic Wisdom (at least in her early mythical form) does not "fall" down into the material world and does not become the "lower" counterimage of her spiritual "idea." This is left to the Christianized Valentinian branch of Gnosticism — and even there, according to Irenaeus's testimony, every effort has been made to spiritualize the lower Wisdom and to bring her back to her proper place in the spiritual world. Accordingly, it is Wisdom herself for whom the task of salvation had originally been reserved; only in the Valentinian Gnosis is this function absorbed by Christ, who deprives Wisdom of her salvific qualities. It would be much later in Judaism that Wisdom would return, fully invested with all of her powers, including the release of evil.

✵ 4 ✵

THE RABBINIC SHEKHINAH

AFTER the destruction of Jerusalem and the Temple in 70 CE, Rabbinic Judaism established itself as the form of "normative" Judaism that succeeded in defining the Jewish religion during the first six centuries of the common era and would influence the religious and cultural character of the Jews far beyond its heyday. It is named after the Rabbis who, as the leading figures of this period, left their mark in the vast literary corpus they created: Mishnah, Talmud (or rather Talmudim: the Jerusalem Talmud and the Talmud of Babylonia), Midrashim, and Targumim. In fact, with their enormous literary output, the Rabbis absorbed and simultaneously tried to suppress all of the other currents prevalent in the rich pre-Rabbinic Jewish tradition. Through their writings they determined what would and would not be deemed worthy of belonging to the Jewish heritage and of being transmitted to future generations. As we will see, their attempt was so successful that most, if not all, of the competing trends either disappeared or can be reconstructed only from the fragments left after their "digestion" by Rabbinic tradition.

WISDOM

The threads tied by biblical and extrabiblical Wisdom traditions, by Philo, and by the "gnostics" were cut, forgotten, or completely transformed. No doubt, Wisdom remained present among the Rabbis, but mainly in her manifestation in Jesus Sirach, with its emphasis on the Torah as the center of the world and of life. (The Rabbis liked Jesus Sirach so much that they elevated the book to a quasi-canonical status, even though it did not belong to the biblical canon.) In their perception, they alone embodied the classical ideal of Wisdom (*hokhmah*), and appropriately they called themselves *hakhamim*, "sages" (lit. "wise men"). The Torah had become Wisdom, and the Rabbis were her true guardians; it was only through them and their interpretation that ordinary mortals could gain access to her.

What then happened to Wisdom, as the daughter, partner, and spouse of God in the process of creation? The Rabbis developed quite a variety of concepts concerning the comprehensibility and description of God in his different manifestations, and prominent among them is God the creator, in Rabbinic terminology *mishe-'amar we-hayyah ha-'olam* ("He, who spoke and the world came into existence").[1] Within the context of God's creative activity, they were well aware of the Wisdom tradition starting with Proverbs 8. Yet the way they interpreted it followed precisely the line established by Jesus Sirach. For example, a famous homiletical Midrash relates the first verse of Genesis to Proverbs 8:30.[2] Addressing the exegetical enigma of Wisdom being God's *amon*, the Midrash first explores the whole range of semantic possibilities of the difficult word *amon*:

> "In the beginning God created" (Gen. 1:1).[3] R. Oshaya commenced [his exposition thus]: "I was with Him as an *amon*, a source of delight every day" (Prov. 8:30).
>
> > *Amon* means tutor;
> > *amon* means covered;
> > *amon* means hidden;
> > and some say, *amon* means great.
>
> *Amon* is a tutor, as you read: "As an *omen* (male nurse/foster father) carries the sucking child" (Num. 11:12).
>
> *Amon* means covered, as you read: "*Ha-'emunim* (they that were clad; i.e., covered) in scarlet" (Lam. 4:5).
>
> *Amon* means hidden, as you read: "And he concealed (*omen*) Hadassah" (Esther 2:7).[4]
>
> *Amon* means great, as you read: "Are you any better than No-amon?" (Nah. 3:8) which is rendered: "Are you any better than Alexandria the Great, that is situated among the rivers?"[5]

None of these possible meanings of *amon* meets with the approval of our (anonymous) author. Rather he offers the following interpretation, illustrated by a parable:

> Another interpretation: *amon* is a workman (*uman*). The Torah declares: I was the working tool of the Holy One, blessed be He. In

human practice, when a mortal king builds a palace, he builds it not with his own skill but with the skill of an architect (*uman*). The architect moreover does not build it out of his head, but employs plans and diagrams to know how to arrange the chambers and the wicket doors. Thus the Holy One, blessed be He, consulted the Torah[6] and created the world, while the Torah declares: "In the beginning (*be-reshit*) God created" (Gen. 1:1), and [the word] *reshit* refers here to the Torah, as you read [in the verse]: "The Lord created me as the beginning (*reshit*) of His way" (Prov. 8:22).

The final, and accepted, understanding of *amon* is "workman, craftsman, architect." Thus our Midrash follows one of the two possible readings that we discussed in the exegesis of Proverbs 8:30,[7] while implicitly rejecting the second one ("child"). Moreover, the Midrash presupposes Jesus Sirach's identification of Wisdom with Torah, since it is the Torah who speaks and who is the object of the parable. The Torah was at the same time God's architect and the building plan that God consulted when he created the world. Accordingly, the first verse of the Bible does not mean, "In the beginning God created," but rather "By means of *reshit*[8] (sc. the Torah) God created." The Torah was God's *amon*, his architect and building plan, through which God created the world. Whoever looks at the Torah thus sees the building plan of the world. It is through the Torah that God reveals the structure of the world — and himself as the Creator — to all human beings.

GOD THE ONLY CREATOR

This is the gist of the Rabbinical concept of Wisdom: the personified Wisdom of previous tradition, the little child/daughter of God, is transformed into the *book* of the Torah that contains all of the possible meanings of creation. A plan, a book, was all that God used, and surely this plan/book was created by him.[9] When interpreting the first verses of Genesis, the Rabbis were at pains to refute the opinion that God, before he started his act of creation, had at his disposal certain "materials" that were already "available" — such as "*tohu*," "*bohu*," "darkness," and the like.[10] Even worse was the insinuation that God might not have been alone when he created heaven and earth: there might have been other personal "gods" or "powers" at his disposal, who assisted him with the creation. The well-known argument that the Hebrew word for "God" in Genesis 1:1, *elohim*, is in the plural could easily be dismissed on philological grounds (for those who knew Hebrew). Despite the plural ending of *elohim*, the verse's subject, the appropriate verb *bara* ("he created"), is in the singular; hence, "*God* created heaven and earth," and not "*the gods* created heaven and earth."[11] Not everybody knew Hebrew and was convinced by philology, however. The idea that God had helpers or assistants during the process of creation appears to have been persistent and widespread, since the Rabbis must argue against it time and again. One classical answer is the following Midrash:

When were the angels created? R. Yohanan said: They were created on the second day, as it is written: "Who sets the rafters of His lofts in the waters" (Ps. 104:3), followed by: "Who makes the spirits His angels" (ibid. 4).[12] R. Hanina said: They were created on the fifth day, for it is written: "And let fowl fly above the earth" (Gen. 1:20), and it is written: "And with two he would fly" (Isa. 6:2).[13]

R. Luliani b. Tabri said in R. Isaac's name: Whether we accept the view of R. Hanina or that of R. Yohanan, all agree that none were created on the first day, lest you should say: Michael stretched [the universe] in the south and Gabriel in the north, while the Holy One, blessed be He, measured it in the middle, but: "I am the Lord, who made all things, who alone stretched out the heavens, who spread out the earth by Myself (*me-'itti*)" (Isa. 44:24): *mi 'itti* ("who was with Me") is written:[14] who was associated with Me in the creation of the world?

Ordinarily, a mortal king is honored in his realm and the great men of the realm are honored with him. Why? Because they bear the burden [of state] with him. The Holy One, blessed be He, however, is not so, because He alone created His world, He alone is glorified in His universe. R. Tanhuma quoted: "For You are great and perform wonders (Ps. 86:10). Why? Because: "You God are alone" (ibid.). You alone did create the world. Hence: "In the beginning *God* created" (Gen. 1:1).[15]

This Midrash makes it unquestionably clear that God is the one and only creator of the world. He had no helper, neither another god nor an angel. Indeed, the Midrash asserts that the angels themselves were created; the later the better. And no one was even present during the process of creation. The play on words *me-'itti/mi 'itti*, which depends on a minor shift in the vocalization, stresses that the angels not only did not participate in the creation, but were not even present when God created the world. Nobody was there; God was alone. There is no hint of another divine power, not even a subordinate divine power that could be interpreted as in any way restricting the omnipotence of God the creator. And there is certainly no hint of a female divine power, who witnessed God's creation or participated in it as his partner. God the creator was alone — and undoubtedly male. This has become the almost dogmatic foundation of Rabbinic Judaism.

ISRAEL, GOD'S SPOUSE, DAUGHTER, SISTER, AND MOTHER

Yet this does not mean that the Rabbis completely eschewed female symbols and metaphors related to the divine world — on the contrary. One of the predominant feminine metaphors already in the Hebrew Bible is the image of Zion — the mountain, city, and Temple of God — as "daughter." Zion, as the holy city Jerusalem, is imagined as a (virgin) daughter who, for instance, despises her enemies[16] or is threatened with destruction by the prophets because she did not obey God.[17] There can be no doubt that this comparison is made on a purely metaphorical level, in no way implying any kind of kinship between God and Zion. This is all the more true for the image of Zion as "mother," which does not occur in the Bible but appears for the first time in the Septuagint[18] and later, with more frequency, in Rabbinic literature.[19] Here, Zion is the personified mother of Israel, who has been exiled because of their sins, and does not signify any particular relationship with God (except that he is the one who punishes her/them).

But the Rabbis like to play with metaphors, and sometimes it is difficult to decide how far they wish to go — in the degree of radicality of their metaphors as well as the degree to which these metaphors blur the line between image and reality. The following

midrash also refers to the mother of Israel, but suddenly establishes a relationship between God as father and Israel as mother:

> R. Hanina b. Papa said: Whoever enjoys this world without a
> benediction is like robbing the Holy One, blessed be He, and the
> community of Israel (*kenesset Yisra'el*), as it [Scripture] says: "He
> who robs his father and his mother and says: 'It is no offense,' is
> the companion of a destroyer" (Prov. 28:24).

> "His father" is none other but the Holy One, blessed be He, as it
> says: "Is not He your father who created you" (Deut. 32:6). And
> "his mother" is none other than the community of Israel (*kenesset
> Yisra'el*), as it says: "Hear, my son, the discipline of your father,
> and do not forsake the instruction of your mother" (Prov. 1:8).[20]

God and the community of Israel are the father and mother of
the one who transgresses their instruction, who robs them of that
to which they are entitled. On the metaphorical level this comes
quite close to the image of God and his spouse (the community of
Israel) begetting the individual members of this community. Only
on the metaphorical level, however, is the connection made and
even there it is conspicuous that only the scriptural proof for God
(father) uses the metaphor of procreation; the scriptural proof
for the community of Israel (mother) refers to the obedience demanded by both, father and mother. Moreover, and more importantly, the text is not interested at all in pursuing the father/
mother metaphor. The message that it wants to convey is that
enjoying the world without the proper benediction is a transgression. It robs God as well as the community of Israel: God because
he is entitled to benedictions (which is made abundantly clear by
the name the Rabbis prefer, "the Holy One, blessed be He") and
the community of Israel, not because its members deserve benedictions themselves, but because withholding a benediction from
God means withholding God's blessing from Israel.

Another Midrash, explaining the biblical verse Canticles 3:11,
plays with the metaphorical meaning of "daughter," "sister," and
"mother":

> "[O maidens of Zion, go forth and gaze upon King Solomon,]
> upon the crown wherewith his mother has crowned him [on his
> wedding day]" (Cant. 3:11). R. Yohanan said: R. Simeon b. Yohai
> asked R. Eleazar b. R. Yose: Have you perhaps heard from your

father what is the meaning of: "upon the crown wherewith his mother has crowned him" (ibid.)? He replied: Yes. How [did he explain it,] he asked. He said:

By a parable of a king who had an only daughter of whom he was exceedingly fond, so that [at first] he called her "my daughter"; till not satisfied with that expression of his fondness he called her "my sister," and still not satisfied with that expression of his fondness he called her "my mother." So the Holy One, blessed be He, loved Israel exceedingly and called them "my daughter," as it says: "Hearken, O daughter, and consider" (Ps. 45:11); till not satisfied with that expression of his love he called them "sister," as it says: "Open to me, my sister, my love" (Cant. 5:2); and still not satisfied with that expression of his love he called them "my mother," as it says: "Hearken to Me, O My people, and give ear to Me, O My nation (*u-le'ummi*)" (Isa. 51:4) — but it is written *u-l'mi*.[21]

R. Simeon b. Yohai rose and kissed him on his head, saying: Had I come only to hear this explanation from your mouth, it would have repaid me.[22]

The subject of this Midrash is God's abundant love for Israel, a well-known theme in Rabbinic literature. What is remarkable here is the designation of Israel as "daughter," "sister," and "mother" — in all three cases with clearly sexual overtones. The first biblical proof for the designation "daughter" (Ps. 45:11) occurs in the context of the royal wedding between a "king" and a Tyrian princess, here interpreted as the royal wedding of God and Israel. The same is true for the second biblical proof for "sister" (Cant. 5:2). That the "lover" in Canticum is God and his "love" (bride) Israel has become the standard interpretation in Rabbinic Judaism.[23] The real surprise is the third proof for "mother" (Isa. 51:4). The Midrash interprets a biblical text that speaks unequivocally of the people and nation of Israel, as "my mother" (again with a minor shift in the vocalization). Since there is a clear intensification from "daughter" to "sister" and, finally, "mother," the designation of Israel as God's mother represents the climax of his love for Israel. It serves also as the climax of the Midrash because it presents the link with the difficult verse Canticles 3:11, prompting R. Simeon b. Yohai's enthusiastic approval. In the light of this interpretation, Canticles 3:11 has to be understood as follows:

upon the crown wherewith his mother (i.e., Israel, God's mother) has crowned him. Israel, as the beloved daughter, sister, and mother of God, is represented in Solomon's crown, upon which the "daughters of Zion" are asked to gaze. Israel's traditional role as the daughter of God has been completely inverted; it has become God's companion (sister) and his mother. The logical consequence for God is even more disturbing: if Israel is the mother of God, he becomes Israel's child! Of course, the Rabbis were not particularly interested in overstretching logical consequences, at least not in haggadic matters. But the game they play here with metaphors expressing the love between God and Israel goes very far—although in the end they seem to keep the boundaries between metaphor and reality: the love is real, but the embodiment of love is metaphorical. It is certainly not by coincidence that precisely this Midrash has been taken up and explored further in the kabbalistic book Bahir.[24]

SHEKHINAH

Yet the Rabbinic use of feminine metaphors in the divine realm is not restricted to Israel in its capacity as God's spouse, daughter, sister, and mother. It is God himself for whom the Rabbis have created a term with a clearly feminine gender: Shekhinah. And here the question immediately arises whether or not the feminine gender of Shekhinah implies an allusion to God's female sexuality or rather, to be more cautious, a female aspect of God. The term is derived from the Hebrew root *shakhan*, "to dwell, reside, abide," and its literal meaning is God's "indwelling" or "presence" among the people of Israel at a certain place, particularly and probably originally in the Temple. (The term may have originated from a verse like Exodus 25:8: "And let them make me a sanctuary that I may dwell (*we-shakhanti*) among them.") Nevertheless, the term "Shekhinah" is distinctively Rabbinic, representing one of the most common designations for God in Rabbinic Judaism.[25]

Let us look now at some selected Midrashim from among the hundreds of texts in which the Shekhinah plays an important role. We will direct our attention particularly to the questions of the gender of the Shekhinah and of her relationship to God.[26]

Most of the relevant Midrashim refer to the triad God/Israel/ Torah, and many of them belong to the literary genre of parables of a king. One prominent example:

> What is the meaning of "testimony"?[27] Said R. Simeon, son of R. Ishmael: It is a testimony to the whole world that there is forgiveness for Israel.[28] Another explanation: It is a testimony to the whole world that he [Moses] was appointed by God [to erect] the Tabernacle.

> R. Isaac said: It can be compared to a king who took a wife whom he loved very dearly. In the course of time he became angry with her and deserted her, and her neighbors taunted her, saying: He will no longer return to you. Subsequently, the king sent her a message: Prepare my palace and make the beds therein, for I am coming back to you on such-and-such a day; and when that day arrived, the king returned to her and became reconciled to her, entering her chamber and eating and drinking with her. Her neighbors at first would not believe all this; but when they scented the fragrant spices, they at once knew that the king had become reconciled to her.

> In like manner did God love Israel, bringing them before Mount Sinai, giving them the Torah, and calling them kings, as it says: "And you shall be to Me a kingdom of priests" (Ex. 19:6), but after only forty days they sinned.[29] The heathen nations then said: God will no longer be reconciled to them, as it is said: "Men said among the nations: They shall no more sojourn here" (Lam. 4:15).[30] But as soon as Moses pleaded for mercy on their behalf, God forgave them, for it says: "And the Lord said: I have pardoned according to your word" (Num. 14:20). Moses then said: Master of the World! I personally am quite satisfied because you have forgiven Israel, but do please announce the fact to all the nations that you have no more resentment against Israel in your heart. The divine reply was: Upon your life, I will cause my Shekhinah to dwell in their midst, for it says: "And let them make Me a sanctuary that I may dwell among them" (Exod. 25:8). By this shall all nations know that I have forgiven them. This is why it says: "The Tabernacle of the Testimony" (Exod. 38:21), because the Tabernacle was a testimony to the Israelites that God had pardoned their sins.[31]

Again, it is Israel that is presented in metaphorical language as the king's (God's) spouse. The king loves his spouse, dismisses her (for reasons not mentioned in the parable), but later returns to her in his palace and installs her in her proper place. Accordingly, God loves Israel and gives them the Torah, but he withdraws when they sin. On Moses' intercession (which has no equivalent in the parable) he forgives Israel and, as a testimony for both the pagan nations and Israel itself, he has them build a Sanctuary as his dwelling place among them. Indeed, the fragrant spices that the neighbors smell from the palace of the king refer to the incense rising from the sanctuary. The parable and its interpretation are closely interrelated. And, as happens very often, not all of the elements are fully worked out in both parts (although in most cases they can be easily completed).

There can be no doubt that God, the king, is male and Israel, his spouse, is female. But whereas the parable uses quite explicit sexual imagery—the king disowns his spouse but returns not only to his palace but also to her bed, and the neighbors smell the fragrances of the loving wife expecting the return of her lover—its interpretation is devoid of sexual overtones. Rather, it expounds the *history* between God and Israel: God's love for and election of Israel, the giving of the Torah, Israel's sin with the Golden Calf, Moses' intercession, God's mercy, the building of the Sanctuary, God's dwelling in the Sanctuary, the fragrant smell of the sacrifices as a sign of reconciliation. In the parable's interpretation, nothing remains of the male/female imagery of the parable, of the marriage partnership between the king and his spouse.

This is not (and cannot be) changed by the introduction of the term "Shekhinah" into the text; in the parable, as well as in the interpretation, the feminine role is occupied by the king's spouse and the people of Israel, respectively. Despite her feminine gender, the Shekhinah is clearly equated with the same male God with no allusion to a female aspect whatsoever. The Shekhinah is identical with the one who speaks (in Exod. 25:8, emphasis added): "And let them make *Me* a sanctuary that *I* may dwell among them." God *is* the Shekhinah, and there is no essential difference between him and the Shekhinah. But is there any distinction? There remains the strange phrase: "I will cause My Shekhinah to dwell in their midst," which sounds as if God sends down something of himself (part of himself?) to dwell in the Sanctuary among Israel. On the other hand, it is he himself who dwells amongs them and who has forgiven them, the same God. The conclusion seems to be unavoidable: As has been reinforced repeatedly by Arnold Goldberg, the Shekhinah is always identical with God,[32] but the term never designates the "undivided divinity," the very essence of God. Rather, it makes a distinction within God's mode of existence ("Daseinsweise") and refers primarily to his presence on earth, as distinct from his presence in heaven.[33] In other words, the concept of the Shekhinah presents a partial idea ("Teilvorstellung") of the divinity that, especially in parables and in poetical dramatization, tends towards a personification of this partial aspect.[34] Although this is certainly true for our midrash, we will have to look carefully whether or not it applies to the whole of Rabbinic Judaism.

The delicate, and momentous, distinction between God's presence in heaven and on earth is made the subject of the following Midrash:

> The Rabbis make a comparison with a king who gave his daughter in marriage to someone in another country. The people of his country said to him: Your majesty, it accords with your honor and it is only right that your daughter should be in the same country with you. He said to them: What does it matter to you? They replied: Perhaps later you will visit her and stay with her on account of your love for her. He then replied: I will give my daughter in marriage out of the country, but I will reside with you in this country.
>
> So when the Holy One, blessed be He, announced His intention of giving the Torah to Israel, the ministering angels said to the Holy One, blessed be He: Sovereign of the Universe, "You are He whose (asher) majesty is over the heaven" (Ps. 8:2); it is Your happiness (ishureka),[35] Your majesty, and Your praise that the Torah should be in the heaven. He said to them: What does it matter to you? They said: Perhaps tomorrow You will cause Your Shekhinah to abide in the lower world. Then the Holy One, blessed be He, replied to them: I will give My Torah to the dwellers on earth, but I will abide with the celestial beings. I will give away My daughter with her marriage portion to another country in order that she may pride herself with her husband in her beauty and charm and

be honored as befits a king's daughter. But I will abide with you in
the upper world. Who stated this clearly? Habakkuk, as it says:
"His majesty (*hodo*) covers the heavens, and the earth is full of His
praise (*tehillato*)" (Hab. 3:3).

R. Simeon said in the name of R. Yoshua b. Levi: Wherever God
made His Torah to abide, there He made His Shekhinah to abide.
Who stated this clearly? David, as it is written: "Let them praise
the name of the Lord, for His name alone is exalted; His majesty
(*hodo*) is on earth and in heaven" (Ps. 148:13)—first on earth and
then in heaven.[36]

Here we have another example of female imagery related to God:
God's daughter is identified with the Torah, which he is about to
give to the daughter's husband, the people of Israel on earth. But
this female imagery is not the major topic of the midrash. Rather,
it is taken for granted—as is the fact that Israel can be God's
spouse, as well as the husband of his daughter. The Midrash is
mainly concerned with the question of whether God, whose primary and natural place is in heaven, can also be present on earth.
This concern is put into the mouth of the angels who, according
to the Rabbis, have a vital interest in God's residence among
them and in heaven. This interest collides with the equally vital
interest of the people of Israel: that God dwells among them as
well and not only among the angels. The suspicious and envious
angels[37] suspect (and rightly so, as we shall see) that God's act of
giving the Torah to Israel will have the consequence of him following his beloved daughter/Torah to take residence among Israel. But God comforts and calms his angels with a verse from
Habakkuk: it is only his praise (*tehillah*; i.e., his Torah) which is
on earth; his majesty (*hod*) remains in heaven.[38]

In reality, however, God betrays his angels. The final dictum by
R. Simeon in the name of R. Yoshua b. Levi clearly expresses the
true opinion of the Rabbis: according to David, of course a more
important prophet than Habakkuk, God's majesty (i.e., his presence) is not restricted to the realm of heaven but extends over the
earth, as well. Moreover, and worse for the poor angels, in establishing the sequence "on earth and in heaven" David makes clear
that God's primary and natural place is among human beings
(specifically Israel) and not among the angels! God does in fact

follow his precious gift, his daughter/Torah, and takes residence among Israel; from now on heaven is only his second home.

Again, there can be no doubt that the Shekhinah is identical with God. More precisely, she is his "mode of existence" on earth and among Israel. The Rabbis do not question God's presence on earth; on the contrary, they regard it as superior to his presence in heaven and among the angels. Indeed, this has become one of the predominant characteristics of Rabbinic theology. Yet there is no trace, however hidden, of a female coloring to this concept of the Shekhinah.

The same is true for the many texts in which the Rabbis, following the anthropomorphic descriptions of God in the Bible,[39] speak of the "face," "mouth," "back," "feet," and "wings" of the Shekhinah.[40] These are the well-known biblical metaphors that do not amount to any literal, visual representation of God's body, let alone to any female representation. If there are at all hints of a divine body, this body is definitely male.[41] Instead of visualizing the Shekhinah in bodily form, the Rabbis prefer the biblical images of cloud, pillar of cloud and fire, or pillar of fire. It is the pillar of cloud going before the people of Israel during the day and the pillar of fire showing them the way at night[42] that have become the favored visual representations of the Shekhinah:

> Aaron shall set them [the lamps] up in the Sanctuary outside the curtain of the testimony (Lev. 24:3). It is a testimony for all human-kind that the Shekhinah is in Israel. But did they [Israel] need the light [of the lamps]? For the whole of the forty years that the Isra-elites travelled in the wilderness they did not need any lamp, as it is said: "For over the Tabernacle a cloud of the Lord rested by day, and fire would appear in it [the Tabernacle][43] by night, (in the view of all the house of Israel throughout their journeys)" (Exod. 40:38). If this is so, why does it [the Bible] say "of the testimony" (Lev. 24:3)? It is a testimony for all humankind that the Shekhinah is in Israel.[44]

Why was the curtain in the Sanctuary called the "curtain of the testimony"? Because the lamps set up in front of the curtain were neither needed nor used as lights, but rather as witnesses: they testified to the presence of the Shekhinah at night in the Sanctu-ary. The Shekhinah is light, and her splendor illuminated the Sanctuary. The splendor of the Shekhinah is so overwhelming, another midrash argues quite ironically, that it even blinds sun and moon: when they go out to illuminate the world they are blinded and cannot see anything. In order to help them God fires flashing arrows in front of them to show them their way.[45] The splendor of the Shekhinah even serves as nourishment: the angels do not need any ordinary food but are nourished on the splendor of the Shekhinah, and this is also the destiny that awaits the blissfully happy righteous in the world to come.[46]

The following Midrash, an interpretation of Exodus 2:4 ("And his [Moses'] sister [Miriam] stood afar off to know what was done to him") illustrates just how farfetched any notion of a female quality of the Shekhinah was for the Rabbis:

> And his sister stood afar off (Exod. 2:4). R. Isaac said: The whole of this verse is spoken with reference to the Shekhinah:[47]
>
> "And she stood" (*wa-tetatzev*),[48] as it is written: "And the Lord came and stood (*wa-yityatzev*) etc." (1 Sam. 3:10).
>
> "His sister" (*ahoto*), as it is written: "Say to wisdom, you are my sister (*ahoti*)" (Prov. 7:4).
>
> "Afar off" (*me-rahoq*), as it is written: "The Lord appeared from afar (*me-rahoq*) unto me" (Jer. 31:3).
>
> "To know" (*le-de'ah*), as it is written: "For the Lord is a God of knowledge (*de'ot*)" (1 Sam. 2:3).
>
> "What" (*mah*), as it is written: "What (*mah*) does the Lord demand of you?" (Deut. 10:12).
>
> "Done" (*ye'aseh*), as it is written: "Indeed, my Lord God does (*ya'aseh*) nothing [without having revealed His purpose to His servants the prophets]" (Amos 3:7).
>
> "To him" (*lo*), as it is written: "[So Gideon built there an altar to the Lord] and called it (*lo*)[49] 'Lord is peace'" (Jud. 6:24).[50]

The major statement of this Midrash is the proof that Miriam, Moses' sister, was a prophet because she foresaw what would happen to the infant Moses who was put into the basket on the Nile; namely that he would be saved and become the savior of Israel. Thus the reference to the Shekhinah or the Holy Spirit; the presence of the Shekhinah makes the gift of the Holy Spirit (i.e., the Spirit of Prophecy) possible. The proof is that every single word of Exodus 2:4, which speaks of Miriam, is related to another biblical verse that contains the same term but refers to God. The key verse for this purpose of the Midrash, of course, is Amos 3:7, since it emphasizes the importance of prophecy.

This line of argument is fairly routine. For our purposes, what makes the Midrash interesting is the fact that its subject is the prophetess Miriam, whose female gender might occasion a female counterpart in the prooftexts referring to God. But, of course, the counterpart is the same male God — the Lord or the Lord God, as he is called in all but one of the verses. This again presents definite proof that the Shekhinah is perceived as identical with the one and male God. Yet there is the one exception: "sister" (*ahot*) in Exodus 2:4 and Proverbs 7:4. Proverbs 7:4 is a brilliant prooftext because it relates Miriam, Moses' "sister," to the divine Wisdom, who is the "sister" of all human beings. Just as Wisdom in the biblical prooftext is clearly perceived as female, so also the only logical conclusion seems to be that, among the many manifestations of God, one takes on female form (and this conclusion suggests itself all the more if one considers the biblical and postbiblical Wisdom tradition). But this is precisely *not* what happens. In hiding Wisdom in a sequence of verses that all speak of the Lord God, the author of our Midrash makes it absolutely clear that he does not even ponder the notion of a female aspect of God. Presumably, he could not find another biblical verse that mentions "sister" together with a designation for "God." Hence he takes the risk of equating "God" with "Wisdom" — without making the necessary next step and speculating about the nature of "Wisdom."[51] Our Midrash contains a distant echo of the older Wisdom tradition, but it only reinforces the conclusion that the Rabbis have moved far away from it.

Personification of the Shekhinah

The Rabbis clung to the uniform and standardized masculinity of their God and did not succumb to the "danger" of opening up again to the potentialities inherent in the text of their Bible. But what about the other "danger" connected with the concept of the Shekhinah, the danger of separating between "God" and "his Shekhinah"? We have already noticed a certain tension between the Shekhinah as being identical with God and simultaneously distinct from him, in so far as the term signifies God's presence on earth, as distinct from his primary place in heaven. The more acute and intense this tension becomes the more difficult it is to maintain the identity, rather than give way to a tendency that aims at turning the Shekhinah into an entity distinct from God. And this is precisely what happens, albeit slowly, becoming apparent only in later midrashic texts (at least in the concurrent opinion of scholars like Goldberg[52] and Scholem[53]). Let us look at some of the relevant texts. The earliest text discussed in this connection is the brief dictum by R. Meir in the Mishnah, with parallels in the Babylonian Talmud:

> R. Meir said: When a man suffers,[54] to what expression does the Shekhinah give utterance? As it were (*kivyakhol*), my head is heavy, my arm is heavy![55] If God (*ha-maqom*) is so grieved over the blood of the wicked that is shed, how much more so over the blood of the righteous.[56]

This is clearly an anthropomorphic personification of the Shekhinah. But nothing indicates that the Shekhinah is conceived as an entity distinct from God; the Shekhinah is God, *ha-maqom* (lit. "the place"), a common Rabbinic designation for the omnipresent God. Neither are anthropomorphic descriptions of God unusual (in either biblical or Rabbinic literature), nor is it exceptional that God is depicted as sharing the human feeling of suffering.[57] That some important and early manuscripts of the Mishnah lack the word "Shekhinah" and instead simply read "When a man suffers, what does the tongue [of God] say?" is no proof to the contrary;[58] it merely shows that some scribes disliked anthropomorphic expressions of God. Precisely for this reason, "Shekhinah" is most likely the correct reading.

A similar case of dramatic personification, which according to Goldberg falls under the category of "poetic personification,"[59] is the following Midrash. It refers to the so-called ten stages of ascent (*ma'alot*) of the Shekhinah when she left the first Temple after its destruction:

R. Aha said: This may be likened to a king who left his palace in anger. After going out, he came back and embraced and kissed the walls of the palace and its pillars, weeping and exclaiming, "Peace upon you, house of my palace, peace upon you, house of my kingship, peace upon you, house of my Glory! Peace upon you, from now onward let there be peace!" Similarly when the Shekhinah went forth from the Temple, she returned and embraced and kissed the walls and pillars of the Temple, wept and said, "Peace upon you, house of my Temple, peace upon you, house of my kingship, peace upon you, house of my Glory! Peace upon you, (from now onward let there be peace!").[60]

This is a "bold personification,"[61] indeed, but clearly of the same God who is identical with his Shekhinah: God, when he leaves his Sanctuary, is in a distressed state because he is giving up his presence among the people of Israel on earth. And, again, there is no hint of any female personification of God. Rather, the Shekhinah is characteristically compared to the king, an unambiguously male figure.

Quite different, however, is the following Midrash:

Another interpretation: "See a man skilled at his work (— he shall attend upon kings)" (Prov. 22:29). When the Sanhedrin sought to include him [Solomon] among the three kings and four commoners [who are denied a place in the world to come],[62] the Shekhinah stood up before the Holy, praised be He, and said to Him: Master of both worlds, have You ever seen anyone as diligent in doing Your work?[63] And yet they wish to count him among those consigned to [eternal] darkness! At that moment a heavenly voice came forth, saying to them: "He shall attend upon kings; he shall not attend upon those consigned to [eternal] darkness" (Prov. 22:29).[64]

The Sanhedrin wanted to count Solomon among those to be condemned in the world to come, presumably because of his immoral behavior and because he was regarded as the author of the book of Kohelet (Ecclesiastes) with its cynical attitudes.[65] Thanks to the intervention of the Shekhinah, who reminds the members of the Sanhedrin of his diligent building of the Temple, Solomon is saved and counted among those having a share in the world to come. In depicting the Shekhinah as standing up before God and speaking to him, the Midrash goes very far in its dramatic and bold personification. As a matter of fact, it draws a clear distinction between God and his Shekhinah: the Shekhinah has become a "persona" different and distinct from God — although still with no female features. The problem, however, is that we have another version of this Midrash in the Babylonian Talmud that omits the Shekhinah and reads quite differently:

> Rab Judah said in Rab's name: They [the Sanhedrin] wished to include another one [Solomon], but an apparition of his father's image [David] came and threw itself down [in supplication] before them, which, however, they disregarded. A heavenly fire descended and its flames licked their seats, yet they still disregarded it. Whereupon a heavenly voice came forth and said to them: "See a man skilled at his work — he shall attend upon kings; he shall not attend upon those consigned to [eternal] darkness" (Prov. 22:29).[66]

Here, it is not the Shekhinah who stands up before God, but the image of David, Solomon's father, which throws itself down before the members of the Sanhedrin. Unlike the version in Midrash Mishle, the Sanhedrin must be forced to comply with the decision of the heavenly voice.[67] Hence this version amends the offensive idea of the Shekhinah and God facing one another in a dialogue; the image of David substitutes for the Shekhinah, and the problem is solved. Or is it the other way around? Might the Bavli version retain the original, earlier text that was later turned into the Midrash Mishle version, with its bold substitution of the Shekhinah for the image of David? This is the opinion of Scholem, who simply asserts the dependence of Midrash Mishle on the Bavli: "Indeed, we can see how the talmudic statement was transposed from its originally innocent context to that of the *Shekhinah*."[68] This is possible, in particular if one considers the presumably late date of the final compilation of Midrash Mishle (ninth century,[69] as opposed to the Bavli's final redaction in the seventh century), although, of course, the date of the final compilation of a given Rabbinic work is by no means decisive for the date of a certain tradition or literary unit within that respective work. And one can quite reasonably argue for the priority of the Midrash Mishle version.

Indeed, the talmudic version, with the *image* of David interven-

ing and throwing itself down before the members of the Sanhedrin, is not as "innocent" as Scholem maintains. It may well be
that the Shekhinah defending Solomon before God represents the
original version, which was changed into the image of David
when the scene was transferred from the heavenly court to the
court of the Sanhedrin on earth. Not only could the Shekhinah
not prostrate herself before the Sanhedrin, as has been observed
by Goldberg,[70] but the emphasis in the earthly scene is put on the
Sanhedrin's (the Rabbis')[71] independence of the heavenly voice (a
point that has nothing to do with Solomon's fate and could easily
be a later elaboration of the original story). Whichever version
can claim priority, we nevertheless have here an unambiguous example within Rabbinic literature of a clear distinction between
the Shekhinah and God, which goes beyond mere poetic personification. Moreover, there can be no doubt that we are dealing
with a later evolution in the process of the formation of the idea
of the Shekhinah—whatever this "later" means in terms of time
(certainly at the end of the classical Rabbinic period, if not later;
that is, not before the seventh century).

There are some more examples of this separation between God
and his Shekhinah that Goldberg tends to view as text corrup-
tions. In one version of the discussion between God and his angels about God's appropriate place—in heaven or on earth—God
says to the angels: "Upon your life, the Shekhinah, she is with me
(*etzli hi'*), as it is said: '(His majesty covereth the heavens,) and
the earth is full of His praise' (Hab. 3:3)."[72] Here again the Shekhinah seems to become independent, an entity separate from
God, and one may well doubt whether this is only because the
text is "unreliable."[73] In the above quotation from Midrash Ekha
Rabba, we saw how the distressed Shekhinah leaves the Temple
immediately before its destruction.

Another Midrash is more complicated. It explains—with *kivyakhol* ("as it were"), the usual caution when expressing some
unexpected opinion—that God in heaven joined Israel on earth
in their weeping for the destruction of the Temple: "As it were,
there is weeping before me[74] because I have deserted my Shekhinah."[75] This strange phrase "because I have deserted my Shekhinah" can either be a corruption (Goldberg asks as rhetorically
as emphatically, "How could God desert his Shekhinah?")[76] or
another example of the "drifting apart" of God and his She-

khinah: in giving up his presence on earth God has not just left the earth but rather, *kivyakhol*, has abandoned his Shekhinah, who perhaps even remains on earth. This is a far-reaching conclusion, but by no means inconceivable.

The following Midrash, also from Pesiqta Rabbati, seems to play with the terms "Glory" and "Shekhinah," both substitutes for God himself — or more:

> Another comment: "If I forget you, O Jerusalem" (Ps. 137:5). When Israel went into exile, the Shekhinah went into exile along with them. The ministering angels said to him [God]: Master of the universe, Your Glory (*kevodkha*) instead of You/in place of You (*bimqomkha*) — don't despise Your Shekhinah! The Holy One, blessed be He, replied: Were not certain things stipulated between Me and Israel? I stipulated with their fathers that at the time they were well off I would be with them, and if they were not well off My Glory (*kevodi*) would be with them, as it is said: "I will be with him in trouble" (Ps. 91:15).[77]

This is another common topic: God, equated with the Shekhinah, follows Israel into exile wherever they go, and he will return with them to Jerusalem at the end of days.[78] The protest of the angels against God's suffering and exile with Israel is also routine; their envy of Israel is proverbial. What is unusual here, however, and difficult, is the strange phrase that translates literally as: "Your Glory (is?) instead of You (or: in place of You) — don't despise your Shekhinah!" Braude translates "[L]et the glory of Thy presence remain in its proper place. Demean not Thy presence." This smoothing translation resorts to the traditional interpretation: the Glory of thy presence (i.e., the Glory of your Shekhinah) shall remain in its (the Glory's, the Shekhinah's) proper place, which is in heaven. The Shekhinah must not stay with Israel in exile! But unfortunately the Hebrew text neither reads "the Glory of your Shekhinah" nor "in its proper place," but rather precisely as translated above.[79] Taken seriously this strange phrase means: your Glory/Shekhinah[80] is on earth instead of you. If you leave her on earth, together with the exiled people of Israel (i.e., outside the land of Israel and outside the Temple), you despise and humiliate her; you must let her return to you in heaven. Needless to say, this presupposes a distinction between God and his Shekhinah. The Shekhinah has become God's deputy on earth, acting on his behalf. Goldberg again doubts the reliability of the textual tradition and ponders the possibility that the author of our midrash simply wanted to say "your Shekhinah, that is you,"[81] but this again only smoothes away the textual problem.

The more radical interpretation can be readily supported by a literal reading of God's answer to the angels: when Israel is doing well, I (God) am with them, but when they are not, my Glory (the Shekhinah) is with them. Here we have the same distinction between God and his Shekhinah. When Israel is in their land, God is present among them in his Temple; when Israel is in exile, it is "only" his Shekhinah who is with them. But there remains a certain ambiguity that cannot be resolved. The prooftext that God's Glory is with Israel (instead of God himself) has again the divine "I": "I will be with him in trouble"; that is, I am my Glory/Shekhinah, I am identical with her. Thus it appears that the author of our Midrash deliberately plays with the possibility of distinguishing between God and the Shekhinah, but simultaneously tries (or rather pretends) to maintain the identity. In doing so, he clearly moves forward toward a decisive distinction.

This final step is taken in an unquestionably late Midrash, Seder Eliyyahu Rabba, which includes God, together with his people Israel, in the process of redemption:

> Nay more, of him who acts justly, [gives] charity, and thus preserves many lives, Scripture says: "He has redeemed My soul through peace" (Ps. 55:19). When such acts are performed, the Holy One, blessed be He, says: Who is the man who redeems Me and My Shekhinah (*oti u-shekhinati*) and Israel from among the worshippers of idols?[82] It is the man exercising justice and giving charity.[83]

The notion that God is redeemed, together with Israel, from exile is a direct consequence of the idea that the Shekhinah stays with Israel even in exile. It is not uncommon in Rabbinic literature, although the Rabbis were aware that it could be regarded as offensive.[84] But what is extremely uncommon is the clear threefold distinction between God, his Shekhinah, and Israel. In fact, this is the only case in Rabbinic literature where God speaks of himself *and* his Shekhinah.[85] Yet we have another version of the difficult phrase, again in the Babylonian Talmud, which reads: "The Holy One, blessed be He, says: If a man occupies himself with the study of the Torah and with works of charity and prays with the congregation, I account it to him as if he had redeemed Me, Me and My children, from among the nations of the world."[86] This reading is much smoother, and its implications fall completely within the confines of the traditional concept. In this particular case, I am inclined to see the Bavli version as the earlier and the Seder Eliyyahu Rabba version as the later stage of development, not only because of the late date of Seder Eliyyahu Rabba but also (and primarily) because of the clear-cut distinction, "Me and My Shekhinah." A similar phrase can be found only in the very late Midrash compilation Bereshit Rabbati by R. Moshe ha-Darshan of Narbonne (first half of the eleventh century),[87] which states that when God saw the horrible deeds of the generation of the Flood, "He withdrew Himself and His Shekhinah (*'atzmo u-shekhinato*) from among them" and ascended to heaven.[88] The unquestionably earlier versions of this text in *Otiyyot de-R. Aqiva*, as well as in the Third Book of Enoch, both have the much more "innocent" rendering: "I withdrew my Shekhinah from among them"—clearly avoiding the offensive doubling of God and his Shekhinah.[89]

Finally a few remarks on the Targumim, the Aramaic translations of the Hebrew Bible. The Targumim are well-known for their various circumlocutions for the name of God, among which are the "Memra" (the Word of God), the "Iqar/a" (the Glory of God, the Aramaic equivalent of the Hebrew *kavod*), and the "Shekhinah" or the "Glory of the Shekhinah." Several of these designations are commonly combined, as in the Targum to Deuteronomy 31:3–8, one of the examples quoted by Scholem.[90] Scholem was intrigued by the translation of verse 3, which reads in Hebrew: "The Lord, your God, He will go over [the Jordan] before you." In the Targum Jonathan to the Torah (the so-called Targum Pseudo-Jonathan) this is translated (emphasis added): "The Lord, your God, *and* His Shekhinah go before you," suggesting a pronounced distinction between God and the Shekhinah. As Scholem also observes, however, this distinction is not kept as clearly in the following verses. In verse 6, the Hebrew, "For the Lord, your God, it is He who goes with you," is translated: "For the Lord, your God, His Shekhinah leads before you." Similarly in verse 8, "And the Lord, it is He who goes before you," is rendered in the Targum as: "And the Word of the

Lord, His Shekhinah, leads before you."[91] Here the Word of God and his Shekhinah are equated, but both are identical with God. This speaks in favor, pace Scholem, of not taking the distinctive "and" in verse 3 too literally, although more research considering all of the evidence, including the respective targumic manuscripts, is necessary in order to get a decisive picture. Nevertheless, a look at the other known versions of the targumic tradition on Deuteronomy 31:3–8 corroborates this preliminary result. Targum Onkelos reads "the Lord, your God, His Word" (v. 3), just "the Lord, your God" (v. 6), and "the Lord, it is he who leads before you" (v. 8), with no further addition. And the so-called Codex Neofiti, the earliest Palestinian Targum, renders "the Lord, your God, the Glory of whose Shekhinah leads before you" (vv. 3, 6) and "the Word of God, the Glory of whose Shekhinah is leading before you" (v. 8), combining "Word," "Glory," and "Shekhinah," and making very clear — through the complicated relative clause *de* — that all of these designations are attributes of God and not, by any means, distinct entities.[92]

But still, Scholem is correct to argue that the wealth of targumic circumlocutions for God can be an easy temptation to understand these various designations as different ("hypostatized") divine entities. That this indeed happened can be proven from the very late midrash compilation Midrash ha-Gadol, dated by most scholars to the thirteenth century[93] (although, again, this particular tradition may be earlier).[94] The Midrash refers to a targumic translation of Exodus 24:10, which is preserved in the so-called Fragment Targum. Here the biblical verse ("And they saw the God of Israel") is rendered "And they saw the Glory of the Shekhinah (*iqar shekhinteh*) of the God of Israel"[95] — quite a common combination, as we have seen. But the unknown author of the following comment did take offense at this translation:

R. Eliezer said: Whoever translates a verse [from the Hebrew Bible] literally is a liar, and whoever adds to it commits blasphemy. For instance, one who translates [the Hebrew verse Exod. 24:10 literally into Aramaic] "And they saw the God of Israel" is a liar, for the Holy One, blessed be He, sees but is not seen. Yet one who translates [the same Hebrew verse into] "And they saw the Glory of the Shekhinah of the God of Israel" commits blasphemy, for he makes here three (a Trinity): the Glory, the Shekhinah, and God![96]

Whatever the precise date of this polemic is, it certainly does not derive from R. Eliezer (b. Hyrkanos), a Rabbi from the second generation of the Tannaim (ca. 90–130 CE). A parallel in the Babylonian Talmud ascribes its origin to R. Judah (the Patriarch?): "R. Judah said: Whoever translates a verse literally is a liar, and whoever adds to it commits blasphemy"[97]—thus making clear that the verdict against too literal as well as too free translations is Rabbinic and that the concrete example is from a later, most probably post-Rabbinic, period. This provides definite proof that the Aramaic Bible translations did serve as evidence for a division between God and some other subordinate, but nevertheless divine, entities. That our author evidently polemicizes against a possible trinitarian understanding of the Aramaic Bible translation does not necessarily imply that his polemics are directed against Christians. On the contrary, they aim at Jews who, in his view, come dangerously close to the Christian attitude of dissolving the unity of the one and only God into a diversity of several Gods.

In conclusion, the classical concept of the Shekhinah represents an attempt to express God's presence among his people Israel on earth in one specific term. Originally the identity between "God" and the "Shekhinah" is maintained: God is his Shekhinah, and the Shekhinah is God. Yet in Rabbinic Judaism we do find a clear tendency toward a personification of the Shekhinah, at first in the form of a poetic dramatization with no particular theological consequences, but later taking the form of a separate entity next to God. The process of distinction begins within Rabbinic literature, albeit in a playful and ambiguous way, and comes to fuller force in the late Rabbinic and post-Rabbinic periods. At this stage, the question of theological "correctness" also arises. But at no point during the development of the concept of the Shekhinah can an inclination be observed to take seriously the feminine gender of the term "Shekhinah." Even when referring to the biblical Wisdom, the Midrash is at pains to ignore any possible female aspect. We do find female metaphors in Rabbinic literature, but these refer to Israel as God's "partner" rather than to the Shekhinah. The Shekhinah, whether identical with God or becoming increasingly distinct from him, remains male. Yet, the more distinct the Shekhinah becomes the greater the possibility that she gains (or rather regains) a female personality.

✾ 5 ✾

THE SHEKHINAH OF THE
PHILOSOPHERS

THE MOST EXTREME STEP in distancing the Shekhinah from God
was taken by the emerging Jewish philosophy of the early Middle
Ages. Its representatives have been labeled "rationalistic," because one of their major concerns was to maintain — or rather
restore — the integrity of the monotheistic and abstract concept of
God. Much more than the Rabbis of the talmudic period they
were worried about the blunt anthropomorphisms in the Bible,
which crudely describe God in human form. They regarded these
as a threat not only to God's otherness and uniqueness, inconceivable by human imagination, but also to his undivided unity —
a threat that led, they feared, back into the horrors of polytheism, against which the Bible and the Rabbis both fought. They
were at great pains to "cleanse" the Bible, and hence God, from
all anthropomorphic tendencies and to restore what they believed
was the original and pure form of Jewish monotheism.

To do so, they took up the Rabbinic concept of the Shekhinah
and equated it with the biblical concept of the Glory of God
(*kavod*), claiming that the Shekhinah and the Kavod respectively
were not identical with God, but rather *created* entities or powers.
The first assumption, the equation of the Shekhinah with the
Kavod, has some historical precedent, since the Rabbis could easily use the term Shekhinah for the biblical Kavod. The second
assumption, the assertion that the Shekhinah/Kavod was created
by God, as a power distinct from God, clearly runs against both
the Rabbinic and biblical tradition. We have seen that, in the
classical talmudic literature, the Shekhinah is always identical
with God and that only in the late talmudic and post-talmudic
periods does a tendency emerge to distance the Shekhinah from
God, giving her a personality of her own. But none of these later
texts suggests that the Shekhinah is created. Although none of
them takes the trouble either to define how precisely this divine

Shekhinah is related to the Godhead, she still remains within the realm of the divinity.

As for the biblical Kavod, there can be no doubt that it was originally identical with God. The quite common phrase *kevod YHWH*, "the Glory of the Lord," always refers to God himself. The most graphic description of the Kavod can be found in the biblical book of Ezekiel, and it is also here that the divine Kavod is explicitly compared to human form: Ezekiel, the prophet, sees the famous divine chariot, carried by the four creatures with their four faces and wings, and upon the chariot a throne upon which someone sits (Ezek. 1):

> (26) Above the expanse over their [the four creatures'] heads was the semblance (*demut*) of a throne, in appearance (*mar'eh*) like sapphire; and on top, upon this semblance (*demut*) of a throne, there was the semblance (*demut*) of a human form.[1] (27) . . . There was a radiance all about him. (28) Like the appearance of the bow which shines in the clouds on a day of rain, such was the appearance of the surrounding radiance. That was the appearance of the semblance of the Glory[2] of the Lord (*kevod YHWH*).

The carefully phrased and cautious language of this vision (the repeated "semblance," "appearance," "likeness") cannot hide the fact that Ezekiel here describes what the philosophers most abhor: God not only makes himself visible to a prophet but, worse, appears in human form. And it is absolutely clear that this "something," the manifestation of God's Glory that appears to the prophet, is God himself, not some created entity.

SAADIA GAON

Not so the philosophers. At some point in the post-talmudic period (the period of the Geonim right after the redaction of the Talmud) a radical shift occurs. The early philosophers give up the close connection between God and his designations like Shekhinah or Kavod, declaring them to be created entities, distinct from God. We do not know exactly when this happened, and we do not know why. We only know that the first evidence we have is from the theologian and philosopher Rav Saadia Gaon (882–942), the famous Gaon of Sura in Babylonia, who was one of the most prominent representatives of the rationalistic Jewish philosophy influenced by the Islamic Kalam. His major philosophical work, written in Arabic but translated very early (even twice) into Hebrew, *Sefer Emunot we-De'ot* ("The Book of Beliefs and Opinions"), is the earliest Jewish philosophical work from the Middle Ages thus far known.

Saadia's God is absolutely transcendent and incorporeal. He is the creator of the world and of all corporeal existence. As such, he is by necessity incorporeal, since if he were corporeal there would have to be a cause of his existence. This also excludes all corporeal attributes like the notorious anthropomorphic descriptions in the Bible. The only attributes Saadia is willing to concede are the three essential qualities, known from the Kalam, of life, wisdom, and power. Yet these attributes are in reality united in God's essence and do not impose any plurality on him.

From this background, it becomes immediately clear that Saadia must dismiss all the biblical anthropomorphisms of God as figurative speech—far from any literal statement about God's visible appearance, let alone his essence. By this he can easily explain away all crude bodily anthropomorphisms, like descriptions of his mouth, eyes, ears, arms, and feet. But there still remains the vision of God that the prophets encountered according to the Bible, and it is certainly not by coincidence that Saadia finds, in texts like Ezekiel 1, the major stumbling block of his cleansing exercise:

> Peradventure however, someone, attacking our view, will ask: "But how is it possible to put such constructions on these anthropomorphic expressions and on what is related to them, when Scripture itself explicitly mentions a form (*demut*) like that of human beings that was seen by the prophets and spoke to them and to which they imputed God's words, let alone the description by it of God's being seated on a throne, and His being borne by the angels on top of a firmament, as Scripture says: "And above the firmament that was over their heads was the likeness (*demut*) of a throne, as the appearance (*mar'eh*) of a sapphire stone; and upon the likeness (*demut*) of the throne was a likeness (*demut*) as the appearance (*mar'eh*) of a man above it" (Ezek. 1:26)? Furthermore, this form (*demut*) is also mentioned as having been seated on a throne with angels on its right and its left, as Scripture says:

"I saw the Lord sitting on His throne, and all the hosts of heaven standing by Him on His right hand and on His left" (1 Kings 22:19).

Our answer to this objection is that this form (*demut*) was something [specially] created (*beru'ah*). Similarly the throne and the firmament, as well as its bearers, were all of them created: the Creator created them out of light (*zohar*)[3] for the purpose of assuring His prophet that it was He that had revealed His word to him, as we shall explain in the third treatise of this book. It is a form (*demut*) nobler[4] even than [that of] the angels, magnificent in character, resplendent with light (*behirat zohar*),[5] which is called "the Glory of the Lord" (*kevod H'*). It is this form, too, that one of the prophets described as follows: "I beheld till thrones were placed, and the Ancient of Days took his seat" (Dan. 7:9),[6] and that the sages characterized as Shekhinah. Sometimes, however, this specially created being consists of light (*zohar*) without the form (*demut*) of a human being. It was, therefore, an honor that God had conferred on His prophet by allowing him to hear the oracle[7] from the mouth of a majestic form (*demut*) created out of light (*zohar*) that was called "the Glory of the Lord" (*kevod H'*), as we have explained.[8]

Saadia here makes the unequivocal and bold distinction between God himself, the unique and incorporeal creator, and the "form" (*demut*) created out of brilliant light (*zohar*), which is called "Kavod" in the Bible and "Shekhinah" by the Rabbis. Hence Kavod/Shekhinah is a created entity that consists of a very fine substance, like the divine throne, the firmament (?)[9] and those who bear them, probably the four creatures (*hayyot*). Apparently this entity is among the very first creations, if not the first creation itself, and it may even well be that Saadia here refers to the biblical distinction—to which the Rabbis attach particular importance—between the "light" (*'or*) created on the first day, and the "lights" (*me'orot*) created on the fourth day.[10] In any case, the ordinary angels are of a less fine substance, subordinate to Kavod/Shekhinah.

It is this very peculiar first creation that is referred to, Saadia argues, in visions granted to prophets such as those mentioned in Ezekiel 1:26, 1 Kings 22:19, and Daniel 7:9. When the prophets Ezekiel, Micah, and Daniel saw the "likeness as the appearance of a man," the "Lord sitting on His throne," and the "Ancient of Days," they did not behold God himself, but rather this first created "form." It can take the form of a human being, as in these three cases, but it can also be formless, without the form of a human being. Interestingly enough, Saadia does not give a biblical prooftext for the latter possibility, although he could easily have referred to the pillar of fire—one of the favored visual representations of the Shekhinah in Rabbinic literature.[11] Clearly, the visual representation of God in the form of a human being is both what predominates in the Bible and what bothers Saadia most. By choosing for this created being the Hebrew word *demut*, with its double meaning of "likeness" and "form," he emphasizes the close proximity to God, while also underlining that this "form" was created, like the first man, Adam: "And God said: Let us make man in our image (*be-tzalmenu*), after our likeness (*ki-demutenu*)."[12]

Hence Ezekiel and Daniel saw this first creature, which was in the likeness of man, who himself is in the likeness of God. But what about Micah's "Lord sitting on His throne"? Here the identification with God seems unmistakable, but Saadia offers a simple philological solution (which is not in itself improbable, but clearly overstretches the confines of Hebrew grammar): "If, again, it [Scripture] uses the phrase 'Glory of the Lord,' that too implies something created. If, however, it mentions the name 'Lord' but does not attach to it the word 'Glory' or 'Angel' but only such expressions as 'vision' or 'throne' or some human attribute, there can be no doubt but that there is something suppressed in the utterance, the full form of which should be 'Glory of the Lord' or 'Angel of the Lord,' in accordance with the practice of the language of Scripture to leave out words by ellipsis."[13] Thus, the "Lord sitting on His throne" is not God but his created "Glory"!

JUDAH BEN BARZILLAI OF BARCELONA

Saadia's bold move of explaining away God's visual manifestation by introducing a created intermediary figure between God and the angels, as well as the human world, would become common property among the philosophically oriented interpreters of the Bible. A true follower of Saadia in this regard in the eleventh century is Judah ben Barzillai of Barcelona (ca. 1035–1105), who in addition to his halakhic works wrote a famous commentary on the *Sefer Yetzirah* ("Book of Creation"). Like Saadia, he was very much concerned to assert God's absolute transcendence and incorporeality; his commentary, although regarded to be a "vast treasury of ancient mysticism and esotericism,"[14] clearly follows the philosophical line of thought established by Saadia:

> When the thought arose in Him [God] of creating His world, He first of all creatures created the Holy Spirit (*ruah ha-qodesh*), to be a sign of His divinity, which was seen by the prophets and the angels. And He created the form (*demut*) of His Throne of Glory, to be the Throne of Glory for the Holy Spirit, called the Glory (*kavod*) of our God, which is a radiant brilliance (*hod boheq*) and a great light (*'or gadol*) that shines upon all the Creator's [other] creatures. And that great light is called the Glory of our Creator, blessed be His name and His Glory and His Kingdom forever. And the Holy Scripture always calls the Holy Spirit Glory of our God . . . And the sages call this great light Shekhinah . . . And no creature can look at this great light in its beginning (*tehillah*),[15] no angel nor seraph nor prophet can behold the beginning of this light, because the great power of the light was at its beginning. And were a prophet to behold it, his soul would immediately separate itself from his body, and he would die.

> Moses, our Master, asked God to behold the beginning of the great light which is called Glory of our God, and this is the Shekhinah, and about this Scripture says: "Oh, let me behold Your Glory!" (Exod. 33:18), and the Creator answered him: "You cannot see My face" (Exod. 33:20), the interpretation of which is: the face [or "front"] of My Glory. . . . Because Moses, our Master, indeed wanted to behold the face of the Glory, as it is written: "[Let me behold] Your Glory" (Exod. 33:18). And the Creator answered him: "You cannot behold the face of the light of My Glory in its very beginning [or 'front']: for man may not see Me and live" (Exod. 33:20). . . . Therefore it is written: "[And the Lord said:] As My Glory passes by, I will put you in a cleft of the rock and shield you with My hand until I have passed by. Then I will take My hand away, and you will see My back [or "end"] (*ahorai*); but My face (*panai*) must not be seen" (Exod. 33:21–23).

For any "seeing" that is spoken of regarding an angel or a prophet, concerning this created light that the Holy One, blessed be He, forever created to show [it] to the angels and prophets, refers to the Holy One, blessed be He, showing the end (*sof*) of this Glory and of this light to whom He wishes, but no man can see the beginning (*tehillah*) of the light and the contents of his Glory and the likeness/form (*demut*) of his brilliance.[16]

This presents a rather complex sequel to Saadia's created Kavod/Shekhinah. Judah ben Barzillai starts, quite surprisingly, with the Holy Spirit as the first created being. In the Bible, as well as in Rabbinic Judaism, the Holy Spirit is a power emanating from God and, as such, is closely related to God—certainly not a created and separate entity.[17] That Judah ben Barzillai takes the Holy Spirit as his starting point is based on Genesis 1: 2, where the "Spirit of God" is mentioned as hovering over the abyss, and, more specifically, on *Sefer Yetzirah*, where the universe is said to be created out of ten numbers and the twenty-two letters of the Hebrew alphabet. There, the act of creation, or rather emanation, is described as follows: "Ten numbers without anything (*belimah*). One: the Spirit of the Living God, blessed and blest is His name, the Holy Spirit."[18] Thus, the first of the ten "numbers" constituting the universe is the Holy Spirit. Since all of the numbers are created (there follow the primordial elements air, water, and fire, and six dimensions of space: height, abyss, east, west, south, and north), the Holy Spirit, too, is created. The Throne of Glory—which in all the earlier Jewish tradition, most prominently in the Hekhalot literature,[19] is the throne of God—now becomes the throne of the created Holy Spirit.

Notably, this remains wholly consistent within Judah ben Barzillai's system: he takes the term "Throne of Glory" literally as denoting the throne on which not God himself sits, but rather his created Glory, the Kavod. Consequently, the Kavod must be identified with the Holy Spirit. The Holy Spirit is the biblical Kavod, as well as the "great light" (an expression that suggests that he most probably has the "light" from Genesis 1:3 in mind). Finally, like Saadia, Judah ben Barzillai identifies the HolySpirit/Kavod/great light with the Shekhinah of the Rabbis.

Now Judah ben Barzillai introduces an important distinction. Whereas, according to Saadia, the prophets saw precisely the created Kavod/light/Shekhinah, Judah distinguishes between the front/back or beginning/end of the Kavod, by playing with the words *tehillah/sof* ("beginning/end") and *panim/ahor* ("face" or "front"/back," derived from Exod. 33:17–23). Moses did not want to see the face of God (this, of course, is completely out of the question), but rather the face/front of the Kavod. And even this was not granted to him: God let him see only the back/end of the Kavod. Hence, even the Kavod could be seen by Moses only partially, from his back. Accordingly, Judah concludes that no created being (even angels or prophets) can see the Kavod in his entirety; it is only the back that is revealed to them. Or, following the beginning/end imagery, it is not the light in its primordial power, but rather a pale reflection of its original brightness.

JUDAH HA-LEVI

The next evidence that we have on our subject derives from the great poet and theologian Judah ha-Levi (before 1075–1141). In his *Kuzari*—a fictitious dialogue between the king of the Khazars, an (Aristotelian) philosopher, a Christian, a Moslem, and a Jew— he has left us a unique attempt to reconcile the traditional concept of the Jewish religion with the new philosophical doctrines, or rather, to defend the traditional concept against philosophical rationalism. (The original title of the *Kuzari* is *Kitāb al-Hujja wal-Dalīl fī Nasr ad-Dīn adh-Dhalīl* ["The Book of Argument and Proof in Defense of the Despised Faith"].)[20] It is clear that Judah ha-Levi knew the *Sefer Yetzirah*, since he provides a summary of the book and a commentary at the end of the fourth part of the *Kuzari*, and it may well be that he knew Judah ben Barzillai's commentary, as well.

Part four begins with a discussion of the names of God, particularly the two major biblical names *Elohim* and the tetragrammaton *YHWH* (pronounced *Adonai*). The former is the God known by the philosophers, while the latter is the God of Israel, known only through revelation and prophecy. But even the prophets, he argues, do not have direct access to God. They comprehend him only by means of intermediaries,[21] such as: "Glory (*kavod*), Shekhinah, dominion (*malkhut*), fire, cloud, image/likeness (*tzelem*), image/form (*temunah*), 'the appearance of the bow'

(Ezek. 1:28)."[22] The name that includes all of these intermediaries is "Glory of God" (*kevod YY'*). It is obvious that these intermediaries are created entities and as such by no means identical with God, although Judah ha-Levi does not say so explicitly, and probably avoids doing so because of his Neoplatonic tendencies. This becomes especially clear when he speaks about the nature of the prophetic vision:

> Nay, a prophet's eye is more penetrating than [philosophical] speculation. His sight reaches up to the heavenly host [the angels] direct, he sees the dwellers in heaven, and the spiritual beings which are near God, and others in human form. They are alluded to in the verse: "Let us make man in our image, after our likeness" (Gen. 1:26). . . . God created man in the form of His angels and servants which are near Him, not in place but in rank, as we cannot speak of place in connection with God.[23]

Here the angels are placed on the same level as the "intermediaries" mentioned above, and it is these angelic intermediaries that the prophet sees—certainly not God himself. Moreover, man is not created in the image and likeness of God, but rather in the "form" of his angels. Hence the Kavod (and by definition also the Shekhinah) becomes identical with the realm of the angels and the heavenly world; they all are created from a "very fine substance" (*guf daq*):

> "Glory of God" (*kevod H'*) is, according to one view, that fine substance (*guf daq*) which follows the will of God, a substance assuming any form God wishes to show to the prophet. According to another view the "Glory of God" means the whole of the angels and spiritual beings, as well as the throne, chariot (*merkavah*), firmament, wheels (*ofannim*), spheres (*galgalim*), and like them among the other imperishable beings. All this is called Kavod, just as the king's retinue is called his splendor (*kevudah*).[24]

The problem that Judah ha-Levi here addresses is whether the Kavod assumes different and ever-changing forms (so that the prophet can see different and changing things), or whether the "fine substance" from which it is generated has taken on just (and only) the various forms that we know from the Bible. He is apparently influenced by the (Rabbinic) tradition that some angels are created only for a specific purpose, after which they perish, whereas other angels are granted everlasting existence,[25] and he leaves the answer to this question deliberately open.[26] Yet whatever form the Kavod assumes, there can be no doubt that it is a created entity that can lose its form and hence vanish in a certain "configuration."

Now Judah ha-Levi turns to the same biblical text Judah ben Barzillai mentioned when discussing Moses' vision:

> Perhaps that was what Moses desired, when he said: "Oh, let me behold Your Glory" (Exod. 33:18). God fulfilled his wish on the condition that he should not see His face which no mortal could endure, as He said: "And you will see My back; but My face must not be seen" (Exod. 33:23). This includes the Glory which the prophet's eye could bear, and there are things in its wake which even our eye can behold, as the "cloud," and the "devouring fire," because we are accustomed to see them. The higher degrees of these are so transcendental that even prophets cannot perceive them. He, however, who boldly endeavors to do so impairs his constitution, even as the power of sight is impaired. People with weak eyes only see by subdued light after sunset, like the bat. Weak-eyed people can only see in the shadow, but people with strong eyes can see in sunlight. No eye, however, can look into the bright sun, and he who attempts to do so is stricken with blindness. Such is the explanation of the "Glory of God," "the Angels of the Lord," and the "Shekhinah of the Lord," as they are called in the Bible.[27]

Hence, according to Judah ha-Levi, Moses could not see God's face: this is taken for granted and follows the established line of argument. What he saw is only the Kavod. In identifying the Kavod with *God's* back, however, Judah ha-Levi moves it closer to God again than Judah ben Barzillai, who interpreted both the "face" and the "back" in terms of the Kavod, instead of God. Whereas for Judah ben Barzillai the prophet can see only part of the Kavod (his "back"), now the Kavod can be perceived in much greater fullness — if only by the prophet, while ordinary people are confined to lesser and more moderate degrees of perception.[28] Not only does Judah ha-Levi seem to be more generous regarding the vision of the Kavod (insofar as ordinary people can see at least parts or degrees of it), but he also reverses Judah ben Barzillai's extreme position regarding the distance between God and the Kavod. Although created, the Kavod is a substance emanating from God, and the closer to God this substance is the finer it becomes. There is, so to speak, a continuous flow of a fine substance "out of" God, from the utmost fineness at one end to a coarser one at the other. The prophet can perceive a degree of fineness that is much finer than ordinary people could bear, but even he cannot reach the finest fineness that is closest to God.

MOSES MAIMONIDES

Turning finally to Moses Maimonides (1138–1204), the great philosopher/theologian and main representative of an Aristotelian theology in the Jewish Middle Ages, we find the same aversion to the notion of God's corporeality we encountered, above all, with Saadiah. As Maimonides states at the very outset of his famous treatise *Dalālat al-Hā'irīn* (*Moreh ha-Nevukhim* in the Hebrew translation, "The Guide of the Perplexed," written around 1190), the unity of God "can have no true reality unless one disproves His corporeality."[29] Indeed, one of the major goals of the *Moreh* is the refutation of the doctrine of God's corporeality. A large section of the first part of this work is devoted to explaining away the worrisome anthropomorphic character of many biblical terms—Maimonides starts right away with the words *tzelem* ("image") and *demut* ("likeness"), which figured so prominently in his predecessors' deliberations.

Another of these problematic words is *la'avor* ("to pass by"), because it clearly presupposes some kind of corporeality when referring to God. Maimonides finds it in the story of Moses carving the two tablets of stone, which immediately follows Moses' abortive request to see God's face. When Moses went up on Mount Sinai with his two tablets, the Bible says, "And the Lord passed before his face" (Exod. 34:6). The plain meaning of this verse is clearly that "his face" refers to Moses' face, and that God passed before Moses. Maimonides, however, makes every effort to explain this literal meaning away: "In my opinion the dictum of Scripture: 'And the Lord passed before his face' (Exod. 34:6), conforms to this last figurative use; the possessive suffix in the third person attached to the Hebrew word 'face' refers to God, may He be exalted [and not to Moses]."[30]

This is a very strange interpretation because it implies that God passed before his own face. But Maimonides has a much more sophisticated justification for his strange exegesis:

> The explanation of this, according to what I think and to what occurs to me, is that Moses, peace be on him, demanded a certain apprehension — namely, that which in its [Scripture's] dictum: "But My face must not be seen" (Exod. 33:23), is named "the seeing of the face" — and was promised an apprehension that is named "the seeing of the back" in its dictum: "And you will see My back" (Exod. 33:23). . . . Scripture accordingly says in this passage that God, may He be exalted, hid from him the apprehension called that "of the face" and made him pass over to something different; I mean the knowledge of the acts ascribed to Him, may He be exalted, which, as we shall explain, are deemed to be multiple attributes.[31]

Here not only is any corporeality taken away from God, but Maimonides does not even resort to the easy strategy, suggested by the biblical text and followed by his predecessors: the Kavod. Rather, for Maimonides, the "face" that Moses could not see is God himself, his essence, while the "back" that Moses did see instead is not the Kavod, but rather God's (accidental) attributes of action. Hence the phrase "And the Lord passed by before His [God's] face" means that God made him (Moses) pass over from his "face" (which he could not apprehend) to his "back" (which he could apprehend). Nevertheless, despite all his effort, Maimonides remains well aware of the traditional way out of the problem posed by this biblical text. At the end of his discussion, he approvingly quotes the targumic translation of the verse Exod. 34:6, which substitutes the Shekhinah for God. Yet he also takes it for granted — quite against the spirit of the Targum — that the Shekhinah, of course, is not identical with God, but created: "He [the targumic translator, Onqelos] does the same thing with regard to the dictum of Scripture: 'And the Lord passed by before his face' (Exod. 34:6), which he translates: 'The Lord caused His Shekhinah to pass before his face.' Thus according to him it was indubitably a created thing that passed by; he considers that in the expression 'his face' the possessive suffix in the third person refers to Moses our Master. . . . This too is an excellent interpretation that may be approved of."[32] Here the plain meaning of the biblical text is preserved — "his face" is Moses', and not God's, face. This generous concession, however, becomes possible only by transforming the targumic Shekhinah into a created being.

Another striking example of Maimonides' readiness to follow the anti-anthropomorphic tradition of Targum Onqelos — and insinuating a rather peculiar reading of Onqelos or pretending that his reading is the most natural one — is his discussion of Exod. 24:10: "And they saw the God of Israel, and there was under his feet, as it were, a work of the whiteness of sapphire stone" (Exod. 24:10). The problem here, of course, is that God is described as having feet and thus seems to be corporeal. Again, Maimonides quotes Onqelos approvingly:

> The interpretation of Onqelos is, as you know, as follows. He considers that the third person suffix, "his," in the words "his feet" refers to God's throne; accordingly he translates: "And under the throne of His Glory." Understand this and admire how far Onqelos was from belief in the corporeality of God and from everything that leads to it even though it be by the longest way. For he does not say: "And under His throne." For should the term "throne" have been referred to God in the sense that has been explained above, this would have entailed the consequence that He would have been conceived of sitting upon an body and thus would have entailed the belief in corporeality. Accordingly [Onqelos] referred the term "throne" to "His Glory," I mean to the Shekhinah, which is a created light.[33]

It is the Kavod (Shekhinah) who is sitting on the throne, not God, and this Kavod/Shekhinah is a created light. This means that it is not only created but also has no recognizable shape — certainly not in human form. In making a clear-cut distinction between God and the created Kavod/Shekhinah, Maimonides conceals that it is by no means self-evident that Targum Onqelos understood the Kavod/Shekhinah as a created being (it is most likely that it did not). Moreover, other Targumim (which Maimonides either ignores or does not know) were much less strict in their attitude to the anthropomorphism of God's feet (as well as other parts of his body). For instance, Targum Pseudo-Jonathan translates Exodus 24:10: "And Nadab and Abihu lifted up their eyes, and saw the Glory of the God of Israel; and under the footstool of His feet which was placed beneath His throne, was like the work of a sapphire stone,"[34] clearly not replacing God's feet with the throne but, on the contrary, depicting God sitting on his throne and resting his feet on a footstool (which, as the continuation explains, is made of a brick stone in memory of the servitude of the children of Israel in Egypt)![35]

According to Maimonides' highly sophisticated definition, the biblical Kavod ("Glory of God") can thus have three different meanings: following Targum Onqelos (but also Saadia, Judah ben Barzillai, and Judah ha-Levi) it can refer to the created light; in the example of Moses, it can refer to God's essence; and, a third and new aspect, it can refer to the praise of God:

> Similarly the "Glory of God" is sometimes intended to signify the created light that God causes to descend in an particular place in order to confer honor upon it in a miraculous way: "And the Glory of God (*kevod YHWH*) abode upon Mount Sinai, and [the cloud] covered it," and so on (Exod. 24:16); "And the Glory of God (*kevod YHWH*) filled the tabernacle" (Exod. 40:34). The expression is sometimes intended to signify His essence and true reality, may He be exalted, as when he [Moses] says: "Oh, let me behold Your Glory" (Exod. 33:18), and was answered: "For man may not see Me and live" (Exod. 33:20). . . . . "Glory" is sometimes intended to signify the honoring of Him, may He be exalted, by all men. . . . It is in view of this notion being named "glory" that it is said: "The whole earth is full of His glory (*kevodo*)" (Isa. 6:3), this being equivalent to the dictum: "And the earth is full of His praise (*tehillato*)" (Hab. 3:3), for "praise" is called "glory." Thus it is said: "Give glory (*kavod*) to the Lord your God" (Jer. 13:16); and it is said: "And in His temple all say: glory (*kavod*)" (Ps. 29:9). This occurs frequently. Understand then likewise the equivocality with reference to "glory" and interpret the latter in accordance with the context. You shall thus be saved from great difficulty.[36]

The third distinction ("glory" = "praise") is certainly philologically correct, although one might wonder whether it applies to all of Maimonides' examples. For instance, the quotation from Isaiah 6:3 was understood by many of his predecessors in terms of the presence of God on earth, not just of his praise (in fact, it has been taken as the prime example of a biblical reference to

God's presence in the Temple, as seen by the prophet). Altogether, it is conspicuous how much Maimonides seems to avoid establishing any relationship between the prophet and the divine Kavod. His prooftexts for the interpretation of Glory as created light are all taken from Exodus (which have nothing to do with prophetic vision), and he does not refer to the visions in Ezekiel and 1 Kings, which were so important (albeit troublesome) for Saadia. And the only case in which Maimonides grants the meaning of God's "essence" for the term Kavod concerns Moses' attempt to see God himself, which he uses only to prove that this is utterly impossible and that Moses saw instead some manifestation of the divine attributes.

In sum, the early medieval Jewish philosophers with their rationalistic attitudes, whether in Aristotelian or (Neo-) Platonic guise, develop a theory of the created Kavod/Shekhinah as consisting of a very fine and sublime material and taking on different forms. It is the first "creature" that God created and can be identified with the mysterious first light that, according to a certain reading of Genesis 1:3,[37] was the first "thing" ever created. As such, it remains far removed from the traditional notion of the Kavod/Shekhinah as God's manifestation on earth. Only Maimonides allows himself to relate the term Kavod to the essence of God, although only to ensure that one can speculate about such things, but certainly not perceive them. Yet he does grant the possibility that "Kavod" *can* refer to God himself, not just to the created light or to God's praise. Moreover, and most importantly for our purpose, none of these interpretations even touch upon the question of God's gender. In effect, by removing any hint of corporeality from the image of God, the early medieval Jewish philosophers were also successful in eliminating any trace of his male or female character left over from the Bible or the subsequent Jewish tradition. The God of the philosophers is completely asexual, and his created Kavod/Shekhinah thus becomes either a formless substance or, if it takes on human form at all, a male human figure. No echo remains of the biblical Wisdom tradition or even of the Rabbis' artful play with gender metaphors, let alone of Philo's subtle relationship between God, his Logos, and his Wisdom.

✿ 6 ✿

THE SHEKHINAH IN THE BAHIR[1]

THE REMOTE AND ASEXUAL God of the philosophers represents the farthest that Jewish tradition could depart from the Wisdom tradition, as developed in the Hebrew Bible and later noncanonical ramifications. It pretends to "restore" a pure, non-anthropomorphic monotheism. But, in reality, it creates concepts quite alien to the much richer biblical and early postbiblical lore. In ignoring (or at least making more difficult) God's presence and accessibility on earth, it weakens the notion of a personal God who reveals himself in visions and listens to prayers. Similarly, in abolishing any trace of human shape (even the traditional all-male image, not to mention some female potentiality), it positions God beyond human apprehension, and desire.

Yet apprehension and desire are powerful forces that cannot be easily suppressed for the sake of abstract philosophical cognition — certainly not within the realm of religion. In fact, precisely at the first peak of Jewish philosophical thinking, a countermovement arose that swept away, or rather completely ignored, all of the philosophical subtleties about the abstract and transcendent God that had so far developed. This is the early Kabbalah, which emerged at the end of the twelfth century CE in Provence in Southern France. Although not very far in terms of time and space from a philosopher like Maimonides, this movement belonged to a completely different realm, both culturally and religiously. When reading the first kabbalistic tractates, one gets the feeling of being transferred to an archaic and mythical world, which seems much closer again to the origins of the Hebrew Bible than to the domain of philosophical speculation. This impression certainly holds true for the very first document of the Kabbalah, the book Bahir.

The book Bahir appeared out of the blue, so to speak, without any warning, in Provence towards the end of the twelfth century. It takes its title from the Bible verse Job 37:21 ("But now one does not see the light [any more], it shines [*bahir hu'*] in the heavens") and is attributed to an early Jewish mystic of the second century CE — a well-tried fiction that intends to guarantee its age and thus its "orthodoxy." Modern scholarship has concluded that the text originated in the Orient in Late Antiquity and that, between 1130 and 1170, sections of this early Bahir reached Provence, "where they were subjected to a final revision and redaction into the form in which the book has come down to us."[2] It takes the form of a traditional Midrash in the strict sense of the term: an anthology of various statements, mostly brief, that are attributed to different Rabbis allegedly of the early Rabbinic period and often expound biblical verses, while following many of the literary patterns characteristic of the Midrash (especially the *mashal*, "parable"). Some of the Rabbis are known from the Rabbinic literature, but others appear to be purely fictional. There is also no definite order in the book. The manuscripts and the traditional printed editions do not contain any systematic division of the text, so that the modern editions and translations unfortunately arrange it into different sections.[3] One can sometimes find a certain line of argument in the arrangement of the various passages/units, but the thread is often broken and is either given up or only reemerges at a later stage.

In its depiction of God, the Bahir goes quite decidedly beyond the Bible and Rabbinic Judaism in Late Antiquity, while having little or nothing in common with medieval Jewish philosophy, either in its Neoplatonic version or (much less) in the form of the emerging Aristotelianism, such as that expounded in the twelfth century by Maimonides.[4] Its ideal in the Bahir is not to assert an unchanging God, the unmoved mover of the philosophers, but rather to present an unfolding depiction of the diverse and dynamic life, which goes on within God himself. It is true that God remains one and one alone, but he nonetheless possesses an incredibly rich inner life; his Godhead unfolds in potencies, energies, emanations (Hebrew *sefirot*),[5] which embody different aspects of his essence that continually interrelate with one another. Whereas the undivided oneness of God belongs to an area about which no statement is possible (this is the hidden God, which the later Kabbalah termed *'En Sof*, literally "Without End"), his inner unfolding into Sefirot (which were very soon fixed at ten) can be described.

In the Bahir the system of the ten inner divine potencies has not yet developed to its full complexity, as we find it, for example, in the Zohar and in the later Kabbalah; it can only be reconstructed from various shreds and fragments. Nevertheless, the essential characteristics are already present: the total of ten; the clear separation between the three upper Sefirot and the seven lower ones; the tension between God's love and his punishing judgment in the fourth and fifth Sefirah, which is balanced out in the sixth; and finally the tenth Sefirah, the Shekhinah, which is defined as an explicitly female principle.

The Ten Sefirot

Let us first look at the system of the ten Sefirot as it is developed in the Bahir. Among these ten, the upper three Sefirot play a prominent role:

> What is the meaning of "Holy, holy, holy" (in Isa. 6:3), [and why is it] followed by "the Lord of hosts, the whole earth is filled with His glory"?
> The [first] "Holy" is the Supreme Crown.
> The [second] "Holy" is the root of the tree.
> The [third] "Holy" is united and special in (= separate from) all of them: "the Lord of hosts, the whole earth is filled with His glory".[6]

The threefold *qadosh* from Isaiah 6:3 is here understood as referring to the three upper Sefirot of the divine pleroma, of which only the first and highest one has a name, the "Supreme Crown" (*keter 'elyion*), precisely the name it gets in all subsequent kabbalistic systems. The second one remains unnamed (although in other sections it is called *hokhmah*, "Wisdom"); it is the root of the divine tree, another symbol of the divine pleroma, which reaches down into the lower world, and is here localized in the second Sefirah. What is striking is that it is the root that is above, not the branches, as one would expect. This can only mean that the divine tree is turned upside down: its roots are above and its branches reach downwards, down to the earthly realm. Most interesting is the third Sefirah, which again is not here named (in other sections, it is called *binah*, "Understanding") but is characterized in a very strange manner as simultaneously "united" (with the other Sefirot) and "special," which here denotes "separate,"[7] namely separate from the divine realm of the other Sefirot. A parable explains what this simultaneously "united" and "separate" nature means:

> And what is that [third] "Holy" which is united [and at the same time separate]? This can be explained by a parable: A King had sons, who in turn also had sons. When these [latter] sons [the grandsons of the King] fulfill his wishes, he enters among them and makes everything exist, and provides them with food and pours goodness upon them, so that both the fathers and the sons will be satisfied. But when the [grand]sons do not fulfill his wishes, he provides for no more than the needs of the fathers.[8]

The King, of course, is God, and his sons are the Sefirot (that is, the divine pleroma, the inner structure of the Godhead), so that the King and his sons together constitute the Godhead. These Sefirot also have sons, who thus are the grandsons of the King/God; these sons no doubt represent the people of Israel on earth. Hence we encounter here the interdependence of the divine and the earthly realm. Israel are the children of God, who are bound to fulfill his will. This is an extremely common, traditional motif that, however, here gets a completely new twist: when Israel fulfills God's will, it is not only Israel that gains advantage, but also their "fathers" — namely the sons of the King, which are the divine pleroma, which is God himself! This implies that even God himself depends on what Israel does on earth. When Israel fulfills God's wishes, by fulfilling the Torah, then God amply provides for both the people on earth *and* the divine realm; God is "united" with Israel. If they do not, however, the divine realm (that is, God's own pleroma) receives the minimum it needs, while the earthly people are punished by God's being "special" (remote and separate). So what we have here is the description of the inner structure of the Godhead (the upper three Sefirot) as it "functions" in relation to Israel, the sons of God.[9] I will return to this later, but first it is necessary to explain in more detail the system of the ten Sefirot, according to the Bahir.

The Bahiric system of the ten Sefirot is outlined in paragraphs 96, 104, 105, and 115, which most probably belonged together originally. The word used here for the Sefirot is *ma'amarot* (lit.

"sayings"; Scholem translates *logoi*, "words," probably thereby alluding to the prologue of the Gospel of John). The upper three, according to paragraph 96, are the Supreme Crown (*keter 'elyion*), Wisdom (*hokhmah*), and the "Quarry of the Torah." The scriptural proof for "Wisdom" is the standard midrashic interpretation that we discussed above.[10] Here, however, it takes on a completely new meaning: "The second one is Wisdom (*hokhmah*), as it is written: The Lord created me at the beginning (*reshit*) of His course, [as the first of His works of old] (Prov. 8:22). 'Beginning' (*reshit*) is nothing other than 'Wisdom,' as it is written: The beginning is Wisdom, [the fear of God] (Ps. 111:10)."[11] Whereas the midrash wants to prove that the very first word of Genesis, "in the beginning" (*bereshit*), means "Wisdom" and that this "Wisdom" is to be equated with the "Torah," (hence: "By means of Wisdom/Torah God created heaven and earth"), our text says that "Wisdom" is the "beginning" of God's act of self-creation, emanation, enfolding himself within the ten Sefirot.[12] "Wisdom" is the second Sefirah in the process of the divine emanation. The name "Quarry of the Torah" for the third Sefirah is unique to the Bahir, which does know the name that is to become the standard designation for this Sefirah: *binah*, "Understanding" or "Intelligence."[13] In the Bahir, however, the third Sefirah is the "Quarry of the Torah," in the sense that it is the place at which the Torah is hewn. It is the place of the Written Torah — in contrast to the Oral Torah, which is located in the tenth Sefirah, the Shekhinah — and from it emanate all of the other "forms," namely the seven lower Sefirot.

The forth and the fifth Sefirah are the Right and the Left Hand of God respectively (the fifth is also called the "Great Fire"), and according to the later systems of the Kabbalah represent the functions of God's "Mercy/Love" (*hesed*) and "Judgement/Strength" (*din/gevurah*). The symbolism of the sixth Sefirah is again unique to the Bahir; it is the "Throne of Glory," quite distinct from "Beauty" (*tif'eret*) or "Compassion" (*rahamim*) in the later systems. With the seventh Sefirah we enter the world of sexual symbolism within the ten Sefirot, which is completely absent from the Jewish literature and religion before the Bahir, although it will play a very prominent role in later kabbalistic texts like the Zohar (where its designation is "Endurance" or "Eternity," *netzah*): "The seventh one is the east of the world. It is from where the Seed of Israel [comes]. The spinal cord originates in man's brain and extends to the sexual organ, where the seed is. It is therefore written: From the east I will bring your seed, [and from the west I will gather you] (Isa. 43:5)."[14] The eighth Sefirah is called the "Righteous One" (*tzaddiq*) or "Foundation" (*yesod*), because it "supports the whole world" (the later name for this Sefirah is "Majesty," *hod*, whereas *yesod* will become the name of the ninth Sefirah).[15] That the righteous one is the foundation of the world (and of all souls) is derived from Proverbs 10:25 and is also an important topic in the Rabbinic literature.[16] But here this motif is again given a clearly sexual connotation. Paragraph 71 describes a "column" that goes from the earth up to heaven and is called "Righteous": "when there are righteous people upon earth, it becomes strong, but when there are not, it grows slack." Finally, as for the ninth and the tenth Sefirah:

> What is the ninth? He said to them: The ninth and tenth are together, one opposite the other. . . . They are like [two] Wheels (*ophannim*). One inclines to the north, while the other inclines to the west. They reach down to the lowest earth. . . . The end of the Shekhinah of the Holy One, blessed be He, is under his feet, as it is written: The heaven is my throne, and the earth is my footstool (Isa. 66:1). The Endurance (*netzah*) of the world is down there, as it is written: From eternity to eternity (*le-netzah netzahim*, forever). (Isa. 34:10).[17]

The two wheels are of course the wheels of the Merkavah,[18] which are here equated with north and west, as well as with the two "endurances," one upper and one lower: the ninth and the tenth Sefirah. The lower one of the two and thus the lowest of the ten Sefirot is the Shekhinah, the Presence of God in the world and his feminine principle. Here it is clearly the partner of the ninth Sefirah, the masculine principle in the normative system of the Kabbalah, and thus contradicts the most likely older location of the masculine principle in the seventh or eighth Sefirah.[19]

Sexual Symbolism

The markedly sexual symbolism for masculinity and femininity in the Bahir warrants some further clarification (in this context I will provide just some basic information and return to the subject of God's androgynous nature in the last chapter). As we have seen, the masculine principle is located in the seventh (or eighth) Sefirah, oriented toward the "east of the world," whereas the tenth Sefirah (the Shekhinah) represents the feminine principle and is oriented toward the west. A parable further explains this relationship:

> Why is [west] called *ma'arav* (lit. "mixture")? Because it is there that all seed is mixed together. A parable: This matter is compared to a prince who had a beautiful and virtuous bride in his chamber. He was accustomed to taking riches from his father's house and always bringing them to her. She, in turn, took everything, always hid it and mixed it all together. Ultimately he wanted to see what he had gathered and accumulated. Therefore it is written: "From the west [mixture] I will gather you" (Isa. 43:5). And what is meant by "his father's house"? It is that about which it is written: "From the east I will bring your seed" (ibid.). This teaches us that he brings [the seed] from the east and sows it in the west. And in the end he gathers what he has sowed.[20]

Here in typical kabbalistic fashion, events in the divine and the earthly realm intersect. The mixing of the seed in the tenth Sefirah draws upon clearly sexual imagery to describe the interaction of male and female potencies within God (the "prince" and his "bride"; that is, the other Sefirot and the tenth Sefirah), as well as the entrance of human souls into the world, which (literally) takes place through the tenth and lowest Sefirah, located at the crossing, so to speak, of the earthly and divine worlds. In his essence God is male and female, and *therefore* man, too, is male and female (and not the other way round), as the following passage quite drastically asserts:

> I have already told you that the Holy One, blessed be He, has seven holy forms,[21] and they all have their counterparts in man, as it is written: "[God created man in his image,] in the image of God he created him, male and female he created them" (Gen. 1:27). And they are the following: the right and left leg, the right and left hand, the trunk with the place of procreation, and the head. These are [however only] six, and you say seven? Seven they are with his wife, [about whom] it is written: "And they shall be one flesh" (Gen. 2:24).[22]

Earthly man is the likeness of the divine "body." His "extremities" (legs, arms, trunk with phallus, and head) correspond to the seven lower divine Sefirot. Just as God is only complete with the female tenth Sefirah, so also does man need the complement of the woman, who becomes an integrated whole with his body. In other words: the female belongs essentially to the male; man is incomplete without woman precisely because *God* is both male and female!

Various images are used to illustrated the feminine quality of the tenth Sefirah. Particularly graphic in its sexual symbolism is the image of the Etrog, the citrus fruit that, along with the palm branch, the willow, and the myrtle, belongs to the "four species" in the bouquet of Sukkot (where the palm branch, willow, and myrtle are tied together and held in the right hand, while the Etrog is carried separately in the left hand). In the following parable, the palm branch is interpreted as male and the Etrog as female: "It is like a King who planned to plant nine male trees in his garden, and all were date palms. What did he do? He said: If they are all of the same kind, it is impossible for them to exist. What did he do? He planted amongst them an Etrog, and this was one of the nine, of which he had [originally] planned that they be male. And what is [the] Etrog? [The] Etrog is female."[23]

THE POSITION OF THE SHEKHINAH IN THE SEFIROTIC SYSTEM

Let us now look more closely at the position of the female Shekhinah in the system of the ten Sefirot. What is most striking is her receptive function, which is emphasized repeatedly and expressed in different images. She is the vessel (*shiddah*) into which all of the powers of the upper Sefirot flow and at the same time the heart (*lev*) of God that points to the 32 hidden paths of wisdom by which the world was created according to the *Sefer Yetzirah*[24] (the numerical value of the Hebrew word *lev* is 32).[25] She is a valuable precious stone that God loves more than his "kings" (a clear hint at the other Sefirot) and that he embraces, kisses, and puts on his head (obviously as a crown) and loves.[26] In a rich but somewhat bizarre image, she is a beautiful, fragrant vessel that he loves, puts on his head or on his arms (obviously an allusion to the Tefillin worn on the forehead and arm), and indeed even lends to his son.[27] This precious stone is itself "crowned," and everything is "contained" in it.²⁸ The latter statement, that it absorbs and "contains everything" within it (that is, the powers of all the other Sefirot), illustrates a further distinctive characteristic of the tenth Sefirah. In an interpretation of Genesis 24:1 ("And God blessed Abraham with all" [*ba-kol*]), this "all" (*kol*) is interpreted as a "beautiful vessel" that holds "beautiful precious stones," "which have no equal" — no doubt a further reference to the tenth Sefirah, which combines within her all of the beauty and power of the other divine Sefirot.²⁹ This explains why, among other things, she is also symbolized by the ocean that contains the water of all of the rivers within it (that is, the forces of all the other Sefirot): "'All the brooks go to the sea, but the sea is not filled' (Eccles. 1:7). What is this sea? Let us say that it is the Etrog."³⁰

The position of the Shekhinah is, however, by no means only that of the lowest Sefirah, nor is her function limited to pure receptivity. It is true that, in the hierarchy of the Sefirot, she is located at the bottom, but she is at the same time connected in a strange way with the third Sefirah, "understanding" (*binah*). The Bahir states explicitly that, in reality, there are *two* Shekhinot: "There is a Shekhinah below, just like there is a Shekhinah above. And what is this Shekhinah [below]? Let us say that it is the light which has emanated from first light."³¹ "Understanding" (*binah*) is the "mother" of the upper world, from which the seven lower Sefirot emanate;³² it is the primordial light to which the natural light corresponds,³³ and also the Written Torah, from which the Oral Torah originates.³⁴ A perfect harmony seems to exist between the third Sefirah (*binah*), as the lowest of the three upper Sefirot, and the tenth Sefirah (Shekhinah), as the lowest of the seven lower Sefirot. Whereas the third Sefirah bundles up the powers of the three upper Sefirot and passes them on to the seven lower Sefirot, the tenth Sefirah bundles up the powers of the seven or ten Sefirot and transmits them down to the earthly world.

Standing on the threshold to the earthly world, the Shekhinah hands over the divine powers assembled within her to this world and at the same time directs them above. As the "crowned precious stone in which all is contained," she is the foundation stone and yet strives to return back to the place whence she originated, the third Sefirah: "'The stone which the builders rejected has become the chief cornerstone' (Ps. 118:22). And it ascends to the place from which it was hewn, as it is written: 'From there is the shepherd, the stone of Israel' (Gen. 49:24)".[35] It is quite clear that the separation of the tenth from the third Sefirah and the strivings of both towards union are not descriptions of chronologically distinct emanations of the divine essence — for instance, in the sense that both became separated as a result of a catastrophic event (the inner divine catastrophe as well-known from the later Kabbalah) and are awaiting their reunion in a better (that is, messianic) future — but a necessary and simultaneous condition. Only in her position at the bottom edge of the divine world can the Shekhinah fulfill her divinely intended task (that is, a task intrinsic to God's nature) for the earthly world; yet according to her own nature she belongs to the three highest divine potencies. We shall later see, however, that the union of the two Sefirot is in no way dependent on these alone, but relies on the involvement of Israel, and thus human beings.

The double function of the tenth Sefirah, her orientation above and below, is very graphically expressed in the Hebrew concept *daveq u-meyuhad* ("united [or connected] and [at the same time] separate)," as mentioned above. Two parables elucidate this special feature through an exegesis from Ezekiel 3:12 ("Blessed be the glory of God from his place"):

What is "the glory of God"? A parable: This matter is comparable to a King in whose chamber the Queen was, and all his hosts delighted in her. They had sons, who came every day to see the King, and they blessed him. They said to him: "Where is our mother?" He replied: "You cannot see her now." They said: "Let her be blessed, wherever she is!"

And what is meant by "from his place"? Because there is no one who knows his place. A parable: There was a King's daughter who came from a faraway place and no one knew whence she had come, but they saw that she was a capable woman, beautiful and refined in everything she did. They then said: "She is certainly taken from the side of light, for the world is illuminated through her deeds." They asked her: "From whence have you come?" She said: "From my place." They said: "If so, the people of your place must be great. Blessed be she and blessed be her place!"[36]

In the first parable the King is God (that is, the totality of all of the Sefirot) and the Queen (Aramaic *matronita*, lit., "[his] spouse") is the Shekhinah, the tenth Sefirah. As the spouse of the King, she clearly assumes a prominent position among the other Sefirot, the "hosts"[37] who take delight in her. The sons of the divine couple are the people of Israel: the King they can see and extol daily, but not the Queen, their mother. They therefore praise the "glory of God," their mother, wherever she is; that is, without knowing her exact whereabouts. The first parable thus describes the position of the Shekhinah within the system of the ten Sefirot: she is *God's* glory and as such "united" (*daveq*) with God in the innermost chamber of the King. To this chamber, humankind, or rather Israel, has no access; the sons cannot see their mother's place of origin.

The second parable tells a different story. Here the Shekhinah is described in her function as the daughter of the King who, from her position as the tenth Sefirah, exerts her powers within the world of human beings. She comes from a faraway land, "from the side of light," which naturally denotes her divine realm. As the King's daughter, she is simultaneously God's messenger, who illuminates the earthly world. Only in this state can human beings see her and speak with her; however, her actual place, the place of her origin, remains hidden from their view. The second parable thus describes the position of the Shekhinah in her state of isolation (*meyuhad*), in her separation from her divine origin and in her dwelling among human beings. Because the Shekhinah is at one and the same time "united" with her divine origin and "separated" from it, she is the outstanding part of the Sefirotic system and, moreover, the power by which the divine sphere exerts influence on the earthly world, by which God communicates with humankind.

Mediatrix between Heaven and Earth

This significant aspect must be explored in more depth. The description of the Shekhinah as mediator (*mediatrix*) between God and human beings, between heaven and earth, represents one of the central concerns of the Bahir and the Kabbalah. In this connection, it is important that she is equated with the Oral Torah, or, to be more precise, the separation between Written and Oral Torah. Whereas, as we have seen, the Written Torah is identified with the third Sefirah (*binah*) and remains inaccessible for humans in the divine sphere, the Oral Torah is equated with the tenth Sefirah and can thus—but only thus—be effective in the earthly world.

This separation between the Written and the Oral Torah flagrantly contradicts the classical Rabbinic tradition, according to which both forms of the Torah, the Written and the Oral, were given to Moses on Mount Sinai. Indeed, the Rabbis set great store by the statement that nothing from the Torah has been left behind in heaven. In contrast, the Bahir takes this idea and radically transforms it into a powerful myth that goes far beyond the accepted tradition. According to the Bahir, the Shekhinah in her divine manifestation is identical with the Written Torah (which stays in heaven), whereas the Shekhinah in her earthly manifestation is identical with the Oral Torah (which comes down to earth). Hence, the Shekhinah, as God's female principle, is located in the innermost essence of the divinity (the Written Torah), while at the same time exposed to the world of human beings (the Oral Torah). That is, the Oral Torah that has been given to Israel is not just a "book," but God himself who enters the world in the form of his daughter.[38] We have already seen this in the parable quoted above, which describes the relationship between the divine daughter and the people on earth. Likewise, the following parable describes the ongoing relationship between the King and his daughter:

> This is comparable to a King who had a daughter who was good and comely, graceful and perfect. And he married her to a prince, and gave her garments and a crown and jewelry and he gave her to him with a great fortune. Can the King now live without his daughter?[39] No! But can he be with her all day long? No! What did he do? He built a window between himself and her, and whenever the daughter had need of her father and the father of the daughter, they would come together[40] through the window. Of this is it written: "All the glory of the King's daughter is inside, her garment is interwoven with gold" (Ps. 45:14).[41]

Here again the King is God and the daughter is the Shekhinah, the tenth Sefirah. Most likely the royal prince is Solomon, to whom God gave wisdom (according to 1 Kings 5:9ff., 26), another symbol for the Oral Torah. As the King's daughter, the Shekhinah belongs to the divine sphere; as the Oral Torah, she is Solomon's bride and thus sent into the lower world. She is separated from the King, her father, but nonetheless is always close to him: through the window they can come together whenever they desire. And, more importantly, she retains the "glory" of her divine origin, that is, her divine essence, even in the earthly realm, also bringing it down to earth.

A further parable describes in more detail how man gains access to God through the Oral Torah, the Shekhinah. It explains the already mentioned 32 paths of wisdom concealed in God, through which he created the world:

> What are [these] thirty-two? He said: These are the 32 paths. This is like a King who was in the innermost chamber [of his palace], and the number of rooms was 32, and there was a path to every chamber. Did it suit the King to allow everyone to enter his chambers by these paths? No! But did it suit him not to display openly his pearls and hidden treasures, jeweled settings and beautiful things at all? No! What did [the King] do? He took [his] daughter and concentrated all paths in her and in her garments, and whoever wishes to enter the interior must look this way [at her]. . . .[42] At times, in his great love for her, he calls her "my sister," for they come from the same place; sometimes he calls her "my daughter," for she is his daughter; and sometimes he calls her "my mother."[43]

This is one of the most important texts about the Shekhinah. The 32 paths of wisdom are the essence of the heavenly as well as of the earthly world; to a certain extent they prefigure in heaven what was transferred to earth in creation.[44] Whoever knows them has access to the King (that is, to God) and to all of the secrets of creation. God did not want to make his heavenly treasures accessible to all, but neither did he want to conceal them from the world (in fact, he ends up creating the earthly world in them). He therefore decided to combine them in his "daughter," the Shekhinah and the Oral Torah. She contains within her all of the paths of wisdom; whoever wants to understand and fathom them must look at her, the Shekhinah, which is the Torah. Consequently, the Torah is the only medium through which God and the secrets of his creation are accessible to all human beings.

Thus here again we have a parable that attempts to describe the paradoxical position of the Shekhinah as part of both the heavenly and the earthly worlds, not by abstract concepts, but in the form of the metaphorical language of the parable — something that is characteristic of Jewish mysticism in general and of the Bahir in particular. Entrusted to Solomon on behalf of all of the people of Israel as the Torah, the Shekhinah is God's daughter; as one of the ten Sefirot she is his sister, a partner with equal rights in the interplay of inner divine potencies; and as the mother of his sons (that is, of Israel) she is his spouse.[45] Only in this last sense, as mother of his sons, can he also call her "mother" in the striking image of the parable (albeit not literally "my mother," of course).

The *Vorlage* for this wording was quite obviously a parable in the Rabbinic literature, and it is only against this background that the Bahir's bold statement really becomes clear. The starting point of the Rabbinic parable is the Bible verse Song of Songs 3:11 ("Go forth, you daughters of Zion, and gaze upon King Solomon wearing the crown with which his mother crowned him on the day of his wedding"):

> This is compared to a King who had an only daughter, whom he loved very greatly and would call "my daughter." Not satisfied with that he called her "my sister." And still not satisfied with that he [finally] called her "my mother." Thus the Holy One, blessed be He, loved Israel above all else and called them "my daughter" . . . Not satisfied with that he called them "my sister." . . . Still not satisfied with that he [finally] called them "my mother".[46]

The subject of this parable is the love of God for Israel; thus "daughter," "sister," and "mother" are nothing but metaphors to express the exceptionality and the intensification of this love. God loves Israel as one loves his daughter, sister, or mother. The highest form of love is mother-love; therefore he calls Israel even "my mother." Totally different, much bolder and more concrete, is the parable in the Bahir. Here the "daughter" of God is literally his daughter, namely the Shekhinah, who has been sent to human beings; his "sister" is literally his sister, and the "mother" is his spouse, as well as the mother of his sons. If one transfers the Rabbinic parable to the parable in the Bahir, one might argue that it is this final function of the Shekhinah, as wife and mother, in which the highest form of the love relationship between God and his female partner takes concrete form. This is certainly implicit, even though the tenor of the Bahir parable is directed primarily at the function of the Shekhinah as daughter and thereby at God's embodiment in the world. With his female force, the Shekhinah, God enters the world.[47]

What precisely is the task of the Shekhinah, as the embodiment and emissary of God in the world? Here, the same holds true as with her role in the system of the inner divine powers: she is not only God's passive presence among the people of Israel, but she also plays an active part in their destiny; she helps Israel gain access to God. This is based, as we would expect, on her capacity as the Oral Torah, which encompasses all of the Commandments that Israel must fulfill.[48] In her dual capacity as the feminine part of the divinity and as the Oral Torah, "she illuminates the world" in a double sense: she makes possible God's presence among human beings, while also enabling Israel to fulfill the Torah. Accordingly, since God has surrendered to Israel through his Shekhinah, it is not only Israel that is affected by whether and how it fulfills the Torah, but God, as well.[49] Therefore, the Shekhinah reacts to Israel's behavior and is herself affected by it. When Israel sins, then the Shekhinah, too, suffers; and when they do God's will, then she also benefits:

> What is this like? Like a King who had a [beautiful] spouse, and he had children from her. He loved them and raised them, but they went astray. He then hated both them and their mother. Their mother went to them and said: "My children, why do you [do] this that your father hates both you and me?" [She spoke to them in this manner] until they had remorse and did again the will of their father. When their father saw this, he loved them as much as he did in the beginning. He then also remembered[50] their mother.[51]

Again the King is God, his spouse the Shekhinah, and the children are Israel. Thus the Shekhinah is again portrayed in her dual role as the female partner in the divine realm and as the mother of the divine couple's children. In the latter function, she is responsible for her children's actions, and accordingly "hated" (a notably strong expression) by her husband as a result of the children's bad behavior. As Israel's mother, she has become — despite her divine origins — part of Israel. In fact, she is identified with

Israel to such a degree that her own destiny stands dependent on them (her children). Therefore, it is she who must persuade Israel to fulfill the Commandments and to atone for their sins, so that God will again love them *and their mother*, since it is only through her that God loves Israel and only through Israel that he loves her. Although this interpretation appears to go too far, the parable almost conveys the impression that God loves Israel more than the Shekhinah and that the most important task of the mother is to reconcile the "children" with their "father"! Only when the children repent and return to their father, does he "remember" their mother; only then does he set her up again in her position as his beloved spouse.

Another mythical image of the three-way relationship between God, his spouse and mother of his children, and Israel rests on the distinction between the primordial light of the creation (Gen. 1:3) and the natural light that separates night from day (Gen. 1:14). As we have seen, the hidden primordial light is identified with the third Sefirah, "Understanding,"[52] while the natural light, which illuminates the earthly world, is identified with the tenth Sefirah, the Shekhinah and the Oral Torah.[53] The following exegesis describes the intimate connection between the two lights and Israel:

> "And the glow (*nogah*) will be like light (*'or*)." One day the glow that was taken from the first light will be like [the] light [itself], if my children keep the Torah and commandments that I gave to teach them, as it is written (Prov. 1:8): "Hear my son, the discipline of your father, and do not abandon the instruction (*torah*) of your mother." And it is written (Hab. 3:4): "Rays go forth from his hand, and his hidden force is there." What is "his hidden force"? This is the light that he stored away and hid, as it is written (Ps. 31:20): "that you have hidden away for those who fear you." What remains for us is that which "you have accomplished for those who find shelter in you (ibid.)" — in this world: who keep your Torah, observe your commandments, and sanctify your great name, uniting[54] it secretly and publicly".[55]

Although the primordial light and the natural light, the third and the tenth Sefirah, are separated, they can nevertheless be united, if Israel keeps the Torah. Israel's fulfillment of the Torah leads to the union — or better still, the *re-union* — of the natural light with the primordial light, the Oral Torah with the Written Torah, the Shekhinah with "Understanding" (*binah*). When Israel sanctifies God's great name, they unite it. Here, this can mean nothing else but that they unite the ten Sefirot: the Shekhinah will return to her original place (the third Sefirah), and all of the Sefirot will become one. Whether this is possible at any time or only in the future (perhaps in the messianic age of redemption) is left unspecified. The accent, however, appears to be placed more on the present, namely on the act of unification of the Sefirot as always possible (as well as the opposite movement, their unfolding anew into the ten divine potencies).[56]

To summarize briefly: The Shekhinah is God's feminine potency and as such is the lowest and, to a certain extent, the weakest of the divine forces in their dynamic interplay with one another. But at the same time, she is the most important and strongest among them, because she unites within herself the flow of all of the other energies. She bridges the heavenly and the earthly realms, not only because of her position on the borderline between the divinity and the human world, but because she is, above all, God's own embodiment in the world. Through her God enters the world, and her only task is to unite Israel with God. If she succeeds in this, she will not only lead Israel to God, but she herself will return to her divine origin. By taking up residence amidst the people of Israel, she has made the destiny of Israel her own. She is responsible for Israel, and Israel likewise for her. Only through her does Israel have access to God, just as her (re-)union with her divine spouse ultimately depends on Israel. Because she alone belongs to both worlds, it is only through her that the earthly world can be reconciled with the heavenly one and only through her that humankind can be united with God. The feminine potency is the key to both worlds. Without her, the heavenly world would be incomplete, and the earthly world would neither exist nor be able to find its way back to its creator.

PART II

THE QUEST FOR ORIGINS

❖ 7 ❖

GNOSIS

MODERN SCHOLARSHIP still stands in astonishment before this powerful myth about God's femininity and has not gotten very far in explaining its origins. The inner Jewish line of tradition from the biblical Wisdom literature through Philo, the Rabbinical Shekhinah, and early medieval Jewish philosophy is certainly inadequate to explain the bahiric concept of a dynamic life of God, including a female potency through which he reaches down to the earth. Some of the ideas developed in the Wisdom literature and in particular in Philo certainly come close to what we encounter in the Bahir, or, to put it differently, one could read these earlier traditions in the light of the Bahir and discover some surprising similarities (for example, there is clearly a "female potency through which God reaches down to earth" in the Wisdom literature). Nevertheless, there are important differences. Nowhere in the Wisdom literature—with the possible exception of Sapientia Salomonis—is the female potency regarded as part of God himself, of his inner divine structure. In contrast to the biblical Wisdom literature, Philo does conceive of the Godhead as including some kind of a feminine dimension, but here the major obstacle remains: No one would want to claim that the authors/editors of the Bahir had any direct or indirect access to the writings of Philo. His ideas were continued and developed further by Christianity, rather than Judaism, and there is no evidence whatsoever that the Bahir, in whichever stage of its redactional process, was influenced by Philo.

What then of Gnosis, the other potential source of influence that immediately comes to mind? This possibility has been propagated vehemently and suggestively by Scholem, the first scholar to deal seriously and extensively with the question of the origin of the Bahir.[1] Scholem sees two potential gnostic sources behind the bahiric tradition of the Shekhinah. One is inspired by the parable of the King's daughter who comes from a faraway place, from the side of light, and who illuminates the world. This parable, he argues, "corresponds in a surprising manner to the 'daughter of light' in the gnostic bridal hymn in the *Acts of Thomas* and similar well-known gnostic texts" (by the latter he means hymns like the Hymn of the Pearl or the Hymn of the Soul, which Hans Jonas had taken to be gnostic). Although he admits that the "daughter of light" in the *Acts of Thomas* can be interpreted not only as the "lower Sophia" (i.e., the embodiment of Wisdom on earth), but also as the gnostic redeemer or the human soul that returns to her original place, he nevertheless sees some close parallels between the bahiric parables and the gnostic myth of Wisdom, therefore favoring its interpretation as the "lower Sophia." Among the close parallels that he mentions are common motifs such as the 32 paths of Wisdom in the Bahir,[2] with the strange and as yet unexplained praise by the "thirty-two" in the Greek text of the bridal hymn,[3] and the notion of the King's daughter as "the reflection which was taken from the primordial light,"[4] as compared to Sophia, of whom it is said: "the reflection (*apaugasma*) of the kings[5] is in her."[6]

Here, the identification of the bride with the lower Sophia is just as problematic as are the motifs allegedly common in both texts. Of the possible identifications of the gnostic bride, the human soul is the most likely, and the common motifs are more than random. The "thirty-two" in the bridal hymn are indeed strange, but the bahiric source for this is clearly the *Sefer Yetzirah* (as Scholem duly acknowledges). Thus, there is no reason to establish any particular link with any gnostic text. And as far as the *apaugasma* in the bridal hymn is concerned, this is obviously inspired by Sapientia Salomonis 7:26.[7] Consequently, one could just as easily argue for the influence of Sapientia Salomonis on the Bahir, as opposed to the gnostic bridal hymn.

The second source that Scholem identifies as the possible background of the bahiric Shekhinah and regards as gnostic must be taken more seriously. It is Irenaeus's version of the Valentinian form of Gnosis, whose notion of the Sophia (or rather the twofold Sophia) he describes as follows: "The Gnostics, especially those of the Valentinian school, developed the idea of two aeons that are both called Sophia. One, the 'upper Sophia,' is high above, in the world of the pleroma; the other, however, which is also related to the symbolism of the 'virgin of light,' is found at its lower end. The gnostic myth of the cosmic drama told of the fall of the lower Sophia, which succumbed to the temptation of the hyle and fell from the pleroma into the lower worlds, where it is either wholly, or at least in certain parts of its luminous being, 'in exile.'"[8] The key words in this description, which is clearly influenced by Hans Jonas's *Gnosis und spätantiker Geist*,[9] are the "upper" and "lower Sophia," the "fall" of the lower Sophia, the "temptation of the hyle," and the subsequent "exile" of the lower Sophia in the material world. Scholem equates the "upper" and the "lower" Sophia with the bahiric location of the Shekhinah in the third and tenth Sefirah respectively, putting a strong emphasis on the "exile" of both the Sophia and the Shekhinah. In fact, the "exile" serves as his major basis for comparison between the gnostic Sophia and the bahiric Shekhinah: "Here it is important to note that the identification of the Shekhinah as a divine hypostasis, with the gnostic Sophia, could make use, as the most important *tertium comparationis*, of the idea of exile in the lower world. This was all the easier once a distinction was established . . . between God and the Shekhinah."[10] From this, he arrives at the final conclusion: "Our investigation therefore constrains us to admit the assumption that Oriental sources originating in the world of gnosticism influenced the elaboration of the symbolism of the Book *Bahir* or that fragments relating to the Shekhinah in that work themselves belong to such a stratum."[11]

As is the case quite often with Scholem, however, he is not as unequivocal as he might first sound. In his article on the Shekhinah, he not only tones down his remark about the exile of the Shekhinah (here, he suddenly declares: "*Sefer ha-Bahir* does not call this an exile of the *Shekhinah*—such a notion is not really developed in this book—but rather seems to imply that it is her destiny to dwell in the lower realms"),[12] but also raises a completely different possibility: "The images used for this relationship [between God and the Shekhinah] in the *Bahir* appear in all their original freshness, whether they were taken from the legacy of Gnostic speculation in late antiquity *or whether they took shape in the course of the creative reflection of anonymous Jewish God-seekers of the twelfth century upon the meaning of the images of their own tradition*."[13] So, in the end—despite his bold declaration that certain passages in the Bahir relating to the Shekhinah (!) may belong to a stratum (!) of early gnostic sources—Scholem leaves himself a way out of his gnostic preoccupation and allows for an inner Jewish line of development, possibly even implying some sort of early Jewish influence on the classical gnostic tradition, a Jewish "precursor" to the Gnosis.[14]

Let us look then more closely at the gnostic systems and compare our findings with Scholem's suggestions and conclusions. I will begin with the Valentinian form of the gnostic myth because this is the only version to which Scholem had access when he wrote about the Bahir (after sources for pre-Valentinian forms of Gnosis later became available through the Nag Hammadi Codices, Scholem never returned to the question of the gnostic origin of the Bahir). First of all, there is clearly an "upper" and "lower" Sophia in Irenaeus's account of the Valentinian Gnosis: Sophia and Achamoth.[15] The upper one remains completely within the divine realm of the aeons, held back and put into her proper place by "Limit"; the lower one is decisively located in the material world. Yet, the "split" between Sophia and Achamoth does not occur because of any "temptation of the hyle," the material world. On the contrary: the "primordial catastrophe" (to put it in terms of the later Lurianic Kabbalah) occurs because of an excessive amount of desire and love on the part of Sophia. In her passion and desire for the Father, she resists the further process of unfolding the aeons; instead, she wants to return to the Father and to be dissolved in his universal and undivided essence. In other words, she wants to become one with the Father again and thus resists the process of creation.[16] Accordingly, Achamoth, the lower Sophia, does not "fall" into the mundane world, but rather is the "materialization" of the upper Sophia's overflowing passion and love — and as such represents the first step in the creation of the material world. To be sure, this is not described in positive terms and certainly not something the Father wanted to happen. Nevertheless, it is not as negative, actively negative, as Scholem seems to propose. One could describe this as an "exile" of the lower Sophia in the material world, but this description is not particularly illuminating. The material world was brought into existence by separating Achamoth from Sophia. Therefore Achamoth is responsible for the material world, and by redeeming and restoring her to her proper place in the divine realm, the material world will be redeemed as well (or to put it differently: the material world will be redeemed *with* and *through* Achamoth).

If Scholem's description of the Valentinian Gnosis, which he uses as his point of comparison with the Bahir, is not entirely concordant with our reading of the sources, then we get an even more different form of the Gnosis when we take into consideration the earlier manifestation of the gnostic myth as we know it from, for instance, the Apocryphon of John. Here again, we have the pattern of a dual appearance of "Wisdom": Barbelo and Sophia. Barbelo is the Second Principle, and as such the first emanation of the Father; Sophia is the very last of the divine aeons, on the borderline between the spiritual and the material world. So there is a distinction between an "upper" and "lower" Sophia, but, in contrast to the Valentinian Gnosis, both Barbelo and Sophia belong to the spiritual realm of the aeons. Unlike the Valentinian Gnosis, where Achamoth is the "excretion" of the upper Sophia's passion and, as such, part of the material world, here the process of the creation of the mundane world starts through the lower Sophia and within the divine realm. Thus, the distinction between the divine and the material world is less sharp and clearcut than in the Valentinian Gnosis. Moreover, in the Valentinian Gnosis, the fatal "mistake" of the upper Sophia occurred because, in her overflowing desire, she was directed backwards, toward the Father. In the Apocryphon of John, however, the break in the cosmic drama happens when the lower Sophia acts without her male partner and without the approval of the Father. It is the product of this disruptive and "independent" nature of Sophia, namely Ialdabaoth, who is cast away from the spiritual world and initiates the process of creating the counterworld of the material universe.

Finally, and most importantly, there is nothing in the earlier gnostic myth that supports the idea of a fall or exile of the lower Sophia. It is doubtful even in the Valentinian Gnosis, but here such an idea is simply wrong. As we have seen, Sophia/Life/Afterthought is sent down into the material world by Barbelo to rectify her "mistake." Thus, it is Sophia herself who acts as healer of the cosmic break, the ultimate redeemer, in contrast to the Valentinian Gnosis where this task is relegated to Christ. When it comes to the task of redemption, the Apocryphon of John may even blur the distinction between Barbelo and Sophia and also have Barbelo descend into the material world. Barbelo and Sophia, the dual manifestation of Wisdom, are reunited, so to speak, in "Wisdom's" attempt to redeem the material world and to lead it back to the spiritual realm of the aeons.

Thus with regard to Scholem's analysis of the Bahir's gnostic background we arrive at a quite paradoxical conclusion. Scholem's results are not particularly convincing, on the one hand, because he relies exclusively on the Valentinian form of the Gnosis (although this is not his fault), and on the other hand, because his interpretation of this strand of the Gnosis is guided by Hans Jonas's very peculiar reading of the texts, overemphasizing, to say the least, the notion of Sophia's "fall" into the material world and her subsequent "exile." If we read the Valentinian Gnosis slightly differently, however, above all taking into account the pre-Valentinian myth of creation, Scholem's results become much more meaningful. So, ironically, Scholem is right, but for the wrong reasons. The "gnostic myth," as it can be reconstructed today, is much closer to the Bahir than he thought or could prove.[17]

If we apply our interpretation of the gnostic myth to the concept of the Shekhinah in the Bahir, we must admit that there are some stunning and rather unexpected similarities. A gnostic exegete like the author of the Apocryphon of John could read the Bahir as follows: There is an upper Shekhinah (Barbelo), who belongs to the uppermost part of the sefirotic system (if we equate the "Father" with the first Sefirah, she is not the first emanation of the Godhead, and thus not located in the second Sefirah, but can be identified with the third Sefirah, *Binah*). And there is a lower Shekhinah (Sophia), the tenth Sefirah, located at the borderline between the divine and the mundane realms. Moreover, it is this Shekhinah that is sent down into the material world to redeem it and to lead it back to its "Father," God. Although her task proves to be difficult, in the end she will no doubt succeed, and will not only have the mundane world returned to its origin, but she herself will also be reunited with her upper manifestation.

As far as the place and function of God's feminine manifestation is concerned, the parallels between the gnostic myth and the Bahir are quite suggestive. There is, however, nothing in the Bahir that resembles the role that the lower Sophia plays in the process of the emanation of the material world. In the Bahir, the Shekhinah is certainly not responsible for the creation of the mundane world. She is crucial in redeeming Israel (and with them "their" world), but she has nothing to do with creation (in contrast to the ancient Wisdom tradition). Yet even here the difference is not as great as it may first seem. As we have seen, in distinguishing between Barbelo and Sophia and holding "only" Sophia responsible for the creation of the material world, the gnostic myth accounts for the origin of evil, which is relegated to a "lower" part of the divine realm, but nevertheless originates within the structure of the aeonic system itself. I have argued that this notion is alien to the ancient Wisdom tradition, which does not concern itself with the (metaphysical) origin of evil.

This is quite in contrast to the Bahir, which goes a step further and does address the question of the origin of evil—in fact, well beyond the biblical or the classical Rabbinical tradition, but again much closer to the gnostic myth. The strict monotheism of the Hebrew Bible, with its emphasis on God's absolute power of creation, has both good and evil equally originating in God's will, as part of his creation. This principle was given its classical formulation by the prophet Isaiah: "I am the Lord, and there is no one else, I form light and create darkness, I make peace and create evil, I the Lord do all these things."[18] Evil, along with its consequences, was deliberately created by God: "The Lord made everything for a purpose, even the wicked for an evil day."[19] Accordingly, Satan in the biblical book of Job is not a demonic counterpower acting of his own will, but on the contrary belongs to the "sons of God" (divine beings, angels), whose only power consists of testing Job on God's behalf.[20] This line has been followed by Rabbinic Judaism, which has a very realistic sense of sin and evil; for instance, the morning *Shema'* praises God as the creator of light *and* darkness. For the Rabbis, evil is part of creation, even of God's plan of creation.[21] Sin and death (as a consequence of sin) belong to history and as such have been integrated in God's creation. To put it differently and more pointedly: sin is what makes history move; it is the "engine" of history. Without the possibility of sin, of deciding for or against sin, there would be no humanity and thus no history.[22] All human beings would still be in the state of purity, like the angels. But this precisely is the difference between angels and humankind according to Rabbinic Judaism: the angels cannot sin—even if they wished so— but human beings have to confront the choice of good and evil. When Adam and Eve decided to follow the evil inclination, they decided in favor of sin—and set history into motion.[23]

Now the Bahir moves evil backwards, so to speak, from creation into God himself. Like the gnostic myth, it tries to answer the question: if God has created the world knowing that this would include sin, how do sin and evil relate to God? The Bahir's answer is not yet very systematic, but it is the first, still archaic and dark attempt in Judaism to locate evil in the sefirotic structure of the Godhead. The first reference to evil is in an interpretation of the famous *tohu* and *bohu in* Genesis 1:2: "When God began to create heaven and earth, the earth was chaotic (*tohu*) and desolate (*bohu*)":[24]

> What is the meaning of the verse (Eccles. 7:14): "Also one opposite the other was made by God"?
>
> He created desolation (*bohu*) and placed it in peace, and he created chaos (*tohu*) and placed it in evil.
>
> Desolation is in peace, as it is written (Job 25:2): "He makes peace in his high places." This teaches us that Michael, the prince of God's right, is water and hail, while Gabriel, the prince of God's left, is fire. The two are reconciled by the prince of peace. This is the meaning of the verse (Job 25:2): "He makes peace in his high places."

tohu	*bohu*
left	right
Gabriel	Michael
fire	water
evil	peace

At first, this seems quite harmless, basically following the interpretation of the classical midrash: Michael is water and hail, and Gabriel is fire, and how do they exist (in heaven) one alongside the other? God, or rather his angel of peace, makes peace among them, so that they can live peacefully with each other.[25] There are, however, some details that go beyond the Rabbinic midrash, in particular the addition of peace versus evil to the contrast between the two sides (in the midrash *God* makes peace between Michael and Gabriel), and the identification of Michael, water and peace with the right side of God, and of Gabriel, fire and evil with the left side, respectively. (This is clearly a further development of the two principles of love/mercy and judgment/justice, which are located in God, according to the midrash, and fight with each other.)[26] Hence, we are speaking in fact about God and not about the angels, as becomes clear also from the following text:[27]

> Strength (*gevurah*) is the officer of all the holy forms to the left of the Holy One, Blessed be He. He is Gabriel. And the officer of the

holy forms to the right is Michael. In the middle is truth. This is
Uriel, the officer of all the holy forms [in the center].

strength (*gevurah*)
Gabriel   Michael
left   right

truth (*emet*)
Uriel
middle

The "holy forms" obviously are the (ten) Sefirot, the emanations
and potencies within God. Thus, the text refers to the distribu-
tion of the divine emanations, and the "left" and "right" side
clearly correspond to the fourth and fifth Sefirah, Love/Mercy
and Judgment/Justice; even the name "Strength" is the name
given to the fifth Sefirah in most of the subsequent systems. Now
we understand also why in the bahiric system of the ten Sefirot
(or "words") the "Great Fire" is located in the fifth Sefirah:[28] it is
the origin of evil, which accordingly originates within God himself! "Truth," located in the middle and under the supervision of
the angel Uriel, seems to be the sixth Sefirah in the subsequent
sefirotic system, later called *Tif'eret* ("Beauty"), which mediates
between "Mercy" and "Judgment."

That evil originates within God, emanating from his fifth Sefirah, is stated even more clearly in the following text:[29]

What is [this attribute of God]? It is the Satan. This teaches us that
the Holy One, Blessed be He, has an attribute whose name is evil.
It is to the north of the Holy One, Blessed be He, as it is written
(Jer. 1:14): "From the north will evil come forth, upon all the inhabitants of the earth." Any evil that comes to "all the inhabitants
of the earth" comes from the north.

What is this attribute [or: principle]? It is the form of the [left]
hand. It has many messengers, and the name of them all is evil,
evil. Some of them are great, and some are small, but they all bring
guilt to the world.

This is because chaos is toward the north. Chaos (*tohu*) is nothing
other than evil. It confounds the world and causes people to sin.
Every evil impulse (*yetzer ha-ra'*) that exists in humankind comes
from there.

This is a difficult text that speaks in strange and mythical images. Some of them we know already: the left hand or side of God, which is identified with chaos (evil). It is made entirely clear, however, that this evil principle, the principle of God's justice and judgment, is one of the emanations of God, which rest in God and through which he acts on the outside world. Most importantly, there exists a close relation between the metaphysical presence of evil rooted in God and the ethical evil that is a consequence of the evil impulse or inclination in human beings: in quite a naïve way the evil impulse of human beings is led back to the evil principle in God ("all evil that comes to the inhabitants of the earth comes from the north"). Thus, the evil impulse, all human evil on earth, is not only created by God (as the Bible and the Rabbis argue), but is the result of the location of evil within God, in the system of the ten Sefirot.

Here we have for the very first time, quite bluntly and straightforwardly, a tone that is to become a keynote of the later Kabbalah: evil belongs not only to the world and to humanity, but also to God. What we do not find, however, is any affiliation of evil with the Shekhinah, the feminine principle. Evil is firmly located in the fifth Sefirah and never connected with the tenth or the third Sefirah, respectively. Thus the Bahir lacks the close connection of evil and the material world with the feminine element in the divine realm, which is so striking in the gnostic myth. This next step is left to the subsequent systems of the Kabbalah, most prominently in the Zohar, where different locations of evil within the Godhead are suggested[30] and the Shekhinah combines in herself the forces of mercy and judgment, good and evil.[31]

Nevertheless, in placing the Shekhinah on the borderline between the divine and the mundane worlds and in locating evil within the divine structure, the Bahir comes very close to the gnostic myth.[32] This makes the question of the possibility of any historical relationship between the two systems all the more pressing and disturbing, taking into consideration the geographical ("Orient" versus Provence) and the temporal gap (first centuries CE versus around 1200). Before returning to this question, I will first address the much more immediate historical context of the Bahir: Christianity in France in the twelfth century CE.

❊ 8 ❊

CHRISTIANITY

UNTIL very recently scholars have hardly paid any attention to the immediate context surrounding late twelfth-century Jewry in Southern France to account for the Bahir's appearance there.[1] Scholem, who so fervently insists on the heretical elements of the Gnosis as the direct source of the Bahir, conspicuously avoids placing the book in the cultural context whence it originated. This is all the more surprising since the Jews of twelfth-century Provence did not live in a ghetto nor in otherworldly conventicles, but in the midst of Christian communities. To be sure, Scholem does consider the "gnostic" movements of the Cathari and the Albigenses, which flourished in Southern France and Provence in the twelfth century, as the missing link between the early Gnosis and the Bahir. He tries very hard to discover evidence of connections between the Cathar movement and the early Kabbalists of the Bahir, but he finds no conclusive proof of mutual influence nor of direct historical connections. Despite some shared assumptions (for example, a higher world separated from the lower one, the coupling of masculine and feminine potencies in the upper world, the problem of evil) and motifs (for instance, the transmigration of souls), he discards the idea of "immediate influences," but rather argues in favor of a "common source in the ancient gnosis."[2] In particular, there is nothing in these heretical Christian movements that resembles the role the Shekhinah plays in the bahiric system of the divine potencies and as God's messenger on earth.[3]

Looking more closely at the Christian environment of Provencal Jewry, one immediately comes across a phenomenon that has been completely ignored by Scholem and his followers: the veneration of the Virgin Mary, which grows in Western Christendom during the tenth and eleventh centuries and almost explodes in the twelfth century, primarily due to the mediation and ardent promulgation of the monks of the Cistercian order. It was the

Cistercians who, with their churches and monasteries dedicated to her and the *Salve Regina, Mater Misericordiae,* sung daily at their vespers, carried the love and veneration of Mary at first through France and then throughout Europe. The service in the monasteries of the Cistercians (and of the Dominicans, from the beginning of the thirteenth century) became the center of the veneration of the Virgin; Mary, the Mother of God and Queen of heaven, was the focus of many of their sermons.

EASTERN CHURCH

The veneration of Mary had long been the domain of Eastern Christendom; only slowly and hesitantly was it accepted by Western theologians, coming into full blossom in the High Middle Ages. The full doctrine of Mary was gradually developed in the East and accepted, albeit with much less excitement, in the West.[4] The first decisive step leading to the exaltation and veneration of Mary was taken at the council of Ephesus (431 CE), which was instigated by the debate between Nestorius, the Patriarch of Constantinople, and Cyril of Alexandria on the divine/human nature of Jesus and the question of whether his mother Mary should appropriately be called *theotokos* (lit. "she who gives birth to God") or *anthrōpotokos* (lit. "she who gives birth to man"). Whereas Nestorius wavered between *theotokos, theodochos, anthrōpotokos,* and *christotokos,* concerned lest the Virgin be seen as a goddess,[5] Cyril, and with him the council of Ephesus, emphasized the complete "union" (*henōsis*) of both the divine and human nature of Jesus; thus, they concluded that Mary gave birth to neither a purely divine nor a purely human being, but rather to the perfect and unique combination of the two: the God made flesh. From this, it follows that Mary is not just *anthrōpotokos,* but truly *theotokos,* and in the full sense of the word: the mother of the God/Man Jesus. After the condemnation of Nestorius as a heretic, Cyril exultantly and triumphantly praises Mary, the *theotokos* and eternal virgin (the two are joined at a very early stage):

> Joyously I see the assembly of the saints, you who have all readily gathered together, called by the holy and God-bearing Mary, the everlasting Virgin. . . . We hail you, God-bearing Mary, venerated

jewel of the whole world, the inextinguishable lamp, the crown of virginity, the scepter of orthodoxy, the indestructible temple, receptacle of the inscrutable, mother and virgin. . . . We hail you, who have limited the Unlimited in the lap of the holy Virgin Mother. Through her the Trinity is honored, through her the cross is held to be revered and honored throughout the whole universe. Through her heaven rejoices; through her the angels and archangels are pleased; through her demons are chased away; through her the devil, the tempter, fell from heaven; through her the fallen creation will be taken up into heaven; through her the whole of creation, which was caught up in idolatry, came to recognize the truth; . . . through her the nations will be led to repentance. . . . Through her the apostles proclaim the salvation of the nations, through her the dead will be resurrected, through her the kings will rule, through the holy Trinity.[6]

This comes, indeed, close to a deification of Mary. Christology moves toward Mariology; through the physical relationship between her and her divine son, Mary partakes in her son's divinity—precisely the development Nestorius tried to prevent. The repeated "through her" can be read "innocently" as a christological statement; that is, it is only because Mary gave birth to God in human form that redemption takes place. But it can also be understood in a more radical way: it is only "through her" that the holy Trinity is venerated; it is only "through her" that the fallen creation returns to heaven; it is only "through her" that the dead rise from death, and so on. This goes far beyond what Nestorius could tolerate and even what the council of Ephesus probably had in mind. Mary begins to acquire a unique position within the redemption process; she becomes the necessary *mediatrix* ("mediator") between God and human beings and assumes, together with her son Jesus Christ, the role of *corredemptrix* ("co-redeemer").[7]

After the councils of Ephesus and Chalcedon (451 CE) devotion to Mary and the process of her deification increased significantly. Building on earlier, pre-Ephesus foundations, popular piety succeeded in gradually integrating the cult of pagan goddesses into the worship of Mary, most notably among them Kybele in Syria, Isis in Egypt, and Artemis in Asia Minor (or some syncretistic combination of major characteristics of all of them).[8] It is her motherhood, her function as intercessor, and her praise as the Queen of Heaven that relate Mary to these goddesses and that facilitate her "usurpation" of their role as the mothers of gods and of their functions. Prayers praise her as *theotokos*, and she is seen more and more as the mediator of the faithful's prayers. Images not only of Jesus, but also of Mary come into fashion. Most notable among them is the depiction of Mary in San Apollinare Nuovo in Ravenna (middle of the sixth century), where she is seated opposite Jesus on almost the same golden throne. Both are flanked by angels, with a procession of female martyrs walking towards her and a procession of male martyrs walking towards him. Moreover, the imperial couple, Justinian and Theodora, here represent the earthly counterparts of the divine "couple," Jesus and Mary. Festivals of Jesus also commemorate Mary, and at the end of the fourth century CE Eastern Christendom even begins to celebrate the first festivals dedicated solely to her.

One decisive step in the veneration of Mary is the tradition of her (bodily) assumption into heaven. The earlier church knew nothing of Mary's bodily assumption, but rather commemorated her death (and at most quarreled over its exact location, namely Jerusalem or Ephesus). The New Testament provides no details about the circumstances of her death, let alone about what happened to her body after she died. It is not before the end of the fifth century that apocryphal traditions appear that deal with this question and hint at the possibility that not just her soul was taken up into heaven, but also her body.[9] The legend, circulated in many languages and various versions, has become known under the common title "De Transitu Beatae Mariae Virginis."[10] The different versions disagree about many details,[11] but the overall structure is more or less the same: Mary prays for her death (in Jerusalem), an angel or Christ himself announces the forthcoming death, and the apostles assemble in her house to accompany her during the last hours of her life. Christ appears and takes her soul, and the apostles carry her body to the burial place (in some versions the valley of Josaphat). Some wicked Jews intervene and try to disturb the funeral or to kidnap the holy body, but a miracle occurs: the hands of the Jews stick to the coffin to be cut off by an angel. The Jews, however, repent their evil deed and are healed by the apostles (Peter). Finally the apostles bury the body, and after some time (here the versions diverge most:

immediately after the funeral, after three days [!], or much later), Christ resurrects the body, which is carried away into heaven. For example, the Latin version published by Tischendorf recounts the following finale:

> Then the apostles laid the body with great honor to rest into the monument, in exceedingly weeping and singing love and sweetness. And suddenly a light from heaven surrounded them and, whereas they fell on the ground, the holy body was taken up by angels into heaven. (*Tunc apostoli cum magno honore posuerunt corpus in monumento, flendo et canendo prae nimio amore et dulcedine. Et subito circumfulsit eos lux de celo, et cadentes in terram, corpus sanctum ab angelis in celum est assumptum.*)[12]

Hence the legend clearly distinguishes between the assumption of the soul and of the body, but it is equally clearly concerned to make sure that, in the end, the body is resurrected and reunited with its soul in heaven. This is particularly true for a sixth-century text, pseudepigraphically ascribed to bishop Melito of Sardis (d. 180 CE), in which Christ asks the apostles what he should do with the body of his mother three days after the funeral. Peter suggests that he should resurrect it and accompany it into heaven (*ita resuscitans matris corpusculum, tecum eam deduceres laetantem in caelum*).[13] The archangel Michael brings her soul, and Jesus resurrects her body by means of a dramatic incantation-like speech: "Raise up, you who are closest to me, my dove, tent of glory, vessel of life, heavenly temple; and since you have not experienced the blemish of guilt (acquired) through intercourse, you will not suffer from the resolution of your body in the grave" (*Surge, proxima mea, columba mea, tabernaculum gloriae, vasculum vitae, templum caeleste; et dum non sensisti labem delicti per coitum, non patiaris resolutionem corporis in sepulcro*).[14] Finally, Christ returns with his resurrected mother to paradise: "*et haec dicens Dominus, cum canentibus angelis et matre sua receptus est in paradiso.*"[15]

In the seventh century the homily on Mary's death by the archbishop John of Thessalonike (d. 649) became so popular that it was integrated into Byzantine liturgy and inspired the frequent depiction of Mary's death in Byzantine art. Here, too, her soul is first taken up into heaven, and the bodily resurrection follows at a separate stage. This last step is described differently. In the

Greek version published by Tischendorf, the apostles stay at the grave for three days and listen to the songs of the angels, praising "Christ, our God, who was born from her" (*ton ex autēs techthenta*). After three days, the singing stops, and they conclude that Christ "had taken up her unblemished and precious body into paradise."[16] Another version, which is probably the oldest and most authentic one[17] and which is part of the Byzantine liturgy for August 15 even today, has a much more dramatic finale, drawing a striking parallel with Jesus' resurrection: when the apostles open the grave after three days they find nothing but the shrouds and understand that God had resurrected her.[18]

It is precisely the close connection between Mary's status as *theotokos* and mother of God (*theomētēr*), without any blemish and original sin, and her final assumption into heaven in both her soul *and* body, that constitutes the foundation of the veneration of Mary as developed in the Eastern church. These characteristics define her relationship with God on the one hand and human beings on the other. For John of Damascus (d. 749), she becomes the bride chosen by the Father, who, as it were, marries her through the mediation of the Holy Spirit;[19] for Germanus of Constantinople, she is the "cause of all salvation," "*mediatrix* of all sinners," because "nobody will be saved but through you, *theotokos*."[20] In the eighth century CE, the cult of the Virgin Mary was well established in the Eastern church and spreading rapidly.[21]

WESTERN CHURCH

The Occident was much less preoccupied with Mary's role in the process of salvation. To be sure, the *theotokos* of the council of Ephesus was confirmed in 430 CE by a Roman synod, and the doctrine of *Dei genetrix* or *Deipara* subsequently entered Western theology and liturgy. Fathers of the church, such as Ambrose and Augustine, were, however, much more concerned about the correct doctrine regarding Christ (by virtue of fending off Arianism and Manichaeism) than belief about Mary. For Ambrose, Mary is certainly not without sin because this can be said of God alone.[22] He even finds it necessary to warn against the adoration of Mary: "Mary was the Temple of God and not the God of the Temple (*Maria erat templum Dei, non Deus templi*); hence He alone has to be worshipped who was present in the Temple."[23] The legend of Mary's bodily assumption into heaven reached the West but here, too, the reaction was much more reserved. Although Gregory of Tours (d. 594) quotes the legend and clearly knows the tradition about the separate assumption of her soul and her body,[24] the belief in her bodily assumption was less than assured even in the eighth century.[25] Things changed gradually and slowly in the ninth and tenth centuries. Hrabanus Maurus (d. 856) praises Mary as the eternal Queen (*regina regnabis in aeternum*), to whom Christ has given sovereignty over the heavens (*regina coelorum*),[26] and he seems to be the first in the Western church to emphasize her mediating role: "she was considered to be worthy of entrusting us with insistent pleading to our Lord Christ in heaven" (*ipsa nos sedula prece Christo domino nostro commendare dignatur in coelis*).[27] The heyday of the veneration of Mary in the Occident would not begin, however, until the eleventh century, reaching its climax in the twelfth century. In what follows, I will survey some of the most important Christian theologians of the eleventh and twelfth centuries, in close proximity in time to the appearance of the Bahir around 1200.

PETER DAMIAN

One of the major figures of the reform movement in the eleventh century, attacking the moral decadence of the clergy and attempting to purify the church (by advocating, among other things, celibacy), was Peter Damian (1007–1072), the Benedictine monk and Cardinal from Italy. According to him, Mary is naturally the *genetrix Dei*, and both *domina mundi* and *coeli regina*.[28] But Peter also speculates about her function in the divine plan of history: she was "chosen and pre-selected before the creation of the world in the deliberations of the eternal wisdom" (*ante constitutionem mundi in consilio aeternae sapientiae electe et praeelecta*).[29] Thus, he clearly establishes a connection between Mary and the biblical Wisdom. It is only after her birth that dawn broke for the human race; she "goes before the true light" (*veri praevia luminis*) and accordingly is called the "morning star within the mist which coruscates in the solstice of heaven in greatest brightness" (*stella matutina in medio nebulae, quae in coeli cardine summo splendore coruscans*).[30]

In particular, her assumption and place in heaven is described in great detail. The "royal Virgin is raised to the throne of God Father and replaced to the seat of the Trinity itself, . . . seated to the right of the Lord of strengths" (*Virgo regalis ad thronum Dei Patris evehitur, et in ipsius Trinitatis sede reposita . . . reginam sedentem a dextris Domini virtutum*).[31] This is an exceptional statement. Mary is not only included in the holy Trinity (she takes her proper place with the Trinity, which was assigned to her from the beginning), but even assumes the role of Jesus, in so far as the second part is obviously a reference to Mark 14: 62 where Jesus says of himself that he will be "seated at the right hand of the Power."[32] Whereas Jesus returns to the right of his Father, Mary returns to the right of her son, Jesus, and hence becomes part of the Trinity! Quite a different, and not less astonishing, image is evoked later on in the same sermon. Here it is said of Mary that she, "reclining upon the golden couch of the divine majesty, rests in the arms of her bridegroom, indeed her son" (*in aureo reclinatorio divinae majestatis incumbens, intra sponsi, imo Filii sui, brachia requiescit*).[33] This imagery, of course, is taken directly from the Song of Songs: Mary and Jesus are the loving couple, reunited in heaven. With his strange combination of *intra sponsi, imo Filii sui, brachia*, however, Peter is at pains to make it very clear that the couple must not be mistaken for a regular bride and bridegroom, but rather ought to be understood as mother and son.

Through her inclusion in the Holy Trinity, Mary becomes part of the process of salvation. It is to her that "all the power in heaven and earth was given" (*et data est tibi omnis potestas in coelo et in terra*)[34] — again a clear transference of power from Jesus to her.[35] She becomes essential for the blessedness of human-kind[36] and for the restoration of humanity, because God listens to her and follows her advice.[37] Moreover, it is only through her that God loves humankind: "I know, Lady, that you are the most blessed one and that you love us with insurmountable love, us whom, within you and through you, your Son and your God loves with greatest love. Who knows how often you cool off the wrath of the Judge when out of the presence of the Deity comes forth the power of judgement?" (*Scio, domina, quia benegnissima es, et amas nos amore invincibili, quos in te et per te Filius tuus et Deus tuus summa dilectione dilexit. Quis scit quotiens refrigeras iram Judicis, cum justitiae virtus a praesentia deitatis egreditur?*).[38]

Mary is the true *mediatrix* and *corredemptrix* through whom the flux of the divine love and blessings is channeled; it is she who ensures that the divine punishment is balanced by divine mercy.

HERMAN OF TOURNAY

Moving to the first half of the twelfth century and to France: Herman of Tournay (ca. 1090–ca. 1147), the Benedictine Abbot of Saint-Martin, presents another outstanding example of the well-educated and well-traveled clergy, often away on important church missions. Herman, too, emphasizes Mary's predetermined role in the salvation history and her identification with Wisdom: "The Lord had planted her from the beginning" (*a principio*), and this "beginning" is explicitly related to Proverbs 8:22 and Wisdom.[39] Mary is the Wisdom of Proverbs, and it is through her that the human race will be restored: "in his foreknowledge God had arranged and declared to restore the human race through her fruit" (*in praescientia sua Deus proposuerat et diffinierat per eius fructum reparare genus humanum*).[40] From this it follows that the incarnation of God through Mary was predetermined from the very beginning of creation. Mary is identified with the paradise of Genesis 2:8 ("The Lord God planted a garden in Eden, in the east, and placed there the man whom He had formed"): "this means, from the beginning he prepared a royal palace, in which he put his Son, co-equal and co-eternal, when he had formed man" (*id est paraverat aulam regiam a principio, in qua poneret Filium suum, coaequalem sibi et coaeternum, cum hominem formaverat*).[41] Immediately after man was created in the Garden of Eden, God "planted" his son Jesus in Mary, the pre-existent, or rather pre-created, Wisdom of Proverbs, to mend man's (Adam's) sin.

Mary's role as *mediatrix* between God and humanity is symbolized by the image of the body of the Church. Whereas Christ personifies the "head" of the Church and the community on earth its "body" from the shoulders downwards, Mary is the "neck," the link between head and body: "By the neck of the holy church our Lady is to be understood, who, as the mediator between God and humankind, while she gave birth to the Word Incarnate of God, as it were connected the head with the body,

Christ with the church, the Deity with our humankind" (*Collum ergo sanctae Ecclesiae competenter domina nostra intelligitur, quae inter deum et homines mediatrix existens, dum Dei Verbum incarnatum genuit, quasi caput corpori, Christum Ecclesiae, divinitatem humanitati nostrae conjuxit*).[42] Herman even goes so far as to put God and Mary on an equal footing, as bride and bridegroom. "God has created everything, and Mary has given birth to God, hence, since Mary gave birth to the Son of God, Mary has become the bride of God" (*Deus omnia creavit, et Maria deum generavit, et quia Dei Filium genuit Maria, sponsa utique Dei facta est Maria*). Accordingly, just as God is called "Father of all created things" (*Pater rerum creatarum*), so Mary can be called "Mother of all recreated things" (*Mater rerum recreatarum*).[43] This is again a very bold statement because it transfers to Mary a quality that is reserved for Jesus and only makes sense in a christological context (Mary can aptly be called *Mater rerum recreatarum* as the mother of Jesus only, and it is of course Jesus, not Mary, who ultimately "recreates" humankind). The way Herman puts it, however, comes very close to the notion of *corredemptrix*, Mary's collaboration in the process of redemption.

Since Mary, in her role as *corredemptrix*, has become the mother of all of humankind, it is because of her that Jesus is "our brother" and God "our Father." This close kinship of God, Mary, Jesus, and humankind is a common topos in many of the sermons. It is used, for instance, by Herman's contemporary Bernard of Clairvaux, as well as by Anselm of Canterbury in England at the end of the eleventh century.[44] The appropriate conclusion resulting from this kin relationship can only be that we do not have to fear God, the judge, because he has become, through Mary, our brother.[45] Therefore Mary, the *mediatrix* and *interventrix*, assumes the role of the one to whom human beings confess their sins — once again a role taken over from Jesus and only thinly disguised by the qualifying *post Deum*: "To you, our mediator, we flee for refuge, you, who is after God our only hope. To you we confess our sins. We beg you urgently to become the mediator and intercessor between us and God" (*Sed ad te confugientes, mediatrix nostra, quae est post Deum spes sola, tibi peccata nostra confitemur: teque inter nos et Deum mediatricem et interventricem fieri exoramus*).[46]

BERNARD OF CLAIRVAUX

The climax of Marian veneration was reached with the Cistercian Bernard of Clairvaux (1091–1153), the major figure of the monastic reform.[47] In his many sermons, particularly his sermons on the Song of Songs delivered between 1135 and 1153, he romanticizes the relationship between Christ, Mary, and humankind. Bernard is the preacher of love, who "uncovers a mystical system by which the Christian is transfigured by love."[48] God is the God of love, and through Christ his love transformed Mary and finally reached us, humankind, to enable us to take part in it.[49] The most appropriate source for this theology of love, of course, is the biblical book Song of Songs, in which Christ is the lover, whereas his bride can be the Church, the individual soul, the monks of Clairvaux, or the Virgin Mary. Bernard takes up many of the motifs that we have encountered so far, most notably in Peter Damian and Herman of Tournay, but probably the most outstanding characteristic of his sermons is his use of blatantly erotic language.

Mary is known in heaven in her "appearance" and "beauty" (*specie sua et pulchritudine sua*) and, appealing to the inhabitants of heaven, she even arouses the desire (*concupiscentia*) of the King himself.[50] The "King" sends a messenger to her (his angel), but when her "nard gave forth its fragrance" (Cant. 1:12), he cannot wait to see her and even arrives before his angel: "in his great desire he came to the Virgin, whom he loved, whom he had chosen for himself, whose beauty he desired, before his messenger arrived" (*nimio tamen pervolans desiderio praevenit suum nuntium ad Virginem quam amaverat, quam sibi elegerat, cuius decorem concupierat*).[51] The most explicit erotic language is used in the following interpretation of Canticles 1:1 in a sermon on Mary's assumption to heaven:

> However, who would even be in a position to imagine how the glorious Queen of the world left us today, with what reverential love the whole host of celestial armies rushed to meet her, with what hymns she was led to the throne of glory, with what radiant face, with what a cheerful expression, with what divine kisses was she taken up by her son and elevated above all creation! . . . Yes

indeed, blessed were the kisses which the mother pressed upon the lips of the infant, while she smiled at him as he sat on her virgin's lap. But shouldn't we deem even much happier those kisses which in blessed greeting she receives today from the mouth of him who sits on the throne to the right of the Father, when she ascends to the throne of glory, sings a nuptial hymn and says (Cant 1:2): "Let him kiss me with the kisses of his mouth."[52]

Mary's reunion with her son in heaven is not just the reunion of mother and son, but also that of bride and bridegroom. The imagery of Canticles overpowers the mother/son relationship; Mary and Jesus become the true lovers of Canticles who celebrate their wedding in heaven.[53]

Like his predecessors, Bernard emphasizes Mary's role in the process of salvation. He also identifies her with biblical Wisdom, who was created before the beginning of creation. The verse from Jesus Sirach 24:8 ("Then the creator of all things commanded me [Wisdom]; he, who created me decreed where I should dwell") is rendered in the Latin translation "he, who created me rested in my tent" (*et qui creavit me requievit in tabernaculo meo*).[54] Bernard applies this to God's "residence" in Mary; that is, his incarnation in her.[55] Mary is crucial and indispensable for the course of history. The salvation of humankind, the restitution of the world corrupted through Adam's and Eve's sin, depends solely on her, on her readiness to accept the conception of the Word Incarnate:

> The angel is waiting for your reply. It is time for him to return to the One who sent him.[56] We, too, are waiting for this merciful word, my Lady, who are miserably weighed down under a sentence of condemnation. The price of our salvation is being offered you. If you consent, we shall immediately be set free. We all have been made in the eternal Word of God, and look, we are dying.[57] In your brief reply we shall be restored and so brought back to life (*reficiendi, ut ad vitam revocemur*). Doleful Adam and his unhappy offspring, exiled from Paradise, implore you, kind Virgin, to give this answer. . . . For it the whole world is waiting, bowed down at your feet. And rightly so, because on your answer depends the comfort of the afflicted, the redemption of captives, the deliverance of the damned; the salvation of all the sons of Adam, your whole race. Give your answer quickly, my Virgin. My Lady, say this word which earth and hell and heaven itself are waiting

for. The very King and Lord of all, he who has so desired your beauty,[58] is waiting anxiously for your answer and assent, by which he no doubt proposes to save the world.[59] Him whom you pleased by your silence, you will please now even more by your words. He calls out to you from heaven:[60] "O fair among women, let me hear your voice!"[61]

From this it becomes clear that God's incarnation is not just a divine decree, but depends on Mary's consent. Salvation would have been impossible if she hadn't agreed to her decisive role in it. In other words: she takes an *active* part in the process of salvation. She is the *corredemptrix* in the true sense of the word: the redeemer together with God. Accordingly, when she receives the message of the angel and accepts it, it is not just Jesus who is with her and awaits her answer, but the holy Trinity altogether: "Not only the Lord, your Son, is with you, whom you clothe with your flesh, but also the Lord, the Holy Spirit, by whom you conceive, and the Lord, the Father, who begets whom you conceive."[62]

Mary is the new Eve. Whereas Eve was the instrument of temptation (*ministra seductionis*), Mary became the instrument of atonement (*ministra propitiationis*): "the former enticed into transgression, the latter became the channel of redemption" (*illa suggessit praevaricationem, haec ingessit redemptionem*).[63] As the true *mediatrix* and *interventrix*, she mediates between heaven and earth, and her mediation benefits not only humankind, but even God himself:

> For she has "become all things to all men,"[64] she has made herself "a debtor to the wise and to the unwise."[65] To all she opens wide the bosom of her mercy so that all may receive of her fullness:[66] captives deliverance, the sick health, the sad consolation, sinners pardon, the just grace, the angels joy, the whole blessed Trinity glory, and the person of the Son the substance of his human nature, so that "there is no one that can hide himself from the heat"[67] of her charity.[68]

Bernard explicitly addresses the problem of Mary's mediating role in relation to Jesus, who is supposed to be the only mediator between God and humankind. True, he argues, Jesus became our brother through Mary, and it is appropriate to use him as our advocate. But still, although he has become man, he nevertheless remained God, and therefore one might fear his divine majesty. What better advocate could there be with him than Mary![69] Mary is the mediatrix of the mediator: "We have need of another mediator to mediate between him [Christ] and us, and for this we can find none so well qualified as Mary."[70] The culmination of Bernard's attempt to describe Mary's mediating role is the image of the aqueduct. Mary is the aqueduct, which channels the divine blessings to all humankind on earth:

> You have already divined, dearest brethren, unless I mistake, to whom I allude under the image of an aqueduct which, receiving the fullness of the fountain from the Father's heart, has transmitted the same to us, if not as it is in itself, at least in so far as we can contain it. Yea, for you know to whom it was said, "Hail, full of grace!"[71] But shall we not wonder how such and so great an aqueduct could have been formed, the top of which—like the ladder which Jacob saw in vision[72]—was to reach to heaven, nay, to be lifted higher than the heavens, and to touch that living fountain of "the waters that are above the heavens"?[73] Even Solomon wondered at this, and, as if despairing of the possibility, cried out, "Who can find a valiant woman"?[74] In fact the reason why the streams of heavenly grace did not begin to flow down upon the human race for so long a time was this: that the precious aqueduct whereof I speak did not as yet mediate between God and humankind.[75]

God's mercy needs Mary in order to be fully channeled down to earth. Without Mary—and her consent to God's plan of salvation—salvation becomes impossible. No wonder that Mary is raised to a quasi-divine position. She is the Queen of heaven, elevated even above the angels, the "throne of grace" of Hebrews 4:16,[76] which humankind approaches "in order that we receive mercy and find grace" (ibid.). This is another bold transference from Jesus to Mary or, to put it differently, a deliberate play with theological fire, because Bernard certainly did not want to substitute Mary for Jesus, but nevertheless does precisely this, if taken literally. Mary is the *stella maris*, the "star under whose guidance and mediation we pass over the sea to our fatherland" (*ipsa est stella, cuius ducatu et interventu ad patriam transfretamus*).[77] Finally, she is identified with the "woman robed with the sun" of Revelation 12:1. Briefly pondering the possibility that the woman may be the Church, Bernard considers Mary a much more appropriate candidate:

> Not without reason, therefore, is Mary represented as clothed with the sun, since she has penetrated the unfathomable abyss of divine wisdom to a degree that is almost incredible; so that we can say of her that she is immersed in that ocean of inaccessible light as utterly as is possible to any created nature not deified by hypostatic union. She is plunged, I say, in that heavenly fire wherewith the prophet's lips were purified,[78] and wherewith the Seraphim are inflamed. For Mary has merited far more than the prophets or the Seraphim. To her it is due not merely to be lightly touched with that fire, but to be completely surrounded with it, to be utterly enveloped and absorbed in it. Most intense, undoubtedly, is the light and heat of this woman's clothing.[79]

The sun, of course, symbolizes divinity. Thus, unlike the angels or the prophets or any other human being, who are only touched by the divine fire, Mary is completely enclosed in it. She is transformed by it and becomes part of it; that is, part of the Godhead, the Trinity. It is certainly not by coincidence that the editor and German translator of this sermon finds it necessary to remark that this paragraph does not imply a "mystical deification (*theōsis*)" of Mary and to insist that her nature does not dissolve itself in God.[80] But this is precisely what seems to be at stake here, despite the translator's cautious remark and despite Bernard's own distinction between Mary's created nature and the splendor of the deity! Bernard, of course, would never use the word "deification" concerning Mary, yet he nonetheless comes very close to it. Again, he plays with the possibility and probably even crosses the border. Mary becomes fully absorbed into the divine light, and by this she is distinguished from any other angelic or human being, a creature of her own, belonging to both the human and the divine worlds.

Bernard's student Guerric (ca. 1070/80–1157), the abbot of Igny, stands in the tradition of his master. According to him, Mary is the "Mother of life" (*mater est vitae*),[81] the "throne of the crowned King" (*thronus Regis coronati*).[82] Ascending to heaven "she resides in gilded apparel as the crowned Queen to the right of the King" (*a dextris Regis Regina coronata consedeat in vestitu deaurato*).[83] At the same time Guerric can describe

Mary's reunion with her divine son in elaborate erotic imagery. She is the "marriage-bed of the bridegroom incarnate" (*thalamus sponsi incarnati*),[84] not just the mother but also the bride of the King (*mater Regis et sponsa*): "Rest then, you blissfully happy [bride], in the arms of [your] bridegroom. He will make you blossom . . . in [his] embrace and kisses, as he rested delightfully in the tent of your body and in the bedchamber of your tender heart" (*Requiesce igitur, o felix, inter brachia Sponsi. Replicabit tibi . . . inter amplexus et oscula, quam suaviter requieverit in tabernaculo corporis tui, quam suavis in cubiculo cordis tui*).[85]

GODFREY OF ADMONT

Another fervent admirer of the Virgin Mary and prominent example of Marian theology in the twelfth century is Godfrey of Admont (ca. 1100–1165), the Benedictine monk and abbot of the monastery of Admont (Styrie, Austria). Mary's role in the process of salvation is a major theme in his theological thought. Again, Mary is identified with the Wisdom of Proverbs 8:22 and is therefore God's pre-created and predestined "helper": "Ardently thirsting for humankind's salvation from the beginning, for this he created her, his beloved, preserving her sinless in the realm of sin . . . that he might have a companion in his desire (*in desiderio participem*) and a helper (*adjutricem*) to fulfil what he desired at the opportune time."[86]

Like Bernard, Godfrey sees the holy Trinity as a whole at work in beginning the process of redemption through Mary; "the holy Trinity, which as a whole was active in the one flesh of the Virgin for the conception and birth of God's son for the redemption of the human race" (*Trinitas sancta, quae tota operata est in una carne Virginis ad concipiendum et pariendum Filium Dei pro redemptione humani generis*).[87] In calling Mary the "matter" (*materia*) out of which the restitution of the human race was made possible, Godfrey, too, attributes to Mary (or comes very close to attributing to her) a soteriological function: "And since Mary, the blessed mother of God, revealed herself as the matter,[88] if I may say so, of the restoration of the human race, nearly all of the Scripture, which commemorates the work of creation and restoration of the human race, lavishes special praise on this very

Virgin as the, as it were, restorer of the human race" (*Et quia beata Dei Genitrix Maria materia, ut ita dicam, humanae reparationis exstitit, omnis pene Scriptura, quae opus creationis et reparationis humanae commemorat, hanc eadem Virginem quasi reparatricem humani generis speciali laude commendat*).[89] Mary is not just the *mediatrix* and *interventrix* — as the *reparatrix humani generis* she indeed assumes her predestined role as *corredemptrix*.

HILDEGARD OF BINGEN

The female counterpart of the Benedictine and Cistercian monks and abbots of the eleventh and twelfth centuries is Hildegard of Bingen (1098–1179), the Benedictine nun, visionary, and abbess of Rupertsberg (opposite Bingen on the river Rhine).[90] Hildegard, after the approval of her literary activities by Pope Eugenius III (himself a Cistercian and disciple of Bernard), became a celebrity and a restless propagator of monastic and clerical reform. Her many published works (six major books and a number of smaller publications) and her vast correspondence with the highest levels of society, clergy and laity alike, made her one of the most influential figures in the twelfth century. One of the luminaries of the age, with whom she corresponded since 1147 (more than three hundred letters are ascribed to her), was Bernard of Clairvaux, who took great interest in her visions and interceded on her behalf with Pope Eugenius III.

Among her writings is a collection of liturgical poetry and music, composed between 1148 and 1158 and arranged in a cycle under the title *Symphonia armonie celestium revelationum* ("Symphony of the Harmony of Celestial Revelations").[91] In her poems extolling the Virgin, Hildegard agrees with the Marian theologians of her time in drawing a close link between Mary and Wisdom, thus relating Mary to the very beginning of creation and to God's predetermined plan of salvation.[92] As a matter of fact, as Barbara Newman observed, the very arrangement of the liturgical pieces in a manuscript of the *Symphonia*, which seems to have been produced under Hildegard's personal supervision, points to Mary's role "as the centerpiece of God's eternal plan, his beloved from before all time."[93] The manuscript begins with two antiphons directed to God the Father, followed by no less

than twelve songs to Mary, three to the Holy Spirit, one to Ca-
ritas, and one to the Trinity. Thus there is no poem at all addressed to Jesus; instead, Mary has taken his place between the
Father and the Holy Spirit—a clear indication that Mary is elevated among the Trinity and assumes the function of Jesus, in the
sense that his work of salvation was made possible only through
her active participation!

Several of the songs emphasize Mary's predetermined status in
God's plan of creation and salvation, wavering between asserting
her creation before all creation and suggesting that God at least
foresaw her when he began his creation. "You are the shining
white lily / on which God gazed before all creation" (*Tu can-
didum lilium / quod Deus ante omnem creaturam inspexit*)[94]
clearly presupposes Mary as "Firstborn before all creation," alluding to Wisdom in Proverbs 8:22. Another hymn, however, is
more cautious and depicts God foreseeing her as the necessary
tool of salvation: "O flower, you did not spring from dew / nor
from drops of rain, / nor did the air fly over you, / but the divine
radiance / brought you forth on a most noble branch. / O branch,
God had foreseen your flowering / on the first day / of his creation" (*Deus in prima die / creature sue previderat*).[95] But this
is probably too rationalistic an alternative. That God "foresees"
Mary does not just mean that he knew that she would be born in
time and history; rather, she was already "there," with him, in
the form of biblical Wisdom. In this sense Hildegard can call
Mary "sister of Wisdom" (*soror Sapientiae*), clearly referring to
Proverbs 7:4 ("Say to Wisdom, 'You are my sister'"). Newman
compares Hildegard's statements on Mary's pre-creational status
with a miniature from the late twelfth century, interestingly
enough an illustration to Josephus's *Antiquitates*.[96] The miniature
shows Christ the creator surrounded by six medallions, which
depict the six days of creation. His right hand is elevated in the
typical gesture of blessing, the left hand holds a seventh medallion depicting Mary with her hands raised in prayer. A diagonal
line connects the Mary medallion with the medallions of the first
(light and darkness) and the sixth day (Adam and Eve), strongly
suggesting that Mary is not just the new Eve, but included in the
creation of the six days. She is the completion of creation and as
such in a very concrete form present at the time of creation.

The union between God and Mary is again described in erotic

language. The "lily" that God "gazed upon before all creation" of course alludes to the bride of Canticles: "Like a lily (*lilium*) among thorns, so is my darling among the maidens" (Cant. 2:2). Mary is this "most beautiful and most tender" (*pulcherrima et dulcissima*) bride: "how greatly God delighted in you / when he set / the embrace of his warmth in you / so that his Son took suck from you" (*cum amplexionem caloris sui / in te posuit*).[97] God, the bridegroom, has singled out Mary because of her beauty: "What a mighty work this is! / God gazed / on his fairest daughter / as an eagle / sets his eye upon the sun: // When the supernal Father / saw the Virgin's splendor / and wished his Word / to take flesh in her."[98]

Most important in Hildegard's Marian theology is Mary's function as *reparatrix* or even *recreatrix*,[99] the one who completes, or rather recreates, creation. Like Godfrey of Admont, Hildegard calls Mary the new matter of the new creation:

O resplendent jewel
and unclouded beauty of the sun
which was poured into you (*qui tibi infusus est*),
a fountain springing
from the Father's heart,
which is his only word,
through which he created
the prime matter of the world (*mundi primam materiam*),
which Eve threw into confusion.

For you the Father fashioned
this Word as man,
and therefore you are that luminous matter (*lucida materia*)
through which his very Word breathed forth
all virtues,
as in the prime matter he brought forth (*ut eduxit in prima materia*)
all creatures.[100]

This beautiful and delicately structured hymn outlines Mary's essential role in the process of creation. The key word is *materia*: through his only Word (Jesus) the Father created the *materia prima* of the world, which, unfortunately, was thrown into disorder (*turbavit*) by Eve. This is the dramatic conclusion of the first strophe. Then begins the new creation—not just of the world but even of the Word! The Word, through which the failed creation was made, had to be recreated in order to enable a new, successful creation: it had to become man. In a bold shift from the Word through which God created the prime matter of the world to the new, "luminous" matter through which the new Word was fashioned, Hildegard assigns Mary an enormous importance in the process of history and salvation. She is the *lucida materia*, which transformed the Word so that it could successfully complete its creation. Only through the *lucida materia* of Mary could the Word take the form that made creation successful; in other words, it is Mary, and only Mary, who guarantees the success of God's creation.

Looking at this from a slightly different angle, one may even go a step further. Since the new creation, which comes into fashion through the union of the Word with the *lucida materia* of Mary, is the desired one—in contrast to the failed creation of the *prima materia*—one could even conclude that the failure of the "first creation" inaugurated by Eve was fortunate or even planned by God. Whether Hildegard "stops just short of affirming that Eve's fall was fortunate,"[101] or whether she crosses the thin borderline to a *felix culpa* theology, there can be no doubt that the new creation is essentially better than the failed first one—and that the Word Incarnate in Mary has become possible only through Eve's failure and Mary's success. In a prose poem in her epilogue to the "Life of St. Rupert" Hildegard is very clear about this:

> O form of women, sister of Wisdom,
> how great is your glory!
> For in you there rose a life unquenchable
> that death shall never stifle.
> Wisdom exalted you to make
> all creatures fairer in your beauty than they were when the world
>   was born.[102]

The same is true for the hymn mentioned above. After calling Mary the "branch God had foreseen on the first day of creation," the hymn continues:

> And he made you for his Word
> as a golden matrix (*auream materiam*),
> O praiseworthy Virgin.

O how great
in its powers is the side of man
from which God brought forth the form of a woman (*de quo Deus
formam mulieris produxit*),
which he made the mirror (*quam fecit speculum*)
of all his beauty (*omnis ornamenti sui*)
and the embrace (*et amplexionem*)
of his whole creation (*omnis creature sue*).

. . . . .

O how greatly we must lament and mourn
because sadness flowed in guilt
through the serpent's counsel
into woman.

For the very woman
whom God made to be the mother of all (*matrem omnium*)
plucked at her womb
with the wounds of ignorance
and brought forth consummate pain
for her kind.

But, O dawn,
from your womb
a new sun has come forth (*novus sol processit*),
which has cleansed all the guilt of Eve
and through you brought a blessing greater (*et maiorem benedic-
tionem per te protulit*)
than the harm Eve did to mankind (*quam Eva hominibus
nocuisset*).

Hence, O saving Lady (*o Salvatrix*),
you who bore the new light (*novum lumen*)
for human-kind:
gather the members of your Son (*membra Filii tui*)
into celestial harmony.[103]

The *materia aurea* takes up the *lucida materia* as opposed to
the *prima materia*: in giving birth to the Word Incarnate Mary is
the "mirror of all his beauty" and the "embrace of his whole
creation." This language strongly calls to mind Sapientia Salomonis 7:25f., where Wisdom is called "a clear affluence from the

glory of the Almighty," the "radiance that streams forth from everlasting light," and the "flawless mirror (*esoptron akēlidō*) of the active power of God." Mary mirrors God's beauty and reflects it to the earth and to humankind. This again emphasizes her creative role, her part in God's creation of the new world and the new humanity. Through her, God reaches down to earth and "embraces" his world. In stating that the blessing brought into the world through Mary is greater than the harm caused by Eve, Hildegard again evokes the *felix culpa* motif and combines it with Mary's eminent status as the predetermined tool of salvation.[104] As a matter of fact, the "original sin" is eradicated from the very beginning, from the time of creation, by Mary, the eternal Virgin without sin.[105] Hence it is only consistent that the hymn finally escalates into the highest possible title for Mary: *salvatrix*, "saving Lady," honoring her salvific function and putting her on one and the same level with Jesus.

Eve's *felix culpa* enabled the process of salvation, put in motion by God becoming man through Mary. The beneficiary of this process, of course, is humankind, but it has its repercussions for the divine world as well. Hildegard is very restrained about this subject, but at least she hints at it:

> O what great felicity is
> in this form [of the femininity],
> for malice,
> which flowed from women —
> women thereafter rubbed it out,
> and built
> all the sweetest fragrance of the virtues,
> and embellished heaven (*ac celum ornavit*)
> more than she formerly troubled earth (*plus quam terram prius turbavit*).[106]

Here again we have the Eve/Mary typology. One woman, Eve, troubled earth, the other, Mary, mended the original fracture caused by Eve. But Mary's "healing power" does not just extend over the earth (that is, humanity), but rather affects heaven (that is, the Godhead itself). Thus, in enabling God to become man, Mary inaugurates a new stage within the Godhead, something that would have been impossible without Eve's failure and Mary's success.

PETER OF BLOIS

Bernard of Clairvaux and Hildegard of Bingen no doubt represent the high point of Marian theology in the twelfth century. I conclude with an example from the second half of the twelfth century, Peter of Blois (ca. 1135–probably 1212), who spent most of his time as an administrator in ecclesiastical and royal governments, at first in France and later in England.[107] In a sermon on Mary's birth, which draws heavily on Bernard's sermons, Peter summarizes Mary's unique position. He interprets the title "rose of Sharon," attributed to the bride in Canticles 2:1, as referring, of course, to Mary:

> "Sharon" is translated by "pre-eminence" (*principatus*): she [Mary] is not just made the mediator (*mediatrix*) between God and humankind but rather the ruler (*princeps*) and Queen of heaven. She was made mistress of the world (*domina mundi*), restorer of the age (*reparatrix saeculi*), destroyer of the netherworld (*destructrix inferni*), glory of the martyrs, honor of the virgins, strength of the just, confidence of the fallen (*lapsorum fiducia*), hope of the fighting, exultation of the angels.[108]

MARY AND THE SHEKHINAH

The major characteristics of the eleventh and twelfth century peak of Marian theology can be summarized as follows:

1. Although all statements about Mary have to be seen and evaluated within the framework of Christology — and from a dogmatic Christian point of view are clearly subordinated to a comprehensive Christology — there can be no doubt that the elite of the church of the eleventh and, in particular, of the twelfth century moved towards the direction of Mary's deification.[109] This deification process extends between two poles: Mary's identification with Wisdom, the "Firstborn before all creation," and her assumption into heaven. The former not only makes her a predetermined participant in the process of salvation, but also elevates her to a heavenly status before her actual birth as a human being on earth. The latter posits her return to a "divine" status after

her death and includes her in the holy Trinity. Transformed by the divine fire and seated to the right of Jesus on the throne of grace, with all of the power given to her, she assumes a salvific function that was originally reserved for Jesus.

2. Several of the statements employ very explicit erotic imagery, drawn mostly from the Song of Songs. The bridegroom is always God and the bride, although she can be identified differently, is often Mary. Due to the complex trinitarian relationship between Father, Son, and Holy Spirit, Mary's bridegroom is either God (in an undifferentiated way) or Jesus. As such, Mary is simultaneously the daughter of God and the mother, as well as the bride, of Jesus. When Jesus and Mary reunite in heaven, it is not just the reunion of mother and son, but also of bride and bridegroom. The heavenly reunion of the divine couple is often described in graphical erotic language.

3. Mary's function as mediator between heaven and earth, God and humankind, is expressed in ever bolder terms. The frequent triad *mediatrix/interventrix/reparatrix* leads to *corredemptrix* and finally (in Hildegard of Bingen) to *salvatrix*. Mary is a necessary and active participant in the process of history (the process of salvation). Without her consent, God's plan for humanity's salvation would have proved futile.

4. Mary is the crucial point around which heaven and earth revolve. All of the divine blessings are channeled through her (for example, the image of the aqueduct). God loves us and reaches down to us through her. This movement from above to below is supplemented by a reciprocal movement from below to above: Mary's intercession on behalf of humanity is so important that we even confess our sins to her. Although she has made God our brother, it is still easier to turn to her, rather than directly to her son.

5. Mary is the new Eve. Whereas Eve spoiled the first creation, Mary made the second successful creation possible. As such she is the new "matter" through which God created his new world. But, in providing the new "matter" for the new world, Mary also provided the "matter" for the new God. Through her not only the new world was created but also, as it were, the new God, the God/Man, the Word Incarnate.

To conclude, let us venture another look at the bahiric concept of the Shekhinah from a Christian point of view (as well as at the

Christian doctrine of Mary from a Jewish point of view). For a Christian observer the myth of the Bahir—and for a Jewish observer the doctrine of Mary—could be read as follows:

God's unity is multiple, threefold in the Christian Trinity and tenfold in the Bahir (which nevertheless puts a clear emphasis on the upper three Sefirot). In his love of humankind God exposes himself to the human world, which has been corrupted by "evil," in order to lead it back to him. In the Bahir, this "evil" originates in God himself—strangely enough from a Christian perspective, although the Christian concept of *felix culpa* is not too far from this (both view evil as something necessary for the subsequent process of salvation). In Christianity, the redeemer is God's son; in the Bahir, it is God's daughter, his feminine potency. In order to perform his task of redemption, the son of God, who has been sent to earth, has to become man (yet remains God); the daughter of God in the Bahir, who has been sent to earth, remains part of the Godhead and does not become a human being: there is no incarnation of God's daughter in Judaism corresponding to the incarnation of God's son in Christianity.

No one, of course, would expect speculations in Judaism about the divine and human nature of God comparable to the dogmatic speculations in Christianity. Certain structural or phenomenological similarities between the concepts of the Shekhinah and Mary/Jesus are obvious, however. True, the feminine aspect of the Godhead is much more dominant in the Bahir than in the Christian doctrine. In the Bahir, the feminine potency is included among the ten Sefirot, and quite prominently so, whereas there is nothing female attached to the three divine powers in Christianity. The Christians let God, as it were, acquire his feminine quality on earth, through a human being. This human being, Mary, however, is related on the one hand to the "pre-existent"[110] Wisdom and on the other hand elevated to heaven to be (re)united with the divine Trinity. Hence she undergoes a process of deification. In her position as simultaneously God's daughter, mother, and bride, she very much resembles the Shekhinah's position in the Bahir.

Both concepts are closest to each other when we consider the function of the Shekhinah and of Mary on earth. It is only through the Shekhinah that humankind has access to their Father. She channels the divine blessings down to earth,[111] and she is responsible for their well-being and well-doing—and her success in the end also affects her and the Godhead. Similarly, Mary is the *mediatrix* and *interventrix* of all human beings. She is the receptacle of the divine blessings and directs humankind's prayers and request for forgiveness to God. Moreover, her active participation in the salvation process not only transforms humankind but also herself — and God.

If we finally consider the development in Judaism from the biblical Wisdom tradition to the Bahir, and in Christianity from the New Testament to the theologians of the twelfth century, we discover a remarkable symmetry. In abandoning the concept of Wisdom and focusing on the Logos, Christianity shifts the figure of the savior from the female Wisdom to the male Logos/Jesus — only to start the process again of gradually reintegrating the feminine through Mary. Likewise Judaism almost completely gives up the feminine dimension of God after Philo — only to "rediscover" it all the more intensely in the Bahir, the first kabbalistic tractate. Whereas the process of reintegration seems to occur more slowly and gradually in Christianity and more suddenly in Judaism, both reach their climax in the second half of the twelfth century in (Southern) France. If this development is not mere coincidence (and it is hard to imagine coincidental parallel phenomena like these) the question of historical links and mutual influences becomes all the more pressing.

❄ 9 ❄

COUNTER-EVIDENCE: MARY

AND THE JEWS

As the mother of Jesus, the Son of God, Mary was certainly known among the Jews for many centuries. Whether or not they wanted to, they could not avoid her growing presence in the Christian world, first in the East and then in the West. Yet it wasn't a particularly pleasant image that arose in front of the eyes of the Jews, at least from their perspective. Being held responsible for the death of her son, they could hardly escape the seemingly inevitable conclusion, on the part of the Christians, that they were only too willing to extend their wicked thoughts and hateful deeds to his mother. This is precisely the connection made by Christian legend and art, and this evidence appears to shed doubt upon the idea that Mary served as a model for the (re)emergence of God's female aspect within the heart of the Jewish mystical tradition. Moreover, concerning Mary's role as mother of the God/Man Jesus, the claim of her perpetual virginity, and the gradual process of her deification, it is clear that these characteristics were quite alien to any "normative" form of Judaism and must have provoked unflattering Jewish responses. Needless to say, such Jewish responses will not have contributed to the positive reception of the image of Mary in Jewish circles. In what follows I will deal, first, with some prominent anti-Jewish legends and images related to the Christian veneration of Mary and, second, with Jewish polemics against the Virgin Mary.

Anti-Jewish Legends and Images

The Jews Disturb Mary's Funeral

The tale about the wicked Jews disturbing the funeral of the Blessed Virgin is presumably our earliest evidence for the proliferation of Christian legends about the Jews' ill-treatment of

Mary. As we noted in the previous chapter, it is related to the budding tradition about Mary's assumption into heaven, which is summarized under the title *De Transitu Beatae Mariae Virginis*. Recent research distinguishes between three major versions of the *Transitus Mariae*, the earliest of which is ascribed to Melito (c. 120–185 CE), bishop of Sardis in Asia Minor and allegedly a disciple of the Apostle John. According to Monika Haibach-Reinisch, the editor of one of the two extant recensions of Pseudo-Melito's *Transitus*, it may well date as early as the beginning of the fifth century CE (and it's "heretical" *Vorlage* to the fourth century).[1] The full account of the Jewish intervention in the solemn funeral procession for Mary conducted by the apostles reads as follows:[2]

> But when the high priests had heard [this], they went out of the city with a great crowd, saying: "What is this sound, so pleasing to hear?" Then [someone] appeared who said to them: "Mary has just now left her bodily condition (*Maria exiit modo de corpore*), and the disciples of Jesus are saying praises around her."[3] When the high priest (*princeps sacerdotum*) of the Jews—who was the priest (*pontifex*) of that year in his turn—saw the wreathed funeral couch (*lectum*) and the disciples of the Lord singing with exultation around the bier (*feretrum*), filled with anger and wrath he said: "Behold the tabernacle of he who threw us and our whole people into disorder, what sort of glory has she[4] received?" And saying these things, he wanted to overturn the funeral couch and bring it down to the ground (*voluit evertere lectum et ad terram deducere*). And at once both of his hands dried up from the very elbows (*et statim aruerunt ambae manus eius ab ipsis cubitis*) and they clung to the bier (*adhaeserunt feretro*).
>
> Then while the apostles were carrying around the bier, part of him was hanging and [the other] part was clinging to the funeral couch (*pars eius pendebat et pars adhaerebat lecto*), and he was tortured by the harsh punishment, while the apostles were walking about with exultation and singing praise to the Lord. The angels who were in the clouds struck the crowd, who had gone out of the city, with blindness (*percusserunt populum caecitate*). Then the high priest, who was clinging to the bier (*princeps sacerdotum qui adhaerebat feretro*) began to shout and say: "I beseech you, Saint Peter, do not despise me in so urgent a moment as this! Remember

when the door servant accused you, it was I who spoke well on your behalf.[5] Rather, now I beg you to have pity on me before the Lord."[6] Then Peter said to him: "We [apostles] have no power to make alterations in the world, but if you believe in God and in him, whom that [woman] carried [in her womb], Jesus Christ, our Lord, [then] your hands will be released from the bier (*solventur a feretro manus tuae*)." He answered him: "Is there anything that we do not believe? But what shall we do? Since the enemy of the human race completely blinded our hearts (*excaecavit corda nostra*), so that we may not confess the wondrous deeds of God, especially when we ourselves have cursed Christ, shouting: 'His blood is upon us and upon our sons.'[7] And the stain of so great a sin clung to us (*adhaeret nobis*)." Peter responded to him: "This curse will harm those who have continued in their unbelief, but mercy will not be denied to those who turn to the Lord."

When Peter caused the bier to stand still, the high priest said: "I believe in the Son of God, whom that [woman] carried in her womb, Jesus Christ, our Lord." And at once his hands were freed from the bier (*statimque solutae sunt manus eius a feretro*), but his forearms were withered[8] (*et erant brachia eius arida*), and the punishment did not leave him [completely]. Then Peter said to him: "Approaching the body, kiss the funeral couch and say: 'I believe in the Son of God, Jesus Christ, our Lord, whom that [woman] carried in her womb and she remained a virgin after the birth.'" When he had done thus, he instantly returned to health (*statim redditus est sanitati*). And he began to praise God magnificently and to bear witness of Mary from the books of the Old Testament, namely that she is the Temple of God, that even the apostles wept with joy and admiration.

The story continues by recounting that Peter gives the High Priest a palm branch to put on the eyes of the Jews struck with blindness (metaphorically and physically). Those who believed in Jesus were healed and regained their vision, but those who "remained in the hardness of their hearts died."

This is a remarkable story, and its moral is disturbingly clear: the Jews hate Jesus, "who threw our whole people in disorder"; all the more so do they hate Mary, his mother, and they begrudge her the glory that awaits her in heaven. Although they did not kill Mary (as they did Jesus), they at least could disturb her funeral and desecrate the holy body. For this disrespect and hatred they receive the punishment they deserve. Their High priest, who himself carries out the despicable deed, gets his hands stuck to the bier, and his people, who are already struck with blindness of the heart, are struck with physical blindness, as well. The only appropriate remedy for them is full submission to the core of the Christian faith: belief in both Jesus Christ as the Son of God *and* in his mother Mary, who remained a virgin after his birth and is now about to be taken up into heaven to be reunited with her divine son!

The story is clearly modeled after certain themes and motifs from the Hebrew Bible as well as from the New Testament. The fate of the High Priest recalls 2 Samuel 6, in which David brings the Ark of the Covenant in a solemn procession from Baalim of Judah to Jerusalem.[9] The Ark was carried on a new cart, accompanied by Abinadab's sons Uzza and Ahio, while "David and all the House of Israel" were dancing before the Lord (vv. 3–5). When they reached the threshing floor of Nakhon, "Uzza reached out for the Ark of God and grasped it, for the oxen had stumbled. The Lord was incensed at Uzza. And God struck him down (*wa-yakkehu*)[10] on the spot for his indiscretion, and he died there beside the Ark of God."[11] Uzza touched the Holy Ark involuntarily and with no bad intention (in fact, his motivation was good, since it was in danger of being overturned!), yet he had to die. The Jewish High Priest deliberately tries to overturn the funeral couch of Mary, who is called the *tabernaculum* and even *templum* of Jesus and represents the new Ark of the new God. Yet, he does not die and is even given the opportunity to convert to the new faith. Ironically, the punishment inflicted upon him is a withered arm (or more precisely two withered arms), the very illness that Jesus is said to have healed on a Sabbath: "there was a man in the synagogue who had a withered arm (*et erat ibi homo habens manum aridam*)" (Mark 3:1)[12]—the exact same word used in our story (*et erant brachia eius arida*).

But what precisely happened to the poor Jewish High Priest? The text says that "his hands dried up from the very elbows" and "clung to the bier." This apparently means that both his forearms were dried up and stuck to the bier; accordingly, "part of him was hanging and [the other] part was clinging to the funeral couch." This suggests a bizarre image: after the failed assault, when the apostles lifted up the bier again and continued their funeral procession, the High Priest wasn't just dragged alongside them, but was literally hanging from the bier, dangling in the air. The other recension (B¹) makes this graphic point even clearer. It says that the apostles "lifted the bier up" again (*elevantibus*[13] *apostolis feretrum*), and later, when the Jew's hands were finally freed, it adds: "he began to stand [again] on his feet" (*coepit stare pedibus suis*), implying that he fell down to his feet from some height.[14]

This must indeed have been a cruel punishment — to have his withered arms stuck to the bier and his body hanging in midair, while the apostles continued with the funeral procession. The redactor of *Transitus A* seems to have wished to ease the Jew's fate somewhat. In this version, the wicked Jew is not the High Priest, but "a certain Jew with the name of Ruben." He, however suffers the same punishment: "his hand dried up all the way down to the elbow (*manus eius aruerunt usque ad cubitum*); until he unwillingly-willingly descended into the Valley of Josaphat, weeping and lamenting because his hands were elevated to the bier (*quia manus eius erant erectae ad feretrum*), and he didn't have the power to draw his hands back."[15] Here, poor Ruben is at least allowed to walk down to the Valley of Josaphat on his own feet without awkwardly (and certainly more painfully) dangling in the air.

Yet there is still another reading of the wicked Jew's fate, which is preserved in the Greek recension of *Transitus A*. This version transmitted by John of Thessalonike, the archbishop of Tessalonike between 610 and 649, has all of the elements known from Pseudo-Melito, with some further embellishments (for example, that Satan went in to the High Priest and tempted him not only to overturn the funeral couch, but also to kill the apostles; the angels struck the Jews with blindness so that they could no longer see the apostles and instead bumped their heads against the wall; only the High Priest retains his vision, in order to carry out his wicked deed). Moreover, when the High Priest tries to overturn the bier, "his hands were immediately glued to the couch (*ekolletēsan tō krabbatō*)[16] and were cut off (*ekopēsan*)[17] from [his] elbows, and they remained hanging from the couch (*kai emeinan kremamenai eis ton krabbaton*)."[18]

This version effectively (if gruesomely) "solves" the problem of having the High Priest stuck by his hands to the bier, while the apostles uncompassionately continue their funeral procession. The body of the Jew was not dangling from the bier, nor was he dragged along on his feet. Rather, his forearms were cut off from his body, and they dangled from the bier, while he remained on his feet. Not a very elegant solution, but certainly effective. Of course, if one adopts this version of events, then another question arises: how did it happen that his hands were cut off from his elbows? This question is answered in a version of the *Koimēsis* that was probably written in the second half of the sixth century and is pseudepigraphically ascribed to the Apostle John.[19] It offers the following account of the Jewish attack on Mary's funeral:[20]

> And behold while [Mary] was being carried, some hefty Jew by the name of Jephonias rushed and attacked the bier, [while] the apostles were holding [it]. And behold, an angel of the Lord by means of some tremendous power cut both his hands (*tas dyo ekopsen cheiras*) from his shoulder with a sword of fire and made them hang in midair round the bier. Since this miracle happened the whole of the crowd of the Jews that was watching exclaimed: "He who was born by you, God bearing and ever virgin Mary, is the true God indeed." And he himself, after Peter exhorted him to accept the miracles of God, rose behind the bier and cried: "Holy Mary, you, who gave birth to Christ the God, have mercy on me." And Peter turned to him and said: "In the name of He, who was begotten by Her, your severed arms shall be rejoined [to your body]." Immediately with Peter's word, the arms that were hanging from the bier of the Lady [Mary], left and rejoined Jephonias' [body]. And he himself believed and praised Christ the God who was begotten by Her.

Pseudo-John does not explicitly mention that the arms of the Jew were stuck to the bier and that he could not remove them, but this is clearly presupposed. Through divine intervention, the poor Jew is freed of the bier, but unfortunately also of his hands! Even though much of this ultimate solution lies in the "logical" consequence of the narrative itself, it may well be that it was inspired by another text from the Hebrew Bible. In Zechariah 11 the "worthless shepherd" is described as abandoning his strayed and injured flock and feasting on the flesh of the fat ones:[21]

> Oh, the worthless shepherd
> Who abandons the flock!
> Let a sword descend upon his arm
> And upon his right eye!
> His arm shall shrivel up;
> His right eye shall go blind.

In our legend, the "worthless shepherd" is interpreted as the leader of the Jews, the High Priest (contrasted, of course, with the "good shepherd," Jesus). He has "abandoned his flock" by foolishly instigating an attack on the funeral of Jesus' mother, and his punishment accordingly involves his arm and his eye. In the biblical text, the descent of the sword upon his arm is explained as his arm "drying up" (in Hebrew *yavosh tivosh*, and in the Vulgate *ariditate siccabitur*, similar to our story!), and the descent of the sword upon his eye is explained as blindness. Our story includes both the withered arms (of the High Priest) and the blinded eyes (of all of the Jews), but in addition it may have taken the sword descending on the arm literally: the arms not only dried up, but were also cut off by a sword!

This is certainly an ingenious interpretation of Zechariah. But is it possible that Jews were familiar with this nasty Christian story and its reading of the biblical prophet? I would like to suggest that they were. First of all, there is no reason to assume that anti-Jewish stories were kept secret from the Jews; on the contrary, the polemical and propagandist purpose demands that they were publicized not just among Christians, but also among Jews. Although clearly meant to strengthen the faith of the Christians, the Jews were also supposed to learn important lessons from them: there are serious consequences for Jewish opposition to Christian beliefs, and there is only one ultimate and desirable solution for them, namely to convert to Christianity and to accept Jesus, the son of God, as their Lord, and his mother, Mary, as their Lady.

The impact of literary sources, however likely, can hardly be proven. Yet we are fortunate enough to have some pictorial evidence. Since the legend that the Jews disturbed Mary's funeral became part of the *koimēsis* and assumption tradition,[22] it is depicted on quite a number of mural paintings and (in the West) on

FIGURE 1. Detail, Wall Painting, Yılanlı Kilise, Cappadocia. Drawing by Annette Yoshiko Reed.

stained glass windows in churches and in book illustrations. The earliest example seems to be the mural painting preserved in an eleventh-century cave church in Cappadocia in Asia Minor (Yılanlı Kilise, close to Ihlara, southeast of the Van Lake).[23] It is unique in that it shows the apostles standing behind an *empty* bier, while Jesus is shown at its right, accompanied by an angel, and holding the soul (*anima*) of Mary—depicted as a tiny person—in his elevated hands. In front of the bier stands the Jew,

FIGURE 2. Fresco, Panhagia Mavriotissa Kastoria, Macedonia. N. Moutsopoulos, *Kastoria: Panagia he Mavriotissa* (1967), plate 70.

pictured as a much smaller figure, with both his arms uplifted and his hands cut off (there is no angel with a sword, and the hands are not stuck to the bier, but this may be due to the bad preservation). The painting then seems to capture the very moment of Mary's death in her bedroom, with Jesus taking her up into heaven; accordingly, the attack of the Jew (which is not shown but presupposed) is moved from the funeral procession to the bedchamber. [Fig. 1]

A late eleventh-, early twelfth-century mural painting in the Panhagia Mavriotissa in Kastoria in Greece (Macedonia) illustrates the funeral procession: Mary is lying on the bier, accompanied by the apostles. In front of the richly decorated bier are an angel and a Jew, again depicted in much smaller figures. The angel is shown with his sword still raised after he had cut off the Jew's hands,[24] while the Jew stands with his back to the bier, facing the observer, raising his mutilated forearms with both his hands clinging to the bier. [Fig. 2]

A similar illustration occurs in a Greek lectionary from Southern Italy from the twelfth or thirteenth century. Here again the funeral procession is depicted, in front of which the angel points with his sword to the Jew (or perhaps is about to put it back into

his sheath?); the Jew stands with his back to the bier, looking to
the angel, with his forearms uplifted in a prayer-like gesture.[25] In
a sequence of four scenes presenting the death, funeral, and assumption of Mary, the bronze gates of the Cathedral of Susdal in
Russia (created between 1227 and 1237)[26] capture the moment
when the hands of the Jew have been cut off and the angel puts
his sword back into his sheath.[27] From precisely the same time
(before 1232), we find the motif in a *Koimēsis* miniature in an
Armenian lectionary from Thargmantchats, which is most lav-
ishly decorated and well- preserved.[28] Here, Mary's body is lying
on the bier, which is surrounded by the apostles and Jesus, accompanied by seven angels and holding Mary's *anima*. In front of
the bier are again two smaller figures: the angel and the Jew with
his hands cut off and sticking visibly to the bier. The angel raises
his sword in a threatening gesture, as if he is ready to attack a
second time. [Fig. 3]

In the fourteenth century, this iconographical motif becomes
even more widespread, with prominent examples including the
frescoes in Staro-Nagoričino, Serbia (ca. 1317),[29] and in Mistra,
Greece.[30]

So far, our examples have all come from Byzantine or Armenian art, which reflects the development and earlier circulation of
the related Marian literary tradition in the East. Both the iconographical tradition surrounding Mary's death and funeral and the
anti-Jewish legend associated with it would, however, eventually
travel to the West and became known there in the twelfth century
at the latest.[31] The earliest evidence for the visual representation of the Jewish attack on Mary's funeral that I have found so
so far is a miniature in the York Psalter, now in the Library of the
Hunterian Museum in Glasgow, which seems to date from the
second half of the twelfth century.[32] It shows Mary's bier surrounded by the apostles and followed by a group of Jews. One of
them, presumably the High Priest, touches the bier with his
hands. The imagery is subtle; without any knowledge of the literary *Vorlage*, one would hardly understand his gesture as an attempt to overthrow the bier.[33] The High Priest seems to be rather
undecided about whether to support the bier, along with the
apostles, or to attack it. The editor of the Psalter has concluded
from this, quite convincingly: "It is clear that the artist had no
model for this scene."[34] He must have known some version of the

FIGURE 3. Armenian Lectionary, Thargmantchats. Christa Schaffer,
Koimesis: Der Heimgang Mariens (1985), plate 5. By permission of
Christa Schaffer.

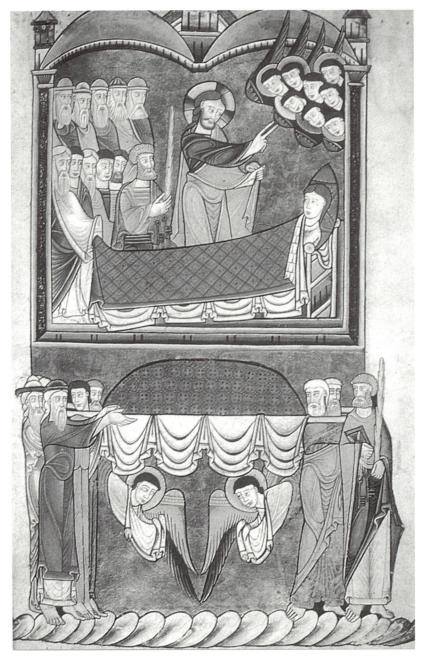

FIGURE 4. York Psalter (Glasgow, MS. Hunter. 229), folio 18r.
By permission of the Glasgow University Library, Department of
Special Collections.

story, but was probably not familiar with any of the earlier Byzantine representations. [Fig. 4]

In comparison, the Berthold missal from the Benedictine Abbey Weingarten in Germany, made between 1215 and 1217 for the abbot Berthold, is much more graphic.[35] The illustration shows Mary lying on her bier, surrounded by the apostles and Jesus, again carrying her *anima*. In front of the bier there is a figure, clearly the Jewish malefactor, who sits on the ground with both hands pressed against the bier — obviously caught at the very moment when he is trying to overthrow the funeral coach with the dead body of the Virgin. In sharp contrast to the depressed and sad looking apostles and Jesus, his face is angry and clearly expresses his malevolent intentions. His hands are not (yet) cut off, however, nor is there an angel threatening him with a sword.[36] [Fig. 5]

Not much later (ca. 1240), in Oxford William de Brailes designed and illustrated the first Book of Hours, a devotional manual for the laywoman (the first owner, probably a nonaristocrat lady with the name Susanna, is depicted in the book). Among its many illustrations is a sequence of episodes relating to the death, assumption, and burial of the Virgin Mary. One of these shows the scene of Mary's funeral, which is framed on either side by scenes of her death and her coronation in heaven.[37] Two apostles carry the bier, which is covered by a pall that hides her body from the viewer, while two Jews disturb the procession. One of them is hanging from the poles of the bier, the other one from the pall covering it. It may well be that this scene captures the moment at which the hands of the Jew are stuck to the bier and he realizes that he will be dragged along with it. [Fig. 6]

The illustration is obviously influenced by Pseudo-Melito's version of the story; additional scenes depict the Jews struck with blindness[38] and one of them begging Saint Peter to cure him.[39] Another English illuminated manuscript, the so-called Holland Psalter, from the second half of the thirteenth century,[40] features *three* Jews with their hands clinging to the bier and clearly dangling in the air (the scene is titled "De Iudeis pendentib[us] ad feretrum b[eata]e V[ir]ginis").[41] [Fig. 7]

In the De Lisle Hours, from early fourteenth-century England, the Jewish villain is depicted twice in the same scene: first grabbing the bier and trying to get hold of it (he is again much smaller

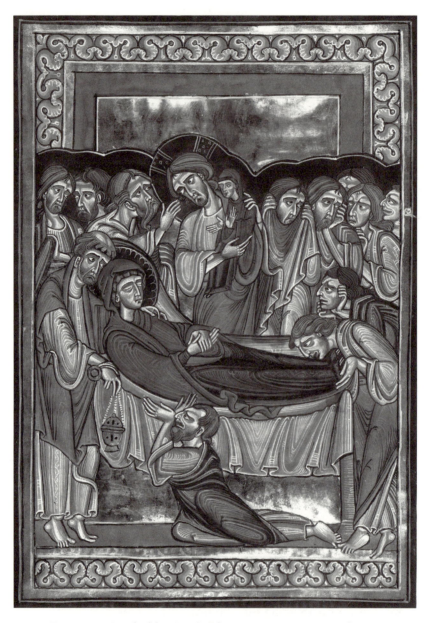

Figure 5. Berthold Missal (The Pierpont Morgan Library, New York, MS. M. 710), folio 107. By permission of the Pierpont Morgan Library.

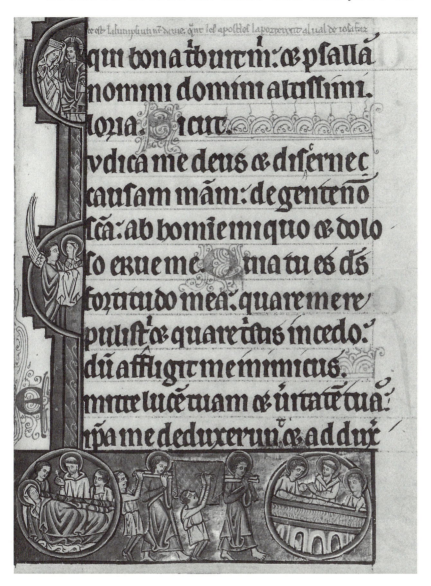

FIGURE 6. Compline of the Virgin, William de Brailes Book of Hours (The British Library, MS ADD. 49999), folio 61. By permission of the British Library.

FIGURE 7. Holland Psalter (St. John's College, K. 26), folio 24r. By
permission of the Master and Fellows of St. John's College,
Cambridge. Photo, The Conway Library, Courtauld Institute of Art.

than the apostles and the bier), then clinging with both of his hands to the bier, with his feet dangling in the air like a clumsy mountain-climber.[42] [Fig. 8]

The Occidental illustrations discussed so far all occur in private liturgical books, which were not meant for broad, public circulation. Hence it is unlikely that many Jews had a chance to see them. There is, however, clear evidence that the story of the wicked Jews disturbing Mary's funeral also found its way into the public sphere. The magnificent stained glass windows from the early thirteenth century in the Cathedral of Chartres are a case in point. Among a long sequence of scenes illustrating the death, funeral, burial, and assumption of the Virgin Mary there is one picture that shows Mary's funeral:[43] Mary, hidden by her splendidly decorated bier, is surrounded by sad-looking apostles. Among them, as if he were one of them, one figure stands out: a figure with no nimbus, touching the bier with one hand. This is obviously the Jewish High Priest, who has a surprised expression in his face, as he looks at his presumably stuck hand.[44] There is nothing (yet?) of the aggression depicted in the liturgical books, nor an angel attempting to cut off his hand. [Fig. 9]

The large medallion with this scene is flanked on both sides with four apostles watching the funeral, one of them (St. John) carrying the palm branch, which will later heal the Jew(s).

The angel, who is missing in all of the earlier Western liturgical books,[45] appears in a glass window from the second half of the thirteenth century in the Freiburg Münster in southwest Germany.[46] As in the other Western works, Mary's bier is carried by the apostles and draped with a pall. Here, however, an angel appears above the bier with a sword drawn in his right hand. The figure of a Jew is clearly identified by his pointed hat; he is lying on the ground, collapsed in front of the bier in an awkward, twisted posture. His hands have apparently just been cut off, but they are neither stuck to the bier nor have they fallen to the ground; they are still part of his body, depicted in the very moment before they fall down (a thin line between his arms and his hands indicates that they have been cut off). [Fig. 10]

This illustration may be less dramatic and less gruesome than the Byzantine representations,[47] but the Jews of Freiburg nevertheless must have been made well-aware of the grim consequences of trying to resist the message of the Christian faith (and,

Figure 8. De Lisle Hours (The Pierpont Morgan Library, New York, MS. G. 50), folio 161r. Photo and permissions, The Conway Library, Courtauld Institute of Art.

FIGURE 9. Detail, Funeral of the Virgin, Chartres Cathedral, nave, south wall, bay 4. Photo and permissions, Centre des Monuments Nationaux, Paris.

in contrast to Chartres, the happy salvation awaiting them, if only they accepted it, is conspicuously missing in the Freiburg window).

The Image of Mary in the Latrine

Another example from Christian literature, which shows Jews acting aggressively and violently against the veneration of Mary, comes to us from the Irish monk Adamnan. Its origin, however, is again Byzantine. Adamnan (ca. 625–704) was the ninth abbot of the monastery on the island of Iona, founded in 563 by St. Col-

FIGURE 10. Schneider-Fenster, Grabtragung Mariae, Freiburg, Münster. Photo and permissions, Corpus Vitrearum Deutschland, Freiburg i. Br. (R. Wohlrabe), Akademie der Wissenschaften und der Literatur Mainz.

umba as the starting point of his Christianization of Scotland. Noted as the biographer of St. Columba, Adamnan wrote another book, *De Locis Sanctis*, mainly about holy places in the Holy Land. It is based on a pilgrimage of the (otherwise unknown) Gaulish bishop Arculf, who visited Adamnan at Iona and provided him with the material for his book. Arculf's pilgrimage apparently took place between 679 and 682, and Adamnan's *De Locis Sanctis* was composed between 683 and 686.[48]

Toward the very end of his pilgrimage, just before coming to Iona,[49] Arculf visited Constantinople, probably around 680–81.[50] The third "book" of *De Locis Sanctis* is dedicated solely to the

marvels of the magnificent Byzantine capital. The final story Adamnan relates in Arculf's name is the following, entitled *De
Imagine Sanctae Mariae*:[51]

> The oft-mentioned Arculf gave us an accurate rendering also of a
> true story about an ikon of the holy Mary, mother of the Lord
> (*sanctae matris Domini Mariae toracida*), which he learned from
> some well-informed witnesses in the city of Constantinople. On the
> wall of a house in the metropolitan city, he said, a picture of the
> blessed Mary used to hang, painted on a short wooden tablet
> (*imago beatae Mariae in brui tabula figurata lignea*). A stupid and
> hardhearted man (*stolidus et duricors homo*) asked whose picture
> it was, and was told by someone that it was a likeness of the holy
> Mary ever virgin. When he heard this that Jewish unbeliever (*ille
> Iudeus incredulus*) became very angry and, at the instigation of the
> devil, seized the picture from the wall and ran to the building near
> by, where it is customary to dispose of the soil from human bodies
> by means of openings in long planks whereon people sit. There, in
> order to dishonor Christ, who was born of Mary, he cast the pic-
> ture of His mother through the opening on the human excrements
> (*humanum stercus*) lying beneath. Then in his stupid folly he sat
> above himself and evacuated through the opening, pouring the ex-
> crements of his own person on the ikon of the holy Mary (*purgans
> proprii stercus uentris super toracidam beatae Mariae*) which he
> had just deposited there. After that disgraceful action the hapless
> creature went away, and what he did subsequently, how he lived,
> or what sort of end he had, is unknown. After that scoundrel had
> gone, one of the Christian community came upon the scene, a for-
> tunate man, zealous for the things of the Lord. Knowing what had
> happened, he searched for the picture of the holy Mary, found it
> hidden in the refuse (*inter humana stercora*) and took it up. He
> wiped it carefully and cleaned it by washing it in the clearest water,
> and then set it up in honor by him in his house. Wonderful to
> relate, there is always an issue of genuine oil from the tablet with
> the picture of the blessed Mary (*ex eadem beatae Mariae imaginis
> tabula uerum ebulliens distillat semper oleum*), which Arculf, as
> he was wont to tell, saw with his own eyes. This wondrous oil
> proclaims the honor of Mary, the mother of the Lord Jesus of
> whom the Father says: "With my oil I have anointed him."[52] Like-
> wise the psalmist addresses the Son of God himself when he says:

"God thy God hath anointed thee with the oil of joy beyond thy companions."[53]

This story about the image of the Virgin Mary is the last of three stories, all dealing with images desecrated or dishonored. The other two concern St. George and depict Christians who disbelieve in the representation of the Saint in his image; hence it is very likely that all three stories "indicate the first rumblings of the Iconoclast controversy,"[54] which became manifest in the eighth century during the reign of Leo III (717–741). The first George story involves a "hardhearted wretch, an unbeliever" (*duricors et incredulus homuncio*); after seeing the image of St. George depicted on a marble column in the city of Diospolis, he becomes "very angry with the insensible object" and strikes with his lance at the likeness of the Saint. Although the unbeliever is not a Jew, the language used is very similar to the one in the Mary story, including the remark that he acts at the instigation of the devil. As a result of his wicked attack, his horse collapses under him, and not only is his lance stuck in the column, but the fingers of both hands are stuck and cannot be removed.[55] Only after he does penance and invokes "the name of the eternal God and of the confessor," the "merciful God" releases him — "not just from the visible marble bond of the moment, but . . . also from the invisible fetters of sin, mercifully succouring him now saved by faith."[56]

The second George story refers to the same marble column with the image of the Saint, but this time the culprit is a believer, who addresses the image as if St. George were present (*ad quam [imaginem] quasi ad praesentem Georgium*). He promises the Saint his horse as a gift if he makes sure that God grants him a safe return from a dangerous trip. After returning safely, however, he tries to cheat the Saint and to offer him money instead of his beloved horse, but the horse doesn't move, so he ends up paying money and giving away his horse. The moral of the story is that St. George is indeed present in his image and cannot be cheated.[57]

The unquestionable presence of the Saint in his or her image is also emphasized in the final story about Mary's image. Any desecration of Mary's image means nothing less than a physical desecration of the holy Virgin herself! The desecrated image needs proper cleansing or rather purification, and the permanent emission of oil from the wooden image confirms that the image has been successfully restored to its previous glory. The oil not only proves that the image is clean/pure again, but also that Mary has been restored to her divine status. This latter point, Mary's divine status, is made graphically clear by the bold use of the two verses from the Psalms. These two verses refer to the oil of kingship with which God, the Father, has anointed his Son Jesus, and it is this very oil that pours out from the image of Mary. Mary is anointed with the same oil as her son and hence included in the holy Trinity!

As for the Jew as an example of the unbeliever (*incredulus*), he is in good company with his Christian fellows—at least as far as his disbelief in the image as the representation of the Saint is concerned. The Jew certainly goes a step further than the Christian unbelievers do, however, because he not only disapproves of Mary's image, but also of her very position as the mother of God. He does not oppose just images, but rather the essence of the Christian faith, that Christ himself is the Son of God born by a virgin. Yet the reaction of our pious author to the deed of the Jew remains conspicuously vague. To be sure, it is disgraceful, and the Jew is a "stupid" (*stolidus*) and "hardhearted" (*duricors*) "unbeliever" (*incredulus*). The Christian who struck with his lance at St. George's image and whose fingers were stuck in it, is, however, similarly *duricors* and *incredulus*, and even *stolidissimus*. The Christian unbeliever eventually repents and is restored to his proper faith, whereas the fate of the Jew remains unknown. There is no hint of any attempt to convert the Jew, and not even a suggestion of the appropriate punishment that the author of our story certainly felt he deserved. Unlike the legend of the Jews disturbing Mary's funeral (and unlike the tale about the Christian unbeliever in St. George's image), there is no punishment for the Jew, but neither is there any salvation.

Adamnan's *De Locis Sanctis* popularized the story of the desecration of Mary's image in the West, and it became incorporated into all of the major collections of the Virgin's miracles. A full history of its development, however, which traces and documents its spread in the Occident, has yet to be written. The earliest evidence cited by Schreiner[58] is in the *Chronica Maiora* of the English Benedictine monk and chronicler Matthew Paris (d. 1259), one of our most important sources for the history of Europe between 1235 and 1259.[59] Paris's version specifies the name of the

Jew ("Abraham") and locates the story in England. More importantly, he tells us the punishment inflicted on the Jew: he was thrown into the "most hideous prison of the London Tower," but was eventually released under the protection of his patron, Richard of Cornwall.

At almost the same time, a Spanish version[60] of the story appears in the *Cantigas de Santa Maria*, composed by Alfonso X (El Sabio, "The Wise"), King of Castile (1252–1284).[61] In Cantiga 34 the pious King relates:[62]

> This is how the Holy Mary got even with the Jew for the dishonor he did to Her image.[63]
>
> *It is right and fitting that he who insults Holy Mary should receive the devil as punishment.*[64]
>
> Concerning this, I shall relate a true miracle, which the Virgin Mother of God performed in the rich city of Constantinople in order to demonstrate that he who goes against Her will is as powerless as a straw against the wind.
>
> There was in the street a well-made image of Holy Mary, painted on wood. It was so beautiful that even if one examined more than a hundred, not another to equal it could be found. A Jew stole it one night, and after he carried it home hidden under his cape, he threw it into the privy, then he sat down there and desecrated it shamefully. The devil killed him, and he went to perdition.
>
> After the Jew was thus killed and condemned and the devil had taken him off without a trace, a conscientious Christian took the image out of the evil-smelling hole. Although the place was foul, the image gave off a beautiful fragrance that spices from the East, balsam or unguent, would not smell as pleasant as the image which I mention. After he took it out of there, he washed it in water at once and took it to his house. He put it in a proper place and made offerings to it for his salvation. When he had done all this, the Mother of God performed a great miracle there. A substance like oil issued from the image in great abundance to serve as a reminder of this wondrous event.

This version is clearly inspired by Adamnan, yet displays some striking differences. There is no longer any hint of the story's (presumably original) context in the Iconoclast controversy, which had long since faded away. Alfonso's Christian has no problem with taking the image for Mary's powerful presence; he even makes "offerings to it for his salvation." Indeed, it is only after this demonstration of his faith that the Mother of God performs her miracle. Moreover, the oil miracle no longer serves as critical testimony for Mary's elevated status, as equal with the Trinity, but is just "a reminder of the wondrous event." Finally and most importantly, the wicked Jew's fate is not longer unknown. On the contrary, it becomes the essential feature of the whole story. This is made abundantly clear by the refrain: anyone who insults the Holy Mary is punished by the devil—and this is precisely what happens to the Jew. His wicked deed is not only instigated by the devil (as Adamnan also has it), but he himself is killed and condemned forever, without having been given a chance to repent and to convert. The inescapable fate of the Jew—and, one might confidently add, of his people—is eternal perdition. This verdict is aptly documented by a series of illustrations in an Escorial manuscript of the *Cantigas*, in which the devil is shown urging the Jew to throw the image of Mary into the latrine and, most graphically, carrying him away to the place of his eternal damnation.[65] [Fig. 11]

The Jewish Boy in the Furnace

The last anti-Jewish legend to be discussed here is the best documented, and certainly the best researched. It differs from the funeral legend and the story about Mary's image in the privy, in so far as it is not the Virgin who is the primary object of the Jews' hatred, but Jesus, and, more precisely, Jesus as embodied in the Holy Communion. This time Mary's role is to protect (at least) one innocent Jewish boy. The two earliest versions of this legend are transmitted by two almost exactly contemporaneous authors, the Antiochan lawyer Evagrius Scholasticus (ca. 536–593/94) and the bishop Gregory of Tours (538/39–594); the former included it in his Greek *Historia Ecclesiastica*,[66] the latter in his Latin *Liber in Gloria Martyrum*.[67] I quote Gregory's slightly more embellished version, which was adopted in the West:[68]

> I will not pass over the events in the East that support the catholic faith.[69] The son of a Jewish glass-worker was studying and learning

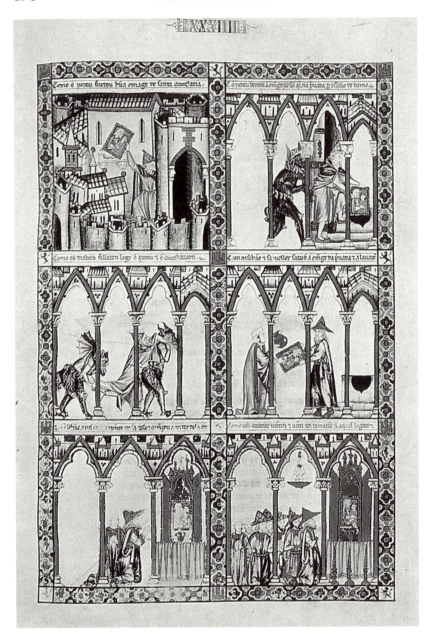

FIGURE 11. Alfonso X el Sabio, Cantigas de S. Maria (Biblioteca S. Lorenzo el Real de El Escorial, Cod. T.I.1), Cantiga 34, folio 15r. Copyright © Patrimonio Nacional, Madrid.

the alphabet with Christian boys. One day while the ritual of the mass was being celebrated in the church of the blessed Mary, this Jewish boy (*infans Iudaeus*) approached with the other young boys to partake the glorious body and blood of the Lord. After receiving the holy [eucharist], he happily returned to his father's house. His father was working, and between embraces and kisses the boy mentioned what he had so happily received. Then his father, an enemy of Christ the Lord and his laws (*Christo domino ac suis legibus inimicus*), said: "If you have communicated with these boys and forgotten your ancestral worship, then to avenge this insult to the law of Moses I will step forward against you as a merciless murderer (*parricida in te durus exsistam*)." And he seized the boy and threw him into the mouth of a raging furnace; he was persistent and added wood so the furnace would burn hotter. But that compassion that had once sprinkled the dew of a cloud on the three Hebrew boys who had been thrown into a Chaldaean furnace[70] was not lacking. For it did not allow this boy, even though lying on a pile of coals in the middle of the fire, to be consumed in the least.

When his mother heard that the father had evidently decided to incinerate their son, she hurried to save him.[71] But when she saw the fire leaping from the open mouth of the furnace and flames raging here and there, she threw her barrette to the ground. Her hair was disheveled; she wailed that she was in misery and filled the city with her cries. When the Christians learned what had been done, they all rushed to such an evil sight; after the flames had been beaten back from the mouth of the furnace, they found the boy reclining as if on very soft feathers. When they pulled him out, they were all astonished that he was unhurt. The place was filled with shouts, and so everyone blessed God. Then they shouted that they should throw the instigator of this crime into these flames. Once he was thrown in, the fire burned him so completely that somehow scarcely a tiny piece of his bones was left.

When the Christians asked the young boy what sort of shield he had had in the flames, he said: "The woman who was sitting on the throne in that church where I received the bread from the table and who was cradling a young boy in her lap covered me with her cloak, so that the fire did not devour me (*mulier, quae in basilicam illam, ubi panem de mensa accepi, in cathedra resedens, parvulum*

*in sinu gestat infantem, haec me pallio suo, ne ignis voraret, oper-
uit).*" There is hence no doubt that the blessed Mary had appeared
to him. Then, having acknowledged the catholic faith, the young
boy believed in the name of the Father and the Son and the Holy
Spirit. After he and his mother had been baptized in the waters of
salvation, they were reborn. In that city many Jews were saved by
this example.

This story of the Jewish boy in the furnace is clearly modeled,
as the text itself indicates, after the story of the three Jewish men
in the book of Daniel. The three men (Shadrach, Meshach, and
Abed-Nego) were thrown into the fiery furnace because they refused to worship the statue of gold set up by King Nebuchadnezzar. All "peoples and nations of every language" (Dan. 3:4)
followed the order of the king, but only "certain Jews" paid no
heed to the king's decree and did "not serve your god or worship
the statue of gold that you have set up" (3:12). The king, "filled
with such rage" that "his visage was distorted," ordered the furnace to be heated up "seven times its usual heat" (3:19) and had
the three Jews thrown into the raging furnace. The heat was so
great that it even killed the poor servants carrying the Jews to the
furnace — but, miraculously, the three Jews could walk around in
the fire unharmed, accompanied by a fourth man, whom the king
immediately identifies as a divine being (3:25). The king recognizes that the God of Shadrach, Meshach, and Abed-Nego has
sent an angel to save his servants, who leave the furnace unharmed, and gives an order that anyone who blasphemes the God
of the Jews "shall be torn limb from limb, and his house confis-
cated, for there is no other God who is able to save in this way"
(3:29).

The Jewish boy in our story clearly takes the place of Shadrach, Meshach, and Abed-Nego in the Daniel story. He is thrown
into the furnace because he does not believe (any longer) in the
idol set up by his father and instead has turned to the true God,
present in the Eucharistic host. His father takes the place of King
Nebuchadnezzar and, at the same time, of those who blaspheme
the true God after the miraculous event. He therefore throws the
boy into the furnace — and must be thrown into the fire himself
(which is the logical conclusion of the story and much easier than
tearing him limb from limb). Mary, of course, here stands for

God and for the angel sent to rescue the endangered believer(s). Most importantly, whereas the Daniel story symbolizes the shift from idolatry to Judaism, the new retelling symbolizes the shift from Judaism to Christianity, from the God of the Jews to Jesus Christ. Jesus is the new and true God, acknowledged by the Jewish boy; his father, who clings to the old faith, must be killed.

This is reminiscent of another story in which the contrast between idolatry and Judaism is similarly displayed.[72] In Genesis 15:7, it is said of Abraham that the Lord took him "out from Ur of the Chaldeans," which could be understood literally as meaning "out of the fire ('ur) of the Chaldeans." This is precisely how the Aramaic Targum rendered the verse.[73] Following this interpretation, the burning question arises: How does Abraham come to be in a "fire" and to need to be taken out of it? This question is answered by a Midrash in Genesis Rabba, which tells the following story about Abraham and his father Terah:[74]

R. Hiyya said: Terah was a manufacturer of idols. He once went away somewhere and left Abraham to sell them in his place. A man came and wished to buy one. "How old are you?" Abraham asked him. " Fifty years," was the reply. "Woe to such a man!" he exclaimed, "you are fifty years old and would worship a day-old object!" At this he became ashamed and departed. On another occasion a woman came with a plateful of flour and requested him, "Take this and offer it to them." So he took a stick, broke them, and put the stick in the hand of the largest. When his father returned he demanded, "What have you done to them?" "I cannot conceal it from you," he rejoined. "A woman came with a plateful of fine meal and requested me to offer it to them. One claimed, 'I must eat first,' while another claimed, 'I must eat first.' Thereupon the largest arose, took the stick, and broke them." "Why do you make sport of me," [his father] cried out; "have they then any knowledge?" "Should not your ears listen to what your mouth is saying," [Abraham] retorted. Thereupon [Terah] seized him [Abraham] and delivered him to Nimrod. "Let us worship the fire!" he [Nimrod] proposed. " Let us rather worship water, which extinguishes the fire," replied [Abraham]. "Then let us worship water!" "Let us rather worship the clouds which bear the water." "Then let us worship the clouds!" "Let us rather worship the winds which disperse the clouds." "Then let us worship the wind!" "Let us rather worship human beings, who withstand the wind." "You are just bandying words," [Nimrod] exclaimed; "we will worship nought but the fire. Behold, I will cast you into it, and let your God whom you adore come and save you from it."

As would be expected, Abraham is saved from the fire. Thus this explains what the verse Genesis 15:7 means that God took him "out of the fire of the Chaldeans." Here again it is the shift from idolatry to Judaism that is at stake, at the very beginning of Judaism, actually at its hour of birth. This midrashic version comes even closer to the Christian story of the Jewish boy, in that Terah is directly responsible for his son Abraham being thrown into the fire. Although the father does not throw him into the furnace himself, he delivers him to Nimrod, who does the nasty job. We can hardly assume that the author of the Christian story knew some kind of a Jewish midrashic version about Abraham and his father Terach—although this possibility need not be excluded. At least the tradition that Abraham was rescued from the fiery furnace is known to the Vulgate of Nehemiah 9:7, which translates Nehemiah 9:7 ("You are the Lord, the God, who chose Abram and brought him out of Ur of the Chaldeans and gave him the name Abraham") as: *tu ipse Domine Deus qui elegisti Abram et eduxisti eum de igne Chaldeorum et posuisti nomen eius Abraham* ("who chose Abram and led him out of the fire of the Chaldeans and gave him the name Abraham").

In her monograph on *Gentile Tales: The Narrative Assault on Late Medieval Jews*, Miri Rubin has examined in detail the further development of the story of the Jewish boy in the furnace from Evagrius Scholasticus and Gregory of Tours up to the High Middle Ages.[75] Through authors like Paschasius Radbertus (d. 859), Botho of Prüfening, Siegbert of Gembloux, and Honorius of Autun (all twelfth century) the story reached England and was codified in several collections of Marian tales (Anselm of Bury St. Edmunds, Dominic of Evesham, William of Malmesbury) as early as the first half of the twelfth century. Even before its inclusion in these collections, the story appears in a Christmas sermon by Herbert de Losinga, Bishop of Norwich (ca. 1050–1119). The sermon follows closely Gregory of Tours, albeit with some variations. It places the story in "a certain Greek city in which Christians and Jews dwelt mingled with one another" and explains that "the children of the Jews were taught the learning of the Christians" (*discebant iudaeorum liberi christianas litteras*). When the Jewish boy tells his mother that he had received the Holy Communion, it is she who "kindles in the father of the child madness and cruelty," whereupon "this most unnatural father" (*hinc nefandissimus pater*) heats the furnace and throws his son into it. The mother then regrets her fury and calls the Christians, who find the child safe and alive. When they ask him who protected him, he answers: "The Lady who sits above the altar of the Christians, and the little one whom she cherishes in her bosom, stood around me (*et paulus quem fovet in sinu suo circumsteterunt me*), and stretching forth their hands they hedged my body round (*et porrectis manibus suis corpus meum vallaverunt*)." Excited about this miracle, the Christians don't just burn the father, but all of the Jews who would not believe in the Word Incarnate.[76]

Most important for the wider circulation of the story, outside of monastic circles, was its translation into the vernacular. The earliest known thus far would seem to be the French translation by the Anglo-Norman poet Adgar in the second half of the twelfth century.[77] The most popular French translation was the one by Gautier de Coincy in his *Les Miracles de Notre Dame*, written between 1223 and 1227.[78] Despite being set in Bourges, Gautier's version follows Gregory in many details, contrasting again the viciousness of the father with the mother's despair and cry for help. Mary's role is emphasized; she not only saves the child, but it is she, not the priest, who gives the Holy Communion to him in person: "the lovely image | which this morning smiled | when she gave me communion (*quant ele me commenioit*) | came with me into the furnace | immediately I fell asleep so was I at ease."[79] The father finds his fitting destiny whereas mother and son, together with many other Jews, receive baptism. At the very end, the author adds his personal voice and expresses his own abhorrence of the Jews: "I am so very hard towards them | that if I were king of the whole kingdom | I would not tolerate even one of them (*un a durer n'en endurroie*)."[80]

Not much later, in the second half of the thirteenth century, a very similar version of the story is told by Alfonso X in his *Cantigas*.[81] The story is set in Bourges, and again the father is the archvillain (Alfonso even knows his name: "Samuel," and mother and son are "Rachel" and "Abel"). As in Gautier, the Virgin her-self gives the sacrament to the Jewish boy, and he recognizes her and her son in the furnace: "I held close to me the one whom the Lady on the altar with her beautiful Son was holding close to her."[82] As a result of the great miracle the Jewish mother and son believe in the Christian faith (although it is only the son who receives baptism "at once"), whereas the father is put to death in the furnace.[83]

As is the case with the other stories, the visualization of the tale of the Jewish boy in the furnace in illuminated manuscripts and stained glass windows added to its popularity and influence among Christians, which couldn't escape the notice of the Jews. Gautier's version in particular was copied in many illuminated manuscripts. The following example, from a Parisian workshop around 1327, shows the mother tearing her hair, while the father pushes his son, seated on a shovel like a piece of bread (like the host!) ready for baking, into the flaming furnace.[84] [Fig. 12]

Dating from slightly earlier (ca. 1310–1320), are the illustra-tions of this tale in the Queen Mary Psalter.[85] In the first scene, the Jewish boy is depicted as kneeling together with his Christian friends, receiving the host from a priest, while a statue of the Virgin and Child observes the scene. The second scene shows the very moment at which the father tosses his poor child into the raging furnace and the Virgin, with her outstretched hand, seems to stop him or at least to protect the child from the flames. [Fig. 13–14]

But the visual representation of our story was not restricted to manuscript illustrations. Already in the mid-thirteenth century, the tale appears on stained glass windows[86] in France and in En-gland. The earliest to date seems to be the representation in Le Mans Cathedral (around 1241). Here, the story is depicted in three scenes: the Jewish boy, in a group of Christian children, prepares to take the Holy Communion; the father throws the child into the blazing furnace with the mother watching in de-spair (her head bowed and her hands placed against her chest); and finally the boy is in the furnace with Mary covering him with her cloak.[87] [Fig. 15]

Two similar stained glass scenes, dating from the middle of the thirteenth century, occur in Lincoln Cathedral. The first shows the father throwing his boy into the furnace, while the second

FIGURE 12. Gautier de Coincy, Miracles de Notre Dame (Bibliothèque Nationale, Paris, MS N.Acq.fr.24541), folio 35r. By permission of Bibliothèque nationale de France, Paris.

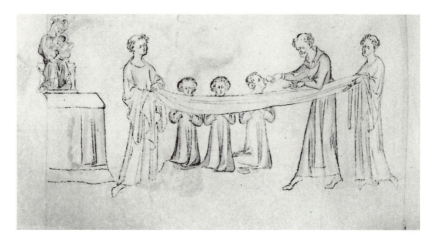

Figure 13. Queen Mary Psalter (The British Library, MS
ROY.2.B.VII), folio 207v. By permission of the British Library.

presents the boy sitting like an icon in the middle of the furnace,
flanked on both sides by the father and the protecting Virgin.[88]
[Fig. 16]

Miri Rubin reads this story primarily in the context of the
Christian accusation of the Jews desecrating the host for ritual
purposes (which again is connected with the accusation of ritual
murder), one of the most popular anti-Jewish tales in the Middle
Ages. Her interpretation evokes the associations between children, danger, pollution, and Jews, concluding: "The tale of the
Jewish Boy thus allows a number of fantasies to be expressed:
return to the mother, rejection of the father, enclosure within the
saving grace of Christ through his mother. *The Jew could have no
part in these.*"[89] No doubt, some powerful fantasies are invoked
here, but I do not believe that the stereotype of the Jewish threat
plays a prominent role among them. On the contrary, the tale
retells the story of salvation through the new Christian faith —
and illustrates how the Jews *can* become part of it! There is a
perfect symmetry between the child Jesus sacrificed by his father
(God) for the salvation of humankind, and the Jewish child killed
by his father because of the stubbornness of the Jews. The only
difference is that the Jewish child isn't actually killed, but is rescued by the mother of God (the mother Mary, who has given

FIGURE 14. Queen Mary Psalter (The British Library, MS
ROY.2.B.VII), folio 208r. By permission of the British Library.

birth to the savior) and becomes a savior of his people, in as
much as his mother and many other Jews convert to Christianity.
So the Jewish boy, thrown into the oven and almost baked like a
host, is compared with Jesus. This is quite the opposite of a threat
posed by the Jews.[90] The message that our story and similar tales
want to convey, albeit with different nuances and different grades
of anti-Semitism, is that the Jews *can* be included "within the
saving grace of Christ through his mother."

To be sure, this is not the whole story. The problem is not, pace
Rubin, whether or not the Jews *can* become part of salvation, but
whether or not they *want* to become part of it. Obviously they
do not want to, at least not voluntarily, and therefore must be
threatened with violence (having their hands chopped off, being
struck with blindness, being thrown into a furnace) until they
finally recognize the blessings of Christian salvation. Hence, the
true message is that the Jews must be *forced* into salvation, and
the best that they can hope for is an innocent Jewish boy to take
the lead. Mary, originally the object of Jewish hatred, finally res-
cues the Jews not only from fire, but from their very Jewishness —
whether or not they want this "salvation" (if they still insist on
not wanting it, despite Mary's miraculous intervention, they must
be exterminated).

FIGURE 15. Detail, Boy in Furnace, Le Mans Cathedral, bay 105.
Photo and permissions, Centre des Monuments Nationaux, Paris.

The Jews were certainly aware of these expressions of Christian concern for their salvation. We do not know exactly how they responded to them, but it seems quite unlikely that such stories aroused their enthusiasm for the Virgin Mary. We do have, however, a few (surprisingly few) Jewish sources that directly address Mary's position in the Christian history of salvation and her emerging cult in late antiquity and the early Middle Ages.

FIGURE 16. Lincoln Cathedral, window S1. By permission of the Dean and Chapter of Lincoln Cathedral.

JEWISH POLEMICS AGAINST MARY

Rabbinical Evidence and Toledot Yeshu

Jesus does not figure prominently in Jewish tradition,[91] and this is all the more true for his mother Mary.[92] The earliest datable evidence comes from Origen's *Contra Celsum*, which quotes extensively from the anti-Christian polemical treatise *Alethēs Logos*, written by the pagan philosopher Celsus in the second half of the second century CE. Most of Celsus's arguments against Christianity are put into the mouth of a Jew, which may be due to the literary genre (cf. Justin's *Dialogue with Trypho*), but certainly does not exclude the possibility of Celsus's familiarity with traditions circulating among Jews. According to Origen, Celsus represents a Jew as having a conversation with Jesus himself and refuting him on many charges, among others that "he fabricated the story of his birth from a virgin." In reality, the Jew argues, Jesus was born "from a poor country woman who earned her living by spinning" and who was driven out by her husband because she was convicted of adultery.[93] More concretely, Jesus' mother was betrothed to a carpenter, but his true father was "a certain soldier named Panthera."[94] Because he was so poor, Celsus's Jewish informant continues, Jesus "hired himself out as a workman in Egypt," from where he returned with "certain magical powers on which the Egyptians pride themselves."[95]

This attack is obviously directed against the Christian claim of Jesus' noble descent from Davidic lineage and particularly against the assertion that he was born from a virgin. Evidently, the charge that Mary committed adultery is the most logical conclusion for anyone, Jewish or pagan, who could not believe in her perpetual virginity and Jesus' virginal birth. A remote echo of this reaction can be found in the famous (and controversial) tradition in the Babylonian Talmud that explains the double patronymic of the magician Ben Stada ben Pandera (obviously a conflation of two originally independent traditions: both Ben Stada and Ben Pandera are traditionally identified with Jesus).[96] The first explanation is that "Stada" was the name of his mother's husband and "Pandera" the name of her lover, clearly presupposing that Jesus was the illegitimate son of her lover Pandera. The second explanation suggests that "Stada" was his mother's name and that her husband was called Papos b. Yehuda, a well-known Palestinian scholar of the first half of the second century CE (unusually inferring a patronymic and a matronymic).[97] Finally the Bavli proposes that his mother was Miriam, "the long-haired,"[98] who was called "Stada" because she was "unfaithful to her husband" (*setat da mi-baʿalah*: a play on words with *stada* and *setat da*). Whether Ben Stada and Ben Pandera or the hybrid Ben Stada ben Pandera originally referred to Jesus or to some earlier magicians who were only later identified with Jesus, as Johann Maier suggests, the passage in the Bavli comes very close to Celsus; the similarity of the names "Panthera" and "Pandera" can hardly be accidental. In both, Jesus' mother Miriam/Mary is an adulteress and her son Jesus an illegitimate child.

The brief talmudic passage is the most prominent reference to Mary in the classical Rabbinical literature[99] and is quite undisguised in its polemical aim. In general, however, the Rabbis seem to have either suppressed polemical remarks against Mary (whether voluntarily, due to censorship, or both) or were simply not particularly interested in polemics against Jesus' mother. The latter possibility is endorsed by the version of Jesus' birth presented in the infamous *Toledot Yeshu* ("The Life of Jesus"), the best known and most widely circulated polemical Jewish tractate. Opinions about the dating of the tractate vary from the first centuries CE to the High Middle Ages. Although the first definite evidence of some version of the existing text appears in Agobard of Lyon's ninth-century *De Iudaicis Superstitionibus*, where he refers directly to a Jewish book about the life of Jesus,[100] there can be no doubt that the book is composed of many different traditions, some of which are much earlier than the ninth century. At what stage the various traditions were compiled into a book bearing the title *Toledot Yeshu* remains an open question.[101]

In most versions of the *Toledot Yeshu* collected by Samuel Krauss, Miriam/Mary is betrothed or married to a nobleman of the house of David; that is, the kingly (messianic!) Davidic dynasty, precisely as claimed in the New Testament![102] Her fiancé or husband,[103] Yohanan,[104] is not only of noble origin, but also God-fearing and a Torah scholar. Unfortunately, Miriam has a wicked neighbor with the name Yosef (b.) Pandera, a notorious adulterer, who pretends to be her fiancé/husband and forces her into sexual intercourse, although she is having her menstruation.[105] Almost all extant versions agree that he acts against Miriam's will; Miriam is the seduced and innocent victim of a wicked villain. The fruit of the adulterous affair is Jesus, the bastard (*mamzer*) and son of a menstruate women (*ben niddah*). Whereas much polemical fervor is directed against Jesus in the subsequent narrative, Miriam/Mary comes off remarkably well: a Rabbinical trial confirms that she does not deserve any punishment because she did not consent to Yosef b. Pandera's seduction.[106] It is only in the much later Slavonic versions of the story that Mary becomes an active partner in the adultery.[107]

Whatever its precise date, the *Toledot Yeshu* tradition reveals a conspicuously restrained attitude towards Mary. Her son Jesus, to be sure, was a bastard and *ben niddah* who, despite his magical power, was finally and successfully sentenced to death. And yet his mother Mary was merely seduced by an unscrupulous adulterer. Thus, at least as far as Mary is concerned, the emerging picture is more complex than the cliché of a wholly negative and spiteful Jewish attitude towards her.[108] If Maier is correct in assuming that the *Toledot Yeshu* motifs are based primarily on the Western Jewish tradition (rather than stemming from Palestine or Babylonia),[109] it may well be that they reflect the less developed veneration of the Virgin in the West. This seems to have allowed the Jews a more relaxed response — quite in contrast to the more blunt polemic in the (albeit fragmentary) Bavli evidence, which answers Eastern Christian attitudes towards Mary.

The Apocalypse of Zerubbavel

A conspicuously different story is told in the Apocalypse of Zerubbavel (*Sefer Zerubbavel*), a Palestinian apocalyptic text from the early seventh century, which clearly reflects a Byzantine background.[110] In fact, as David Biale has pointed out, it is the most powerful counterhistory of the Christian narrative of the savior Jesus born from the Virgin Mary.

The book's name is derived from Zerubbavel, the Davidic governor of Judah, who played an essential role in the rebuilding of the (second) Temple in the late sixth century BCE.[111] This Zerubbavel is taken in a vision to "Niniveh, the great city, which is the city of blood," later identified with "Rome the Great" and clearly alluding to Constantinople, the Eastern Rome.[112] The apocalypse is quite a hodgepodge of various motifs, some traditional, some bold and new. The dramatis personae on the Jewish side are Menahem son of Ammiel, identified with the Messiah son of David, the Davidic Messiah (he is also called the son of Hezekiah, echoing the Rabbinical association of King Hezekiah with the Messiah);[113] and Nehemiah son of Hushiel, son of Ephraim, son of Joseph, undoubtedly the Messiah son of Joseph of the

Rabbinical tradition. These well-known heroes are destined to wage the eschatological war; according to the Rabbinical tradition, the Messiah son of Joseph will die in the first attempt to bring about salvation whereas the Messiah son of David will successfully fight the final battle.[114] The text, however, also adds a completely new and surprising figure: Hefzibah, the mother of the Davidic Messiah Menahem son of Ammiel! In the Bible Hefzibah is the name of the mother of the wicked King Manasseh[115] and also appears as a name for Zion at the end of time.[116] Here she is not only the mother of the Davidic Messiah, but the wife of the prophet Nathan as well.

These Jewish heroes are counterbalanced on the Christian side with just one Messiah: Armilos, who is the son of Satan and of a statue of stone.[117] His birth is graphically described as follows:

> He [the angel] seized me [Zerubbavel] and took me to the house of disgrace and merrymaking[118] and showed me a marble stone in the shape of a virgin (*even ahat shayyish bi-demut ishah betulah*).[119] The beauty of her appearance was wonderful to behold. "This statue[120] is the wife of Belial," he said, "and Satan will come and lie with her, and she will bear a son named Armilos. He will destroy the people."[121]

Armilos, of course, is Jesus, or rather the "Antichrist," the inverted counterimage of the Jewish Messiah.[122] It has long been observed that the marble stone, his mother, is the inverted image of Mary.[123] Not only is Mary *not* a virgin, but she even has intercourse with Belial/Satan, obviously the counterimage of God! It is difficult to imagine a nastier and more obscene counternarrative of the New Testament birth story, much less one that moreover can be firmly put into a historical context. The last incarnation of Christ on earth, according to the anonymous author of our Zerubbavel Apocalypse, is the Byzantine Emperor Heraclios (610–641 CE), who lost, among other things, Palestine to the Arab Muslims. As we have seen, the cult of the Virgin Mary is well established in the seventh century and integrated in Byzantine liturgy and art. Martha Himmelfarb has pointed out that icons of Mary were prominent among the images used to protect cities or armies and that Heraclios was even known to have "carried a statue of the Virgin into battle with him."[124] Thus Mary must have seemed omnipresent at the time of the composition of the

Zerubbavel Apocalypse, and its nasty story of Armilos's birth is clearly a contemporary Jewish answer to the increasing Christian veneration and deification of the Virgin, which was reaching its climax in the East.[125]

But this is only one side of the coin. It is obvious that Hefzibah, the Jewish mother of the Jewish Messiah, is portrayed as the counterpart of Mary, the Christian mother of the Christian Messiah.[126] She assumes a very active role in the redemption as described in the Zerubbavel Apocalypse, receiving the "staff of salvation" (*matteh yeshu'ot*) that was given to Adam, Moses, Aaron, Joshua, and David, the same staff that "blossomed and sprouted in the tent at the time it belonged to Aaron."[127] Moreover, "a great star (*kokhav gadol*) will shine before her" — clearly an allusion to the star in Numbers 24:17 ("a star rises from Jacob, a scepter comes forth from Israel"), a verse with long and infamous history of messianic interpretation.[128] In the first stage of the salvation process, Hefzibah will kill the two evil kings of Yemen and Antioch, and her staff will help the first Messiah, Nehemiah son of Hushiel, against Shiroi, the king of Persia. Then Armilos is born, who will kill the Messiah ben Joseph, Nehemiah son of Hushiel, but Hefzibah "will stand at the east gate [of Jerusalem] so that that wicked man will not come there."[129] When her son Menahem son of Ammiel, the Messiah ben David, takes over, the slain Messiah will be awakened, and Hefzibah will hand the staff over to him so that he, together with the Messiah ben David and the prophet Elijah, can complete the work of salvation (among other things, Armilos will be finally killed by Menahem son of Ammiel).

This is indeed, as David Biale observes, "an unprecedented role" given "to a Jewish woman in the redemptive process." Some stories in the Rabbinic literature do mention the mother of the Messiah,[130] but none of them comes even close to Hefzibah's *active* messianic role. Together with the slain Messiah ben Joseph, with her son, the Messiah ben David, and — to a certain extent — with the prophet Elijah, she forms the messianic triad (or quadrad) that brings about redemption. She is fully invested with the messianic insignia, most notably the staff of salvation and the star, and enjoys equal rights with her male companions. In the true sense of the word, she becomes the *corredemptrix* with her son, the dominant figure of the redemptive process—precisely like Jesus and Mary in the comparable Christian literature.

What we have here, then, is a double Jewish counterhistory to the Christian narrative of birth and redemption. On the one hand, the Apocalypse of Zerubbavel polemicizes against and parodies Christian claims about the birth of the Messiah Jesus from the Virgin Mary. It is difficult to imagine a more drastic and polemical counternarrative than the birth of Armilos from a statue inseminated by Satan. But this is not the full story. At the same time and in the same text, the author adapts and usurps the Christian story, transforming it into a powerful Jewish counternarrative; for the first time in Jewish history, the mother of the Messiah gains an active role in the redemption process. True, "the figure of the Virgin aroused strong but ambivalent feelings" in the author of the Apocalypse because the stone statue is "the mother of the Antichrist" and yet "surpassingly beautiful."[131] Yet I would even go a step further and argue that we not only encounter an ambivalence between (physical) attraction and (theological) denial but also, and more forcefully, between theological attraction and theological denial. The author fights on two fronts: he tells the same story twice, deliberately rejecting and accepting it simultaneously. His level of engagement is ambivalent, both negatively polemical and positively affirmative.[132]

With this we have come full circle. We began with Christian legends that portray the Jews as filled with hatred against Mary and her veneration, yet assert that they are still eligible for salvation (in most of the sources), even if they must be forced into it. Such legends (and images!) hardly made the Jews prone to any affectionate feelings towards the Virgin—and certainly do not suggest a positive Jewish adaptation of the Christian model and its transformation into a comparable Jewish narrative. Our second topic, the Jewish polemics against Mary, displayed a more complex picture. To be sure, the relevant sources reveal quite a dose of polemics. This dose, however, is unequally distributed, with more in the East and less in the West, nicely matching the different levels of enthusiasm for Mary and the different progress in her veneration in the Eastern and Western parts of the Roman/Byzantine Empire. Moreover, its most negative embodiment, the Zerubbavel Apocalypse, simultaneously proves to be the most positive one. The Mary/Hefzibah story in the Zerubbavel Apocalypse is clear evidence that the Jewish response to the Christian veneration of Mary could be *at the same time* negative and positive. Or to put it differently: that the polemical rejection of Mary's function in the process of the salvation of humankind does not necessarily exclude the positive adaptation of her role and attributes through the transformation of the Christian narrative into a bold Jewish counternarrative.

✤ 10 ✤

HOW MUCH "ORIGINS," OR: THE

ANXIETY OF INFLUENCE

WITHIN THIS FINAL CHAPTER, we return to the pressing issues that we have left lingering for some time, taking up questions that we have carefully circumvented or, to put it more gently, held in suspense. In the previous chapters, I have proposed that we may indeed discern a parallel development in Judaism and Christianity, beginning with God's feminine manifestation in the biblical Wisdom tradition, progressing to the suppression of the feminine, and culminating in its gradual, and eventually triumphant, reintegration in God. At this point, we must further ask: if this development is not merely coincidental, is it possible to identify the historical channels and the trajectories of mutual influence(s)? These are, of course, the "serious" questions that true historians desire to have answered, before allowing themselves to speculate further. But such questions raise major methodological problems, which cannot be ignored if one does not want to follow an all too simplistic path of historical inquiry.

I will begin by considering how the question of "origins" has shaped previous research into the Kabbalah, showing how the common assumption that a concept has only one point of origin determines historical reasoning. More often than not this assumption is linked with the "myth of the priority of origins"; that is, the notion of the ontological priority of the ultimate derivation of an idea, compared with its subsequent historical ramifications. This will lead us to examine again the nature of the "feminine" as expressed in the Bahir, particularly with regard to the relationship between the metaphorical and ontological levels of meaning. If we conclude that the feminine imagery in the Bahir clearly transcends a purely metaphorical plane, then the parallels with Christian Mariology become all the more important. In order to reach a more balanced judgement about the possible interaction between Judaism and Christianity, the category of "influence" will be discussed at greater length. The essentialist notion of "influence" that is prevalent in most historical research will be contrasted with a more dynamic model of interaction. Such a more nuanced theory of historical influence leads us to question how scholars appeal to the categories of "proof" and "truth" on the so-called phenomenological or structural level, as opposed to a historical level. Finally, I will turn to the historical milieu of late twelfth-century Provence, inquiring into possible points of contact between Jews and Christians that may help us to understand the emergence of the concept of the Shekhinah in the Bahir.

MYTHICAL ORIGIN

As we have seen, the reemergence of the feminine in the bahiric concept of the Shekhinah marks a new and quite unexpected twist in the long history of an old topic. Clearly the most impressive motif within the (new) kabbalistic system of the ten Sefirot, this concept is inextricably linked with the question of the origin of the Kabbalah as such. In fact, the literary complex of the Shekhinah traditions in the Bahir serves as Scholem's most decisive proof for his hypothesis that "Oriental sources originating in the world of gnosticism"[1] found their way, through the winding paths of history, into the first kabbalistic tractate. No doubt, it is this quest for origins, for the ultimate derivation of the Kabbalah, which constitutes the driving force behind much (if not most) of Scholem's scholarly fervor; to this question, he dedicated the only major monograph he wrote in German — with the very German title *Ursprung und Anfänge der Kabbala*. The book attempts to achieve precisely what the title promises: to uncover the "origins" of the Kabbalah and to describe its "early stages."[2] This goal is stated very clearly in the programmatic "beginning" of the first chapter, aptly entitled "The Problem": "The question of the origin and early stages of the Kabbalah, that form of Jewish mysticism and theosophy that appears to have emerged suddenly in the thirteenth century, is indisputably one of the most difficult in the history of the Jewish religion after the destruction of the Second Temple. Just as indisputably, it is one of the most important."[3]

With his impassioned search for "origins," Scholem reveals himself as a true heir to German Romanticism, particularly to the later stages of this movement, which applied romantic ideals to all areas of nature, history, and society, including sciences and arts, thereby laying the foundations for the emergence of disciplines such as literary studies, German studies, religious studies, and linguistics. The founding fathers of these modern disciplines all shared the conviction that the ideal of the "perfect," and accordingly of the "authentic," was to be found in the past rather than in the present or the future, and the more remote and "mythical" this past proved to be, the better.[4] Thus conceived, the historian of literature, language, or religion — and Scholem definitely understood himself as a historian of religion — uncovers the mythical source of something and describes its early stages until it firmly and visibly manifests itself as an established phenomenon.[5]

Thus the romantic quest for origins is coupled with a firm sense of historical development. It is the task of the historian, first, to reconstruct the origins of something, and then, to trace the stages of its unfolding. In many cases, and certainly in the case of the Kabbalah, this "something" is hidden in a mythical past, because nothing can be more "ancient," "original," and "authentic" than a myth. In locating the kabbalistic myth in the mysterious and vaguely defined "Orient," and in identifying it with the "Gnosis," Scholem, however, was forced to deviate from his romantic model: whereas the German romantics discovered the mythical origin of their own nation — and systematically collected and analyzed this national treasure — Scholem was faced with the problem of assuming a "foreign" and "external" origin of something that became, as he repeatedly emphasizes, one of the most powerful forces in the history of the Jewish religion. The tension caused by the allegedly alien origin of an intrinsically Jewish phenomenon can be detected in quite a number of his subtle and sometimes contradictory formulations. Scholem wavers between positing plainly external "gnostic" sources (predominantly from Valentinian Gnosticism),[6] internal "subterranean levels of the Jewish society"[7] (i.e., some indigenous but marginal Jewish sources?), and "vestiges of an ancient *Jewish*[8] gnosis," in which "anonymous Jewish gnostics sought to express their mystical conception without impairing their Jewish monotheism."[9] Altogether, his argument seems to imply that he favors some kind of "Jewish gnostic system," which developed in parallel to the classical gnostic systems of late antiquity and would eventually find its way to the Jews in medieval Provence.[10] Of course, the tension between the external and internal elements of the alleged origin remains, because Scholem does not explain how the (Valentinian) "Gnosis" was transformed in the respective Jewish sources.[11]

Once the ancient myth—whether in its original "foreign" form or in its Jewish adaptation—has seen the light of day, it finally sets off to generate the Kabbalah. This birth, at a given historical moment towards the end of the twelfth century, can be described as the result of a *linear historical process*—although, to be sure, few traces of its evolution have been left for the historian to "discover." Here again, Scholem wavers between two poles. On the one hand, he is fully aware that the Kabbalah "constitutes a phenomenon of Jewish life in the Christian Occident" and that, accordingly, we must locate the Provencal Jews within their particular "environmental context and not remain content with an analysis of the internal factors active at the time."[12] The two major factors that shape this environment are the poetry of the troubadours and the "dualistic religion" of the Cathars and Albigenses. He mentions the former only in passing. The latter, in contrast, is discussed quite at length, but the result, as we have seen,[13] proves to be largely negative. Nevertheless Scholem suggestively plays with the possibility that some gnostic ideas were mediated to the Provencal Jews through the heretical sects of the Cathars and Albigenses. Such modes of transmission, he muses, may have been facilitated by the fact that the Cathars and the Jews shared an opposition to Catholic orthodoxy (despite the "metaphysical anti-Semitism" prevalent in the Cathar movement).[14] In the end, he is left with the vague conclusion that the Cathar sect was "linked at least by its structure and perhaps also by its history to the world of Gnosticism and Manichaeism"[15] and the speculation that the Jews were connected with this gnostic-Cathar world either "openly or invisibly."[16]

The theory of an invisible and direct line of contact between the *ancient* Gnosis and Provencal Jewry, transmitted through subterranean channels, is the other pole that Scholem considers—and ultimately favors. Repeatedly he conjures up ancient "notebooks" and "fragmentary leaves," "vestiges of old literary material," that contained originally gnostic ideas (or bits of ideas) and eventually reached the editors of the Bahir.[17] Here, then, we are confronted with the claim of a direct *literary* link between the "Gnosis" and the Bahir, fragmentarily preserved in certain literary strata of the Bahir and particularly prominent in the material about the She-khinah.[18] We have seen the strong phenomenological and structural similarities between some important gnostic and bahiric motifs, which are indeed most salient with regard to the concepts of Sophia and the Shekhinah. Nevertheless, the proof in support of some textual connection between the "Gnosis" and the Bahir, or even their interdependence, has yet to be produced. The theory that Scholem suggests is itself a powerful myth: the birth of the Kabbalah out of the spirit of Gnosis. But this mythical origin remains as indefinite as its early historical stages: it mediates itself through yellowed leaves that no one has seen, through historical links that no one has established.[19]

The most recent attempt to break away from Scholem's romantic quest for a mythical origin and linear evolution has been presented by Elliot Wolfson in his programmatic article on "Hebraic and Hellenic Conceptions of Wisdom in *Sefer ha-Bahir*."[20] Wolfson analyzes the bahiric concept of the Shekhinah within the broader context of the emergence of the first kabbalistic system in the Bahir. In contrast to Scholem's rather static developmental model, he wants to draw a dynamic and dialectic picture of the concept of Wisdom/Sophia/Shekhinah, which does not rely on a linear trajectory from origin X to historical manifestation Y. Rather, Wolfson proposes a binary structure deeply ingrained in Judaism since the Hellenization of Palestine, already apparent in the later stages of the biblical canon. The generative dichotomy, he argues, is the structure of "Hebraism" versus "Hellenism," "Scripture" versus "philosophy," "Jerusalem" versus "Athens." While the extreme poles are in constant tension and conflict with each other, the two opposites nevertheless merge from time to time, producing creative syntheses such as the thought of Philo or the "religious philosophy" of the Middle Ages. The early concept of Wisdom falls neatly into these categories: the "Hebraic" version is "mythical" and portrays Wisdom as a (feminine) "divine hypostasis," whereas the "Hellenic" version is "philosophic," and depicts Wisdom as the (masculine) "demiurgical Logos."[21] Later however, in a process of philosophical adaptation extracted from Neoplatonic sources, Hellenic elements penetrate into the bahiric concept of Wisdom (which is essentially "Hebraic" and

"mythical") and create a new Hebraic/Hellenic synthesis that fa-
cilitates "the bridging of the transcendent and the immanent, the
metaphysical and the physical." In short: "the philosophical layer
superimposed on the mythopoeic provided the mechanism by
which the abstract symbolism could be concretized in the empirical realm of space and time."[22]

This idea of a structural, if not ontological, dichotomy between
mythical "Hebraism" and philosophic "Hellenism," proves much
more dynamic than Scholem's theory of the gnostic origins of the
Kabbalah in general and the bahiric Shekhinah in particular. At
the same time, it certainly avoids the historical problems that
plague Scholem's model. Indeed, Wolfson explicitly distances
himself from Scholem's origin theory[23] and the historical trap in
which it is caught: "With respect to the question of the provenance of the mythopoeic image of wisdom in the *Bahir*, I adopt a
functionalist as opposed to an historicist perspective. That is, I
am not concerned with tracing the historical origins of the concept since it may be well-nigh impossible to establish this fact
with any certainty. I am concerned with the way that the term
functions in the given intellectual environment, which is reflected
in a specific literary context."[24]

Scholars of religion commonly find a comfortable retreat in the
withdrawal to a "functionalist" approach, all the more so since
one can easily accuse one's opponent of "historicist" reductionism. But is this approach any more sound? To begin with, Wolfson's notion of a bipolar structure is highly problematic. This
essentialist bifurcation fatally smacks of the old (Christian theologian) prejudice of "Hebrew" versus "Greek thinking" à la Thorleif Boman (*Hebrew Thought Compared with Greek*),[25] which
has been long superseded in the study of early Judaism (and
Christian origins) by the much more nuanced research of Elias
Bickerman, Martin Hengel, and others.[26] Furthermore, Wolfson
still cannot escape the inevitable historical question. There is no
such thing as pure "Hebraism" and pure "Hellenism," but only
varying grades and shades—or, better yet, different configurations—of what might be called, for strictly heuristic purposes,
"Hebraic" and "Hellenic." Whenever we seriously grapple with a
"specific literary context," as Wolfson himself has put it, we find
ourselves confronted with the historical context in which a text
was composed and transmitted. A term or concept that "func-

tions" in a "given intellectual environment" necessarily functions in a historical environment. In other words, Wolfson's structural dichotomy can not save us from the lowly spheres of historical inquiry.

The problem at stake becomes clearer when we examine Wolfson's main argument more closely. Briefly summarized, it proceeds as follows: In the late Second Temple and early Rabbinic literature, the concept of Wisdom already reflected a merging of the "mythic" Hebraic notion of Wisdom and the "philosophic" Hellenic doctrine of the Logos. By the Middle Ages, this Hebraic/ Hellenic admixture became so fully absorbed into "Jewish" thought that its originally Hellenic components completely lost their mark of identity. In the Bahir, and more precisely in its later redactional strata, the process of "Hellenization" begins again: the Hebraic/Hellenic amalgam, with its strong "mythic" substratum, is again exposed to a "philosophic" discourse. Since the divine *hypostasis* is characteristic of the Hebraic notion of Wisdom and the *demiurgical* Logos of its Hellenic counterpart, we are confronted with a repeated (and repeatedly successful) penetration of the demiurgical/cosmological Logos into the realm of hypostatic Wisdom.

But this bipolar opposition of the hypostatic Wisdom and the demiurgical/cosmological Logos, does not stand up to historical scrutiny. As we have seen, both the canonical and noncanonical "Hebraic" Wisdom tradition features Wisdom not just as a divine hypostasis, but always oriented towards the earthly realm of human beings. We observed this in Proverbs' depiction of Wisdom as playing in front of God before and during the creation of the world, but nevertheless finding her delight with humankind. We found this, too, in Jesus Sirach's image of Wisdom taking residence among the people of Israel on earth, and in Sapientia Salomonis's notion of Wisdom as simultaneously God's beloved *parhedros* and the medium by which divine energy is refracted down to the human world. In none of these cases is Wisdom's demiurgical or cosmological role separated from her hypostatic "essence." Even for Philo, who distinguishes between the (albeit overlapping) concepts of Wisdom and Logos, it is primarily the Logos that is connected with the archetypal world of ideas in the divine mind, while Wisdom's task is to mediate these ideas for the world of human beings — quite the opposite of Wolfson's bipolar model! Thus his clear-cut distinction between the "Hebraic" and the "Hellenic" does not work, either as a fundamental binary opposition or in its neat division of labor between the hypostatic/transcendent Wisdom and the cosmological/immanent Logos.[27]

Just as Scholem's romantic quest for the authentic origins (of the Kabbalah, as well as of the feminine manifestation of God) becomes entangled in insoluble historical problems, so Wolfson's notion of bipolar opposites forsakes the historical dimension in favor of playing with philosophical glass beads. But the short-comings of both models expose what is needed: a dynamic struc-ture that takes the historical questions seriously. The former an-swers Wolfson's legitimate appeal for dynamism, while the latter follows Scholem's demand for a rigorous historical inquiry. Even if questions of origins and derivation cannot entirely be excluded, we should be less concerned to find "the" mythical origins, and instead examine the interplay of various factors in their particular historical dimensions. These factors are not necessarily or essen-tially structured in a dichotomous fashion. Nevertheless, the shared source of the Hebrew Bible/Old Testament and their largely par-allel development (in attraction and repulsion) makes Judaism and Christianity the natural candidates for a more careful inquiry into how the bahiric concept of the Shekhinah was shaped by the dynamic interaction between two seemingly opposite systems of thought. Our investigation has shown that, with regard to the feminine aspect of God, both religions indeed share a common storehouse of motifs, which stem mainly from the canonical and noncanonical Wisdom tradition and thus encourage very similar modes of thinking. Before returning to the question of how this similarity can be further described and explained, we should ven-ture another look at the nature of the feminine as depicted in the Bahir and in Christianity.

FEMININITY

In the Bahir the images of the feminine are conveyed through parables, which follow the Rabbinic paradigm of parables about a mortal king ("a king of flesh and blood") who metaphorically represents his divine counterpart, God. Like their Rabbinic pre-cursors, the bahiric parables provide the "king" with a "queen" (i.e., a "spouse") and with "sons," as well as with a "daughter" (i.e., the couple's "children"). What at first glance seems to be a strong similarity between the Bahir and Rabbinic literature, turns out, on closer inspection, to be very different. As a rule the Rabbinic parables use the royal family, like the king himself, as symbols for something else (e.g., the king's spouse = Israel, the daughter = the Torah, the son = Israel); they distinguish explicitly between what they call the *mashal* and the *nimshal*, the "illustrative" part of the parable and its moral, the "explanatory" part. In other words, they display a clear awareness of the difference between metaphorical language about God and the "reality" of God's relationship with his people Israel on earth. Quite in contrast to their Rabbinic predecessors, the bahiric parables completely conflate the distinction between *mashal* and *nimshal*. Even as they retain the appropriate linguistic marker for the parable (*mashal le* . . . or the full formula, *mashal le-mah ha-davar domeh*: "this resembles" or "a parable, to what can this be compared"), preserving the appearance of its traditional structure, they collapse the distinction between the metaphor and the reality that it expresses. Or, more accurately, the two levels are united, and metaphor becomes reality.

This renunciation of the metaphorical character of the parable has far-reaching consequences for the meaning of the images used in the Bahir. True, the images remain "images" or "symbols," but they acquire a degree of reality that far exceeds their Rabbinic counterparts.[28] It seems now that the queen *is* the king's spouse and the mother of his children, that the sons *are* his sons, and the daughter *is* his daughter. The images no longer function to designate something different, but they have become quasi-ontological statements about the "essence" of God. This means that we cannot simply explain away the force of the Bahir's images of the feminine, dismissing them as nothing but bold similes.

In reconsidering the role of the feminine in the Bahir, we must first emphasize the ontological unity of the male and female "aspects" of God. This is, among other things, graphically depicted in the parable of the nine palm trees and the Etrog, which guarantees that the system of the ten divine potencies can exist,[29] and in the no less graphic interpretation of the biblical verses Genesis 1:27 and 2:24.[30] God is constituted in primordial androgyny, and the dynamic interplay among his nine male and one female potencies can be described in terms of a sexual intercourse (cf. the parable of the king's son who mixes the "seed" in the "west"; namely, the Shekhinah).[31] The most striking evidence for the fundamentally androgynous nature of God is the parable of the palm tree and the date:

> Why was she called Tamar[32] and not by any other name? For she was female. You think [this is so] because she was female? Rather say, because she comprised both male and female, for all palm trees comprise both male and female. How is this? The palm-branch (*lulav*) is male, and the fruit is male from the outside and female from the inside. How is this? The kernel of the date is split like [the vagina] of a woman, and corresponding to her is the power of the moon above.[33]

The androgynous nature of the palm tree is well known in the Jewish tradition,[34] but, as Scholem correctly observes, it is the palm tree that is androgynous (or rather either male or female)[35] and not the fruit (date). The split kernel of the date is described accurately, however, and Scholem concludes from this that the author of our section did know dates from his own experience, but not palm trees (and accordingly must have lived in a northern environment).[36] In any case, the phallus-shaped date and her vagina-shaped kernel symbolize for our author the inherently androgynous nature of the divinity.[37]

The primordial androgyny of God, however, was only an ideal state that did not last forever. Just as human beings did not remain in their androgynous state and were split into their male and female components, so even God himself had to suffer from the separation of his male and female components. His feminine part, so essential for the nourishment and vitality of the inner divine life, was split off from its masculine companion. The Bahir does not explicitly inform us about when and why this happened, but this split is clearly associated with the creation of the mundane world of human beings. It is the image of the Shekhinah as the king's daughter or the mother of his children that predominates in the Bahir and depicts God's relationship with his created world. Quite a number of the parables try to express the continuous tension between the Shekhinah as essentially belonging to the divine realm and simultaneously becoming part of the mundane world: the king cannot always live with his daughter, but neither can he exist without her. Therefore, he meets her from time to time through a "window";[38] he wants to display his pearls and hidden treasures openly rather than to hide them;[39] the princess on earth is of mysterious, "far-away" origin;[40] everybody "desires" the beautiful daughter of the king.[41] This tension emerges most explicitly in the parables about Solomon, the king's "son." The biblical verse 1 Kings 5:26, according to which "God gave wisdom to Solomon," is here explained through a parable of a king, "who marries his daughter to his son. He gave her to him as a gift and said to him: do with her as you wish."[42] This imagery is obviously not as innocent as it seems. To begin with, the king marries his daughter not to a son in law but literally to *his* son. He thus establishes an "incestuous" relationship between his "daughter" and his "son." Furthermore, he invites his "son" to do whatever he wishes with his "daughter," clearly raising some sexual undertones that one would not expect from a decent father. The matter is further complicated by the fact that the "daughter" is already married:

> The Holy One, blessed be he, said [to Solomon]: Since your name is like the name of my glory,[43] I will marry you to my daughter. But she is [already] married![44] Let us say that he gave her to him as a gift, as it is written: God gave wisdom to Solomon (1 Kings 5:26). [The nature of that wisdom] is [here] not explained. Where, then, is it explained? In the following [when it is written]: For they saw that he possessed the wisdom of God to execute justice (1 Kings 3:28). We then see that the very wisdom, which was given to God and which is with him in his chamber,[45] that [this very wisdom] is in his [Solomon's] midst to execute justice. What is [the meaning of] "to execute justice"? As long as a person executes justice, this wisdom of God assists him and brings him close [to God]. If not, she keeps him at a distance [from God] and even punishes him, as it is written: I, for my part, will discipline you (Lev. 26:28).[46]

This parable depicts a puzzling threefold relationship: the king is married to his spouse, whom he marries as his daughter to his son. Since it is always the same Wisdom, who is the spouse of the king and, in her capacity as his daughter, the bride of his son, we end up with a multiple incestuous relationship. The dramatic exclamation in the parable — "But she is [already] married!" — points to this paradoxical situation. It can be easily solved, of

course, on the metaphorical level. If we take the king as a metaphor for God and Wisdom for the Torah, we avoid any problem
(even though, in comparison with classical Rabbinical parables,
God's "marriage" with the Torah still remains odd): God gives
his Torah to Solomon, his son, who represents Israel. Thus the
degree of Israel's closeness to God depends on the degree to
which they fulfill the Torah. Yet the Bahir again takes these concepts far beyond the metaphorical level; it explicitly does *not*
draw the line from the *mashal* to the *nimshal*, even as it certainly
presupposes the equation of his daughter (much less of his wife)
with the Torah. More precisely, it adopts this equation, but transforms it into an ontological statement about God's feminine quality, which remains part of the divinity at the same time that it
becomes part of the human world. In order to fulfill his task on
earth, God must "split up" with his feminine quality or, to put it
more pungently: to enable God to become part of humanity, a
"gender difference" must be introduced into the originally androgynous and unified nature of God. It is this "gender difference" within the divine essence, I venture to suggest, which is
God's "gift" to humanity.[47] If he had not split off from himself
what essentially belongs to him, humanity would not be able to
get close to him.

Nevertheless, the separation of his feminine dimension from
himself disrupts the original unity of God's masculinity and femininity and thus needs to be mended. Since humanity is the cause
of this disruption, its mending becomes possible only through humanity. This is the gist of the many parables that portray the
Shekhinah as "mother" and is expressed most graphically in the
parable in which the king hates his spouse because her children
behave badly.[48] When the people of Israel fulfill the will of their
father, not only are they brought closer to God, but they empower the Shekhinah to return to her original state. More precisely, when Israel unites God's name (in the *Shema‘*), the tenth
Sefirah will be reunited with the third Sefirah, the place of her
origin.[49] God will be made one again; his original androgyny will
be restored. What happens to humanity remains unexplained, but
we may assume that the restoration of God's original androgyny
means the abolition of creation or, rather, the inclusion of creation in God's eternal unity.

As we have seen,[50] it is precisely in the earthly dimension of the

divine — the poignant image of the divine reaching down to earth
through its feminine aspect — that the early Kabbalah most resembles Christianity. To be sure, there is nothing comparable in
the Christian Trinity to the Bahir's assertion of an ontological
unity in God's masculinity and femininity; on the contrary, quite
in contrast to the Bahir, Christianity always presupposes the pri-
macy of the masculine over the feminine. Nevertheless, the
wholly male God is felt to be deficient, and this deficiency involves his creation. As Hildegard of Bingen most distinctly expresses it, the primordial creation that was accomplished solely
through the divine Logos failed — one might add: *because* it was
accomplished solely through the (male) Logos. Of course, it was
Adam and Eve who technically spoiled the harmony of creation,
but they probably could not have done so if it had not been deficient in the first place. In any case, the rupture that was caused or
laid open through Adam and Eve, could only be mended through
a woman. This woman, Mary, made possible the new and successful creation because she enabled God to become man. God
acquires his human status through a woman, and this woman in
turn acquires a divine status among the Trinity. The images of
mother and son, bride and bridegroom, king and queen blur —
another case of divine "incest." It is at the end of a long process
of salvation history, which leads through the turmoil of the world
of human beings, that Christianity integrates the feminine into
the divinity.

INFLUENCE

Historians of religion employ various terms to describe models of
interaction between related textual, discursive, and, above all,
cultural phenomena. Among them belong, for example, "development," "dependence," and "borrowing," but the most cherished no doubt (at least in modern Kabbalah studies) is, as Gil
Anidjar has observed, the category of "influence."[51] It is directly
connected with "proof": the more and better proof is provided,
the more likely we may assume that a given text or cultural phenomenon X has influenced a given Y. Consequently, "influence"
and its companion "proof" presuppose the following: What is
compared in order to determine whether — and to which degree —

the one exerted influence on the other, are static entities, "enshrined notions of essence"[52] that are well-defined. They dwell in some kind of "monadic isolation" — just from time to time to put out feelers that reach into the other monad and communicate to it something of the first monad's essence. This "something" changes the second monad and adapts it to the first monad. How this happens is difficult to describe, but *that* it happens must be proved. The proof, then, is the materialized link between the two entities X and Y, and it materializes itself preferably in physical evidence such as manuscripts or objects of art. If we cannot come up with such a "proof,"[53] we must reject the idea of any contact between the components and phenomena that we set out to compare. Since it is very difficult to provide the necessary "proof" for the alleged "influence," "influence" more often than not serves as a category to inhibit rather than to encourage any fruitful comparison.

This essentialist notion of influence is clearly determined by the categories of cause and effect, firmly established by scholastic philosophy.[54] Thus, for example, the pseudo-Aristotelian *Liber de causis* proposes a hierarchy of causes: the higher a cause, the greater the influence it exerts on its effect.[55] According to Thomas Aquinas, it is the temporal and spatial proximity between cause and effect that is decisive and determines the degree of influence: "The closer something received is to the cause which exerts influence on it, the more it participates in its influence. The influence, however, of the grace comes from God."[56] But the static and almost mechanical interpretation of influence in terms of cause and effect does not convey the original meaning of the Latin *influentia* or *influxus*, nor has Thomas's pious attempt to trace it back to God anything to do with the original usage. Originally *influentia* or *influxus* are terms of late antique astrology, which refer to the "influence" of stars on the fate of human beings,[57] and this is precisely the meaning "influence" regains in the early modern period.[58]

The astrological derivation of the term "influence" and its early modern adaptation allows for a less quantitative and mechanical understanding than the scholastic equation of cause and effect. Despite their deterministic quality, the stars do not operate automatically, but rather require our imagination and mind to have an effect on us. Thus "influence" can adopt the meaning of "inspiration,"[59] emphasizing the *active* participation of the "influenced" during the process of "influencing." As such, "influence" does not describe the relationship of two entities, one of which is the "original" and "active" partner, while the other is its "passive" counterpart, a receptacle that receives and imbibes material without changing it. Rather, this model of "influence" outlines a dynamic relationship in which the influenced actively and creatively "digests" what it receives, creating something that is new, no longer identical with its "origin." As a consequence of this process of active adaptation, the notion of the priority of origins dissolves and becomes constantly fluent. In short, there is no such thing as *the* cause or *the* origin, in which the "derived" only participates in different grades or shades of intensity.

Following Shakespeare's understanding of "influence" as "the flowing from the stars upon our fates and our personalities,"[60] Harold Bloom has developed his famous theory of the "anxiety of influence." This theory is decidedly *poetic* and concerned solely with the relationship between literary works and their writers. Bloom defines "influence" and the "anxiety of influence" as follows:

> "Influence" is a metaphor, one that implicates a matrix of relationships — imagistic, temporal, spiritual, psychological — all of them ultimately defensive in their nature. What matters most . . . is that the anxiety of influence *comes out of* a complex act of strong misreading, a creative interpretation that I call "poetic misprision." What writers may experience as anxiety, and what their works are compelled to manifest, are the *consequence* of poetic misprision, rather than the *cause* of it. The strong misreading comes first; there must be a profound act of reading that is a kind of falling in love with a literary work. That reading is likely to be idiosyncratic, and it is almost certain to be ambivalent, though the ambivalence may be veiled.[61]

It is not my intention to evaluate Bloom's poetic theory of influence, but it seems to me that his dynamic interpretation of influence has ramifications far beyond the confines of poetic theory. If we transfer it to the realm of cultural history — despite the gap in translation from literature to history — we can describe historical processes and cultural connections in similar terms: the exchange of never-changing essences between "enshrined" entities gives way to a continual and dynamic interplay of active and constantly changing partners. Thus conceived, historical influence is a creative and mutual process that affects both partners, so that neither is simply "source" or "recipient." As in the poetic theory, the recipient actively digests the transmitted tradition, transforms it, and creates something new. Similarly, the act of re-creation is tantamount to "killing" the transmitted; thus the inevitable feeling of anxiety toward the "source" that is transformed and recreated, the ambivalence of attraction and repulsion.

To be sure, the dynamic notion of "influence" as a category of cultural history does not exempt us from "proof." But just as "influence" changes its character and is viewed differently, "proof" must be assessed differently, as well. "Proof" is not so much, or not only, the tangible physical evidence, materialized in this and that quotation adduced from this and that manuscript (preferably a long-overlooked quotation from a known manuscript, a long-neglected manuscript, or, even better, a completely new manuscript), but the realization of a close relationship between intertwined components in constantly changing configurations. If we stop comparing static entities and instead attempt to describe connections and relations between factors that have always been intermingled, whose very "essence" emerges from this interconnection, then the character of "proof" changes, as well. The possibility of "exchange" is a priori much greater, or rather the process of exchange becomes the essence. Of course, the relationship between the factors under consideration is not necessarily and not always a positive one. On the contrary, as we have seen, it is a constant movement between attraction and repulsion. More precisely, the very act of experiencing "influence," of digesting and recreating the received, is ambivalent because it simultaneously preserves and destroys the transmitted tradition.

If we now apply this theory of cultural/historical influence to both of our religions, Judaism and Christianity, and their view of God's femininity, the result is a much more complex picture. To begin with, we are less concerned with discerning the origin of these ideas in *one* religion; rather we consider both religions not as two essentialized self-contained entities, but as two poles of one spectrum or as two components of one religious discourse constantly engaged in active relationship.[62] This relationship produces various configurations — positive and negative, friendly and hostile, attracting and rejecting—but it is always a relationship, which (consciously or unconsciously) never obliterates their common origin. Despite all of their efforts to the contrary, this shared origin never collapses into the mythical legitimization of either one. Rather, it is continually realized in their historical relationship and in the identities that they must constantly secure for themselves.[63]

As such, the Jewish and Christian articulation of feminine aspects of the divine represents a process that gains its vitality through the mutual exchange. In so far as we can trace it back, it begins with the biblical Wisdom tradition, which inaugurates the theme of God's feminine manifestation, and finds its first climax in Philo's interplay of Sophia and Logos. In the Gnostic drama, Christianity—or rather Christianity and Judaism—develop structures that are essentially Jewish and reach far back into the Jewish Wisdom tradition. These structures continue in different ways in Judaism and Christianity, yet at the same time influence each other. In Christianity, the suppressed femininity becomes triumphant in Mary, who, at the end of a long process, is included in the divinity. Judaism develops an ambivalent relationship with the Christian veneration of Mary. On the one hand, it mockingly disapproves of the idea of the mother of God; on the other hand it treats Mary considerately and by no means only polemically. The talmudic and post-talmudic discussions about the Virgin Mary are classic examples of the simultaneous attraction and repulsion that the Christian veneration of Mary exerted on the Jews. Most impressively, the author of the Zerubbavel apocalypse succeeds in a "creative misreading" that manages to polemicize graphically against the birth of the Christian Messiah from the Virgin Mary, while at the same time providing the Jewish Messiah with a mother who absorbs a great many of her son's messianic qualities.

The common denominator of the Christian Mary and the Jewish Shekhinah is their salvific function. Both play a decisive role in the historical process that finally leads to the salvation of humankind and of God (an intrinsic part of which is the reintegration of the feminine into the Godhead). Mary saves humanity (including the Jews!), while the Shekhinah saves Israel/humanity (including the Christians?). In both cases the salvific function grows out of the biblical Wisdom tradition, which expresses

God's desire to reach down to the mundane world. Both Judaism and Christianity refer back to the biblical Wisdom, as well as making use of the transformations of this Wisdom/Sophia/Mary/Shekhinah during their common history and through their mutual "creative misreading." Surveying the whole historical process from the Bible up to the High Middle Ages, it seems that Christianity "suffered" from the anxiety of (Jewish) influence primarily in antiquity, whereas Judaism "suffered" from the anxiety of (Christian) influence predominantly in Late Antiquity and in the Middle Ages.

The dynamic theory of historical influence finally liberates us from the sterile opposition of a proof/truth on the phenomenological or structural level and on the historical level. It has become a popular game in scholarly reasoning about the origins of the Kabbalah or of particular kabbalistic ideas to distinguish the so-called phenomenological or structural from the historical level of argumentation. The two require different grades of "proof": a "phenomenological" similarity between certain ideas can generously be granted (because it does not require the "proof" of "influence" or "dependency," or at least much less "proof"). The matter, however, becomes much more grave if we approach the question from the historical level; in front of the tribunal of history we had better come up with "hard-core" evidence to buttress our claim!

One case in point is Moshe Idel's answer to Scholem's theory regarding the connection between Gnosis and the Bahir. Idel argues that Scholem is certainly right on the phenomenological level, but on the historical level he is wrong: "Instead of assuming gnostic influence on the Bahir, I suggest to assume that there were early Jewish esoteric traditions that influenced the early Gnosis. They were accordingly preserved in the Jewish framework and afterwards included in the Bahir and other kabbalistic works."[64] As to Idel's two assumptions, Scholem would certainly have agreed to the first one (the possibility of an ancient Jewish Gnosis).[65] The problem, however, is the second one (Jewish esoteric traditions preserved in Jewish sources that found their way into the Bahir). Idel discusses some interesting terms and concepts that appear in the early Jewish literature, alongside both the gnostic tradition and the Bahir, but he neglects to address the crucial question of how concretely and through which channels these Jewish traditions reached the Bahir. Thus the "historical proof" provided in the end does not prove anything, but remains on the same level as the despised "phenomenological" proof.[66] The only difference is that the one comes from gnostic and the other from equally ancient (or even more ancient) Jewish sources, yet the historical gap between the ancient source and the Bahir has yet to be bridged.[67] Something must be wrong, indeed, with our concept of "influence" and historical proof of such influence.

HISTORY

In the end, what do we know, then, about the Bahir and its historical circumstances? What is it that we can adduce *historically* about the Bahir and its Jewish environment in late twelfth-century Provence? Scholem aptly summarized his influential view in his famous article "Kabbalah" in the *Encyclopaedia Judaica*: "*Sefer ha-Bahir*, ostensibly an ancient Midrash, appeared in Provence some time between 1150 and 1200 but no earlier; it was apparently edited there from a number of treatises which came from Germany or directly from the East. An analysis of the work leaves no doubt that it was not originally written in Provence . . . , and to a large extent confirms the mid-13th-century kabbalistic tradition concerning the history of the book and its sources before it reached the early Provencal mystics in a mutilated form."[68] Here two things are important: First, the Bahir was not *written* in Provence, but rather *edited* there, and second, it comes from the East via Germany (Ashkenaz). The kabbalistic tradition, which confirms the latter, stems from the Spanish Kabbalist Isaac ben Jacob Cohen of Soria, who wrote around 1260–70. According to Isaac ben Jacob Cohen, the Bahir

is the book, more precious than gold, which Rabbi Nehunya ben Haqqana revealed through mysterious and concealed allusions to those "gifted with understanding" (i.e., the mystics) of Israel, the group of sages and the academy of old and holy men. And this book came from Palestine to the old sages and Hasidim, the Kabbalists in Germany (*Allemannia*), and from there it reached several of the old and eminent scholars among the Rabbis of Provence, who went in pursuit of every kind of secret science, the possessors of a higher knowledge. However, they only saw a part of it and not the whole of it, for its full and complete text did not come into their hands. In any case, it came to them from a distant land, whether from Palestine or from abroad, from old sages and holy Kabbalists, who possessed a well-ordered tradition (*Kabbalah*) transmitted to them orally by their fathers and forefathers.[69]

This quotation provides the only evidence so far for the "Eastern" origin of the Bahir and its mode of transmission; it serves as the foundation for Scholem's "Gnostic" theory, as well as for the more recent hypothesis, which wants to make Ashkenaz (or rather the Ashkenazi Hasidim) the source of some of the major new ideas expressed in the Bahir.[70] Attempts to distinguish between clearly identifiable layers of the Bahir — both in terms of time and space — have, however, yielded very limited results, if not outright failure. Scholem discovered quotations from the lost *Sefer Raza Rabba* ("The Book of the Great Mystery") in a late thirteenth-century Ashkenazi Hasidic commentary on the *Shi'ur Qomah*, which may well have served as a kind of proto-version of the Bahir.[71] Most conspicuously, however, the very elements in the doctrine of the Bahir that are new and that distinguish it as the first kabbalistic tractate are *not* part of the *Raza Rabba* and thus cannot have been adopted by the Bahir through the *Raza Rabba*. This definitely applies to the idea of the feminine potency of God as proposed by the Bahir. The alleged Cathar layer of the Bahir is very thin, if not nonexistent, despite Scholem's and, more recently, Shulamit Shahar's attempts to find some affinities in the doctrine of Satan and evil.[72] The same is true for the Provencal layer identified by Haviva Pedaya.[73] And finally, many of our problems could be solved if Mark Verman were correct in arguing that the Bahir stemmed, not from Provence, but from Catalonia and was composed, not before 1225, by either Ezra or Azriel of Gerona.[74] But unfortunately, the one philological argument on which Verman's theory rests,[75] does not provide grounding solid enough for such a far-reaching hypothesis.

The intellectual climate of the Provencal Jews of the second half of the twelfth century also does not help much in pinpointing the emergence of the Bahir's kabbalistic doctrine in general and its feminine dimension in particular. Scholem meticulously traced all of the possible "mystical" elements in the early kabbalistic or rather proto-kabbalistic circles around scholars like Abraham b. Isaac of Narbonne (1110–1176), Abraham b. David of Posquières, the Rabad (1125–1198), and Jacob Nazir of Lunel (second half of the twelfth century).[76] Many important details emerged — but nothing remotely comparable to the bahiric system of the Sefirot and its feminine component. A major factor in the development of the cultural life of Provencal Jewry was the emigration of Spanish scholars to Provence following the destruction of Jewish centers in Spain, in the wake of the invasion of Spain by the Almohades in the middle of the twelfth century. One of the most famous scholars to emigrate from Granada to Lunel was Judah ibn Tibbon (ca. 1120–ca. 1190), whose translations of philosophical books into Hebrew brought distinctively Neoplatonic ideas to the Rabbis of Provence. Among his many translations was Judah ha-Levi's *Kuzari*, which clearly exhibits Neoplatonic influence and must have opened up a new world to the Jews of Provence. Yet Judah ha-Levi's presentation of the Kavod or the Shekhinah respectively as a created substance that may take on human form — to be sure male human form — does not lead directly or indirectly to the Bahir's powerful image of the Shekhinah as God's spouse, sister, daughter, and mother. No one will doubt that the early Kabbalah that surfaces in the Bahir is a "polymorphous entity informed by distinct patterns and structures conveyed in symbolic and mythical images," as Wolfson has eloquently put it,[77] and that Neoplatonic ideas belong to the distinct patterns and structures that shaped the Bahir. But these Neoplatonic ideas appear sporadically in certain terms and phrases; they cannot be identified with a distinct stratum in the Bahir's redactional process, let alone recognized as the channels that transported the notion of God's femininity to the editors of the Bahir. That the Bahir is the legitimate child of (Jewish) Gnosticism and Neoplatonism, as Scholem wants us to believe,[78] may well be the case in a very general sense, but this insight does not help us to locate historically the emergence of some of the Bahir's most daring ideas.

What, then, about Christianity and its (direct or indirect) historical impact on the Bahir? Wolfson has discovered certain traits of ancient Jewish/Christian traditions in the Bahir. More precisely, he suggests "that perhaps within the framework of Jewish-Christianity older Jewish mythologoumena were preserved that are discernible in the Hebrew text of the *Bahir*."[79] He finds such a mythologoumenon in the bahiric image of the "tree that is all," but is well aware that he is discussing isolated motifs without being "able to explain the precise avenue of transmission of these motifs into the hands of those Jews responsible for the redaction of the *Bahir* in the different stages."[80] As such, we are dealing again, as is the case with Scholem's Gnosticism and Idel's Jewish esotericism, with presumably ancient motifs that found their way mysteriously, through underground channels, to the Jews of Provence. Although there is nothing wrong with this concept in itself, its articulation follows the same problematic, linear pattern of "ancient origins," "(defective) transmission," and "late end-result."

The proposition to consider the *immediate* Christian context in which the Bahir saw the light of day, and to point to the parallels between the Christian veneration of Mary and the bahiric image of the Shekhinah, has the obvious advantage of focusing on *contemporary* evidence. Instead of searching for a remote point of origin, which must materialize in mysterious ways, this approach is content with what happens in the direct environment of the phenomenon under question. At first glance, this seems to come as a relief. At second glance, however, it appears that we have not gained much, because it remains almost impossible to "prove" — in the usual sense of the term — any *direct* contact between Christians and Jews in Provence with respect to religious matters such as the manifold and dynamic shape of the divinity, let alone its female potency. To be sure, the Provencal Jews did not live in a ghetto, and we may assume numerous and varied forms of daily contact with their Christian environment. It is, however, more than bold to suggest that they might have discussed similarities between the Trinity and the Sefirot or between Mary and the Shekhinah. At least we do not have any "proof" for such an encounter.

Yet, it is as positivistic as it is naïve to approach the question by looking for direct textual evidence of Christian "influence" on the Jewish doctrine of the Shekhinah — or rather, to regard direct textual evidence as the only conceivable proof for any kind of religious exchange between Christians and Jews. The Jews certainly did not convene in their synagogues or schools to hatch out ideas that they had heard from their Christian neighbors, which they liked so much that they set out to imitate them consciously and purposefully. This is quite a naïve model of cultural interaction. But Jews and Christians did live in the same world, rather than in two separate worlds rigorously sealed off one from the other. Jews could not avoid seeing and hearing their Christian fellow-countrymen, and even if they did not report to us what they saw and heard, we can assume that they did see and hear a lot of what was happening on both sides.

As for our topic, I would like to propose that the Jews of Provence could not escape the explosion in Marian theology and the veneration of the Virgin, which was taking place literally before their eyes. Even if they did not visit Christian churches to listen to the sermons of the preachers, they are likely to have seen processions with the Virgin Mary in the streets, and they may have heard preachers in the marketplace. Indeed, why are we so sure that they did not? Perhaps we too readily adopt a static, one-dimensional picture of the encounter between Christians and Jews, accepting the traditional model of the eternal enmity between the two separate "religions." There has certainly been a great deal of enmity on both sides, but this is not the full picture, as even the Jewish polemics against the veneration of Mary have taught us. We would not have legends about Jewish children partaking in the Holy Communion together with their Christian friends and being punished by their parents if not for the possibility that Christian and Jewish children may have not just played together, but even gone together to their respective services (indeed, why is it so hard to imagine Christian children participating in Synagogue services — and Christian parents reacting similarly to the Jewish parents in the Marian legends?). I would even go a step further and propose that it is by no means impossible that Jewish children participated in school lessons of Christian children. There is no proof for such an assumption in Southern France in the second half of the twelfth century, but still one wonders why Gregory of Tours — in his version of the legend of the Jewish boy partaking of the host — passingly mentions that "the son of a Jewish glass-worker was studying and learning the alphabet with Christian boys"?[81]

We are not completely lost, however, with regard to the much-desired "hard-core" evidence. One case in point is Bernard of Clairvaux, of all people: the fervent preacher of the Virgin Mary.[82]

We know that Bernard visited Southern France in 1145 to preach against Henry of Lausanne, the advocate of a proto-Cathar heresy. He even visited Albi, which was already a center of heretical doctrines and soon to become the stronghold of the Albigenses. The sermon that he delivered in Albi on August 1, 1145 was enthusiastically received by the inhabitants of the city and led him to believe that he had taken them back to the true Catholic faith — quite mistakenly, as the subsequent history of Albi would prove.[83] Whatever he preached against the heresy, it is quite unlikely that he forgot to mention his ardor for the Virgin, especially since the festival of her assumption into heaven (August 15) was near. And if the whole city was in turmoil, it is hard to imagine that this escaped the attention of the Jews.

The Jews, as a matter of fact, had reason to listen to him carefully. Soon after his visit to Provence he began his campaign for the Second Crusade, instigated by the Cistercian Pope Eugenius III. Bernard began his preaching activity in the spring of 1146, traveled widely in Northern France and Germany, and showered all of Europe with letters and pamphlets calling upon Christians to fight against the Muslim infidels in the Holy Land. The Jews of France and Germany were directly involved in all of this and in constant danger of pogroms, since some preachers found it appropriate to direct the wrath of their co-religionists against the Jews, who were much more obvious and proximate victims than the remote and unknown Muslims. The most outstanding example of this zeal is the monk Radulf, who preached in the Rhineland with considerable success. Bernard went to Germany to preach against Radulf, and finally met him in Mainz to forbid him his preaching activity.

Much has been written about Bernard's encounter with Radulf and his attitude towards the Jews.[84] It is clear that Bernard did not act out of any particular sympathy for the Jews; this would have been completely incongruous with the spirit of his time. And yet, as David Berger convincingly argues, within the parameters of his time and faith Bernard seems to have showed an unusual degree of understanding.[85] True, much of his zeal to take action against Radulf may have been motivated by his highly developed sense of church hierarchy, insofar as Radulf's sermons presumptuously ignored strict instructions from the archbishop of Mainz who, in accordance with customary church policy, attempted to protect the Jews as an important source of income.[86] The Jews nevertheless perceived Bernard as their benefactor and savior. At least, this is what we learn from the *Sefer Zekhirah* ("Book of Remembrance") of Ephraim b. Jacob of Bonn (b. 1132) on the sufferings of the Jews during the Second Crusade. Ephraim of Bonn explicitly mentions Bernard's intervention against Radulf and quotes him as saying: "You do well to go against the Ismaelites [Muslims], but whoever touches a Jew to take his life acts as if he touches Jesus himself. My student Rudolf, who spoke against them [the Jews] that they should be wiped out, has preached wrongly because it is written of them in the Book of Psalms: 'Do not kill them lest my people be forgotten' (Ps. 59:12)." And he continues: "They [the Christians] all regard this monk among their saints, and we never found out that he was taking bribes for his talking well of the Jews."[87]

In interpreting Psalms 59:12 as a reference to the Jews, Bernard follows the general theological practice of his time: the Jews are not to be killed off, but rather to be dispersed all over the world as the biblical verse continues "only with your power make wanderers of them." According to this classical theological paradigm, the Jews are the living witness of the triumph of the Christian faith and thus must be saved for their final salvation. From one of the propaganda letters that Bernard sent out to call upon his fellow Christians to kill the Muslims (dated 1146), we know that he indeed used this Psalm verse to make his case. Here, he argues that the Jews (quite unlike the pagans) are neither to be killed nor to be forcefully converted because the Christians need them as the witnesses to their redemption and for the fulfillment of the promise that all Israel shall be saved at the end of time.[88] Thus Ephraim clearly knows what he is talking about. He must have seen one of Bernard's letters, or even may have heard him preaching as a young boy, and he most likely gives a reliable account of the Jewish feelings toward Bernard and his attitude to them in the wake of the Second Crusade. Nothing proves the possibility that the Jews of Provence were well-aware of what happened to their co-religionists in the Rhineland and of the role Bernard played in all of this, but nothing excludes it.

In Bernard of Clairvaux, who has been assigned a prominent place in Dante's paradise and became the "Doctor Marianus" in the final scene of Goethe's *Faust*, we find one possible trajectory of approach for the Provencal Jews to the Christian veneration of Mary as it developed in the late twelfth century. Future research may yield more potential points of contact.[89] I wish, however, to reiterate that my argument does not rely on this kind of "proof," as welcome as such "evidence" may be. The Jews of Southern France were surrounded by a Christian society that was impregnated by a completely new view of the feminine (or to be more cautious, by a view of the feminine that had already been developing for some time and reached its climax in the twelfth century), both in the religious and in the secular realm. In the religious realm it was the veneration and divination of Mary; in the secular realm it was the love poetry of the Troubadours — which most likely influenced each other.[90] The prevalent intellectual climate of the place and of the time — in other words, a shared Zeitgeist — makes it highly probable that the strong emphasis put on the feminine image of God in the Bahir was the product of the final editor of the book, or of a circle of editors who flourished in the late twelfth century.

This is not to say that I want to exclude the prehistory of the feminine dimension of God as it manifests itself in the Bahir. But I wish to argue that this daring concept, even if it predates the final redactional layer of the Bahir and belongs to an earlier stratum from elsewhere, was shaped by the constant interaction between Judaism and Christianity just as much as it was defined by its ultimate "origin" in the Jewish Wisdom tradition. Or to put it differently: neither was the Jewish Wisdom tradition purely Jewish from the outset, nor did it remain purely Jewish in the course of history. Rather, "Wisdom" became entangled in various cultural configurations, Jewish and Christian, which molded each other through continuous attraction and repulsion. This dynamic pattern of attraction and repulsion was certainly not restricted to the twelfth century. Indeed, even if a case can successfully be made for earlier strata of the Bahir that include the book's doctrine of God's femininity, the presumed transmission of the book from an "Eastern" origin to the "West" (through Ashkenaz or directly via Italy to Provence) fits quite well with the route taken by the veneration of the Virgin Mary, from Byzantine Christianity to the Western church. In other words, there may have been many points of contact through which Byzantine Jews could have come across the gradually developing process of Mary's veneration and deification. There is not much that can be "proved" here either, but Mary's visibility in the Byzantine cultural context may well have found its expression in earlier layers of the Bahir, as well.

Wherever the Bahir acquired its idea of the feminine manifestation of God, one thing remains undisputed. The book traveled from Provence to the Spanish Kabbalists, who regarded it as an ancient and authoritative source. It was in Christian Spain, about a hundred years after the appearance of the Bahir, that the Jewish mystics of the Zohar developed the notion of God's femininity further, in ever bolder sexual terms:

> "I am a lily (*havatzelet*) of Sharon, a rose (*shoshanah*) of the valleys (Cant. 2:1)."[91] . . . Come and see. At first [before divine intercourse] she [the Shekhinah] is green like a lily, whose leaves are green; afterward "a rose" (*shoshanah*), she is red with white colors.[92] *Shoshanah*, with six leaves;[93] *shoshanah* because she changes (*ishtaniat*) from color to color, and varies (*shaniat*) her colors. *Shoshanah* — first a lily; when she wishes to unite with the king, she is called "lily"; after she has become united with him, with the king, with those kisses, she is called "rose," since it is written: "His lips are as roses (*shoshanim*)" (Cant. 5:13).[94]

❋ NOTES ❋

INTRODUCTION

1. On the Ashera see, for example, Saul M. Olyan, *Ashera and the Cult of Yahweh in Israel*, Atlanta: Scholars Press, 1988; Christian Frevel, *Aschera und der Ausschließlichkeitsanspruch YHWHs. Beiträge zu literarischen, religions-geschichtlichen und ikonographischen Aspekten der Ascheradiskussion*, Weinheim: Beltz Athenäum, 1995; Bob Becking, Meindert Dijkstra, Karel Vriezen and Marjo C. A. Korpel, eds., *Only One God: Monotheism in Ancient Israel and the Veneration of the Goddess Ashera*, Sheffield: Sheffield Academic Press, forthcoming.

2. See the brief summary in Tikva Frymer-Kensky, *In the Wake of the Goddesses: Women, Culture, and the Biblical Transformation of Pagan Myth*, New York: The Free Press, 1992, p. 156 (with bibliography in the notes).

3. The last known Jewish document from Elephantine dates from 399 BCE.

4. Scholars use the category of "syncretism" for this phenomenon, which poorly veils the fact that there is no such thing as "monotheism," even toward the end of the monarchy.

5. See, for example, Odo Marquardt, "Lob des Polytheismus: Über Mono-mythie und Polymythie," in: *Philosophie und Mythos. Ein Kolloquium*, ed. Hans Poser, Berlin: Walter de Gruyter, 1979, pp. 40–58; Jacob Taubes, "Zur Konjunktur des Polytheismus," in: *Mythos und Moderne: Begriff und Bild einer Rekonstruktion*, ed. Karl Heinz Bohrer, Frankfurt a.M.: Suhrkamp, 1983, pp. 457–470.

6. See Frymer-Kensky, *In the Wake of the Goddesses*, p. 1.

7. Jan Assmann, *Moses the Egyptian: The Memory of Egypt in Western Monotheism*, Cambridge, Mass.: Harvard University Press, 1997, p. 217.

8. See for example, as far as early Christianity and Gnosis are concerned, the pioneering article by Elaine Pagels, "Irenaeus, the 'Canon of Truth,' and the Gospel of John: 'Making a Difference' through Hermeneutics and Ritual," forthcoming in *Vigiliae Christianae*.

9. See in particular his magnum opus *Major Trends in Jewish Mysticism*, first published in 1941 by Schocken Publishing House and then in many editions and translations, and his *Origins of the Kabbalah*, originally published in German as *Ursprung und Anfänge der Kabbala*, Berlin: Walter de Gruyter, 1962.

10. Thus the dynamic model that I propose, with its continuous shift between two extreme poles, differs considerably from Scholem's progressive (Hegelian) triad, polytheism — radical monotheism — return of myth in mysticism (see the introductory chapter of his *Major Trends*, pp. 7ff.).

11. For the name, see Chapter 6, pp. 118f.

12. See the full quotation from Isaac Cohen in Chapter 10, pp. 235f.

13. On the translation of this passage, see Scholem, *Origins*, p. 43, n. 74, and Mark Verman, *The Books of Contemplation: Medieval Jewish Mystical Sources*, Albany, N.Y.: State University of New York Press, 1992, pp. 168f.

14. Hebrew text in Adolf Neubauer, "The Bahir and the Zohar," *JQR* 4, 1892, p. 358; the translation follows Scholem, *Origins*, pp. 42f.

15. By "her" I refer to the feminine gender of *hokhmah/sophia* in both Hebrew and Greek and to her personified status in most texts.

16. See, for example, Israel J. Yuval, "Easter and Passover as Early Jewish-Christian Dialogue," in: Paul F. Bradshaw and Lawrence A. Hoffmann, eds., *Passover and Easter: Origin and History to Modern Times*, South Bend, Ind.: University of Notre Dame Press, 1999, pp. 98–124; id., "Passover in the Middle Ages," ibid., pp. 127–160; id., *"Two Nations in Your Womb": Perceptions of Jews and Christians*, Tel Aviv: Am Oved, 2000 [in Hebrew]; Ivan Marcus, *Rituals of Childhood: Jewish Acculturation in Medieval Europe*, New Haven and London: Yale University Press, 1996; Susan Einbinder, *Beautiful Death: Jewish Poetry and Martyrdom in Medieval France*, Princeton University Press, forthcoming. Just before the manuscript of my book went to press, my Berlin colleague Johannes Heil kindly presented to me the very useful collection of articles *Maria — Tochter Sion? Mariologie, Marienfrömmigkeit und Judenfeindschaft*, edited by himself and Rainer Kampling, Paderborn: Ferdinand Schöningh 2001. Characteristically enough for the state of the field in Germany, the Christian veneration of Mary is viewed almost exclusively as the vehicle for hatred of Jews and anti-Semitism. An exception is Heil's more nuanced article on pp. 37–57.

17. *Rituals of Childhood*, pp. 11f.

CHAPTER ONE

1. Later addition to the Book of Job.

2. The passage belongs to the latest parts of the book.

3. The Hebrew version of Jesus Sirach can be safely dated to the early second century BCE (about 190).

4. All translations from the Hebrew Bible follow the Jewish Publication Society (JPS) edition: *Tanakh: A New Translation of the Holy Scriptures According to the Traditional Hebrew Text*, Philadelphia: The Jewish Publication Society, 1985. Major deviations are recorded.

5. Literally, "There is a path which no bird knows . . . ," but it is obviously the path that leads to the gold and precious stones hidden in the depths of the earth.

6. The JPS translation reads misleadingly, "source."

7. The JPS translation reads misleadingly, "We have only a report of it."

8. The JPS translation has again "source."

9. Literally, "counted it."

10. Or "established it"; the JPS translation reads misleadingly, "measured it."

11. JPS translation: "probed it."

12. The Hebrew text wavers between *enosh* ("humankind") and *adam* ("man"); see vv. 13 and 28. In the following I use the generic "humankind."

13. It is certainly by coincidence, but some of these verbs are used for God's creation and Abraham's imitation of it in the much later *Sefer Yetzirah* ("Book of Creation"); see *Sefer Yetzirah*, ed. Ithamar Gruenwald, in: *IOS* 1, 1971, pp. 132–177 (§§ 19 and 61).

14. Gerhard von Rad, *Wisdom in Israel*, London: SCM Press, 1972, p. 148.

15. See also von Rad, *Wisdom in Israel*, p. 147, n. 3.

16. The picture drawn by man ruling the earth makes it quite clear that our author indeed is preoccupied with men rather than with women.

17. Note the similar juxtaposition with *binah* in Job 28:12, 20.

18. Proverbs 8:1–11.

19. The JPS translation has instead "rejoicing before Him at all times," playing down the literal meaning.

20. JPS has "rejoicing."

21. The Septuagint has *ektisen* ("created"), which Aquila, Symmachus, and Theodotion translate *ektēsato* ("acquired").

22. As apparently the JPS translation does.

23. A good summary is provided by Bernhard Lang, *Frau Weisheit. Deutung einer biblischen Gestalt*, Düsseldorf: Patmos-Verlag, 1975, pp. 93–95 (the English version: *Wisdom and the Book of Proverbs: A Hebrew Goddess Redefined*, New York: Pilgrim Press, 1986, unfortunately does not contain the discussion of *amon*); Otto Plöger, *Sprüche Salomos (Proverbia)*, Neukirchen-Vluyn: Neukirchener Verlag, 1984, pp. 94–96. And see already the various philological interpretations in Bereshit Rabba 1:1.

24. See in particular Christa Kayatz, *Studien zu Proverbien 1–9. Eine form- und motivgeschichtliche Untersuchung unter Einbeziehung ägyptischen Vergleichmaterials*, Neukirchen: Neukirchener Verlag, 1966, pp. 93ff.; Burton L. Mack, *Logos und Sophia. Untersuchungen zur Weisheitstheologie im hellenistischen Judentum*, Göttingen: Vandenhoek & Ruprecht, 1973, pp. 34–42; Jan Assmann, *Ma'at. Gerechtigkeit und Unsterblichkeit im Alten Ägypten*, München: C. H. Beck, 1990.

25. Assmann emphasizes that Maat, in addition to her classical definition as the immanent order of creation, embodies the categories of "justice" and "truth" (*Ma'at*, pp. 33f., 164ff.). This brings her very close to "Wisdom" in Proverbs: since the order, implanted by God in his creation, is the order that human beings are expected to follow, Maat/Wisdom acquires a social and ethical dimension. Thus it is not a question of either "cosmic order" or "justice";

rather, the ethical dimension is a consequence of Maat/Wisdom's function as the cosmic order of the world.

26. More precisely, she is the daughter, as well as the spouse and the mother, of Re; her three roles are closely interlinked (Assmann, *Ma'at*, pp. 161ff.).

27. Assmann, *Ma'at*, pp. 168f.; Kayatz, *Studien*, p. 96.

28. Kayatz, ibid., pp. 97ff.

29. Hans Bonnet, art. *"Maat,"* in: *Reallexikon der ägyptischen Religionsgeschichte*, Berlin: Walter der Gruyter, 1952, p. 430; see also Wolfgang Helck, art. *"Maat,"* in: *Lexikon der Ägyptologie*, ed. Wolfgang Helck and Wolfhart Westendorf, vol. 2, Wiesbaden: Otto Harrassowitz, 1980, cols. 1110–1119.

30. Assmann, *Ma'at*, p. 172. The parallel with the biblical and postbiblical Wisdom tradition is more striking than with the prologue of the Gospel of John as Assmann suggests.

31. See Kayatz, *Studien*, pp. 94ff.

32. *Wisdom in Israel*, p. 153.

33. The translation follows the Greek text. English Translation: *The Wisdom of Ben Sira*, a new translation with notes by Patrick W. Skehan, introduction and commentary by Alexander A. di Lella, New York: Doubleday, 1987.

34. Literally, "all these things are the book of the covenant . . . ".

35. 6:22; translation *The Revised English Bible: with Apocrypha*, Oxford: Oxford University Press, 1989.

36. Literally, "creator."

37. Literally, "Wisdom, the craftswomen of all these things, taught me (this)."

38. "Word" and "Wisdom" are used almost as synonyms in Sap. Sal. 9:1f.

39. The Greek text continues to refer to "her" in the feminine, although the subject is *pneuma*.

40. 9:17 probably shouldn't be understood too literally as Wisdom and the Holy Spirit being two distinctive entities.

41. The resemblance of some of these epithets to Stoic philosophy has long been observed; see, for example, Chrysostome Larcher, *Le Livre de la Sagesse ou la Sagesse de Salomon*, vol. 2, Paris: Gabalda, 1984, pp. 479–514; Helmut Engel, *" 'Was Weisheit ist und wie sie entstand, will ich verkünden',"* in: Georg Hentschel and Erich Zenger, *Lehrerin der Gerechtigkeit*, Leipzig: Benno-Verlag, 1991, pp. 67–102 (pp. 74f.).

42. Literally, "she is the steam (*atmis*) of the power of God."

43. Or "a pure emanation."

44. Or "efflux, effulgence."

45. Literally, "because of her living together with God."

46. The Revised English Bible translation "has accepted her" is unacceptable.

47. *Logos und Sophia*, pp. 66–72; see also John S. Kloppenborg, "Isis and Sophia in the Book of Wisdom," *HTR* 75, 1982, pp. 57–84; Engel, Weisheit, pp. 76–85, 95–102.

48. Julian, Epist. 47.

49. Plutarch, *De Iside* 53.

50. Ibid., 43.

51. Ibid., 59: "the ideas, forms, and emanations of the god remain in heaven and in the stars."

52. Ibid., 43: "thus they locate the power of Osiris in the moon and say that Isis, as the creative principle, has intercourse with him."

53. Ibid., 53.

54. Ibid., 64.

55. Cf. Konrat Ziegler, art. "Plutarchos," in: *PW*, vol. 21.1, 1951 (reprint 1990), col. 716.

56. *Logos und Sophia*, p. 70.

57. Ibid., 71.

CHAPTER TWO

1. The most comprehensive analysis of Philo's work is still Harry A. Wolfson, *Philo. Foundations of Religious Philosophy in Judaism, Christianity, and Islam*, 2 vols., Cambridge, Mass.: Harvard University Press, 1948, ³1962.

2. See lately Peter Schäfer, *Judeophobia: Attitudes toward the Jews in the Ancient World*, Cambridge, Mass., and London: Harvard University Press, 1997, pp. 136ff.

3. See on our subject John Dillon, "Female Principles in Platonism," *Itaca* 2, 1986, pp. 108–123 (on Philo, pp. 117ff.).

4. See in particular Wolfson, *Philo*, pp. 200–294; still very useful is the brief summary of Philo's concept of Wisdom by Hans Leisegang, art. "Sophia," in: *PW*, III A,1, 1927, cols. 1031–1034.

5. Jean Laporte, "Philo in the Tradition of Biblical Wisdom," in: Robert L. Wilken, ed., *Aspects of Wisdom in Judaism and Early Christianity*, South Bend, Ind. and London: University of Notre Dame Press, 1975, pp. 103–141 (106).

6. Ibid., 135.

7. *De Ebrietate* 30f. All translations from Philo follow, with some corrections, the Loeb Classical Library edition.

8. The same notion also in *De Virtutibus* 62: "Now Wisdom's years are from old, before not only I, but the whole universe was born."

9. *Origenis Hexaplorum . . . Fragmenta*, ed. Fridericus Field, vol. 2, Oxford, 1875 (reprint Hildesheim: Georg Olms, 1964), p. 326.

10. See also *De Confusione Linguarum* 49: Wisdom, "mother" and "nurse" (*tithēnē*). And cf. Plato, *Timaeus* 49a and the reference in Plutarch, *De Iside* 53 (Chapter 1, p. 37).

11. See Chapter 1, p. 26.

12. *De Opificio Mundi* 19f.

13. Ibid., 24.

14. For a detailed discussion see Mack, *Logos und Sophia*, pp. 108ff. (Mack exaggerates, however, the influence of the Isis/Osiris myth). Carsten Colpe, who gives a thorough account of Logos and related terms, is surprisingly laconic about Wisdom: "Von der Logoslehre des Philon zu der des Clemens von Alexandrien," in: *Kerygma und Logos. Festschrift für Carl Andresen zum 70. Geburtstag*, ed. Adolf M. Ritter, Göttingen: Vandenhoek & Ruprecht, 1979, pp. 89–107 (p. 96).

15. *Legum Allegoriae* I, 63–65.

16. Ibid., 64.

17. Ibid., 65.

18. In *De Fuga et Inventione* 97, the "supreme divine Logos" (*ton anōtatō logon theion*) is even called the "fountain of Wisdom" (*sophias pēgē*), "Logos" probably referring to the ontological quality of Logos/Wisdom, and "Wisdom" to the epistemological quality (Wolfson, *Philo*, p. 259, relates "Logos" to the "antemundane Logos" and "Wisdom" to the "revealed Law of Moses"). Quite to the contrary, in *De Somniis* II, 241f. (another interpretation of Gen. 2:10), it is the "divine Logos," who descends from the "fountain of Wisdom" (*apo pēgēs tēs sophias*), turning "Logos" into an epistemological quality! — The controversial passage in *De Fuga et Inventione* 108f. does not state that the Logos is the son of God and of Wisdom, but rather that the High Priest, who is *comparable* to the Logos, is the child of God and Wisdom, the parents of the universe; see also Ursula Früchtel, *Die kosmologischen Vorstellungen bei Philo von Alexandrien*, Leiden: Brill 1968, pp. 175, 178.; Wolfson, ibid.

19. See also Wolfson, *Philo*, vol. 1, p. 258: "Wisdom, then, is only another word for Logos, and it is used in all the senses of the term Logos. Both these terms mean, in the first place, a property of God, identical with His essence, and, like His essence, eternal. In the second place, they mean a real, incorporeal being, created by God before the creation of the world. Third, . . . Logos means also a Logos immanent in the world, and so, also Wisdom . . . is used in that sense." I would qualify the somewhat oversimplistic first sentence (the terms "Wisdom" and "Logos" aren't just interchangeable), and I would add that the *reason* for the distinction of the first and the second meaning is the epistemological quality of Wisdom (the third meaning).

20. Notice the play of words with *akrotomos*.

21. *Legum Allegoriae* II, 86.

22. *Quod Deterius Potiori Insidiari Solet* 118.

23. The LXX version of Jeremiah 3:4 differs considerably from the Hebrew text; Philo substitutes *archēgon* ("chief/guide of your virginity") in the LXX with *andra* ("man/husband") in order to make the husband/wife comparison.

24. *De Cherubim* 49f.

25. Ibid., 51f.

26. *Quod Deterius Potiori Insidiari Solet* 54.

27. *Legum Allegoriae* II, 49.

28. Ibid.

29. *Quod Deterius Potiori Insidiari Solet 54.*

30. In *De Fuga et Inventione* 109 God is the "father of all" (*tōn sympantōn patēr*), and Wisdom is the mother, "through whom the universe (*ta hola*) came into existence."

31. Ibid., 115–117.

32. On the metaphor of Wisdom as nourisher, see in particular Karl-Gustav Sandelin, *Wisdom as Nourisher. A Study of an Old Testament Theme, its Development within Early Judaism and its Impact on Early Christianity*, Åbo: Åbo Akademi, 1986, pp. 82ff. (on Philo).

33. More traditional is the comparison of the effect Wisdom exerts on the mind with sun's rays (*De Congressu* 47). Wisdom's rays in the soul are "spiritual rays," sown by the Father (*De Vita Contemplativa* 68).

34. *Legum Allegoriae* II, 49f.

35. See also *De Migratione Abrahami* 27–30, where man is called upon leaving sense-perception and bodily existence and returning to the "land of your father" (Gen. 31:3), which is Logos/Wisdom (not explicitly called mother here). He will then acquire the "companionship of the bountiful God," which is the "fountain from which the good things are poured forth."

36. *Quis Rerum Divinarum Heres Sit* 52f.

37. We will encounter the same problem in the Bahir.

38. See also *Legum Allegoriae* 64, and note 10 above.

39. *bat el.*

40. *De Fuga et Inventione* 50.

41. See pp. 45f. above.

42. *De Fuga et Inventione* 51.

43. See also Laporte, *Philo in the Tradition of Biblical Wisdom*, p. 118: "Feminine in regard to God, Wisdom becomes masculine with regard to man, who is made masculine by her, and begets . . . "

44. See above p. 45.

45. *De Fuga et Inventione* 52.

46. The male quality of the "daughter" defuses the simultaneous use of the spouse/mother and daughter metaphors.

47. And here, too, in her function she is again male: "For in the bodily marriage the male sows the seed and the female receives it; on the other hand in the matings within the soul, though virtue seemingly ranks as wife, her natural function is to sow good counsels and excellent words . . . " (*De Abrahamo* 101).

48. *De Plantatione* 65.

49. Ibid., 23f.

50. One of her effects is "drunkenness which is soberness itself" (*Quod Omnis Probus Liber Sit* 13; 117).

51. *De Sacrificiis Abelis et Caini* 78f.

52. *De Posteritate Caini* 78.

53. See Chapter 1, pp. 36f., above.

54. *Quod Deus Immutabilis Sit* 92.

55. *De Congressu Quaerendae Eruditionis Gratia* 14. See also ibid. 36f. where "living together in concubinage with the slavish arts" is opposed to being enrolled as the "husband of the queen and mistress virtue." In ibid. 79 the hierarchy is culture of the schools — philosophy — Wisdom: "And therefore just as the culture of the schools (*hē egkyklios mousikē*) is the bond-servant of philosophy, so must philosophy be the servant of Wisdom (*doulē sophias*)."

56. *Quod Deus Immutabilis Sit* 143.

57. *De Somniis* II, 13: "In the same way the pleasures of the body descend upon us in gathered force like a cataract deluging and obliterating one after another all the things of the mind; and then, after no long interval, Wisdom with strong and vehement counterblast both slackens the impetus of pleasures and mitigates in general all the appetites and ambitions which the bodily senses kindle in us."

58. "Unaided" means, as the editor of this volume correctly observes (referring to *De Migratione Abrahami* 142), "without needing the midwife's skill." But the "midwife", of course, is the "handmaid" of Wisdom, human knowledge (*epinoias kai epistēmas anthrōpōn*), as the text in *De Migratione* explicitly states.

59. *De Vita Contemplativa* 68.

60. The embodiment of Wisdom.

61. *De Cherubim* 50. See also *Quaestiones in Exodum* II, 3.

62. If Sapientia Salomonis is to be dated later, as some scholars assume, one would have to argue that the Wisdom/spouse tradition goes back to Philo and that it is Philo who influenced Sapientia Salomonis.

63. Rev. ed., Wilmette, Illinois: Chiron Publications, 1994, pp. 95–106.

64. *Feminine Dimension*, p. 96.

65. Ibid., 98.

66. Here she follows Mack; see above [n. 14].

67. *De Somniis* II, 241f. [above, n. 18].

68. *Feminine Dimension*, p. 100.

69. Ibid., 102.

70. Ibid.

71. Ibid., 103 and more often.

72. *De Fuga et Inventione* 50–52.

73. *Feminine Dimension*, p. 105.

74. And also, the metaphors are used by Philo rather interchangeably and in multiple ways.

75. See Chapter 8, pp. 144f., below.

CHAPTER THREE

1. Strange, because in classical Greek the adjective *gnōstikos* did not refer to persons, but rather to human capacities. Thus, what is meant by *gnōstikos* is that the follower of the group has the capacity, which leads to knowledge.

2. The terms "gnosis" and "Gnosticism" were defined at the famous Messina congress as follows: "In order to avoid an undifferentiated use of the terms *gnosis* and Gnosticism, it seems to be advisable to identify, by the combined use of the historical and the typological methods, a concrete fact, 'Gnosticism,' beginning methodologically with a certain group of systems of the Second Century A.D. which everyone agrees to be designated with this term. In distinction from this, *gnosis* is regarded as 'knowledge of the divine mysteries reserved for an élite.'" See Ugo Bianchi, ed., *Le Origini dello Gnosticismo. Colloquio di Messina, 13–18 Aprile 1966*, Leiden: Brill, 1967, p. XXVI.

3. See, most elaborately, the sweeping attack by Michael Allen Williams, *Rethinking "Gnosticism": An Argument for Dismantling a Dubious Category*, Princeton, N.J.: Princeton University Press, 1996.

4. Williams (ibid., pp. 51–53) suggests, instead of "Gnosticism," the category "biblical demiurgical traditions." As with most of these substitutes (another example is "ritual" instead of "magic"), "biblical demiurgical" is too narrowly defined to capture the much broader phenomenon expressed by "Gnosis" or "Gnosticism" and to become generally accepted.

5. For a still useful summary of the literary and historical evidence see Bentley Layton, *The Gnostic Scriptures. A New Translation with Annotations and Introductions*, New York: Doubleday, 1987, pp. XV–XXVII; 5–22.

6. On Valentinus and his system, see most recently Christoph Markschies, *Valentinus Gnosticus? Untersuchungen zur valentinianischen Gnosis mit einem Kommentar zu den Fragmenten Valentins*, Tübingen: J.C.B. Mohr (Paul Siebeck), 1992. Markschies suggests that the disciples of Valentinus developed the mythological system we attribute to him, not Valentinus himself.

7. Without adopting his problematic use of language ("the gnostic myth" or "the gnostic sect").

8. *The Gnostic Scriptures*, p. 8.

9. See, for example, Gedaliahu A. G. Stroumsa's programmatic monograph *Another Seed: Studies in Gnostic Mythology*, Leiden: Brill, 1984, or the more specific articles by Edwin M. Yamauchi, "Jewish Gnosticism? The Prologue of John, Mandaean Parallels, and the Trimorphic Protennois," in: *Studies in Gnosticism and Hellenistic Religions*, presented to Gilles Quispel on the Occasion of his 65th Birthday, ed. Roeloef van den Broek and Marten J. Vermaseren, Leiden: Brill, 1981, pp. 467–497, and Birger A. Pearson, "Pre-Valentinian Gnosticism in Alexandria," in: *The Future of Early Christianity: Essays in Honor of Helmut Koester*, ed. Birger A. Pearson, Minneapolis: Fortress Press,

1991, pp. 455–466. Layton in the Preface to his *Gnostic Scriptures* (p. XII) avoids explicitly addressing this question; yet this reservation does not prevent him from more or less working with the presupposition "that the gnostic myth emerged from Christianity" (ibid., p. 20). He not only claims that the (majority of) gnostic works have the distinctive features of Christian Scriptures, but even argues that the (few) gnostic works, in which Christian features are completely absent, were written as part of a Christian (rather than extra- or pre-Christian) literary corpus. Just as the former is a hasty a conclusion, so the latter proves problematic.

10. I quote from the translation by Waldstein and Wisse in: *The Apocryphon of John: Synopsis of Nag Hammadi Codices II,1; III,1; and IV,1 with BG 8502,2*, ed. Michael Waldstein and Frederik Wisse, Leiden: Brill, 1995. If not stated otherwise, I follow the longer version, which is the Coptic translation of a long Greek recension. The structuring of the quotations follows, with some variations, Waldstein and Wisse.

11. NHC II 2:14ff.

12. BG 25:10; NHC II 3:36.

13. NHC II 4:19f.

14. NHC II 4:24–26; BG 27:2–4.

15. NHC II 4:12.

16. NHC II 4:27–5:4.

17. Cf. George W. MacRae, "The Jewish Background of the Gnostic Sophia Myth," *NT* 12, 1970, pp. 86–101; Sergio La Porta, "Sophia-Mētēr: Reconstructing a Gnostic Myth," in: *The Nag Hammadi Library after Fifty Years*, ed. John D. Turner and Anne McGuire, Leiden: Brill, 1997, pp. 188–207.

18. Layton, *Gnostic Scriptures*, p. 15.

19. NHC III 7:13f.; BG 27:6.

20. Michael Waldstein, "The Primal Triad in the *Apocryphon of John*," in: *The Nag Hammadi Library after Fifty Years*, pp. 154–187 (165).

21. Waldstein, ibid., p. 166.

22. Sapientia Salomonis 7:26; see Chapter 1, pp. 35f., above.

23. NHC II 5:4–11.

24. This part is missing in the shorter version.

25. Jorunn Jacobsen Buckley, *Female Fault and Fulfilment in Gnosticism*, Chapel Hill: University of North Carolina Press, 1986, p. 41.

26. *De Fuga et Inventione 50–52*; see Chapter 2, pp. 49f.

27. NHC II 6:2f.

28. NHC II 6:8f.

29. NHC II 6:15f.

30. NHC III 9:17; BG 30:6 (*autogenētos*); not here in NHC II but, for example, in II 7:11.

31. NHC III 9:18; BG 30:7; not in NHC II.

32. NHC II 6:10–13.

33. NHC III 9:10–13; BG 29:18–30:2.

34. BG 29:3 reads "her."

35. NHC II 6:14f.

36. The uncertainty of this reading results from the Greek abbreviation *ChRS* in the Coptic text, which can be resolved either as *Christos* or as *chrēstos*, or, more precisely, the abstract nouns *christotēs*, "christhood," and *chrēstotēs*, "goodness." See Waldstein, The Primal Triad, pp. 174f., who argues for a pun that plays with both anointing/annointed and goodness. The Christian influence here is obvious, but this does not necessarily mean that "the anointing scene in *Ap. John* presupposes a specifically Christian setting" (Waldstein, ibid., p. 174), neither is it unequivocal proof that the Apocryphon of John is "an example of a Christian work that discusses the preexistent Christ but not the incarnation" (Layton, *Gnostic Scriptures*, p. 23). It may as well have originated in a Jewish context that was later revised in a Christian spirit.

37. NHC II 6:18–26.

38. NHC II 6:33f.

39. NHC II 7:11.

40. NHC II 7:22–30.

41. NHC II 9:19–22.

42. (1) Grace (*charis*), (2) Truth (*alētheia*), (3) Form (*morphē*), (4) Reflection or Afterthought (*epinoia*), (5) Perception (*aisthēsis*), (6) Memory (*mnēmē*), (7) Understanding (*synēsis*), (8) Love (*agapē*), (9) Idea (*idea*), (10) Perfection (*teleios*), (11) Peace (*eirēnē*), (12) Wisdom (*sophia*).

43. NHC II 8:20.

44. I follow now the shorter version in BG 36:16ff., because of its better structured and more poetical character.

45. NHC II 9:27: "invisible Spirit."

46. BG 36:16–37:11.

47. Anne Pasquier, "Prouneikos: A Colorful Expression to Designate Wisdom," in: *Images of the Feminine in Gnosticism*, ed. Karen L. King, Philadelphia: Fortress Press, 1988, pp. 47–66 (56f.).

48. La Porta, "Sophia-Mētēr," p. 194, has pointed out that already her "dislocation" in the arrangement of the twelve aeons indicates a disharmony and instability within the system.

49. BG 37:12–18.

50. BG 37:18–38:6.

51. Layton, *Gnostic Scriptures*, pp. 74f., n. 95b. But see the more recent discussion by Joseph Dan, "Yaldabaoth and the Language of the Gnosis," in: *Geschichte—Tradition—Reflexion. Festschrift für Martin Hengel zum 70. Geburtstag*, vol. 1: *Judentum*, ed. Peter Schäfer, Tübingen: J.C.B. Mohr (Paul Siebeck), 1996, pp. 557–564: "Yaldabaoth" is a kind of acronym, consisting of the letters "Y," "L," "D," and "Baoth" in the phrase *Yah Elohim Adonai Tzebaoth* (which is common in the literature of Merkavah mysticism).

52. Compare also Isa. 45:21.

53. NHC II 14:12f. The "ninth heaven" seems to be the ninth from the bottom of the twelve aeons; that is, the fourth from the top: the place of "Reflection" or "Afterthought" (Layton, *Gnostic Scriptures*, p. 39, n. 14c); but see La Porta, "Sophia-Mētēr," p. 200.

54. With the translation of *epinoia* by "Afterthought" I follow Layton; Waldstein and Wisse have "reflection" (see above notes 42 and 53).

55. Waldstein and Wisse have "him," and Layton has "it." Since "Afterthought/Reflection" belongs to the twelve aeons which originate from Barbelo, I have substituted "her" for "him/it."

56. Following Layton; Waldstein and Wisse have "it."

57. NHC II:20:9–28.

58. NHC II 10:18.

59. NHC II 23:20–25.

60. NHC II 4:32: *pronoia*, the realization of the invisible Spirit's thought (*ennoia*), translated by Waldstein and Wisse as "Providence."

61. See also La Porta, "Sophia-Mētēr," pp. 195ff.

62. Cf. Prov. 2:16–19; 5:1–23; 6:20–26.

63. La Porta, "Sophia-Mētēr," pp. 195–207.

64. See Michael A. Williams's response in the same volume, pp. 217–220.

65. La Porta, "Sophia-Mētēr," p. 201.

66. It may not be by coincidence that the poem is missing in the shorter version of the book.

67. Following Layton; Waldstein and Wisse have "wickedness."

68. NHC II 30:11–31:28.

69. See Chapter 7, n. 9, below.

70. NHC II 14:9–13.

71. As to Ialdabaoth in the Apocryphon of John, there is no compelling reason to identify him with the Platonic demiurge (Layton, *Gnostic Scriptures*, p. 15, n. 4), neither to argue in favor of his equation with the Jewish God as opposed to the First Principle. To be sure he calls himself a "jealous god" and boasts that there is no other god apart from him (NHC II 13:8f.), but this does not mean that there is an absolute caesura between him and the upper world. He is the source of evil but still, he also remains to be the son of Sophia. The Kabbalah will show that and how even evil can be integrated into the realm of the divinity.

72. *Adversus Haereses*, 1.1.1–1.8.5. I follow, with some variations, the translation by Layton, *Gnostic Scriptures*, pp. 281ff.

73. *Adversus Haereses*, 1.1.3.

74. Also called "First-Father" (*propatōr*) and "Deep" (*bythos*).

75. Also called "Grace" (*charis*) or "Silence" (*sigē*).

76. *Apeskēpse*, literally "was hurled from above."

77. The perfect "First-Father."

78. *Adversus Haereses*, 1.2.2.

79. *Adversus Haereses*, 1.2.4.

80. *Adversus Haereses*, 1.2.5.

81. *Adversus Haereses*, 1.4.2.

82. It is called the "midpoint"; that is, "above the demiurge but below or outside the fullness"; *Adversus Haereses*, 1.5.3.

83. *Adversus Haereses*, 1.7.1.

CHAPTER FOUR

1. On this designation of God, see Arthur Marmorstein, *The Old Rabbinic Doctrine of God*, vol. 1, *The Names and Attributes of God*, London: Milford, Oxford University Press, 1927 (reprint New York: Ktav, 1968), p. 89.

2. Bereshit Rabba 1:1; all translations from Bereshit Rabba follow *Midrash Rabbah: Genesis*, 2 vols., trans. H. Freedman, London: Soncino Press, 1939. On the interpretation of the Midrash, see, for example, Alexander Samely, "Between Scripture and its Rewording: Towards a Classification of Rabbinic Exegesis," *JJS* 42, 1991, pp. 39–67; Philip S. Alexander, "Pre-Emptive Exegesis: Genesis Rabbah's Reading of the Story of Creation," *JJS* 43, 1992, pp. 230–245.

3. This is the traditional interpretation of Genesis 1:1. As we will see, the Midrash understands the Hebrew text (*bereshit bara' elohim*) differently.

4. JPS translation: "He was foster father to Hadassah," but this comes close to Numbers 11:12. The Midrash probably understands the verse to mean that Mordecai concealed her from the public gaze.

5. This is the translation of the Aramaic Targum of Nahum 3:8 which renders "No-amon" by "Alexandria the Great."

6. Literally, "looked into the Torah."

7. See Chapter 1, p. 26, above.

8. *Be* in *be-reshit* can be temporal ("in the beginning") as well as instrumental ("by means of, through").

9. See the use of Proverbs 8:22 in the parable and other midrashim that make clear that the Torah was created before the creation of the world (e.g., Bereshit Rabba 1:4).

10. Bereshit Rabba 1:5. This interpretation presupposes the following reading of the first three verses of Genesis that is, following Rashi, the translation of the Jewish Publication Society: "(1) When God began to create heaven and earth — (2) the earth being unformed (*tohu*) and void (*bohu*), with darkness over the surface of the deep (*tehom*) and a wind from God sweeping over the water — (3) God said, 'Let there be light'; and there was light." According to this translation/interpretation the first "thing" God created is the light; what is mentioned in the parenthesis (*tohu, bohu*, darkness, and *tehom*) was already present

and therefore "available." The (or rather, most) Rabbis in Bereshit Rabba of course refute this interpretation.

11. Bereshit Rabba 1:7.

12. Psalms 104:3 refers to the firmament that was created on the second day (Gen. 1:6–8); since it is followed in Psalms 104:4 by the angels, this is taken as proof that the angels were created on the same day as the firmament.

13. All winged creatures were created on the fifth day (Gen. 1:20–23); since according to Isaiah 6:2 the angels have wings they must have been created on the fifth day, too.

14. The Midrash vocalizes *mi 'itti* instead of *me-'itti* in the Masoretic text.

15. Bereshit Rabba 1:3.

16. Isaiah 37:22; 2 Kings 19:21.

17. In particular in the Book of Lamentations (2:1,8,10,13,18; 4:22).

18. Septuagint Psalms 86:5.

19. Compare, for example, Pesikta Rabbati 26, ed. Friedmann, fol. 129a–132a; Targum Canticles 8:5.

20. b Berakhot 35b.

21. That is, defectively (without the *waw*), and therefore can be read as *u-le'immi* ("and to my mother").

22. Shir ha-Shirim Rabba 3,11:2; the translation follows *Midrash Rabbah: Song of Songs*, trans. Maurice Simon, London: Soncino Press, 1939, ³1961.

23. See, for example, the Rabbinic interpretation of the Song of Songs in Shir ha-Shirim Rabba and in the Targum: devoid of any sexual implications, so characteristic of the biblical text, it expounds the *history* of God and the people of Israel.

24. See Chapter 6, p. 131, below.

25. The most comprehensive and unsurpassed evaluation of the concept of the Shekhinah is Arnold Goldberg, *Untersuchungen über die Vorstellung von der Schekhinah in der frühen rabbinischen Literatur*, Berlin: Walter de Gruyter, 1969. Unfortunately, the book has not been translated into English, and the English reader is still confined to the outdated monograph by Joshua Abelson, *The Immanence of God in Rabbinical Literature*, London: Macmillan, 1912 (reprint New York: Hermon Press, 1969).

26. Interestingly and characteristically enough, there is no discussion at all in Goldberg's book of the gender of the Shekhinah.

27. In the verse Exodus 38:21: "These are the records of the Tabernacle, the Tabernacle of the Testimony."

28. The Tabernacle was to serve as an atonement to Israel after having made the Golden Calf.

29. And made the Golden Calf.

30. The next verse in Lamentations reads: "The Lord's countenance has turned away from them."

31. Shemot Rabba 51:4 (see also Tanhuma Buber, *pequde* 2, p. 127); the

translation follows *Midrash Rabbah: Exodus*, trans. S.M. Lehrman, London: Soncino Press, 1939, [3]1961.

32. Goldberg speaks of the "Subjektsidentität von Schekhinah und Gottheit"; that is, of the identity of the subject of the Shekhinah and God (*Untersuchungen*, pp. 457f.; 534ff.).

33. Ibid., 534.

34. Ibid., 536.

35. A play of words with the root *'shr*.

36. Shir ha-Shirim Rabba 8:11.

37. On this topic, see my monograph *Rivalität zwischen Engeln und Menschen. Untersuchungen zur rabbinischen Engelvorstellung*, Berlin and New York: Walter de Gruyter, 1975.

38. This implies another dig at the angels: it is only human beings, not the angels, who can praise God properly!

39. For example, Exodus 33:20 (face); Numbers 12:8 (mouth and face); Exodus 33:23 (back and face); Psalms 17:8 (wings); Isaiah 66:1 (feet).

40. See the summary in Goldberg, *Untersuchungen*, pp. 463f.

41. Even the later, prekabbalistic *Shi'ur Qomah* speculations, that is, the descriptions of the measurement of the divine body and its limbs that follow the depiction of the lover in Canticles 5:10–16, leave no doubt that this is a male body. Cf. Peter Schäfer (with Margarete Schlüter and Hans Georg von Mutius), *Synopse zur Hekhalot-Literatur*, Tübingen: J.C.B. Mohr (Paul Siebeck), 1981, §§ 695ff.; 948ff.

42. Exodus 13:21ff.

43. This is apparently how the midrash understand the verse. In the Bible, "in it" most likely refers to the cloud.

44. Sifra *emor* 17, p. 103d.

45. Wayyikra Rabba 31:9.

46. See the texts in Goldberg, *Untersuchungen*, pp. 281ff.

47. The parallels in y Sota and Shemot Rabba have "Holy Spirit" instead of "Shekhinah."

48. The interpretation follows the sequence of the Hebrew text.

49. Literally, "called to him/it."

50. b Sota 11a; y Sota 1:9; Shemot Rabba 1:22. The translation follows *The Babylonian Talmud: Seder Nashim*, vol. 3, trans. Isidore Epstein, London: Soncino Press, 1936.

51. This is left to the English translator of our Midrash, who adds the note: "Wisdom is an emanation from God" (p. 52, n. 4). This is obviously a possibility to solve the problem, but most certainly not the one our Midrash would have chosen.

52. *Untersuchungen*, pp. 458, 462.

53. "Shekhinah," pp. 147–154.

54. Capital punishment.

55. Literally, "I am lighter than my head, I am lighter than my arm," a euphemistic expression for feeling grief and weakness.

56. m Sanhedrin 6:5; b Sanhedrin 46a/b; b Hagiga 15b.

57. See Peter Kuhn, *Gottes Trauer und Klage in der Rabbinischen Überlieferung*, Leiden: Brill, 1978.

58. Compare Scholem, "Shekhinah," p. 150.

59. *Untersuchungen*, p. 462.

60. Ekha Rabba, Pet. 25, ed. Buber, fol. 15a; Pesiqta deRav Kahana, 13:11, ed. Mandelbaum, p. 235. The translation follows *Midrash Rabbah: Lamentations*, trans. A. Cohen, London: Soncino Press, 1939, ^{3}1961.

61. Scholem, "Shekhinah," p. 150.

62. The three kings are Jeroboam, Ahab, and Manasseh; the four commoners are Balaam, Doeg, Ahitophel, and Gehazi; compare m Sanhedrin 10:2.

63. Solomon was diligent in doing God's work because he built the Temple in seven years, although it took him thirteen years to build his own house: this is the interpretation immediately preceding our Midrash in Midrash Mishle.

64. Midrash Mishle 22, ed. Visotzky, p. 156. The translation follows *The Midrash on Proverbs*, trans. from the Hebrew with an introduction and annotations by Burton L. Visotzky, New Haven and London: Yale University Press, 1992, pp. 99f.

65. Cf. Wayyiqra Rabba 19:2 and Visotzky, *Midrash on Proverbs*, p. 145, n. 9.

66. b Sanhedrin 104b. The translation follows I. Epstein, ed., *Hebrew-English Edition of the Babylonian Talmud: Sanhedrin*, London: Soncino Press, 1969.

67. This is in line with the Rabbinic attitude to the heavenly voice (*bat qol*): the Rabbis don't regard the decision of the heavenly voice as superior to their own decision. On the heavenly voice, see Peter Kuhn, *Offenbarungsstimmen im Antiken Judentum. Untersuchungen zur Bat Qol und verwandten Phänomenen*, Tübingen: J.C.B. Mohr (Paul Siebeck), 1989.

68. Scholem, "Shekhinah," p. 152. Goldberg, *Untersuchungen*, p. 350, follows him somewhat hesitantly and ambiguously.

69. Visotzky, *Midrash on Proverbs*, p. 10.

70. *Untersuchungen*, p. 350. But even this could become possible, although much later. Scholem, "Shekhinah," p. 152, quotes the version transmitted by Judah he-Hasid of Regensburg (d. 1217): "The Shekhinah threw herself down before the Holy One blessed be He," which is clearly a secondary combination of the Midrash Mishle and Bavli Sanhedrin versions.

71. According to the Rabbinic view the Sanhedrin is controlled by Rabbis.

72. Midrash Tehillim 8:2, ed. Buber, p. 76.

73. Goldberg, *Untersuchungen*, p. 67.

74. This awkward circumlocution means that God wept.

75. Pesiqta Rabbati 29, ed. Friedmann, p. 136b.

76. *Untersuchungen*, p. 184, n. 1.

77. Pesiqta Rabbati 31, ed. Friedmann, p. 144b. The translation follows *Pesikta Rabbati*, trans. from the Hebrew by William G. Braude, New Haven and London: Yale University Press, 1968, vol. 2, p. 609.

78. Compare Goldberg, *Untersuchungen*, pp. 160ff., 493ff.

79. Scholem, too, translates "Your Glory is in its place," ignoring the suffix *bimqomkha*. Of the two possible translations of *kevodkha bimqomkha* suggested by Goldberg (*Untersuchungen*, p. 165, n. 2), namely either "the Glory is like you" or "on behalf of you," I can follow only the second one. Israel Yuval draws my attention to b Bekhorot 30b (*kevod zaqen yehe munah bimqomo*), where *bimqomo* clearly means "in its [proper] place" (as Braude translates). The problem, however, remains that Pesiqta Rabbati reads *bimqomkha* and not *bimqomo* ("Your Glory shall remain in Your place"). Thus even if this translation is correct, the text suggests a distinction between God and his Glory/Shekhinah.

80. The equation of "Glory" (*kavod*) and "Shekhinah" is fairly routine in Rabbinic literature; compare Goldberg, *Untersuchungen*, pp. 468–470.

81. *Untersuchungen*, p. 166: "deine Schekhinah, das bis du."

82. My translation follows what I regard as the *lectio difficilior* in the printed edition; Friedmann's edition has: "Who redeems Him from the place of His Shekhinah, and redeems Israel from among the nations of the world," which doesn't make any sense. Braude and Kapstein in their translation (*Tanna debe Eliyyahu: The Lore of the School of Elijah*, trans. from the Hebrew by William G. Braude and Israel J. Kapstein, Philadelphia: The Jewish Publication Society of America, 1981, p. 162) try to combine both readings and arrive at the following hybrid version: "Who is the man who ransoms Me from whatever place of exile [My] presence abides in, and ransoms Israel from exile among the peoples of the world."

83. Seder Eliyyahu Rabba, ed. Jerusalem 1962–63, p. 129; ed. Friedmann, p. 53. The translation follows Braude and Kapstein, *Tanna debe Eliyyahu*, p. 162.

84. Compare, for example, Mekhilta deRabbi Yishmael, ed. Horovitz-Rabin, p. 51: God redeems himself, together with Israel, from exile and returns with them to Jerusalem. This "dangerous" idea is couched in the cautious formula *kivyakhol*, "as it were." See Goldberg, *Untersuchungen*, pp. 160ff.

85. Pace Scholem who declares: "God frequently speaks about the *Shekhinah*, but never to it; never does the expression 'I and My *Shekhinah*' appear" ("Shekhinah," p. 149). We have already seen that the first part of his assertion is incorrect (since at least the Shekhinah speaks to God), and we now see that the second part is also problematic — although, admittedly, this applies to later Midrashim only, and Scholem correctly distinguishes between what he calls "the ancient exoteric aggadah" and "later midrash."

86. b Berakhot 8a.

87. Günter Stemberger, *Einleitung in Talmud und Midrasch*, München: C. H. Beck, [8]1992, p. 345.

88. Chanoch Albeck, *Midrash Bereshit Rabbati ex libro R. Mosis Haddarshan collectus . . .* , Jerusalem: Mekize Nirdamim 1940, p. 27.

89. *Otiyyot de-R. Aqiva*, in: Shlomo A. Wertheimer, *Batei Midrashot*, second ed. . . . by Abraham J. Wertheimer, vol. 2, Jerusalem: Mosad ha-Rav Kook, ²1954, p. 351; Third Enoch, in: *Synopse zur Hekhalot-Literatur*, § 72. On the date of *Otiyyot de-R. Aqiva* and its relationship to the Hekhalot literature, see Stemberger, *Einleitung*, pp. 339f.

90. Scholem, "Shekhinah," p. 154.

91. Scholem, who was always extremely critical with regard to other scholars' knowledge of Hebrew and Aramaic, falls into the typical lapse of confusing the Aramaic Pa'el *dabbar* ("to lead, guide") with the Hebrew Pi'el *dibber* ("to speak") and translates in both verses "speaks" instead of "leads."

92. Targum Onkelos and Targum Pseudo-Jonathan are translated from the text in the Biblia Rabbinica; Codex Neofiti is translated from the edition by Alejandro Díez Macho, *Neophyti 1. Targum Palestinense MS de la Bibliotheca Vaticana*, Madrid: Consejo Superior de Investigaciones Científicas, 1978 (the translation follows Martin McNamara, *Targum Neofiti 1: Deuteronomy*, Edinburgh: T. & T. Clark, 1997).

93. Stemberger, *Einleitung*, p. 344.

94. Scholem, who quotes this tradition ("Shekhinah," p. 157), dates the passage itself to the "eighth to tenth century?".

95. Translated from the edition by Michael L. Klein, *The Fragment Targums of the Pentateuch According to their Extant Sources*, vol. 1, Rome: Biblical Institute Press, 1980, p. 87.

96. Midrash ha-Gadol Exodus 24:10, ed. Mordecai Margulies, Jerusalem: Mosad ha-Rav Kook, ²1966, p. 555. The first to quote this Midrash was Solomon Schechter in his *Some Aspects of Rabbinic Theology*, London: Black, 1909, p. 40, n. 1.

97. b Qiddushin 49a.

CHAPTER FIVE

1. Literally, "the semblance (*demut*) in appearance (*mar'eh*) like a man."

2. JPS translation: "Presence."

3. Here I deviate from Rosenblatt's translation (see n. 8, below), which reads: "were all of them produced for the first time by the Creator out of fire." Rosenblatt unfortunately translates *zohar* sometimes by "fire" and sometimes by "light."

4. Or "more sublime," as Scholem translates in "Shekhinah," p. 154.

5. Scholem, ibid., translates: "more enormous in its creation, bearing splendor and light." Literally it means, "powerful in its creation being the splendor of light."

6. Here I follow the JPS translation rather than Rosenblatt's somehow awkward rendering.

7. Literally, "to hear the vision."

8. Saadia, *Emunot we-De'ot*, Chap. III, ed. Yosef D. Kafach, Jerusalem: Sura, 1970, pp. 103f.; translation Samuel Rosenblatt, *Saadia Gaon. The Book of Beliefs and Opinions*, New Haven: Yale University Press, [4]1958, pp. 120f.

9. It is not clear whether *ha-moshav ha-nissa* actually refers to "firmament" (*raqia'*), as has been translated already by Yehuda ibn Tibbon.

10. See, for example, Bereshit Rabba 3:6.

11. See Chapter 4, pp. 91f., above.

12. Genesis 1:26.

13. *Emunot we-De'ot*, p. 104; translation Rosenblatt, *The Book of Beliefs and Opinions*, p. 122.

14. Joseph Dan, *Gershom Scholem and the Mystical Dimension of Jewish History*, New York and London: New York University Press, 1987, p. 88.

15. Scholem has "in its primal existence," which is certainly correct, but does not follow the play on words with "beginning" and "end."

16. Salomon J. Halberstam, ed., Yehūda Ben-Barzillay, *Perush Sefer Yesīra*, Berlin: M'kize Nirdamim, 1885 (reprint Jerusalem: Maqor, 1970), pp. 16f.; partly translated in Scholem, "Shekhinah," p. 155.

17. See Peter Schäfer, *Die Vorstellung vom Heiligen Geist in der Rabbinischen Literatur*, München: Kösel-Verlag, 1972, p. 62: although never directly identified with God, the Holy Spirit is nevertheless the mode through which *God* reveals himself.

18. *Sefer Yetzirah* 1:9 (ed. Gruenwald 1:10, p. 144).

19. See Peter Schäfer, *The Hidden and Manifest God: Some Major Themes in Early Jewish Mysticism*, Albany, N.Y.: State University of New York Press, 1992, pp. 11ff.

20. In the translation by Judah ibn Tibbon: *Sefer ha-hokhahah weha-re'ayah le-hagganat ha-dat ha-bezuyah*.

21. The Hebrew word he uses for "intermediary" is *mitzua'*, from the root *matza'*, "to place in the middle."

22. *Kuzari*, IV:3.

23. *Kuzari*, ibid. The translation follows *Sefer ha-Kuzari. Book of Kuzari by Judah Hallevi*, trans. from the Arabic by Hartwig Hirschfeld, New York: Pardes, 1946, pp. 184f.

24. A play on words with *kavod* ("Glory") and *kevudah* in Judges 18:21 (the "retinue" or "household"). *Kuzari* IV:3; Hirschfeld, p. 186.

25. BerR 78:1.

26. See *Kuzari*, ibid.: "Some angels are only created for the time being from fine elementary substances, others are lasting angels, and are perhaps those spiritual beings of which the prophets speak. We have neither to refute nor to adopt their views."

27. *Kuzari*, ibid. (Hirschfeld, pp. 186f.).

28. This distinction between the prophet's and ordinary people's vision be-

comes even clearer if one follows the Hebrew translation by Judah ibn Tibbon (Yehudah Even-Shemuel, ed., *The Kosari of R. Yehuda haLevi*, Tel Aviv: Dvir, 1972, p. 164): "So with regard to this Kavod, as there is something which the sight of the prophet alone can bear, there are likewise things in its wake which even our sight can bear, as the 'cloud' and the 'devouring fire,' because we are accustomed to see them. Yet beyond these [forms] things are getting so fine, until a degree [of fineness] is reached which even a prophet cannot perceive."

29. *Moreh* I:1; Moses Maimonides, *The Guide of the Perplexed*, trans. by Shlomo Pines, Chicago and London: The University of Chicago Press, 1963, p. 21.

30. *Moreh* I:21; Pines, p. 48.

31. Ibid.; Pines, pp. 48f.

32. Ibid.; Pines, p. 49.

33. *Moreh* I:28; Pines, p. 60.

34. The translation follows John W. Etheridge, *The Targums of Onkelos and Jonathan ben Uzziel on the Pentateuch* . . . , *Genesis and Exodus*, London: Longman, Green, Longman, and Roberts, 1862, p. 526.

35. As the text adds, this particular brick includes the abortion of a young woman as a result of the hard labor the people of Israel suffered in Egypt. At the time of redemption this brick will disappear, and this is what is meant by the continuation of the verse in Exodus 24:10: "like the very sky in purity."

36. *Moreh* I:64; Pines, pp. 156f.

37. See Chapter 4, n. 10.

CHAPTER SIX

1. Earlier versions of this chapter appeared in German in *Saeculum* 49, 1998, pp. 259–279, and in English in *JAAR* 68, 2000, pp. 221–242.

2. Scholem, *Origins*, p. 123.

3. I use the Hebrew edition by Daniel Abrams, *The Book Bahir: An Edition Based on the Earliest Manuscripts*, Los Angeles: Cherub Press, 1994 (which divides the text, following Scholem's translation, into 141 paragraphs). My translation follows Scholem's German translation (his Munich doctoral thesis): *Das Buch Bahir. Ein Schriftdenkmal aus der Frühzeit der Kabbala auf Grund der kritischen Neuausgabe von Gerhard Scholem*, Leipzig: W. Drugulin, 1923 (reprint Darmstadt: Wissenschaftliche Buchgesellschaft, 1970), as well as *The Bahir* . . . , Translation, Introduction and Commentary by Aryeh Kaplan, York Beach, Maine: Samuel Weiser, 1979, paperback 1989 (198 paragraphs).

4. I am aware that a clear-cut dichotomy between "philosophy" and "Kabbalah" can be contested and that more recent research questions the usefulness of these two categories as two distinct units, and there is certainly some justification for such an approach. Nevertheless, in order to cast the Bahir's concept

of God into sharper profile—particularly with regard to the feminine side—it is no doubt helpful to contrast it with a more "rationalistic" (another problematic category) philosophical approach.

5. The technical term *sefirot* does appear in the Bahir (*Bahir*, 87), but is not very prominent there; the book prefers the terms *ma'amarot* ("words": Scholem translates "logoi") and *middot* ("qualities, potencies").

6. *Bahir*, 89 (Kaplan, 128).

7. Scholem, *Bahir*, 89, translates: "verbunden und geeint" ("connected and united"), and Kaplan, 128, has "attached and unified." This is linguistically possible, but makes no sense in this particular context. *Meyuhad* means here rather "special, individual," in the sense of "isolated, separated." A similar view is offered by Joseph Dan and Ronald C. Kiener (*The Early Kabbalah*, New York: Paulist Press, 1986, p. 62): "'united' and 'special' (meaning here: separated)."

8. *Bahir*, 89 (Kaplan, 129).

9. Israel is at the same time the sons and grandsons, the sons of the fathers and the grandsons of the King, because the parable distinguishes between "God" and his Sefirot, although both are identical.

10. See Chapter 4, above.

11. *Bahir*, 96 (Kaplan, 142).

12. This also changes the plain meaning of the Psalm verse which is: "The beginning of Wisdom is the fear of God"!

13. For example, *Bahir*, 74 (Kaplan, 104).

14. *Bahir*, 104 (Kaplan, 155).

15. *Bahir*, 105 (Kaplan, 157f.). Because of the almost identical masculine symbolism attached to both the seventh and the eighth "word," the continuation of our § 105 asks whether the eighth is not in reality the seventh "word," and answers this question in the affirmative: "Yes, it is the seventh." Thus, we are obviously dealing here with two different layers of the *Bahir*, which ascribe the masculine principle to the seventh and the eighth Sefirah, respectively.

16. b Hagiga 12b.

17. *Bahir*, 115 (Kaplan, 169).

18. The divine chariot of Ezekiel 1 (although the technical term *merkavah* is not mentioned there: it appears for the first time in 1 Chron. 28:18 and is used in Sirach 49:8 for the content of Ezekiel's vision).

19. Moreover, to make the confusion complete, both the ninth and the tenth Sefirah seem to be called "Endurance" (*netzah*), in clear contradiction to the normative system where "Endurance" is the seventh Sefirah.

20. *Bahir*, 104 (Kaplan, 156).

21. The "forms" refer to the Sefirot, in particular the lower seven ones.

22. *Bahir*, 116 (Kaplan, 172).

23. *Bahir*, 117 (Kaplan, ibid.).

24. See *Sefer Yetzirah*, 1:1.

25. *Bahir*, 43 (Kaplan, 63); cf. also 67, 75, 97.

26. *Bahir*, 49 (Kaplan, 72).

27. *Bahir*, 101 (Kaplan, 152).

28. *Bahir*, 61 (Kaplan, 91).

29. *Bahir*, 52 (Kaplan, 78).

30. *Bahir*, 120 (Kaplan, 178). Similarly, Isaiah 6:3 ("the whole earth is full of his glory") is interpreted as referring to the tenth Sefirah: the "earth," which is a symbol of the Shekhinah, is full of God's glory; that is, she is the combined power of all the other Sefirot (*Bahir*, 90; Kaplan, 130).

31. *Bahir*, 116; Kaplan, 171 (the following "which is Wisdom" is most probably a gloss: cf. Scholem, *Bahir*, p. 124, n. 4). And see Scholem, *Origins*, pp. 173–176 and 178–180 (on the double Shekhinah).

32. *Bahir*, 74 (Kaplan, 104f.).

33. *Bahir*, 97 (Kaplan, 147).

34. *Bahir*, 97, 98f.; 131 (Kaplan, 147–149, 190).

35. *Bahir*, 61 (Kaplan, 91).

36. *Bahir*, 90, Kaplan, 131f. (according to Scholem's translation: *Bahir*, 90 α and β); the English translation follows Scholem, *Origins*, p. 166.

37. On the heavenly hosts as a term for the Sefirot, see also *Bahir*, 90; Kaplan, 133 (Scholem, *Bahir*, 90 γ).

38. It seems as if the Bahir reverses the equation of Wisdom with the (book of the) Torah in Jesus Sirach and "returns" to Proverbs' personified Wisdom (God's little daughter).

39. Literally, "can he live outside his daughter"?

40. Or "join one another."

41. *Bahir*, 36 (Kaplan, 54); the English translation follows Scholem, *Origins*, p. 164.

42. The sentence left out seems to be a gloss that doesn't belong here; see Scholem, *Bahir*, p. 45, n. 7.

43. *Bahir*, 43 (Kaplan, 63); the English translation follows Scholem, *Origins*, 162f.

44. On the thirty-two paths, see also *Bahir*, 62, 67, 75, 97 (the source is *Sefer Yetzirah* 1:1).

45. See also *Bahir*, 51 and 90; Kaplan, 76 and 131 (Scholem, *Bahir*, 51 α and 90 α).

46. Shir ha-Shirim Rabba 3,11:2. See above, pp. 84–86.

47. The verse Song of Songs 3:11 would then need to be understood in the sense of the Bahir: Solomon was crowned by his mother, the third Sefirah, with the crown of the Torah, the tenth Sefirah.

48. Compare, for example, *Bahir*, 131 (Kaplan, 190).

49. *Bahir*, 90; Kaplan, 132 (Scholem, *Bahir*, 90 β).

50. A gloss in the Munich manuscript (see Abrams, *Bahir*, pp. 146 and 147, n. 1) reads "and loved their mother."

51. *Bahir*, 51; Kaplan, 76 (Scholem, *Bahir*, 51 α).

52. *Bahir*, 131, 133 (Kaplan, 190, 193).

53. *Bahir*, 97–99 (Kaplan, 147–149).

54. *Meyahadin*, "confess as one (name)."

55. *Bahir*, 98 (Kaplan, 147f.).

56. What speaks for this view is the phrase "in this world"; compare also Scholem, *Bahir*, 137, where likewise no eschatological connotation is indicated.

CHAPTER SEVEN

1. At first in his Munich doctoral dissertation (see above Chapter 6, n. 3) and then in *Origins*, pp. 68ff., as well as in "Shekhinah," pp. 140–196.

2. *Bahir*, 43 (Kaplan, 63).

3. Erwin Preuschen, *Zwei gnostische Hymnen*, Giessen: Ricker, 1904, p. 10.

4. *Bahir*, 98 (Kaplan, 147f.).

5. Interestingly enough, Scholem translates "of the king" (in the singular) whereas the Greek text clearly has the plural, "of the kings."

6. Preuschen, ibid.

7. See Chapter 1, p. 35, above.

8. Scholem, *Origins*, p. 91.

9. Published for the first time in 1934 (first volume) and 1954 (second volume). See vol. 1: *Die mythologische Gnosis*, Göttingen: Vandenhoek & Ruprecht, ³1964, pp. 362ff.; id., *The Gnostic Religion*, Boston: Beacon Press, ²1958, pp. 174ff.

10. Scholem, *Origins*, p. 93.

11. Ibid., 96f.; see also p. 123.

12. Scholem, "Shekhinah," p. 167

13. Ibid., 170f. Emphasis mine.

14. See also Elliot Wolfson, "Hebraic and Hellenic Conceptions of Wisdom in *Sefer ha-Bahir*," *Poetics Today* 19, 1998, p. 155.

15. See also Gospel of Philip, 60 (Wesley W. Isenberg, trans., "The Gospel of Philip (II,3)," in: James M. Robinson, ed., *The Nag Hammadi Library in English*, Leiden: Brill, 1978, paperback HarperSanFrancisco, 1990, p. 146: "Echamoth is one thing and Echmoth another. Echamoth is Wisdom simply, but Echmoth is the Wisdom of death which is the one which knows death, which is called 'the little Wisdom.'"

16. Another very close parallel to the Lurianic Kabbalah!

17. With this I qualify considerably my argument in *JAAR*, p. 236f. A new evaluation of the gnostic evidence should include other texts such as, for example, the Gospel of Philip and the Tripartite Tractate.

18. Isaiah 45:6f.

19. Proverbs 16:4.

20. Job 1:6–12.

21. See, for example, Bereshit Rabba 8:4ff.

22. See, for example, b Avodah Zarah 5a.

23. See on this my *Rivalität zwischen Engeln und Menschen*, particularly pp. 225f.

24. *Bahir*, 9 (Kaplan, 11).

25. See Devarim Rabba 5:12; and cf. Schäfer, *Rivalität*, p. 57.

26. Bereshit Rabba 8:4; 12:15.

27. *Bahir*, 77 (Kaplan, 108).

28. *Bahir*, 96 (Kaplan, 145).

29. *Bahir*, 109 (Kaplan, 162f.).

30. See *The Wisdom of the Zohar: An Anthology of Texts*, ed. Isaiah Tishby, vol. 2, Oxford: Oxford University Press, 1989, pp. 458–461.

31. See, for example, Zohar I, 1a; 221a (Tishby, *The Wisdom of the Zohar*, vol. 1, pp. 391f.). And see already the "Treatise of the Left Emanation," in: Dan and Kiener, *The Early Kabbalah*, pp. 165–182.

32. Interestingly enough, Scholem does not particularly emphasize the gnostic/bahiric line in his discussion of evil, neither in *Origins* nor in his article "*Sitra Ahra*: Good and Evil in the Kabbalah," in: *On the Mystical Shape of the Godhead: Basic Concepts in the Kabbah*, New York: Schocken Books, 1991, pp. 56–87.

Chapter Eight

1. The first attempt is my article "Tochter, Schwester, Braut und Mutter. Bilder der Weiblichkeit Gottes in der frühen Kabbala," *Saeculum* 49, 1998, pp. 259–279 (slightly different English version in *JAAR* 68, 2000, pp. 221–242). Since the publication of this article, my colleague Arthur Green was kind enough to share with me an early draft of an article dealing with the Shekhinah in the Kabbalah, in which he comes to similar conclusions regarding the "influence" of the veneration of Mary.

2. Scholem, *Origins*, p. 236.

3. Despite all of his efforts to establish a link between the Bahir and the Cathar movement, Scholem remains surprisingly indifferent to the contemporaneous theological developments in Christian doctrine, which shape Christianity so decisively in the twelfth century. One might even venture the argument that his desperate attempt to connect the origins of the Kabbalah with the mythical East is what allows him to sidestep a comparison that he never seriously considered. For Scholem, Christianity was either a negative foil of Judaism, to be approached at most as Judaism's counterimage, or apologetically, something of which could be shown that it existed in Judaism, as well (and, no doubt, in a better form). With regard to our subject, he remained conspicuously silent. The

reasons why he chose to remain silent are beyond the scope of our investigation, but it is difficult to imagine that a scholar of Scholem's caliber did not discern the strong structural parallels. For the time being, we may speculate that he did not *want* to see the parallels because he was so occupied with the uniqueness and independence of the Kabbalah as an intrinsically Jewish phenomenon. See on this Amnon Raz-Krakotzkin, "Without Other Accounts: The Question of Christianity in the Writings of Yitzchak Baer and Gershom Scholem," *Jewish Studies* 38, 1998, pp. 73–96 (I thank my friend and colleague Israel Yuval for having drawn my attention to this important article); Peter Schäfer, "Gershom Scholem und das Christentum," forthcoming.

4. A still very useful description of the development of the veneration of Mary is Walter Delius, *Geschichte der Marienverehrung*, München and Basel: Reinhardt, 1963. And see more recently Marina Warner, *Alone of All Her Sex: The Myth and the Cult of the Virgin Mary*, London: Weidenfeld and Nicolson, 1976; Michael P. Carroll, *The Cult of the Virgin Mary: Psychological Origins*, Princeton: Princeton University Press, 1986; Vasiliki Limberis, *Divine Heiress: The Virgin Mary and the Creation of Christian Constantinople*, London: Routledge, 1994; Jaroslav Pelikan, *Mary Through the Centuries: Her Place in the History of Culture*, New Haven: Yale University Press, 1996.

5. Nestorius, in: Friedrich Loofs, ed., *Nestoriana. Die Fragmente des Nestorius*, Halle: Max Niemeyer, 1905, pp. 167/4f., 263/12, 276/4f., 337/11f., 353/19f. (*monon mē poieitō tēn parthenon thean*); and see the index on p. 402, s.v. "Maria."

6. Cyril, Homiliae Diversae 4, MPG 77, cols. 991/992, and *Acta Conciliorum Oecumenicorum*, ed. Eduard Schwartz, tomus primus, volumen primum, pars altera, Berlin: Walter de Gruyter, 1927, pp. 102f.

7. Delius, *Marienverehrung*, p. 110.

8. The 1999 senior thesis by Marisa F. Gonzalez, *The Road to Ephesus: the Rise of Marian Devotion in the Eastern Mediterranian*, Princeton University, Department of Religion, investigates the pre-Ephesus evidence.

9. For a helpful summary, see Christa Schaffer, *Koimesis. Der Heimgang Mariens: Das Entschlafungsbild in seiner Abhängigkeit von Legende und Theologie*, Regensburg: Friedrich Pustet, 1985; Karoline Kreidl-Papadopoulos, art. "Koimesis," in: Klaus Wessel and Marcell Restle, eds., *Reallexikon zur Byzantinischen Kunst*, vol. 4, Stuttgart 1990, cols. 136–182.

10. Ed. K. von Tischendorf, *Apocalypses Apocryphae*, Leipzig: Mendel, 1866 (reprint Hildesheim: Georg Olms, 1966), pp. 113–123.

11. See in particular Hans-Rudolf Peters, *Die Ikonographie des Marientodes*, Diss. Bonn 1950.

12. Tischendorf, *Apocalypses Apocryphae*, p. 119.

13. Monika Haibach-Reinisch, *Ein Neuer "Transitus Mariae" des Pseudo-Melito*, Rome: Pontifica Academia Mariana Internationalis, 1962, p. 85.

14. Ibid., 85f.

15. Ibid., 87.

16. Tischendorf, *Apocalypses Apocryphae*, "Iohannis Liber de Dormitione Mariae," p. 111.

17. Martin Jugie, *La mort et l'assomption de la Sainte Vierge*, Città del Vaticano: Bibliotheca Apostolica Vaticana, 1944, p. 140 with n. 6.

18. Text with German translation in Schaffer, *Koimesis*, pp. 56–58.

19. Johannes Damascenus, Homilia in Nativitatem B.V. Mariae, MPG 96, col. 666B.

20. Germanus Const., In Praesentationem SS. Deiparae I, MPG 98, col. 300C/D; In Annunciationem SS. Deiparae, MPG 98, col. 321B; In Dormitionem BMV II, MPG 98, col. 349B.

21. Delius, *Marienverehrung*.

22. Ambrosius, De Spiritu Sancto III, 11:74, MPL 16, col. 827A.

23. Ibid., III, 11:80, MPL 16, col. 829A/B.

24. Gregory of Tours, *Liber in Gloria Martyrum*, c. 4, in: *Monumenta Germaniae Historica, Scriptores Rerum Merovingicarum* 1:2, ed. Bruno Krusch, Hannover: Hahn, 1969, p. 39: "*Et ecce iterum adstetit eis Dominus, susceptumque corpus sanctum in nube deferri iussit in paradiso.*"

25. Delius, *Marienverehrung*, pp. 150ff.; Kreidl-Papadopoulos, Koimesis, col. 144.

26. Hrabanus Maurus, Homilia 29, In Assumptione Sanctae Mariae Virginis, MPL 110, col. 55D.

27. Hrabanus Maurus, Homilia 149, In Assumptione Sanctae Mariae, MPL 110, col. 435B. Another author, whose Mariology needs to be explored further, is Paschasius Radbertus (786–ca. 860); see his *De Partu Virginis*, ed. E. Ann Matter, and *De Assumptione S. Mariae Virginis*, ed. Albert Ripberger, in: Corpus Christianorum Continuatio Mediaeualis, LVI C, Turnholt: Brepols, 1985.

28. Petrus Damianus, Sermo 40, In Assumptione Beatissimae Mariae Virginis, MPL 144, col. 717A.

29. Sermo 45, In Nativitate Beatissimae Virginis Mariae, MPL 144, col. 747D.

30. Sermo 40, In Assumptione Beatissimae Mariae Virginis, MPL 144, col. 719D.

31. Ibid., col. 717B.

32. The Greek word used for "power" is *dynamis*, which is rendered in Latin *virtutes*. The New Testament verse itself alludes to Ps. 110:1: "God's oracle to my lord: Sit at my right hand."

33. Sermo 40, MPL 144, col. 722C.

34. Sermo 44, MPL 144, col. 740B.

35. Matthew 28:18 (Vulgate): *data est mihi omnis potestas in caelo et in terra.*

36. Sermo 44, MPL 144, col. 740B: *Nil tibi impossibile, cui possibile est desperatos in spem beatitudinis relevare.*

37. Ibid., col. 740C: *Accedis enim ante illud aureum humanae reconciliationis altare, non solum rogans, sed imperans, domina, non ancilla.*
38. Ibid.
39. Herman of Tournay, De Incarnatione Christi, cap. 8–11, MPL 180, col. 28C.
40. Ibid.
41. Ibid., col. 28D.
42. Ibid., col. 30A.
43. Ibid., col. 36.
44. Bernard: see below; Anselm: "If you, Lady, are his mother, then are not your other sons his brothers? . . . Therefore our judge is our brother. The savior of the world is our brother. Finally our God is made our brother, through Mary (*denique deus noster est factus per Mariam frater noster*)" (Oratio 7:132–141, in: *S. Anselmi . . . Opera Omnia*, vol. 2, ed. Franciscus Salesius Schmitt, Stuttgart-Bad Cannstatt: Frommann-Holzboog, 1968, p. 23); Clarissa W. Atkinson, *The Oldest Vocation: Christian Motherhood in the Middle Ages*, Ithaca and London: Cornell University Press, 1991, p. 118.
45. Herman of Tournay, De Incarnatione Christi, MPL 180, col. 37: *Per Mariam Deus judex noster, factus est frater noster.*
46. Ibid., col. 38A.
47. Only slightly earlier and another important link in the chain of Marian theology is the *Speculum Virginum*, ascribed to Conrad of Hirsau (ca. 1070–ca. 1150); cf. Constant J. Mews, "Hildegard, the Speculum Virginum and Religious Reform in the Twelfth Century," in: Alfred Haverkamp, ed., *Hildegard von Bingen in ihrem historischen Umfeld. Internationaler wissenschaftlicher Kongreß zum 900jährigen Jubiläum, 13.–19. September 1998, Bingen am Rhein*, Mainz: Philipp von Zabern, 2000, pp. 237–267. Constant Mews was kind enough to make available to me the manuscript of Kim E. Power, "From Ecclesiology to Mariology: Patristic Traces and Innovation in the *Speculum Virginum*," to be published as Chapter 4 in: *Listen Daughter: the Speculum Virginum and the Formation of Religious Women in the Middle Ages*, New York: St. Martin's Press, forthcoming. Power emphasizes the, in her opinion, radical and new Mariology in the *Speculum Virginum* with its nuptial symbolism, Mary's equation with pre-existent Wisdom ("Lady Wisdom incarnate"), her inclusion in the Trinity, and her role as *reconciliatrix*, *reparatrix*, and *operatrix*. As new as these theologoumena may be in comparison with the patristic sources, they are certainly not new in eleventh- and twelfth-century theology.
48. Warner, *Alone of All Her Sex*, p. 129.
49. Bernard of Clairvaux, Sermones super Cantica Canticorum, Sermo 29, IV:8, in: Bernhard von Clairvaux, *Sämtliche Werke lateinisch/deutsch*, ed. Gerhard B. Winkler, Innsbruck: Tyrolia-Verlag, vol. 5, 1994, p. 465.
50. In Laudibus Virginis Matris, Homilia II:2; ibid., vol. 4, 1993, p. 50.
51. Ibid., Homilia III:2, p. 80.

52. In Assumptione Beatae Mariae, Sermo 1:4, in: Bernhard von Clairvaux, *Sämtliche Werke lateinisch/deutsch*, vol. 8, 1997, pp. 530–532.

53. See also the sixth parable (vol. 4, 1993, pp. 860ff.) about the King's son and the Ethiopian bride, which in some details resembles the gnostic Hymn of the Pearl.

54. Vulgate Jesus Sirach 24:12.

55. Sententiae III:111, in: Bernhard von Clairvaux, *Sämtliche Werke lateinisch/deutsch*, vol. 4, 1993, p. 190. Although in the following he refers to the "city of God," from the beginning of the paragraph it becomes clear that he is talking about Mary.

56. Compare Tobit 12:20.

57. Compare 2 Corinthians 6:9.

58. Compare Psalms 45:11.

59. The salvific function of Jesus, the Son (cf. John 3:17: "God sent his Son into the world that through him the world might be saved") is again applied to Mary, his mother. Without her consent Jesus' mission would have been impossible.

60. Compare Canticles 1:8, 8:13.

61. In Laudibus Virginis Matris, Homilia IV:8, in: Bernhard von Clairvaux, *Sämtliche Werke lateinisch/deutsch*, vol. 4, 1993, pp. 112–114. The English translation follows *Homilies in Praise of the Blessed Virgin Mary by Bernard of Clairvaux*, trans. by Marie-Bernard Saïd, Kalamazoo, Mich.: Cistercian Publications, 1993, p. 53.

62. Homilia III:4, in: Bernhard von Clairvaux, *Sämtliche Werke lateinisch/ deutsch*, vol. 4, 1993, p. 82. The English translation follows, with modifications, Saïd, *Homilies*, p. 36.

63. Dominica infra Octavam Assumptionis 2, in: Bernhard von Clairvaux, *Sämtliche Werke lateinisch/deutsch*, vol. 8, 1997, p. 596.

64. Compare 1 Corinthians 9:22 where Paul is speaking of himself.

65. Compare Romans 1:14.

66. Compare John 1:16, referring to Jesus!

67. Compare Psalms 19:7, referring to God!

68. Dominica infra Octavam Assumptionis 2, in: Bernhard von Clairvaux, *Sämtliche Werke lateinisch/deutsch*, vol. 8, 1997, p. 596. The English translation follows *St. Bernard's Sermons on the Blessed Virgin Mary*, trans. from the original Latin by a Priest of the Mount Melleray, Chulmleigh, Devon: Augustine Publishing Company, 1984 (reprint 1987), p. 208.

69. In Nativitate Beatae Mariae: De Aquaeductu, 7, in: Bernhard von Clairvaux, *Sämtliche Werke lateinisch/deutsch*, vol. 8, 1997, p. 628.

70. Dominica infra Octavam Assumptionis 2, in: ibid., vol. 8, 1997, p. 596; translation *St. Bernard's Sermons on the Blessed Virgin Mary*, p. 207.

71. Luke 1:28.

72. Compare Genesis 28:12.

73. Compare Psalms 148:4.

74. Proverbs 31:10.

75. In Nativitate Beatae Mariae: De Aquaeductu, 4, in: ibid., p. 624; the translation follows *St. Bernard's Sermons on the Blessed Virgin Mary*, pp. 82f.

76. Sententiae III:87, in: Bernhard von Clairvaux, *Sämtliche Werke lateinisch/deutsch*, vol. 4, 1993, p. 129.

77. Ibid. See also De Laudibus Virginis Matris Hom. 17, MPL 183, cols. 70ff. (Delius, *Marienverehrung*, pp. 158f.), where Mary, the *stella maris*, is identified with the star rising from Jacob (Numbers 24:17), a verse traditionally associated with the Messiah!

78. Compare Isaiah 6:6f.

79. Dominica infra Octavam Assumptionis 3, in: Bernhard von Clairvaux, *Sämtliche Werke lateinisch/deutsch*, vol. 8, 1997, p. 598. The English translation follows *St. Bernard's Sermons on the Blessed Virgin Mary*, pp. 209f.

80. Bernhard von Clairvaux, *Sämtliche Werke lateinisch/deutsch*, vol. 8, 1997, p. 1011, n. 49.

81. Sermones in Assumptione Beatae Mariae, Sermo I, MPL 185, col. 188B.

82. Ibid., col. 189D.

83. Ibid., Sermo II, col. 193B.

84. Ibid., Sermo I, col. 189D.

85. Ibid., Sermo III, col. 195B/C.

86. Homilia 31 in Annunciatione BMV, MPL 174, col. 770B/C (translation Barbara Newman, *Sister of Wisdom: St. Hildegard's Theology of the Feminine*, Berkeley and Los Angeles: University of California Press, 1987, paperback 1989, p. 161). See also Newman's quotation from a manuscript of Speculum Virginum (London BL Arundel 44, fol. 41a), in which Mary is described as "ordained from old, from eternity," united with her Son "in a mysterious unity": "For did not the primal origin of all divine works lie hidden in them invisibly, with the perfect fullness of the eternal will and the supreme goodness, to be unfolded at the foreordained time?"

87. Homilia Dominicam I Adventus IV, MPL 174, col. 41A. Warner, *Alone of All Her Sex*, p. 131, presumably refers to this passage when she, somewhat offhandedly, states: "Godfrey of Admont . . . suggested all three persons of the Trinity were Mary's lovers."

88. It may well be, as Ivan Marcus suggests (written communication), that we have here a deliberate play on words with *materia* and *mater*.

89. Homiliae Festivales 75: Homilia in Nativitatem Beatae Mariae Virginis secunda, MPL 174, col. 1006C.

90. See a brief sketch of her life and work in Newman, *Sister of Wisdom*, pp. 4–34.

91. German edition: *Hildegard von Bingen. Lieder*, ed. Pudentiana Barth, Maria I. Ritscher, and Joseph Schmidt-Görg, Salzburg: Müller, 1969. I quote from the English edition by Barbara Newman, *Saint Hildegard of Bingen: Symphonia. A Critical Edition of the Symphonia armonie celestium revelationum [Symphony of the Harmony of Celestial Revelations]*, Ithaca and London: Cornell University Press, 1988.

92. On Hildegard as a theological thinker in general, see Constant Mews, "Religious Thinker: 'A Frail Human Being' on Fiery Life," in: *Voice of the Living Light: Hildegard of Bingen and her World*, ed. Barbara Newman, Berkeley: University of California Press, 1998, pp. 52–69.

93. Newman, *Sister of Wisdom*, p. 161.

94. *Symphonia*, ed. Newman, 17:3, pp. 122f.

95. Ibid., 20:2b–3a, pp. 128, 131.

96. *Sister of Wisdom*, pp. 104f. (Paris, BN lat. 5047, fol. 2a).

97. *Symphonia*, ed. Newman, 17:4, pp. 122f.

98. Ibid., 21/3–11, pp. 132f. (quoted also in Newman, *Sister of Wisdom*, p. 162).

99. The term has been introduced by Newman, *Sister of Wisdom*, p. 163.

100. *Symphonia*, ed. Newman, 10, pp. 114f.

101. Newman, *Sister of Wisdom*, p. 164.

102. *Ad Vitam S. Ruperti Epilogus*, 6, in: *Analecta Sanctae Hildegardis*, ed. Jean-Baptiste Pitra: *Analecta sacra*, vol. 8, Monte Cassino, 1882 (reprint Farnborough: Gregg, 1966), p. 364 (translation Newman, *Sister of Wisdom*, p. 165).

103. *Symphonia*, ed. Newman, 20, pp. 128–131.

104. See Newman's similar remark on Hildegard's epilogue to the "Life of St. Rupert," *Sister of Wisdom*, p. 165.

105. That Mary was with no sin starts earlier but becomes established in the twelfth century (Delius, *Marienverehrung*, p. 159).

106. *Symphonia*, ed. Newman, 16, pp. 120f.

107. Edward J. Keale, art. "Peter of Blois," in: *New Catholic Encyclopedia*, New York: McGraw-Hill Book Company, 1967, vol. 11, p. 212.

108. Sermo 38 In Nativitate Beatae Mariae, MPL 207, col. 674A.

109. It is revealing that Delius, after having emphasized over and over again how close Mary comes to a divine status (he even approves of Harnack's statement that Mary becomes the "halbgöttische Vermittlerin zwischen Gott und Menschen") in the end concludes about Bernard: "Aber alle diese Stellen lassen keine direkte Mitwirkung der Maria am Heilswerk Christi zu, sondern sie bedeuten lediglich, dass Maria durch die Geburt des Sohnes der Menschheit den Erlöser und durch ihn die Erlösung geschenkt hat" (*Marienverehrung*, p. 162). He could have spared himself several chapters, if it all comes down to just this.

110. For want of a better term I reluctantly use here the term "pre-existent," however not in the literary sense of the word (eternally existent before all creation), but in the sense of "created before all creation."

111. I deliberately evoke the image of Mary as the aqueduct.

CHAPTER NINE

1. *Ein Neuer "Transitus Mariae,"* pp. 9f., 46. She calls her recension *Transitus B²*, to distinguish it from the other recension (*Transitus B¹* according to Haibach-Reinisch), which was published by Tischendorf in his *Apocalypses*

Apocryphae, pp. 124–236. The two other versions are *Transitus A*, according to Haibach-Reinisch's nomenclature, composed approximately in the seventh century (published in Tischendorf's *Apocalypses Apocryphae*, pp. 113–123), and *Transitus C*, probably the latest Latin adaptation (published by André Wilmart, "L'ancien récit latin de l'Assomption," in: *Analecta Reginensia. Extraits des Manuscrits Latins de la Reine Christine Conservés au Vatican*, Città del Vaticano: Biblioteca Apostolica Vaticana, 1933, pp. 323–362); see Haibach-Reinisch, pp. 24ff. A more complex (but not very clear) picture of the various versions is drawn by Kreidl-Papadopoulos (Koimesis, col. 140), who dates the Pseudo-Melito *Transitus* to the sixth century CE.

2. Haibach-Reinisch, *Ein Neuer "Transitus Mariae,"* pp. 79–83. On pp. 102–105, she gives a synoptic edition of both the B^1 and B^2 recensions.

3. *Circa eam*, most likely "around her dead body," not "saying praises about her."

4. The tabernacle is equivalent with Mary.

5. Compare Matthew 26:69–71; Mark 14:66–69; Luke 22:56f.

6. That is, be my patron and speak for me before the Lord.

7. Compare Matthew 27:25.

8. Literally, "dry."

9. Emphasized by Klaus Schreiner, "Antijudaismus in Marienbildern des späten Mittelalters," in: *Das Medium Bild in historischen Ausstellungen. Beiträge . . . zur Sektion 6 des 41. Deutschen Historikertags in München 1996*, Augsburg: Haus der Bayerischen Geschichte, 1998, p. 10.

10. Literally, "he smote him"; Vulgate 2 Samuel 6:7: *et percuisset eum*.

11. 2 Samuel 6:6f.

12. Compare Matthew 12:10 (*et ecce homo manum habens aridam*); Luke 6:6 (*et erat ibi homo et manus eius dextra erat arida*).

13. Instead of just *portantibus* in A^2.

14. Haibach-Reinisch, *Ein Neuer "Transitus Mariae,"* pp. 102, 104.

15. Tischendorf, *Apocalypses Apocryphae*, pp. 118f.

16. Latin translation: *manus eius grabato adhaeserunt*.

17. Latin translation: *succisae sunt*.

18. Martin Jugie, "Homélies Mariales Byzantines (II)," in: *PO* 19, 1925, p. 399.

19. Published by Tischendorf in his *Apocalypses Apocryphae*, pp. 95–112, under the title *Iohannis Liber de Dormitione Mariae*.

20. Ibid., 110f.

21. Zechariah 11:17.

22. The Byzantine church begins to depict Mary's death and funeral in the early eleventh century (Ludmila Wratislaw-Mitrovic and Nikolaj Okunev, "La dormition de la sainte Vierge dans la peinture médievale orthodoxe," *Byzantinoslavica* 3, 1931, pp. 134–180), or even already before the tenth century (Kreidl-Papadopoulos, Koimesis, col. 145).

23. Nicole and Michel Thierry, *Nouvelles Églises Rupestres de Cappadoce,*

Région du Hasan Daği (*New Rock-Cut Churches of Cappadocia*), Paris: Librairie C. Klincksieck, 1963, pp. 105f., plates 51 a and b, 52 a and b, 53; Marcell Restle, *Byzantine Wall Painting in Asia Minor*, vol. 1, Recklinghausen: Verlag Aurel Bongers, 1967, pp. 67, 69f., 72f.; vol. 3, plate 498. Restle, p. 73, argues strongly in favor of dating the *Koimesis* painting to the second half of the eleventh century. Iconographically, he sees a "more provincial Armenian flavour" at work, probably influenced by Egypt and Syria (p. 69).

24. Stylianos Pelekanides, *Kastoria*, vol. 1, *Byzantinai Toichographiai: Pinakes*, Thessalonike 1953, plate 74; and see Ann Wharton Epstein, "Frescoes of the Mavriotissa Monastery Near Kastoria: Evidence of Millenarianism and Anti-Semitism in the Wake of the First Crusade," *Gesta* 21, 1982, p. 26.

25. Maria L. Gengaro, Francesca Leoni, Gemma Villa, *Codici Decorati e Miniati dell'Ambrosiana: Ebraici e Greci*, Milano: Casa Editrice Ceschina, 1959, p. 201 and plate LXXXVIII.

26. Georgij K. Vagner, *Alte russische Städte*, München: Deutscher Kunstverlag, 1980, pp. 384–386.

27. Ivan I.Tolstoj and Nikodim P. Kondakov, *Russkija Drevnosti v pamjatnikach iskusstva*, vol. 6, St. Petersburg: Benke, 1899, p. 67; Wratislaw-Mitrovic and Okunev, La Dormitio, p. 151.

28. Schaffer, *Koimesis*, pp. 81f., plate 5.

29. Wratislaw-Mitrovic and Okunev, Dormitio, pp. 153ff., plate VII.

30. Ibid., 162ff., plate XVI.

31. The earliest example of a representation of Mary's assumption into heaven seems to stem from the eighth century CE already (Cathedral of Sens), but an important role in the transmission of the assumption motif was played by the school of Reichenau in the early eleventh century. See Josef Hecht, "Die frühesten Darstellungen der Himmelfahrt Mariens. Eine ikonographische Studie," in: *Das Münster* 4, 1951, pp. 1–12.

32. Thomas S. R. Boase, *The York Psalter in the Library of the Hunterian Museum, Glasgow*, London: Faber and Faber, 1962, p. 5, suggests a date before or shortly after 1173.

33. Ibid., 24f., plate 5.

34. Ibid., 13.

35. *Vollständige Faksimileausgabe im Originalformat des Berthold-Sakramentars, Ms. M.710 der Pierpont Morgan Library in New York*, Graz: Akademische Druck- und Verlagsanstalt, 1995, fol. 101.

36. This seems to be one major difference between the Byzantine representations of the scene and their adaptations in the Western tradition: the angel makes his appearance much later, probably not before the first half of the fourteenth century. See, however, the Freiburg Münster.

37. Claire Donovan, *The de Brailes Hours: Shaping the Book of Hours in Thirteenth-Century Oxford*, Toronto and Buffalo: University of Toronto Press, 1991, plate 5: The British Library, London, Ms. Add. 49 999, fol. 61r.

38. Ibid., 99, fol. 61v.

39. Ibid., fol. 62v.

40. The Index of Christian Art gives the date 1270–1280.

41. Cambridge, St. John's College, Ms. K.26, fol. 24r.

42. De Lisle Hours, Ms. G. 50, Pierpont Morgan Library, New York, fol. 161r. A quite unusual story is told in the Hungarian-Italian legendary from 1325–1335 (Rome, Biblioteca Vaticana, Ms. Lat. 8541, fol. 2v). Here one scene shows the High Priest with his hands raised to the bier, and the other one depicts the same High Priest with the healing palm branch in one hand and a group of Jews kneeling or standing in front of him, obviously begging to be healed. They are not only struck with blindness, but some are bleeding from wounds inflicted on them by a sword that an angel flying above them holds in his hands.

43. Colette Manhes-Deremble, *Les vitraux narratifs de la cathédrale de Chartres*, Paris: Le Léopard d'Or, 1993, pp. 175–177, fig. 76 and plate 42:11 (pp. 360f.).

44. Manhes-Deremble, ibid., 175, describes the scene as follows: "Au cours de la procession, le grand-prêtre . . . touche le cercueil et garde sa main collée."

45. The first example I found is the Hungarian/Italian legendary from the first half of the fourteenth century.

46. Fritz Geiges, *Der mittelalterliche Fensterschmuck des Freiburger Münsters*, Freiburg im Breisgau: Breisgau-Verein Schau-ins-Land, 1931, p. 42 (thirteenth century), plates 148 and 149 (p. 49); Ingeborg Krummer-Schroth, *Glasmalereien aus dem Freiburger Münster*, Freiburg im Breisgau: Rombach, 1967, p. 116 (around 1320–30); Schreiner, Antijudaismus, p. 17, ill. 9 (second half of the thirteenth century).

47. Schreiner, ibid., 19.

48. Denis Meehan, ed., *Adamnan's De Locis Sanctis*, Dublin: The Dublin Institute for Advanced Studies, 1958, p. 11.

49. It is unclear in the first place what business he had to be in Iona. He traveled back to Gaul via Sicily, and the only explanation is that a storm in the Bay of Biscay drove him off his course home and eventually to the Scottish coast (Meehan, *Adamnan's De Locis Sanctis*, p. 7).

50. Meehan, ibid.

51. Meehan, ibid., 118f. The English translation follows Meehan. German translation in: *Arculf: Eines Pilgers Reise nach dem heiligen Lande (um 670)*, aus dem Lateinischen übersetzt und erklärt von Paul Mickley, Zweiter Teil: Heilige Staetten im Lande, Damaskus, Tyrus, Alexandrien, Leipzig: J. C. Hinrichs'sche Buchhandlung, 1917, pp. 53f.

52. Psalms 89:21 (Vulgate 88:21).

53. Psalms 45:8 (Vulgate 44:8).

54. Meehan, *Adamnan's De Locis Sanctis*, p. 119, n. 1.

55. This may well be a faint echo of the *Transitus* story.

56. Meehan, *Adamnan's De Locis Sanctis*, pp. 112f.

57. Ibid., 114–117.

58. Schreiner, Antijudaismus in Marienbildern, p. 23.

59. Henry R. Luard, ed., *Matthaeus Parisiensis Chronica Maiora*, London: Her Majesty's Stationary Office, 1880, pp. 114f.

60. Actually Galician-Portuguese; see Kulp-Hill (n. 62, below), pp. XI and XV.

61. Alfonso X, el Sabio, *Cantigas de Santa Maria*: Cantigas 1 a 100, ed. Walter Mettmann, Madrid: Edilan, 1986, Cantiga 34, pp. 143f.

62. Translation: *Songs of the Holy Mary of Alfonso X, The Wise: A Translation of the* Cantigas de Santa Maria, trans. Kathleen Kulp-Hill, with an introduction by Connie L. Scarborough, Tempe, Arizona: Arizona Center for Medieval and Renaissance Studies: 2000 [Medieval and Renaissance Texts and Studies, vol. 173], p. 45.

63. This serves as the title of the poem.

64. This serves as the refrain of the poem.

65. Ms. Escorial T.I.1 (Códice Rico), fol. 15r. A facsimile edition of the manuscript: *El "Códice Rico" de las Cantigas de Santa Maria*, 2 vols., Madrid: Edilan, 1980. On the codex, see Connie L. Scarborough, *Women in Thirteenth-Century Spain as Portrayed in Alfonso X's Cantigas de Santa Maria*, Lewiston: The Edwin Mellen Press, 1993, pp. 1–16. On the image of the Jews in the Cantigas, see Albert I. Bagby, "The Jew in the *Cántigas* of Alfonso X, El Sabio," *Speculum* 46, 1971, pp. 670–688; id., "The Figure of the Jew in the *Cantigas* of Alfonso X," in: *Studies on the Cantigas de Santa Maria: Art, Music, and Poetry*, Proceedings of the International Symposium on the *Cantigas de Santa Maria* of Alfonso X, el Sabio (1221–1284) in Commemoration of its 700th Anniversary Year—1981, ed. Israel J. Katz and John E. Keller, Madison: Hispanic Seminary of Medieval Studies, 1987, pp. 235–245.

66. Evagrius, *Historia Ecclesiastica*, IV:36, ed. Joseph Bidez and Léon Parmentier, London: Methuen, 1898 (reprint Amsterdam: Hakkert, 1964), pp. 185f.; French translation by André-Jean Festugière, in: *Byzantion* 45, 1975, pp. 399f.

67. Gregorii Episcopi Turonensis Liber in Gloria Martyrum, *Monumenta Germaniae Historica, Scriptores Rerum Merovingicarum*, 1:2, p. 44.

68. Translation: Gregory of Tours, *Glory of the Martyrs*, trans. with an introduction by Raymond van Dam, Liverpool: Liverpool University Press, 1988 [Translated Texts for Historians, Latin Series III], pp. 29–31.

69. Evagrius places the story in the capital Constantinople.

70. Compare Daniel 3:8–30.

71. In Evagrius's version, the mother calls for her son, and he answers from the furnace.

72. I owe this reference to my research assistant, Annette Reed.

73. See, for example, Codex Neofiti Genesis 11:31; 15:7: "And Terah took his son Abram and his grandson Lot and his daughter-in-law Sarai, Abram's wife, and [he] went out with them from the Chaldeans' fiery furnace to go to the

land of Canaan. [Later, God said to Abraham:] 'I am the Lord who took you out of the fiery furnace of the Chaldeans to give you this land to inherit.'" Translation James L. Kugel, *Traditions of the Bible: A Guide to the Bible as it was at the Start of the Common Era*, Cambridge, Mass. and London: Harvard University Press, 1998, p. 253.

74. Bereshit Rabba 38:13.

75. New Haven and London: Yale University Press, 1999, pp. 8–27.

76. Edward Meyrick Goulburn and Henry Symonds, eds., *The Life, Letters, and Sermons of Bishop Herbert de Losinga*, vol. 2: *The Sermons*, Oxford and London: James Parker and Co., 1878, pp. 30–33. The translation follows Goulburn and Symonds.

77. Rubin, *Gentile Tales*, p. 203, n. 25 (Lit.!).

78. Gautier de Coincy, *Les Miracles de Notre Dame*, ed. V. Frederic Koenig, vol. 2, Genève: Librairie Droz, and Paris: Librairie Minard, 1961, pp. 95–100.

79. Ibid., p. 98, lines 94–98; translation Rubin, *Gentile Tales*, p. 13.

80. Ibid., p. 100, lines 140–142; translation Rubin, *Gentile Tales*, p. 14. What is new here is not so much the fact that not *all* of the Jews convert (we have this, for example, in Herbert de Losinga's sermon, as well as in other stories), but rather the expression of the author's individual voice (pace Rubin, *Gentile Tales*, pp. 13f.).

81. Kulp-Hill, *Songs of the Holy Mary*, no. 4, pp. 6f.

82. Ibid., 7.

83. I therefore don't think that "here the traditional mood of the tale is restored, with a happy ending as mother and son convert and father is put to death" (Rubin, *Gentile Tales*, p. 15). The ending here is as "happy" as in Gautier; Alfonso merely does not express his personal attitude toward the Jews.

84. Paris, Bibliothèque Nationale, Ms. N.Acq. fr. 24541, fol. 35r (ICA, no. 0066079).

85. London, British Library, Ms. Roy. 2B.Vii, fols. 207v and 208r.

86. Interestingly enough, in many of the versions the father is a glazier!

87. Figure 15 reproduces what is allegedly the restored version. The unrestored (and much different) version, which is described above, can be found in Henry Kraus, *The Living Theatre of Medieval Art*, Bloomington and London: Indiana University Press, 1967, pp. 160f., figures 112–114. See also Meredith Parsons Lillich, "Gothic Glaziers: Monks, Jews, Taxpayers, Bretons, Women," in: *JGS* 27, 1985, p. 73.

88. Nigel J. Morgan, *The Medieval Painted Glass of Lincoln Cathedral*, London: Oxford University Press, 1983, p. 11, 1C. Image in Rubin, *Gentile Tales*, p. 17 (fig. 2). See also the thus far unique representation of the story in a sculptured ceiling boss in the cloister of Norwich Cathedral, in: Montague Rhodes James, *The Sculpture Bosses in the Cloisters of Norwich Cathedral*, Norwich: Goose and Son, 1911, p. 25, VI.5.

89. *Gentile Tales*, p. 27. My emphasis.

90. There are some other remarkable aspects to be emphasized; for example, the Jewish mother and the mother Mary—the Jewish mother resists the father, and Mary complies with the will of the father/God, and both rescue the child.

91. Most of the widely discussed talmudic evidence has been contested in Johann Maier's comprehensive analysis of the sources; compare his *Jesus von Nazareth in der Talmudischen Überlieferung*, Darmstadt: Wissenschaftliche Buchgesellschaft, 1978. Whether or not Maier's extremely critical and minimalist interpretation stands up to criticism is a different question.

92. See Klaus Schreiner, *Maria*, München: Hanser, 1994, pp. 417–423.

93. Origenes, *Contra Celsum* I, 28. The translations follows *Origen*: Contra Celsum, trans. with an introduction and notes by Henry Chadwick, Cambridge: Cambridge University Press, 1953, pp. 28–31.

94. Ibid., I, 32. Compare also Tertullian, *De Spectaculis*, 30, who calls Jesus the son of a carpenter and a prostitute (*fabri aut quaestuariae filius*).

95. Ibid., I, 28.

96. b Shabbat 104b and b Sanhedrin 67a.

97. Although the alleged relationship between "Papos b. Yehuda" and "Pandera" is more than remote.

98. *Megadla se'ar neshya*, mostly explained as "plaiting the hair of [other] women." It makes much more sense, however, that *megadla* refers to the fact the she was letting her own hair grow long, thus alluding to her dubious status. See Maier, *Jesus von Nazareth*, p. 241.

99. The "son of a prostitute" in Pesikta Rabbati, 21 (Friedmann, fol. 100b), presumably refers to idolatry in general, rather than to Jesus; compare Maier, *Jesus von Nazareth*, pp. 244–247.

100. Samuel Krauss, *Das Leben Jesu nach jüdischen Quellen*, Berlin: Calvary, 1902 (reprint Hildesheim and New York: Georg Olms, 1977), p. 5; William Horbury, *A Critical Examination of the Toldedoth Jeshu*, Ph.D. dissertation, Cambridge 1971. And see most recently Yaacov Deutsch, "New Evidence of Early Versions of *Toldot Yeshu*," *Tarbiz* 69, 1999–2000, pp. 177–197 [in Hebrew].

101. The most comprehensive treatments of the history of the *Toledot Yeshu* are still the monograph by Krauss and Horbury's unpublished Ph.D. thesis; despite Krauss' undeniable merit, a new analysis of all of the available evidence is highly desirable. See also the useful summary by Joseph Dan, art. "Toledot Yeshu," in: *EJ* 15, 1971, cols. 1208f.

102. Matthew 1:1–16.

103. In some versions she is just betrothed to him, in others they are actually married.

104. In most versions; sometimes the names of the husband and of the villain are exchanged.

105. The Firkovitch manuscript of the *Toledot Yeshu* published by Deutsch in Tarbitz (pp. 183f.) does not mention Miriam/Mary as *niddah*, and Deutsch

suggests that this belongs to the earliest versions of the story (p. 182). If this is correct, Miriam is completely innocent: she is even not accused of having illicit intercourse with her husband because of her menstruation!

106. Krauss, *Leben Jesu*, pp. 38ff., 64ff., 118ff.

107. Ibid., 131ff.

108. See also David Biale, "Counter-History and Jewish Polemics against Christianity: The *Sefer toldot yeshu* and the *Sefer zerubavel*," *JSocS* N.S. 6, 1999, p. 135: "The text's [*Toledot Yeshu*'s] treatment of key figures is also more complex than one might expect from a pejorative counter-history. Although Mary is not the holy virgin of Christian tradition, neither is she portrayed with quite the same venom as in later medieval texts."

109. *Jesus von Nazareth*, p. 255. I don't think, however, pace Maier, that all of the talmudic passages—which he believes originally didn't have to do anything with Jesus or Mary—were only later, in the post-talmudic period, reinterpreted as referring to Jesus (and Mary).

110. Martha Himmelfarb, "Sefer Zerubbabel," in: David Stern and Mark J. Mirsky, eds., *Rabbinic Fantasies: Imaginative Narratives from Classical Hebrew Literature*, Philadelphia and New York: The Jewish Publication Society, 1990, p. 67.

111. Haggai 2:20–23; Zechariah 3:8, 6:9–15.

112. The translation follows Martha Himmelfarb, who used the Bodleian manuscript MS. Heb. d. 11, fol. 248r–251r as her primary source, but also consulted the printed editions by Jellinek (Adolph Jellinek, *Beit ha-Midrash*, vol. 2, Leipzig: Nies, 1855, reprint Jerusalem: Wahrmann Books, 1967, pp. 54–57), Wertheimer (Shlomo A. Wertheimer, *Batei Midrashot*, second ed. . . . by Abraham J. Wertheimer, vol. 2, Jerusalem: Mosad ha-Rav Kook, ²1954, pp. 497–505), and Even-Shmuel (Yehudah Even-Shmuel, *Midreshe Ge'ullah*, Jerusalem and Tel Aviv: Mosad Bialik, ²1954, pp. 55–88).

113. Menahem son of Hezekiah in b Sanhedrin 98b; Hezekiah as the Messiah in y Berakhot 2:4, fol. 5a; b Sanhedrin 94a, Berakhot 28b, Shir ha-Shirim Rabba 4,8:3; Lamentations Rabba 1:16.

114. Compare Joseph Heinemann, "The Messiah of Ephraim and the Premature Exodus of the Tribe of Ephraim," *HThR* 68, 1975, pp. 1–15; Arnold Goldberg, *Erlösung durch Leiden. Drei rabbinische Homilien über die Trauernden Zions und den leidenden Messias Efraim (PesR 34. 36. 37)*, Frankfurt am Main: Selbstverlag der Gesellschaft zur Förderung Judaistischer Studien in Frankfurt am Main e.V., 1978, pp. 55f.

115. 2 Kings 21:1.

116. Isaiah 62:4.

117. In Hebrew, *tzalmat ha-even*, an "image" or "statue" of stone.

118. This is a church.

119. So the Oxford manuscript.

120. Literally "stone."

121. Even-Shmuel, *Midreshe Ge'ullah*, p. 79; MS. Oxford, fol. 249r.

122. Or rather: the two Jewish Messiahs who mirror the qualities of the Christian Messiah.

123. See already Israel Lévi, "L'apocalypse de Zorobabel et le roi de Perse Siroès," *REJ* 71, 1920, p. 60, and Himmelfarb, "Sefer Zerubbabel," p. 69.

124. Himmelfarb, ibid.; critically Paul Speck, "The Apocalypse of Zerubbabel and Christian Icons," *JSQ* 4, 1997, pp. 183–190.

125. At the end of the Apocalypse, the perverted echo of Mary's veneration is emphasized again: "This Armilos will then take his mother, the stone from which he was born, out of the house of disgrace of the scoffers. From all over, the nations will come to worship that stone, burn incense, and pour libations to her. No one will be able to look upon her face because of her beauty. Whoever does not bow down to her will die, suffering like an animal" (Himmelfarb, "Sefer Zerubbabel," p. 80; MS. Oxford, fol. 251a).

126. This was first observed by Himmelfarb, ibid.

127. Himmelfarb, ibid., p. 74.

128. Septuagint Numbers 24:17; TO ibid.; y Ta'anit 4:8, fol. 68d.

129. Himmelfarb, "Sefer Zerubbabel," p. 75.

130. Most notably the famous story of the birth of the Messiah at the time of the destruction of the Temple in Lamentations Rabba 1:16 and y Berakhot 2:4, fol. 5a; see on this Galit Hasan-Rokem, *Web of Life: Folklore and Midrash in Rabbinic Literature*, Stanford: Stanford University Press, 2000, pp. 152ff.; Israel Knohl, *The Messiah before Jesus: The Suffering Servant of the Dead Sea Scrolls*, Berkeley: University of California Press, 2000, pp. 72–74, and, most recently, Martha Himmelfarb, "The Mother of the Messiah in the Talmud Yerushalmi and Sefer Zerubbabel," in: *The Talmud Yerushalmi and Graeco-Roman Culture*, vol. 3, ed. Peter Schäfer, Tübingen: Mohr Siebeck, forthcoming.

131. Himmelfarb, "Sefer Zerubbabel," p. 69.

132. To a very different conclusion comes Stephen J. Shoemaker, "'Let Us Go and Burn Her Body': The Image of the Jews in the Early Dormition Traditions," *Church History* 68, 1999, p. 821. Shoemaker reads the image of Mary in the Apocalypse of Zerubbavel as marking "a major boundary between Christianity and its Jewish source."

CHAPTER TEN

1. *Origins*, pp. 96f.

2. The English translation skips, not by accident, the seemingly redundant "Anfänge" ("beginnings, early stages"), and has simply *Origins of the Kabbalah*.

3. Scholem, *Origins*, p. 3.

4. The English word "origin," stemming from Latin *origo* (*oriri*— "to arise"), denotes both the act of arising or springing from something and that from which something arises or springs, its source; see *The Oxford English Dictio-*

nary, vol. 7, reprint Oxford 1961, p. 202. The same is true for the German "Ursprung," which literally means "that which rises or springs from something"; that is, a source (in the literal as well as in the metaphorical sense of the word). It is no coincidence that the most comprehensive article about the word "Ursprung" can still be found in the famous *Deutsches Wörterbuch* by the brothers Jacob and Wilhelm Grimm (vol. 11.3, bearbeitet von Karl Euling, Leipzig 1936, cols. 2538–2545).

5. On Scholem's concept of "origins," see also Elliot Wolfson, *Along the Path: Studies in Kabbalistic Myth, Symbolism, and Hermeneutics*, Albany, N.Y.: State University of New York Press, 1995, p. 70: "In general, it can be said that this search for origins was clearly mediated by the specific cultural concerns of Scholem and his generation and may not be shared by scholars writing in an age that has challenged in fundamental ways the whole notion of origins as some fixed, absolute beginning in time or place."

6. Scholem, *Origins*, pp. 66f., 90f.

7. Ibid., 45. And see the sentence in Scholem, "Shekhinah," pp. 170f., in which he wavers between the "legacy of Gnostic speculation" and the "creative reflection of anonymous Jewish God-seekers . . . upon the meaning of the images of their own tradition."

8. My emphasis.

9. Scholem, ibid., 86.

10. See Scholem, *Origins*, pp. 90f., 93.

11. Which nevertheless "largely [detached] themselves, of course [!], from their organic connection with gnostic mythology" (ibid., p. 90). The quoted part of the sentence is again a masterpiece of Scholem's art of simultaneous giving and taking.

12. Ibid., 12f.

13. Chapter 8, p. 147.

14. Scholem, *Origins*, p. 16.

15. Ibid., 15.

16. Ibid., 18.

17. Ibid., 18, 45.

18. Ibid., 96f.

19. I therefore disagree with Gil Anidjar's analysis of the roles played by the category of "myth" and the dichotomy between "East/Orient" and "West" in Scholem's work (Gil Anidjar, "Jewish Mysticism Alterable and Unalterable: On *Orient*ing Kabbalah Studies and the 'Zohar of Christian Spain,'" *JSocS*, N.S. 3, 1996–97, pp. 110ff.). I do not think that terms such as "old," "archaic," or even "primitive," which most commonly are used as markers of myth, remain negatively charged in Scholem's value system, therefore serving to maintain or even reinforce the negative connotation of "myth" (and, by extension, of the origin of Kabbalah). Nor am I convinced that the East, the embodiment of "archaic" and "primitive" myth, retains a negative connotation in Scholem's system. It seems to me that the opposite is true, at least as far as Scholem's view

of the Bahir and the origins of the Kabbalah are concerned. Scholem does not want to distance himself from the East and the Orient. On the contrary, by seeking the origins of the Kabbalah in the mysterious and mythically creative "Orient," he strives to revalue the Kabbalah and to enhance its status. Springing from the living source of the "Orient," the origin of all vitality and truth, the Kabbalah embodies the true inner life of Judaism. This is Scholem's message, deeply anchored in German Romanticism, which Anidjar's zeal against the Jewish version of "Orientalism" fails to recognize.

20. *Poetics Today* 19, 1998, pp. 147–176.

21. The last dichotomy on pp. 154f.

22. "Hebraic and Hellenic Conceptions," p. 168.

23. Ibid., 155: "By applying the term *Hebraism* to the mythic representation of *hokhmah*, I am deliberately eschewing Scholem's theory regarding the gnostic origin of the bahiric images of Sophia."

24. Ibid.

25. Philadelphia: Westminster Press, 1960; originally in German: *Das hebräische Denken im Vergleich mit dem griechischen*, Göttingen: Vandenhoek & Ruprecht 1952, [5]1968.

26. Also, Wolfson unfortunately does not remain consistent in his taxonomy, but seems to become entangled with his own complicated system when at the end of his article he suddenly declares the mythical depiction of Wisdom in the Bahir a product of an "originally *Hellenic* context" ("Hebraic and Hellenic Conceptions," p. 173; emphasis mine).

27. That Wolfson is aware of the problematic nature of his schematic dichotomy becomes apparent in a tell-tale subordinate clause. When discussing the merging of the "Hebraic notion of Wisdom" with the Hellenic doctrine of the Logos, he suddenly qualifies the Hebraic notion of Wisdom as "itself perhaps [!] betraying some influence of the Hellenistic concept of Sophia" ("Hebraic and Hellenic Conceptions," p. 154).

28. Since this applies to *all* of the bahiric parables, the shift was clearly intentional and not accidental; and there is no reason to believe that the Bahir, somehow "forgetting" its more sophisticated precursor, regressed to a more "primitive" or "naïve" stage of the art of parable.

29. *Bahir*, 117 (Kaplan, 172); see Chapter 6, p. 125, above.

30. Ibid., 116 (Kaplan, ibid.); see Chapter 6, pp. 124f., above.

31. Ibid., 104 (Kaplan, 156); see Chapter 6, p. 124, above.

32. Literally "palm tree."

33. *Bahir*, 139 (Kaplan, 198).

34. Compare b Pesahim 56a and Scholem, *Bahir*, pp. 153f.

35. Accordingly, strictly speaking not each tree is androgynous, but rather the gender difference is distributed among different trees (some are male and others are female).

36. Scholem, *Bahir*, p. 154.

37. I therefore don't see any basis for Wolfson's repeated claim that God's allegedly primordial androgyny is only superficial, that in reality the feminine emanates from and depends on the masculine. To prove this claim, he strangely reads a lot of phallic symbolism into the bahiric sources and maintains, without much evidence, that not only is the upper Shekhinah (the third Sefirah = *binah*) essentially male, but also her lower counterpart, the tenth Sefirah — although the latter is always portrayed as female ("Hebraic and Hellenic Conceptions," pp. 160–167)! The "proofs" that he adduces are all weak or forced interpretations. For instance, from the depiction in one parable of the seven lower Sefirot (including the tenth Sefirah, the Shekhinah) as the seven *sons* of the king, he concludes the "ontic containment of the feminine in the masculine" (ibid., p. 166). I would argue that this is a clear overinterpretation of a parable that is not concerned with the ontic status of the Shekhinah, but simply includes her among the king's sons. The same is true for the parable of the nine male palm trees supplemented by the female Etrog (*Bahir*, 117). When the text says that the Etrog "was one of the nine, of which he had [originally] planned that they be male," it certainly does not want to tell us, as Wolfson maintains, that "the female aspect of the divine pleroma . . . is itself part of the masculine" (ibid., p. 167). Again, the plain meaning of the text suggests that God simply changed his mind; he originally planned "his garden" to be completely male, but realized that an all-male garden (i.e., an all-male God) would not be able to survive.

38. *Bahir*, 36 (Kaplan, 54); see Chapter 6, p. 129, above.

39. Ibid., 43 (Kaplan, 63); see Chapter 6, p. 130, above.

40. Ibid., 90 β (Kaplan, 132); see Chapter 6, pp. 127f., above.

41. Ibid., 108 (Kaplan, 162).

42. Ibid., 3 (Kaplan, 3).

43. One of God's names is *ha-melekh she-ha-shalom shelo* ("the king to whom peace belongs"; compare b Shavu'ot 35b) which sounds similar to *she-lomo*. God's "glory" (*kavod*) is the Shekhinah.

44. This is the correct translation, pace Scholem's harmonizing "Aber sie ist [ihm] doch bereits vermählt" (*Bahir*, p. 46), which misses the point of the parable. The daughter is not married already to Solomon, but to the king! In *Origins*, pp. 92f., he gives the correct interpretation.

45. The translation follows Ms. Munich; see Abrams, *The Book Bahir*, p. 142f.

46. *Bahir*, 44 (Kaplan, 65).

47. Pace Wolfson's speculations, following Derrida, about the secrecy and the incestuous nature of the "gift" ("Hebraic and Hellenic Conceptions," pp. 158ff.). The incestuous relationship, on which Wolfson feasts, is the "logical" conclusion of the daring imagery, but not its essence.

48. *Bahir*, 51 α (Kaplan, 76); see Chapter 6, p. 132, above.

49. Ibid., 98 (Kaplan, 148); see Chapter 6, pp. 133f., above.

50. Chapter 8.

51. "Jewish Mysticism Alterable and Unalterable," n. 25, pp. 141f.

52. Anidjar, ibid., 142.

53. Which, accordingly, is "definitive," as much as the influence is "direct": see Wolfson, regarding the Bahir and the Cathar movement (*Along the Path*, p. 64): "no scholar has yet demonstrated direct influence in a definitive manner" (quoted also by Anidjar, ibid., 142).

54. Compare Rainer Specht, art. "Einfluß," in: *Historisches Wörterbuch der Philosophie*, ed. Joachim Ritter, vol. 2, Darmstadt: Wissenschaftliche Buchgesellschaft, 1972, cols. 395f.

55. Otto Bardenhewer, ed., *Die pseudoaristotelische Schrift über das reine Gute, bekannt unter dem Namen Liber de causis*, Freiburg i.Br.: Herder, 1982, § 1: *Omnis causa primaria plus est influens super causatum suum quam causa universalis secunda.*

56. *Summa Theologica* III q. 7 art. 1c (cf. q. 7 art. 9c): *Quanto enim aliquod receptivum propinquius est causae influenti, tanto magis participat de influentia ipsius. Influxus autem gratiae est a Deo.*

57. Compare in detail Julius Firmicus Maternus, *Mathesis* I, book 1 (Pierre Monat, ed. and trans., Firmicus Maternus, *Mathesis*, Tome I, Livres I–II, Paris: Les Belles Lettres, 1992). The book was composed around 335–337 CE.

58. Martin Ruland in his *Lexicon Alchemiae sive Dictionarium Alchemisticum* (Frankfurt 1612) defines *influentia* as the nature and virtue of the superior stars and planets, which we attract or absorb with our imagination and mind: *Influentia est, quando imaginatione ac mente superiorum siderum atque planetarum naturam ac virtutes in nos attrahimus* (*Lexicon Alchemiae*, p. 267, s.v. "influentia."

59. See Harold Bloom, *The Anxiety of Influence: A Theory of Poetry*, New York and Oxford: Oxford University Press, [2]1997, p. XII, with reference to Shakespeare.

60. Ibid.

61. Ibid., XXIII.

62. See also Yuval, *Two Nations in Your Womb*, pp. 40–45.

63. Compare the interesting parallel with Walter Benjamin's theory of translation, suggested by Emil Angehrn in his "Ursprungsmythos und Geschichtsdenken," in: *Der Sinn des Historischen. Geschichtsphilosophische Debatten*, ed. Herta Nagl-Docekal, Frankfurt a. Main: Fischer Taschenbuch Verlag, 1996, p. 319: "Wie eine radikale Theorie der Übersetzung davon ausgeht, daß kein letztes Original, kein durchgehender Referent gegeben ist, an dem sich alles mißt, sondern ein Sinnzusammenhang der Überlieferung, der fortwährenden Auflösung und Neuinterpretation, so kann historische Erinnerung als etwas verstanden werden, das nicht einen gründenden Anfang vergegenwärtigt und doch in der verwandelnden Aneignung einer Tradition geschichtliche Identität konstituiert."

64. Idel, "The Problem of the Sources of the Bahir," in: *Jerusalem Studies in*

Jewish Thought 6, 3–4, 1986/87, p. 57 [in Hebrew]; compare also id., *Kabbalah: New Perspectives*, New Haven and London: Yale University Press, 1988, pp. 122–128.

65. This has been observed also by Wolfson, *Along the Path*, p. 64.

66. No one would want to argue, for example, against the observation that the bahiric phrase "forms of God" has a prehistory in Qumran literature.

67. Note the underlying assumption that intra-Jewish "influence" needs less proof of historical channels than extra-Jewish "influence."

68. *EJ*, vol. 10, Jerusalem: Keter, 1971, col. 518, reprint in G. Scholem, *Kabbalah*, New York: Schocken, 1978, p. 42.

69. Quotation and translation from Scholem, *Origins*, p. 41 (Hebrew text in: "Qabbalot R. Ya'aqov we-R. Yitzhaq bene R. Ya'aqov ha-Kohen," *Madda'e ha-Yahadut* 2 , 1926–27, pp. 276–280).

70. Abrams, *The Book Bahir*, pp. 14ff., 27ff.

71. Scholem, *Origins*, pp. 106–123.

72. Ibid., 234–237; Shulamit Shahar, "Catharism and the Beginnings of the Kabbalah in Languedoc: Elements Common to the Catharic Scriptures and the Book *Bahir*," *Tarbiz* 40, 1971, pp. 483–507 [in Hebrew].

73. Haviva Pedaya, "The Provençal Stratum in the Redaction of *Sefer ha-Bahir*," in: *Jerusalem Studies in Jewish Thought* 9, 1990, pp. 139–164 [in Hebrew].

74. *Books of Contemplation*, pp. 168ff.

75. The vocalization of *hbr* as *hibber* ("was composed by") instead of *hubbar* ("was composed for") in the famous quotation from Meir b. Simon's *Milhemet Mitzwah*; see Scholem, *Origins*, p. 43 with n. 74; Verman, *Books of Contemplation*, pp. 168f.; Wolfson, *Along the Path*, p. 196, n. 28.

76. Scholem, *Origins*, pp. 35ff.

77. Wolfson, *Along the Path*, p. 69.

78. See, for example, *Kabbalah*, p. 45: "The encounter between the Gnostic tradition contained in the *Bahir* and neoplatonic ideas concerning God, His emanation, and man's place in the world, was extremely fruitful, leading to the deep penetration of these ideas into earlier mystical theories. The Kabbalah, in its historical significance, can be defined as the product of the interpenetration of Jewish Gnosticism and neoplatonism."

79. Wolfson, *Along the Path*, p. 66.

80. Ibid., 67.

81. See Chapter 9, pp. 197–199, above.

82. The most comprehensive recent biography on Bernard is by Peter Dinzelbacher, *Bernhard von Clairvaux. Leben und Werk des berühmten Zisterziensers*, Darmstadt: Primus Verlag, 1998.

83. Dinzelbacher, *Bernhard*, p. 280.

84. Dinzelbacher, *Bernhard*, pp. 289–293 and the literature mentioned there, particularly David Berger, "The Attitude of St. Bernard of Clairvaux toward the

Jews," in: *PAAJR* 40, 1972, pp. 89–108. More recently, see Jeremy Cohen, "'Witnesses of our Redemption': The Jews in the Crusading Theology of Bernard of Clairvaux," in: Bat-Sheva Albert, ed., *Medieval Studies in Honour of Avrom Saltman*, Ramat-Gan: Bar-Ilan University Press, 1995, pp. 67–81; Johannes Rauch, "Die anderen im Menschenbild Bernhards: Juden, Heiden, Ketzer," in: *Bernhard von Clairvaux und der Beginn der Moderne*, ed. Dieter R. Bauer and Gotthard Fuchs, Innsbruck and Wien: Tyrolia Verlag, 1996, pp. 235–261; Friedrich Lotter, "The Position of the Jews in Early Cistercian Exegesis and Preaching," in: Jeremy Cohen, ed., *From Witness to Witchcraft: Jews and Judaism in Medieval Christian Thought*, Wiesbaden: Harrassowitz, 1996, pp. 163–185.

85. Berger, "The Attitude of St. Bernard," pp. 95ff.

86. Dinzelbacher, *Bernhard*, p. 290.

87. *Hebräische Berichte über die Judenverfolgung während der Kreuzzüge*, ed. Adolf Neubauer and Moritz Stern, trans. by Seligmann Baer, Berlin: Verlag von Leonhard Simion, 1892 (reprint Hildesheim: Olms, 1997), p. 59 (my translation; and see the translation by Shlomo Eidelberg, trans. and ed., *The Jews and the Crusaders: The Hebrew Chronicles of the First and Second Crusades*, Madison, Wis.: University of Wisconsin Press, 1977, p. 122).

88. *Epistola* 363:6f., in: *S. Bernardi Opera*, ed. Jean Leclercq and Henri M. Rochais, vol. 8, Rome: Editiones Cistercienses, 1977, pp. 316f.; Berger, "The Attitude of St. Bernard," pp. 90ff.

89. Constant Mews has drawn my attention to Sigebert of Gembloux (ca. 1030–1112), who is said to have won Jewish friends in Metz (ca. 1080) because of his zeal for the *Hebraica veritas*; cf. Ludwig Bethmann, ed., *Sigeberti Gemblacensis Chronigraphia*, in: *Monumenta Germaniae Historica SS*, vol. 6, Hannover 1844 (reprint Stuttgart: Anton Hiersemann, 1980), p. 269.

90. On this, see Warner, *Alone of All Her Sex*, pp. 134ff.

91. The text plays with the double designation of the beloved (Shekhinah) in the Song of Songs as *havatzelet* and *shoshanah*. Whatever the original, that is, biblical, meaning of these two terms is (*havatzelet* is usually translated as "rose" and *shoshanah* as "lily"), the symbolism of colors used here requires the change from "white" to "red," thus from "lily" to "rose." The author of our piece clearly relies on a European/medieval understanding of the names of flowers, and not on any "original" biblical meaning.

92. That is, "white" and "red" are combined, and the divine judgement is sweetened with mercy.

93. The six lower Sefirot from Hesed to Yesod.

94. *Zohar* I, 221a; the translation follows Tishby, *The Wisdom of the Zohar*, vol. 1, p. 392.

❀ BIBLIOGRAPHY ❀

Abelson, Joshua, *The Immanence of God in Rabbinical Literature*, London: Macmillan, 1912 (reprint New York: Hermon Press, 1969).

Abrams, Daniel, *The Book Bahir: An Edition Based on the Earliest Manuscripts*, Los Angeles: Cherub Press, 1994.

Albeck, Chanoch, *Midrash Bereshit Rabbati ex libro R. Mosis Haddarshan collectus . . .* , Jerusalem: Mekize Nirdamim, 1940.

Alexander, Philip S., "Pre-Emptive Exegesis: Genesis Rabbah's Reading of the Story of Creation," *JJS* 43, 1992, pp. 230–245.

Angehrn, Emil, "Ursprungsmythos und Geschichtsdenken," in *Der Sinn des Historischen. Geschichtsphilosophische Debatten*, ed. Herta Nagl-Docekal, Frankfurt a. Main: Fischer Taschenbuch Verlag, 1996; pp. 305–332.

Anidjar, Gil, "Jewish Mysticism Alterable and Unalterable: On *Orient*ing Kabbalah Studies and the 'Zohar of Christian Spain,'" *Jewish Social Studies*, N.S. 3, 1996–97, pp. 89–157.

Assmann, Jan, *Ma'at. Gerechtigkeit und Unsterblichkeit im alten Ägypten*, München: C. H. Beck, 1990.

——, *Moses the Egyptian: The Memory of Egypt in Western Monotheism*, Cambridge, Mass.: Harvard University Press, 1997.

Atkinson, Clarissa W., *The Oldest Vocation: Christian Motherhood in the Middle Ages*, Ithaca and London: Cornell University Press, 1991.

Bagby, Albert I., "The Jew in the *Cántigas* of Alfonso X, El Sabio," *Speculum* 46, 1971, pp. 670–688.

——, "The Figure of the Jew in the *Cantigas* of Alfonso X," in: *Studies on the Cantigas de Santa Maria: Art, Music, and Poetry*, Proceedings of the International Symposium on the *Cantigas de Santa Maria* of Alfonso X, el Sabio (1221–1284) in Commemoration of its 700th Anniversary Year—1981, ed. Israel J. Katz and John E. Keller, Madison: Hispanic Seminary of Medieval Studies, 1987, pp. 235–245.

Bardenhewer, Otto, ed., *Die pseudoaristotelische Schrift über das reine Gute, bekannt unter dem Namen Liber de causis*, Freiburg i.B.: Herder, 1882.

Barth, Pudentiana, Maria I. Ritscher, and Joseph Schmidt-Görg, eds., *Hildegard von Bingen. Lieder*, Salzburg: Müller, 1969.

Becking, Bob, Meindert Dijkstra, Karel Vriezen, and Marjo C.A. Korpel, eds., *Only One God: Monotheism in Ancient Israel and the Veneration of the Goddess Ashera*, Sheffield: Sheffield Academic Press, forthcoming.

Berger, David, "The Attitude of St. Bernard of Clairvaux Toward the Jews," in: *Proceedings of the American Academy for Jewish Research* 40, 1972, pp. 89–108.

Bethmann, Ludwig, ed., *Sigeberti Gemblacensis Chronigraphia*, in: *Monumenta Germaniae Historica SS*, vol. 6, Hannover 1844 (reprint Stuttgart: Anton Hiersemann, 1980).

Biale, David, "Counter-History and Jewish Polemics against Christianity: The *Sefer toldot yeshu* and the *Sefer zerubavel*," *Jewish Social Studies*, N.S. 6, 1999, pp. 130–145.

Bianchi, Ugo, ed., *Le Origini dello Gnosticismo*, Colloquio di Messina, 13–18 Aprile 1966, Leiden: Brill, 1967.

Bidez, Joseph, and Léon Parmentier, eds., *The Ecclesiastical History of Evagrius: With the Scholia*, London: Methuen, 1898 (reprint Amsterdam: Hakkert, 1964).

Bloom, Harold, *The Anxiety of Influence: A Theory of Poetry*, New York and Oxford: Oxford University Press, ^{2}1997.

Boase, Thomas, S. R., *The York Psalter in the Library of the Hunterian Museum, Glasgow*, London: Faber and Faber, 1962.

Boman, Thorleif, *Hebrew Thought Compared with Greek*, Philadelphia: Westminster Press, 1960 (originally in German: *Das hebräische Denken im Vergleich mit dem griechischen*, Göttingen: Vandenhoek & Ruprecht, 1952, ^{5}1968).

Bonnet, Hans, art. "Maat," in: *Reallexikon der ägyptischen Religionsgeschichte*, Berlin: Walter de Gruyter, 1952, pp. 430–434.

Braude, William G., *Pesikta Rabbati*, trans. from the Hebrew, vol. 2, New Haven and London: Yale University Press, 1968.

Braude, William G., and Israel J. Kapstein, *Tanna debe Eliyyahu: The Lore of the School of Elijah*, trans. from the Hebrew, Philadelphia: The Jewish Publication Society of America, 1981.

Buckley, Jorunn Jacobsen, *Female Fault and Fulfilment in Gnosticism*, Chapel Hill: University of North Carolina Press, 1986.

Carroll, Michael P., *The Cult of the Virgin Mary: Psychological Origins*, Princeton: Princeton University Press, 1986.

Chadwick, Henry, *Origen: Contra Celsum*, trans. with an introduction and notes, Cambridge: Cambridge University Press, 1953.

Cohen, Jeremy, "'Witnesses of Our Redemption': The Jews in the Crusading Theology of Bernard of Clairvaux," in Bat-Sheva Albert, ed., *Medieval Studies in Honour of Avrom Saltman*, Ramat-Gan: Bar-Ilan University Press, 1995, pp. 67–81.

Colpe, Carsten, "Von der Logoslehre des Philon zu der des Clemens von Alexandrien," in *Kerygma und Logos. Festschrift für Carl Andresen zum 70. Geburtstag*, ed. Adolf M. Ritter, Göttingen: Vandenhoek and Ruprecht, 1979, pp. 89–107.

Dan, Joseph, art. "Toledot Yeshu," in: *EJ* 15, Jerusalem: Keter, 1971, cols. 1208f.

———, *Gershom Scholem and the Mystical Dimension of Jewish History*, New York and London: New York University Press, 1987.

————, "Yaldabaoth and the Language of the Gnosis," in: *Geschichte — Tradition — Reflexion. Festschrift für Martin Hengel zum 70. Geburtstag*, vol. 1: *Judentum*, ed. Peter Schäfer, Tübingen: J.C.B. Mohr (Paul Siebeck), 1996, pp. 557–564.

Dan, Joseph, and Ronald C. Kiener, *The Early Kabbalah*, New York: Paulist Press, 1986.

Delius, Walter, *Geschichte der Marienverehrung*, München and Basel: Reinhardt, 1963.

Deutsch, Yaacov, "New Evidence of Early Versions of *Toldot Yeshu*," *Tarbiz* 69, 1999–2000, pp. 177–197 [in Hebrew].

Díez Macho, Alejandro, *Neophyti 1. Targum Palestinense MS de la Bibliotheca Vaticana*, Madrid: Consejo Superior de Investigaciones Científicas, 1978.

Dillon, John, "Female Principles in Platonism," *Itaca* 2, 1986, pp. 108–123.

Dinzelbacher, Peter, *Bernhard von Clairvaux. Leben und Werk des berühmten Zisterziensers*, Darmstadt: Primus Verlag, 1998.

Donovan, Claire, *The de Brailes Hours. Shaping the Book of Hours in Thirteenth-Century Oxford*, Toronto and Buffalo: University of Toronto Press, 1991.

Eidelberg, Shlomo, ed., *The Jews and the Crusades: The Hebrew Chronicles of the First and Second Crusade*, Madison, Wis.: University of Wisconsin Press, 1977.

Einbinder, Susan, *Beautiful Death: Jewish Poetry and Martyrdom in Medieval France*, Princeton: Princeton University Press, forthcoming.

El "Códice Rico" de las Cantigas de Santa Maria, 2 vols., Madrid: Edilan, 1980.

Engel, Helmut, " '"Was Weisheit ist und wie sie entstand, will ich verkünden',," in: *Lehrerin der Gerechtigkeit*, ed. Georg Hentschel and Erich Zenger, Leipzig: Benno-Verlag, 1991.

Engelsman, Joan Chamberlain, *The Feminine Dimension of the Divine*, rev. ed., Wilamette, Ill.: Chiron Publications, 1994.

Epstein, Ann Wharton, "Frescoes of the Mavriotissa Monastery Near Kastoria: Evidence of Millenarianism and Anti-Semitism in the Wake of the First Crusade," *Gesta* 21, 1982, pp. 21–29.

Epstein, Isidore, ed., *Hebrew-English Edition of the Babylonian Talmud: Sanhedrin*, London: Soncino Press, 1969.

Etheridge, John W., *The Targums of Onkelos and Jonathan ben Uzziel on the Pentateuch* . . . , *Genesis and Exodus*, London: Longman, Green, Longman, and Roberts, 1862.

Even-Shemuel, Yehudah, ed., *Midreshe Ge'ullah*, Jerusalem and Tel Aviv: Mosad Bialik, ²1954.

———— ed., *The Kosari of R. Yehuda haLevi*, Tel Aviv: Dvir, 1972.

Festugière, André-Jean, "Evagre, *Histoire Ecclésiastique*," in: *Byzantion* 45, 1975, pp. 187–488.

Frevel, Christian, *Aschera und der Ausschließlichkeitsanspruch YHWHs. Beiträge zu literarischen, religionsgeschichtlichen und ikonographischen Aspekten der Ascheradiskussion*, Weinheim: Beltz Athenäum, 1995.

Früchtel, Ursula, *Die kosmologischen Vorstellungen bei Philo von Alexandrien*, Leiden: Brill, 1968.

Frymer-Kensky, Tikva, *In the Wake of the Goddesses: Women, Culture, and the Biblical Transformation of Pagan Myth*, New York: The Free Press, 1992.

Geiges, Fritz, *Der mittelalterliche Fensterschmuck des Freiburger Münsters*, Freiburg im Breisgau: Breisgau-Verein Schau-ins-Land, 1931.

Gengaro, Maria L., Francesca Leoni, and Gemma Villa, *Codici Decorati e Miniati dell'Ambrosiana: Ebraici e Greci*, Milano: Casa Editrice Ceschina, 1959.

Goldberg, Arnold, *Untersuchungen über die Vorstellung von der Schekhinah in der frühen rabbinischen Literatur*, Berlin: Walter de Gruyter, 1969.

Gonzalez, Marisa F., *The Road to Ephesus: the Rise of Marian Devotion in the Eastern Mediterranian*, Princeton University, Department of Religion, senior thesis.

Goulburn, Edward Meyrick, and Henry Symonds, eds., *The Life, Letters, and Sermons of Bishop Herbert de Losinga*, vol. 2: *The Sermons*, Oxford and London: James Parker and Co., 1878.

Grimm, Jacob and Wilhelm, *Deutsches Wörterbuch*, vol. 11.3, bearbeitet von Karl Euling, Leipzig 1936, cols. 2538–2545.

Gruenwald, Ithamar, ed., *Sefer Yetzirah*, in: *Israel Oriental Studies* 1, 1971, pp. 132–177.

Haibach-Reinisch, Monika, *Ein Neuer "Transitus Mariae" des Pseudo-Melito*, Rome: Pontifica Academia Mariana Internationalis, 1962 [Bibliotheca Assumptionis B. Virginis Mariae, 5].

Halberstam, Salomon J., ed., Yehūda Ben-Barzillay, *Perush Sefer Yesīra*, Berlin: M'kize Nirdamim, 1885 (reprint Jerusalem: Maqor, 1970).

Hasan-Rokem, Galit, *Web of Life: Folklore and Midrash in Rabbinic Literature*, Stanford: Stanford University Press, 2000.

Hecht, Josef, "Die frühesten Darstellungen der Himmelfahrt Mariens. Eine ikonographische Studie," in: *Das Münster* 4, 1951, pp. 1–12.

Heil, Johannes, and Rainer Kampling, eds., *Maria — Tochter Sion? Mariologie, Marienfrömmigkeit und Judenfeindschaft*, Paderborn: Ferdinand Schöningh 2001.

Helck, Wolfgang, art. "Maat," in: *Lexikon der Ägyptologie*, ed. Wolfgang Helck and Wolfhart Westendorf, vol. 2, Wiesbaden: Otto Harrassowitz, 1980, cols. 1110–1119.

Himmelfarb, Martha, "Sefer Zerubbabel," in: David Stern and Mark J. Mirsky, eds., *Rabbinic Fantasies: Imaginative Narratives from Classical Hebrew Literature*, Philadelphia and New York: The Jewish Publication Society, 1990, pp. 67–90.

———, "The Mother of the Messiah in the Talmud Yerushalmi and Sefer Zerubbabel," in: *The Talmud Yerushalmi and Graeco-Roman Culture*, vol. 3, ed. Peter Schäfer, Tübingen: Mohr Siebeck, forthcoming.

Hirschfeld, Hartwig, *Sefer ha-Kuzari. Book of Kuzari by Judah Hallevi*, trans. from the Arabic, New York: Pardes, 1946.

Horbury, William, *A Critical Examination of the Toldedoth Jeshu*, Ph.D. dissertation, Cambridge 1971.

Idel, Moshe, "The Problem of the Sources of the Bahir," in: *Jerusalem Studies in Jewish Thought* 6, 3–4, 1986–87, pp. 55–72 [in Hebrew].

———, *Kabbalah: New Perspectives*, New Haven and London: Yale University Press, 1988.

Isenberg, Wesley W., trans., "The Gospel of Philip (II,3)," in: James M. Robinson, ed., *The Nag Hammadi Library in English*, Leiden: Brill, 1978 (paperback HarperSanFrancisco, 1990).

James, Montague Rhodes, *The Sculptures Bosses in the Cloisters of Norwich Cathedral*, Norwich: Goose and Son, 1911.

Jellinek, Adolph, *Beit ha-Midrash*, vol. 2, Leipzig: Nies, 1855 (reprint Jerusalem: Wahrmann Books, 1967).

Jonas, Hans, *Gnosis und spätantiker Geist*, vol. 1: *Die mythologische Gnosis*, Göttingen: Vandenhoeck & Ruprecht, 1934 (^{3}1964); vol. 2: *Von der Mythologie zur mystischen Philosophie*, Göttingen: Vandenhoeck & Ruprecht, 1954.

———, *The Gnostic Religion*, Boston: Beacon Press, ^{2}1958.

Jugie, Martin, "Homélies Mariales Byzantines (II)," in: *PO* 19, 1925, pp. 289–526 [171–409].

———, *La mort et l'assomption de la Sainte Vierge*, Città del Vaticano: Bibliotheca Apostolica Vaticana, 1944.

Kafach, Yosef D., ed., Saadia, *Emunot we-De'ot*, Jerusalem: Sura, 1970.

Kaplan, Aryeh, *The Bahir* . . . , Translation, Introduction and Commentary, York Beach, Maine: Samuel Weiser, 1979 (paperback 1989).

Kayatz, Christa, *Studien zu Proverbien 1–9*, Neukirchen-Vluyn: Neukirchener Verlag, 1966.

Keale, Edward J., art. "Peter of Blois," in *New Catholic Encyclopedia*, New York: McGraw-Hill Book Company, 1967.

Klein, Michael L., *The Fragment Targums of the Pentateuch According to their Extant Sources*, vol. 1, Rome: Biblical Institute Press, 1980.

Kloppenborg, John S., "Isis and Sophia in the Book of Wisdom," *HTR* 75, 1982, pp. 57–84.

Knohl, Israel, *The Messiah before Jesus: The Suffering Servant of the Dead Sea Scrolls*, Berkeley: University of California Press, 2000.

Koenig, V. Frederic, ed., Gautier de Coincy, *Les Miracles de Notre Dame*, vol. 2, Genève: Librairie Droz, and Paris: Librairie Minard, 1961.

Kraus, Henry, *The Living Theatre of Medieval Art*, Bloomington and London: Indiana University Press, 1967.

Krauss, Samuel, *Das Leben Jesu nach jüdischen Quellen*, Berlin: Calvary, 1902 (reprint Hildesheim and New York: Olms, 1977).

Kreidl-Papadopoulos, Karoline, art. "Koimesis," in Klaus Wessel and Marcell

Restle, eds., *Reallexikon zur Byzantinischen Kunst*, vol. 4, Stuttgart 1990, cols. 136–182.

Krummer-Schroth, Ingeborg, *Glasmalereien aus dem Freiburger Münster*, Freiburg im Breisgau: Rombach, 1967.

Krusch, Bruno, ed., Gregory of Tours, *Liber in Gloria Martyrum*, in *Monumenta Germaniae Historica, Scriptores Rerum Merovingicarum*, Hannover: Hahn, 1969.

Kugel, James L., *Traditions of the Bible: A Guide to the Bible as It Was at the Start of the Common Era*, Cambridge, Mass., and London: Harvard University Press, 1998.

Kuhn, Peter, *Gottes Trauer und Klage in der Rabbinischen Überlieferung*, Leiden: Brill, 1978.

———, *Offenbarungsstimmen im Antiken Judentum. Untersuchungen zur Bat Qol und verwandten Phänomenen*, Tübingen: J.C.B. Mohr (Paul Siebeck), 1989.

Kulp-Hill, Kathleen, trans., *Songs of the Holy Mary of Alfonso X, The Wise: A Translation of the* Cantigas de Santa Maria, with an introduction by Connie L. Scarborough, Tempe, Ariz.: Arizona Center for Medieval and Renaissance Studies, 2000 [Medieval and Renaissance Texts and Studies, vol. 173].

Lang, Bernhard, *Frau Weisheit. Deutung einer biblischen Gestalt*, Düsseldorf: Patmos-Verlag, 1975 (English version: *Wisdom and the Book of Proverbs : A Hebrew Goddess Redefined*, New York: Pilgrim Press, 1986).

La Porta, Sergio, "Sophia-Mētēr: Reconstructing a Gnostic Myth," in: *The Nag Hammadi Library after Fifty Years: Proceedings of the 1995 Society of Biblical Literature Commemoration*, ed. John D. Turner and Anne McGuire, Leiden: Brill, 1997, pp. 188–207.

Laporte, Jean, "Philo in the Tradition of Biblical Wisdom," in *Aspects of Wisdom in Judaism and Early Christianity*, ed. Robert L. Wilken, Notre Dame and London: University of Notre Dame Press, 1975, pp. 103–141.

Larcher, Chrysostome, *Le Livre de la Sagesse ou la Sagesse de Salomon*, vol. 2, Paris: Gabalda, 1984.

Layton, Bentley, *The Gnostic Scriptures. A New Translation with Annotations and Introductions*, New York: Doubleday, 1987.

Leclercq, Jean, and Henri M. Rochais, eds., *S. Bernardi Opera*, vol. 8, Rome: Editiones Cistercienses, 1977.

Leisegang, Hans, art. "Sophia," in: *PW*, III A,1, 1927, cols. 1031–1034.

Lévi, Israel, "L'apocalypse de Zorobabel et le roi de Perse Siroès," *REJ* 68, 1914, pp. 129–160; 69, 1919, pp. 108–121; 71, 1920, pp. 57–65.

Lillich, Meredith Parsons, "Gothic Glaziers: Monks, Jews, Taxpayers, Bretons, Women," *Journal of Glass Studies* 27, 1985, pp. 72–92.

Limberis, Vasiliki, *Divine Heiress: The Virgin Mary and the Creation of Christian Constantinople*, London: Routledge, 1994.

Loofs, Friedrich, ed., *Nestoriana. Die Fragmente des Nestorius*, Halle: Max Niemeyer, 1905.

Lotter, Friedrich, "The Position of the Jews in Early Cistercian Exegesis and Preaching," in Jeremy Cohen, ed., *From Witness to Witchcraft: Jews and Judaism in Medieval Christian Thought*, Wiesbaden: Harrassowitz, 1996, pp. 163–185.

Luard, Henry R., ed., *Matthaeus Parisiensis Chronica Maiora*, London: Her Majesty's Stationary Office, 1880.

Mack, Burton L., *Logos und Sophia. Untersuchungen zur Weisheitstheologie im hellenistischen Judentum*, Göttingen: Vandenhoek & Ruprecht, 1973.

MacRae, George W., "The Jewish Background of the Gnostic Sophia Myth," *NT* 12, 1970, pp. 86–101.

Maier, Johann, *Jesus von Nazareth in der Talmudischen Überlieferung*, Darmstadt: Wissenschaftliche Buchgesellschaft, 1978.

Manhes-Deremble, Colette, *Les vitraux narratifs de la cathédrale de Chartres*, Paris: Le Léopard d'Or, 1993.

Marcus, Ivan, *Rituals of Childhood: Jewish Acculturation in Medieval Europe*, New Haven and London: Yale University Press, 1996.

Markschies, Christoph, *Valentinus Gnosticus? Untersuchungen zur valentinianischen Gnosis mit einem Kommentar zu den Fragmenten Valentins*, Tübingen: J.C.B. Mohr (Paul Siebeck), 1992.

Marmorstein, Arthur, *The Old Rabbinic Doctrine of God*, vol. 1: *The Names and Attributes of God*, London: Milford, Oxford University Press, 1927 (reprint New York: Ktav, 1968).

Marquardt, Odo, "Lob des Polytheismus: Über Monomythie und Polymythie," in: *Philosophie und Mythos. Ein Kolloquium*, ed. Hans Poser, Berlin: Walter de Gruyter, 1979, pp. 40–58.

Matter, E. Ann, and Ripberger, Albert, eds., Paschasius Radbertus, *De Partu Virginis* and *De Assumptione S. Mariae Virginis*, in: *Corpus Christianorum Continuatio Mediaeualis*, LVI C, Turnholti: Brepols, 1985.

McNamara, Martin, trans., *Targum Neofiti 1: Deuteronomy*, Edinburgh: T. & T. Clark, 1997.

Meehan, Denis, ed., *Adamnan's De Locis Sanctis*, Dublin: The Dublin Institute for Advanced Studies, 1958 [Scriptores Latini Hiberniae, vol. 3].

Mettmann, Walter, ed., Alfonso X, el Sabio, *Cantigas de Santa Maria*: Cantigas 1 a 100, Madrid: Edilan, 1986.

Mews, Constant, "Religious Thinker: 'A Frail Human Being' on Fiery Life," in: *Voice of the Living Light: Hildegard of Bingen and her World*, ed. Barbara Newman, Berkeley: University of California Press, 1998, pp. 52–69.

———, "Hildegard, the Speculum Virginum and Religious Reform in the Twelfth Century," in: Alfred Haverkamp, ed., *Hildegard von Bingen in ihrem historischen Umfeld. Internationaler wissenschaftlicher Kongreß zum 900jährigen Jubiläum, 13.–19. September 1998, Bingen am Rhein*, Mainz: Philipp von Zabern, 2000, pp. 237–267.

Mickley, Paul, *Arculf: Eines Pilgers Reise nach dem heiligen Lande (um 670)*, aus dem Lateinischen übersetzt und erklärt, Zweiter Teil: Heilige Staetten im

Lande, Damaskus, Tyrus, Alexandrien, Leipzig: J. C. Hinrichs'sche Buchhandlung, 1917.

Monat, Pierre, ed. and transl., Firmicus Maternus, *Mathesis*, Tome I, Livres I–II, Paris: Les Belles Lettres, 1992.

Morgan, Nigel J., *The Medieval Painted Glass of Lincoln Cathedral*, London: Oxford University Press, 1983.

Neubauer, Adolf, "The Bahir and the Zohar," *JQR* 4, 1892, pp. 357–368.

Neubauer, Adolf, and Moritz Stern, eds., *Hebräische Berichte über die Judenverfolgung während der Kreuzzüge*, trans. Seligmann Baer, Berlin: Verlag von Leonhard Simion, 1892 [Quellen zur Geschichte der Juden in Deutschland, II, vol. 2], reprint Hildesheim etc.: Olms, 1997.

Newman, Barbara, *Sister of Wisdom: St. Hildegard's Theology of the Feminine*, Berkeley: University of California Press, 1987 (paperback 1989).

———, *Saint Hildegard of Bingen: Symphonia. A Critical Edition of the Symphonia armonie celestium revelationum [Symphony of the Harmony of Celestial Revelations]*, Ithaca and London: Cornell University Press, 1988, ²1998.

Olyan, Saul M., *Ashera and the Cult of Yahweh in Israel*, Atlanta: Scholars Press, 1988.

Pagels, Elaine, "Irenaeus, the 'Canon of Truth,' and the Gospel of John: 'Making a Difference' through Hermeneutics and Ritual," *Vigiliae Christianae*, forthcoming.

Pasquier, Anne, "Prouneikos: A Colorful Expression to Designate Wisdom," in: *Images of the Feminine in Gnosticism*, ed. Karen L. King, Philadelphia: Fortress Press, 1988, pp. 47–66.

Pearson, Birger A., "Pre-Valentinian Gnosticism in Alexandria," in: *The Future of Early Christianity: Essays in Honor of Helmut Koester*, ed. Birger A. Pearson, Minneapolis: Fortress Press, 1991, pp. 455–466.

Pedaya, Haviva, "The Provençal Stratum in the Redaction of *Sefer ha-Bahir*," in: *Jerusalem Studies in Jewish Thought* 9, 1990, pp. 139–164 [in Hebrew].

Pelekanides, Stylianos, *Kastoria*, vol. 1, *Byzantinai Toichographiai: Pinakes*, Thessalonike 1953.

Pelikan, Jaroslav, *Mary Through the Centuries: Her Place in the History of Culture*, New Haven: Yale University Press, 1996.

Peters, Hans-Rudolf, *Die Ikonographie des Marientodes*, Diss., Bonn 1950.

Pines, Shlomo, trans., Moses Maimonides, *The Guide of the Perplexed*, Chicago and London: The University of Chicago Press, 1963.

Pitra, Jean-Baptiste, ed., *Analecta Sanctae Hildegardis*, in: *Analecta sacra*, vol. 8, Monte Cassino, 1882 (reprint Farnborough: Gregg, 1966).

Plöger, Otto, *Sprüche Salomos (Proverbia)*, Neukirchen-Vluyn: Neukirchener Verlag, 1984.

Power, Kim E., "From Ecclesiology to Mariology: Patristic Traces and Innovation in the *Speculum Virginum*," in: *Listen Daughter: the Speculum Virginum and the Formation of Religious Women in the Middle Ages*, ed. Constant Mews, New York: St. Martin's Press, forthcoming.

Preuschen, Erwin, *Zwei gnostische Hymnen*, Giessen: Ricker, 1904.

Rad, Gerhard von, *Wisdom in Israel*, London: SCM Press, 1972.

Rauch, Johannes, "Die anderen im Menschenbild Bernhards: Juden, Heiden, Ketzer," in *Bernhard von Clairvaux und der Beginn der Moderne*, ed. Dieter R. Bauer and Gotthard Fuchs, Innsbruck and Wien: Tyrolia Verlag, 1996, pp. 235–261.

Raz-Krakotzkin, Amnon, "Without Other Accounts: The Question of Christianity in the Writings of Yitzchak Baer and Gershom Scholem," *Jewish Studies* 38, 1998, pp. 73–96 [in Hebrew].

Restle, Marcell, *Byzantine Wall Painting in Asia Minor*, vol. 1, Recklinghausen: Verlag Aurel Bongers, 1967.

Rosenblatt, Samuel, *Saadia Gaon. The Book of Beliefs and Opinions*, trans. from the Arabic and the Hebrew, New Haven: Yale University Press, [4]1958.

Rubin, Miri, *Gentile Tales: The Narrative Assault on Late Medieval Jews*, New Haven and London: Yale University Press, 1999.

Ruland, Martin, *Lexicon Alchemiae sive Dictionarium Alchemisticum*, Frankfurt 1612.

Saïd, Marie-Bernard, trans., *Homilies in Praise of the Blessed Virgin Mary by Bernard of Clairvaux*, Kalamazoo, Mich.: Cistercian Publications, 1993 [Cistercian Fathers Series: Number Eighteen-A].

Samely, Alexander, "Between Scripture and its Rewording: Towards a Classification of Rabbinic Exegesis," *JJS* 42, 1991, pp. 39–67.

Sandelin, Karl-Gustav, *Wisdom as Nourisher: A Study of an Old Testament Theme, its Development within Early Judaism and its Impact on Early Christianity*, Åbo: Åbo Akademi, 1986 [Acta Academiae Aboensis, Ser. A, Humaniora, vol. 64 nr 3].

Scarborough, Connie L., *Women in Thirteenth-Century Spain as Portrayed in Alfonso X's Cantigas de Santa Maria*, Lewiston: The Edwin Mellen Press, 1993.

Schäfer, Peter, *Die Vorstellung vom Heiligen Geist in der Rabbinischen Literatur*, München: Kösel-Verlag, 1972.

———, *Rivalität zwischen Engeln und Menschen. Untersuchungen zur rabbinischen Engelvorstellung*, Berlin and New York: Walter de Gruyter, 1975.

———, (with Margarete Schlüter and Hans Georg von Mutius), *Synopse zur Hekhalot-Literatur*, Tübingen: J.C.B. Mohr (Paul Siebeck), 1981.

———, *The Hidden and Manifest God: Some Major Themes in Early Jewish Mysticism*, Albany, N.Y.: State University of New York Press, 1992.

———, *Judeophobia: Attitudes toward the Jews in the Ancient World*, Cambridge, Mass., and London: Harvard University Press, 1997 (paperback 1998).

———, "Tochter, Schwester, Braut und Mutter. Bilder der Weiblichkeit Gottes in der frühen Kabbala," *Saeculum* 49, 1998, pp. 259–279.

———, "Daughter, Sister, Bride and Mother: Images of the Femininity of God in the Early Kabbalah," *JAAR* 68, 2000, pp. 221–242.

———, "Gerschom Scholem und das Christentum," forthcoming.

Schaffer, Christa, *Koimesis. Der Heimgang Mariens: Das Entschlafungsbild in seiner Abhängigkeit von Legende und Theologie*, Regensburg: Friedrich Pustet, 1985.

Schechter, Solomon, *Some Aspects of Rabbinic Theology*, London: Black, 1909.

Schmitt, Franciscus Salesius, ed., *S. Anselmi Cantuariensis Archiepiscopi Opera Omnia*, vol. 2, Stuttgart-Bad Cannstatt: Frommann-Holzboog, 1968.

Scholem, Gershom, *Das Buch Bahir. Ein Schriftdenkmal aus der Frühzeit der Kabbala auf Grund der kritischen Neuausgabe von Gerhard Scholem*, Leipzig: W. Drugulin, 1923 (reprint Darmstadt: Wissenschaftliche Buchgesellschaft, 1970).

———, "Qabbalot R. Ya'aqov we-R. Yitzhaq bene R. Ya'aqov ha-Kohen," *Madda'e ha-Yahadut* 2, 1926–27, pp. 165–293.

———, *Major Trends in Jewish Mysticism*, Jerusalem: Schocken Publishing House, 1941 (reprint New York: Schocken, 1995).

———, *Ursprung und Anfänge der Kabbala*, Berlin: Walter de Gruyter, 1962. (English translation: *Origins of the Kabbalah*, ed. R. J. Zwi Werblowsky, trans. Allan Arkush, Princeton: The Jewish Publication Society and Princeton University Press, 1987).

———, art. "Kabbalah," in: *EJ*, vol. 10, Jerusalem: Keter, 1971, cols. 489–653.

———, *Kabbalah*, New York: Schocken, 1978.

———, "Shekhinah: the Feminine Element in Divinity," in: *On the Mystical Shape of the Godhead: Basic Concepts in the Kabbalah*, ed. and rev., acc. to the 1976 Hebrew edition, by Jonathan Chipman, trans. from German by Joachim Neugroschel, New York: Schocken Books, 1991, pp. 140–196, 293–300.

———, "Sitra Ahra: Good and Evil in the Kabbalah," in: *On the Mystical Shape of the Godhead: Basic Concepts in the Kabbalah*, ed. and rev., acc. to the 1976 Hebrew edition, by Jonathan Chipman, trans. from German by Joachim Neugroschel, New York: Schocken Books, 1991, pp. 56–87, 281–283.

Schreiner, Klaus, "Antijudaismus in Marienbildern des späten Mittelalters," in: *Das Medium Bild in historischen Ausstellungen. Beiträge . . . zur Sektion 6 des 41. Deutschen Historikertags in München 1996*, Augsburg: Haus der Bayerischen Geschichte, 1998, pp. 9–34.

———, *Maria*, München: Hanser, 1994.

Schwartz, Eduard, ed., *Acta Conciliorum Oecumenicorum*, tomus primus, volumen primum, pars altera [Concilium Universale Ephesenum], Berlin: Walter de Gruyter, 1927.

Shahar, Shulamit, "Catharism and the Beginnings of the Kabbalah in Languedoc: Elements Common to the Catharic Scriptures and the Book *Bahir*," *Tarbiz* 40, 1971, pp. 483–507 [in Hebrew].

Shoemaker, Stephen J., "'Let us Go and Burn Her Body': The Image of the Jews in the Early Dormition Traditions," *Church History* 68, 1999, pp. 775–823.

Specht, Rainer, art. "Einfluß," in: *Historisches Wörterbuch der Philosophie*, ed.

Joachim Ritter, vol. 2, Darmstadt: Wissenschaftliche Buchgesellschaft, 1972, cols. 395f.

Speck, Paul, "The Apocalypse of Zerubbabel and Christian Icons," *JSQ* 4, 1997, pp. 183–190.

St. Bernard's Sermons on the Blessed Virgin Mary, trans. from the original Latin by a Priest of the Mount Melleray, Chulmleigh, Devon: Augustine Publishing Company, 1984 (reprint 1987).

Stemberger, Günter, *Einleitung in Talmud und Midrasch*, München: C. H. Beck, ⁸1992.

Stroumsa, Gedaliahu A.G., *Another Seed: Studies in Gnostic Mythology*, Leiden: Brill, 1984.

Tanakh: A New Translation of the Holy Scriptures According to the Traditional Hebrew Text, Philadelphia: The Jewish Publication Society, 1985.

Taubes, Jacob, "Zur Konjunktur des Polytheismus," in: *Mythos und Moderne: Begriff und Bild einer Rekonstruktion*, ed. Karl Heinz Bohrer, Frankfurt a.M.: Suhrkamp, 1983, pp. 457–470.

The Oxford English Dictionary, vol. 7, reprint Oxford 1961.

The Revised English Bible: With Apocrypha, Oxford: Oxford University Press, 1989.

Thierry, Nicole and Michel, *Nouvelles Églises Rupestres de Cappadoce, Région du Hasan Daği* (New Rock-Cut Churches of Cappadocia), Paris: Librairie C. Klincksieck, 1963.

Tischendorf, Konstantin von, *Apocalypses Apocryphae*, Leipzig: Mendel, 1866 (reprint Hildesheim: Olms, 1966).

Tishby, Isaiah, ed., *The Wisdom of the Zohar: An Anthology of Texts*, with extensive introductions and explanations, English translation by David Goldstein, vols. 1–3, Oxford: Oxford University Press, 1989 (reprint 1994).

Tolstoj, Ivan I., and Nikodim P. Kondakov, *Russkija Drevnosti v pamjatnikach iskusstva*, vol. 6, St. Petersburg: Benke, 1899.

Vagner, Georgij K., *Alte russische Städte*, München: Deutscher Kunstverlag, 1980.

van Dam, Raymond, Gregory of Tours, *Glory of the Martyrs*, trans. with an introduction, Liverpool: Liverpool University Press, 1988 [Translated Texts for Historians, Latin Series III].

Verman, Mark, *The Books of Contemplation: Medieval Jewish Mystical Sources*, Albany, N.Y.: State University of New York Press, 1992.

Visotzky, Burton L., *The Midrash on Proverbs*, trans. from the Hebrew with an introduction and annotations, New Haven and London: Yale University Press, 1992.

Vollständige Faksimileausgabe im Originalformat des Berthold-Sakramentars, Ms. M.710 der Pierpont Morgan Library in New York, Graz: Akademische Druck- und Verlagsanstalt, 1995.

Waldstein, Michael, "The Primal Triad in the *Apocryphon of John*," in: *The Nag Hammadi Library after Fifty Years: Proceedings of the 1995 Society of*

Biblical Literature Commemoration, ed. John D. Turner and Anne McGuire, Leiden: Brill, 1997, pp. 154–187.

Waldstein, Michael, and Frederik Wisse, eds., *The Apocryphon of John: Synopsis of Nag Hammadi Codices II,1; III,1; and IV,1 with BG 8502,2,* Leiden: Brill, 1995.

Warner, Marina, *Alone of All Her Sex: The Myth and the Cult of the Virgin Mary,* London: Weidenfeld and Nicolson, 1976.

Wertheimer, Shlomo A., *Batei Midrashot,* second ed. . . . by Abraham J. Wertheimer, vol. 2, Jerusalem: Mosad ha-Rav Kook, ²1954.

Williams, Michael A., *Rethinking "Gnosticism": An Argument for Dismantling a Dubious Category,* Princeton, N.J.: Princeton University Press, 1996.

———, "Response to the Papers of Karen King, Frederik Wisse, Michael Waldstein and Sergio La Porta," in: *The Nag Hammadi Library after Fifty Years: Proceedings of the 1995 Society of Biblical Literature Commemoration,* ed. John D. Turner and Anne McGuire, Leiden: Brill, 1997, pp. 208–220.

Wilmart, André, "L'ancien récit latin de l'Assomption," in: *Analecta Reginensia. Extraits des Manuscrits Latins de la Reine Christine Conservés au Vatican,* Città del Vaticano: Biblioteca Apostolica Vaticana, 1933, pp. 323–362.

Winkler, Gerhard B., ed., Bernhard von Clairvaux, *Sämtliche Werke lateinisch/ deutsch,* Innsbruck: Tyrolia-Verlag, vol. 4, 1993; vol. 5, 1994; vol. 8, 1997.

Wolfson, Elliot, *Along the Path: Studies in Kabbalistic Myth, Symbolism, and Hermeneutics,* Albany, N.Y.: State University of New York Press, 1995.

———, "Hebraic and Hellenic Conceptions of Wisdom in *Sefer ha-Bahir,*" *Poetics Today* 19, 1998, pp. 147–176.

Wolfson, Harry A., *Philo. Foundations of Religious Philosophy in Judaism, Christianity, and Islam,* 2 vols., Cambridge, Mass.: Harvard University Press, 1948, ³1962.

Wratislaw-Mitrovic, Ludmila, and Nikolaj Okunev, "La dormition de la Sainte Vierge dans la peinture médievale orthodoxe," *Byzantinoslavica* 3, 1931, pp. 134–180.

Yamauchi, Edwin M., "Jewish Gnosticism? The Prologue of John, Mandaean Parallels, and the Trimorphic Protennois," in: *Studies in Gnosticism and Hellenistic Religions,* pres. to Gilles Quispel on the Occasion of his 65th Birthday, ed. Roeloef van den Broek and Maarten J. Vermaseren, Leiden: Brill, 1981, pp. 467–497.

Yuval, Israel, "Easter and Passover as early Jewish-Christian dialogue," in: Paul F. Bradshaw and Lawrence A. Hoffmann, eds., *Passover and Easter: Origin and History to Modern Times,* South Bend, Ind.: University of Notre Dame Press, 1999, pp. 98–124.

———, "Passover in the Middle Ages," ibid., pp. 127–160.

———, *"Two Nations in Your Womb": Perceptions of Jews and Christians,* Tel Aviv: Am Oved, 2000 [in Hebrew].

Ziegler, Konrat, art. "Plutarchos," in: *PW,* vol. 21.1, 1951 (reprint 1990), cols. 636–962.

❖ INDEX ❖